PENGUIN BOOKS

THE VALMIKI RAMAYANA VOLUME 3

Bibek Debroy is a renowned economist, scholar and translator. He has worked in universities, research institutes, industry and for the government. He has widely published books, papers and articles on economics. As a translator, he is best known for his magnificent rendition of the Mahabharata in ten volumes, and additionally the *Harivamsha*, published to wide acclaim by Penguin Classics. He is also the author of *Sarama and Her Children*, which splices his interest in Hinduism with his love for dogs.

PRAISE FOR *THE MAHABHARATA*

'The modernization of language is visible, it's easier on the mind, through expressions that are somewhat familiar. The detailing of the story is intact, the varying tempo maintained, with no deviations from the original. The short introduction reflects a brilliant mind. For those who passionately love the Mahabharata and want to explore it to its depths, Debroy's translation offers great promise . . .'—*Hindustan Times*

'[Debroy] has really carved out a niche for himself in crafting and presenting a translation of the Mahabharata . . . The book takes us on a great journey with admirable ease'—*Indian Express*

'The first thing that appeals to one is the simplicity with which Debroy has been able to express himself and infuse the right kind of meanings . . . Considering that Sanskrit is not the simplest of languages to translate a text from, Debroy exhibits his deep understanding and appreciation of the medium'—*The Hindu*

'Debroy's lucid and nuanced retelling of the original makes the masterpiece even more enjoyably accessible'—*Open*

'The quality of translation is excellent. The lucid language makes it a pleasure to read the various stories, digressions and parables'—*Tribune*

'Extremely well-organized, and has a substantial and helpful Introduction, plot summaries and notes. The volume is a beautiful example of a well thought-out layout which makes for much easier reading'—*Book Review*

'The dispassionate vision [Debroy] brings to this endeavour will surely earn him merit in the three worlds'—*Mail Today*

'Debroy's is not the only English translation available in the market, but where he scores and others fail is that his is the closest rendering of the original text in modern English without unduly complicating the readers' understanding of the epic'—*Business Standard*

'The brilliance of Ved Vyasa comes through, ably translated by Bibek Debroy'—*Hindustan Times*

THE VALMIKI RAMAYANA 3

Translated by Bibek Debroy

PENGUIN BOOKS

An imprint of Penguin Random House

PENGUIN BOOKS

USA | Canada | UK | Ireland | Australia
New Zealand | India | South Africa | China

Penguin Books is part of the Penguin Random House group of companies
whose addresses can be found at global.penguinrandomhouse.com

Published by Penguin Random House India Pvt. Ltd
7th Floor, Infinity Tower C, DLF Cyber City,
Gurgaon 122 002, Haryana, India

First published in Penguin Books by Penguin Random House India 2017

Translation copyright © Bibek Debroy 2017

All rights reserved

10 9 8 7 6

ISBN 9780143428060

Typeset in Sabon by Manipal Digital Systems, Manipal
Printed at Replika Press Pvt. Ltd, India

www.penguin.co.in

For Professor Shailendra Raj Mehta

Contents

Acknowledgements

This journey, with Penguin, started more than a decade ago. It is a journey of translating Sanskrit texts into English, in unabridged form. It commenced with the Bhagavad Gita in 2006, followed by the Mahabharata (2010 to 2014) and the Harivamsha (2016). It continues with the Valmiki Ramayana and will be followed by the Puranas. To the best of my knowledge, the great translator, Manmatha Nath Dutt (1855–1912), is the only other person who has accomplished the 'double' of unabridged translations of both the Valmiki Ramayana and the Mahabharata in English. In this journey with Penguin, special thanks to Meru Gokhale, Ambar Sahil Chatterjee and Paloma Dutta. All three have made this journey easier to traverse.

My wife, Suparna Banerjee (Debroy), has not only been *patni*, she has been *grihini* and *sahadharmini* too. Had she not provided an enabling and conducive environment, juggling professional commitments and carving out the time required for translating would have been impossible. यः तया सह स स्वर्गो निरयो यस्त्वया विना (2.27.16).

This translation is based on the Critical Edition brought out (between 1951 and 1975) by the Oriental Institute, now part of Maharaja Sayajirao University, Baroda. When I started work on translating the Mahabharata in 2009, there was a thought, however hazy, of attempting the Valmiki Ramayana too. Therefore, one had to acquire the seven published volumes of the Critical Edition. Those who have tried this acquisition will testify this is no mean task. Multiple channels and multiple efforts failed. The Oriental Institute is not known for its marketing and distribution successes.

The context changed in 2015, because I joined the government. By then, I had still not been able to get copies of the Critical Edition. What with joining the government, which made finding time difficult, and an inability to get the text, I remarked to my wife that destiny willed otherwise. A few months later, on a flight, I found myself seated next to Shailendra Mehta, economist, scholar, friend, and currently president, director and distinguished professor at MICA, Ahmedabad. 'What next, after the Mahabharata?' asked Shailendra and I described my frustration. A few weeks down the line, Shailendra Mehta walked into my office, lugging a trolley bag, with all seven volumes in them. 'All yours,' he said. What destiny willed was clear enough. The dedication of this three volume set to Shailendra is a paltry attempt to say thank you.

'What next, after the Valmiki Ramayana?' Life moves on to the Puranas, beginning with the Bhagavata Purana. At one point, the Mahabharata translation seemed like a mammoth task, stretching to infinity. With the major Puranas collectively amounting to four times the size of the Mahabharata, they are more monumental than the mammoth. But as always, if it so wills, destiny finds a way.

Introduction

The Ramayana and the Mahabharata are known as *itihasa*s. The word itihasa means 'it was indeed like that'. Therefore, the word is best rendered as legend or history, and not as myth. This does not mean everything occurred exactly as described. In a process of telling and retelling and oral transmission, embellishments are inevitable. However, the use of the word itihasa suggests a core element of truth. There were two great dynasties—*surya vamsha* and *chandra vamsha*.[1] The first proper king of the surya vamsha was Ikshvaku and the Ramayana is a chronicle of the solar dynasty, or at least a part of its history. Similarly, the first king of the chandra vamsha was Ila and the Mahabharata is a chronicle of the lunar dynasty. The Puranas also describe the histories of the solar and lunar dynasties. Though there are some inconsistencies across genealogies given in different Puranas, the surya vamsha timeline has three broad segments: (1) from Ikshvaku to Rama; (2) from Kusha to Brihadbala; and (3) from Brihadbala to Sumitra. In that stretch from Ikshvaku to Rama, there were famous kings like Bharata (not to be confused with Rama's brother), Kakutstha, Prithu, Yuvanashva, Mandhata, Trishanku, Harishchandra, Sagara, Dilipa, Bhagiratha, Ambarisha, Raghu, Aja and Dasharatha. These ancestors explain why Rama is referred to as Kakutstha, Raghava or Dasharathi.

Rama had two sons—Lava and Kusha. Ikshvaku and his descendants ruled over the kingdom of Kosala, part of today's Uttar Pradesh. The Kosala kingdom lasted for a long time, with

---

[1] The solar and the lunar dynasty, respectively.

the capital sometimes in Ayodhya and sometimes in Shravasti. When Rama ruled, the capital was in Ayodhya. After Rama, Lava ruled over south Kosala and Kusha ruled over north Kosala. Lava's capital was in Shravasti, while Kusha's capital was in Kushavati. We don't know what happened to Lava thereafter, though he is believed to have established Lavapuri, today's Lahore. The second segment of the surya vamsha timeline, from Kusha to Brihadbala, doesn't have any famous kings. Brihadbala was the last Kosala king. In the Kurukshetra War, he fought on the side of the Kouravas and was killed by Abhimanyu. The third segment of the surya vamsha timeline, from Brihadbala to Sumitra, seems contrived and concocted. Sumitra is described as the last king of the Ikshvaku lineage, defeated by Mahapadma Nanda in 362 BCE. Sumitra wasn't killed. He fled to Rohtas, in today's Bihar.

The Ramayana isn't about these subsequent segments of the timeline. Though there are references to other kings from that Ikshvaku to Rama stretch, it isn't about all of that segment either. Its focus is on Rama. It is difficult to date the poet Kalidasa. It could be anytime from the first century CE to the fifth century CE. Kalidasa wrote a *mahakavya*[2] known as *Raghuvamsha*. As the name of this mahakavya suggests, it is about Raghu's lineage, from Dilipa to Agnivarna, and includes Rama. But it isn't exclusively about Rama. Ramayana is almost exclusively about Rama. That's the reason it is known as रामायण = राम + अयण. अयन means travel or progress. Thus, Ramayana means Rama's progress. There is a minor catch though. अयन means travel or progress and अयण is a meaningless word. The word used in Ramayana is अयण, not अयन. This transformation occurs because of a rule of Sanskrit grammar known as internal *sandhi*. That is the reason रामायन becomes रामायण.

Who is Rama? The word राम means someone who is lovely, charming and delightful. There are Jain and Buddhist versions (*Dasharatha Jataka*) of the Rama account and they differ in significant details from the Ramayana story. For instance, in Jain accounts, Ravana is killed by Lakshmana. In *Dasharatha Jataka*,

[2] Epic.

Sita is Rama's sister. In Ramayana and Purana accounts, Rama is Vishnu's seventh *avatara*.[3] Usually, ten avataras are named for Vishnu, though sometimes, a larger number is also given. When the figure is ten, the avataras are *matsya*,[4] *kurma*,[5] *varaha*,[6] *narasimha*,[7] *vamana*,[8] Parashurama, Rama, Krishna, Buddha and Kalki (Kalki is yet to come). In the cycle of creation and destruction, *yugas*[9] follow each other and one progressively goes down *krita yuga* (alternatively *satya yuga*), *treta yuga*, *dvapara yuga* and *kali yuga*, before the cycle starts again. In the list of ten avataras, matysa, kurma, varaha and narasimha are from the present krita yuga; Vamana, Parashurama and Rama are from the present treta yuga; Krishna is from dvapara yuga; and Buddha and Kalki are from kali yuga. Rama was towards the end of treta yuga. (In the 'Uttara Kanda', dvapara yuga has started.) Just as Krishna's departure marked the transition from dvapara yuga to kali yuga, Rama's departure marked the transition from treta yuga to dvapara yuga.

When did these events occur? It is impossible to answer this question satisfactorily, despite continuous efforts being made to find an answer. At one level, it is an irrelevant question too. There is a difference between an incident happening and it being recorded. In that day and age, recording meant composition and oral transmission, with embellishments added. There was noise associated with transmission and distribution. It is impossible to unbundle the various layers in the text, composed at different points in time. Valmiki is described as Rama's contemporary, just as Vedavyasa was a contemporary of the Kouravas and the Pandavas. But that doesn't mean today's Valmiki Ramayana text is exactly what Valmiki composed, or that today's Mahabharata text

[3] Incarnation, or descent.
[4] Fish.
[5] Turtle.
[6] Boar.
[7] Half-man, half-lion.
[8] Dwarf.
[9] Eras.

is exactly what Krishna Dvaipayana Vedavyasa composed. Therein lies the problem with several approaches to dating.

The first and favoured method of dating is undoubtedly the astronomical one, based on positions of *nakshatra*s and *graha*s,[10] or using information about events like eclipses. However, because layers of the text were composed at different points in time, compounded by precession of the equinoxes, this leads to widely divergent dates for an event like Rama's birth, ranging from 7323 BCE to 1331 BCE. Second, one can work with genealogies, notwithstanding problems of inconsistencies across them. One will then obtain a range of something like 2350 BCE to 1500 BCE. Third, one can work with linguistics and the evolution of language, comparing that of the Ramayana to other texts. Fourth, one can work with the archaeological evidence, such as the pottery discovered in sites known to be associated with the Ramayana. Even then, there will be a wide range of dates, from something like 2600 BCE to 1100 BCE. Fifth, one can consider geography, geology, changes in the course of rivers. Finally, there are traditional views about the length of a *manvantara*[11] or yuga. Given the present state of knowledge, it is impossible to impart precision to any dating of the incidents in the Ramayana. Scholars have grappled with the problem in the past and will continue to do so in the future. This may be an important question. But from the point of view of the present translation, it is an irrelevant one.

The present translation is about the Ramayana text. But what is the Ramayana text? After a famous essay written by A.K. Ramanujan in 1987 (published in 1991), people often mention 300 Ramayanas. It is impossible to fix the number, 300 or otherwise, since it is not possible to count satisfactorily—or even define—what is a new rendering of the Ramayana story, as opposed to a simple retelling, with or without reinterpretation. Contemporary versions, not always in written form, are continuously being rendered. There are versions of the Ramayana story in East Asia (China, Japan),

[10] Constellations/stars and planets.
[11] Lifespan of a Manu.

South-East Asia (many countries like Thailand, Indonesia and Malaysia), South Asia (Nepal, Sri Lanka) and West Asia (Iran). As mentioned earlier, there are Buddhist and Jain versions. Every state and every language in India seems to have some version of the Rama story. Our impressions about the Rama story are often based on such regional versions, such as, the sixteenth-century *Ramcharitmanas* by Goswami Tulsidas. (Many of these were written between the twelfth and seventeenth centuries CE.) Those depictions can, and will, vary with what is in this translation. This translation is about the Sanskrit Ramayana. But even there, more than one text of the Sanskrit Ramayana exists—Valmiki Ramayana, Yoga Vasishtha Ramayana, Ananda Ramayana and Adbhuta Ramayana. In addition, there are versions of the Ramayana story in the Mahabharata and in the Puranas. With the exception of the Ramayana story in the Mahabharata, the Valmiki Ramayana is clearly the oldest among these. This is a translation of the Valmiki Ramayana and yes, there are differences between depictions in the Valmiki Ramayana and other Sanskrit renderings of the Rama story.

If one cannot date the incidents of the Ramayana, can one at least conclusively date when the Valmiki Ramayana was written? Because of the many layers and subsequent interpolations, there is no satisfactory resolution to this problem either. The Valmiki Ramayana has around 24,000 *shloka*s, a shloka being a verse. The Mahabharata is believed to have 100,000 shlokas, so the Valmiki Ramayana is about one-fourth the size of the Mahabharata. These 24,000 shlokas are distributed across seven *kanda*s—'Bala Kanda' (Book about Youth), 'Ayodhya Kanda' (Book about Ayodhya), 'Aranya Kanda' (Book of the Forest), Kishkindha Kanda (Book about Kishkindha), 'Sundara Kanda' (Book of Beauty), 'Yuddha Kanda' (Book about the War) and 'Uttara Kanda' (Book about the Sequel). Kanda refers to a major section or segment and is sometimes translated into English as Canto. 'Canto' sounds archaic, 'Book' is so much better. This does not mean the kanda-wise classification always existed. For all one knows, initially, there were simply chapters. In this text itself, there is a reference to the Valmiki Ramayana possessing 500 *sarga*s. The

word sarga also means Book, but given the number 500, is more
like a chapter. (For the record, the text has more than 600 chapters.)
Most scholars agree 'Uttara Kanda' was written much later. If one
reads the 'Uttara Kanda', that belief is instantly endorsed. The 'Uttara
Kanda' doesn't belong. This isn't only because of the content, which
is invariably mentioned. It is also because of the texture of the text,
the quality of the poetry. It is vastly inferior. To a lesser extent, one
can also advance similar arguments for the 'Bala Kanda'. Therefore,
the earlier portions were probably composed around 500 BCE. The
later sections, like the 'Uttara Kanda', and parts of the 'Bala Kanda',
were probably composed around 500 CE. It isn't the case that all later
sections are in 'Uttara Kanda'.

There is a mix of earlier and later sections across all kandas.
The word kanda also means trunk or branch of a tree. The
Mahabharata is also classified into such major sections or Books.
However, in the Mahabharata, these major sections are known as
parvas. The word parva also means branch. However, parva suggests
a smaller branch, one that is more flexible. Kanda suggests one that
is more solid, less flexible. There may have been slight variations
in shlokas across different versions of the Sanskrit Mahabharata,
but fundamentally the Sanskrit Mahabharata is a single text. The
original text expanded, like a holdall, to include everything. Those
different versions have been 'unified' in a Critical Edition published
by the Bhandarkar Oriental Research Institute, Poona (Pune). In the
case of the Valmiki Ramayana, with its kanda-kind of classification,
the evolution seems to have been different. If someone was unhappy
with what Valmiki had depicted, he simply composed another
Ramayana. In Sanskrit, mention has already been made of the Yoga
Vasishtha Ramayana, Ananda Ramayana and Adbhuta Ramayana.
This continued to happen with vernacular versions.

This translation is of the Valmiki Ramayana. It is necessary to
stress this point. Both the Ramayana and the Mahabharata are so
popular that one is familiar with people, stories and incidents. That
doesn't necessarily mean those people, stories and incidents occur in
the Valmiki Ramayana in the way we are familiar with them. Just
as the Bhandarkar Oriental Research Institute produced a Critical

Edition of the Mahabharata, between 1951 and 1975, the Oriental Institute, Baroda, produced a Critical Edition of the Valmiki Ramayana. This translation is based on that Critical Edition, published sequentially between 1958 and 1975. Producing a Critical Edition meant sifting through a large number of manuscripts of the Valmiki Ramayana. The editors had around 2000 manuscripts to work with. Not all of these were equally reliable. Therefore, in practice, they worked with fifty to hundred manuscripts, the specific number depending on the kanda in question. It is not that there were significant differences across the manuscripts and broadly, there was a Southern Recension (version) and a Northern one, the latter sub-divided into a North-Western and a North-Eastern one. The earliest of these written manuscripts dates to the eleventh century CE. In passing, the language may have been Sanskrit, but the script wasn't always Devanagari. There were scripts like Sharada, Mewari, Maithili, Bengali, Telugu, Kannada, Nandinagari, Grantha and Malayalam. Since this translation is based on the Baroda Critical Edition, it is necessary to make another obvious point. Even within the Sanskrit Valmiki Ramayana, not everything we are familiar with is included in the Critical text. For instance, the configuration of nakshatras and planets at the time of Rama's birth is not part of the Critical text. Nor is the bulk of one of the most beautiful sections of the Valmiki Ramayana, Mandodari's lamentation. Those are shlokas that have been excised. That's also the case with a shloka that's often quoted as an illustration of Lakshmana's conduct. नाहं जानामि केयूरं नाहं जानामि कुण्डलं। नूपुरं तु अभिजानामि नित्यं पादाभिवन्दनात॥ This is a statement by Lakshmana to the effect that he cannot recognize the ornament on Sita's head or her earrings. Since he has always served at her feet, he can only recognize her anklets. This too has been excised. There are instances where such excision has led to a break in continuity and inconsistency and we have pointed them out in the footnotes.

There are two numbers associated with every chapter. The first number refers to the kanda, while the second number, within brackets, refers to the number of the chapter (sarga) within that kanda. Thus, Chapter 1(33) will mean the thirty-third chapter in

'Bala Kanda'. The table below shows the number of chapters and shlokas we have in the Critical Edition. The Critical text has 606 chapters, 106 more than the 500 sargas mentioned in the text itself. And there are 18,670 shlokas. If one considers chapters and shlokas from non-Critical versions, irrespective of which version it is, there are almost 650 chapters and just over 24,000 shlokas. Compared to such non-Critical versions, very few chapters have been excised from 'Bala', 'Ayodhya', 'Aranya', 'Kishkindha' or 'Sundara' kandas. The excision is primarily from 'Yuddha' and 'Uttara' kandas. The excision of shlokas is uniformly spread throughout the kandas, though most excision, relatively speaking, is from the 'Ayodhya', 'Yuddha' and 'Uttara' kandas.

Name of kanda	Number of chapters	Number of shlokas
Bala Kanda	76	1941
Ayodhya Kanda	111	3160
Aranya Kanda	71	2060
Kishkindha Kanda	66	1898
Sundara Kanda	66	2487
Yuddha Kanda	116	4435
Uttara Kanda	100	2689
Total	606	18,670

Valmiki is the first poet, *adi kavi*. By the time of classical Sanskrit literature, some prerequisites were defined for a work to attain the status of mahakavya. Kalidasa, Bharavi, Magha, Shri Harsha and Bhatti composed such works. Though these notions and definitions came later, the Valmiki Ramayana displays every characteristic of a mahakavya and is longer than any of these subsequent works. The story of how it came about is known to most people who are familiar with the Ramayana. The sage Valmiki had gone, with his disciple Bharadvaja, to bathe in the waters of the River Tamasa. There was a couple of *krouncha*[12] birds there, in the act of making

[12] Curlew.

love. Along came a hunter[13] and killed the male bird. As the female
bird grieved, Valmiki was driven by compassion and the first shloka
emerged from his lips. Since it was composed in an act of sorrow—
shoka—this kind of composition came to be known as shloka. So
the Ramayana tells us. Incidentally, this first shloka doesn't occur in
the first chapter. It isn't the first shloka of the Valmiki Ramayana.
The incident and the shloka occur in the second chapter. More
specifically, it is the fourteenth shloka in the second chapter and is
as follows. मा निषाद प्रतिष्ठां त्वमगमः शाश्वतीः समाः। यत्क्रौंचमिथुनादेकमवधी
काममोहितम् ॥ 'O nishada! This couple of curlews was in the throes of
passion and you killed one of them. Therefore, you will possess ill
repute for an eternal number of years.'

Till a certain period of history, all Sanskrit works were in poetry
or verse, not in prose. The Vedangas are limbs or auxiliaries and
the six Vedangas are shiksha,[14] chhanda,[15] vyakarana,[16] nirukta,[17]
jyotisha[18] and kalpa.[19] These are needed to understand not just the
Vedas, but also Sanskrit works. Chhanda is one of these. Chhanda
can be translated as metre and means something that is pleasing
and delightful. Chhanda shastra is the study of metres or prosody.
Sanskrit poetry wasn't about what we tend to identify as poetry
today, the act of rhyming. Chhanda begins with the concept of
akshara, akin to, but not exactly identical with, the English concept
of syllable, that is, part of a word with a single vowel sound. Other
than possessing a single vowel sound, an akshara must not begin
with a vowel. Aksharas can be hrasva or laghu—light or L—and
guru—heavy or G. Simply stated, with a short vowel, the akshara is
L and with a long vowel, the akshara is G. There are some additional
conditions, but we needn't get into those. Every verse consists of
four padas, the word pada meaning one quarter. Depending on how

[13] Nishada.
[14] Articulation and pronunciation.
[15] Prosody.
[16] Grammar.
[17] Etymology.
[18] Astronomy.
[19] Rituals.

many aksharas there are in a pada and the distribution of those
aksharas into L and G, there were a variety of metres. Depending
on the subject and the mood, the poet consciously chose a metre.
Analysing in this way, there were more than 1300 different metres.
One of the most popular was *anushtubh*. This figures prominently
in the Valmiki Ramayana, the Mahabharata and the Puranas. The
anushtubh structure meant eight aksharas in each pada, with a total
of thirty-two aksharas. In addition, for anushtubh, in every pada,
the fifth akshara would have to be L and the sixth akshara would
have to be G. In classical Sanskrit literature, conditions were also
applied to the seventh akshara, but such refinements came later. For
that first verse, the decomposition runs as follows: (1) L L L G L G
L G; (2) L G L G L G L G; (3) L L G G L G G L; (4) G G L L L G
G L. (1) *ma ni sha da pra tish tham*; (2) *tva ma ga mah shash vati sa
mah*; (3) *yat kroun cha mi thu na de ka*; (4) *ma va dhi ka ma mo hi
tam*. It is not that Valmiki only used anushtubh. There are actually
sixteen different metres in the Valmiki Ramayana.

It is impossible to capture the beauty of chhanda in an English
translation. One can attempt to do a translation in verse, but it will
fail to convey the beauty. If the original text is poetry, one starts with
an initial question. Should one attempt a translation in verse or in
prose? This translation is based on the premise that the translation
should be as close as possible to the original Sanskrit text. One
should not take liberties with the text. This translation is therefore
almost a word-to-word rendering. If one sits down with the original
Sanskrit, there will be almost a perfect match. In the process,
deliberately so, the English is not as smooth as it might have been,
had one taken more liberties, and this is a conscious decision. Had
one attempted a translation in verse, one would perforce have had
to take more liberties. Hence, the choice of prose is also a deliberate
decision. As composers, there is quite a contrast between Valmiki
and Vedavyasa. Vedavyasa focuses on people and incidents. Rarely
does the Mahabharata attempt to describe nature, even if those
sections are on geography. In contrast, Valmiki's descriptions of
nature are lyrical and superlative, similar to Kalidasa. A translation
can never hope to transmit that flavour. There is no substitute to

reading the original Sanskrit, more so for the Valmiki Ramayana than for the Mahabharata.

Which occurred earlier, the incidents of the Ramayana or the Mahabharata? Which was composed earlier, the Ramayana or the Mahabharata? The Ramayana incidents occurred in treta yuga, the Mahabharata incidents in dvapara yuga. Rama was an earlier avatara, Krishna a later one. Hence, the obvious deduction is that the Ramayana incidents predated those of the Mahabharata—an inference also bolstered by the genealogy and astrological arguments mentioned earlier. However, and not just for the sake of being perverse, consider the following. Geographically, the incidents of the Mahabharata mostly occur along an east–west axis, along either side of what used to be called Uttarapath, the northern road, more familiar as Grand Trunk Road or National Highway (NH) 1 and 2. The incidents of the Ramayana often occur along a north–south axis, along what used to be called Dakshinapath, the southern road. Sanjeev Sanyal[20] has made the point that while Uttarapath remained stable over time, the Dakshinapath during Rama's time was different from the subsequent Dakshinapath, with the latter more like today's NH 44. To return to the point, the geographical terrain of the Mahabharata was restricted to the northern parts of the country, with the south rarely mentioned. The Aryan invasion theory has been discredited because of a multitude of reasons, but myths and perceptions that have lasted for decades are difficult to dispel. However, regardless of the Aryan invasion theory, the Ramayana reveals a familiarity with the geography of the southern parts of the country that the Mahabharata does not. The fighting in the Mahabharata, in the Kurukshetra War, is cruder and less refined. In the Ramayana, bears and apes may have fought using trees and boulders, but humans did not. A human did not tear apart another human's chest and drink blood. The urbanization depicted in the Ramayana is rarely found in the Mahabharata. We have cited these counter-arguments to make a simple point. Which incident

[20] *Land of the Seven Rivers: A Brief History of India's Geography,* Sanjeev Sanyal, Penguin, 2012.

occurred earlier and which text was composed earlier are distinct questions. They should not be confused. Even if the Ramayana incidents occurred before the incidents of the Mahabharata, that doesn't automatically mean the Ramayana was composed before the Mahabharata. The Rama story occurs in the Mahabharata, known as the 'Ramopakhyana' section. There is no such reference to the Mahabharata incidents in the Ramayana. This is the main reason for arguing that the Ramayana was composed before the Mahabharata.

The relationship between the 'Ramopakhyana' and the Valmiki Ramayana is also of scholarly interest. Which was earlier? Did one borrow from the other, or did both have a common origin? That need not concern us. What should be stressed is the obvious—the Valmiki Ramayana wasn't composed at a single point in time and there is a difference between the original composition and the present text, as given to us say in the Critical Edition. If bears and apes fought with the help of trees and boulders, and Angada suddenly kills someone with a weapon, that part is probably a later composition, with the composer having deviated from the original template. If a verse is in anushtubh, but deviates from the L–G pattern, this may have been a conscious decision, but in all probability, reflects the inferior skills of a subsequent poet. If we take the Critical text as it stands, while there are no direct references to the incidents of the Mahabharata, there are plenty of indirect allusions. There are shlokas reminiscent of the Bhagavatgita. When Bharata comes to Rama to inform him about Dasharatha's death, Rama asks him about the welfare of the kingdom, reminiscent of similar questions asked by Narada to Yudhishthira. In the Valmiki Ramayana, there are references to kings of the lunar dynasty (Yayati) and incidents (Ilvala and Vatapi) that are only described in the Mahabharata. The evidence may be circumstantial and speculative, but it is the following. It is as if the later composers knew about the Mahabharata incidents and the text, but consciously avoided any direct references.

Why is another translation of the Valmiki Ramayana needed? Surely, there are plenty floating around. That's not quite true. Indeed, there are several translations of the Valmiki Ramayana, including some recent ones, but they are abridged. In any act of abridgement, some sections are omitted or summarized. Abridged translations, no matter how good they are, are not quite a substitute for unabridged translations, which bring in the nuances too. To the best of my knowledge, the list of unabridged translations of the Valmiki Ramayana is the following: (1) Ralph T.H. Griffith;[21] (2) Manmatha Nath Dutt;[22] (3) Hari Prasad Shastri;[23] (4) Desiraju Hanumanta Rao and K.M.K. Murthy;[24] and (5) Robert P. Goldman.[25] Given the timelines, the Goldman translation is the only one based on the Critical Edition. Having translated the Mahabharata,[26] it was natural to translate the Valmiki Ramayana. The intention was to do a translation that was popular in style. That meant a conscious decision to avoid the use of diacritical marks, as would have been the case had one used IAST (International Alphabet of Sanskrit Transliteration). If diacritical marks are not going to be used, there may be problems rendering names, proper and geographic. We have sought to make the English renderings as phonetic as is possible. Thus, we use 'Goutama' to refer to the sage of that name—although others have often referred to him elsewhere as 'Gautama'. We have chosen Goutama on the logic that if Gomati is not Gamati, why should Goutama be rendered as Gautama? There remains the question of what one does with vowel sounds. How does one differentiate the short sound from the long? Should Rama be written as Raama and Sita as Seeta? That seemed to be too artificial and contrary to popular usage. On rare occasions, this does

---

[21] *The Ramayana of Valmiki, translated into English verse*, Ralph T.H. Griffith, E.Z. Lazarus and Company, London, 1895.

[22] *Valmiki Ramayana*, Manmatha Nath Dutt, R.K. Bhatia, Calcutta, 1891–92. Manmatha Nath Dutt (Shastri) was one of India's greatest translators (in English). He also translated the Mahabharata and several Puranas.

[23] *The Ramayana of Valmiki*, Hari Prasad Shastri, Shanti Sadan, London, 1952.

[24] This is net based, on the site http://www.valmikiramayan.net/ and leaves out 'Uttara Kanda'.

[25] *The Ramayana of Valmiki: An Epic of Ancient India*, Robert P. Goldman, Princeton University Press, 1984 to 2016.

[26] *The Mahabharata*, Bibek Debroy, Penguin (India), 10 volumes, 2010–2014, boxed set 2015.

cause a problem, with a danger of confusion between the ape Taara and his daughter Taaraa, Vali's wife. Such occasions are however rare and we have explained them. However, there are also instances where we have deviated from popular usage. Hanumat is a case in point, where Hanuman seemed to be too contrary to grammatical principles. There are some words that defy translation, *dharma* is an example. Hence, we have not even tried to translate such words. The Goldman translation is academic in style. This translation's style is more popular. Therefore, there is no attempt to overburden the reader with extensive notes. However, a straight translation may not be self-explanatory. Hence, we have put in footnotes, just enough to explain, without stretching the translation.

As with the Mahabharata, the Valmiki Ramayana is a text about dharma. Dharma means several different things—the dharma of the four *varna*s and the four *ashrama*s, the classes and stages of life; the governance template of *raja dharma*, the duty of kings; principles of good conduct, *sadachara*; and the pursuit of objectives of human existence, *purushartha*—dharma, *artha* and *kama*. As with the Mahabharata, the Valmiki Ramayana is a *smriti* text. It has a human origin and composer, it is not a *shruti* text. Smriti texts are society and context specific. We should not try to judge and evaluate individuals and actions on the basis of today's value judgements. In addition, if the span of composition was one thousand years, from 500 BCE to 500 CE, those value judgements also change. The later composers and interpreters may have had problems with what the earlier composers authored. A case in point is when Sita is being abducted by Ravana. At a certain point in time, men and women universally wore an upper garment and a lower one. When she is being abducted through the sky, Sita casts aside and throws down not just her ornaments, but her upper garment too. As this translation will illustrate, this caused problems for subsequent composers and interpreters.

To return to the notion of dharma—transcending all those collective templates of dharma—there is one that is individual in nature. Regardless of those collective templates, an individual has to decide what the right course of action is and there is no universal answer as to what is right and what is wrong. There are always contrary pulls of dharma, with two notions of dharma pulling in different directions. It is not immediately obvious which is superior. Given the trade-offs, an individual makes a choice and suffers the consequences. Why is there an impression that these individual conflicts of dharma are more manifest in the Mahabharata than in the Ramayana?

The answer probably lies in the nature of these two texts. What is the difference between a novel and a long story, even when both have multiple protagonists? The difference between a novel and a long story is probably not one of length. A novel seeks to present the views of all protagonists. Thus, the Mahabharata is a bit like a novel, in so far as that trait is concerned. A long story does not seek to look at incidents and actions from the point of view of every protagonist. It is concerned with the perspective of one primary character, to the exclusion of others.

If this distinction is accepted, the Valmiki Ramayana has the characteristics of a long story. It is Ramayana. Therefore, it is primarily from Rama's point of view. We aren't told what Bharata or Lakshmana thought, or for that matter, Urmila, Mandavi or Shrutakirti. There is little that is from Sita's point of view too. That leads to the impression that the Mahabharata contains more about individual conflicts of dharma. For the Valmiki Ramayana, from Rama's point of view, the conflicts of dharma aren't innumerable. On that exile to the forest, why did he take Sita and Lakshmana along with him? Was Shurpanakha's disfigurement warranted? Why did he unfairly kill Vali? Why did he make Sita go through tests of purity, not once, but twice? Why did he unfairly kill Shambuka? Why did he banish Lakshmana? At one level, one can argue these are decisions by a personified divinity and therefore, mere humans cannot comprehend and judge the motives. At another level, the unhappiness with Rama's decisions led to the composition of alternative versions of the Ramayana. Note that Sita's questions about dharma remained unanswered. If you are going to the forest as an ascetic, why have you got weapons with you? If the *rakshasas*[27]

---

[27] Demons.

are causing injuries to hermits, punishing the rakshasas is Bharata's job, now that he is the king. Why are you dabbling in this? Note also Rama's justification at the time of Sita's first test. It wasn't about what others would think, that justification came later. The initial harsh words reflected his own questions about Sita's purity. Thus, Rama's conflicts over dharma also exist. It is just that in the Valmiki Ramayana, it is about one individual alone.

In conclusion, this translation is an attempt to get readers interested in reading the unabridged Valmiki Ramayana. Having read abridged versions, and there is no competition with those, to appreciate the nuances better, one should read the unabridged. And, to appreciate the beauty of the poetry, one should then be motivated to read the text in Sanskrit. A translation is only a bridge and an unsatisfactory one at that.

CHAPTER SIX

Yuddha Kanda

Chapter 6(1)

Hanumat spoke those words in a proper way. Hearing them, Rama was filled with delight and replied in the following words. 'O Hanumat! You have performed a great task that is extremely difficult to accomplish. There is no other person on earth who is capable of doing this, not even in his mind. I do not see anyone other than Garuda, Vayu and Hanumat who can cross the great ocean. The city of Lanka is protected extremely well by Ravana, and the gods, the *danavas*,[1] the *yakshas*,[2] the *gandharvas*,[3] the serpents and the *rakshasas*[4] find it impossible to penetrate it. Even if someone enters, how can he emerge with his own life? It is unassailable and is protected extremely well by the rakshasas. Other than someone who possesses a valour and strength that is equal to Hanumat's, who is capable of doing this? Hanumat has performed a great act of service for Sugriva. He has exhibited a strength and valour that is worthy of him. A person who is engaged as a servant and lovingly performs an extremely difficult task for his master, is said to be superior among men. If a capable person is engaged in a royal task and does not perform it attentively, he is said to be worst among men. Hanumat has accomplished the task he was appointed to do. He has satisfied Sugriva and has not diminished his own self. Through obtaining sight of Vaidehi, I, the lineage of Raghu, and the immensely strong Lakshmana have been protected, in accordance with *dharma*. However, my mind is still distressed and I am suffering. He has performed a good deed for me and I am unable to perform an equally good deed in return. But let me embrace Hanumat, who is everything to me. At the present time, that is all I can do for the great-souled one. The task of searching out Sita's trail has been accomplished in every possible way. But when I think of the ocean, my mind is distressed yet again. How can

[1] Demons.
[2] Yakshas are semi-divine species, described as companions of Kubera, the lord of riches.
[3] Semi-divine species, companions of Kubera, celestial musicians.
[4] Demons.

one cross to the other shore of this ocean, the great store of water? How will these attentive apes cross over to the southern shore? I have heard the account about Vaidehi. How will the apes now cross over to the other shore of the ocean?' Apprehensive and grieving, the mighty-armed Rama, the destroyer of enemies, told Hanumat this and became immersed in thought.

Chapter 6(2)

Rama, Dasharatha's handsome son, was filled with grief. To dispel his sorrow, Sugriva addressed him in these words. 'O brave one! Why are you tormented, like an ordinary person? Like an ungrateful person abandons friendship, give up this torment. O Raghava! I do not see any reason for this torment now. After all, we have got to know where the enemy resides. O Raghava! You are persevering, knowledgeable about the sacred texts, wise and learned. Discard this ordinary sentiment, like a person with a cleansed soul gives up what destroys the objective. We will cross the ocean, populated by large crocodiles. We will invade Lanka and slay your enemy. If a person is distressed and without enterprise, with his soul enveloped in sorrow, all his objectives suffer and he faces a hardship. In every way, all these leaders of the apes are brave and capable. They are full of enterprise. For your sake, they will even enter a fire. I can discern this through their delight, and reasoning adds firm conviction to this. You must use your valour to get Sita back and slay the enemy. We will construct a bridge and see that city. O Raghava! You must act in this way towards the king of the rakshasas. You will see the city of Lanka, located on the summit of Trikuta. When you see him, you must certainly kill Ravana in the encounter. When a bridge is constructed over the ocean and all our soldiers reach Lanka, it is certain that they will be victorious. In a battle, these brave apes can assume any form at will. O king! Therefore, get rid of this confused intelligence that destroys all objectives. In this world of men, sorrow destroys all valour. If a man valiantly engages in a task, capability will follow. O immensely wise one! At this time, resort to spirit and energy. Even for brave and great-souled people like you, sorrow over something lost or destroyed renders all objectives unsuccessful. You are best among intelligent ones. You are skilled in the teachings of all the sacred texts. With advisers like me, you are certain to vanquish the enemy. O Raghava! When you wield your bow, I do not see anyone in the three worlds who can stand before you in a battle. The task that you have entrusted to the apes will not suffer. You will soon cross over the eternal ocean and see Sita. O lord of the earth! Therefore, enough of resorting to grief. Resort to anger. *Kshatriyas* who do not make efforts are wicked. All of them are terrified of terrible ones. Use your subtle intelligence and, together with us, think about how the terrible ocean, the lord of the rivers, can be crossed. These apes are brave in battle and can assume any form at will. They will shower down rocks and trees and destroy their enemies. Through some means, we will cross over Varuna's abode. What is the need to speak a lot? In every possible way, you will be victorious.'

Chapter 6(3)

Sugriva's words were full of great meaning and reasoning. Kakutstha accepted them and told Hanumat, 'In every possible way, I am extremely competent to cross over the ocean, quickly building a bridge over the ocean, or drying it up. How many impenetrable forts exist in Lanka? Tell me that. O ape! I wish to know everything about them, as if I have seen them myself. You have comfortably seen, exactly as it exists, the size of the army, the gates, forts and arrangements, the preparations made for guarding and the residences of the rakshasas in Lanka. Tell me the truth about all this. You are accomplished in every possible way.'

Hanumat, the son of the wind god, was best among those who were accomplished in the use of words. Hearing Rama's words, he again addressed him in these words. 'Listen to everything—the forts, the preparations, the arrangements, the manner in which the city of Lanka is guarded and the soldiers. Lanka is supremely prosperous and the ocean is terrible. The large number of soldiers are divided into formations and the mounts have been instructed. Lanka is happy and full of joy. It is full of crazy elephants. It is full of large chariots and large numbers of rakshasas. The firm gates are closed and sealed with large beams. There are large gates and four extremely large ones. There are large and extremely strong machines.[5] When enemy soldiers arrive, they are rebuffed by these. Large numbers of brave rakshasas have fashioned hundreds of terrible *shataghni*s[6] and the gates are protected exceedingly well with these. They are sharp and made out of black iron. There is a giant rampart made out of gold and it is extremely difficult to penetrate. At intervals, this is decorated with gems, coral, lapis lazuli and pearls. There are extremely terrible moats everywhere. These are fathomless and are filled with extremely auspicious and cool water. They are also filled with crocodiles and fish. Along the gates, there are four extensive drawbridges. These have firm fortifications and many machines are placed atop these. In every direction, the moats are covered with machines. When invading enemy soldiers escape, these are used to fling them away. One of these drawbridges is strong and cannot be shaken. It is extremely firm. It is decorated with many golden pillars and platforms. O Rama! Ravana is naturally inclined to fight. He is ready and not distracted. He is powerful and ready to command. The city of Lanka is like a fort of the gods and is impregnable. It generates fear. It has four kinds of fortifications—water, mountains, forests and artificial ones. O Raghava! It is located on the distant other shore of the ocean. There is no approach in any direction and it cannot be reached by a boat either. The fortification has been constructed on the summit of a mountain and it is like a fortification of the gods. Lanka is extremely difficult to conquer and is full of horses and elephants. There are trenches, shataghnis and many kinds of machines. The city of Lanka, which belongs to the evil-

---

[5] Like catapults.
[6] A shataghni is a weapon that can kill one hundred at one stroke.

souled Ravana, is radiant. There are ten thousand rakshasas along
the western gate. All those unassailable ones wield spears in their
hands. They are the best among warriors who fight with swords.
There are one hundred thousand rakshasas along the southern gate.
Those excellent warriors possess four kinds of forces.[7] There are
one million[8] rakshasas along the eastern gate. All of them are skilled
in the use of all weapons and wield swords and shields. There are
one hundred million rakshasas along the northern gate. They are
extremely revered and are the sons of noble lineages. They are on
chariots, or have horses as their mounts. There are hundreds of
thousands in battle formations in the middle. There are more than
one crore rakshasas, *yatudhanas*[9] who are invincible. I shattered
the drawbridges and filled up the moats. I burnt the city of Lanka
and demolished the ramparts. Through whatever means possible,
we must cross Varuna's abode. Once that is done, it is certain that
the apes will destroy the city of Lanka. With Angada, Dvivida,
Mainda, Jambavat, Panasa, Nala and the commander Nila, why
will you need the rest of the army? We will leap and go to Ravana's
great city. We will destroy the ramparts and residences and bring
Maithilee back. Therefore, quickly command all the forces to be
gathered. We will be delighted to leave in a short while.'

Chapter 6(4)

In due order, Hanumat described it, exactly as it was. Hearing his
words, the immensely energetic Rama, with truth as his valour,
said, 'You have described the city of Lanka, belonging to the terrible
rakshasas. I am telling you truthfully that I will quickly destroy it. O
Sugriva! The idea of leaving immediately appeals to me. The sun has
reached midday and this is an auspicious moment for victory. The

[7] Chariots, horses, elephants and foot soldiers.
[8] *Ayuta* is ten thousand, *niyuta* is one hundred thousand, *prayuta* is one million and
arbuda is one hundred million.
[9] A yatudhana is an evil spirit or demon.

nakshatra[10] is Uttara Phalguni today and tomorrow, there will be a conjunction with Hasta. O Sugriva! Surrounded by all the soldiers, let us leave. Auspicious portents are manifesting themselves before me. I will slay Ravana and bring back Sita Janakee. This upper eyelid of mine is twitching. It seems to be telling me that my desire of obtaining victory will be fulfilled. Examining the path, let Nila proceed ahead of the army. Let him be surrounded by one hundred thousand spirited apes. O Nila! O commander! Quickly lead the army along a path that is full of honey, with roots, fruits, cool groves and water. You must always be ready to protect yourself against the rakshasas. Along the path, those evil-souled ones will seek to destroy the roots, fruits and water. Let the residents of the forest leap into low grounds, fortifications in the forests, and forests to check if the soldiers of the enemy are hidden there. Let immensely strong ones be ahead of the terrible army, which will have the complexion of waves in the ocean. Let it be led by hundreds and thousands of lions among apes. Gaja is like a mountain. Gavaya is immensely strong. Let them and Gavaksha proceed in front, like proud bulls in front of a herd of cows. As the army of apes advances, let the ape Rishabha, bull among apes and a lord of the apes, protect the right flank. Gandhamadana is as spirited and invincible as an elephant in musth. As the army of the apes advances, let him be stationed along the left flank. I will proceed in the middle of the army, delighting the flood of soldiers. I will be astride Hanumat, like the lord[11] on Airavata. Let Lakshmana, who is like Death, be astride Angada, like the lord of creatures and the lord of riches astride Sarvabhouma.[12] Jambavat, the great spirited lord of the bears, Sushena and the ape named Vegadarshi—let these three protect the rear.' Hearing Raghava's words, Sugriva, the lord of the army and the immensely brave bull among apes, commanded the apes.

Desiring to fight, all the large numbers of apes leapt up. They quickly jumped from the caves and the summits. Rama, with dharma in his soul, and Lakshmana were worshipped by the king of the apes

---

[10] There are twenty-seven nakshatras, which are stars/constellations.

[11] Indra.

[12] The comparison is with Kubera, Kubera's elephant being named Sarvabhouma.

and proceeded in a southern direction, with the soldiers. As they
proceeded, they were surrounded by hundreds, tens of thousands,
hundreds of thousands and crores of apes that possessed the
complexion of elephants. The large army of apes followed them. All
of them were protected by Sugriva and were delighted and happy.
Those apes jumped, leapt and roared. They sported and played
on musical instruments, proceeding southwards. They devoured
extremely fragrant honey and fruits. They carried large trees that
were full of many clusters of flowers and buds. Proud, they suddenly
carried each other and flung each other down. They leapt down and
leapt up. Others flung down others. In Raghava's presence, the apes
roared, 'Ravana and all the roamers in the night deserve to be killed
by us.' With many apes, Rishabha, the brave Nila and Kumuda
cleared the path in front. King Sugriva, Rama and Lakshmana were
in the middle. Those destroyers of enemies were surrounded by many
strong and terrible ones. The brave ape, Shatabali, was surrounded
by tens of crores. Single-handedly, he protected the entire army of
apes. Surrounded by one hundred crores, Kesari, Panasa, Gaja and
the extremely strong Arka protected one flank. With Sugriva in the
front, Sushena and Jambavat, surrounded by many bears, protected
the rear. The brave Nila, the commander, was a bull among apes.
He was best among those who could leap, and protected the army.
Darimukha, Prajangha, Jambha and the ape Rabhasa proceeded,
urging the brave apes on all sides to hurry. In this way, proud of
their strength, the tigers among apes proceeded. They saw Sahya,
best among mountains and full of trees and creepers. That large and
terrible army of apes was like waves in the ocean. They marched
with a great roar, like the terrible force of the ocean. Those brave
elephants among apes were alongside Dasharatha's son. Swiftly,
all of them leapt forward, like well-trained horses when they are
goaded. Borne aloft by those two apes,[13] those two bulls among
men were radiant. They were like the moon and the sun, when they
touch the two large planets.[14]

[13] Hanumat and Angada.
[14] Jupiter and Venus.

The learned and talented Lakshmana, astride Angada, addressed Rama in auspicious words that were full of meaning. 'We will swiftly kill Ravana and get back Vaidehi, who has been abducted. Successful in your objective, you will return to Ayodhya, which is full of prosperity. O Raghava! I can see great portents in the sky and on the ground. I see all these auspicious omens, indicating success in your objective. An auspicious and favourable wind is blowing, gentle, beneficial and pleasing to the soldiers. The animals and birds are speaking in full and gentle tones. All the directions are clear and the sun is sparkling. Ushanas,[15] descended from Bhrigu, is following you, with a pleasing light. The sacred and supreme *rishi*s, born in a pure way from Brahma, are all circling around Dhruva, manifesting their rays.[16] The royal sage Trishanku, our supreme and great-souled grandfather from the lineage of the Ikshvakus is radiant and sparkling, with his priest.[17] The nakshatra Vishakha is sparkling, without anything to mar it. This is the supreme nakshatra for the great-souled Ikshvakus. The terrible nakshatra of the *nairittas*[18] is suffering. This is Mula and its foundation has been touched and is suffering from a comet. All this has presented itself for the destruction of the rakshasas. It is time and, suffering from the planet,[19] it is as if their nakshatra has been seized by death. The tasty waters are pleasant and the forests are full of fruit. An extremely fragrant breeze is blowing. There are seasonal flowers on the trees. O lord! Arrayed in battle formations, the soldiers of the apes seem to be even more resplendent. They are like the soldiers of the gods at the time of

[15] Meaning Shukra (Venus).

[16] The *saptarshi*s are the seven great sages. The list varies, but the standard one is Marichi, Atri, Angira, Pulastya, Pulaha, Kratu and Vasishtha. In the sky, the saptarshis are identified with the constellation of Ursa Major (Great Bear). The saptarshis were Brahma's mental sons. Dhruva is the Pole Star.

[17] Trishanku was born in the solar dynasty and his priest (Vishvamitra) gave him the boon that he would be in the sky, after Trishanku started to fall down from heaven. Astronomically, Trishanku is identified as the Southern Cross. Depending on the location in India, this can usually be seen on the southern horizon between April and June.

[18] Demons.

[19] This means the comet.

the *tarakamaya* battle.[20] O noble one! Look at all this. You should be delighted.' Happy, Soumitri spoke to his brother, comforting him in this way.

The giant army proceeded, covering the entire earth. It was full of tigers among bears and apes, using nails and teeth as weapons. With the tips of their hands and the tips of their feet, the apes raised a terrible dust that entered inside the world and took away the sun's radiance. Through night and day, the great army of apes marched. Protected by Sugriva, the soldiers were happy and cheerful. All the spirited apes marched, delighted at the prospect of war. Desiring to free Sita, they did not tarry even for an instant. They reached Mount Sahya and Mount Malaya, full of trees and populated by many animals. There were wonderful groves, rivers and waterfalls. Rama also went and saw Sahya and Malaya. The apes enjoyed themselves, among the *champaka*, *tilaka*, mango, *ashoka*, *sinduvaraka*,[21] *karavira* and *timisha* trees. Intoxicated in their strength, the apes enjoyed fruits that tasted like *amrita*, roots and flowers from the trees. Cheerfully, honey-brown in complexion, they drank honey from long honeycombs that were one *drona*[22] in size and proceeded. They broke the trees and pulled out the creepers. As they proceeded, the bulls among apes flung away excellent boulders. Insolent because of the honey, some apes roared among the trees. Some reached out to the trees. Others leapt down. The entire earth was full with those bulls among apes, just as when the earth is full of ripened paddy.

The lotus-eyed Rama reached Mahendra. The mighty-armed one ascended the summit, which was ornamented with trees. Having ascended the summit, Rama, Dasharatha's son, saw the abode of the waters, filled with turtles and fish. They progressively crossed over the giant mountain of Malaya and reached the ocean, which roared terribly. Rama, supreme among those who cause pleasure, with Sugriva and Lakshmana, descended quickly to the excellent forest along the shore. There were rocks underneath and it was

[20] Famous battle between the gods and the demons. It took place after Chandra, the moon, abducted Tara, Brihaspati's wife.

[21] The five-leaved chaste tree (*Vitex negunda*), but this should read *sindhuvaraka*.

[22] A drona is a wooden vessel, as well as an unit of measurement.

washed with waves of water that suddenly arose. Having reached the extensive shoreline, Rama spoke these words. 'O Sugriva! We have reached Varuna's abode. We must now think about what we pondered earlier.[23] The other shore of the ocean, the lord of the rivers, cannot be discerned. Without a proper means, we are incapable of crossing this ocean. Therefore, let us reside here while we have consultations about how this army of apes can cross over to the other shore.' The mighty-armed one was afflicted because of Sita's abduction. Having reached the ocean, Rama instructed that they should camp there. 'The time for consultations about how we should cross the ocean has arrived. Let no one leave his battalion and go off anywhere else. However, let the brave apes proceed and ascertain whether there is any danger for us.'

Hearing Rama's words, Sugriva and Lakshmana made the soldiers set up camp on the extensive shore of the ocean, filled with trees. Near the ocean, that army was radiant. It looked like a beautiful second ocean, filled with water that had a honey-brown complexion. The bulls among apes reached the forest along the shore. They settled down there, desiring to cross over to the other shore of the great ocean. Having reached the great ocean, the army of the apes was delighted. They looked at the great ocean, turbulent because of the force of the wind. The distant other shore was populated by large numbers of rakshasas. The leaders among the apes sat down and looked at Varuna's abode. At the end of the day and the beginning of the night, it was terrible, filled with horrible crocodiles and alligators. When the moon arose, it turned turbulent and reflected the moon's image. There were giant crocodiles that were as terrible as the wind. It was populated with whales and *timingila*s.[24] Varuna's abode was filled with blazing serpents and snakes. There were gigantic creatures and many kinds of mountains in the deep. It was extremely difficult to cross. It was impenetrable. It was impassable. It was fathomless and was the abode of asuras. The impenetrable depths was agitated by the wind and were filled

---

[23] A means of crossing the ocean.

[24] Timingila is a fish that devours whales (*timi*).

with *makara*s,[25] serpents and snakes. Large torrents of water rose
and fell. There were radiant and large serpents in the water, speckled
with dots that seemed to be made out of fire. The ocean reached
down to the region of *patala*,[26] the dominion of the enemies of the
gods. The ocean was like the sky. The sky was like the ocean. No
distinction could be seen between the ocean and the sky. The water
mixed with the sky and the sky mixed with the water. With stars in
the sky and jewels in the water, both seemed to be the same. One
was filled with rising clouds and the other was filled with rising
waves. There was no particular distinction between the two, the
ocean and the sky. Each making its own terrible noise, they seemed
to clash against each other. The waves of the king of the rivers and
the great clouds seemed to be engaged in a battle. In the grip of
the wind, the jewels and waves in the water roared. Filled with a
large number of creatures, it seemed to angrily rise up. The great-
souled ones saw the abode of the waters, lashed by the wind. A
wind arose in the sky and the waves seemed to be conversing with
it. Waves roared and whirled around in the water, as if the ocean
was intoxicated.

Chapter 6(5)

Self-controlled, Nila protected the virtuous army in the proper
way and it camped itself on the northern shore of the ocean.
Mainda and Dvivida, bulls among apes, roamed around in all the
directions, protecting the soldiers.

When the army had settled down along the shore of the lord
of the male and female rivers, Rama saw that Lakshmana was by
his side and addressed him in these words. 'Indeed, as time passes,
my sorrow is becoming less. However, the grief at not being able to
see my beloved is increasing from one day to the next day. I am not

---

[25] Mythical aquatic creatures, which can be loosely translated as sharks or crocodiles.
[26] One of the seven nether regions.

distressed that my beloved is far away. Nor am I distressed that she
has been abducted. I am grieving that her age is passing. O wind!
Blow where my beloved is. Touch her and touch me. It is through
you that I can touch her body. It is through the moon that our eyes
meet. As she was being abducted, my beloved must have spoken to
me. "Alas, lord!" That thought is scorching my body, as if I have
imbibed some poison. Night and day, the fire of desire is consuming
my body. It is acting as kindling to the great flames of my thoughts.
O Soumitri! Without you, I will immerse myself in the ocean and
sleep. When I sleep in this way, perhaps the water will somehow
quench my blazing desire. Burnt by this desire, I am capable
of remaining alive only because I and the one with the beautiful
thighs are located on the same earth. A paddy field without water
survives by imbibing water from an adjacent paddy field that is
full of water. In that way, I am alive by being sprinkled, having
heard that she is alive. When will I defeat the enemies and see the
beautiful-hipped and lotus-eyed Sita, extensive in her prosperity?
Her beautiful lips are like the *bimba* fruit. Her face is like a lotus.
When will she raise it slightly and I drink from it, like a diseased
person drinking medicine? Her thick breasts are close together, they
are like palm fruit. They are delightful. When will they tremble and
press against me? The dark-eyed one has left and is in the midst of
the rakshasas. I am her protector. But she is without a protector and
cannot find anyone to save her. In the autumn, the moon's outline
drives away dark clouds. Like that, when will she appear, driving
away and agitating the rakshasas? Sita is naturally slender. Because
of sorrow, fasting and the adversity faced from the time and the
place, she has become even more slender. When will I strike the
Indra among rakshasas with arrows in his chest and bring Sita back,
thereby dispelling the sorrow in my heart? When will the virtuous
and anxious Sita, who is like a daughter of the immortals, cling to
my neck and release tears of joy? When will I suddenly free myself
from this terrible sorrow that has resulted from the separation with
Maithilee, like one casts away a soiled garment?' In this way, the
intelligent Rama lamented there. At the end of the day, the sun's
form diminished and sunset arrived. Remembering the lotus-eyed

one, he was overwhelmed with grief. However, comforted by Lakshmana, Rama worshipped the *sandhya*.[27]

Chapter 6(6)

The Indra among rakshasas was like the great-souled Shakra. Having seen the terrible deeds, which caused fear, wrought by Hanumat in Lanka, he lowered his face and a bit ashamed, spoke to all the rakshasas. 'The city of Lanka is impossible to assail. But he entered and destroyed it, despite being only an ape. He saw Sita Janakee. He destroyed the palace and the *chaitya*.[28] The best among rakshasas were killed. Hanumat agitated the entire city of Lanka. O fortunate ones! What should be done? What is our subsequent task? Speak about what we are capable of doing, so that we can take appropriate action. Spirited and noble ones have said that consultations are the foundation of victory. O immensely strong ones! Therefore, the idea of consulting about Rama appeals to me. There are three types of people in the world—superior, inferior and mediocre. Let me tell you about the qualities and bad traits they possess. A supreme man is said to be one who consults capable ministers and undertakes beneficial acts after the advice, doing the same with friends who have a similar objective and relatives who are favourably inclined. He performs an act after such collective consultations, paying due attention to destiny. A man is said to be mediocre if he determines an objective alone, uses only his mind to decide what constitutes dharma and undertakes the task alone. If a man does not distinguish between the good and the bad, depending on destiny alone, and decides that he will undertake an act, such a man is said to be inferior. Just as men are always classified into superior, inferior and mediocre, advice is also known to be superior, inferior and mediocre. Superior advice is said to be

---

[27] Sandhya is any conjunction of day and night. Hence, it is dawn, as well as dusk.

[28] The word chaitya has several meanings—sacrificial shed, temple, altar, sanctuary and a tree that grows along the road.

that discussed and arrived at by ministers through unanimity, in conformity with the foresight of the sacred texts. When seeking the objective, the ministers have many kinds of views and one finally has to be chosen through consensus, this is said to be mediocre advice. When they debate with each other and discuss different points of view, without being able to arrive at a consensus, that advice is said to be inferior. O supreme among ministers! You are virtuous. Consult well and decide on the course of action. I will undertake that. Rama is surrounded by thousands of brave apes. He is approaching the city of Lanka and will lay siege to us. It is evident that the spirited Raghava will easily cross the ocean, with his younger brother, his soldiers and his followers. Our enmity with the apes has commenced. Therefore, consult and tell me what is beneficial for the city and the soldiers.'

Chapter 6(7)

The Indra among rakshasas said this to the immensely strong rakshasas. Having heard this, all of them joined their hands in salutation to Ravana, the lord of the rakshasas, and said, 'O king! Our extremely large army is full of clubs, spears, swords, javelins and spikes. Why are you distressed? The lord of wealth[29] resides on the summit of Kailasa and is surrounded by many yakshas. You created a great carnage and brought him under your subjugation. O lord! He boasted of his friendship with Maheshvara. He is extremely strong and is a guardian of the world. However, you angrily defeated him in a battle. You killed, agitated and oppressed large numbers of yakshas. From the summit of Kailasa, you seized the *vimana*[30] and brought it here. Out of fright, Maya, Indra among the danavas, desired your friendship. O bull among the rakshasas! He bestowed his daughter[31] on you as a wife. There was an Indra

[29] Kubera.
[30] Pushpaka.
[31] Mandodari.

among danavas. His name was Madhu and he brought pleasure to Kumbhinasa.[32] He was insolent about his valour and invincible. However, you subjugated him and brought him under control. O mighty-armed one! You went to *rasatala*[33] and subjugated and seized the *nagas*[34] Vasuki, Takshaka, Shankha and Jati. O lord! There were brave danavas who were infinitely strong. In addition, they had also obtained a boon. In an encounter, you fought against them for an entire year. O scorcher of enemies! Using your own strength, you brought them under subjugation. O lord of rakshasas! There are many kinds of *maya* you learnt there. Varuna's sons were brave and valiant in battle. Their followers possessed the four kinds of forces. O mighty-armed one! You defeated them. O king! You immersed yourself in the ocean of Yama's army. The staff of death was like a giant crocodile there and the region was full of silk-cotton trees. You countered Death and obtained a great victory. Through that great battle, you made all the worlds extremely content. The earth was full of many brave kshatriyas, as if with large trees, who were like Shakra in their valour. In a battle, Raghava is not equal to them in valour, qualities or enterprise. They were extremely difficult to vanquish. O king! However, you overcame them and killed them. O king! The calamity that has arisen is due to an ordinary person. You should not take this to heart. You will kill Raghava.'

Chapter 6(8)

There was a rakshasa named Prahasta and he possessed the complexion of a dark cloud. He was a brave commander. He joined his hands in salutation and spoke these words. 'There are

---

[32] Kumbhinasa was Ravana's sister, married to Madhu.

[33] One of the seven nether regions.

[34] Throughout the translation, we have generally used serpents for nagas and snakes for *sarpa*s. Nagas are not quite snakes. They are semi-divine, can assume human forms and live in specific regions.

no gods, danavas, gandharvas, *pishacha*s,[35] birds or serpents whom you are incapable of afflicting in a battle, not to speak of apes. All of us were distracted and trusting and were thus deceived by Hanumat. Otherwise, that dweller in the forest would not have left with his life. Command me and I will remove apes from the entire earth, its mountains, forests and groves, right up to the frontiers of the ocean. O roamer in the night! I will arrange for your protection from the apes. Because of the crime you have committed,[36] there will not be the slightest bit of misery for you.'

There was a rakshasa named Durmukha. Extremely angry, he said, 'He[37] oppressed all of us and that cannot be forgiven. This is an additional attack unleashed on the prosperous Indra among the rakshasas, his city and his inner quarters, by the Indra among the apes. From this instant, I will single-handedly repulse and kill the apes, whether they enter the terrible ocean, the sky or rasatala.'

Seizing a terrible club that was smeared with flesh and blood, extremely angry, the immensely strong Vajradamshtra said, 'What do we have to do with the pitiable ascetic Hanumat? The invincible Rama, Sugriva and Lakshmana exist. I will single-handedly agitate the army of the apes, approach Rama, Sugriva and Lakshmana and kill them with this club.'

The brave and valiant Nikumbha was Kumbhakarna's son. Extremely enraged, he spoke to Ravana, the one who made the worlds shriek. 'All of you remain here with the great king. I will single-handedly slay Raghava and Lakshmana.'

There was a rakshasa named Vajrahanu and he was like a mountain. He angrily licked his lips with his tongue and spoke these words. 'All of you get rid of your anxiety and perform your own tasks. I will single-handedly devour all the leaders of the apes. Rest assured and sport. Be at ease and drink *madhu* and *varuni*.[38] I will single-handedly slay Sugriva, Lakshmana, Angada, Hanumat, Rama and all the elephants in the battle.'

[35] Malevolent beings.
[36] Sita's abduction.
[37] Hanumat.
[38] Forms of liquor.

Chapter 6(9)

Nikumbha, Rabhasa, the immensely strong Suryashatru, Suptaghna, Yajnakopa, Mahaparshva, Mahodara, the invincible rakshasas Agniketu and Rashmiketu, Indrajit, Ravana's extremely energetic and strong son, Prahasta, Virupaksha, the immensely strong Vajradamshtra, Dhumraksha, Atikaya and the rakshasa Durmukha became angry and seized clubs, spears, javelins, spikes, tridents, battleaxes, bows, arrows and large and sharp swords. All of them blazed in their energy. Those rakshasas stood up and told Ravana, 'Today we will slay Rama, Sugriva, Lakshmana and the pitiable Hanumat who attacked Lanka.'

Vibhishana restrained all those who had seized weapons. He joined his hands in salutation, made them sit down again and spoke these words. 'O father![39] The learned ones have said that if the objective cannot be attained through the three modes, only then is it the time to display valour.[40] O father! Following the tested methods, valour is only successful against those who are distracted, engaged with someone else, or those who are suffering on account of misfortune. How can you resort to strength and defeat someone who is attentive? How can you wish to attack him in that way? He has conquered his rage and is invincible. Hanumat has performed the extremely difficult deed of crossing the terrible ocean, the lord of the male and female rivers. Who can dispute that? O those who roam around in the night! The valour and strength of the enemy is immeasurable. One should never be rash and take them lightly. The illustrious Rama's wife was abducted. Earlier, what did he do to the king of the rakshasas in Janasthana? Khara crossed his limits and was killed by Rama in a battle. Depending on one's strength, one must certainly protect the lives of creatures. That is the reason an extremely great fear has arisen on account of Vaidehi. She was abducted and must be abandoned. What is the purpose in provoking

[39] The word used is *tata*, which can be translated as either father or son, depending on whom Vibhishana is addressing. Since words are primarily addressed to Ravana, we have translated it as father.

[40] That is, use *danda* only if *sama, dana* and *bheda* do not work.

a quarrel? He is full of valour and follows dharma. A pointless enmity with him is futile. Let Maithilee be given to him. Maithilee should be given to him before he uses his arrows to shatter this city, with its elephants, horses and many kinds of jewels. Let Sita be given before the extremely terrible and large army of invincible apes attacks Lanka. If Rama's beloved wife is not voluntarily returned, the city of Lanka and all the brave rakshasas will be destroyed. As a relative, I am seeking to pacify you. Act in accordance with my words. I am speaking about a beneficial medication. Let Maithilee be given back. The son of the king will release invincible arrows with new heads and tufts. They will be like the rays of the autumn sun. Before Dasharatha's son does that, let Maithilee be given to him. Abandon rage. It destroys the dharma of happiness. Serve the dharma that extends pleasure and deeds. Be pacified, so that our sons and relatives remain alive. Give Maithilee back to Dasharatha's son.'

Chapter 6(10)

Vibhishana uttered those extremely well-articulated and beneficial words. However, goaded by destiny, Ravana replied in harsh words. 'One can reside with an enemy or an angry and virulent serpent, but one cannot dwell with an enemy who states himself to be a friend. O rakshasa! I know about the conduct of relatives in all the worlds. Relatives are always delighted at the hardships their relatives face. O rakshasa! They disrespect and seek to bring down relatives who are important, successful, learned, devoted to dharma in their conduct and brave. They are like assassins and are always delighted at each other's hardships. They conceal their terrible thoughts and therefore bring fear to relatives. In earlier times, in a pond full of lotuses, some elephants were heard to chant a shloka when they saw men with nooses in their hands. Hear my words. "Fire, other weapons and nooses aren't as fearful to us as terrible relatives who are engaged in their own selfish pursuits and bring us fear. There is no doubt that they will speak about the means whereby we can be captured. Out of all kinds of fear, we know that the hardship which results from relatives is the most fearful. It is evident there is wealth in cows. It is evident there is self-control in *brahmana*s. It is evident there is fickleness in women. It is evident there is reason for fear in relatives."[41] O amiable one! You do not desire that I should be honoured by the world, nor my prosperity, nobility of birth and the fact that I stand on the heads of enemies. O roamer in the night! Had anyone else spoken such words, this very instant, he would have ceased to exist. O worst of the lineage! Shame on you.'

Vibhishana spoke about good policy. Being addressed in these harsh words, he rose up into the sky with a club in his hand, along with four rakshasas. The handsome Vibhishana was in the sky. Having conquered his rage, he spoke to his brother, the lord of the rakshasas. 'O king! Since you are my brother, you can tell me whatever you wish. However, I cannot pardon these harsh and false words that you have spoken. O Dashanana! Those who have not cleansed their souls and have come under the subjugation of destiny do not accept well-articulated and beneficial words addressed to them. O king! Men who always speak what is pleasant are easy to get. But for disagreeable words that are like medication, a speaker and a listener are both extremely rare. You are bound in the noose of destiny, which takes away all creatures. This destruction could not be ignored, just as a burning house cannot be. I do not wish to see you slain by Rama's sharp arrows, decorated with gold and like a blazing fire. In the field of battle, brave and strong people who are accomplished in the use of weapons sink down when destiny comes upon them, like a bridge made with sand. Using whatever means, protect yourself, the city and these rakshasas. May you be fortunate. I am leaving. Without me, be happy. Desiring your welfare, I tried to restrain you. O roamer in the night! But my words were not to your liking. When their time and lifespan is over, men do not accept the beneficial words spoken by their well-wishers.'

[41] It is not clear from the text where the elephant quote ends. This seems to be the right place. Wild elephants are referring to domesticated elephants being used to trap and capture them.

Chapter 6(11)

Ravana's younger brother spoke these harsh words to Ravana.
Having said them, in an instant, he reached the spot where
Rama and Lakshmana were. His form was like the summit of
Meru and he blazed like a flash of lightning. From the ground, the
lords of the apes saw him standing in the sky. With the apes, the
invincible Sugriva, lord of the apes, saw this fifth person.[42] With the
other apes, the intelligent one started to think. Having thought for
a while, he addressed all the apes, with Hanumat at the forefront,
in these excellent words. 'He possesses all the weapons and he is
with four rakshasas. Behold. There is no doubt that the rakshasas
are advancing so as to kill us.' Hearing Sugriva's words, all those
excellent apes raised *sala* trees and boulders and spoke these words.
'O king! Quickly command us, so that we can kill these evil-souled
ones. They have limited lifespans. Let us bring them down on the
ground and kill them.' While they were conversing in this way,
Vibhishana reached the northern shore and stationed himself in the
sky. The immensely wise and great Vibhishana stationed himself
in the sky. On seeing them, he addressed them in a loud voice.
'The rakshasa named Ravana is wicked in conduct and is the lord
of the rakshasas. I am his younger brother and am known by the
name of Vibhishana. Having slain Jatayu, he abducted Sita from
Janasthana. Incapacitated and distressed, she has been imprisoned
and is exceedingly well-protected by the *rakshasi*s.[43] I repeatedly
entreated him in many kinds of virtuous words filled with reason
that Sita should be returned to Rama. But he did not heed them.
Goaded by destiny, Ravana did not accept them. Though those
beneficial words that were spoken were like medication, he acted
in a contrary way. He spoke harshly to me and disrespected me, as
if I was a servant. Abandoning my sons and my wife, I am seeking
refuge with Raghava. Quickly inform the great-souled Raghava, the
refuge of all the worlds, about Vibhishana presenting himself.'

---

[42] There were four other rakshasas.
[43] Rakshasa lady.

Sugriva was dexterous in his valour. Hearing these words, he swiftly went to the presence of Rama and Lakshmana and said, 'Ravana's younger brother is known by the name of Vibhishana. With four other rakshasas, he is seeking refuge with you. Know that Vibhishana has been sent by Ravana. O supreme among those who know what is proper! I think it proper that he should be captured. This rakshasa is deceitful in intelligence and has come here because he has been instructed. O Raghava! When you trust him, he will hide himself and strike you with maya. Using severe chastisement, he and his advisers should be killed. This Vibhishana is the cruel Ravana's brother.' Wrathful, the leader of the army told Rama this. He was accomplished in the use of words and skilled in speech. Having said this, he was silent. The immensely strong Rama heard Sugriva's words. He spoke to Hanumat and the foremost apes who were near him. 'You have heard what the king of the apes has said about Ravana's younger brother. These words are full of deep meaning and reasoning. In a time of hardship, a capable well-wisher who desires eternal prosperity must use purposeful and intelligent words of advice. What do you think?' Asked in this way, they attentively articulated their own views. Desiring Rama's welfare, they addressed him politely. 'O Raghava! There is nothing in the three worlds that is unknown to you. O Rama! You are asking us as well-wishers and showing us honour. You possess the vow of truth. You are brave and follow dharma. You are firm in your valour. You take action after due examination. You can remember. You have devoted your soul to well-wishers. Therefore, one by one, your advisers will speak to you. They are capable and full of intelligence. One by one, they will give you their reasons.'

After this, the intelligent Angada spoke first to Raghava. The ape's words were that Vibhishana should first be tested about his intentions. 'Since he has come from the enemy, there is every reason to be suspicious of him. One should not hastily believe that Vibhishana is a trustworthy person. Those who are deceitful in intelligence roam around, hiding their own sentiments. They strike at a weakness and can lead to an extremely great calamity. One must decide on one's conduct after judging the pros and the cons. If there is an accumulation of qualities, one must follow that course. If there are evils, one must discard it. If there are extremely great evils, without any hesitation, one must discard it. O king! If one knows that there is a great accumulation of qualities, one must act accordingly.'

Sharabha spoke determined words that were full of meaning. 'O tiger among men! As a counter, let us quickly send spies after him. Let a spy who is subtle in intelligence ascertain the exact nature of the truth. After examining the different courses of action, if it is proper, he can be accepted.'

Jambavat was accomplished in intelligence and knew about the sacred texts. Considering the objective, he proclaimed the following words, which were full of qualities and devoid of demerits. 'Vibhishana has come from the wicked Indra among rakshasas, who is bound in enmity towards you. He has come at the wrong time and place. He must be suspected in every possible way.'

Mainda was accomplished in distinguishing between good and bad policy. He was skilled in speaking and spoke words that were full of excellent reasons. 'O lord of the supreme among men! Vibhishana has said that he is Ravana's younger brother. Let him be questioned, sweetly and slowly. Let his true sentiments be ascertained. Act thereafter. O bull among men! Use your intelligence to decide whether he is evil or not evil.'

Hanumat was supreme among advisers and full of purity. Slowly, sweetly and briefly, he spoke these words. 'You are best in intelligence. You are capable and supreme among eloquent ones. When speaking, even Brihaspati is incapable of surpassing you. O king! O Rama! I am not speaking so as to rival the others, nor do I desire superiority over the others. I am speaking these words because it is an important matter. Your advisers have spoken about determining the pros and the cons. I see a problem in this and that kind of action cannot be pursued. Short of engaging someone, it is not possible to determine his capability. To me, there seems to be a problem in suddenly engaging someone. Your advisers have spoken about employing a spy. This is impossible to achieve and I do not see how that can be brought about. This Vibhishana has arrived at the wrong time and place. I will tell you what my thoughts are about this. Listen to me. For him, this is the right time and place and that is the reason he has come here. He has come from one person to another person,[44] having judged their respective qualities and sins. He has seen the wickedness in Ravana and the valour in you. This is according to his intelligence and that is the reason he has come here. O king! It has been suggested that he should be questioned by men who are in disguise. Having considered it, here is my view on that. If an intelligent person is suddenly questioned, he will be suspicious. Thus, a person who has come happily may be falsely questioned and the friendship may be destroyed. O king! It is impossible to suddenly ascertain the inclinations of someone else. Without possessing a great deal of skill, it is impossible to determine what there is in someone's inner mind. I do not detect any evil sentiments in what he has spoken. His face is also pleasant. Therefore, I do not doubt him. A deceitful person does not approach in such a self-assured way, unsuspecting in his mind. His words are not evil. Therefore, I do not doubt him. Even if one hides it, it is impossible not to reveal something in one's form. Even if men try forcibly, the inner sentiments are revealed. O supreme among those who know what must be done! You know what must be done. If appropriate to the time and the place, a task that should be undertaken must be done quickly, so that it is successful. Considering your enterprise and Ravana's false conduct and hearing about the slaying of Vali and Sugriva's consecration, he must have first turned his mind to seeking the kingdom[45] and has come here. With this consideration at the forefront, he should be added to our side. To the best of my ability, I have spoken about this rakshasa's uprightness. O supreme among intelligent ones! Having heard, you must finally decide on what is proper.'

[44] From Ravana to Rama.
[45] Of the rakshasas.

Chapter 6(12)

Hearing what Vayu's son had said, Rama was pleased in his mind. The invincible and learned one replied, stating what he had decided. 'I also wish to speak about my attitude towards Vibhishana. All of you are interested in our welfare and therefore, I wish that all of you should hear this. Someone who has arrived as a friend must never be discarded, even if there are taints in him. The virtuous ones condemn that.'

Hearing Rama's words, Sugriva, the lord of the apes, was goaded by his affection and replied to Kakutstha. 'O one who knows about dharma! O lord of the worlds! O one who is like the jewel on a crest! How wonderful. You have spoken like a spirited and noble one, established along the path of virtue. My inner thoughts are also that this Vibhishana is pure. On the basis of his inclinations, this is my surmise and I have examined it in every possible way. O Raghava! Therefore, let him quickly become one of our equals. We will then obtain the friendship of the immensely wise Vibhishana.'

Rama examined the words that had been spoken by Sugriva. He then addressed the bull among apes in words that were even more auspicious. 'How does it matter whether this roamer in the night is extremely wicked or not wicked? He is incapable of causing the slightest bit of injury to me. O lord of large numbers of apes! If I so wish, I can kill pishachas, danavas, yakshas and all the rakshasas on earth with the tips of my fingers. It has been heard that an enemy arrived and sought refuge. As is proper, a dove honoured and invited him and offered him his own flesh. He received someone who had come to kill his wife. O best among apes! If a dove did that, what about a person like me?[46] The rishi Kanva's son was Kandu and he was a supreme sage. He was full of dharma and spoke the truth. Listen to the chant he had recited in ancient times. "O scorcher

---

[46] This is a story from the Mahabharata. A fowler captured a she-pigeon or she-dove. Since the fowler was hungry and a guest, the he-pigeon or he-dove offered his body to the fowler as food.

of enemies! Even if an enemy wishing to cause injury arrives in a distressed state, with his hands cupped, and seeks refuge, he should not be killed. Even if an enemy is insolent, if he seeks refuge in a distressed state, a person who has cleansed his soul should protect that enemy, even at the cost of his own life. Because of fear, confusion or desire, if he does not protect, despite possessing the capacity and the spirit, he commits a sin and is condemned by the worlds. If a potential protector sees someone who seeks refuge being destroyed, when the person who should have been protected departs, he takes away all the good deeds of the potential protector. There is a great sin in not protecting someone who seeks refuge. It destroys heaven and fame. It destroys strength and valour." I will truly follow the meaning of Kandu's excellent words. It leads to the following of dharma. It leads to fame. It leads to the fruit of heaven being obtained. If a person seeks refuge and says, "I am yours", against all creatures, I will grant him freedom from fear. That is my vow. O best among the apes! Bring him here. Whether it is Vibhishana or whether it is Ravana himself, I will grant him freedom from fear.' After hearing Sugriva's words, the lord of men addressed the lord of the apes in this way. Vibhishana quickly arrived to meet him, like the king of the birds meeting Purandara.

Chapter 6(13)

When Raghava granted him freedom from fear, Ravana's younger brother, lowered himself, and with his faithful companions, descended on to the ground. Vibhishana, with dharma in his soul, descended and sought refuge at Rama's feet, with the four rakshasas. Vibhishana addressed Rama in these words. They were appropriate and full of dharma, causing delight. 'I am Ravana's younger brother and I have been humiliated by him. You are the refuge of all creatures and I am seeking refuge with you. I have abandoned Lanka, my friends and my riches. My kingdom, my life and my happiness are now vested in you. I will help you in killing the rakshasas and attacking Lanka. As long as I am alive, I will attack and penetrate that army.'

Thus addressed, Rama embraced Vibhishana. Rejoicing, he told Lakshmana, 'Fetch water from the ocean. O one who shows honours! Using that, quickly consecrate the immensely wise Vibhishana as the king of the rakshasas, so that I am pleased.' Thus addressed, following Rama's instruction, in the midst of the foremost apes, Soumitri consecrated Vibhishana as the king. Seeing that Rama was pleased, the apes immediately emitted a loud roar and uttered words praising him.[47]

Hanumat and Sugriva spoke to Vibhishana. 'The ocean cannot be agitated. How can we cross Varuna's abode? We must swiftly find a means so that all the soldiers can cross over Varuna's abode, the lord of the male and female rivers.' Addressed in this way, Vibhishana, who knew about dharma, replied, 'To proceed, King Raghava should seek refuge with the ocean. The immeasurable and great ocean was dug by Sagara. Knowing that Rama is a relative, the great ocean should perform this task.'[48] The learned rakshasa, Vibhishana, spoke in this way. Raghava was naturally devoted to dharma and this appealed to him, since it was a good deed to accomplish the purpose. He first smiled and then spoke to the immensely energetic Lakshmana and Sugriva, the lord of the apes. 'O Lakshmana! Vibhishana's advice appeals to me. With Sugriva, tell me if the idea appeals to you. Sugriva is always learned and you are skilled in offering counsel. Both of you decide whether what has been said appeals to you.' Thus addressed, both those brave ones, Sugriva and Lakshmana, spoke these words with humility. 'O tiger among men! O Raghava! Why will it not appeal to us? At this time, what Vibhishana has spoken will bring us joy. Varuna's abode is terrible. Without building a bridge across the ocean, not even Indra, with the gods and the *asura*s, is capable of reaching Lanka. Let us act exactly in accordance with the brave Vibhishana's words. We have spent an excessive amount of time already. Let us engage with

[47] Praising Rama.
[48] Sagara was Rama's ancestor.

the ocean.' Thus addressed, Rama spread out *kusha* grass on the shores of the lord of the male and female rivers, like a sacrificial altar laid out for a fire.

Chapter 6(14)

Having spread out kusha grass on the ground, Rama controlled himself and attentively lay down there, spending three nights. But the careless ocean did not show himself to Rama,[49] despite Rama making every effort to show him the honour that he deserved and worshipping him. At this, Rama became angry at the ocean and the corners of his eyes turned red.

Lakshmana, with the auspicious marks, was near him and he said, 'O Lakshmana! Behold. An ignoble one has been worshipped. The ocean has not shown himself. This is arrogance. The qualities of virtuous ones—tranquility, forgiveness, uprightness and pleasantness in speech, are incapable of yielding fruits when directed at those devoid of qualities. The world regards a man who praises himself, is wicked and shameless, proceeds in a contrary direction and raises the rod of chastisement everywhere as someone who is virtuous. Conciliation is not capable of ensuring deeds. Conciliation is not capable of ensuring fame. O Lakshmana! Nor, in this world, can one obtain victory in the field of battle through that. Today, the makaras in this abode of makaras will be mangled with my arrows. O Soumitri! Behold. Everywhere, I will obstruct the flow of the water. O Lakshmana! Behold. I will mangle the giant snakes, the fish, the trunks of elephants[50] and the serpents. In the great encounter today, I will use my arrows to dry up the ocean, with its conch shells, nets of oysters, fish and makaras. This abode of makaras takes me to be someone who is forgiving. He considers me to be incapable. Shame on those who are forgiving towards such

[49] In personified form.
[50] Elephants in the water.

people. O Soumitri! Bring me my bow and the arrows that are like virulent serpents. Even if he cannot be agitated, I am angry and will agitate the ocean. The turbulent waves do not cross the shoreline. However, with my arrows, I will make Varuna's abode cross all boundaries.'

Saying this, with the bow in his hand, he dilated his eyes in rage. The invincible Rama looked like the blazing fire of destruction at the end of a *yuga*. He stretched his bow and made the world tremble with a terrible arrow. He released the fierce arrow, like Shatakratu does with the *vajra*. That excellent arrow blazed in its energy and was immensely forceful. It entered the waters of the ocean and terrified the serpents. With the large crocodiles and makaras and an extremely terrible wind, there was great turbulence in the ocean. A large garland of waves, filled with conch shells and oysters, spread out in every direction. Everywhere in the great ocean, there were violent waves full of smoke. With mouths flaming and eyes blazing, the serpents suffered. So did the immensely valiant danavas who resided in patala. Thousands of waves, like Vindhya and Mandara, leapt up in the king of the waters, filled with crocodiles and makaras. The torrent of waves whirled around, terrifying the serpents and the rakshasas. Giant crocodiles leapt up from the abode of the waters.

Chapter 6(15)

After this, from the middle of the ocean, Sagara[51] himself arose, like the sun arising atop the great mountain of Meru. The ocean was seen, together with serpents with flaming mouths. He was dressed in red garlands and garments and his eyes were like the petals of lotuses. He was adorned with molten gold and his complexion was like that of mild lapis lazuli. After having taken the valiant one's permission first, Sagara approached Raghava, with the bow and arrow in his hand. He joined his hands in salutation

---

[51] The personified form of the ocean.

and spoke these words. 'O Raghava! O amiable one! The earth, the wind, the sky, water and light are stationed in their natural states, following their eternal paths. I am also in my natural state. I am fathomless and cannot be leapt across. I am telling you that it will be unnatural for me not to be fathomless. O son of a king! My water is full of crocodiles and sharks and out of desire, avarice or fear, it is impossible for me to stupefy it. O Rama! I will arrange it so that you can cross over me. While the soldiers are crossing, the crocodiles will not strike. O amiable one! This one, named Nala, is Vishvakarma's son. Thanks to the boon bestowed on him by his father, he is Vishvakarma's equal. This ape, great in endeavour, will build a bridge over me and I will bear it. He is just like his father.' Having said this, the ocean vanished.

The immensely strong Nala, supreme among apes, arose and addressed Rama in these words. 'I will construct an extensive bridge over Varuna's abode. The great ocean has spoken the truth. I can resort to my father's capability. On Mandara, Vishvakarma granted my mother a boon. Vishvakarma said, "The son born through you will be my equal." Since I had not been asked, I had not spoken to you about my qualities. Therefore, let the bulls among the apes now fashion the bridge.'

Given their leave by Rama, hundreds of thousands of delighted leaders of the apes left in every direction and went to the great forest. The bulls among the apes resembled boulders and dragged boulders. The apes shattered these and started to drag them towards the ocean. The apes filled the ocean with salas, *ashvakarnas*, *dhavas*, bamboos, *kutajas*, *arjunas*, *talas*, tilakas, timishas, *bilvas*, *saptaparnas*, blossoming *karnikaras*, mangos and ashoka trees. The supreme among apes brought some trees with roots, others without roots. Like Indra's standard, the apes raised up and dragged trees. Large boulders were violently hurled in and the waters surged up, touching the sky and then falling back again. In the middle of the lord of the male and female rivers, Nala constructed a gigantic bridge that was ten *yojanas* wide and one hundred yojanas long. Boulders were flung in. Boulders were thrown in there. At that time, a tumultuous sound arose within that great ocean. Thus, Nala

constructed a beautiful and handsome bridge across the abode of
the makaras. It was as radiant as Svati's path in the firmament.[52]
Wishing to see this extraordinary sight, the gods, the gandharvas,
the siddhas[53] and the supreme rishis arrived and stood there, in
the sky. The apes roared. They leapt up and leapt down. This was
unthinkable. This was impossible to believe. This was extraordinary
and made the body hair stand up. All the creatures witnessed the
bridge being built over the ocean. There were thousands of crores
of greatly energetic apes. Having constructed the bridge across the
ocean, they crossed over to the other shore of the great ocean. It was
beautiful, large and constructed well. It was planned well and the
path was smooth. The radiant and grand bridge could be seen like
a line drawn through the ocean.

With a club in his hand, Vibhishana stood on the shore of
the ocean. He stood there with his advisers, waiting to attack the
enemy. The handsome Rama and Lakshmana were in front of the
soldiers. With dharma in their souls, the archers were with Sugriva.
Some apes passed along the middle, others passed through the
sides. Others did not use that path, but leapt into the water. Some
resorted to the sky and leapt across, like Suparna. The giant roar
of the ocean was surpassed by their loud roars. The terrible army
of the apes crossed over the terrible ocean. Using the bridge built
by Nala, the army of the apes crossed. The king[54] made them camp
at a spot on the shore where there were many roots and fruits
and a lot of water. Raghava performed an extraordinary task that
was very difficult to accomplish. On seeing this, the gods, together
with the siddhas, the charanas[55] and the maharshis, approached
Rama and separately sprinkled him with auspicious water. 'O god
among men on earth! Defeat the enemy. Rule up to the frontiers
of the ocean for an eternal number of years.' Thus was Rama,
god among men, honoured and worshipped with many kinds of
auspicious words.

[52] Meaning, not just the path of Svati nakshatra, but the entire Milky Way.
[53] Successful sages.
[54] Sugriva.
[55] Celestial bards.

Chapter 6(16)

Rama, Dasharatha's son, crossed the ocean with the army. The prosperous Ravana spoke to his two advisers, Shuka and Sarana. 'The entire army of the apes has crossed over the ocean, which is extremely difficult to cross. Rama's act of constructing a bridge across the ocean is unprecedented. I would never have been able to believe that a bridge could be constructed across the ocean. I must certainly pay attention to this army of the apes. Without being detected, the two of you penetrate the army of the apes and ascertain the number and valour of the foremost among the apes. Which advisers of Rama and Sugriva have assembled? Which brave apes are striding around in front? How was a bridge constructed over the ocean, full of water? Where have the great-souled apes camped? You must ascertain the truth about Rama's conduct, valour and weapons and those of the brave Lakshmana. Who are the commanders of the immensely energetic apes? To find the truth out about all this, the two of you must swiftly depart and return.' The two rakshasas, Shuka and Sarana, were commanded in this way. Those two brave ones adopted the forms of apes and entered the army of the apes. They found that army of apes to be unthinkable and their body hair stood up. Shuka and Sarana were unable to count their number. Everywhere, there were some who had crossed, some who were crossing and some who wished to cross. Some had camped, others were setting up camp. There was a terrible roar from that loud army.

Though those two immensely energetic ones, Shuka and Sarana, were disguised, Vibhishana detected and captured them and spoke to Rama. 'O destroyer of enemy cities! These two are spies and have come here from Lanka.' Seeing Rama, those two were distressed and lost all hopes of remaining alive. Terrified, they joined their hands in salutation and spoke these words. 'O amiable one! Sent by Ravana, the two of us have come here. O descendant of the Raghu lineage! We were to find out everything about your army.'

Hearing their words, Rama, Dasharatha's son, engaged in the welfare of all beings, laughed and said, 'Have you seen the entire army? Have you examined us well? Have you accomplished the task

you were told to? If you have, return at ease. When you enter the
city of Lanka, exactly recount the words I speak to the king of the
rakshasas, the younger brother of the lord of riches. "When you
abducted Sita, you resorted to your strength. As you wish, display
that, with your soldiers and your relatives. When it is tomorrow, you
will see me use my arrows to destroy the city of Lanka, with its gates
and ramparts, and the army of the rakshasas. O Ravana! Use all your
strength to free yourself from my rage. When it is tomorrow, I will
be like Vasava with his vajra, unleashing his vajra on the danavas.'"

Having been thus commanded, the two rakshasas, Shuka and
Sarana, praised Raghava for being devoted to dharma and said, 'May
you be victorious.' They went to the city of Lanka and spoke to the
lord of the rakshasas. 'O lord of the rakshasas! We were captured
by Vibhishana and deserved to be killed. However, on seeing us,
the infinitely energetic Rama, with dharma in his soul, freed us. The
four bulls among men are in the same place. They are brave, like the
guardians of the world. They are accomplished in the use of weapons
and are firm in their valour. They are Rama, Dasharatha's son, the
handsome Lakshmana, Vibhishana and the greatly energetic Sugriva,
who is like the great Indra in his prowess. Even if all the other apes
remain standing, these are capable of uprooting and flinging away
the city of Lanka, with its gates and its ramparts. Rama's weapons
are just as his form is. Even if the other three remain standing, he
can single-handedly destroy the city of Lanka. The army is protected
by Rama, Lakshmana and Sugriva. All of them are invincible, even
to the gods and the asuras. The forms of the residents of the forest
are joyous and they have standards. The residents of the forest have
arrived, desiring to fight. Enough of this enmity. Peace is indicated.
Give Maithilee back to Dasharatha's son.'

Chapter 6(17)

Not scared, Sarana spoke these words, which were like
medication. King Ravana heard them and replied to Sarana.

'Even if the gods, the gandharvas and the danavas attack me, even if there is fear from all the worlds, I will not give Sita away. O amiable one! You have been severely oppressed by the apes and are terrified. That is the reason you now think that returning Sita will be a virtuous deed. What is the name of the enemy who is capable of defeating me in a battle?' Ravana, the lord of the rakshasas, spoke these harsh words. Having spoken them, he ascended to the top of his palace, as white as snow in complexion. It was as tall as many palm trees put together. Ravana wished to see for himself. Ravana was senseless with rage and he was with the two spies. He looked at the ocean, the mountains and the forests. He saw that the entire ground was filled with apes. He saw that the end of that large army of innumerable apes could not be seen.

Beholding this, King Ravana asked Sarana, 'Among the foremost of apes, who are the brave and extremely strong ones? In every direction, which ones, great in enterprise, will advance in front? Whom will Sugriva listen to? Who are leaders among the leaders? O Sarana! Tell me everything. Who are the chiefs among the apes?'

Using these words, the Indra among the rakshasas asked Sarana. Among the residents of the forest, he[56] told him about the ones who were foremost among the foremost. 'There is an ape standing there, facing Lanka. He seems to be dancing. He is surrounded by hundreds and thousands of leaders. Everything in Lanka, the walls and the ramparts, the mountains, the forests and the groves, are trembling because of his loud roar. He is stationed in front of all the Indras among the apes in Sugriva's army. This brave and great-souled leader is named Nila. There is another valiant one whose arms are raised upwards. He is stamping on the ground with his feet. He is yawning and is looking towards Lanka with rage. He is like the summit of a mountain and his complexion is like the filament of a lotus. In great anger, he is repeatedly lashing his tail. The ten directions are resounding with the sound of his tail. Sugriva has instated him as the heir apparent in the kingdom of the apes. His name is Angada and he is challenging you in the encounter.

[56] Sarana.

There are some apes who are tightening their bodies and slapping them. They are roaring. These bulls among apes have got up and are yawning in anger. They are terrible and impossible to withstand. They are fierce and awesome in valour. There are ten billion and one million of these brave ones, camped in that sandalwood grove. They are following one who wishes to attack Lanka and crush it with his own army. He possesses the complexion of silver and he is Shveta. He has his army and he is terrible in valour. This intelligent and brave ape is famous in the three worlds. He is the one who swiftly approached Sugriva and has gone back again, dividing his army into many separate battalions and delighting them. In front of the banks of the Gomatee, there is Mount Ramya. It is also named Samkochana and that mountain is full of many kinds of trees. A leader named Kumuda used to rule over that kingdom. He is the one who is followed by one lakh of apes. He possesses a long tail and his extensive body hair is extremely long, coppery brown, yellow, black and white. He is the performer of terrible deeds. He is spirited, angry and terrible and desires to fight. He hopes that he will crush Lanka with his own army alone. There is one who is like a lion, with a long and tawny mane. Standing alone, he is looking at Lanka, as if he will burn it down with his eyes. O king! This handsome one always dwells on Vindhya, the dark mountain, and Mount Sahya. This is the leader named Rambha. There is one whom four hundred thousand leaders among apes have surrounded and are following, as the energetic one advances to crush Lanka. He is shaking his ears and repeatedly yawning. He does not abandon his herd and death cannot defeat him. He is immensely strong and without fear. O king! He always dwells on the beautiful Salvyeya mountain. He is the leader named Sharabha. O king! All these powerful leaders are known as *viharas*.[57] There are one lakh and forty thousand of them. They are stationed there, like giant clouds that have covered the sky. The great sound of drums can be heard in the midst of those brave apes. Those foremost and terrible apes desire to fight. In their midst, like Indra among the gods, there is the

---

[57] Those who wander around.

leader named Panasa, who is impossible to withstand in a battle. He always resides on the supreme mountain of Pariyatra. He is foremost among all leaders and in different formations, there are one lakh and fifty thousand who serve him. He is in the midst of that terrible and radiant army that is marching along, looking like a second ocean along the shores of the ocean. This is the leader named Vinata, who is like Dardara.[58] He roams around, drinking the waters of the river Parnasha, supreme among rivers.[59] The leader named Krathana is summoning six lakh ape soldiers to come and do battle. That ape nourishes a body that is ochre in complexion. This is the energetic Gavaya and he is angrily advancing against you. There are seven lakh and seventy thousand who serve him. He is saying that he will crush Lanka with his army alone. These are the foremost leaders among leaders. They are terrible and impossible to withstand. They are strong and can assume any form at will. They cannot be numbered.'

Chapter 6(18)

'I[60] will tell you about the brave leaders you are looking at. For Raghava's sake, they are ready to give up their lives. There is one who has a lot of thick and soft hair on his tail—coppery, yellow, black and white. He is terrible in his deeds. This is a leader named Hara, who seems to be dragging the earth and seizing the radiant rays of the sun. There are one hundred thousand following him at the rear, holding up trees and eager to climb into Lanka. O destroyer of enemy cities! There are thousands of crores of greatly energetic apes. They wish to fight against you and be victorious. You can see the ones who are stationed there, like dark and large clouds. They are like masses of black collyrium. They possess the valour of truth

---

[58] The mountain, also known as Dardura.
[59] Parnasha is identified with the river Banas, in Rajasthan. That is, Vinata used to reside in that region earlier.
[60] This is a continuation of Sarana speaking.

in an encounter. Those brave ones use nails and teeth as weapons.
They are fierce in their anger and lead to fear. They are innumerable
and cannot be discerned, like another shore to the distant shore of
the ocean. O king! There is one who is in the midst of extremely
terrible bears who reside in mountains, uneven regions and rivers.
O king! He is like Parjanya, surrounded in every direction by
clouds. He is the one who resides in the supreme mountain known
as Rikshavanta, drinking the waters of the Narmada. He is the lord
of all the bears and he is the leader named Dhumra. Behold his
younger brother, who is like a mountain. He is like his brother in
beauty and superior to him in valour. He is the great leader of the
forces, named Jambavat. He may be truculent towards his seniors,
but he is intolerant in striking. When the gods and the asuras fought,
Jambavat helped and performed an extremely great deed for the
intelligent Shakra. Consequently, he obtained many boons. Having
ascended the summits of mountains, they[61] hurl down gigantic
boulders that are huge in size, resembling large clouds. They are
not scared of dying. They possess hair and are like rakshasas and
pishachas. A large number of his soldiers are wandering around,
as energetic as the fire. That wrathful one is stationed amidst the
apes. Stationed there, all the apes are looking towards this leader
among leaders. O king! This lord of apes worships the one with the
one thousand eyes. With an army of strong soldiers, he is the leader
named Rambha. There is the one who has advanced for one yojana
along that mountain and has hauled his body up the mountain for
one yojana. He is supreme in his beauty and his four feet can be seen.
He is known by the name of Samnadana and he is the grandfather
of the apes. In a battle, he fought against the intelligent Shakra, but
was not defeated in that encounter. He is a leader among leaders.
His valour is like Shakra's prowess. In former times, to help the
residents of heaven in the battle between the gods and the asuras, this
one, with a black tail, was born from a gandharva maiden. O lord
of the rakshasas! King Vaishravana,[62] your brother, always sports

---

[61] Jambavat's soldiers.
[62] Kubera.

happily on an Indra among mountains, frequented by *kinnaras*.[63]
This handsome and bull among apes resides there, seated under a
jambu tree. He never indulges in boasting in an encounter and he
is the leader named Krathana. He is stationed there, surrounded by
one thousand crore apes. He hopes that he will crush Lanka with
his own army. There is the one who wanders around the Ganga,
terrifying the leaders of elephants and remembering the old enmity
between elephants and apes. This leader and commander of a herd
is advancing, uprooting trees. He is the one who resides in caves in
mountains. This foremost leader in the army of the apes resides on
Mount Ushirabija, along the river Haimavati, and is like Mandara.
This best among apes finds pleasure, like Shakra himself in heaven.
O king! There is the extremely intolerant leader named Pramathi
and one hundred thousand follow him. You can see him, like a
cloud that has been raised by the wind. As he circles around, a
large quantity of dust is raised. There are extremely strong and
terrible *golangulas*[64] with black faces. You can see that one crore
of them have crossed the bridge. The extremely swift Gavaksha
is the leader of the golangulas. Surrounding him, those energetic
ones are advancing towards Lanka, to crush it. There is a place
where trees yield all the fruits that one desires and are worshipped
by the bees. He resides on that mountain, which has a complexion
like the hue of the sun. Its[65] radiance always dazzles and thus lends
its hue to the birds and the animals. The great-souled maharshis
never forsake its slopes. O king! He finds pleasure on that beautiful
Mount Kanchana. He is foremost among the foremost apes and he
is the leader named Kesari. There are sixty thousand peaks in the
beautiful Mount Kanchana. O unblemished one! Like you among
the rakshasas, there is an excellent peak among them. Tawny
brown, white and copper-coloured, with honey-brown faces, they
reside on that excellent peak, with teeth and nails as weapons. They
possess four teeth, like lions. They are as invincible as tigers. All

---

[63] Kinnara, also known as *kimpurusha*, is a semi-divine species, described as Kubera's
companions.

[64] With a tail like that of a cow, langur.

[65] The mountain's.

of them blaze like the fire and are like virulent poison. Like crazy elephants, they raise their extremely long tails. They are like giant mountains and their roar is like that of large clouds. There is a valiant leader who is stationed amidst them. O king! He is famous on earth by the name of Shatabali. He hopes to crush Lanka with his army alone. Gaja, Gavaksha, Gavaya, Nala and the ape Nila—each one of these leaders is surrounded by ten crores. That apart, there are other foremost apes who reside on Mount Vindhya. They are dexterous in their valour and it is impossible to enumerate their large numbers. O great king! All of them are extremely powerful. All of them have bodies that are like large mountains. In an instant, all of them are capable of hurling down boulders and shattering the earth.'

Chapter 6(19)

Hearing Sarana's words, Ravana, the lord of the rakshasas, looked at the entire army. Shuka then addressed him in these words. 'You can see them stationed there, like large and crazy elephants. O king! They are like *nyagrodha* trees[66] along the Ganga or sala trees in the Himalayas. They are extremely difficult to counter. They are strong and can assume any form at will. They are like *daitya*s and danavas. In a battle, their valour is like that of the gods. There are twenty one thousand crores, one thousand *shanku*s and one hundred *vrinda*s of them.[67] These are Sugriva's advisers and they always make their homes in Kishkindha. These apes have been born from gods and gandharvas and they can assume any form at will. You can see two young ones stationed there and they are like the gods in their forms. These two are Mainda and Dvivida and no one can equal them in battle. With Brahma's permission, these two have partaken of amrita. In the battle, they hope to crush

---

[66] The Indian fig tree.
[67] These numbers are explained later.

Lanka with their energy alone. You can see an angry ape stationed
there, like an elephant with a shattered temple.[68] He can agitate the
ocean with his strength. O lord! He is the one who came to Lanka
and met Vaidehi and you. This is the ape you saw earlier and he has
come again. He is the eldest son of Kesari and is known to be the
son of the wind god. He is famous as Hanumat and he is the one
who leapt across the ocean. This best among apes can assume any
form at will and he is full of strength and beauty. Everywhere, his
progress is always unimpeded, like that of the lord.[69] When he was
a child, he saw the rising sun and wished to drink it up. He leapt
up three thousand yojanas and descended again. "I will seize the
sun and thus satisfy my hunger." Intoxicated by his strength, this
was his thought in earlier times. The sun god, rising above Mount
Udaya, cannot be touched by the gods, the rishis and the danavas.
Unable to reach it, he fell down. When the ape fell down, his jaw
was broken on a slope of the mountain. Since his jaw was firm, it
was broken only a little. That is the reason he is Hanumat. I know
the truth about the ape through *yoga* and *agama*.[70] I am incapable
of describing his strength, beauty and power. Using his energy,
he hopes to single-handedly crush Lanka. After him, there is the
brave and dark one, with eyes like the petals of lotuses. He is an
atiratha[71] of the Ikshvaku lineage, famous in the world because of
his manliness. He never deviates from dharma and never crosses
dharma. He knows about *brahmastra*[72] and he is supreme among
those who possess knowledge about the Vedas. He shatters the sky
with his arrows and even shatters mountains. His anger is like that
of Death and his valour is like that of Shakra. From Janasthana,
you abducted his wife, Sita. O king! He is Rama and he has come
to fight against you in the encounter. There is one on his right, with
a complexion like that of pure molten gold. His chest is broad and
his eyes are coppery red. His hair is black and curled. This is his

---

[68] An elephant in musth.
[69] Vayu.
[70] Keeping it simple, agama is a class of sacred texts that are outside the mainstream.
[71] An atiratha is a great warrior, greater than a *maharatha*.
[72] Brahma's weapon.

brother Lakshmana and he loves him more than his own life. He is accomplished in good policy and fighting and he is learned in all the sacred texts. He is intolerant, impossible to defeat, victorious, valiant, intelligent and strong. He has always been like Rama's right arm, as if his[73] breath of life is coursing outside his body. For Raghava's sake, he does not bother about preserving his own life. He hopes that in the battle, he will slay all the rakshasas. There is one who is standing on Rama's left flank. He is protected by rakshasas and he is King Vibhishana. This prosperous one was consecrated as a king of kings in Lanka.[74] He is angry with you and is advancing in the battle. You can see someone stationed in the middle, like an immobile mountain. He is the unvanquished master of all the foremost apes, possessing energy, fame, intelligence, learning and noble birth. This ape is as radiant as the Himalaya mountains. He resides in Kishkindha, with its impenetrable caves and trees. He dwells there, with the foremost apes, in a fortification in the mountains that is impossible to penetrate. He wears a golden and radiant garland, with one hundred lotuses. Lakshmi, loved by gods and humans, is established in him. After slaying Vali, Rama gave this Sugriva this garland, Tara and the eternal kingdom of the apes. One hundred thousand crores is said to be a shanku and such numbers are advancing to fight in the cause of Sugriva, Indra among the apes.[75] O great king! Look at this army, which has presented itself, like a flaming planet. Therefore, great efforts are recommended, so that we are victorious and the enemy is defeated.'

Chapter 6(20)

Ravana saw the leaders of the apes who were indicated by Shuka, his own brother Vibhishana, stationed near Rama,

---

[73] Rama's.

[74] By Rama.

[75] The Critical Edition excises shlokas where one hundred thousand shankus are said to be a *mahashanku* and one hundred thousand mahashankus are said to be a vrinda.

the immensely valorous Lakshmana who was like Rama's right
arm and Sugriva, the king of the apes, terrible in his valour.
Somewhat anxious in his mind, he became angry. After the end of
the conversation, he reprimanded the two brave ones, Shuka and
Sarana. In an angry voice that was full of intolerance, he addressed
them in these harsh words. 'Those like you should not earn a living
as advisers. You have spoken disagreeable words to the king, the
lord who can reward and punish you. The enemy is acting against
us and has invaded, seeking a battle. Both of you have uttered
words of praise about those who should not be applauded. Your
service to your preceptors, seniors and the aged has been futile.
Though you earn a living from the sacred texts on royal policy,
you have not grasped the essence. Even if you have grasped, you
have not understood. Or the burden of knowledge has confused
you. With such foolish advisers, it is fortunate that I am still here.
Are you not scared of death that you have addressed me in these
harsh words? This is the tongue that commands you and confers
good and bad on you. Even if they are touched by a fire, trees
may remain in a forest. However, if one is touched by a crime
committed against the king, the criminal no longer remains. These
two wicked ones have praised the side of the enemy and I should
kill them. However, the former good deeds done by them have
made my anger mild. Go far away from here and do not be seen
near me. Remembering the good deeds you have done to me, I do
not wish to kill you. Though you are ungrateful and have turned
your faces away from me, because of my affection, I am going
to treat you as if you are already dead.' Thus addressed, Shuka
and Sarana were ashamed. Saying, 'May you be victorious,' they
withdrew from Ravana's presence.

Mahodara was near him and Dashagriva spoke to him.
'Quickly bring spies, who are accomplished in good policy, here.'
Following the command of the king, spies were swiftly summoned.
They joined their hands in salutation and presented themselves,
pronouncing benedictions of prosperity and victory. Those spies
were faithful, brave, devoted and bereft of fear. Ravana, the lord of
the rakshasas, addressed them in these words. 'Leave this place. Go

and test Rama's behaviour towards his close ministers and among
those who have assembled, the ones who are pleased with him.
When does he sleep? When is he awake? What else does he do?
Use your skills to ascertain everything completely and then return.
If kings get to know about the enemy through learned spies, in the
course of the encounter, the enemy can be restrained with only a
little bit of effort.' The spies were delighted and agreed. Placing
Shardula at the forefront, they circumambulated the lord of the
rakshasas. They then left for the spot where Rama and Lakshmana
were.

Disguising themselves, they approached Mount Suvela and
saw Rama, Lakshmana, Sugriva and Vibhishana. However, those
rakshasas were detected by Vibhishana, the Indra among rakshasas,
with dharma in his soul. He had them easily captured. They were
afflicted by the brave ones who were dexterous in their valour and
lost their senses.[76] Sighing, they reached Lanka again. These spies
roamed around in the night and always wandered around outside.[77]
They presented themselves before Dashagriva and told him that an
extremely large body of soldiers were camped near Mount Suvela.

Chapter 6(21)

The spies informed the lord of Lanka that an army that could not
be agitated was camped near Mount Suvela. They also told him
about Raghava. Ravana heard from the spies that the immensely
strong Rama had arrived. Somewhat anxious, he addressed
Shardula in these words. 'O one who roams around in the night!
Your complexion is distressed and not what it should be. I hope you
did not come under the subjugation of the wrathful enemy.'

Thus asked, Shardula became senseless with fear. He softly
addressed the tiger among rakshasas. 'O king! I was incapable of

[76] The dexterity in valour refers to the apes. The Critical Edition excises shlokas
where Rama orders for the release of the spies.

[77] That is, outside the city.

spying on those bulls among apes. They are valiant and strong and are protected by Raghava. I was incapable of conversing with them or questioning them. The apes, resembling mountains, protected the path in every direction. In disguise, no sooner had I penetrated that army, than I was forcibly captured by many and they oppressed me in diverse ways. I was severely struck with thighs, fists, teeth and palms. Those powerful and intolerant apes paraded me around. Conveyed all over the place, I was taken to Rama's presence. All my limbs were covered in blood. I was distracted and my senses were in a whirl. When the apes sought to kill me, I joined my hands in salutation and beseeched them. Raghava saved me and gave me scope to live as I chose. Rama has filled the great ocean with rocks and boulders. With his weapons, he has reached Lanka's gate and is stationed there. Everywhere, he is surrounded by the apes, who are arranged in the form of a Garuda *vyuha*.[78] Having released me, the immensely energetic one is advancing towards Lanka. Before he reaches the ramparts of the city, quickly do something. Either swiftly give him Sita, or grant him an excellent fight.' Hearing this, the lord of the rakshasas was tormented in his mind. Ravana addressed Shardula in these great words. 'Even if the gods and the gandharvas fight against me and even if there is fear from all the worlds, I will not return Sita.'

Having said this, the immensely energetic Ravana spoke again. 'When you spied on the army, who were the brave apes who were present there? What kind of power do those invincible apes possess? Whose sons and grandsons are they? O rakshasa! Tell me the truth about this. One should certainly decide to fight after knowing about their strengths and weaknesses and about the size of the army.' Shardula, the excellent spy, was addressed by Ravana in this way. In Ravana's presence, he started to speak these words. 'O king! Riksharaja's son[79] is extremely difficult to vanquish in a battle. Gadgada's son is known by the name of Jambavat. There is another one of Gadgada's sons. There

---

[78] A vyuha is a battle formation, this one shaped in the form of Garuda.
[79] Sugriva.

is another one who is the son of Shatakratu's preceptor.[80] It is his son who single-handedly created the carnage among the rakshasas. Sushena, with dharma in his soul, is the valiant son of Dharma.[81] O king! The amiable ape, Dadhimukha, is Soma's son. Sumukha, Durmukha and the ape Vegadarshi are like Death in the form of apes. Indeed, they were created by Svayambhu himself. Nila, the commander, is the son of the fire god himself. The son of the wind god is famous by the name of Hanumat. The young, invincible and strong Angada is Shakra's grandson. The powerful Mainda and Dvivida have been born from the two Ashvins. Vaivasvata[82] has five sons there and they are like Death, the destroyer—Gaja, Gavaksha, Gavaya, Sharabha and Gandhamadana. Shveta and Jyotirmukha have been born from the sun god. The ape Hemakuta is Varuna's son. The brave Nala, supreme among apes, is Vishvakarma's son. The brave and swift Sudurdhara is the son of the Vasus. There are ten crore apes who desire to fight. I am incapable of recounting the other handsome sons of the gods. Dasharatha's young son can withstand a lion. He is the one who killed Dushana, Khara and Trishira. There is no one on earth who is Rama's equal in valour. He is the one who killed Viradha and Kabandha, who was like Death. There is no man on earth who can narrate Rama's qualities. The rakshasas who went to Janasthana were slain by him. Lakshmana, with dharma in his soul, is a bull among elephants. Someone who comes in the path of his arrows, even if it is Vasava, will not remain alive. Your brother, Vibhishana, is supreme among the rakshasas. Having accepted the city of Lanka,[83] he is engaged in ensuring Raghava's welfare. I have thus told you everything about the army of the apes. They have camped on Mount Suvela. You should decide what needs to be done next.'

[80] Shatakratu's preceptor is Brihasapati and Brihaspati's son is Kesari. Hanumat is Kesari's son.

[81] Meaning Yama.

[82] Yama.

[83] As a gift from Rama, when Rama consecrated Vibhishana as the king of Lanka.

Chapter 6(22)

The spies told the king of Lanka that Raghava and an army that could not be agitated was camped on Mount Suvela. Through the spies, Ravana heard that the immensely strong Rama had arrived. He was somewhat anxious and spoke to his advisers. 'O advisers! All of you control yourselves and come quickly. O rakshasas! The time for consultations has arrived.' Hearing his words, the ministers swiftly arrived. He consulted with his rakshasa advisers. The invincible one consulted about what should be done next. Then, having granted permission to the advisers to leave, he entered his own residence.

He summoned the immensely strong rakshasa, Vidyujjihva.[84] With the one who was skilled in maya, the one who was great in the use of maya[85] entered the spot where Maithilee was. The lord of the rakshasas told Vidyujjihva, who knew about maya. 'Use your maya to confound Sita, Janaka's daughter. O one who roams around in the night! Use your maya to create Raghava's head. Fashion a great bow and arrows and present yourself before me.' Thus instructed, Vidyujjihva, who roamed around in the night, agreed. He used his maya well and showed Ravana the result. The king was satisfied at this and gave him some ornaments.

The immensely strong one entered Ashokavana. The younger brother of the lord of riches saw the one who was in distress, though she did not deserve to be distressed. Overwhelmed by grief, she was seated on the ground, with her face lowered down. She sorrowed in Ashokavana, thinking about her husband. Near her, terrible rakshasis tended to her. Having approached Sita, he happily pronounced his name. He spoke these insolent words to Janaka's daughter. 'O fortunate one! You comforted yourself by thinking about your husband Raghava, the slayer of Khara. However, he has been killed in the battle. I have killed him and the foundation of your pride has been severed in every possible way. O Sita!

---

[84] Vidyut-Jihva.
[85] Respectively Vidyujjihva and Ravana.

Because of the calamity you face, you will now become my wife.
O foolish one! You pride yourself on being learned. Withdraw
from something that has little merit. O Sita! Hear the account of
your husband being killed, as terrible as Vritra's death. Indeed,
Raghava crossed the ocean and attacked, so as to kill me. He was
surrounded by a large army that had been brought together by the
Indra among the apes. This reached and camped on the southern
shore of the ocean. Rama arrived with this large army when the sun
was about to set. They were exhausted at the end of the journey.
The army was stationed there, happily asleep. In the middle of
the night, the first spies approached it. My large army was led by
Prahasta and reached the spot where Rama and Lakshmana were.
His large army was destroyed at night. The attacking rakshasas
repeatedly raised their weapons—spears, clubs, swords, *chakra*s,
large iron staffs, nets of arrows, javelins, radiant and spiked maces,
daggers, lances, spikes, chakras[86] and bludgeons to bring down
the apes. While Rama was asleep, Prahasta struck him. Without
anyone restraining his hand, he used a large sword to sever his
head. Vibhishana was attacked and captured easily. It is through
good fortune that Lakshmana and all the soldiers of the apes fled
in different directions. O Sita! Sugriva, the lord of the apes, had
his neck broken. With his jawbone shattered, Hanumat was slain
by the rakshasas and is lying down. Just as Jambavat rose up on
his knees, he was killed in the battle. He was severed with many
javelins, just as a tree is cut down. Mainda and Dvivida, the bulls
among the apes, have been killed. They sighed and wept and were
covered in blood. Struck in the middle, those slayers of enemies
were killed with the sword. Lying down on the ground, Panasa
screamed. Mangled by many iron arrows, Darimukha is lying down
in a pit. While he was shrieking, the greatly energetic Kumuda was
killed by arrows. The rakshasas struck Angada's body with many
arrows. With blood flowing from his body, Angada fell down on
the ground. Some apes were crushed, caught in the nets of elephants
and chariots. Lying down, they were dispersed, like clouds by the

---

[86] The word chakra is mentioned twice.

force of the wind. Others were terrified and fled, but were pursued and killed by the rakshasas while they fled, like large elephants by lions. Some fell down in the ocean. Some resorted to the sky. The bears, mingling with the apes, climbed trees. There were many with tawny eyes and disfigured eyes who were killed by the rakshasas along the shores of the ocean, in mountains and in forests. Thus, my soldiers killed your husband and his soldiers. This head, wet with blood and smeared with dust, has been seized.'

After this, the extremely unassailable Ravana, lord of the rakshasas, spoke to the rakshasis in Sita's hearing. 'Fetch the rakshasa Vidyujjihva, the performer of cruel deeds. He is the one who himself collected Raghava's head from the field of battle.' Vidyujjihva brought the head and the bow and arrows. He bowed his head down and stood in front of Ravana. King Ravana spoke to the rakshasa Vidyujjihva, the one with a large tongue, who was stationed there, asking him to come closer. 'Quickly place the head of Dasharatha's son in front of Sita. It is best that the pitiable one sees the final state of her husband.' Thus addressed, the rakshasa flung down the beloved head before Sita and quickly vanished. Ravana flung down the large and radiant bow and said, 'This is Rama's, famous in the three worlds. This is truly Rama's bow, which makes a sound when it is twanged. After having killed the human in the night, Prahasta brought it here.' With the head flung down by Vidyujjihva, Ravana flung the bow down on the ground. He told the illustrious daughter of the king of Videha, 'Submit yourself to me.'

Chapter 6(23)

Sita saw the head and the excellent bow. She heard about the destruction of Sugriva and Hanumat. The eyes and the complexion of the face were just like her husband's face. So were the tips of the hair, the forehead and the auspicious *chudamani*.[87]

---

[87] Jewel worn on the top of the head.

She was convinced because of all these signs and became extremely
miserable. She shrieked like a female curlew and condemned
Kaikeyee. 'O Kaikeyee! May your wishes come true. The delight
of the lineage has been killed. O one who is devoted to dissensions!
You have destroyed the entire lineage. O Kaikeyee! What harm
did the noble Rama do to you? Why did you exile him to the
forest, with bark as garb?' Trembling, the ascetic Vaidehi said
this. Like a severed plantain tree, the young one fell down on the
ground. In a short while, she regained her senses and comforted
herself. The large-eyed one inhaled the fragrance of the head and
lamented. 'Alas! O mighty-armed one! I have been destroyed. I
have followed one who was brave in his vows. This is your final
state and I have become a widow. It is said that if a husband dies
first, that is a bad quality in a woman. However, since you are
good and virtuous in your conduct, you have departed before me.
From one sorrow, I have moved to another sorrow. I am immersed
in an ocean of grief. The one who stirred himself to save me has
himself been brought down. O Raghava! You are the son of my
mother-in-law, Kousalya. You were like a calf and she was like a
cow. She is like a cow without her calf. O one whose valour is
unthinkable! There are those who said that you would live for a
long time. They uttered a lie. O Raghava! Your lifespan has been
limited. Perhaps your wisdom was destroyed. Perhaps, despite your
wisdom, your virtue was destroyed.[88] Perhaps this is the power of
destiny, which cooks creatures. You knew about the sacred texts of
good policy. How could your death not have been foreseen? You
were skilled in discerning hardships and accomplished in avoiding
them. Thus, you have been embraced by the terrible and extremely
violent night of destruction. O lotus-eyed one! You have been
killed and have been taken away from me. O mighty-armed one!
Abandoning me, the ascetic one, you are lying down. O bull among
men! Like a beloved woman, you are embracing the auspicious
earth. I have always worshipped your beloved bow carefully, with
fragrances and garlands. O brave one! This is it, decorated with

---

[88] Thus the destruction.

gold. O unblemished one! In heaven, it is certain that you have met your father and my father-in-law, Dasharatha, together with the earlier ancestors. Having performed great and beloved deeds, you have become a nakshatra in the sky. But in the process, you have neglected your own auspicious lineage of royal sages.[89] O king! Why are you not looking at me? Why are you not replying to me? I am your wife and have been your companion, since the time you were a boy and obtained me, as a girl. You accepted my hand and took a pledge, "I will travel with you." O Kakutstha! Remember that. I am extremely miserable. Take me with you. O supreme among those who reach their destinations! Why have you departed, leaving me? I am extremely miserable. I have been left in this world and you have gone to that world. This body was embraced by me and deserves to be adorned with fortunate objects. It is certainly being dragged by predatory beasts now. Why have you not obtained *agnishtoma*, *agnihotra* and other sacrifices and rites, with plenty of *dakshina*,[90] and not been honoured properly?[91] In her grief, Kousalya wishes to see us. Three of us left on the exile and she will only see Lakshmana return. When she asks him, he will certainly tell her how the army of your friends and you were killed by the rakshasas in the night. She will hear that you have been killed while asleep and that I am in the residence of the rakshasas. O Raghava! Her heart will be shattered. O Ravana! It is best that you bring me down on top of Rama. Perform this excellent and fortunate deed and unite the husband with the wife. Join my head with his head and my body with his body. O Ravana! I will follow and reach the destination obtained by my great-souled husband. I do not wish to remain alive even for an instant, because that would be a wicked life. In my father's house, I have heard brahmanas who are learned in the Vedas speak about this. Those women who love their husbands obtain great worlds. He possessed forgiveness, self-control, truthfulness, dharma, gratefulness and non-violence towards all beings. When he is dead, what will happen to me?' Tormented by grief, thus did the

[89] Presumably, by not leaving a descendant.
[90] Sacrificial fee. These were donated symbolically.
[91] As funeral rites.

large-eyed one lament, as Janaka's daughter beheld her husband's
head and the bow there.

While Sita was lamenting there, a rakshasa joined his hands in
salutation and approached his master. He said, 'O son of a noble
one! May you be victorious.' He greeted him, obtained his favours
and informed him that Prahasta, the commander of the army, had
arrived. 'O lord! All the advisers are well and Prahasta has come
with them. Please see them. There is some urgent task that needs to
be undertaken.' Hearing what the rakshasa had said, Dashagriva
left Ashokavana to go and see the ministers. He entered the
assembly hall. Knowing about Rama's valour, he consulted with all
his capable ministers about what he should himself do next. Within
a short while after Ravana's departure, the head and the excellent
bow vanished. The Indra among rakshasas held consultations
with his capable ministers, who were terrible in their valour. He
determined what he should do about Rama. Ravana, the lord of the
rakshasas, was like Death. Wishing his welfare, the commanders
of the battalions were stationed near him. He told them, 'Quickly
beat a drum with a stick. Make the sound be heard and summon
the soldiers. Do not tell them the reason.' The commanders of the
battalions followed his instructions and swiftly assembled a large
army. They informed their master, who desired to fight, that the
forces had been summoned.

Chapter 6(24)

On seeing that Sita was confounded, her beloved friend, a
rakshasi named Sarama,[92] quickly approached her beloved
Vaidehi. Ravana had asked her to protect Sita and contract her
friendship. However, she was compassionate and was firm in her
vows and actually protected her. Sarama saw that her friend, Sita,

[92] Sarama is believed to have been Vibhishana's wife, although nothing like that is
clearly stated.

had lost her senses. Having rolled around on the ground like a mare, she had just arisen and was covered with dust. Affectionately, the one who was good in her vows comforted her friend. 'O timid one! Because of my affection towards you as a friend, I have myself overheard everything that Ravana told you and what you said in reply. I abandoned all fear of Ravana and hid myself in the desolate sky. O large-eyed one! That was because of you and I do not care for my own life. There is a reason why the lord of the rakshasas was scared and left. O Maithilee! I know everything about the reason for his departure. Rama knows about his soul. It is not possible to approach the tiger among men when he is asleep and kill him. The apes fight with trees and it is not possible to kill them, even by the gods. They are extremely well protected by Rama and the bull among the gods.[93] The handsome one has long and rounded arms. He is powerful and his chest is broad. He is an archer who can withstand everything. He possesses dharma in his soul and is famous on earth. He is valiant and always protects himself and others. He is with his accomplished brother, Lakshmana, who knows the sacred texts about good policy. He is the one who slays large tides of enemy soldiers. His strength and manliness are unthinkable. O Sita! It is not possible for the handsome Raghava, the slayer of enemies, to be killed. The one who acts against all creatures has done this with his perverted intelligence. The one who knows about maya has invoked a terrible maya on you. All your miseries have now gone and your good fortune has presented itself. It is certain that prosperity will now serve you. Hear the most pleasant tidings of all. With the army of the apes, Rama has crossed the ocean. Having reached the southern shore of the ocean, they have camped there. I have seen Kakutstha, with Lakshmana, accomplish this objective. Protected by the army, the two of them are stationed there, near the ocean. He[94] sent some rakshasas who were dexterous in their valour. They have brought the news here, that Raghava has crossed the ocean. O large-eyed one! Having heard this, Ravana, the lord

[93] Indra.
[94] Ravana.

of the rakshasas, is consulting all his advisers about what should be done.'

While the rakshasi Sarama was telling Sita this, a terrible sound was heard, signifying that the soldiers were making all kinds of efforts. The sound of sticks struck against musical instruments was heard and the loud sound of drums. Sweet in speech, Sarama told Sita, 'O timid one! The terrible sound of drums is indicative of a war starting. Listen to the deep rumbling of drums, like the sound of clouds. Crazy elephants are being readied. Horses are being yoked to chariots. Here and there, foot soldiers are arming and preparing themselves. The royal roads are full of soldiers who are extraordinary to behold. The forceful ones are roaring, like waves of water in the ocean. There are sparkling weapons, armour and shields. The chariots, horses, elephants and the rakshasas have been ornamented. Behold the many kinds of radiance, of different hues, that have been created. It has the form of the fire, when it burns down a forest during the summer. Hear the sound of the bells. Hear the clatter of the chariots. Hear the horses neighing. Hear the blaring of the trumpets. A tumultuous sound has been created by the rakshasas preparing themselves and it makes the body hair stand up. Shri, the destroyer of sorrow, serves you. A fear has arisen for the rakshasas from the lotus-eyed Rama, like for the daityas from Vasava. He has conquered his rage and his valour is unthinkable. Having defeated and killed Ravana in the battle, your husband will come before you. With Lakshmana, your husband will exhibit his valour against the rakshasas. Among the enemy, he will be like Vishnu, the slayer of enemies, accompanied by Vasava. Rama will quickly arrive and you will be on his lap. With the enemy brought down, I will see you accomplish your objective. O beautiful one! When the one with the broad chest approaches you and embraces you against his chest, you will shed tears of joy. O queen! You have sported this single braid for a long time and it has reached your hips. O Sita! The immensely strong Rama will soon loosen it for you. O queen! You will see his face, resembling a full moon that has arisen. You will be freed from these tears of misery, like a female snake that sheds its skin. O Maithilee! Ravana will soon be slain in the battle. You deserve all the happiness that you love. You will obtain that happiness. United with the great-souled Rama, you will be delighted, like the earth, full of crops, rejoices when it has excellent rains. O queen! He is like the fearless sun that circles around the excellent mountain,[95] driving its steeds swiftly along its path and exhibiting its powers to all creatures. You will soon find refuge with him.'

Chapter 6(25)

She had been confounded by his[96] words and tormented. Sarama brought her delight, like the water from the sky does to the earth. She[97] desired to ensure the welfare of her friend and knew about the right time. At the right time, she smiled first and then addressed her friend in these words. 'O dark-eyed one! I am capable of conveying your words to Rama and telling him that you are well. I can return, hiding myself. When I course through the sky, without any support, no one is capable of following my path, not even the wind god or Garuda.'

Addressed yet again, Sita spoke to Sarama in sweet and gentle words, her former sorrow having been dispelled. 'You are capable of coursing through the sky and even going to rasatala. But understand what must not be done and what must be done now. If you wish to do what is agreeable to me and if your mind is made up about this, I desire that you should go and find out what Ravana is doing now. I wish to know that. Ravana is cruel and possesses the strength of maya. He makes the enemy scream. The one with evil soul confounded me, like someone is instantly affected by drinking varuni. He used the rakshasis, who always guard me, to constantly censure me and reprimand and slight me. I am anxious and scared. My mind is not at peace. In Ashokavana, I am anxious

[95] Meru.
[96] Ravana's.
[97] Sarama.

because of my fear. If I get to know everything that he has decided and if you report all that to me, it will be a great favour to me.' As Sita said this, Sarama, gentle in her speech, replied to her in these words, wiping away the tears of sorrow. 'O Janakee! If that is your intention, I will go. I will go and see what the enemy's intention is and return.'

Having said this, she approached that rakshasa. She heard what Ravana was telling his ministers. Accomplished in discerning, she heard what the evil-souled one had decided. She then quickly returned to Ashokavana. Having entered the place again, she saw Janaka's daughter. She was waiting for her, like a lotus that is faded and has lost its beauty.[98] Sarama, soft in her speech, returned again and Sita embraced her extremely gently, offering her own seat to her. 'Be seated here comfortably. Tell me the truth. What has the cruel and evil-souled Ravana decided to do?' Sarama was thus addressed by the trembling Sita. She told her everything about the conversation between Ravana and his ministers. 'O Vaidehi! The mother of the Indra of the rakshasas[99] and the aged and understanding minister, Aviddha, spoke great words, urging for your release. "Let Maithilee be honoured and given to the Indra among men. The extraordinary event that transpired in Janasthana[100] should be sufficient. Which man on earth could have performed the crossing of the ocean, the sighting by Hanumat[101] and the slaying of the rakshasas in an encounter?" The aged ministers addressed him in many kinds of ways. However, he is not interested in freeing you, like a person who is excessively addicted to riches. O Maithilee! Before he dies in the battle, he is not interested in freeing you. With his advisers, that is what the cruel one has decided. Because of his addiction to death and his greed, his mind is quite made up. He is incapable of freeing you out of fear, not until he is restrained in a battle. He

---

[98] It is possible to interpret and translate this as Shri separated from the lotus on which she is seated.

[99] Ravana's mother was Kaikasi.

[100] The destruction of the rakshasas.

[101] Of Lanka and Sita.

will destroy himself and all the rakshasas. O dark-eyed one! In the battle, Rama will slay Ravana with his arrows and use every possible means to take you back to Ayodhya.'

At this time, the sound of drums and conch shells was heard. All the soldiers heard the ground tremble. The servants of the king of the rakshasas in Lanka heard the sound created by the soldiers of the apes. They lost their energy and their enterprise and were filled with distress. Because of the sins of their king, they could no longer see what was beneficial for them.

Chapter 6(26)

To the sound of conch shells mixed with that of drums, the mighty-armed Rama Raghava, the conqueror of enemy cities, advanced. Ravana, the lord of the rakshasas, heard the sound. He thought for a while and glanced at the advisers. In the assembly hall, the immensely strong Ravana spoke to all the advisers in a voice that echoed. 'I have heard what you have said about Rama crossing the ocean, his valour and his collection of forces. I also know that you possess the valour of truth in a battle.'

There was a rakshasa named Malyavat and he was extremely wise. He was Ravana's maternal grandfather and hearing his words, he said, 'O king! A king who is learned, humble and a follower of good policy obtains prosperity for a long time and keeps his enemies under his subjugation. At the right time, if he contracts peace with the enemy, or fights against them, or extends his own alliances, he obtains great prosperity. A king who is inferior or equal must seek peace. An enemy must not be underestimated and there must be war only if one is superior. O Ravana! That is the reason an agreement of peace with Rama appeals to me. Give Sita, the reason for the conflict, back to him. All the divine rishis and the gandharvas desire his victory. Do not engage in a conflict with him. An alliance with him is preferable. The illustrious grandfather created two parties—gods and asuras, and they resort to dharma and *adharma*. O Ravana! It has been heard that dharma is on the side of the great-souled gods and adharma is on the side of the rakshasas and the asuras. When dharma devours adharma, *krita yuga* results.[102] When adharma devours dharma, there is the onset of *tishya*. While you roamed around the worlds, you caused great damage to dharma and accepted adharma. That is the reason the enemies are stronger than us. Indeed, it is because of your distractions that adharma is devouring us. The side of the gods and those who seek to enhance the gods is prospering. You are addicted to material pursuits and do whatever you like. This has engendered great anxiety among the rishis, who are like the fire. Their invisible powers are blazing like the fire. They have cleansed their souls through austerities and are devoted to propagating dharma. Those brahmanas always officiate at the principal sacrifices. They follow the rituals and offer oblations into the fire, loudly reciting the Vedas. Through chanting the name of the *brahman*, they overcome the rakshasas and like clouds during the summer, all of them are forced to flee in different directions. The rishis are like the fire and a smoke arises from their agnihotras, dispelling the energy of the rakshasas in the ten directions. In diverse sacred regions, firm in their vows, they observe fierce austerities and scorch the rakshasas. Having seen many ominous signs and diverse terrible portents, I can discern the terrible destruction of all the rakshasas. Clouds are thundering in terrible tones in the sky, giving rise to fear. Everywhere in Lanka, they are showering down warm blood. The mounts are weeping and shedding drops of tears. The standards are pale and faded and no longer shine as they used to. Predatory beasts, jackals and vultures are shrieking in extremely hideous voices. They are incessantly entering Lanka and gathering in droves. In dreams, dark women with white teeth are laughing, stationed in front of the houses and robbing them. Dogs are eating the sacrificial offerings in houses. Cows are giving birth to donkeys and mongooses are giving birth to rats. Cats are

---

[102] There are four yugas—krita (*satya*), *treta, dvapara* and *kali*. As one progressively moves from krita yuga to kali yuga, dharma declines. Tishya yuga is another name for kali yuga.

having intercourse with leopards and pigs with dogs. Kinnaras are having intercourse with rakshasas and humans. There are pigeons and other birds, pale and with red feet. Urged by destiny, they are roaming around, for the destruction of the rakshasas. There are *sharikas*[103] in houses, chirping away. They are fighting in groups and those which are defeated, are falling down. On several occasions, in the form of a dark brown and monstrous man with a shaved head, Death is looking at the houses. There are other evil portents that are manifesting themselves. I think that Rama is Vishnu, who has adopted a human body. This Raghava, firm in his valour, is not a mere man. He has performed the supremely wonderful act of building a bridge across the ocean. O Ravana! Have a treaty of peace with Rama, king of men.' Malyavat, supreme among the supreme in manliness and strength, spoke these words there. Wishing to again test what was in the mind of the lord of the rakshasas, he became silent and looked at Ravana.

Chapter 6(27)

Malyavat spoke these beneficial words. However, the evil-souled Dashanana was under the subjugation of time and could not tolerate them. He was under the subjugation of rage and he furrowed his forehead. His eyes rolled around and he spoke to Malyavat, 'With benefit in your mind, you have uttered harsh and injurious words. You have spoken in favour of the enemy and the words have not penetrated my ears. Rama is a pitiable human. He is alone and has sought refuge with apes. He has been abandoned by his father and has made a home in the forest. Why do you take him to be capable? I am the lord of the rakshasas and cause fear to the gods. I am not inferior in all kinds of valour. Why do you think that I am inferior? I think that you spoke these harsh words because you detest my valour, because you are partial

[103] The bird *Turdus salica*.

towards the enemy, or because you have been urged by the enemy. I am powerful and I am instated in my position. Which learned person, who knows about the truth of the sacred texts, will speak harsh words against such a person, unless he has been urged by the enemy? I have brought Sita from the forest. She is like Shri, without her lotus. Why will I be scared and return her to Raghava? Wait for a few days. You will see Raghava, with Sugriva and Lakshmana and surrounded by crores of apes, killed by me. In a battle, the gods cannot stand before me in a duel. Why should such a Ravana bear the burden of fear in an encounter? I will never bend down. I would rather be sliced into two. This is my innate nature. By nature, I am impossible to cross. If Rama has easily been able to build a bridge across the ocean, what is the marvel in that? Why should that give rise to fear? With his army of apes, Rama has crossed the ocean. I truthfully pledge before you that he will not return with his life.' Angry and agitated, Ravana spoke those words. Realizing this, Malyavat was ashamed and did not utter any words in reply. As is proper, he pronounced benedictions so that the king's victories might increase. Having taken his permission, Malyavat left for his own residence.

To decide what should be done, Ravana had consultations with his advisers. The rakshasa made arrangements so that Lanka could be protected in an unmatched way. He assigned the eastern gate to the rakshasa Prahasta, the southern to Mahavirya, Mahaparshva and Mahodara and the western gate to his son, Indrajit, who was well versed in maya and was surrounded by many rakshasas. He assigned the city's northern gate to Shuka and Sarana and told his ministers that he would also be there himself. The rakshasa Virupaksha, greatly valiant and brave, was placed at the centre of the army, together with many rakshasas. In this way, the bull among rakshasas made arrangements for Lanka and, under the subjugation of destiny, thought that he had succeeded. Having instructed the preparations for the entire city, he then gave his ministers permission to leave. He was worshipped by large numbers of ministers, who pronounced benedictions for victory. He then entered his great and prosperous inner quarters.

Chapter 6(28)

The king of men, the king of apes, the ape who was Vayu's son, Jambavat, the king of bears, the rakshasa Vibhishana, Angada, Vali's son, Soumitri, the ape Sharabha, Sushena, with his sons Mainda and Dvivida, Gaja, Gavaksha, Kumuda, Nala and Panasa reached. They assembled and discussed what should be done about the enemy. 'It can be seen that this city of Lanka is protected by Ravana. It is extremely difficult for even the asuras, the serpents, the gandharvas and the immortals to vanquish it. Placing the objective at the forefront, we must consult and decide. Ravana, the lord of the rakshasas, is always inside it.'

While they were conversing in this way, Ravana's younger brother, Vibhishana, uttered the best of words, articulated properly and full of meaning. 'My advisers, Anala, Sharabha, Sampati and Praghasa, went to the city of Lanka and have returned here again. All of them assumed the forms of birds and penetrated the enemy's forces. They controlled themselves and observed the arrangements that have been made. I have been precisely told about the arrangements made by the evil-souled Ravana. O Rama! I will tell you everything exactly. Listen. With his forces, Prahasta has reached the eastern gate and is stationed there. Mahavirya, Mahaparshva and Mahodara are towards the south. Surrounded by many rakshasas, Indrajit is at the western gate. They wield spears, swords, bows, javelins and clubs in their hands. Ravana's son is protected by brave ones armed with many kinds of weapons. There are many thousands of rakshasas, with weapons in their hands. Extremely anxious and surrounded by many rakshasas, Ravana is himself stationed at the northern gate. With a large army of rakshasas, Virupaksha, with a large spear, sword and bow, is stationed at the centre of the army. They saw many kinds of battalions thus arranged in Lanka. After that, all my advisers quickly returned here again. There are thousands of elephants and tens of thousands of chariots in the city. There are twenty thousand horses and more than one crore of rakshasas. They are brave and strong, like assassins in a battle. These roamers in the night are always engaged in ensuring the welfare of the king of the rakshasas. O lord of the earth![104] For each rakshasa who is going to fight, there are one hundred thousand to tend and support him.' The ministers had spoken about these arrangements in Lanka and Vibhishana repeated them to the lotus-eyed Rama. He again said, 'O Rama! When Ravana fought against Kubera, six hundred thousand rakshasas advanced with him. They were like the evil-souled Ravana in valour, bravery, energy, spirit, pride and insolence. There is no reason to be intolerant. I am trying to anger you, not frighten you. In your valour, you are capable of restraining even the gods. You are surrounded by a large army with the four kinds of forces. With the vyuhas of this army of the apes, you will crush Ravana.'

After Ravana's younger brother had spoken these words, so that the enemy could be countered, Raghava spoke these words. 'Surrounded by many apes, Nila, bull among apes, should be at Lanka's eastern gate, so that he can fight against Prahasta. Surrounded by a large army, Angada, Vali's son, should cause obstructions to Mahaparshva and Mahodara, at the southern gate. Surrounded by many apes, Hanumat, the son of the wind god, immeasurable in his soul, should attack the western gate and penetrate there. The inferior Ravana, is full of strength because he has obtained a boon. He loves to do unpleasant things to large numbers of daityas, danavas and great-souled rishis. He roams around all the worlds, scorching the subjects. I will myself try to kill that Indra among rakshasas at the northern gate, accompanied by Soumitri. I will enter and crush Ravana and his forces there. Let the powerful Indra among apes, Jambavat, the king of the bears, and the younger brother of the Indra among the rakshasas be at the centre of the army. In the battle, the apes should not assume the form of men. That way, in the midst of the army and the battle, we will be able to make out the apes. Among our people too, that will be means of identifying the apes. There are only seven of us humans who will fight against the enemy—I, my greatly energetic brother, Lakshmana, my friend, Vibhishana, and with him, his four advisers.' Desiring to accomplish

[104] Rama.

success in the objective, Rama spoke these words to Vibhishana. He
saw the beautiful slopes of Mount Suvela. The intelligent one made
up his mind to ascend Suvela. The great-souled Rama covered the
entire earth with his large army. Rejoicing, he advanced towards
Lanka. The great-souled one made up his mind to slay the enemy.

Chapter 6(29)

Having made up his mind to ascend Suvela and with Lakshmana
following him, Rama addressed Sugriva in these gentle and
supreme words. Vibhishana, the roamer in the night, knew about
dharma, counsels and rites, and was devoted to him. He also spoke
to him. 'Suvela, the virtuous Indra among mountains, is colourful
with hundreds of minerals. Let all of us climb it and spend the
night there. From there, we will see the residence of that evil-souled
rakshasa, who abducted my wife for the sake of ensuring his own
death. He doesn't know about dharma. He doesn't possess good
conduct or lineage. The rakshasa is inferior in intelligence and that
is the reason he has performed that reprehensible deed. When the
worst among rakshasas is mentioned, my rage increases. Because of
the crime committed by that inferior one, I will see the destruction
of all the rakshasas. Having come under the noose of destiny, one
commits a sin. Because of the crime committed by a person who is
inferior in his soul, his lineage is destroyed.' Extremely angry with
Ravana, he spoke in this way. To dwell there, Rama then started to
climb Suvela's colourful summit. Controlling himself, Lakshmana
followed him at the rear. He was addicted to performing great
acts of valour and held up his bow and arrows. Sugriva and his
advisers and Vibhishana followed him. So did Hanumat, Angada,
Nila, Mainda, Dvivida, Gaja, Gavaksha, Gavaya, Sharabha,
Gandhamadana, Panasa, Kumuda, Rambha, the leader of the
herd, and many other apes who were swift in their speed. They[105]

---

[105] The apes.

roamed around in mountains and with Raghava, hundreds of them
ascended that mountain with a speed like that of the wind. From
every direction, they climbed the mountain within a short while.

From the summit, they saw the city, as if it was suspended in
the air. It was auspicious, with the best of gates and adorned with
supreme ramparts. The leaders among the apes saw that Lanka was
full of rakshasas. The best among apes saw the dark roamers in
the night also stationed there, adding to the collection of ramparts,
since they seemed to form another rampart. The apes saw that all
the rakshasas desired to fight and while Rama looked on, they
emitted a loud roar. The evening was red and the sun set. There was
the radiance of the full moon and night arrived. Rama, the lord of
the army of the apes, was welcomed and honoured by Vibhishana,
together with Lakshmana, the leader of the herds[106] and the herds.
They happily resided on the slopes of Suvela.

Chapter 6(30)

The bulls among the apes spent the night on Suvela. The brave
ones saw Lanka, with its forests and groves. These were flat,
peaceful and beautiful, extremely large in size. Witnessing the
beauty, they were filled with wonder. It was full of champakas,
ashokas, *punnaga*s, salas and talas. It was shrouded with *tamala*
groves and dense with *nagakeshara* trees.[107] There were flowering
*hintala*s,[108] arjunas, *neepa*s and saptaparnas. There were tilakas,
karnikaras and *patala*s[109] in every direction. It was beautiful, with
creepers, with flowers at the tips, enveloping the many kinds of
divine trees, making Lanka resemble Indra's Amaravati. There
were wonderful blossoms and red and delicate leaves. There were
blue grasslands and colourful groves and forests. The lovely trees

---

[106] Sugriva.
[107] Flowering tree, the text uses the word *nagamala*.
[108] Variety of palm.
[109] *Bignonia suaveolens*.

were bedecked with fragrant flowers and fruits, just as men wear ornaments. Like Chaitratha and like Nandana, it was pleasing to the mind. The forests were beautiful in all the seasons and were radiant with bees. Gallinules and lapwings called, peacocks danced. Cuckoos could be heard in the waterfalls in the forests. The birds were always excited and bees buzzed around. There were clumps that were full of birds like cuckoos. Large bees sang and smaller bees swarmed. There was the chirping of wagtails and the calling of cranes.

Delighted and happy, the brave apes, who could assume any form at will, entered those forests and groves.[110] The extremely energetic apes entered there and an extremely pleasant and fragrant breeze began to blow, mixed with the fragrance of flowers. Some other brave apes, leaders of their herds, took Sugriva's permission and emerging from their herds, advanced towards Lanka, which was adorned with flags. As those supreme among those who roar roared in loud voices, the birds were scared and animals and birds terrified. Lanka trembled. They crushed the ground with their feet and created a great force. A dust was created by their feet and suddenly rose up. Frightened by that sound, bears, lions, boars, buffaloes, elephants and deer fled in the ten directions. The single tall peak of Trikuta rose up and touched the sky. It was enveloped with flowers everywhere and seemed to be made out of gold. It sparkled and was beautiful to see, extending for one hundred yojanas. It was lovely, handsome and gigantic and even the birds found it difficult to approach. It was impossible to climb, even in one's thoughts, not to speak of people who sought to ascend. Protected by Ravana, Lanka nestled on that peak. The city had towering gates that were like white clouds. These were made out of gold and there were beautiful silver ramparts. Lanka was supremely adorned with palaces and storeyed mansions. Nestled in between,[111] it was like the sky, Vishnu's region, at the end of the summer. There was a palace ornamented with one thousand pillars there. It resembled the peak of Kailasa and could

---

[110] Clearly having descended from Suvela.
[111] Between heaven and earth.

be seen, as if it was an etching in the sky. This sanctuary of the
Indra among the rakshasas was a supreme ornament for the city.
One hundred rakshasas always protected all of it. With the apes,
Rama, Lakshmana's prosperous elder brother, saw the prosperous
city, which had accomplished its objective of being wealthy. It was
full of jewels and possessed diverse arrangements. It was decorated
with garlands of palaces. There were large machines and huge doors
in the city. With his great force, Rama saw it.

Chapter 6(31)

Having seen various signs, Lakshmana's elder brother addressed
Lakshmana, who possessed all the auspicious signs, in these
words. 'O Lakshmana! Let us gather cool water and groves full of
fruits. Let us divide this army into vyuhas and wait. We can see that
a terrible fear has presented itself and that it will cause a destruction
of creatures. There will be death for the best of bears, apes and
rakshasas. A harsh wind is blowing and the earth is trembling. The
summits of mountains are quivering and falling down on the ground.
Like harsh and cruel predatory beasts, the clouds are rumbling in
harsh tones. They are showering down cruel drops of water mixed
with blood. The evening is extremely terrible and resembles red
sandalwood. A blazing ball of fire is falling down from the sun.
Birds and animals are miserable. In their distress, they are facing
the sun and calling in terrible tones. This is ominous and generates
great fear. Though its radiance cannot be seen in the night, the
moon is scorching us. Its beams are black and red, just as it is at the
time of the destruction of the world. O Lakshmana! Behold. A blue
mark can be seen in the sun's disc. It is small, harsh and ominous
and the extremities are extremely red. The nakshatras can no longer
be seen to be circling as they used to. O Lakshmana! Behold. All
this seems to be telling us that the end of the yuga and the world
has arrived. Crows, hawks and vultures are circling below. Jackals
are also howling in loud and inauspicious voices. This invincible

city is protected by Ravana. Surrounded by the apes on all sides, let us swiftly attack with force.' Lakshmana's brave elder brother spoke to Lakshmana in this way. The immensely strong one quickly descended from the summit of the mountain.

Raghava, with dharma in his soul, descended from the mountain. He looked at his own army, which was extremely difficult for the enemy to assail. Raghava knew about the right time. With Sugriva, since the time was right, he urged the great army of the king of the apes. Surrounded by the large army and leading from the front, with a bow in his hand, the mighty-armed one advanced towards the city of Lanka. Vibhishana, Sugriva, Hanumat, Jambavat, the king of the bears, Nala, Nila and Lakshmana followed him. The extremely large army of bears and residents of the forest was at the rear. As they followed Raghava, they covered the entire ground on earth. The apes, the restrainers of the enemy, were like excellent elephants. They seized hundreds of peaks from the mountains and gigantic trees. After an extremely long period of time, the two brothers who were scorchers of enemies, Rama and Lakshmana, approached Ravana's city of Lanka. It had garlands of flags, with beautiful gardens. It was decorated with groves. There was a wonderful rampart that was very difficult to breach. There were tall gates and turrets. It was extremely difficult for even the gods to attack. Commanded and urged by Rama's words, the residents of the forest attacked it.

Lanka's northern gate was as tall as a mountain peak. Ravana and his younger brother, the archer, laid siege to it and stationed themselves there. Rama, Dasharatha's son, with the brave Lakshmana as his companion, stationed himself there, at the city of Lanka, protected by Ravana. Ravana himself was stationed at the northern gate. Protected by him, no one other than Rama was capable of attacking that gate. Ravana was stationed there, like Varuna is in the terrible ocean. In every direction, it was protected by terrible rakshasas wielding weapons, like the danavas in patala. Inferior ones would have been scared away. He[112] saw many kinds of warriors spread around and masses of weapons and armour.

---

[112] Rama.

Nila, the commander of the army reached the eastern gate and with Mainda and the valiant Dvivida, remained there. With Rishabha, Gavaksha, Gaja and Gavaya, the extremely strong Angada assumed control over the southern gate. Hanumat, the strong ape, protected the western gate. He was with Pramathi, Praghasa and other brave ones. Sugriva was himself stationed in the centre of the army. He sighed like Suparna and was with all the best among the apes. Thirty-six crores of famous leaders of the apes were where the ape Sugriva was, crushing the enemy present there. On Rama's command, Lakshmana, with Vibhishana, placed one crore of apes at every gate. Towards Rama's rear and not far from him, were Sugriva and Jambavat, in the centre of the army and with many soldiers following. Those tigers among apes possessed teeth like those of tigers. Seizing trees and peaks of mountains, they were happy, waiting to fight. All of them stretched and lashed their tails. All of them used teeth and nails as weapons. All of them quivered in their colourful limbs. All of them had grim visages. Some possessed the strength of ten elephants, others that of one hundred. Some possessed valour that was equal to that of one thousand elephants. There were those with the strength of a multitude of elephants, others with ten times that. There were others whose strength could not be measured. All the leaders among the apes were there. Their gathering together was wonderful and extraordinary. The soldiers of the apes were like a swarm of locusts. They seemed to cover the sky and envelop the earth. There were apes who had reached and settled down in front of Lanka. There were one hundred thousand separate divisions of bears and residents of the forest. Some reached Lanka's gates. Others spread around, to fight on every side. In every direction, the apes covered all the mountains. One crore of them advanced towards the city. The forces of the apes wielded trees in their hands. Even the wind found it extremely difficult to penetrate Lanka and they surrounded it from every side. Suddenly besieged in this way, the rakshasas were surprised. The apes resembled clouds and were like Shakra in their valour. As the waves of soldiers advanced, a tumultuous sound arose. It was like the sound of the water when the ocean is agitated. As a consequence of that great sound, Lanka, with all its ramparts, gates, mountains, forests and groves, started to tremble. The army was protected by Rama, Lakshmana and Sugriva. It was more invincible than all the gods and the asuras put together.

Having himself arranged the soldiers in this way, with a view to slaying the rakshasas, he repeatedly consulted with his ministers and decided what should be done. He knew about the truth and was eager to undertake what should be done next. With Vibhishana's sanction, he remembered the dharma of kings. He summoned Angada, Vali's son, and spoke to him. 'O amiable one! O ape! Go to Dashagriva and convey my words to him. Without any fear or distress, enter the city of Lanka. Go to the one who has lost his prosperity and wealth. Bereft of his senses, he is about to die. "O one who roams around in the night! O rakshasa! Because of your delusion and insolence, you have committed crimes against rishis, gods, gandharvas, *apsaras*, serpents, yakshas and kings. The insolence you derived from a boon granted by Svayambhu, the one who uses the rod of chastisement, will certainly be dispelled today. I am afflicted because you abducted my wife. I am stationed at the gates of Lanka, wielding the rod of chastisement. O rakshasa! Slain by me, you will obtain the destinations meant for gods, maharshis and all the royal sages and go there. O worst among rakshasas! In abducting Sita, you used your strength and maya. Exhibit those now and surpass me. I will use my sharp arrows to destroy all rakshasas on earth, unless you seek refuge with me and return Maithilee. Vibhishana, with dharma in his soul and supreme among rakshasas, has come here. Without any thorns, the handsome one will certainly obtain the prosperity of Lanka. Resorting to adharma, you do not have the capacity to enjoy the kingdom even for an instant. You have not cleansed your soul and have foolish and wicked aides. O rakshasa! Resort to your fortitude and valour and fight. In the battle, I will pacify and purify you with my arrows. Even if you assume the form of a bird and course through the three worlds with the speed of thought, when you come within the range of my vision, you will not be able to retain your life. I am speaking these beneficial words to you.

Prepare for your funeral rites. Make the proper arrangements in Lanka. Your life depends on me."'

Rama was unblemished in his deeds. Having been thus addressed by him, Tara's son took to the sky, like the lord of oblations.[113] In a short instant, the handsome one descended within Ravana's residence. He saw Ravana seated there with his advisers, without any anxiety. The bull among apes descended close to him. Angada, with golden bracelets, looked like the fire. In the hearing of the advisers, he made himself known and reported all of Rama's words, without adding or taking anything away. 'I am the messenger of Rama, the Indra of Kosala who is unblemished in his deeds. I am Angada, Vali's son. You may have heard of me. Raghava Rama is the extender of Kousalya's delight. He tells you, "O worst of beings! O cruel one! Come and fight against me. With your advisers, sons, kin and relatives, I will kill you. After I have killed you, there will no longer be any fear in the three worlds. Today, I will uproot the enemy and the thorn of the gods, the danavas, the yakshas, the gandharvas, the rakshasas and the rishis. Once you are killed, Vibhishana will obtain the prosperity, unless you bow down before me and respectfully return Vaidehi."'

The bull among apes addressed him in these harsh words. Hearing them, the lord of large numbers of those who roam around in the night was filled with intolerance. His eyes turned copper-red with rage and he commanded his aides, 'Seize this one, inferior in intelligence. Dishonour him and kill him.' He[114] blazed in his energy, like the fire. Hearing Ravana's words, four terrible roamers in the night seized him. Knowing his own nature, Tara's son allowed himself to be captured. The brave one wished to exhibit his strength to the large numbers of yatudhanas. Like a bird, Angada seized the ones who clung on to his arms and leapt on to the palace that resembled a mountain. While the Indra among rakshasas looked on, all those rakshasas were whirled around by the force of the leap and fell down on the ground. The top of the palace was as tall as

---

[113] The fire god.
[114] Angada.

the peak of a mountain. While Dashagriva looked on, he attacked it. Having destroyed the top of the palace, he announced his own name. He uttered a loud roar and leapt into the sky.

When the palace was destroyed, Ravana was filled with great rage. Able to see his own destruction, he sighed deeply.

Rama was surrounded by many delighted apes. Desiring to slay the enemy, he advanced to fight. The ape Sushena was very brave and was like the summit of a mountain. He was there, surrounded by many apes who could assume any form at will. On Sugriva's instructions, this invincible ape progressively marched around all the gates, like the moon amidst the nakshatras.

There were hundreds of *akshouhini*s[115] of the residents of the forest. Having crossed the ocean, they were camped in Lanka. On seeing them, some rakshasas marvelled. Others were terrified. There were others who were delighted at the prospect of a battle and leapt up. The apes covered the entire area between the ramparts and the moat. The apes were like a second rampart. On seeing this, the rakshasas were distressed. At this great and terrible occurrence, there was an uproar in the capital of the rakshasas. The rakshasas seized large weapons and advanced, like winds that blow at the end of a yuga.

Chapter 6(32)

After this, the rakshasas went to Ravana's residence and reported that Rama, with the apes, had laid siege to the city. On hearing that the city had been besieged, the roamer in the night was filled with anger. He doubled the arrangements and ascended to the top of the palace. He saw that in every direction, Lanka, with its mountains, forests and groves, had been surrounded by innumerable bands of apes who wished to fight. He saw that

---

[115] An akshouhini is an army, consisting of 21,870 chariots, 21,870 elephants, 65,610 horse riders and 109,350 foot soldiers.

because of the apes, the entire earth was brown. He began to think, 'How can they be destroyed?' Having thought for a long period of time, Ravana resorted to his fortitude. With dilated eyes, he looked at Raghava and the leaders among the apes.

While the Indra among rakshasas looked on, wishing to bring pleasure to Raghava, the different parts of the army began to climb into Lanka. Their faces were coppery. Their complexions were golden. For Rama's sake, they were ready to give up their lives. With salas, talas and boulders as weapons, they attacked Lanka. The apes used trees, the peaks of mountains and fists as their weapons. Using these, they broke down the tops of the palaces and the turrets. The moats were filled with clear water. The apes filled these up with earth, the tops of mountains, grass and wood. Other leaders of herds climbed into Lanka with herds of thousand, herds of crores and herds of hundreds of crores. The apes shattered the golden gates. They destroyed the arches that possessed the hue of the summit of Kailasa. The apes leapt up, leapt down and roared. With complexions like those of gigantic elephants, they attacked Lanka. The apes could assume any form at will and attacked Lanka's ramparts. They shouted, 'Victory to the extremely strong Rama and the immensely strong Lakshmana. Victory to King Sugriva, protected by Raghava.' They shouted and roared in this way. The leaders of the apes—Virabahu, Subahu and Nala—the residents of the forest, stationed themselves at the ramparts and crushed them. Looking for an opportunity, they stationed their formations there.

Kumuda was at the eastern gate, surrounded by ten crore of strong apes who desired victory. The brave ape, Shatabali, attacked the southern gate, surrounded by twenty crore of strong ones. The ape Sushena, Tara's father, was at the western gate. He was surrounded by sixty crore of strong ones. With Soumitri, Rama attacked the northern gate and barricaded it. He was with the strong Sugriva, the lord of the apes. Surrounded by one crore of immensely brave ones, the gigantic Golangula and Gavaksha, terrible to behold were by Rama's side. Dhumra, the destroyer of enemies, was surrounded by one crore of immensely brave and extremely forceful bears and was

by Rama's side. The immensely brave Vibhishana was armoured
and had a mace in his hand. He was surrounded by his advisers and
was also where the immensely strong one[116] was. Gaja, Gavaksha,
Gavaya, Sharabha and Gandhamadana rushed around on all sides,
protecting the army of the apes.

Ravana, the lord of the rakshasas, was filled with rage. He
instructed all the soldiers to quickly emerge. Urged by Ravana,
those soldiers cheerfully attacked. They were like the force of the
great ocean at a time when it is full. A terrible engagement took
place between the rakshasas and the apes, like that between the
gods and the asuras in ancient times. Proclaiming their own valour,
those terrible ones[117] used blazing clubs, spears, javelins and
battleaxes to slay the apes. The forceful apes used gigantic trees, the
peaks of mountains and nails and teeth to slay the rakshasas. Some
terrible rakshasas were stationed on the ramparts and used spears
and javelins to strike at the apes who were on the ground. The apes
became angry and leapt on to the ramparts. The apes attacked the
rakshasas and brought them down. As a result of that tumultuous
engagement, mud was created from the flesh and the blood of the
rakshasas and the apes. It was extraordinary.

Chapter 6(33)

The great-souled apes fought with the rakshasas. Both sides
were strong and enraged and it was extremely terrible. The
rakshasas, terrible in their valour, desired Ravana's victory. They
were on horses with golden harnesses, with standards that were like
the flames of the fire. They were on chariots that were like the sun,
adorned in beautiful armour. The tigers among rakshasas emerged
and roared in the ten directions. The large army of the apes, who
could assume any form at will, also desired victory. They attacked

[116] Rama.
[117] The rakshasas.

the rakshasa soldiers. At that time, when they attacked each other, there were duels between the rakshasas and the apes.

The immensely energetic rakshasa, Indrajit, fought against Angada, Vali's son, like Andhaka against Tryambaka.[118] Sampati, always intolerant in a battle, fought against Prajangha. The ape Hanumat angrily attacked Jambumali. Extremely angry, Vibhishana, the rakshasa who was Ravana's younger brother, clashed against Mitraghna,[119] who possessed a fierce force in an encounter. Gaja fought against the extremely strong rakshasa, Tapana. The greatly energetic Nila fought against Nikumbha. Sugriva, Indra among apes, clashed against Praghasa. In the encounter, the handsome Lakshmana fought against Virupaksha. The invincible Agniketu, the rakshasa Rashmiketu, Suptaghna and Yajnakopa clashed against Rama. Vajramushti fought against Mainda and Ashaniprabha against Dvivida. The two foremost apes clashed with those two extremely terrible rakshasas. The brave and terrible rakshasa, Pratapana, could bear great burdens in battles. He fought against Nala, who had a fierce force in battle. The powerful Sushena was famous as Dharma's[120] son. That great ape fought against Vidyunmali. Other terrible apes fought against other rakshasas. Many duels took place and there were many kinds of fights. There was a great and tumultuous engagement and it made the body hair stand up. Desiring victory, the brave rakshasas and apes fought. Blood flowed from the bodies of the apes and the rakshasas and a river was created from this, with the bodies like dams and the hair like moss. Like Shatakratu with his vajra, Indrajit angrily struck Angada, who could shatter the soldiers of the enemy, with a club. In the battle, the handsome and forceful ape, Angada, shattered his gold-embellished chariot and killed his horses and charioteer. In the field of battle, Sampati was struck by Prajangha with three arrows, but used an ashvakarna tree to kill Prajangha. In the encounter, the enraged and immensely strong Jambumali was

[118] Shiva.
[119] Also known as Shatrughna. Indeed, Shatrughna is a more appropriate name. One slays the enemy (*shatru*), not one's friends (*mitra*).
[120] Yama's.

on his chariot and used a javelin to strike Hanumat between the breasts. Hanumat, the wind god's son, climbed on to the chariot and used the palm of his hand to swiftly crush that rakshasa. The rakshasa Tapana was swift in the use of his hands and used sharp arrows to strike Gaja and mangle his limbs. However, Gaja used the summit of a mountain and his fists to slay him. Praghasa seemed to be devouring the soldiers. But Sugriva, the lord of apes, used a saptaparna tree to pierce and kill him. Lakshmana oppressed the rakshasa Virupaksha, who was terrible to behold, with a shower of arrows and then used a single arrow to kill him. The invincible Agniketu, the rakshasa Rashmiketu, Suptaghna[121] and Yajnakopa pierced Rama with arrows. Enraged in the battle, Rama used four terrible arrows that were like the flames of a fire to severe their four heads. In the encounter, Mainda struck Vajramushti with his fist and killed him. Like a city turret that falls down, with his chariot and his horses, he fell down on the ground. While all the rakshasas looked on, Dvivida used the summit of a mountain, which was like the vajra to the touch, to strike Ashaniprabha. In the battle, Dvivida, Indra among apes, used a tree as a weapon and Ashaniprabha struck him with arrows that were like the vajra. With his body deeply pierced by the arrows, Dvivida became senseless with rage. Using a sala tree, he killed Ashaniprabha, together with his charioteer and his horses. Nila had the complexion of a mass of blue collyrium and in the battle, Nikumbha pierced him with sharp arrows that were like lightning in the clouds. Nikumbha, the roamer in the night, was swift in the use of his hands. In the encounter, he laughed and again struck Nila with one hundred arrows. In the battle, Nila was like Vishnu. In the encounter, he used the wheel of a chariot to sever the heads of Nikumbha and his charioteer. Vidyunmali was on his chariot. He used arrows that were ornamented with gold to strike Sushena. He then roared repeatedly. Sushena, supreme among apes, saw that he was on his chariot. He used the summit of a mountain to quickly bring down the chariot. Vidyunmali, the roamer in the night, was dexterous. He swiftly descended from the chariot and

---

[121] This should probably be Shatrughna.

stood on the ground, with a club in his hand. At this, Sushena, bull among apes, was filled with rage. He seized an extremely large boulder and rushed towards the roamer in the night. Vidyunmali, the roamer in the night, saw that he was descending. He swiftly used the club to strike Sushena, supreme among apes, in the chest. Struck by that terrible club in the great battle, the supreme among apes, did the unthinkable. He struck him in the chest with the boulder and brought him down. Vidyunmali, the roamer in the night, was severely struck by the boulder. With his heart shattered, he lost his life and fell down on the ground. Thus, the brave apes fought against the brave roamers in the night. They crushed each other in the duels, like the daityas against the residents of heaven.

The place was littered with shattered and fragmented javelins, swords, clubs, spears, spikes and darts and chariots and warhorses. Crazy elephants, apes and rakshasas were killed. Wheels, axles, yokes and poles were shattered and fell down on the ground. There was a terrible fight and large numbers of jackals gathered. In different directions, there were headless torsos of apes and rakshasas. It was a tumultuous engagement, like a battle between the gods and the asuras. Crushed by the bulls among the apes, the bodies of the roamers in the night oozed out blood. However, they resorted to their spirits and fought again, desiring for the time when the sun would set.[122]

Chapter 6(34)

While the apes and the rakshasas fought in this way, the sun set. Night, which would take away lives, arrived. They were bound in terrible enmity towards each other and fought, desiring victory. A nocturnal fight ensued between the apes and the rakshasas. 'You are a rakshasa,' said the apes. 'You are an ape,' said the rakshasas. In the battle that took place in that

---

[122] The powers of rakshasas increase at night.

terrible night, they fought against each other and killed each other.
'Kill.' 'Shatter.' 'Come here.' 'Why are you running away?' These
extremely tumultuous sounds were heard in the darkness. In the
darkness, the dark rakshasas were clad in golden armour and could
be seen, like blazing herbs in an Indra among mountains. That
darkness was extremely difficult to cross and the rakshasas were
senseless with anger. They descended on the apes with great force
and devoured them. The terrible apes used their sharp teeth, leaping
on to the horses with golden harnesses and standards that were
like the flames of the fire and crushing them in their rage. They
used elephants to climb on to other elephants. They brought down
the standards and flags from their chariots. Senseless with anger,
they shattered them with their teeth. Rama and Lakshmana used
arrows that were like venomous serpents to kill the best among
rakshasas, those who could be seen and those who could not be
seen. The earth was enveloped in a dust that arose from the hooves
of horses and the rims of chariots. As they fought, this blocked
the ears and the eyes. A terrible encounter raged and it made the
body hair stand up. The blood created a river of blood that was
extremely swift in its flow. There was the sound of drums, smaller
drums, tambourines, conch shells and flutes and it was wonderful.
There was the sound of slain and injured rakshasas and that of apes
being struck by weapons. It was extremely terrible. Because of the
fighting, the earth was offered gifts of weapons instead of flowers.
There was mud created by the blood. It was impossible to penetrate
and impossible to discern. The terrible night brought destruction to
the apes and the rakshasas. It was like the night of destruction that
all creatures find extremely difficult to cross.

In the terrible darkness, the delighted rakshasas attacked Rama
and showered down arrows on him. They descended angrily, roaring
and creating a noise that resembled the rumble created by the seven
oceans. In the twinkling of an eye, Rama used six arrows that
were like the flames of a fire to strike six roamers in the night—the
invincible Yajnashatru, Mahaparshva, Mahodara, Vajradamshtra
and the gigantic Shuka and Sarana. They were struck in their inner
organs by the torrent of Rama's arrows. Saving their lives, they

withdrew from the battle. The immensely strong one used arrows that were like the flames of the fire, with golden and colourful shafts, to make the directions and the sub-directions clear again. There were other brave rakshasas who were stationed in front of Rama. When they approached, like insects before a fire, they were also destroyed. Thousands of gold-shafted arrows descended and the night became colourful, like the autumn sky with fireflies.

There was the shouting of rakshasas and the roaring of apes. This made the terrible night become even more terrible. That loud sound spread in every direction and Mount Trikuta, filled with caverns, seemed to become distressed. There were golangulas large in size, with a radiance like that of the darkness. They crushed the roamers in the night with their arms and devoured them.

In the battle, Angada was stationed, ready to slay the enemy. He swiftly killed the charioteer and horses of Ravana's son. A horrible and extremely terrible encounter ensued. With his horses and chariot slain by Angada, Indrajit abandoned his chariot. He used his great maya and vanished. Ravana's wicked son vanished, but was harsh in fighting. Ravana's brave son became senseless with rage and used the boon given to him by Brahma. Though he was invisible, he released sharp arrows that were as radiant as the vajra. Against Rama and Lakshmana, he used arrows that became terrible serpents. In the battle, he angrily used these to pierce the two Raghavas all over their bodies.

Chapter 6(35)

Rama, the powerful prince, commanded ten extremely strong leaders of the apes to search for his[123] trail. The scorcher of enemies instructed Sushena's two sons, Nila, bull among apes, Angada, Vali's son, the spirited Sharabha, Vinata, Jambavat, the immensely strong Sanuprastha, Rishabha and the bull

---

[123] Indrajit's.

Rishabhaskandha. Delighted, those terrible apes seized trees and all of them leapt up into the sky, searching the ten directions. However, Ravana's son knew about weapons and was supreme in the use of weapons. Though they were swift, his arrows were swifter and he used those to restrain their speed. Those apes, terrible in their force, were deeply mangled by iron arrows. Because of the darkness, they could not see him, just as the sun is shrouded in clouds.

Ravana's son, the one who was victorious in assemblies, pierced all the inner organs of Rama and Lakshmana with arrows. They were severely struck. The brave and angry Indrajit incessantly pierced the bodies of the two brother, Rama and Lakshmana, with arrows that were in the form of serpents. Copious quantities of blood flowed out from their wounds. Both of them assumed the appearance of flowering kimshukas.[124] Ravana's son was like a mass of collyrium mixed with oil and his eyes were red. Though he was invisible, he spoke to the two brothers. 'When I render myself invisible and fight, not even Shakra, the lord of the gods, is capable of seeing and approaching me, not to speak of those like you. O descendants of the Raghu lineage! I have covered you in this net of arrows shafted with heron feathers. Overcome with rage, I will now convey you to Yama's abode.' He spoke in this way to the two brothers, Rama and Lakshmana, who knew about dharma. He pierced them with sharp arrows and roared in delight. He was dark, like a mass of black collyrium mixed with oil. In that great encounter, he stretched his large bow and repeatedly struck them with terrible arrows. He knew about inner organs and those sharp arrows struck deep into the inner organs of the brave Rama and Lakshmana. He roared repeatedly. In the field of battle, both of them were bound by nets of arrows. In the twinkling of an eye, they were not even capable of looking. They looked like the great Indra's standard, when it is loosened from its ropes and is quivering. Afflicted by their inner organs being mangled, those two brave ones trembled. The lords of the earth cast aside their large bows and fell down on the ground. Exuding blood, those two brave ones lay down on beds meant for

[124] Tree with red blossoms.

heroes. All their limbs were entwined by those arrows and they were severely afflicted. On their bodies, there was not even the space of a single finger that was not pierced, mangled and wounded by arrows, from the fingers to the feet. They were cruelly struck by the rakshasa who could assume any form at will. Fearful streams of blood started to flow, like water from springs. Pierced in his inner organs by the arrows, Rama fell down first. This was the result of Indrajit's rage, who had vanquished Shakra earlier. He was pierced by *narachas*,[125] half-narachas, *bhallas*,[126] *anjalikas*,[127] *vatsadantas*,[128] *simhadashtras*[129] and *kshuras*.[130] He lay down on that bed meant for heroes, flinging away from his hand his stringed bow, which was bent in three places and was decorated with gold. Rama, bull among men, fell down at a distance that was the range of one arrow away from him. On seeing this, Lakshmana lost all hope of remaining alive. Those two brave ones were bound and lay down, having fallen down. With Vayu's son at the forefront, the apes assembled and surrounded them. They were afflicted and suffered from great misery.

Chapter 6(36)

The residents of the forest looked everywhere on earth and in the sky and saw the two brothers, Rama and Lakshmana, covered with arrows. The rakshasa had accomplished his task and withdrew, like the god with the rains.[131] With Hanumat, Sugriva, Vibhishana, Nila, Dvivida, Mainda, Sushena, Sumukha and Angada quickly came to that spot and started to grieve for the two

---

[125] A naracha is an iron arrow.
[126] Arrows with broad heads.
[127] Arrows with heads shaped like crescents.
[128] Arrows with heads shaped like a calf's tooth.
[129] Arrows with heads shaped like a lion's tooth.
[130] Kshura or *kshurapra* is an arrow with a sharp edge.
[131] The image is of Indra withdrawing after showering down.

Raghavas. They were not moving and breathed faintly. They were covered in streams of blood. They were pierced with nets of arrows and were immobile. They were lying down on beds of arrows. They were sighing like snakes that couldn't make any efforts, their valour exhausted. Blood flowed from their limbs and they looked like two golden standards. Those two brave ones were lying down on beds meant for heroes. They were lying down and not making any efforts. The leaders surrounded them, their eyes filled with tears. They saw that the two Raghavas had fallen down, enveloped in the nets of arrows. All the apes, with Vibhishana, were distressed. The apes searched in all the directions of the sky. But because he was enveloped in his maya, they could not see Ravana's son in the battle. Vibhishana used his own maya to cut through the maya and looking around, saw his brother's son stationed there. He[132] was unmatched in his deeds and could not be countered in an encounter. Vibhishana saw the brave one, invisible because of the boon he had obtained.

Indrajit saw that the two were lying down because of the deed he had performed. Extremely delighted and happy, he told all the nairittas, 'These two extremely strong ones are the slayers of Dushana and Khara. The two brothers, Rama and Lakshmana, have been killed by my arrows. Even if all the large numbers of rishis, gods and asuras come together, they are incapable of freeing these two from the bonds of arrows. It was because of what they did that my father was afflicted by grief and was immersed in thoughts. He was incapable of laying his body down on a bed and the three *yama*s of the night passed.[133] It is because of them that the city of Lanka is as turbulent as a river during the monsoon. I have taken the foundation of the calamity away and have destroyed it in every possible way. Like clouds during the autumn,[134] all the valour of Rama, Lakshmana and all the residents of the forest will be fruitless.' He said this to all the rakshasas who were by

---

[132] Indrajit.

[133] A yama is a period of three hours. Since it is made up of three yamas, the night is known as *triyama*.

[134] Because clouds don't rain during the autumn.

his side. Ravana's son then struck all the leaders of the herds. He afflicted them with torrents of arrows and terrified the apes. The mighty-armed one laughed and spoke these words. 'O rakshasas! In front of the army, I have bound them down with terrible bonds of arrows. All of you look at those two brothers.' The one who fought in mysterious ways said this to all the rakshasas. They were filled with great wonder and satisfied at his deed. Like clouds, all of them emitted a loud roar. They said, 'Rama has been killed,' and worshipped Ravana's son. Seeing that those two, Rama and Lakshmana, were not moving and were lying down on the ground and not breathing, he also thought that they had been killed. Filled with delight, Indrajit, the conqueror of assemblies, entered the city of Lanka and caused happiness to all the nairittas.

The bodies of Rama and Lakshmana were pierced with arrows, in all the limbs and smaller limbs. On seeing this, Sugriva was filled with fear. Vibhishana spoke to the terrified Indra among apes, whose face was distressed and full of tears and whose eyes were also overflowing with tears. 'O Sugriva! Enough of this scare. Control this flow of tears. This is usually what happens in battles. Victory is uncertain. O brave one! Even if there is a bit of good fortune left with us, the two brothers, Rama and Lakshmana, will fling aside this unconsciousness. O ape! I am without a protector. Therefore, steady yourself. For those who are devoted to truth and dharma, death cannot give rise to fear.' Saying this, Vibhishana wet his hand with water and wiped Sugriva's auspicious eyes. The intelligent one wiped the face of the king of the apes. Without any fear, he spoke these words. 'The time has come. O Indra among kings of apes! This is not the time to indulge in lassitude. This is not the time to indulge in excessive affection. That can give rise to death. Therefore, cast aside this lassitude. It destroys all tasks. Think of the welfare of the soldiers who have had Rama at their forefront. As long as Rama suffers from the catastrophe of losing consciousness, they have to be protected. When the two Kakutsthas regain their senses, they will drive away our fear. This is nothing for Rama. Nor will Rama die. This will not diminish his prosperity. The lifespan, extremely difficult to obtain, has not deserted him. Therefore, comfort yourself and resort to your own strength, until I place all the soldiers back in their ranks. O bull among the apes! They are scared and have dilated their eyes in fear. The apes are speaking into each other's ears. On seeing me run around, instilling happiness in the army, let the apes give up their terror, just as one casts aside a garland that has been enjoyed.' Vibhishana, Indra among the rakshasas, reassured Sugriva. Thereafter, he comforted the soldiers of the apes, who were running away.

Indrajit, great in his use of maya, was surrounded by all the soldiers. He entered the city of Lanka and went before his father. Ravana was seated. He joined his hands in salutation and greeted him, telling his beloved father that Rama and Lakshmana had been killed. In the midst of the rakshasas, Ravana heard that the enemy had been brought down. Delighted, he leapt up and embraced his son. He inhaled the fragrance of his head. Happy in his mind, he asked questions. Asked, he told his father everything, just as it had occurred. On hearing the maharatha's[135] words, his heart was filled with floods of joy. The fever caused by Dasharatha's son passed. He praised his son in joyous words.

Chapter 6(37)

Having accomplished his objective, Ravana's son entered Lanka. Distressed, the bulls among the apes surrounded Raghava and protected him. Hanumat, Angada, Nila, Sushena, Kumuda, Nala, Gaja, Gavaksha, Gavaya, Sharabha, Gandhamadana, Jambavat, Rishabha, Sunda, Rambha, Shatabali and Prithu collected trees and constructed vyuhas in every direction. The apes glanced in all the directions, upwards and diagonally. Even if a blade of grass moved, they thought that it might be a rakshasa.

---

[135] Great warrior, more specifically, a maharatha is someone who can single-handedly fight ten thousand warriors.

Ravana was delighted and gave his son, Indrajit, permission to leave. He summoned the rakshasis who were entrusted with the task of protecting Sita. Commanded by him, the rakshasis presented themselves, including Trijata. Delighted, the lord of the rakshasas spoke to the rakshasis. 'Tell Vaidehi that Rama and Lakshmana have been killed by Indrajit. Make her ascend Pushpaka and show her that they have been killed in the battle. She was insolent because she sought refuge with her husband. She did not serve me. In the field of battle, he and his brother have been restrained. Maithilee need not be uncertain now. She need not be anxious. She has no hope. Adorned in all the ornaments, Sita can present herself before me. In the battle today, Rama and Lakshmana have come under the subjugation of death. Having seen this, with her hopes destroyed, she will find no other recourse.' Having heard the words of the evil-souled Ravana, the rakshasis agreed and went to where Pushpaka was. Following Ravana's commands, the rakshasis brought Pushpaka and conveyed it to Ashokavana, where Maithilee was. On account of her husband, she was overcome by sorrow. The rakshasis seized Sita and made her ascend Pushpaka vimana. With Trijata, Sita ascended Pushpaka. Ravana caused Lanka to be decorated with flags, standards and garlands. Delighted, the lord of the rakshasas arranged for it to be proclaimed in Lanka that Raghava and Lakshmana had been killed by Indrajit in the battle.

With Trijata, Sita left on the vimana and saw all the soldiers of the apes who had been brought down. Her mind was happy to see the devourers of flesh.[136] However, she was miserable and grieved to see the apes standing by the side of Rama and Lakshmana. Sita saw that both of them were lying down on beds of arrows and that, afflicted by arrows, Rama and Lakshmana were unconscious. Their armour was cast away. The two brave ones had flung away their bows. Pierced by arrows in all their limbs, they were lying down on the ground, on beds of arrows. She saw the two brave brothers, bulls among men. Extremely miserable with grief, Sita started to lament piteously. Looking at them, the two brothers, whose power

[136] The rakshasas who had been killed.

was like that of the gods, she sorrowed and her eyes filled with tears. She believed that they had been killed and filled with sorrow, she spoke these words.

Chapter 6(38)

On seeing that her husband and the extremely strong Lakshmana had been killed, Sita was overcome with great sorrow. She lamented piteously. 'Those who can read signs[137] said that I would have sons and would not be a widow. They did not know. Since Rama has been killed today, all of them have uttered a falsehood. They said that I would be the queen at a great sacrifice and that I would be the wife supporting such a sacrifice. They did not know. Since Rama has been killed today, all of them have uttered a falsehood. Those learned ones told me that I was blessed. I would be the wife of a brave king. They did not know. Since Rama has been killed today, all of them have uttered a falsehood. In my hearing, those brahmanas spoke the auspicious words that I would be close to my husband. They did not know. Since Rama has been killed today, all of them have uttered a falsehood. Indeed, I have marks of the lotus on the soles of my feet. Because of that, women are consecrated on a throne, with their husbands, who are Indras among men. The inauspicious signs on women who become widows and are limited in fortune are missing. As I look at myself, those signs cannot be discerned. The signs of the lotus on women convey a truth. Since Rama has been slain today, that has been rendered false. My hair is extremely fine, black and smooth. My eyebrows do not touch each other. My hips are round and possess no hair. There are no gaps between my teeth. My temples, eyes, hands, feet, ankles and thighs are perfect in proportion. My fingers are smooth and my nails are delicate and well rounded. My breasts are plump and there is no gap between them. My nipples are depressed. My navel is turned inwards.

[137] Astrologers, soothsayers.

My flanks and breasts are smooth. My complexion is like that of a jewel. My body hair is soft. It is said that I possess the auspicious signs and stand on twelve limbs.[138] Those who are learned about the signs of maidens have spoken of me as one who has the complexion of barley, with no gaps in the hands and the feet,[139] and as one who smiles gently. The brahmanas who are skilled and know about what will happen said that I would be consecrated on the throne with my husband. Everything has been rendered false. Having got to know what had happened, those two brothers searched in Janasthana and crossed the ocean that cannot be agitated. Thereafter, they have been slain in a puddle.[140] Indeed, the two Raghavas knew about the use of Varuna, Agneya, Aindra, Vayavya and Brahmashira weapons. They were like Vasava. Rama and Lakshmana have been killed by someone who used maya to remain invisible in the battle. They were my protectors and I have no protector now. Having come within the range of vision of Raghava in an encounter, no enemy could return with his life, even if he possessed the speed of thought. The burden of destiny is extremely heavy. Death is extremely difficult to vanquish. That is the reason Rama and his brother are lying down, having been brought down in the battle. I am not grieving over the death of my husband and Lakshmana or for myself or my mother, as I am over my ascetic mother-in-law. She incessantly thinks about the time when the vow will be over and about when she will be able to see Sita, Rama and Lakshmana return.'

While she was lamenting, the rakshasi Trijata spoke. 'O queen! Do not grieve unnecessarily. Your husband is alive. O queen! Let me tell you about the great signs whereby one knows that these two brothers, Rama and Lakshmana, are alive. When leaders are killed in a battle, the faces of the warriors do not show any rage. Nor are they filled with joy.[141] O Vaidehi! This vimana has the name of Pushpaka.

---

[138] Ten toes and two soles.

[139] No space between the fingers and the toes.

[140] The text uses the word *goshpada*. This literally means the mark of a cow's foot in the soil and the small puddle of water that fills up such a mark, that is, a trifle.

[141] This is not very clear. It probably means that the other warriors do not stand around, but do something instead.

Had they been killed, it would not have brought you here, through the sky. When the foremost and valiant warrior has been killed, the soldiers lose all eagerness and enterprise. They wander around in the battle, like a boat in the water that has lost its rudder. O spirited ones! These ones are without fear and show no anxiety. The soldiers are protecting the two Kakutsthas, who have been vanquished in the battle through the use of maya. These signs should give rise to joy and you should be devoid of your anxiety. You will see that the two Kakutsthas have not been killed. Out of my affection, I am telling you this. I have never uttered a falsehood in the past, nor will I ever speak it. Because of your character and good conduct, you have found a place in my heart. Indra, with the gods and the asuras, is incapable of defeating these two in a battle. Having looked at their faces, this is what I can tell you. O Maithilee! Gently look at the great signs. They are still breathing and their beauty has not deserted them. In general, when men lose their breath of life and their lives, their faces are seen to be greatly distorted. O Janaka's daughter! Give up your misery, grief and confusion. It is impossible for Rama and Lakshmana not to remain alive.' Hearing her words, Sita Maithilee, who was like a daughter of the gods, joined her hands in salutation and said, 'May it be that way.' With the speed of thought, Pushpaka vimana returned. The distressed Trijata and Sita entered Lanka. With Trijata, she got down from Pushpaka and the rakshasis made her enter Ashokavana. Sita entered the pleasure ground of the Indra-among the rakshasas, filled with many clumps of trees. Having seen the two princes, she thought about them and was filled with great sorrow.

Chapter 6(39)

Dasharatha's two sons were tied down in the terrible bonds of arrows. They were lying down, covered with blood and sighing like serpents. All the foremost and immensely strong apes, with Sugriva, were filled with sorrow and surrounded the great-souled ones.

At this time, the valiant Rama regained his senses. Despite being bound down by the arrows, he used yoga to steady his spirit. He saw his brother, covered in blood and severely unconscious, lying down on the ground. Suffering and with a distressed face, he lamented. 'What will I do with Sita? What is the point of remaining alive? Today, I can see my brother vanquished in a battle, lying down. If I search the world, I am capable of finding a woman like Sita. But one cannot find a brother, adviser and companion like Lakshmana. If he, the extender of Sumitra's delight, returns to the five elements,[142] while these apes look on, I will give up my life. What will I tell my mother, Kousalya? What will I tell Kaikeyee? What will I tell the mother, Sumitra, who desires to see her son? If I return without you, how will I comfort her? Without her calf, she will tremble and shriek like a female osprey. What will I tell Shatrughna and the illustrious Bharata? He went to the forest with me, but I will return without him. Sumitra is firm in her vows and I will not be able to approach her. I will give up my body here. I am not interested in remaining alive. Shame on me. Shame on my evil and ignoble deeds, since this has happened. Lakshmana has fallen down and is lying on a bed of arrows, as if he has lost his life. O Lakshmana! When I was greatly distressed, you always comforted me. Now that you have lost your life, when I am distressed, you will be incapable of speaking to me. In the battle today, he killed many rakshasas who are lying down on the ground. Slain by the enemy, the brave one is now lying down on the ground. He is lying down on this bed of arrows, covered in his own blood. He is radiant in this net of arrows, like the sun when it is about to set. Your inner organs have been pierced by arrows and you are incapable of seeing. Though you are not speaking, the dust and red tinge in your eyes are eloquent. When I went to the forest, the immensely radiant one followed me. In that way, I will follow him to Yama's abode. He was always devoted to the welfare of his relatives. He always followed me. He has been reduced to this state because of my ignoble and evil policy. I do not remember any words the brave Lakshmana spoke

---

[142] The text uses the word *panchatva*. This simply means death, that is, when the body is separated into the five elements.

in rage. I have never heard any harsh or disagreeable words. With one shot, he was capable of releasing five hundred arrows. In the use of weapons, Lakshmana was thus superior to Kartavirya.[143] With his weapons, the great-souled one could destroy Shakra's weapons. He deserved to lie down on an extremely expensive bed, but is lying down on the ground. There is no doubt that the false words I have uttered will destroy me. I have not made Vibhishana the king of the rakshasas. O Sugriva! You should return this instant. O king! Without me, the powerful Ravana will overwhelm you. O Sugriva! Use the bridge across the ocean again and with Angada at the forefront and with your soldiers and well-wishers, return. I am content with the extremely difficult tasks that have been accomplished in the battle by Hanumat and the others, the king of the bears and the lord of the golangulas. Deeds have been done by Angada, Mainda and Dvivida. Kesari and Sampati fought fiercely in the battle. For my sake, Gavaya, Gavaksha, Sharabha, Gaja and other apes were ready to give up their lives in the battle. O Sugriva! It is impossible for humans to cross their destiny. O scorcher of enemies! As a friend and a well-wisher, you have done everything you could. O Sugriva! O one scared of adharma! You have done everything you could. O bulls among the apes! You have performed the acts of friends. With my permission, all of you should now go where you wish.'

All the apes heard his lamentations. Tears flowed from their dark-rimmed eyes. Vibhishana steadied all the formations. With a club in his hand, he quickly went to the spot where Raghava was. He resembled a mass of dark collyrium. Seeing him advance swiftly, all the apes took him to be Ravana's son and fled.

Chapter 6(40)

The immensely energetic and immensely strong king of the apes asked, 'Why is this army distressed, like a boat in the water

---

[143] Kartavirya Arjuna.

that has been rendered immobile because of the wind?' Hearing
Sugriva's words, Angada, Vali's son, replied, 'Do you not see the
immensely strong Rama and Lakshmana? Those two brave sons
of Dasharatha are tied down in nets of arrows. Covered in blood,
those two great-souled ones are lying down on the ground on beds
of arrows.' At this, Sugriva, Indra among the apes, told his son[144]
Angada, 'I do not think that is the reason why there are scared.
Their faces are distressed. They are fleeing in different directions,
abandoning their weapons. The apes have dilated their eyes in terror
and are rambling incoherently. They are not ashamed of each other
and are not glancing back. They are jostling against each other and
are jumping over the ones who have fallen down.'

At this time, holding a club in his hand, the brave Vibhishana
approached Sugriva, looked at him and said, 'May Raghava be
prosperous.' Sugriva saw that Vibhishana had caused terror among
the apes.[145] He told Jambavat, the king of the bears, who was near
him, 'Vibhishana has come here. On seeing him, the bulls among
the apes are running away in fear, suspecting him to be Ravana's
son. They are terrified and are fleeing in many directions. Quickly
steady them and tell them that it is Vibhishana who has come.' Thus
addressed by Sugriva, Jambavat, the king of the bears, assured the
apes and made the ones who were fleeing return. Abandoning their
fear, all the apes returned, after hearing the words of the king of the
bears and seeing Vibhishana.

Vibhishana, with dharma in his soul, saw that Rama's body
was pierced with arrows and so was that of Lakshmana. His
senses were afflicted. He dipped his hands in water and wiped
his eyes. His mind suffered from grief and he wept and lamented.
'These two brave and spirited ones loved to fight. They have
been brought to this state by rakshasas who fight in mysterious
ways. My brother's son is a wicked son and is evil in his soul.
That rakshasa is deceitful in his intelligence and has dislodged
two who are upright in their valour. They have been pierced a lot

[144] Son by extension.
[145] Because they took him to be Indrajit.

with arrows and blood is flowing. They can be seen, sleeping on
the ground like porcupines. Depending on their valour, I desired
a status for myself. However, these two bulls among men are
asleep, waiting for their bodies to be destroyed. With their lives
under threat now, my desire for the kingdom will be destroyed.
My enemy, Ravana, will accomplish his pledge and his wishes will
be satisfied.' When Vibhishana lamented in this way, the spirited
Sugriva embraced him. The king of the apes spoke these words.
'O one who knows about dharma! There is no doubt that you
will obtain the kingdom of Lanka. Ravana and his son will not
obtain this kingdom. These two, Raghava and Lakshmana, are
not badly wounded. Once they get out of their confusion, they will
slay Ravana and his companions in the battle.' He comforted and
assured the rakshasa in this way.

His father-in-law, Sushena, was by his side and Sugriva addressed
him. 'With the large numbers of brave apes go to Kishkindha. Take
these two brothers, Rama and Lakshmana, the scorchers of enemies,
with you. Until they have regained their senses, remain there. I will
kill Ravana, together with his sons and his relatives. Like Shakra
got his lost prosperity back, I will bring back Maithilee.' Hearing
the words of the Indra among the apes, Sushena spoke these words.
'There was a great and extremely terrible battle between the gods
and the asuras. The danavas were skilled in avoiding the touch of
the arrows. Despite the gods knowing about the use of weapons,
they repeatedly struck them. They were afflicted and destroyed.
They lost their senses and almost lost their lives. Brihasapti used
his knowledge of mantras and herbs to treat them. Let apes who
are swift in their speed, Sampati, Panasa and the others, quickly
go to the ocean with milky waters and fetch those herbs. The apes
know about the great herbs in the mountains— *sanjivakarani* and
the divine *vishalya*, created by the gods.[146] In the excellent ocean,
there are two mountains named Chandra and Drona. Amrita was
churned there and the supreme herbs are there. The gods placed

---

[146] Sanjivakarani means something that imparts life, vishalya means something that
removes stakes.

the supreme herbs in the mountains there. O king! Let Hanumat, Vayu's son, go there.'

At this time, a wind arose, accompanied by clouds tinged with lightning. This agitated the water in the ocean and seemed to make the mountains tremble. As a result of the strong wind resulting from the wings, all the large trees on the island fell down. Their branches and roots were shattered and flung into the salty waters. The snakes and serpents that resided there[147] were terrified. All of them quickly submerged, deep into the salty ocean. In a short while, all the apes saw Garuda, Vinata's immensely strong son, blazing like a fire. In the form of arrows, snakes had tied down the two immensely strong men.[148] On seeing him arrive, these fled. Seeing the two Kakutsthas, Suparna honoured them. He touched their faces, which possessed the radiance of the moon, with his hands. Their wounds were healed by the touch of Vinata's son. Their bodies quickly became smooth and excellent in complexion. The great qualities of their energy, valour, strength, endurance and enterprise, as well as their foresight, intelligence and memory were doubled. Garuda raised those two extremely valiant ones, who were Vasava's equal. He cheerfully embraced them.

Rama said, 'It is through your favours that we have been able to overcome the great calamity caused through the powers of Ravana's son. We have swiftly become strong. My heart is as pleased at meeting you as with meeting my father Dasharatha and my grandfather, Aja. O handsome one! Who are you, adorned with divine garlands and pastes? Your garments sparkle and you are adorned with divine ornaments.'

The immensely radiant and immensely strong king of the birds was pleased in his heart. With delight in his eyes, Vinata's son replied, 'O Kakutstha! I am your friend, as loved by you outside your body as your breath of life is inside. I am Garuda and I have come here to help the two of you. The asuras are immensely valiant and the danavas are immensely strong. But they, and all the gods

---

[147] In the ocean.
[148] Rama and Lakshmana.

and gandharvas, even if they placed Shatakratu at the forefront, were incapable of freeing you from this extremely terrible bondage of arrows fashioned through the strength of maya by Indrajit, cruel in deeds. These nagas are Kadru's offspring. Their fangs are sharp and filled with virulent poison. Because of the strength of maya of the rakshasa, they assumed this form of arrows. O one who knows about dharma! O Rama! O one who has truth as his valour! With your brother, Lakshmana, the slayer of enemies in the battle, you are fortunate. Having heard what happened, out of affection for the two of you and observing my friendship, I quickly came here. The two of you have now been freed from the extremely terrible bondage of arrows. However, you must always remain vigilant. In all encounters, the rakshasas naturally fight in deceitful ways. But for brave ones like you, pure in sentiments, uprightness constitutes your strength. In the field of battle, you must never trust the rakshasas. He is an example to show that the rakshasas are always deceitful.' Having told Rama this, the extremely strong Suparna affectionately embraced him and prepared to leave. 'O friend! O Raghava! O one who knows about dharma! O one who is affectionate even towards his enemies! I desire your leave, to return where I came from. With arrows that are like waves, you will only leave the young and the aged in Lanka, killing your enemy, Ravana. You will get Sita back.' Having said this, Suparna, swift in his valour, removed the wounds from Rama. In the midst of those residents of the forest, he circumambulated and embraced the valiant one. Like the wind, Suparna then penetrated the sky.

The leaders of the apes saw that the wounds on the two Raghavas had healed. They roared like lions and lashed their tails. Kettledrums and drums were sounded. Delighted, they blew on conch shells. As was the case earlier, they started to jump around. Some brave apes, who fought with trees, boasted. Hundreds and thousands of them uprooted trees and stood there. They emitted loud roars and scared the roamers in the night. Desiring to fight, the apes assembled before Lanka's gates. A terrible and tumultuous roar arose among the herds of apes, like the extremely terrible roar of the clouds in the night, when summer is over.

Chapter 6(41)

The spirited apes created an extremely tumultuous sound. Ravana, together with the rakshasas, heard the sounds of their roaring. They heard that terrible, deep and rumbling sound. In the midst of his advisers, he spoke these words. 'It is evident that the apes are delighted. An extremely loud roar, like the thunder of the clouds, has arisen amidst them. There is no doubt that there is a reason for their great joy. That is the reason this loud roar is agitating Varuna's abode. The two brothers, Rama and Lakshmana, were bound down with sharp arrows. Because of this extremely loud roar, a doubt has arisen in me.' Having said this to his ministers, the lord of the rakshasas spoke to the nairittas who were near him. 'Go and quickly find out everything about the roamers in the forest. At this time of grieving, how has a reason for delight arisen?' Thus addressed, they swiftly climbed up the ramparts and saw the army protected by the great-souled Sugriva. They saw that the two Raghavas had been freed from the extremely terrible bondage of arrows and that the two immensely fortunate ones had got up. The rakshasas were distressed. With their hearts full of fear, they descended from the ramparts. With pale faces, all of them presented themselves before the Indra among the rakshasas. With distress in their faces, the roamers in the night, accomplished in the use of words, told Ravana everything about that disagreeable and unpleasant news. 'In the battle, Indrajit had bound down the two brothers, Rama and Lakshmana, in bonds of arrows and had disabled their arms. They can be seen in the field of battle, freed from the bondage of arrows. In their valour, they are like Indras among elephants and, like elephants, have severed their bonds.'

Hearing their words, the immensely strong Indra among the rakshasas was overcome by thoughts and sorrow. With a distressed face, he said, 'Indrajit was granted a terrible boon and tied them down with arrows, invincible and like the sun, in the form of virulent serpents. He crushed them in the encounter. Despite the bondage of that weapon, if my enemies have freed themselves, I can see a great danger presenting itself before all my soldiers. They were

shrouded in arrows that possessed Vasuki's energy. However, that
has been rendered unsuccessful. Despite having faced that in the
battle, my enemies are still alive.' Having said this, he sighed like
an enraged serpent. In the midst of the rakshasas, he spoke to the
rakshasa named Dhumraksha. This rakshasa was filled with great
strength and was terrible in his deeds. 'Leave and kill Rama and the
apes.' Thus addressed by the intelligent Indra among the rakshasas,
Dhumraksha prostrated himself. Delighted, he emerged from the
king's residence.

Emerging through the gate, he told the commander of the
forces, 'Ask the forces to hurry. Why delay in fighting?' Following
Ravana's command and hearing Dhumraksha's words, the
commander of the forces told the soldiers who followed him to
quickly ready the army. Those roamers in the night were terrible in
form and bells were tied to their bodies. They roared happily and
surrounded Dhumraksha. They wielded many kinds of weapons
in their hands. There were spears and clubs in their hands. There
were bludgeons, lances, staffs and extremely terrible iron maces.
There were clubs, *bhindipala*s,[149] javelins, spikes and battleaxes.
The terrible rakshasas emerged, roaring like clouds. Some were
on chariots. Others carried decorated standards and readied nets
made out of gold. These[150] were yoked to mules with many kinds
of faces, extremely swift steeds and excellent elephants that were
crazy and excited. As unassailable as tigers, the tigers among
rakshasas emerged. Dhumraksha ascended a divine chariot that
roared like a mule. It was decorated with gold and yoked to mules
that had faces like wolves and lions. Surrounded by rakshasas,
the immensely valorous Dhumraksha emerged laughingly through
the western gate, where Hanumat, the leader of the herd, was
stationed.

The extremely terrible rakshasa left and he was terrible to
behold. From the sky, terrible birds tried to restrain him.[151] An
extremely terrible vulture descended on the top of his chariot and

---

[149] Catapults or javelins that are like blowpipes, with arrows shot through them.
[150] The chariots.
[151] These were ominous portents.

seated itself on the top of his flag. Others that fed on corpses also descended. A giant torso, wet with blood, fell down on the ground near Dhumraksha and emitted a harsh roar. A god showered down blood and the earth trembled. The wind blew in a contrary direction, with a sound like that of a storm. The directions were enveloped in waves of darkness and could not be discerned. The rakshasas saw these ominous signs, the harbingers of fear. These extremely terrible portents manifested themselves and Dhumraksha was distressed. However, the strong one was eager to fight and emerged. He was surrounded by many extremely terrible roamers in the night. He saw the army of several apes. It was like the ocean and was protected by Raghava's arms.

Chapter 6(42)

With a terrible roar, the rakshasa Dhumraksha emerged. All the apes desired to fight. On seeing this, they were delighted and roared. A terrible fight ensued between the apes and the rakshasas. They fought against each other and slew each other with terrible trees and spears and clubs. In every direction, the apes were struck down by the terrible rakshasas. Using trees, the apes also felled the rakshasas down on the ground. Enraged, the rakshasas pierced the apes with sharp and terrible arrows that were shafted with the feathers of herons. They used clubs, terrible spears, heavy bludgeons, terrible maces and colourful tridents. The immensely strong apes also routed the rakshasas. They were excited because of their intolerance and fearlessly performed these deeds. Their bodies were mangled by arrows. Their bodies were struck by spears. However, the leaders among the apes seized trees and boulders. Terrible in their force, the apes roared here and there. They announced their names and crushed the terrible rakshasas. An extraordinary and terrible battle ensued between the apes and the rakshasas. Many boulders and trees with many branches were used. Some rakshasas were crushed by apes who wished for victory. Some

who subsisted on blood[152] vomited blood from their mouths. Some
were struck along the flanks. There were piles of those who had
been struck by trees. Some were shattered with boulders and some
were torn apart with teeth. Standards were crushed and shattered.
Mules were brought down. Chariots were fragmented. The roamers
in the night were brought down. The apes, terrible in their valour,
repeatedly flung themselves on the rakshasas, tearing their faces
apart with the sharp nails on their hands. Their faces turned pale,
their hair was torn out.[153] Senseless because of the smell of blood,
they fell down on the ground. This made the rakshasas, terrible
in their valour, extremely angry. In the battle, they rushed against
the apes with palms that possessed the touch of the vajra. When
they were attacked with force, the apes retaliated with greater force.
They brought the enemy down with fists, feet, teeth and trees.

Dhumraksha, bull among the rakshasas, saw that the soldiers
were being made to flee. In his anger, he fought and created carnage
among the apes. Some were crushed with lances, other apes began
to ooze out blood. Some others were struck with clubs and fell down
on the ground. Some were struck with maces, others shattered with
bhindipalas. Others were struck with spears and, senseless, lost their
lives. Some residents of the forest were killed and, wet with blood,
fell down on the ground. Some were driven away and destroyed,
as the angry rakshasas fought. The hearts of some were shattered
and they lay down on one side. Some were struck with tridents
and their entrails came out. That encounter between the apes and
the rakshasas was great and extremely terrible. Many kinds of
weapons were used and so were boulders and trees. There was the
sweet sound of bowstrings being twanged. Other sounds seemed to
possess a rhythm. It was as if a song was gently being sung by the
gandharvas. In the field of battle, Dhumraksha laughed. With a bow
in his hand, he drove away the apes in all the directions, showering
arrows over them. Maruti saw that the soldiers were distressed and
afflicted because of Dhumraksha. He seized a gigantic boulder and

---

[152] Rakshasas.
[153] A description of the rakshasas.

angrily attacked. His eyes were coppery red. He was like his father in valour and his anger doubled the strength. He flung that boulder towards Dhumraksha's chariot. On seeing that boulder descend, he quickly raised a club, leapt down with great force from the chariot and stood on the ground. Having crushed the chariot, its wheels, *kubara*,[154] horses, standard and the bows, the boulder fell down on the ground. Hanumat, the wind god's son, destroyed the chariot. He then used trees with trunks and branches to create carnage among the rakshasas. The rakshasas were covered with blood, their heads crushed. Others were mangled by the trees and fell down on the ground. Hanumat, the son of the wind god, drove away the rakshasa soldiers. He seized the summit of a mountain and rushed towards Dhumraksha. As he descended, the valiant Dhumraksha raised his club. Roaring, he violently attacked Hanumat. The club was studded with many spikes. With force and anger, Dhumraksha brought it down on Hanumat's head. But the ape possessed the strength of the wind god. Though he was struck by a club that was terrible in form, he paid no heed to the blow. Instead, he brought down the summit of the mountain on Dhumraksha's head. Struck by the summit of the mountain, all his limbs were shattered. He suddenly fell down on the ground, like a mountain that has been fragmented. Seeing that Dhumraksha had been killed, the remaining roamers in the night were frightened. Slain by the apes, they entered Lanka. The son of the wind god killed the enemy. From their wounds, a river of blood started to flow. Exhausted from having slain the enemy, the great-souled one was delighted and was worshipped by the apes.

Chapter 6(43)

Ravana, the lord of the rakshasas, heard that Dhumraksha had been killed. The commander of the forces was present there, his hands joined in salutation. He told him, 'Let invincible rakshasas,

[154] Kubara is the pole for attaching the yoke to the chariot.

terrible in their valour, quickly emerge. Let them place Akampana, skilled in the use of all weapons, at the forefront.'

Terrible in appearance, with horrible eyes, the best among rakshasas seized many kinds of weapons. Urged by the commander of the forces, they attacked. Akampana left, surrounded by terrible rakshasas. He was astride a large chariot that had the complexion of a cloud and made a loud clatter, like the rumbling of a cloud. He himself possessed the complexion of a cloud and was adorned with ornaments made out of molten gold. In a great battle, even the gods were incapable of making him quake. Among the others, Akampana's energy was like that of the sun. He rushed forward angrily, wishing to fight. But suddenly, the horses that bore his chariot along seemed to be struck with lassitude.[155] Though he took joy in fighting, his left eye started to twitch. The complexion of his face paled and his voice became tremulous. Though it was an excellent day, it turned into a bad day and a harsh wind started to blow. All the animals and birds shrieked in cruel tones and this signified fear. However, his shoulders were like those of a lion and he was like a tiger in his valour. Without thinking about these omens, he rushed forward into the field of battle. As the rakshasa emerged with the other rakshasas, there was an extremely loud roar that seemed to agitate the ocean. The large army of the apes was terrified by this sound. With trees and boulders as weapons, they stationed themselves for the battle. An extremely fierce battle ensued between the apes and the rakshasas. For the sake of Rama and Ravana, they were ready to give up their lives. All of them were extremely strong and brave. All of them were like mountains. The apes and the rakshasas desired to slay each other. There was the sound of those extremely spirited ones roaring as they clashed. One could hear them roaring at each other in great rage. As the apes and the rakshasas fought, an extremely terrible dust that was red in hue arose and spread in the ten directions. Like a white silken garment waving in the wind, this dust covered all creatures and they could no longer distinguish each other on the field of battle.

[155] Ominous portents.

Because of the dust, standards, flags, armour, horses, weapons and chariots could not be seen. There was only the extremely loud and tumultuous sound of roaring and clashing. This could be heard in the battle, but nothing could be seen. Exceedingly angry, apes killed other apes in the battle. Because of the darkness, rakshasas also killed other rakshasas. The apes and the rakshasas killed the enemy and also those from their own side. Wet with blood, the earth smeared itself with mire. The dust was sprinkled with waves of blood and settled down. The earth was seen to be strewn with dead bodies. The energetic apes and rakshasas quickly struck each other with trees, spears, boulders, lances, clubs, bludgeons and javelins. The apes were like mountains and terrible in their deeds. With arms like clubs, they fought against the rakshasas and killed them in the battle. The rakshasas were also angry and had spears and javelins in their hands. With those extremely terrible weapons, they slew the apes who were there. The apes used large trees and large rocks to attack and rout the rakshasas, using their valour to counter those weapons.

At this time, the brave apes, Kumuda, Nala and Mainda became supremely angry and displayed excellent force. In the field of battle, those extremely swift leaders among the herds of apes seemed to be sporting as they created great carnage, using trees against the rakshasas.

Chapter 6(44)

Witnessing the extremely great deeds performed by those excellent apes in the battle, Akampana was filled with fierce rage. His form became senseless with rage and he seized his supreme bow. Witnessing the deeds performed by the enemy, he addressed his charioteer in these words. 'O charioteer! Quickly drive the chariot there, where a large number of rakshasas are being slain in the battle. The strong apes, terrible in form, are there. With trees and boulders as weapons, they will stand before me there. They pride themselves on fighting and I wish to slay them. It can be seen that they are crushing all the rakshasa soldiers.' The chariot of the supreme among warriors was drawn by swift horses. In his anger, Akampana attacked the apes and enveloped them in nets of arrows. The apes were incapable of standing there, not to speak of fighting in the battle. They were routed by Akampana's arrows and all of them ran away.

The immensely strong Hanumat saw that his relatives had come under the subjugation of death and were being subdued by Akampana. He attacked and all the leaders among the apes saw that great ape. All those brave apes assembled in the battle and surrounded him. The leaders among the apes saw that Hanumat was stationed there. Because he was strong, the strong ones also sought succour in him. Hanumat was stationed there, with a complexion like that of a mountain. Akampana showered down arrows on him, like the great Indra pouring down rain. Torrents of sharp arrows descended on his body, but he paid no heed to them. The immensely strong one had made up his mind to slay Akampana. The immensely energetic Hanumat, the son of the wind god, laughed. He made the earth quake and attacked the rakshasa. He roared and blazed in his energy. His invincible and radiant form was like that of the fire. The bull among the apes knew that he possessed no weapons. Filled with anger, he used his force to uproot a mountain. Maruti seized that great mountain in one of his hands. The valiant one emitted an extremely loud roar and whirled it around. With that, he attacked Akampana, Indra among the rakshasas, the way Purandara had used his vajra to attack Namuchi in a battle. Akampana saw that the summit of the mountain had been raised up. From a distance, he used arrows that were in the shape of a half-crescent to shatter it. In the sky, the summit of the mountain was shattered by the rakshasa's arrows and, fragmented, fell down. On seeing this, Hanumat became senseless with rage. Full of anger and intolerance, the ape approached an ashvakarna tree. He swiftly uprooted it and like a great mountain, held it up. The immensely radiant one seized the ashvakarna tree, which possessed a gigantic trunk. Greatly happy, he seized it and whirled it around in the battle. Full of great rage, he rushed forward with it. The trees were quickly shattered from the force of his thighs. The earth was shattered from the force of his footsteps. Elephants climbed atop elephants and chariots atop chariots. The intelligent Hanumat slew rakshasa foot soldiers with this. In the battle, he was as angry as Death and destroyed lives. Hanumat saw that the rakshasas were running away. He descended angrily and caused fear to the rakshasas.

Seeing this, the brave Akampana became angry and roared. He used fourteen sharp arrows that could tear the body apart. Using these, the immensely valiant Akampana pierced Hanumat. He was pierced with many showers of arrows. The brave Hanumat could be seen, like a tall mountain. Using supreme speed, he uprooted another tree and used this to quickly strike Akampana, Indra among rakshasas, on the head. In rage, the great-souled Indra among apes struck the rakshasa and he died and fell down in the battle. Akampana, Indra among rakshasas, was slain and lay down on the ground. On seeing this, all the rakshasas were pained, like trees during an earthquake. All the rakshasas were defeated and cast aside their weapons. Terrified and pursued by the apes, they fled towards Lanka. Their hair was dishevelled and they were scared. They were defeated and their pride was destroyed. Sweat dripped from their limbs. As they fled, they sighed. As they entered the city in their fright, they trampled over each other. Confounded, they repeatedly looked back towards the rear. Those immensely strong rakshasas entered Lanka. All the apes assembled together and worshipped Hanumat. He was also delighted and worshipped all the apes back, as they respectively deserved. Hanumat was spirited and kindly disposed towards them. Desiring victory, according to their capabilities, the apes roared. They again dragged away the rakshasas who were still alive.

Maruti killed the assembled rakshasas. The great ape dazzled in his valour. In the field of battle, he was like the powerful Vishnu, when he destroyed the terrible enemy that was in the form of the great asuras. The large number of gods worshipped the god. So did Rama himself and the extremely strong Lakshmana. So did Sugriva, foremost among the apes, and the immensely strong Vibhishana.

Chapter 6(45)

Hearing that Akampana had been killed, the Indra among the rakshasas became angry. With a slightly crestfallen face, he glanced towards his advisers. He thought for a while and consulted with his ministers. He went all around Lanka and inspected all the battalions. He saw the city of Lanka, with garlands of flags and standards. It was protected by large numbers of rakshasas and many battalions covered it. Ravana, the lord of the rakshasas, saw that the city was barricaded. At that time, intolerant, he spoke to Prahasta, who was skilled in fighting. 'O one who is accomplished in fighting! The city will be suddenly besieged and attacked. I do not see any other means of escaping from a battle. With the exception of I, Kumbhakarna, you, my general, Indrajit and Nikumbha, there is no one else who can bear a burden like this. Therefore, quickly collect some forces and gather them together. For the sake of victory, advance to the spot where the residents of the forest are. When you advance, it is certain that the army of the apes will prove to be fickle. Hearing the roars of the Indras among the rakshasas, they will run away. Apes are fickle and insolent, their minds waver. They will not be able to tolerate the roar, like elephants can't stand the sound of lions roaring. O Prahasta! When those soldiers run away, Rama and Lakshmana will be helpless and without a support, easily subjugated. It is better to make certain a danger that is uncertain.[156] Whether favourable or unfavourable, what do you think is a better course of action for us?' Thus addressed by Ravana, the general, Prahasta, replied to the Indra among the rakshasas, the way Ushanas spoke to the Indra among the asuras. 'O king! Earlier, we have held consultations with the skilled ministers on this. After consulting with each other, there was a dispute among us about what should be done. I think that the best course of action is to return Sita. If she was not returned, we foresaw that there would be a battle. I have always been honoured by you, with gifts, respect

---

[156] The sense seems to be the following. If the rakshasas wait for the attack, the danger is uncertain. If the rakshasas attack, the danger is certain.

and many kinds of conciliation. When the time arrives, why will
I not do what is agreeable to you? I will not protect my life, sons,
wives or riches. For your sake, behold. I will give up my life in the
battle and offer it as an oblation.' The general spoke in this way to
Ravana, his master.

Having said this, Prahasta spoke to the commanders who
were standing in front of him. 'Quickly assemble a large army of
rakshasas. In the field of battle, I will use arrows that possess the
force of the vajra to kill the residents of the forest and satisfy birds
with their flesh.' In the rakshasa's[157] residence, the immensely strong
commanders heard his words. They swiftly readied an army. In a
short while, there were brave rakshasas, armed with various kinds
of sharp weapons, and elephants in Lanka. Some satisfied the fire
with oblations. Others bowed down before brahmanas. A fragrant
breeze started to blow, carrying the smell of clarified butter. There
were many kinds of garlands. With mantras, oblations were offered.
Cheerfully, the rakshasas prepared many kinds of equipment
required for the battle. Speedily, the rakshasas brought bows and
armour. While King Ravana looked on, they surrounded Prahasta.
With the king's permission, terrible battledrums were sounded.
Prahasta ascended a divine chariot that had been prepared. It was
yoked to swift horses and there was a well-trained charioteer. It
roared like a large cloud and was as radiant as the sun and the
moon. There was an invincible standard with the mark of a serpent.
There were excellent bumpers and excellent wheels. There were nets
of gold and it seemed to smile in its prosperity. Commanded by
Ravana, he ascended this chariot. Surrounded by a large army, he
quickly emerged from Lanka. Battledrums were sounded, with a
sound like that of clouds. As the commanders of the army departed,
the sounds of conch shells could be heard. With the sound of these
terrible roars, the rakshasas advanced towards the front. They were
terrible in form and gigantic in size. Prahasta was at the front.
Arrayed in an extremely terrible formation, he emerged through
the eastern gate, surrounded by a large army that was like a herd

[157] Ravana's.

of elephants. He was surrounded by an army that resembled waves
in the ocean. Like an enraged Death, Prahasta quickly emerged.
There was the sound of his departure and the rakshasas roared.
All the creatures in Lanka howled in hideous voices. In a sky that
was devoid of clouds, birds that fed on flesh and blood circled the
chariot in a counterclockwise direction.[158] Horrible jackals vomited
fires with flames. Meteors descended from the sky. Harsh winds
started to blow. The planets seemed to clash against each other
and lost their lustre. Blood showered down and sprinkled those
who were towards the front. A vulture descended on the standard
and faced the southern direction. The charioteer had taken part
in several clashes. However, when he was urging the horses, the
goad fell down from the *suta*'s[159] hand. As he emerged, there was
a radiance and prosperity that was extremely difficult to obtain.
However, this vanished in an instant and though the ground was
even, the horses lost their footing.

Prahasta, famous for his strength and manliness, emerged. With
many kinds of weapons, the soldiers of the apes countered him in
the battle. An extremely tumultuous sound arose among the apes.
They uprooted heavy trees and seized boulders. The soldiers on
both sides, large numbers of rakshasas and residents of the forest,
rejoiced. They were forceful and capable and desired to slay each
other. A large sound of their challenging each other was heard. For
the sake of victory, the evil-minded Prahasta headed in the direction
of the army of the king of the apes. He entered that army with great
force, like an insect that is about to die heads towards the fire.

Chapter 6(46)

The terrible Prahasta, terrible in his valour, emerged. He was
surrounded by extremely large rakshasas who roared. The

---

[158] Regarded as inauspicious.
[159] The sutas were charioteers and bards.

large army of the apes saw him and, filled with anger, roared
back at Prahasta. The rakshasas, desiring victory, seized glittering
weapons—swords, spikes, daggers, spears, clubs, maces, bludgeons,
javelins, many kinds of battleaxes and different kinds of bows—
and rushed against the apes. Desiring to fight, the bulls among the
apes seized flowering trees and long and large boulders. As they
rushed against each other, there was an extremely great encounter.
There were many showers of rocks, and showers of arrows also
rained down. In the battle, many rakshasas killed many leaders
among the apes. Many apes also killed many rakshasas. Some
were crushed through spears, some through supreme weapons.
Some were struck with clubs, some were severed with battleaxes.
Some lost all enterprise and fell down on the ground. The hearts
of some were shattered, pierced by arrows aimed at them. Some
were sliced into two with swords and, writhing, fell down on the
ground. The rakshasas used spears to rip apart the sides of the apes.
Angry, hordes of apes surrounded the rakshasas from all directions.
Using trees and the summits of mountains, they crushed them down
on the ground. They severely struck them with palms, hands and
fists that were like the vajra to the touch. They[160] vomited blood
from their mouths and their teeth and eyes were smashed. As the
apes and the rakshasas fought in the battle, there was a tumultuous
sound. There was the sound of those in distress and roars, like the
roaring of lions. Enraged, apes and rakshasas followed the path
meant for heroes. They dilated their eyes and fearlessly performed
these cruel deeds.

Narantaka, Kumbhahanu, Mahanada and Samunnata—
these advisers of Prahasta killed the residents of the forest. They
descended swiftly and killed the apes. With a single strike of the
summit of a mountain, Dvivida killed Narantaka. Swift in the use
of his hands, the ape Durmukha uprooted a large tree and brought
down the rakshasa Samunnata. The wrathful Jambavat seized a
large boulder and used this to strike the energetic Mahanada on
the chest and bring him down. Tara clashed against the valiant

---

[160] Rakshasas.

Kumbhahanu and struck him on the head with a tree. The rakshasa
lost his life. Prahasta was astride his chariot and could not tolerate
these deeds. With a bow in his hand, he created terrible carnage
among the residents of the forest. There was turbulence in both
the armies. They roared like the immeasurable ocean, when it is
agitated. Prahasta was skilled in fighting. In that great battle, he
wrathfully used a great flood of arrows to afflict the apes. The earth
was covered with the bodies of apes and rakshasas, like terrible
mountains that had fallen down. The earth was seen to be covered
with floods of blood, as if it was covered with flowering *palasha*
trees in the month of Madhava.[161] The bodies of slain warriors were
like banks. The shattered weapons were like large trees.[162] There
was a large river with waves of blood that headed for the ocean that
was Yama. Livers and spleens were its great mire. The scattered
entrails were the moss. The severed heads and torsos were the fish,
the flesh was the lichen. The vultures were like large numbers of
swans. The herons were like geese. The fat was the foam, the shrieks
of the afflicted were its roar. There was such a river in the field of
battle and it was impossible for cowards to cross. It was like a river
at the end of the summer, frequented by swans and cranes. The best
among the rakshasas and apes found that river extremely difficult
to cross. They were like devastated lotuses in a lotus pond when a
herd of elephants has crossed over it.

Stationed on his chariot, Prahasta shot floods of arrows.
Nila saw that the spirited one was slaying the apes. As Prahasta,
the extremely invincible one, descended, the great and valiant
ape uprooted a tree and struck him with this. Struck by this, the
enraged bull among the rakshasas roared. He rained down showers
of arrows on the commanders of the apes. He[163] was unable to
counter these and received them with closed eyes, like a bull receives
a sudden and swift autumn downpour. In that way, Nila closed
his eyes and received the extremely terrible shower of Prahasta's

[161] Madhava is a name for the month of Magha (January–February). Palasha trees
have red flowers.
[162] Along the banks.
[163] Nila.

arrows, which were very difficult to resist. But this shower of
arrows enraged him. The great Nila seized an extremely large sala
tree and slew Prahasta's horses, which were as swift as thought,
with this. Prahasta, the commander of the army, found that his
bow had been shattered. He seized a terrible club and leapt down
from his chariot. Those two leaders of the respective armies were
spirited and angry. Though there were wounds on all their limbs,
they stood there, like elephants with shattered temples. They tore
at each other like a lion and a tiger attacking each other with their
extremely sharp teeth. They were like a lion and a tiger in their
efforts. Those two brave and valiant ones desired victory and did
not retreat from the field of battle. Desiring fame, they were like
Vritra and Vasava. With supreme ease, Prahasta struck Nila on the
forehead with the club and blood started to flow from this blow.
Blood covered the great ape's limbs. He seized an extremely large
tree and angrily hurled it towards Prahasta's chest. This blow was
unthinkable. However, the strong one seized the giant club and
rushed towards Nila, the strong ape. He descended with great force
and anger. On seeing this, the great ape, extremely swift, seized
a large boulder. Prahasta desired to fight and in the encounter,
was ready to fight with the club. However, Nila quickly brought
the boulder down on his head. Nila, the foremost ape, released
this giant boulder and it shattered the terrible Prahasta's head into
many fragments. He lost his life. He lost his beauty. He lost his
spirits. He lost his senses. He suddenly fell down on the ground,
like a tree severed at the roots. With his head shattered, a lot of
blood started to flow and ooze out from his body, like a waterfall
from a mountain.

When Prahasta was killed by Nila, that large army of rakshasas
was distressed and wavered. It left for Lanka. With the leader
killed, they were incapable of remaining there, like water is driven
back on confronting a dam. With the leader of the army killed, the
rakshasas lost their enterprise. They were benumbed and went to
the residence of the lord of the rakshasas. The immensely strong
Nila was victorious. He met Rama and Lakshmana and was praised
for his own deeds. The leader of the herd was delighted.

Chapter 6(47)

In the battle, the protector of the rakshasa soldiers was slain by the bull among the apes. Armed with terrible weapons, the army of the king of the rakshasas was like the ocean in its force. But they ran away. They went to the lord of the rakshasas and told him that the commander had been killed by the son of the fire god.[164] Hearing their words, the lord of the rakshasas was filled with rage. He heard that Prahasta had been killed in the battle. He was afflicted by grief and his senses were overcome by anger. Like Indra speaking to the foremost warriors of the immortals, he spoke to the foremost warriors among the nairittas. 'My commander[165] has killed Indra's forces. However, he, with his companions and his elephants, has been killed. This enemy should not be taken lightly. I will not hesitate. For the sake of victory and to destroy the enemy, I will myself go to the wonderful field of battle. With a flood of arrows, I will burn down that army of apes, together with Rama and Lakshmana, like a blazing fire burns down a forest.'

Having said this, the enemy of the king of the immortals, with a dazzling and shining form, ascended a radiant and blazing chariot which was yoked to excellent steeds. Conch shells, drums and cymbals were sounded. Palms were slapped and there were leonine roars. The foremost king of the rakshasas departed, worshipped with auspicious benedictions. The foremost king of the rakshasas was surrounded, like the Rudra, the lord of the immortals, by demons.[166] They were like dark clouds in their forms. They subsisted on flesh and their eyes blazed like the fire. The immensely energetic one suddenly emerged from the city and saw that the army of the apes was stationed in front. He saw that it was roaring like the giant ocean or like a cloud. There were upraised trees and boulders in their hands.

---

[164] Nila.
[165] Prahasta.
[166] *Bhutas.*

The army of the rakshasas was extremely terrible. Seeing this, Rama, followed by the soldiers and extensive in his prosperity, with arms resembling an Indra among serpents, spoke to Vibhishana, supreme among those who knew how to use weapons. 'There are many flags, standards and weapons. There are spikes, swords, spears, chakras and other weapons. The army possesses elephants that are as large as mountains. It cannot be agitated and is full of fearless ones. Whom does it belong to?' Vibhishana was Shakra's equal in valour. Hearing the words Rama had spoken, he told him about this excellent army, which consisted of great-souled bulls among the rakshasas. 'There is a great-souled one astride that elephant. He is like a sun that has just arisen and his face is coppery red in complexion. His being astride it is making the elephant's head tremble. O king! Know him to be Akampana.[167] There is one on a chariot, with a standard bearing a lion on it. He is stretching a bow that is as radiant as Shakra's bow. He is as radiant as a fierce elephant with extended tusks. He is named Indrajit, supreme among excellent ones.[168] There is an archer astride that chariot. He is like Vindhya, Asta or Mahendra. He is the atiratha Atikaya. He is drawing a bow that is unmatched in size. He is name Atikaya because his body is exceedingly large.[169] There is one whose eyes are coppery red and he resembles the newly risen sun. Astride an elephant with jangling bells, that great-souled one is roaring harshly. He is the brave one named Mahodara. He is astride a chariot with a colourful and golden harness. He resembles an evening cloud or a mountain. He has raised a spear that is blazing in its rays. This is Pishacha and he is like the lightning in his speed. That one has seized a sharp spear. He is astride an Indra among bulls that is like a mountain. This *kimkara*[170] is like thunder in his speed and his radiance is like that of lightning. That one who is advancing

---

[167] Unless there was more than one Akampana, there is a consistency problem. Akampana has already been killed by Hanumat.

[168] Alternatively, one who has obtained an excellent boon.

[169] *Kaya* means body and *ati* means exceedingly.

[170] As in, Ravana's servant.

is the illustrious Trishira.[171] That one has the form of a cloud. His chest is broad, firm and formed well. His standard has the king of the serpents. Controlled, he is twanging his bow. He is Kumbha. That one has seized a blazing and smoking club encrusted with molten gold and diamonds. He is advancing with the standard of the army of the rakshasas. That is Nikumbha, the performer of terrible and extraordinary deeds. That one is on a chariot that is shining brightly, as dazzling in form as the fire. There are bows, swords, masses of arrows and flags on the chariot. That one is Narantaka and he fights with the summits of mountains.[172] That one can assume many kinds of terrible forms. He is surrounded by large-eyed and radiant demons[173] with faces like tigers, camels, large serpents and lions. He is the one who destroyed the pride of even the gods. His lustre is like that of the moon. A white umbrella with slender spokes is held above his head. This is the great-souled lord of the rakshasas. He is advancing like Rudra surrounded by bhutas. He wears a diadem and his earrings are moving. His terrible form is like that of Vindhya, Indra among mountains. He is the one who destroyed the pride of the great Indra and of Vaivasvata. As radiant as the sun, the lord of the rakshasas is advancing.'

Rama replied to Vibhishana, the scorcher of enemies. 'The dazzling and great energy of Ravana, the lord of the rakshasas, is amazing. Ravana is blazing like the sun and like the sun's rays, he is extremely difficult to look at. From the signs on his form it is evident that he is full of energy. The bodies of the brave gods and danavas are not like this. They do not dazzle as much as the body of the Indra among the rakshasas. All of them resemble mountains. All of them fight with mountains. All of them are wielding lustrous weapons. All the warriors are extremely energetic. The king of the rakshasas is radiant. He shines in his terrible valour. He is surrounded by fierce ones, like Death is by embodied bhutas.' Saying this, the

---

[171] Since Rama killed Trishira in Janasthana, there may be another consistency problem.

[172] Narantaka has already been killed by Dvivida.

[173] Bhutas.

valiant Rama seized his bow and picked up an excellent arrow, with Lakshmana following him.

The great-souled lord of the rakshasas spoke to those immensely strong rakshasas. 'Have no fear. Station yourselves properly and tend to the gates, the houses and turrets.' He swiftly gave them permission to leave and the rakshasas went to their appointed places. He then shattered the apes, which were like waves in the ocean, filled with large fish. The Indra among rakshasas was ready to fight and descended violently with his blazing bow and arrows. On seeing this, the lord of the apes[174] uprooted the summit of a large mountain and attacked the lord of the rakshasas with this. The summit of the mountain was full of many trees and peaks and seizing it, he hurled it towards the roamer in the night. On seeing it violently descend, he pierced it with arrows with golden tufts. The excellent and large summit of the mountain was full of trees. With the summit shattered, it fell down on the ground. The protector of the world of the rakshasas then picked up an arrow that was like a gigantic snake, with a hue like that of Death. He seized it and it was like the fire in its force. With sparks flying, it possessed a flaming form. That arrow was like the great Indra's vajra in its speed. To kill Sugriva, he angrily released it. The arrow was released from Ravana's arm. It was sharp at the tip and had an excellent form, like Shakra's vajra. It approached Sugriva and pierced him with force, like Guha's fierce spear shattering the Krouncha mountain.[175] Afflicted by the arrow, he lost his senses. Shrieking, the brave one fell down on the ground. Seeing that he had lost his senses and had fallen down on the ground, the yatudhanas who were fighting roared in delight.

Gavaksha, Gavaya, Sudamshtra, Rishabha, Jyotimukha and Nala raised boulders that were gigantic in size and rushed towards the Indra among the rakshasas. The lord of the rakhasas used innumerable arrows that were sharp at the tips to rend this attack fruitless. With nets of arrows that were made out of gold and were

[174] Sugriva.
[175] Kartikeya shattered Mount Krouncha with his spear.

colourfully tufted, he pierced the Indras among the apes. Pierced by the arrows of the enemy of the gods, the Indras among the apes, terrible in form, fell down on the ground. He then enveloped the army of the apes with nets of fierce arrows. Those foremost among brave ones were struck. Pierced by the arrows, they were scared and shrieked. They ran away and sought refuge with Rama.

The great-souled Rama seized his bow and, with his bow, started to swiftly leave. However, Lakshmana approached him, joined his hands in salution, and spoke words that were full of great meaning. 'O noble one! If I wish, I am capable of killing this evil-souled one. I will destroy this inferior one. O lord! Grant me permission.' For Rama, truth was valour and the immensely energetic one said, 'O Lakshmana! Go. Take care against the enemy in the encounter. Ravana is extremely brave. In an encounter, his valour is extraordinary. If he is enraged, there is no doubt that the three worlds are incapable of standing before him. Seek out his weak spots. Hide your own weak spots. Control yourself and make efforts, using your eyes and your bow to protect yourself.' Hearing Raghava's words, he embraced and worshipped him. Honouring Rama, Soumitri set out to do battle. He saw Ravana, with arms that were like the trunks of elephants. He blazed as he held aloft his terrible bow. He enveloped the apes, showering them with nets of arrows and mangling and scattering their bodies.

The immensely energetic Hanumat, son of the wind god, saw this. He sought to counter this net of arrows and attacked Ravana. To scare Ravana, the intelligent Hanumat approached his chariot, raised his right hand and uttered these words. 'You cannot be routed by gods, danavas, gandharvas, yakshas and rakshasas. But you face fear from apes. I have raised my right hand and this has five branches. I will destroy the life that has been in your body for a very long time.' Hearing Hanumat's words, the eyes of Ravana, terrible in his valour, turned red with anger and he spoke these words. 'Without any hesitation, strike me quickly. Be steady and obtain fame. O ape! After ascertaining your valour, I will destroy you.' Hearing Ravana's words, the son of the wind god spoke these words. 'Remember that I have already killed your son Aksha.'

Thus addressed, the immensely energetic Ravana, the lord of the rakshasas, struck the valiant son of the wind god on the chest with his palm. Struck by the palm, he wavered repeatedly. However, enraged, he struck the enemy of the immortals with his palm instead. Struck by the palm of the great-souled ape, Dashagriva was whirled around, like the earth during an earthquake. Seeing that Ravana had suffered in the battle because of the blow from the palm, the rishis, the apes, the siddhas, the gods and the asuras roared. After this, the immensely energetic Ravana regained his composure and spoke these words. 'O ape! Excellent. Though you are my enemy, your valour is praiseworthy.' Thus addressed by Ravana, Maruti replied in these words. 'O Ravana! Since you are still alive, shame on my valour. Those with good deeds speak through their blows. O one evil in intelligence! Why are you boasting? In truth, my fist will convey you to Yama's abode.' At Maruti's words, he blazed in rage. With reddened eyes, the valiant one carefully raised his right fist and brought it down with force on the ape's chest. Struck severely on the chest, Hanumat reeled again.

Seeing that the immensely strong Hanumat was distracted, the atiratha quickly steered his chariot and advanced towards Nila. The lord of the rakshasas used terrible arrows that were like serpents and could penetrate extremely deep into the inner organs. He used these blazing arrows against Nila, the commander of the army of the apes. Nila, the commander of the army of the apes, was struck by this flood of arrows. He picked up the summit of a mountain with one hand and hurled it towards the lord of the rakshasas. The great-souled and energetic Hanumat also regained his composure. Seeing this and wanting to fight, he spoke these angry words to Ravana, the lord of the rakshasas, who was engaged in fighting with Nila. 'When you are fighting with someone, it is not proper to attack someone else.' The immensely strong Ravana struck the summit with seven arrows that were extremely sharp. Struck in this way, the summit shattered and fell down. The commander of the army of the apes saw that the summit of the mountain had been fragmented. The slayer of enemy heroes blazed in anger, like the fire of destruction. In the battle, Nila hurled ashvakarna, dhava, sala,

flowering *chuta*s[176] and many other kinds of trees. Ravana severed
all the trees that were hurled at him. He rained down extremely
terrible showers of arrows on the son of the fire god.[177] He was
showered by these torrents of arrows, like a cloud raining down on
a large mountain. He made his form extremely small and leapt on to
the top of the standard.[178] The son of the fire god stationed himself
on the top of the standard. Seeing this, Ravana blazed in anger,
while Nila roared. The ape leapt from the top of his standard to the
top of his bow and then to the top of his diadem. Witnessing this,
Lakshmana, Hanumat and Rama were astounded. The immensely
energetic Ravana was also amazed at the ape's dexterity. He picked
up the blazing and wonderful Agneya weapon. The apes rejoiced
and shouted at Nila having fearlessly countered Ravana in the
battle and on seeing that he had accomplished his objective. Ravana
was provoked by the roar of the apes. His heart was disturbed and
he wasn't sure about what he should do. Ravana thus picked up
and affixed the Agneya arrow. The roamer in the night aimed in
the direction of Nila, who was stationed atop the standard. The
immensely energetic Ravana, the lord of the rakshasas said, 'O ape!
You are dexterous and supreme in the use of maya. O ape! But if
you are capable, protect your life. Create numerous forms that are
exactly like you. Even then, you will not be able to escape from the
arrow that I have affixed. Protect your life. Even if you are alive,
you will be destroyed.' Saying this, the mighty-armed Ravana, the
lord of the rakshasas, aimed the arrow and struck the commander
of the army. In the form of the arrow, the weapon struck Nila on
his chest. Violently scorched, he fell down on the ground. However,
because of his father's greatness and because of his own energy, he
did not lose his life. He sank down on his knees on the ground.

Dashagriva saw that the ape was unconscious. But he was
eager to fight. On a chariot that roared like the clouds, he attacked
Soumitri. When he brandished his immeasurable bow, with an
undistressed spirit, Soumitri spoke to him. 'O Indra of the roamers

[176] Mango trees.
[177] Nila.
[178] Ravana's standard.

in the night! Advance against me. You should not fight against apes.' The king heard these loudly proclaimed words and the fierce twanging of his bow. He approached the spot where Soumitri was stationed. The rakshasa spoke words that were filled with anger. 'O Raghava! It is good fortune that you have come within the range of my vision. O one perverse in intelligence! You will now meet your end. You will proceed to the land of the dead this very instant. My net of arrows will envelop you.' Though he roared with his white-tipped teeth, Soumitri wasn't disturbed. He replied, 'O king! Those who are great in their powers do not roar. O supreme among those who are wicked in their deeds! Why are you indulging in self-praise? O Indra among the rakshasas! I know your valour, strength, power and prowess. Come. I am stationed here, with a bow and arrows in my hand. Why indulge in pointless self-praise?' When he said this, the lord of the rakshasas became angry and shot seven well-tufted arrows. However, Lakshmana severed these with gold-tufted and colourful arrows that were sharp at the tips and edges. The arrows of the lord of Lanka were violently countered, like serpents repulsed by Indras among serpents. Seeing this, he became angry and shot other sharp arrows. He rained down showers of terrible arrows. However, Rama's younger brother was not agitated. He affixed excellent kshura, *ardhachandra*, *karni* and bhalla arrows[179] and severed those. Lakshmana swiftly affixed arrows that were sharp at the tips. They were like the great Indra's vajra in their force and were blazing in form. To slay the lord of the rakshasas, he released them. The Indra among the rakshasas countered and severed them. He then struck Lakshmana on the forehead with an arrow that was like the fire of destruction in its powers and had been given to him by Svayambhu. Lakshmana was afflicted by Ravana's arrow and wavered. As he trembled, he leaned on his bow. He regained his senses with difficulty and severed the bow of the enemy of the Indra among the gods. When his bow was severed, Dasharatha's son struck him with three arrows that were sharp at

---

[179] Kshurapras (kshuras) are arrows with sharp edges, ardhachandras are in the shape of a half-moon, karnis are barbed and bhallas have broad heads.

the tips. Afflicted by those arrows, the king wavered, but regained his senses with difficulty. His bow was severed and he suffered from those arrows. He was wet with sweat and there was blood on his body. In the battle, summoning up all his fierce energy, the enemy of the gods seized a spear that had been given to him by Svayambhu. It was like the fire and emitted smoke. It terrified the army of the apes. The protector of the kingdom of the rakshasas quickly hurled this blazing spear towards Soumitri. As that weapon descended, Bharata's younger brother struck it with his arrows, like oblations being offered into the fire. Despite this, the spear penetrated into the broad chest of Dasharatha's son. Brahma's spear struck Soumitri between the breasts. However, he remembered whose portion he himself was and thought of Vishnu. Thus, the thorn of the gods was unable to oppress and raise the lord who destroyed the insolence of the danavas with his arms.[180] In a battle, Bharata's younger brother was like the Himalayas, Mandara or Meru, and the three worlds, together with the immortals, were incapable of afflicting him with their arms. He was born from Vishnu's portion, although he had resorted to a human body. On seeing the state of the unconscious Lakshmana, Ravana was amazed.

The son of the wind god was enraged and attacked Ravana. With a fist that was like the vajra, he angrily struck him on the chest. As a result of that blow with the fist, Ravana, the lord of the rakshasas, trembled and fell down. He sank down on his knees on the ground. Seeing that Ravana, terrible in his valour, was unconscious in the battle, the rishis, the apes and the gods, with Vasava, roared. Lakshmana had been afflicted by Ravana. The energetic Hanumat raised him up with his arms and took him to Raghava. The son of the wind god was a well-wisher and supremely devoted. The ape was light in his stride and the enemies were unable to make him quake. Soumitri was extremely difficult to vanquish in a battle. The spear left him and returned to its place in Ravana's chariot. In the great battle, the immensely energetic Ravana also regained his

---

[180] The Critical Edition excises a few shlokas where Ravana tries to pick up the unconscious Lakshmana with his arms.

senses. He picked up sharp arrows and seized his great bow. The
stake was removed from Lakshmana, the slayer of enemies, and he
regained his composure. He remembered his own self and that he
had been born from Vishnu's portion.

Brave warriors from the great army of the apes had been
brought down. In the battle, seeing this, Raghava attacked Ravana.
At this, Hanumat approached him and spoke these words. 'If you
ascend my back, you will be able to chastise the rakshasa.' Rama
heard the words spoken by the son of the wind god. The brave one
quickly climbed on to the great ape, Hanumat. In the encounter, the
lord of men saw that Ravana was astride his chariot. Seeing this, the
immensely energetic one rushed against Ravana, just as an angry
Vishnu raised his weapon against Virochana's son.[181] He twanged his
bow fiercely, with a sound that was like the clap of thunder. In a deep
voice, Rama spoke these words to the Indra among the rakshasas.
'Stay. O tiger among the rakshasas! Stay. Having performed such a
disagreeable act towards me, how can you possibly escape? Even if
you go to the worlds of Indra, Vaivasvata, the sun god, Svayambhu,
the fire god, Shankara or the different directions, you will not be
able to escape from me today. You struck down someone with your
spear today, but he overcame his distress and quickly arose. O king
of large numbers of rakshasas! In the battle today, death will come
to you and to your sons and wives.'[182] Hearing Raghava's words,
the Indra among the rakshasas used sharp arrows that were like the
flames of the fire of destruction to strike the great ape. In the battle,
he was struck by the rakshasa's arrows. However, because of his
natural energy, his energy increased in consequence. The greatly
energetic Rama saw that the tiger among apes had been wounded by
Ravana and was overcome with rage. Rama approached and used
arrows that were sharp at the tips to sever his chariot, its wheels, the
horses, the standard, the umbrella, the large flag, the charioteer, the
javelins, the spears and the swords. He then used an arrow that was
like the thunder and the vajra to swiftly strike Indra's enemy in his

[181] Bali.
[182] The use of the word wives is odd. Non-Critical versions say grandsons instead.

broad and beautiful chest, like the illustrious Indra striking Meru
with his vajra. The king was incapable of being agitated or made
to waver by the thunder or the vajra. However, struck by Rama's
arrow he was severely afflicted. The brave one wavered and let go
of his bow. Rama saw that he was reeling and picked up a blazing
ardhachandra arrow that had the complexion of the sun. The great-
souled one swiftly severed the diadem of the lord of the rakshasas.
The setting on the diadem lost its lustre. It was as resplendent as the
sun, but seemed to lose its rays. It was like a venomous serpent that
had lost its poison. In the battle, Rama spoke to the Indra among
the rakshasas. 'You have accomplished great and terrible deeds.
You have killed brave ones on my side. Therefore, it is evident that
you are exhausted. In this state, I will not use my arrows to convey
you to the land of the dead.' He was addressed in this way and lost
his pride and his joy. He lost his bow, and his horses and charioteer
were slain. He was afflicted by the arrows and his great diadem was
shattered. The king swiftly entered Lanka.

When the immensely strong Indra among the roamers of the
night, the enemy of the gods and the danavas, had left, in the field
of that great battle, Rama, with Lakshmana, arranged for the stakes
to be removed from the apes. The Indra of the enemies of the gods
was routed in this way. The gods, the asuras, the large number of
bhutas, the directions, the oceans, the rishis, and all creatures on
land and in the water rejoiced.

Chapter 6(48)

Frightened and afflicted by Rama's arrows, the king lost his
pride and his senses suffered. He entered the city of Lanka. Like
an elephant by a lion or a serpent by Garuda, the king had been
overcome by the great-souled Raghava. Raghava's arrows were like
Brahma's staff and as radiant as lightning. The lord of the rakshasas
suffered because of these and remembered them. He seated himself
on a supreme and divine throne made out of gold. Ravana looked

at the rakshasas and spoke these words. 'All the supreme austerities
I have performed have become useless. I am like the great Indra,
but I have been vanquished by a human. Brahma spoke terrible
words to me. "Know that you will face fear from humans." That
has now come to be true. I asked that I could not be killed by gods,
danavas, gandharvas, yakshas, rakshasas and serpents, but I did not
ask the same about humans. Since this is evident, all of you should
make the best efforts. Let the rakshasas station themselves on the
tops of the turrets and patrol there. Awake Kumbhakarna, who
suffers because of Brahma's curse. He is unmatched in his gravity
and is one who removes the insolence of the gods and the danavas.'
Knowing that he had been defeated and that Prahasta had been
killed, the immensely strong one commanded the terrible army of
the rakshasas. 'Take care at the gates and climb atop the walls.
Awake Kumbhakarna, who is deep in slumber. That rakshasa
sleeps for nine, six, seven or eight months. Quickly wake up the
immensely strong Kumbhakarna. In a battle, the mighty-armed one
is the support of all the rakshasas. He will swiftly slay the apes and
the two princes. The foolish Kumbhakarna sleeps all the time, he
is devoted to ordinary pleasures.[183] He will engage in an extremely
terrible clash against Rama. If he wakes up, there will no longer be
any sorrow for me. If he cannot help me in this terrible catastrophe
I now face, what is the point of his possessing a strength that is like
that of Shakra?'

Hearing the words of the Indra among the rakshasas, the
rakshasas, in great fear, went to Kumbhakarna's residence. The
devourers of flesh and blood were commanded by Ravana. Taking
fragrances, garlands and food with them, they quickly went. They
entered through the great gate into an area that was one yojana
wide on all sides. This was Kumbhakarna's cave and all kinds of
scents wafted in all directions. Those immensely strong ones entered
the cave and could only remain there with a great deal of difficulty,
because of Kumbhakarna's breathing. They entered that beautiful
and auspicious cave, encrusted with gold and jewels. They saw the

[183] Literally, the pleasures of villagers.

tiger among nairittas lying down and he was terrible to behold. His
sleeping and disfigured form was spread out like a mountain.

Kumbhakarna was deep in slumber and together, they tried to
wake him up. The hair on his body stood up upright and he sighed
like a serpent. He was terrible to behold. As he slept, his great
breaths terrified them. His nostrils were horrible and his mouth was
as large as patala. They saw the immensely strong Kumbhakarna,
tiger among the nairittas. As a supreme offering, they placed a
pile of flesh that was as large as Meru in front of the great-souled
Kumbhakarna. Those tigers among nairittas had gathered an
extraordinary heap from the meat of deer, buffaloes and boars.
There were many pots filled with blood and liquor. They placed these
in front of Kumbhakarna, the enemy of the gods. They smeared the
scorcher of enemies with excellent unguents and sandalwood paste.
They covered him with divine garlands, fragrances and perfumes.
They ignited fragrant incense and praised the scorcher of enemies.
Thousands of yatudhanas roared like thundering clouds. They
blew on conch shells that were as radiant as the moon. Together,
those intolerant ones roared and made a tumultuous sound. The
roamers in the night roared and clapped their hands. Seeking to
wake Kumbhakarna up, they created this tumultuous sound. There
were conch shells, drums, kettledrums and gongs. They clapped and
slapped and roared like lions. The sound spread in the directions
and up into the sky. Hearing this sudden sound, flying birds fell
down. But despite this terrible noise the great-souled Kumbhakarna
did not wake up from his slumber. Therefore, all the large numbers
of rakshasas seized catapults, clubs, maces, summits of mountains,
pestles and bludgeons. Kumbhakarna was sleeping happily, lying
down on the ground. The fierce rakshasas used these and their fists
to strike him on the chest. The rakshasa Kumbhakarna's breathing
was like a gale. Despite being strong, the rakshasas were incapable
of standing before him. Those rakshasas, terrible in their valour,
stationed themselves there. Together, ten thousand rakshasas
started to make a sound with drums, smaller drums, kettledrums,
conch shells and trumpets. He was like a mass of dark collyrium
and did not awake. Though they created a noise and struck him, he

did not realize any of this. Using these means, they were incapable of waking him up. They then started to make greater and extremely terrible efforts. They struck horses, camels, donkeys and elephants with rods and goads.[184] They applied all their strength to drums, conch shells and kettledrums. They struck his body with large pieces of wood that had spikes on them. They applied all their strength to clubs and maces. Lanka was filled with that great sound, with all its mountains and its forests. Even then, he did not awake. One thousand drums were sounded simultaneously in every direction, using sticks fashioned out of refined gold. However, he continued to sleep on and did not wake up, because he was controlled by the curse. The roamers of the night became angry. All of them, terrible in their valour, were suffused with great rage. The rakshasas used all their valour to wake him up. Some beat on drums. Others emitted loud roars. Some pulled out his hair. Others bit his ears with their teeth. But Kumbhakarna was deep in slumber. He did not move. They struck him on the head, the chest and all over the body with solid clubs. Everywhere, they tied him up with ropes and shataghnis. But though he was struck, the rakshasa, gigantic in size, did not wake up. Thousands of elephants were made to run around all over his body. At this touch, Kumbhakarna awoke from his deep slumber.

Summits of mountains and trees had been brought down on his body. He had been subjected to great blows. Having awoken from his sleep, he sprang up. Suffering from hunger, he yawned. His arms were like the hoods of coiled serpents, as firm in essence as the summits of mountains. He flung these around. His disfigured mouth gaped like the subterranean fire. The roamer in the night opened this and yawned. When he yawned, his mouth was like patala. It was seen to be like the sun arising atop Meru's peak. Having woken up, the extremely strong roamer in the night yawned. When he woke up, his breathing was like a storm raging in a mountain. When Kumbhakarna stood up, his form was like that of a cloud with cranes, raining down at the end of summer. His large eyes

---

[184] So that they would make a noise.

blazed like giant planets. They were as radiant as the fire, dazzling like the glitter of lightning. Hungry, he ate the flesh and thirsty, drank the blood. Shakra's enemy drank from the pots filled with fat and liquor. Knowing that he was satisfied, all the roamers in the night approached him. They bowed their heads down in prostration and surrounded him from all directions.

The bull among the nairittas comforted all the nairittas. Surprised at having been woken up, he spoke to all the rakshasas. 'Why have you suddenly woken me up? Is the king well? Has some kind of fear arisen? I think it is clear that some kind of grave danger has presented itself. Why else would you have suddenly woken me up? Today, I will uproot the fear that the king of the rakshasas faces. I will shatter the great Indra and pacify the fire god. I would not have thus been woken up from my sleep because of a trifling reason. Therefore, tell me the truth about why I have been woken up.'

The enraged Kumbhakarna, the scorcher of enemies, spoke in this way. Yupaksha, the king's adviser, joined his hands in salutation and said, 'There is not the slightest bit of fear that has arisen for us on account of the gods. Nor is there any kind of fear from the daityas or the danavas. O king! The fear that has presented itself is due to a human. Apes who are like mountains have surrounded Lanka. Since Rama is tormented on account of Sita's abduction, there is a tremendous fear that has arisen from him. Earlier, a single ape burnt down the great city and killed Prince Aksha, his companions and his elephant. The lord of the rakshasas, Poulastya, the thorn of the gods, himself went out to fight and escaped from Rama, who is like the sun in his energy. The king has never suffered from gods, daityas or danavas. However, that act has been done by Rama. His life was in danger, but he managed to escape.' He heard Yupaksha's words to the effect that his brother had been defeated in the battle. Kumbhakarna widened his eyes and told Yupaksha, 'O Yupaksha! Today, in the battle, I will vanquish all the soldiers of the apes, together with Lakshmana and Raghava. I will only see Ravana after that. I will satisfy the rakshasas with the flesh and the blood of the apes. I will myself drink Rama and Lakshmana's blood.' His proud words were laced with his enhanced rage.

Hearing his words, Mahodara, the foremost among the nairitta warriors, joined his hands in salutation and spoke these words. 'First hear Ravana's words and the pros and cons. O mighty-armed one! After that, defeat the enemy in the battle.' Hearing Mahodara's words, the immensely energetic and immensely strong Kumbhakarna departed, surrounded by the rakshasas. His eyes were horrible and he was terrible in appearance and valour. Having woken him up, the rakshasas swiftly headed for Dashagriva's residence. They went to Dashagriva, seated on his supreme throne. Joining their hands in salutation, all the roamers in the night said, 'O bull among rakshasas! Your brother, Kumbhakarna, has woken up. Will he leave? He has come here to meet you.' Rejoicing, Ravana spoke to the rakshasas who had presented themselves. 'I wish to see him. After showing him the due honours, bring him here.'

Thus addressed, all the rakshasas returned to Kumbhakarna and reported the words uttered by Ravana. 'The king, the bull among all the rakshasas, desires to see you. You should make up your mind to go and delight your brother.' The invincible Kumbhakarna agreed to the command issued by his brother. The immensely valiant one leapt up from his bed. He washed his face. He bathed and happily adorned himself in excellent ornaments. Thirsty, he quickly had a drink that would enhance his strength. Following Ravana's command, the rakshasas quickly brought him liquor and many kinds of food, so that they might take him back swiftly. He drank from two thousand pots and prepared to leave. He was slightly intoxicated and maddened with his energy and strength. Kumbhakarna was cheerful and resembled Death. Surrounded by the army of rakshasas, he went to his brother's residence. At Kumbhakarna's footsteps, the earth trembled. His form illuminated the royal road, like the radiance of the one with one thousand rays lights up the earth. He left, surrounded by those who joined their hands in salutation, like Shatakratu going to Svayambhu's residence. Some sought refuge with Rama, the one who grants refuge.[185] Some walked with him, or were distressed and

---

[185] This refers to those along the road. Presumably, there were apes among them too, not just rakshasas.

fell down. Some were distressed and ran away. Some were terrified and lay down on the ground. He was diademed, like the summit of a mountain. In his energy, he seemed to touch the sun. On seeing this extraordinary sight, the residents of the forest were afflicted by fear and fled here and there.

Chapter 6(49)

On seeing the diademed Kumbhakarna, gigantic in size, the valiant and immensely energetic Rama picked up his bow. He saw the best among rakshasas, who looked like a mountain. The lord[186] himself looked like Narayana in ancient times, ready to stride. He looked like a cloud full of rain, adorned in armlets made out of gold. On seeing him, the great army of apes ran away. The army fled and the rakshasa increased his size. Witnessing this, Rama was astounded and spoke to Vibhishana. 'Who is this? He resembles a cloud. He wears a diadem and his eyes are tawny. He is like a cloud tinged with lightning. Who is this brave one, who can be seen in Lanka? Who is the one who has suddenly surfaced on earth like a meteor? His giant and solitary form can be seen. On seeing him, all the apes are running away, here and there. Tell me. Who is this extremely large person? Is he a rakshasa or an asura? I have never seen such a creature earlier.'

Vibhishana was asked by the prince who was unblemished in his deeds. The immensely wise one replied to Kakutstha in these words. 'He is the powerful Kumbhakarna and he is the son of Vishravasa. He is the one who defeated Vaivasvata[187] and Indra in a battle. O Raghava! In encounters, he has routed thousands of gods, danavas, yakshas, serpents, those who survive on flesh, gandharvas, vidyadharas[188] and snakes. The immensely strong Kumbhakarna wielded a spear in his hand and his eyes were

---

[186] Rama. The allusion is to Vishnu's vamana (dwarf) incarnation.
[187] Yama.
[188] Vidyadharas are semi-divine, occupying the region between heaven and earth.

distorted. The confused gods thought that he was Death and were incapable of killing him. The immensely strong Kumbhakarna is naturally energetic. The other Indras among rakshasas obtain their strength because of boons. As soon as he was born, the great-souled one was afflicted by hunger and ate up many thousand creatures. Seeing that they were being devoured, the suffering creatures were terrified. They went and told Shakra this and sought refuge with him. The great Indra was enraged. The wielder of the vajra struck Kumbhakarna with his sharp vajra. Struck by Shakra's vajra, the great-souled one wavered and roared loudly in rage. Hearing the intelligent Kumbhakarna's roar, the terrified creatures on earth were scared again. The immensely strong Kumbhakarna became angry at the great Indra. He uprooted one of Airavata's tusks and struck Vasava on the chest with this. Struck by Kumbhakarna and afflicted, Vasava trembled. All the gods, the rishis and the danavas were suddenly distressed. With Shakra, the subjects went to the spot where Svayambhu was. They told Prajapati about Kumbhakarna's depredations, about how he had devoured the subjects and oppressed the gods. "If he continues to incessantly devour subjects in this fashion, within a short space of time, the world will be empty." Hearing Vasava's words, the grandfather of all the worlds summoned all the rakshasas and also saw Kumbhakarna. Seeing Kumbhakarna, Prajapati was also terrified. Visualizing the emptiness, Svayambhu said, "Poulastya[189] has certainly created you for the destruction of the worlds. Therefore, from now on, you will lie down, as if you are dead." Succumbing to Brahma's curse, he fell down before the lord.[190] Extremely frightened, Ravana spoke these words. "O Prajapati! You are cutting down a grown and golden tree at the time when it will yield fruit. It is not proper for you to curse your own great-grandson. There is no doubt that your words cannot be false. Let him sleep. But designate a time for him to be awake and for him to lie down." Hearing Ravana's words, Svayambhu again said, "Let him sleep for six months and let him

---

[189] That is, Vishravasa.
[190] Brahma.

remain awake for a single day. On that single day, this brave one will be hungry and will roam around the earth. His mouth will be open and he will angrily devour the worlds, like a fire." Faced with a calamity and dreading your valour, King Ravana has now woken up Kumbhakarna. The brave one, terrible in his valour, has emerged from his camp. Extremely angry, he is rushing towards us, devouring the apes. Seeing Kumbhakarna, the apes have fled. When he is angry in a battle, how can the apes counter him? Let all the apes be told that this is a mechanical contrivance that has turned up. Once the apes know this, they will not be scared.'

The words that emerged from Vibhishana's mouth were full of reasoning. Hearing them, Raghava spoke these words to Nila, the commander. 'O son of the fire god! Go and station all the soldiers in vyuhas. Seize the gates, roads and passages to Lanka. Gather the summits of mountains, trees and boulders. Let all the apes be stationed with their weapons, with boulders in their hands.' Nila, the commander of the army of the apes, was instructed by Raghava. The elephant among the apes issued the appropriate instructions to the army of the apes. Seizing the summits of mountains and with the complexion of mountains themselves, Gavaksha, Sharabha, Hanumat and Angada advanced towards the gates. With boulders and trees raised up in their hands, that fierce army of the apes was resplendent. It looked like a great mass of gigantic and fierce clouds, filled with water, approaching a mountain.

Chapter 6(50)

The tiger among rakshasas was intoxicated and still drowsy. Handsome and pervasive in his valour, he proceeded along the royal road. The extremely invincible one was surrounded by thousands of rakshasas. As he proceeded, from the houses, flowers were showered down on him. He saw the large and beautiful residence of the Indra among the rakshasas. It was as radiant as

the sun to behold and it was decorated with nets of gold. Like the
sun penetrates a mass of clouds, he entered the residence of the
lord of the rakshasas. From a distance, like Shakra seeing the seated
Svayambhu, he saw his brother seated on his throne. He went to
his brother's residence and then entered his chamber. He saw his
anxious brother seated, inside Pushpaka vimana. Dashagriva saw
that Kumbhakarna had presented himself. Delighted, he quickly
arose and brought him close to him. His brother was seated on
the couch. The immensely strong Kumbhakarna worshipped his
feet and asked, 'What is to be done?' Delighted, Ravana arose and
embraced him. He was embraced by his brother and duly honoured.
Kumbhakarna then seated himself on an auspicious, divine and
supreme seat. The immensely strong Kumbhakarna sat down on
that seat. With eyes red with anger, he addressed Ravana in these
words. 'O king! Why did you make efforts to wake me up? Tell
me. Who has caused you fear? Who should now become a dead
person?' His angry brother, Kumbhakarna, was there.

With his eyes rolling around in rage, Ravana addressed him in
these words. 'O immensely strong one! You have been asleep for
an extremely long period of time. Since you have been asleep, you
do not know about the fear that Rama has caused to me. Rama,
Dasharatha's son, is strong and he is with Sugriva. He has crossed
the ocean with his army and has attacked our foundation. Alas!
Look at Lanka, with its forests and groves. Having crossed easily
by means of a bridge, it is now covered with an ocean of apes. In
the battle, the apes have killed the foremost among the rakshasas. I
do not see any way of destroying the apes in the battle. My treasury
is completely exhausted and you must save me and this terrified
city of Lanka, which only has children and old ones left. O mighty-
armed one! For the sake of your brother, perform this extremely
difficult deed. O brother! O scorcher of enemies! I have never had
to utter such words earlier. I have affection and supreme respect for
you. O bull among rakshasas! In many battles with the gods and the
asuras, you have countered the battle formations of the gods and
vanquished the asuras in encounters. Among all creatures, no one
who is your equal in strength can be seen. Therefore, perform this

supremely agreeable task for me. O one who loves to fight! O one who loves his relatives! This will appeal to you. Use your energy to shatter the enemy's army, like a strong wind drives away a cloud during the autumn.'

Chapter 6(51)

Kumbhakarna heard the lamentations of the king of the rakshasas. He laughed and spoke these words. 'We had foreseen this evil earlier, when we had held consultations about what we should do. However, you did not accept the beneficial words that were spoken to you. Indeed, you have quickly reaped the consequences of your evil deeds, just as the perpetrators of wicked acts descend into hell. O great king! At first, you acted without thinking. Because of your valour and insolence, you did not reflect on the consequences. If a person bases himself on his prosperity and does what should be done later, earlier, and what should be done earlier, later, he does not know the difference between good policy and bad policy. If an act is undertaken that is contrary to the time and the place, those acts become tainted, like oblations that haven't been prepared properly. After having an agreement with his advisers, if a person does three kinds of acts and follows five kinds of modes, he is the one who is along the right path.[191] A king is on the right path if he adheres to agreements, uses his intelligence and the intelligence of his advisers and looks towards his well-wishers. O lord of the rakshasas! At the right time, a man must pursue all three of dharma, *artha* and *kama*, or any two of these.[192] If a king or a prince hears which of

---

[191] The three kinds of acts are seeking peace through an alliance, surrendering and swearing allegiance and fighting. The five kinds of modes are starting an act, ensuring the means to accomplish it, deciding on the time and place for the action, guarding against failure and ensuring the chances of success.

[192] Either one pursues dharma, artha and kama together, or dharma and artha, dharma and kama, or artha and kama. The idea is not to pursue one to the exclusion of the other two.

the three is best, but nevertheless, does not comprehend, even if he is extremely learned, he is a failure. O best among the rakshasas! At the right time, if a person uses gifts, conciliation, bheda and valour,[193] he knows both good policy and bad policy. If one consults with advisers and follows dharma, artha and kama at the right time, such a person does not face any hardships in the world. If a king considers the beneficial consequences that will follow and what is good and bad for himself, he knows the true nature of objectives and lives, together with his advisers. Men who do not know the purport of the sacred texts are like animals in their intelligence. Because of their insolence, they do not desire consultations, nor do they internalize them. The task of those who do not know about the sacred texts is to speak words that are not beneficial. Despite desiring great prosperity, they are ignorant about the sacred texts on wealth.[194] There are audacious and eloquent men who converse about what is not beneficial, pretending that it is beneficial. Even if they outwardly consider consultations, in practice, they perform evil acts. Some learned ones are in connivance with the enemy and ensure the destruction of their master. Such ministers ensure the performance of perverse deeds. The master must be able to identify those who pretend to be friends, but are actually enemies when it comes to offering advice. Through their conduct, he must be able to discern advisers who speak of what is harmful. Fickle deeds enable the swift finding out of those who are perverse. Their weaknesses can be detected, just as birds find out holes in Mount Krouncha. If a person ignores the enemy and does not protect himself, he faces a calamity and is dislodged from his own position.'

Dashagriva heard what Kumbhakarna had to say. He knit his eyebrows in rage and spoke these words. 'Do you take yourself to be my senior preceptor that you are instructing me in this way? Why are you exhausting yourself through words? This is the time for appropriate action. What is the point of repeating now what has already been done because of confusion, delusion, strength, energy

---

[193] Respectively, dana, sama, bheda and danda.
[194] The text uses the word *arthashastra*.

or prosperity? This is the time to think about what is appropriate now. Use your valour to dispel my present misery. If you indeed feel any affection for me because I am your brother, if your heart feels it should be done and if your intelligence also agrees on the act, this is what you should do. If a person helps someone who faces a hardship and removes that distress, he is a true well-wisher. If he helps when the need arises, he is a true relative.' Though spoken patiently, these were extremely terrible words.

Kumbhakarna noticed that his brother's senses were excessively agitated. He also realized that he was angry. Therefore, softly and gently, he uttered these kind words of assurance. 'O king! O destroyer of enemies! Listen to my words. O Indra among rakshasas! Enough of this torment. Abandon this rage. You should return to your normal state. O king! As long as I am alive, you should not think about such things. I will destroy the person because of whose deeds you are being tormented. Whatever be your state, I must speak beneficial words to you. O king! I spoke those words as a relative and because of brotherly affection. This is the time for a relative to act gently. Behold. Therefore, in the battle, I will create carnage amidst the enemy. O mighty-armed one! Behold me today in the field of battle. Rama and his brother will be slain and the army of the apes will be driven away. In the battle today, you will see me bring back Rama's head. O mighty-armed one! Be happy. May Sita be miserable. Behold the extremely desired objective today, of Rama being killed. He is the one who killed all the relatives of the rakshasas in Lanka. They are overcome by sorrow because they are grieving over their relatives having been killed. Today, after the enemy is destroyed in the battle, I will wipe away their tears. Sugriva, the lord of the apes, is like a mountain. Behold. In the battle today, I will disperse him, like the sun scatters away a cloud. O one whose valour in battle is unmatched! You do not have to look for anyone else to send. I will uproot your extremely strong enemies. I will even fight against Shakra, Yama, the wind god, Kubera and Varuna. My body is as large as a mountain. When I roar with my pointed teeth and wield a sharp spear, even Purandara is terrified. Otherwise, the enemy can quickly turn mild and throw the weapons away. As long as someone faces me, he is incapable of remaining alive. I do not need a spear, a club, a sword or sharp arrows. If I am angry, with my bare hands, I can slay the wielder of the vajra. Today, if Raghava can withstand the force of my fists, I will bring him down with my torrents of arrows and drink Raghava's blood. O king! Why are you tormented by thoughts? I am standing in front of you. I am here to destroy your enemies. I am ready to leave. Give up this fear of Rama. O king! I will kill him in the battle and also Raghava Lakshmana and the immensely strong Sugriva. I wish to give you great and extraordinary fame. I will bring you happiness by slaying Dasharatha's son. I am leaving, so that I can bring you something pleasant. After killing Rama and Lakshmana, I will eat all the chief leaders among the apes. O king! Sport as you will and drink the best of varuni. Cast away your fever and do all that you must. Today, after I have sent Rama to Yama's abode, Sita will come under your subjugation, for a long period of time.'

Chapter 6(52)

Kumbhakarna, the powerful one with strong arms, spoke in this way. Hearing his words, Mahodara said, 'O Kumbhakarna! Though you have been born in a noble lineage, you are audacious and your perspective is ordinary.[195] Because you are insolent, you are incapable of knowing what should be done at all times. O Kumbhakarna! It is not that the king cannot differentiate between good policy and bad policy. Because of childish folly and audacity, you only desire to speak. The bull among rakshasas does know about enhancing and diminishing,[196] he knows how the apportionment of time and place needs to be done and he can distinguish between those on one's own side and the enemy's. A strong person who is ordinary in intelligence and does not respect

---

[195] Mahodara's arguments are difficult to understand and we have taken some liberties.
[196] Of alliances and relationships.

his seniors is capable of undertaking acts. Why should a learned person act in that way? You have spoken as if dharma, artha and kama are separate objectives. Their nature is such that there are no signs to distinguish between them. Whatever be the consequences, action must always be undertaken. It is better to undertake even wicked deeds. Those also have consequences. It is not necessary that the fruits of dharma and artha are superior. Adharma and *anartha*[197] can also give rise to unintended consequences. Even if a man indulges in acts of kama, in this world and in the next, he obtains the fruits of those deeds. The king set his heart on this act[198] and our views coincided with his. If one displays bravery against an enemy, what is there to condemn in that? Because of your ordinary nature, you have cited reasons for advancing alone. I will tell you why that is inappropriate and not virtuous policy. Earlier, in Janasthana, Raghava killed many extremely strong rakshasas. How will you defeat him alone? Look at all the immensely energetic rakshasas in the city. They are terrified because they have been vanquished earlier. Rama, Dasharatha's son, is like an enraged lion. He is like a snake that is asleep. Ignorantly, you wish to wake him up. He always blazes in his energy and anger and is impossible to assail. He is as intolerable as Death. Who wants to approach him? When one faces an enemy, the outcome is always in doubt. The idea of your advancing alone does not appeal to me. Whether one is superior or inferior and even if the enemy is ordinary, who wishes to take a chance that the life may be given up and one may come under subjugation? O supreme among rakshasas! There is no man who is his equal. He is like Indra and the sun god. How can you speak of fighting against him?'

Having thus angrily spoken to Kumbhakarna, in the midst of the rakshasas, Mahodara spoke to Ravana, the one who made the worlds scream. 'After having already obtained Vaidehi, why are you conversing? If you so desire, Sita will come under your

---

[197] The reverse of artha.
[198] Of kama.

subjugation. O lord of the rakshasas! I have thought of a means whereby Sita might be persuaded. If it appeals to your intelligence, listen to this. Announce that five of us—I, Dvijihva, Samhradi, Kumbhakarna and Vitardana—are setting out to kill Rama. Having gone, we will make efforts and fight against him. If we defeat the enemy, you need not think of any other devices. However, even after we have fought, if the enemy survives, let us implement the strategy that has come to my mind. We will return from the battle with blood all over and our bodies pierced by sharp arrows that have Rama's name inscribed on them. We will fall at your feet and say, "Raghava and Lakshmana have been devoured by us. Fulfil our wishes." O king! Astride elephants, get it proclaimed everywhere in the city that Rama, his brother and his soldiers have been killed. O destroyer of enemies! Being pleased, bestow on your servants objects of pleasure, servants, objects of desire and riches. Give many warriors garlands, garments and unguents meant for heroes. Rejoicing, you yourself indulge in drinking. This rumour will spread thick and fast and reach everywhere. Then go to Sita alone and comfort her. Tempt her with riches, grain, objects of desire and jewels. O king! Using this means, generate fear and grief. Even if she does not desire it, with her protector destroyed, Sita will come under your subjugation. She will believe that her beloved husband has been killed. Because of her hopelessness and the fickleness of feminine nature, she will come under your subjugation. Earlier, she has been reared in happiness. She deserves happiness, but is afflicted by misery. Knowing that she will obtain happiness with you, she will go to you in every possible way. This is the good policy I have thought of. If you see Rama, a calamity may befall you.[199] Remain here and do not suffer from anxiety. You will obtain great gains without taking part in a fight. O lord of the earth! If a king defeats the enemy without fighting, without the soldiers being destroyed and without facing any uncertainty, he obtains great fame, merits, prosperity and deeds for a long period of time.'

[199] In a battle.

Chapter 6(53)

Thus addressed, Kumbhakarna rebuked Mahodara. He spoke to his brother, Ravana, best among rakshasas. 'I will slay the evil-souled one who has caused you this terrible fear. Today, I will wipe Rama away. Without any enemies, you will be happy. Like clouds without water, brave ones do not unnecessarily roar. Behold. As I obtain my objective, my deeds in the battle will roar. Brave ones demonstrate by performing extremely difficult deeds. They do not praise themselves, nor do they think highly of themselves. O Mahodara! When they hear words spoken by the likes of you, only kings who pride themselves on their learning, but are actually feeble in intelligence, find them to be appealing. Those who are cowards in a battle are always pleasant in speech. They always seek to follow the king and thereby, ensure destruction. Possessing access to the king, well-wishers behave like enemies. The treasury is exhausted, the soldiers have been killed. The king is the only one left in Lanka. I am leaving. I am ready for battle, to defeat the enemy. In the great battle today, I will rectify your bad policy.'

When the intelligent Kumbhakarna spoke these words, the lord of the rakshasas laughed and replied in these words. 'There is no doubt that Mahodara is terrified of Rama. O son![200] O one who is accomplished in fighting! The idea of fighting does not appeal to him. As a well-wisher and in strength, there is no one who is equal to you. O Kumbhakarna! For the sake of slaying the enemy and for victory, depart.'

The destroyer of enemies[201] quickly picked up a sharp spear. It was made entirely out of iron. It blazed and was embellished with molten gold. It was as terrible as Indra's vajra. It was as heavy as the vajra and could devastate gods, danavas, gandharvas, yakshas and kinnaras. It was bound with giant ropes and adorned with red garlands. It naturally emitted sparks of flame and was coloured with the blood of enemies. Having seized this sharp spear, the immensely

---

[200] The word used is tata,
[201] Kumbhakarna.

energetic Kumbhakarna addressed Ravana in these words. 'I am going alone. Let this large army remain here. I am hungry and angry now. I will devour the apes.' Hearing Kumbhakarna's words, Ravana addressed him in these words. 'Depart, but surround yourself with soldiers with spears and clubs in their hands. The great-souled apes are swift in their conduct. They are crazy and will destroy anyone who is alone, distracted or inattentive. Therefore, go, but surround yourself with an extremely invincible army. Destroy the party of the enemy, which has caused injury to us rakshasas.' The immensely energetic Ravana arose from his seat. He slung a necklace studded with gems at the ends around Kumbhakarna's neck. The great-souled one also fixed armlets, rings, other excellent ornaments and a chain that resembled the moon. Ravana also arranged that his body would be smeared with divine perfumes and garlands, with beautiful earrings on his ears. The large-eared Kumbhakarna was adorned with golden armlets, braclets and breastplates. He was like a fire that had been fed with excellent oblations. A large and black thread adorned his loins. He looked like Mandara at the time when amrita was obtained, coiled around by the serpent.[202] Capable of bearing a great burden, he bore the burden of the golden armour. He resembled the brilliant lightning, radiant in its own illuminations. After fixing the armour, he was resplendent. He looked like a king of mountains, enveloped by clouds in the evening. The rakshasa had ornaments on all his limbs and a spear in his hand. He was as resplendent as Narayana, exerting himself while taking his three strides.[203]

He embraced his brother and circumambulated him. Bowing his head down before him, the immensely strong one departed. To the sound of praises and benedictions, Ravana sent him off. Conch shells and drums were sounded. There were soldiers with excellent weapons. The sound of elephants, horses and chariots was like the thunder of clouds. The great-souled one, supreme among charioteers, was followed by charioteers. The immensely strong Kumbhakarna was followed by terrible ones who were mounted on snakes, camels,

---

[202] A reference to the churning of the ocean.
[203] A reference to Vishnu's vamana incarnation.

donkeys, horses, lions, wolves, other animals and birds. He held
a sharp spear in his hand and flowers were showered down. An
umbrella was held above his head. He was intoxicated by his pride
and maddened by the smell of blood. The enemy of the danavas and
the gods departed. There were many immensely strong foot soldiers
and they roared loudly. These terrible rakshasas followed him. Their
eyes were horrible and they held weapons in their hands. Their eyes
were red and their forms were extremely gigantic. They were like
masses of dark collyrium. They held aloft spears, swords and sharp
battleaxes. There were many clubs, maces and bludgeons. They
bore extremely invincible and large palm trees on their shoulders.
These were meant to be hurled. Thus, the immensely energetic and
immensely strong Kumbhakarna descended. He emerged from the
city in this terrible form and it made the body hair stand up. His
breadth was that of one hundred bows and his height was that of
six hundred bows. He was fierce. His eyes were like the wheels of a
cart. He resembled a large mountain. Resembling a giant mountain
that has been burnt, he approached the rakshasas. Kumbhakarna,
with the gigantic mouth, laughed and spoke these words. 'Today, I
will angrily burn down the foremost apes and their different herds,
like insects before a fire. Those apes reside in the forest as they will
and have not committed a crime. For those like us, that species
is like an ornament in the city's groves. Raghava, together with
Lakshmana, are the foundation for this siege of the city. When he
is killed, all of them will be killed. I will slay him in the battle.'
When Kumbhakarna spoke in this way, the rakshasas emitted an
extremely terrible roar and this seemed to make the ocean tremble.

As the intelligent Kumbhakarna swiftly descended, in every
direction, many terrible portents manifested themselves. Clouds,
filled with meteors and lightning, thundered in extremely terrible
tones. The earth, with its oceans and forests, trembled. With blazing
pieces of flesh in their mouths, hideous jackals howled. Birds flew
around in an anticlockwise direction.[204] As he[205] proceeded along

---

[204] The anticlockwise direction is inauspicious.
[205] Kumbhakarna.

the road, a vulture descended on the top of his spear. His left eye twitched and his left arm throbbed. A blazing meteor fell down with a terrible sound. The sun lost its lustre. The pleasant breeze stopped to blow. These great omens made the body hair stand up. However, Kumbhakarna was urged by the strength of Death. He did not think about these and departed.

Resembling a mountain, he used his feet to scale over the rampart. He saw the extraordinary army of the apes, resembling a mass of clouds. The apes saw the best among the rakshasas, who was like a mountain. Like clouds dispelled by the wind, they fled in all the directions. Like a net of clouds that has been dispersed, that extremely fierce army of the apes fled in all directions. On seeing this, Kumbhakarna was delighted. He roared like the thunder of the clouds in the sky. On hearing his terrible roar, like sala trees severed at the roots, many apes fell down on the ground. For the sake of slaying the enemy, the great-souled Kumbhakarna emerged with his large club. The large number of apes were filled with a great dread, as if the lord[206] had arrived with the staff of chastisement at the end of a yuga.

Chapter 6(54)

He roared loudly and it resounded in the ocean. He seemed to generate a storm and seemed to shatter the mountains. The apes saw the one with the terrible eyes advance. Maghavan, Yama and Varuna were incapable of killing him. On seeing him, they fled in different directions. On seeing that they were fleeing, Vali's son, Angada, spoke to Nala, Nila, Gavaksha and the immensely strong Kumuda. 'Terrified because of your fear, where are you running away, behaving like ordinary apes? You have forgotten yourselves, your valour and the nobility of your births. O amiable ones! It is best to return. Why are you protecting your lives? This rakshasa is a

---

[206] Yama.

great terror, but he cannot fight.[207] This great terror has arisen and
has been fashioned by the rakshasas. O apes! Return and we will
destroy him with our valour.'

Here and there, the apes reassured themselves with difficulty
and assembled. In the field of battle, they picked up trees and the
summits of mountains in their hands. Having returned, the residents
of the forest were angry. In great rage, like maddened elephants,
they struck him. The immensely strong ones used lofty summits of
mountains, boulders and trees that flowered at the top. However,
he did not tremble. Descending on his body, boulders shattered
into one hundred fragments. Trees that flowered at the top were
shattered and fell down on the ground. Extremely angry, like a fire
that has arisen in the forest, he made supreme efforts and crushed
the immensely energetic soldiers of the apes. Wet with blood, many
bulls among apes lay down. They were restrained and fell down on
the ground, like trees with coppery red blossoms. Some apes leapt
and ran away, without looking back. Some fell into the ocean and
some sought refuge in the sky. Superior in strength, the rakshasa
slew those brave ones. Some fled along the path they had used to
cross the ocean. In fear, their faces turned pale and some resorted
to low ground. Bears climbed up trees and some sought refuge in
mountains. Some were submerged in the ocean. Some sought refuge
in caves. Some apes were distressed, while some helplessly stood
there.

On seeing that the apes were routed, Angada said, 'O apes!
Return. Let us stay and fight. If you are routed and go to any place
on earth, I do not see a spot for all of you. Return. Why are you
protecting your lives? You are running away, casting aside your
weapons. This does not befit your manliness. Your wives will laugh
at you and even if you live, it is as good as being dead. All of us
have been born in noble lineages and are great and pervasive. This
act of being scared is indeed ignoble. Why are you giving up your
valour and running away? At that time, you boasted in assemblies

---

[207] The suggestion is that the terror is an imagined one and even that Kumbhakarna
is a mechanical contrivance.

of people. You said that you were fierce and great. Where have those words gone? If you hear aspersions of being cowards, shame on your lives. Tread the path followed by virtuous people and cast aside this fear. If there is a short lifespan on earth, let us lie down after being killed. It is difficult for those who suffer from lassitude in the field of battle to obtain Brahma's world. Alternatively, obtain fame by killing the enemy in the battle. Once Kumbhakarna sees Kakutstha, he will not return with his life intact. He will be like an insect that approaches a blazing fire. If we have this urge to run away and protect our lives and a single person routs all of us, our fame will be destroyed.' The brave Angada, wearing golden armlets, spoke these words. Those who were running away replied in words that are condemned by brave ones. 'The rakshasa Kumbhakarna is creating great carnage. This is not the time or the place. We love our lives and are leaving.' Speaking these words, all of them fled in different directions. The leaders of the apes had seen the terrible one, with terrible eyes, approach. At the head of the army, the brave ones who were running away were comforted and assured a lot by Angada. Then, all of them returned. Rishabha, Sharabha, Mainda, Dhumra, Nila, Kumuda, Sushena, Gavaksha, Rambha, Tara, Dvivida and Panasa, with the son of the wind god leading the way, quickly advanced in the direction of the fighting.

Chapter 6(55)

On hearing Angada's words, gigantic in form, they returned. All of them made up their minds and desired to fight. Their valour was invoked and their bravery was enhanced. Because of Angada's words, they stationed themselves at the head of the army. They advanced happily, making up their minds to die. The apes, ready to give up their lives, engaged in a tumultuous battle. They used extremely large trees and huge mountains. The apes quickly raised these and rushed towards Kumbhakarna. The valiant Kumbhakarna was enraged and raised a club. In every direction, gigantic in size, he oppressed and dispersed the foe. Uprooted by Kumbhakarna, fifteen hundred and thousands of apes were strewn around and lay down on the ground. He used his hands to pick up sixteen, eight, ten, twenty and thirty apes at a time, fling them into his mouth and eat them. Extremely angry, he devoured them, like Garuda does to serpents.

Stationed in the sky, Hanumat showered down summits of mountains and many kinds of trees on Kumbhakarna's head. He shattered those summits of mountains with his spear. The immensely strong Kumbhakarna shattered that shower of trees. Seizing the sharp spear, he rushed towards the fierce army of the apes. As he advanced, Hanumat seized a giant mountain and stood in front of him. He angrily struck Kumbhakarna, terrible in form, with force, using that excellent mountain. Thus attacked, he was agitated. His body became wet with fat, sprinkled with blood. The spear was like a flash of lightning and was like a mountain that blazed at the summit. Using this, he struck Maruti in the chest, just as Guha struck Mount Krouncha with the tip of his spear. When he was struck in the chest with this spear, his senses were afflicted and he vomited blood from his mouth. In that great battle, Hanumat roared terribly, like the thunder of the clouds at the end of a yuga. Seeing that he[208] was distressed, the large number of rakshasas rejoiced and suddenly roared. The apes were distressed and afflicted by fear. They ran away from Kumbhakarna.

Nila hurled the summit of a mountain towards the intelligent Kumbhakarna. On seeing that it was descending, he struck it with his fist. Struck by the fist, the summit of the mountain was shattered. Blazing with sparks, it fell down on the ground. Rishabha, Sharabha, Nila, Gavaksha and Gandhamadana—these five tigers among apes attacked Kumbhakarna. Those immensely strong ones struck Kumbhakarna, gigantic in size, everywhere with boulders, trees, palms, feet and fists. These blows were like a gentle touch and he did not feel any pain. He embraced the immensely swift Rishabha in his arms. The bull among apes suffered from being squeezed in

[208] Hanumat.

Kumbhakarna's arms. The terrible bull fell down, vomiting blood from his mouth. In the battle, Indra's enemy struck Sharabha with his fist, Nila with his knee and Gavaksha with his palm.[209] Suffering from the blows they had received, they repeatedly oozed out blood. They fell down on the ground, like kimshuka trees that had been cut down. Those great-souled and foremost apes fell down. Thousands of apes attacked Kumbhakarna. He was like a mountain and all those bulls among apes possessed the complexion of mountains. Those immensely strong ones leapt on him, climbed up his body and bit him. Those bulls among apes, struck Kumbhakarna, gigantic in form, with their nails, teeth, fists and thighs. He was like a mountain and was covered with thousands of apes. The tiger among rakshasas was as radiant as an overgrown mountain.[210] The immensely strong one seized all the apes with his hands. He angrily devoured them, like Garuda does to serpents. They were flung into Kumbhakarna's mouth, which resembled patala. However, the apes emerged through his nostrils and his ears. Angry and resembling a mountain, he devoured the apes. Enraged, the supreme among rakshasas mangled all the apes. Because of the flesh and the blood, the rakshasa created a mire on the ground. He roamed around amidst the army of the apes, like the raging fire of destruction. With the spear in his hand, the immensely strong Kumbhakarna was like Shakra with the vajra in his hand, or Yama with the noose in his hand. Just as the fire consumes a dry forest during the summer, like that, Kumbhakarna scorched the soldiers of the apes. Without leaders, the herds were slain. The apes were terrified and anxious and wailed in extremely piteous tones. Kumbhakarna killed many apes. Distressed and with their senses afflicted, they sought refuge with Raghava.

Seeing that the immensely strong Kumbhakarna was descending, the brave Sugriva, lord of the apes, leapt up. The giant ape raised the summit of a mountain and attacked him. With great force, he rushed towards the immensely strong Kumbhakarna. Kumbhakarna

---

[209] Inexplicably, the Critical Edition excises a shloka where he struck Gandhamadana with his feet.

[210] Overgrown with trees.

saw that the ape was descending. He tightened his limbs and faced
the Indra among the apes. He was devouring giant apes and his body
was covered with the blood of apes. On seeing that Kumbhakarna
was stationed there, Sugriva addressed him in these words. 'You
have struck down brave ones and have performed an extremely
difficult deed. You have devoured the soldiers and obtained supreme
fame. Abandon this army of apes. What will you do with ordinary
ones? O rakshasa! Withstand this mountain that I am hurling
towards you.' Full of spirit and patience, the king of the apes spoke
these words. Hearing them, Kumbhakarna, tiger among rakshasas,
spoke these words. 'You are Prajapati's grandson and the son of
Riksharaja. You possess fortitude and manliness. O ape! Why are
you roaring?' Hearing Kumbhakarna's words, he suddenly released
the mountain and struck Kumbhakarna in the chest with it. That
mountain was like the vajra or thunder. The summit of the mountain
smacked against his broad chest and was violently shattered. The
apes were suddenly distressed and the large number of rakshasas
roared, rejoicing. Struck by the summit of the mountain, he was
enraged. He opened his mouth and roared in anger. To kill the lord
of the apes, he hurled that spear that glittered like lightning.

The sharp spear was bound with golden ropes and was hurled
from Kumbhakarna's hand. With the speed of the wind, the son of
the wind god swiftly leapt up, seized it in his hands and broke it.
The giant spear was made out of iron and weighed one thousand
*sahasra*s.[211] The bull among apes broke it on his thighs and was
delighted. On seeing that the spear had been broken, the great-
souled lord of the rakshasas became angry. Malaya was near Lanka.
He uprooted its peak and struck Sugriva with this. In the battle,
struck by the summit of the mountain, the Indra among apes lost his
senses and fell down on the ground. On seeing that he had lost his
senses and had fallen down, all the yatudhanas who were fighting
were delighted and roared. Kumbhakarna displayed a terrible and
extraordinary valour in the battle. He seized Sugriva and raised him
up, just as a terrible wind disperses a cloud. His form was like that

---

[211] A sahasra is a measure of weight.

of a giant cloud. In the battle, Kumbhakarna raised him up and
roamed around. He was radiant, resembling Meru in his beauty.
He looked like Meru, with its tall and terrible peak raised up. In the
battle, the brave one raised him up and walked away, being praised
by the Indras among the rakshasas. When the king of the apes was
seized, the residents of heaven were astounded and a roar was heard
in their residences. Indra's enemy was like Indra and resembled Indra
in valour. Having seized the king of the apes, he thought, 'If this
one is killed, Raghava and all the soldiers will be killed.' Hanumat
saw that, here and there, the army of the apes was running away.
Kumbhakarna had seized the ape Sugriva. The intelligent son of the
wind god thought, 'Now that Sugriva has been seized, what should
I do? In every situation, I should do what is proper. I can assume
the size of a mountain and destroy this rakshasa. I can advance
against the immensely strong Kumbhakarna and shatter his body
with a blow of my fists. The king of the apes will be freed and on
seeing this, all the apes will be delighted. Alternatively, the king can
also free himself, even though he has been seized by the residents of
heaven, the asuras and the serpents. Since Kumbhakarna has struck
him with a mountain in the battle, I think that the lord of the apes
has still not gained consciousness. The instant Sugriva regains his
consciousness in this great battle, he will do what is best for himself
and for the apes. If the great-souled Sugriva is freed by me, his
eternal fame will be destroyed and he will find this unpleasant and
suffer from it. Therefore, I will wait for some time, so that the king
can exhibit his valour. My task is to reassure the army of the apes
that has been routed.' Having thought in this way, Hanumat, the
son of the wind god, steadied the great army of the apes. The great
ape[212] was writhing and Kumbhakarna entered Lanka with him.
Those who were in the mansions, houses and turrets worshipped
him and showered down flowers in front of him. The great-souled
one[213] regained his consciousness with difficulty. He was still stuck
between his[214] arms. He looked at the city and the royal road and

[212] Sugriva.
[213] Sugriva.
[214] Kumbhakarna's.

thought repeatedly. 'Having been seized by him, what should I do now? Right now, I am capable of undertaking an act that can bring the desired benefit to the apes.' Thinking this, the king of the apes violently used his hands. He used his nails to rip apart the ears of Kumbhakarna, the enemy of the Indra of the immortals. He used his teeth to bite his nose and struck his sides with his feet. Kumbhakarna's ears and nose were torn apart, bruised and mangled. There was blood from the wounds and he became full of rage. He flung Sugriva down and crushed him on the ground. He was crushed on the ground with that terrible force and struck by the enemy of the gods. However, he leapt up into the sky with force and went to Rama's presence again. The immensely strong Kumbhakarna was deprived of his ears and nose. Wet with blood, he was radiant, like a mountain with waterfalls. From the city, the great-souled one violently emerged in front of the army of the apes. In the battle, the rakshasa Kumbhakarna devoured them, like the blazing fire of destruction does to the subjects. He was hungry and desired flesh and blood. He entered the vanguard of that army of the apes. Because he was confused in the battle, Kumbhakarna ate up rakshasas, apes, pishachas and bears.[215] In a single hand, he angrily held one, two, three and many apes and rakshasas at the same time and hurled them into his mouth. As the immensely strong one devoured the apes, they struck him back with the summits of mountains and his body was covered with fat and blood.

As they were being devoured, the apes sought refuge with Rama. At that time, Lakshmana, Sumitra's son, the afflicter of enemy armies and the conqueror of enemy cities, angrily started to fight. He pierced the valiant Kumbhakarna's body with seven arrows. Lakshmana affixed and shot some other arrows too.

However, the immensely strong Kumbhakarna passed over Lakshmana. As if causing an earthquake, he rushed towards Rama. Rama, Dasharatha's son, invoked the *roudra* weapon and shot sharp arrows towards Kumbhakarna's chest. As he violently rushed towards Rama, he was pierced by him. He became so angry that

---

[215] He also ate up those who were on his own side.

flames mixed with coal started to emerge from his mouth. Arrows tufted with the feathers of peacocks were embedded in his chest. The giant club was dislodged from his hand and fell down on the ground. The immensely strong one thought that he had been deprived of all his weapons.[216] He created great carnage with his fists and his feet. His limbs were struck by arrows and blood started to flow. He oozed out blood, like waterfalls in a mountain. Because of his terrible anger and because of the blood, he became senseless. He rushed around, devouring apes, rakshasas and bears.

At that time, Lakshmana, with dharma in his soul, spoke to Rama, after having reflected on many techniques that could be used to kill Kumbhakarna. 'He cannot distinguish the apes from the rakshasas. Crazy with the smell of blood, he is devouring those on his own side, as well as those on the enemy's side. Let bulls among apes climb on to his body from all directions and properly cover it. Let the leaders of the herds lead their herds and surround him from every direction. Through this means, the evil-minded one will suffer from a heavy burden. The rakshasa will fall down on the ground and will not be able to kill the apes.' Hearing the words of the intelligent prince, the apes were delighted and started to climb up Kumbhakarna. Kumbhakarna was angry at these apes climbing up. He shook himself with great force, like a wicked elephant tries to shake off an elephant rider. Seeing that he was shaking himself, Rama realized that the rakshasa was enraged. He grasped an excellent bow and rushed towards him with great force. He grasped a bow that was like a serpent. It was strung firmly and fiercely and was colourful with gold. Rama comforted the apes and descended, with a quiver full of arrows fixed. A large number of apes surrounded the one who was extremely difficult to vanquish. The immensely strong Rama advanced, followed by Lakshmana. He saw the great-souled and extremely strong Kumbhakarna. The slayer of enemies was diademed and all his limbs were covered with blood. Like an angry *dishagaja*,[217] he was rushing around in all the directions. Surrounded

---

[216] The Critical Edition excises a shloka where his other weapons also fell down.

[217] Four (sometimes eight) elephants are believed to hold up the four (or eight) directions.

by rakshasas, he was angrily searching for apes. He was like Vindhya and Mandara and was decorated with golden armlets. Blood flowed from his mouth and he was like a cloud that had arisen during the monsoon. He licked the blood along the corners of his mouth. Like Yama the Destroyer, he trampled the army of the apes. The best among rakshasas blazed like the flames of the fire.

On seeing him, the bull among men stretched his bow. The bull among nairittas became enraged at the twanging of the bow. He couldn't tolerate the sound and rushed towards Raghava. He was like a storm or a cloud. His arms were like the coils of the supreme king of serpents. His complexion was like that of a mountain. Seeing him descend in the battle, Rama spoke to Kumbhakarna. 'O lord of the rakshasas! Come. Do not be distressed. Having grasped the bow, I am standing before you. O Shakra's enemy! Know me to be Rama. In a short while, you will lose your senses.' Knowing that this was Rama, he laughed in a distorted voice, as if he was shattering the hearts of all the residents of the forest with that sound. The terrible one laughed in that distorted tone, resembling the thunder of the clouds. The immensely energetic Kumbhakarna addressed Raghava in these words. 'Know that I am not Viradha, Kabandha or Khara. Nor am I Vali or Maricha. It is Kumbhakarna who has arrived. Behold my large and terrible club that is completely made out of iron. In earlier times, I have used this to vanquish the gods and the danavas. Just because I do not possess ears and a nose, you should not take me lightly. I do not feel the slightest bit of pain at my ears and nose having been severed. O tiger among the Ikshvakus! Display your valour and dexterity on my body. After having witnessed your manliness and valour, I will devour you.'

Hearing Kumbhakarna's words, Rama released tufted arrows. They were like the vajra in their force. However, even after being struck by them, the enemy of the gods was not agitated or distressed. Those arrows had cut down the best of sala trees and had slain Vali, bull among the apes. But Kumbhakarna's body was like the vajra and they could not pain him. The shower of arrows rained down on his body. However, the enemy of the great Indra seemed to drink them up. He countered the force of Rama's arrows and struck back with the fierce force of his club. The club was smeared with blood and could terrify the large army of the gods. The rakshasa used the fierce force of the club to strike and drive away the army of the apes. Rama then released the supreme vayavya weapon towards the roamer in the night. It severed his arm, which was still holding on to the club. With his arm severed, he roared loudly. The arm was like the summit of a mountain and was severed by Raghava's arrow, while still holding on to the club. It fell down on the army of the king of the apes and killed many apes who were in that army. The apes who had not been maimed or killed were distressed and sought refuge in the extremities of the army. Suffering in all their limbs, they witnessed an extremely terrible encounter between the lord of the rakshasas and the Indra among men. Kumbhakarna's arm had been severed by the weapon, like the summit of an excellent mountain severed by a large sword. He used his other arm to uproot a tree and in the battle, attacked the Indra among men with this. With the sala tree that had been violently uprooted, this arm looked like the coils of a serpent. Using an arrow that was colourful with molten gold, Rama invoked the *aindrastra* and severed this. Kumbhakarna's arm was like a mountain. Severed, it fell down on the ground. Writhing there, it shattered trees, boulders, rocks, apes and rakshasas. In the battle, Rama saw that his arms had been severed and had fallen down and roared loudly. He seized two sharp ardhachandra arrows and severed the rakshasa's feet. His arms had been severed. His feet had been severed. With a gaping mouth that resembled the mouth of the subterranean fire, he roared violently and rushed towards Rama, like Rahu advancing towards the moon in the sky.[218] Rama used arrows that were sharp at the tips and were tufted with gold to fill up his mouth. His mouth filled with these, he was unable to speak. Because of this great misery, he lost his senses. Rama picked up an arrow that was like the wind in its speed. It was like the rays of the sun and was like the staff of Brahma or Yama. He invoked aindrastra on his sharp and well-tufted arrow. Encrusted colourfully with tufts of diamonds and molten gold, it blazed like the

---

[218] The foot had been severed, he still possessed his thighs.

radiant sun. Its force was like that of the great Indra's vajra. Rama shot this towards the roamer in the night. The arrow was released from Raghava's arm and illuminated the ten directions with its radiance. It could be seen to blaze, like a fire without smoke. Like Shakra's vajra in its powers, it advanced. The head of the lord of the rakshasas resembled the summit of a huge mountain. The teeth were excellently formed and the beautiful earrings were moving. Like Vritra's head severed by Purandara in earlier times, this head was severed. The rakshasa's head was like a mountain. Struck by Rama's arrow, it fell down. As it fell down, it shattered the arches, houses, turrets and ramparts. Gigantic in size, the rakshasa was like the Himalayas and fell into the ocean, crushing the crocodiles, giant fish and serpents and then submerging into the ground there.[219]

The extremely strong Kumbhakarna, the enemy of brahmanas and gods, was killed in the battle. The earth and all the mountains trembled. Delighted, the gods roared loudly. The *devarshis*,[220] the maharshis, the serpents, the gods, the creatures, the birds, the *guhyakas*,[221] the yakshas and the large number of gandharvas who were in the sky rejoiced at Rama's valour. The several apes were delighted, their faces resembling blooming lotuses. Raghava had slain the enemy, who was terrible in valour and impossible to be assailed. The beloved one was worshipped. Kumbhakarna had crushed the soldiers of the gods. He was never exhausted and had never been defeated in great battles. Having slain him in the encounter, Bharata's elder brother rejoiced, just as the lord of the immortals did when the great asura, Vritra, had been killed.

Chapter 6(56)

The rakshasas saw that Kumbhakarna had been killed by the great-souled Raghava. They went and reported this to Ravana,

---

[219] The torso fell into the ocean.
[220] Divine sages.
[221] Semi-divine species, companions of Kubera.

Indra among the rakshasas. Hearing that the immensely strong Kumbhakarna had been killed in the battle, Ravana was tormented by grief. He lost his senses and fell down on the ground. Hearing that their paternal uncle had been killed, Devantaka and Narantaka, and Trishira and Atikaya,[222] were oppressed by grief and wept. Hearing that their brother had been slain by Rama, the performer of unblemished deeds, Mahodara and Mahaparshva were filled with sorrow. Ravana, bull among the rakshasas, regained his senses with difficulty. Distressed because Kumbhakarna had been killed, he lamented. 'Alas! O brave one! O destroyer of the insolence of enemies! O Kumbhakarna! O immensely strong one! Having tormented the soldiers of the enemy, why have you left me and departed? You were my right arm and depending on that, I was not scared of gods and asuras. With that fallen down, I can no longer exist now. How could this have happened! The brave one robbed the gods and the danavas of their insolence. He was like the fire of destruction. He has now been slain by Raghava in the battle. The strike of the vajra could never cause him any suffering. He is sleeping on the ground. How could he have been afflicted by Rama's arrows? These large numbers of gods, stationed in the sky with the rishis, are roaring in delight on seeing you killed in the battle. Having accomplished their objective, it is certain that the apes will rejoice today. From all directions, they will clamber up the fortifications and gates of Lanka. What will I do with the kingdom? What will I do with Sita? Without Kumbhakarna, I have no attachment towards remaining alive. Raghava killed my brother today. If I do not kill him in an encounter, it is better for me to be dead. My life will be fruitless. Today, I will go to the region where my younger brother is. Without my brother, I am not interested in remaining alive, not even for an instant. Considering the injury I have caused to them in the past, the gods will laugh at me. O Kumbhakarna! With you killed, how will I triumph over Indra? The great-souled Vibhishana came to me and spoke auspicious words. Because of my ignorance, I did not accept them then. A terrible shame

---

[222] All four were Ravana's sons. Mahodara and Mahaparshva were Ravana's brothers.

has come over me because of Vibhishana's words and the death of Kumbhakarna and Prahasta. The handsome Vibhishana followed dharma and was banished by me. The wicked deed that I did has brought this sorrow on to me.' His soul was greatly disturbed and extremely piteously, he lamented over Kumbhakarna in many kinds of ways. Knowing that Indra's enemy had been killed, Dashanana fell down, severely afflicted.

Chapter 6(57)

The evil-souled Ravana lamented in this way, tormented by grief. Hearing this, Trishira spoke these words. 'O king! The immensely valiant one, my uncle in the middle,[223] has been killed in this way. Virtuous people do not lament in the way you are doing. O lord! You are alone sufficient to take care of the three worlds. Therefore, why are you sorrowing in this fashion, like an ordinary person? You possess a spear given to you by Brahma, armour, a bow and arrows and a chariot that is yoked to one hundred donkeys, clattering like the thunder of a cloud. With your weapons, you have chastised the gods and the danavas. You possess all the weapons and are in a position to chastise Raghava. O great king! It is best that you remain. I will go out and fight. Like Garuda against the serpents, I will destroy the enemies. Just as the king of the gods did to Shambara and Vishnu did to Naraka, today, brought down by me in the battle, Rama will lie down.' Hearing Trishira's words, Ravana, the lord of the rakshasas, goaded by destiny, regarded this as if he had been born again. Hearing Trishira's words, Devantaka, Narantaka and the energetic Atikaya were delighted at the prospect of fighting. Ravana's brave sons were like Shakra in their valour. Those bulls among nairittas roared, 'I', 'I'. All of them roamed around in the sky. All of them were accomplished in the use of maya. All of them had robbed the gods of their insolence. All of them were unassailable in

---

[223] The text uses the word tata. Literally, my father in the middle.

the field of battle. All of them possessed the strength of weapons. All of them were extensive in their deeds. It had never been heard that any of them had been defeated in a battle. All those brave ones knew about the use of weapons. All of them were accomplished in fighting. All of them were superior in knowledge. All of them had obtained boons. They were the equal of the sun in radiance. Surrounded by these sons, who could crush the army of an enemy in a battle, the king was as radiant as Maghavan, surrounded by immortals who could crush the insolence of great danavas. He embraced his sons and adorned them in ornaments. He pronounced benedictions over them and sent them out to fight. Ravana also sent the two brothers, Mahodara and Mahaparshva, to protect the princes in the battle. They honoured the great-souled Ravana, who made his enemies shriek. Having circumambulated him, those gigantic ones departed.

Those immensely strong ones smeared themselves with fragrances from all the herbs. Those six supreme nairittas emerged, desiring to fight. There was an elephant named Sudarshana and it was like a dark cloud. It had been born in Airavata's lineage. Mahodara ascended this. He had all the weapons with him and was also adorned with quivers. He was radiant astride the elephant, like the sun atop Mount Asta. Trishira, Ravana's son, ascended an excellent chariot that was yoked to excellent horses and stocked with all the weapons. Wielding a bow, Trishira was radiant astride the chariot. He looked like a rainbow amidst the clouds, tinged with lightning and blazing meteors. With three diadems, Trishira was radiant on that excellent chariot.[224] He looked like the Himalayas, Indra among mountains, with its three golden peaks. The energetic Atikaya was the son of the Indra among rakshasas. He was supreme among all archers and ascended a supreme chariot. It possessed excellent wheels and axles, was yoked well and possessed an excellent seat and pole. It blazed with quivers, arrows, seats, spears, swords and clubs. He was radiant because of his colourful and golden diadem. Because of his ornaments, he dazzled like the

---

[224] Literally, Trishira means one with three heads. The three diadems make it clear that he did possess three heads.

illumination of Meru. The extremely strong son of the king was
radiant astride the chariot. He was surrounded by tigers among the
nairittas, like the wielder of the vajra by the immortals. Narantaka
was astride an excellent white horse that was like Uchchaishrava.
It was gigantic in size and possessed the speed of thought. It had
a golden harness. Grasping a spear that had the complexion of a
meteor, Narantaka dazzled. Like the energetic Guha, he seized a
spear, for using it against the enemy in the battle. Devantaka seized
a club that was encrusted with diamonds. He resembled Vishnu's
form, when he had held up a mountain in his arms.[225] The immensely
energetic and valiant Mahaparshva seized a club. With the club in
his hand, he was as radiant as Kubera in a battle. Surrounded by an
unmatched army, those great-souled ones set out. They were like the
gods leaving Amaravati, surrounded by an unmatched army. The
elephants, horses and chariots rumbled like thunder. Rakshasas, the
best of warriors, followed the great-souled ones. Like the rays of the
sun, those great-souled princes were radiant. They blazed because
of their diadems, like shining planets in the firmament. An array
of white umbrellas was held aloft their heads. They resembled an
autumn cloud in the sky, adorned with an array of swans. They had
made up their minds to defeat the enemy or die. The brave ones
departed, resolving to fight.

They roared and shouted, shooting arrows. Indomitable in
battle, those great-souled ones departed, desiring victory. The earth
seemed to tremble because of the slapping[226] and clapping. The
leonine roars of the rakshasas seemed to penetrate the sky. Those
immensely strong Indras among the rakshasas rejoiced as they
emerged. They saw the army of the apes, holding aloft boulders
and trees. The great-souled apes also saw the army of the nairittas.
There were arrays of elephants, horses and chariots and hundreds of
bells tinkled. With great weapons raised, it looked like a dark cloud.
Surrounded by nairittas in every direction, it looked like a blazing
fire or the sun. The apes saw that army advance, fixed in its aim.

---

[225] This is probably a reference to Mount Mandara.
[226] Of chests.

They raised giant boulders and roared repeatedly. The large number of rakshasas could not tolerate the roar emitted by the leaders of the apes. They could not tolerate this fierce and supreme delight. Therefore, those immensely strong ones roared back in more terrible tones. The leaders of the apes penetrated that terrible army of the rakshasas. They raised the summits of mountains and trees and roamed around. Some apes took to the sky, others remained on the ground. With trees and boulders as weapons, they angrily roamed around amidst the soldiers of the rakshasas. The apes, terrible in their valour, were countered with torrents of arrows. However, they produced an excellent shower of trees, mountains and boulders. In the battle, the rakshasas and the apes roared like lions. The apes used boulders to crush the yatudhanas. In the encounter, some angrily killed those who were covered with armour. Some climbed on to chariots, elephants and horses and killed those brave ones. The yatudhanas were violently attacked by the apes. They were brought down with the summits of mountains. Their eyes were gouged out with fists. Those bulls among rakshasas wavered, were brought down and roared. The apes and the rakshasas released boulders and swords. In an instant, the earth was covered with these and flooded with blood. There were piles of dead bodies of rakshasas who could crush their enemies. With their spears shattered, they had been flung down, or were being flung down, by the apes. The roamers in the night killed the apes with the dead bodies of apes. The apes also killed the rakshasas with the dead bodies of rakshasas. The rakshasas seized the boulders and killed the apes with these. The apes also seized the weapons and killed the rakshasas with these. They attacked and killed each other with rocks, spears and other weapons. In the battle, the apes and the rakshasas roared like lions. With their armour and bodyguards shattered, the rakshasas were killed by the apes. Blood began to flow there, like sap from trees. In the battle, some apes destroyed chariots with chariots, elephants with elephants and horses with horses. Using kshurapras, ardhachandras, bhallas and sharp arrows, the rakshasas fragmented the trees and the boulders of the Indras among the apes. In the encounter, the earth was strewn with shattered summits of mountains, severed trees and slain apes and rakshasas. It became impossible to traverse. There was a tumultuous clash and in the forefront of the armies, the rakshasas were brought down. The maharshis and large numbers of gods rejoiced and roared at this.

Narantaka was astride a horse that was like the wind in its speed. He seized a sharp spear and penetrated the army of the king of the apes, the way a fish enters the great ocean. With that blazing spear, the brave and great-souled enemy of Indra killed seven hundred apes in an instant. He slew the soldiers and the bulls among the apes. The vidyadharas and maharshis saw the great-souled one astride the back of the horse, roaming around amidst the army of the apes. They saw that there was a mire of flesh and blood in his path. There were bodies of apes who had fallen down, resembling mountains. Whenever the bulls among apes thought of showing their valour, Narantaka overcame and pierced them. At all ends of the battlefield, Narantaka raised his blazing spear and burnt the soldiers of the apes, the way a fire consumes a forest. By the time the residents of the forest raised trees and boulders, they were struck and brought down, like the vajra shattering mountains. The powerful Narantaka roamed around in all directions. Like the wind during the monsoon, he extensively covered all parts of the battlefield. Among all the brave ones whom the valiant one pierced, not a single one was capable of running away, remaining in one place, moving, rising up or leaving. Though he was alone, with the spear that was as energetic as the sun, he seemed to be like many. He routed the soldiers of the apes and brought them down on the ground. When the spear descended on them, it was like being crushed by the vajra. The apes were incapable of withstanding it and shrieked in loud voices. As the brave apes fell down, they assumed the forms of mountains, with their peaks shattered by the vajra. The best among the apes were reduced to the state they were in when they were brought down by the great-souled Kumbhakarna. They presented themselves before Sugriva.

Sugriva saw that, terrified by their fear of Narantaka, the army of the apes was running away, here and there. He saw the soldiers running away. He also saw Narantaka advancing, astride the back

of the horse and holding the spear. Having seen him, Sugriva, lord
of the apes, spoke to the brave Prince Angada, who was Shakra's
equal in valour. 'O brave one! This rakshasa is astride a horse and is
agitating the army of the apes. Go and take away his life.' Hearing
his master's words, Angada descended. The army[227] was like a mass
of clouds and it was as if a cloud with rays had emerged from that
army. Angada, supreme among the apes, was like a mass of rocks.
He was radiant with his armlets and looked like a mountain with
minerals. The immensely strong one possessed no weapons, only
his nails and teeth. Approaching Narantaka, Vali's son spoke these
words. 'Stay. What are you doing to these ordinary apes? This
spear has the touch of the vajra. Hurl it towards my chest.' Hearing
Angada's words, Narantaka became angry. He bit his lips with his
teeth and sighed like a serpent. He suddenly hurled the blazing spear
and pierced Angada. But striking the chest of Vali's son, which was
as firm as the vajra, it shattered and fell down on the ground. He[228]
saw that the spear had been shattered, as if the coils of a serpent
had been severed by Garuda. Vali's son raised his palm and struck
the horse on the head. The horse's head was shattered by the slap
of the palm and it fell down on the ground. Its feet were broken
and its pupils were gouged out. Though it was like a mountain, its
tongue stuck out. On seeing that the horse had been killed and had
fallen down, Naranataka was overcome with rage. In the battle, the
immensely powerful one raised his fist and struck Vali's son on the
head. Angada's head was smashed by the fierce fist and he oozed
out blood that was extremely warm. For an instant, there was a
blazing loss of consciousness. When he regained consciousness, he
was astounded. Angada's fist was like the summit of a mountain
and his force was like that of the vajra. Vali's great-souled son
brought it down on Narantaka's chest. Crushed by the fist, his chest
was shattered. He seemed to be in flames. He vomited blood and
blood covered his body. Narantaka fell down on the ground, as if
a mountain had been shattered by the vajra and had been brought

---

[227] Of the apes.
[228] Angada.

down. In the forefront of the field of battle, Narantaka, supreme among brave ones, was slain by Vali's son. The supreme gods in the sky and the residents of the forest roared loudly. Angada performed an extremely difficult act of valour and this delighted Rama's heart. He was himself surprised at this extremely brave and valiant act and, rejoicing, started to fight again.

Chapter 6(58)

Seeing that Narantaka had been killed, the bulls among the nairittas, Devantaka, Trimurdha,[229] Poulastya[230] and Mahodara, shrieked. Mahodara mounted an Indra among elephants that was like a cloud. The immensely brave one attacked Vali's valiant son. The powerful Devantaka was tormented, suffering hardship on account of his brother. He seized a blazing club and attacked Angada. The brave Trishira was astride a chariot that was like the sun, yoked to excellent horses. He rushed towards Vali's son. Those three Indras among the nairittas were the destroyers of the pride of the gods and attacked. Angada uprooted a giant tree with branches. The brave Angada violently hurled it towards Devantaka. The giant tree, with the giant branches, blazed like Shakra's vajra. Trishira shattered it with arrows that were like virulent serpents. Seeing that the tree had been severed, Angada leapt up. The elephant among apes showered down trees and boulders. Angrily, Trishira used sharp arrows to shatter these. Surantaka[231] shattered the trees with the tip of his club. Trishira attacked the brave Angada with arrows. Mahodara rushed towards Vali's son on an elephant and struck him on the chest with javelins that were like the vajra. Devantaka angrily approached and struck Angada with a club. However, having done this, he swiftly retreated some distance away. He was simultaneously attacked by those three foremost nairittas.

[229] The same as Trishira.
[230] Meaning Mahaparshva.
[231] The same as Devantaka.

However, despite this, Vali's powerful and immensely energetic son wasn't distressed. He raised his palm and struck that great elephant severely.[232] With its eyes jutting out, the elephant shrieked and fell down.[233] In the battle, Vali's immensely strong son plucked out a tusk and attacked and struck Devantaka. Like a tree in the wind, all his limbs trembled. With the complexion of the sap of lac, copious quantities of blood emerged from his mouth. With difficulty, the powerful and greatly energetic Devantaka got a grip on himself. He firmly struck Angada with that terrible club. Struck by the club, the son of the Indra among the apes sank to his knees on the ground. However, he leapt up again. As he was jumping up, Trishira struck him with three arrows that were like venomous serpents. Those terrible arrows struck the son of the king of the apes on his forehead.

Angada was attacked by three bulls among nairittas. Discerning this, Hanumat and Nila went there. Nila hurled the summit of a mountain towards Trishira, but the intelligent son of Ravana shattered this with sharp arrows. That flat rock was fragmented with hundreds of arrows and emitting sparks and flaming, the summit of the mountain fell down. Seeing this, Devantaka was delighted. In the encounter, he seized a club and advanced and attacked the son of the wind god. Seeing that he was descending, Hanumat, the son of the wind god, leapt up. With a fist that was as forceful as the vajra, he struck him on his head. His head was crushed and shattered by the blow of the fist. His teeth fell out. His eyes jutted out. His tongue hung down. Devantaka, the son of the king of the rakshasas, lost his life and suddenly fell down on the ground.

When he was killed, the immensely strong Trimurdha, the foremost among rakshasa warriors and the enemy of the gods, was angry and attacked. He showered down arrows, fierce and sharp at the tips, on Nila's chest. When torrents of arrows were rained down, the body of the commander of the ape army was mangled. But Nila increased the size of his body and repulsed this with his great strength. When Nila regained his senses, he uprooted

---

[232] The context makes it clear that this was Devantaka's elephant, not Mahodara's.
[233] It died.

a mountain that had clumps of trees. Having uprooted it, with a terrible and fierce force, he used it to strike Mahodara on the head. The mountain descended and shattered Mahodara and the elephant. He was uprooted and, losing his life, fell down on the ground. He fell down, like a mountain struck by the vajra.

Seeing that his paternal uncle had been slain, Trishira became angry. He seized a bow and pierced Hanumat with sharp arrows. Hanumat uprooted Trishira's horse and angrily tore it apart with his nails, like the king of deer against an Indra among elephants. Trishira, Ravana's son, seized a javelin that was like Death on the night of destruction and hurled it towards the son of the wind god. It sped through the sky like a meteor. However, the tiger among apes seized it as it descended, broke it and roared. The terrible javelin was shattered by Hanumat. On seeing this, the large number of apes rejoiced and roared like clouds. Trishira, supreme among rakshasas, raised a sword and in anger, thrust this down into the chest of the Indra among apes. Hanumat, the son of the wind god, was struck by the blow of the sword. He struck the valiant Trishira on the chest with his palm. Struck by the palm, the immensely energetic Trishira lost his senses. The weapon was dislodged from his hands and he fell down on the ground. As the sword was falling down, the great ape seized it. Like a mountain in size, he roared and terrified all the nairittas. The roamer in the night was unable to tolerate this roar. He leapt up and struck Hanumat with his fist. Because of that blow of the fist, the great ape became wrathful. He seized the bull among rakshasas by his diadem. Angry, the son of the wind god used that sharp sword to sever his heads,[234] with the diadems and earrings, just as Shakra severed the head of Tvashta's son.[235] Like stellar bodies dislodged from the sun's path, the heads of Indra's enemy, with eyes that were as large as mountains and as fiery as the fire, fell down on the ground. Trishira, the enemy of the gods, was like Shakra in his valour and was killed by Hanumat. The apes roared and made the earth tremble. The rakshasas fled in different directions.

---

[234] Trishira possessed three heads.

[235] Indra killed Trishira (a different Trishira) or Vishvarupa, the son of Tvashtri/Tvashtra/Tvashta.

Trishira and Mahodara had been killed and so had the invincible Devantaka and Narantaka. On seeing this, the immensely strong Mahaparshva became extremely intolerant and angry. He seized an auspicious club that emitted sparks and was completely made out of iron. It was bound in a golden garment and was smeared with flesh and blood. Its form was radiant, decorated with the blood of enemies. He wore red garlands and was fiery and blazed in his energy. He was as terrifying as Airavata, Mahapadma and Sarvabhouma.[236] The immensely strong Mahaparshva became greatly enraged and seized a club. Like the blazing fire that arises at the end of a yuga, he attacked the apes. The ape Rishabha leapt up. The powerful one approached and stood in front of Mahaparshva, Ravana's younger brother. Seeing the ape standing in front, resembling a mountain, he angrily struck him on the chest with the club that was like the vajra. The bull among apes was struck by the club. His chest was mangled and copious quantities of blood oozed out. After a long period of time, Rishabha, bull among apes, regained his senses. He bit his lips in rage and glanced towards Mahaparshva. In the field of battle, he seized the terrible club and repeatedly struck Mahaparshva, the crazy leader of the army. He was mangled by the club and his eyes and teeth fell off. Like a mountain shattered by the vajra, Mahaparshva fell down. Thus, Ravana's brother was killed. The army of nairittas resembled the ocean. Wishing to only protect their lives, they abandoned their weapons and ran away, like the ocean when it crosses the shoreline.

Chapter 6(59)

Atikaya was like a mountain and was one who robbed the gods and the danavas of their pride. He saw the tumultuous sight of

[236] There are eight elephants who guard the eight directions—Airavata, Pundareeka, Vamana, Kumuda, Anjana, Pushpadanta, Sarvabhouma and Suprateeka. Airavata is also regarded as the king of elephants and is Indra's mount. Mahapadma is another name for Pundareeka.

his own army being distressed and it made the body hair stand up. He saw that his brothers, who possessed a valour that was equal to that of Shakra's, had been killed. He saw that his paternal uncles, the brothers Mahodara and Mahaparshva, bulls among rakshasas, had also been killed in the battle. In the encounter, the immensely energetic one, the beneficiary of a boon from Brahma, became angry. Shakra's enemy mounted a chariot that was as radiant as an array of one thousand suns and attacked the apes. Adorned in a diadem and polished earrings, he twanged his giant bow. He announced his name and roared loudly. There was the terrible sound of his roaring like a lion, announcing his name and twanging his bow. The apes were terrified. They saw his form, which was like that of Vishnu engaging in his three strides. Afflicted by fear, all the apes fled in the ten directions. Seeing that Atikaya was attacking, the apes lost their senses. In the battle, they sought refuge with the one who grants refuge, Lakshmana's elder brother. From a distance, Kakutstha saw Atikaya astride a chariot that was like a mountain. He was brandishing a bow and was roaring like a cloud of destruction.

On seeing the great-souled one, Raghava was extremely surprised. He assured the apes and spoke to Vibhishana. 'Who is this? He is like a mountain. He wields a bow and his eyes are tawny. He is mounted on a giant chariot that is yoked to one thousand horses. He possesses sharp spears and exceedingly sharp javelins and spikes. With the rays of the weapons, he looks like Maheshvara, surrounded by the bhutas. He is radiant and dazzling, like the tongue of Death. Surrounded by javelins, he is like a cloud tinged with lightning.[237] On his excellent chariot, all the bows that have been arranged have golden backs, resembling Shakra's bow[238] in the sky. Who is this tiger among rakshasas who is roaming around in the field of battle? This best among charioteers is advancing on a chariot that is as energetic as the sun. The radiant top of his standard has a mark of Rahu on it. His arrows are shining like the rays of

[237] Javelin is only partly correct. The text uses the word *rathashakti*. While *shakti* is a javelin, rathashakti is the pole that holds up the standard in a chariot. Hence, these were special kinds of javelins.

[238] The rainbow.

the sun and are illuminating the ten directions. His bow is curved in
three places and roars like a cloud. It is ornamented with a golden
back. His bow is as dazzling as Shatakratu's excellent bow. His
giant chariot has a standard, flags and a seat. With four drivers, it
is roaring like thunder. There are thirty-eight quivers on his chariot.
There are bows with terrible bowstrings, golden and brown. Two
swords are slung from the sides of the chariot, illuminating the sides.
Each of them is beautiful and clearly ten cubits long, with handles
that are four cubits.[239] The patient one is like a giant mountain and
wears a red garland around his neck. He is like Death. He possesses
a large mouth, like Death. He is like the sun, inside a cloud. Golden
armlets adorn both his arms. He is as radiant as the excellent
mountain of the Himalayas, with its two peaks. With two earrings,
his face is shining and possesses auspicious eyes. He is like the full
moon between the two stars in Punarvasu.[240] O mighty-armed one!
Tell me. Who is this supreme rakshasa? On seeing him, all the apes
are afflicted by grief and are running away in different directions.

Vibhishana was asked by Prince Rama, infinite in his energy.
The greatly energetic one replied to Raghava. 'The immensely
energetic Dashagriva is the younger brother of King Vaishravana.[241]
Ravana, terrible in his deeds and great in his enterprise, is the lord
of the rakshasas. He has a valiant son who is Ravana's equal in
battles. He serves the aged and is learned. He is supreme among
those who are accomplished in the use of all weapons. He is
skilled in mounting the backs of horses, elephants and chariots,
in wielding the bow and the sword, in bheda, conciliation, dana
and good policy. Resorting to the strength of his arms, Lanka is
free from fear. He is the son of Dhanyamali and he is known by
the name of Atikaya.[242] Cleansing his soul, he worshipped Brahma
and performed austerities. He obtained weapons and defeated the

---

[239] The text doesn't clearly state what is four cubits long, the handle or the scabbard.

[240] A nakshatra is not a star, but can be a constellation too. Punarvasu is the
constellation of Gemini (Mithuna), with the two stars, Gemini and Pollux.

[241] Kubera.

[242] Dhanyamali/Dhanyamalini has been mentioned before. At that time, we weren't
told that she was Ravana's wife.

enemies. Svayambhu granted him the boon that he cannot be killed by the gods and the asuras. He obtained this divine armour and this chariot that is as radiant as the sun. Hundreds of gods and danavas have been defeated by him. He has protected the rakshasas and slain yakshas. The intelligent one used his arrows to stupefy Indra's vajra. In a battle, he countered the noose of the king of the waters.[243] This powerful Atikaya is a bull among the rakshasas. He is Ravana's intelligent son and has destroyed the pride of the gods and the danavas. O bull among men! Therefore, let us act quickly, before he uses his arrows to destroy the soldiers of the apes.

The powerful Atikaya entered the army of the apes. He stretched his bow and roared repeatedly. He saw the supreme among charioteers, terrible in his form, stationed on the chariot. The foremost among the apes attacked the great-souled one. Kumuda, Dvivida, Mainda, Nila and Sharabha used trees and the summits of mountains and simultaneously attacked him. The immensely energetic Atikaya, supreme among those who knew about all weapons, used his gold-tufted arrows to sever those trees and mountains. In the forefront of the battle, the powerful roamer in the night, terrible in his form, used arrows that were completely made out of iron to pierce those apes. Those apes were afflicted by those showers of arrows and their bodies were mangled. In that great battle, they were incapable of countering Atikaya. The rakshasas terrified the soldiers and the brave ones among the apes, just as a young and angry lion drives away herds of deer. In the midst of the ape soldiers, the Indra among the rakshasas did not kill anyone who was not fighting.

Wielding the bow, he went up to Rama and proudly spoke these words. 'I am stationed on my chariot, with a bow and arrow in my hands. I never fight with an ordinary person. Let anyone who possesses strength and enterprise swiftly grant me a duel now.' Hearing his words, Soumitri, the slayer of enemies, became angry and intolerant and attacked. He smiled and seized his bow. In front of Atikaya, he stretched his great bow. Having angrily attacked, Soumitri picked up an arrow from his quiver. The twang

[243] Varuna.

of Lakshmana's fierce weapon terrified the roamers in the night and filled the earth, the mountains, the sky, the ocean and the directions. Hearing the terrible roar of Soumitri's bow, the powerful and immensely energetic son of the Indra among the rakshasas was astounded. Seeing that Lakshmana had presented himself before him, Atikaya was angry. He picked up a sharp arrow and spoke these words. 'O Soumitri! You are a child. You are not accomplished in fighting. Go away. I am like Death. Why do you wish to fight with me? The Himalayas, the sky or the earth are unable to withstand the force of weapons released from my arm. You desire to awake a fire of destruction that is happily asleep. Cast aside your bow and return. If you fight against me, you will lose your life. Or perhaps your obstinacy doesn't allow you to retreat. In that case, remain and give up your life. Go to Yama's abode. Behold my sharp arrows. They destroy the pride of enemies. They are embellished with molten gold and are like Ishvara's[244] weapons. This arrow is like a serpent and will drink blood, just as an enraged king of deer drinks the blood of a king of elephants.' Hearing Atikaya's proud and angry words in the battle, the extremely strong prince and prosperous one was also enraged. He spoke words that were full of great import. 'One doesn't become powerful only through the use of words. One doesn't become a virtuous person only through self-praise. I am stationed here, with a bow and arrow in my hands. O evil-souled one! Show me your valour. Demonstrate it through your deeds. You should not indulge in self-praise. Only a person who possesses manliness is said to be brave. You are an archer and are astride a chariot that has all the weapons. Demonstrate your valour through arrows or other weapons. Thereafter, I will use sharp arrows to bring down your head, just as at the right time, the wind brings down a palm fruit from its stem. My arrows are embellished with molten gold. Today, they will drink the blood that oozes out from the wounds created in your body by these stakes. Taking me to be a child, you should not take me lightly. Whether I am a child or whether I am aged, in the encounter you will know me as Death.'

[244] Probably meaning Shiva.

He heard Lakshmana's words, full of great meaning. Enraged, Atikaya picked up a supreme arrow. The vidyadharas, bhutas, gods, daityas, maharshis, guhyakas and great-souled ones witnessed that encounter. Angry, Atikaya affixed the arrow to his bow. As if eating up the sky that was in between them, he shot this at Lakshmana. The sharp arrow descended, like a venomous serpent. Lakshmana, the slayer of enemy heroes, severed this with an ardhachandra arrow. That arrow was like the hood of a serpent and was splintered. Seeing this, Atikaya became extremely angry and affixed five arrows. The roamer in the night shot these towards Lakshmana. However, Bharata's younger brother severed them with his sharp arrows. Lakshmana, the slayer of enemy heroes, severed these with his sharp arrows. He then picked up a sharp arrow that blazed in its energy. Lakshmana affixed this to his excellent bow. He stretched it with force and released the arrow. He drew the bow all the way back and released the arrow with drooping tufts. It struck the forehead of the brave and supreme rakshasa. The arrow penetrated the forehead of the terrible rakshasa. In the battle, with blood streaming from him, he looked like an Indra among the serpents. The rakshasa trembled, just like the turrets of Tripura when they were struck by Rudra's terrible arrow. Lakshmana made him tremble. Having reassured himself and regained his breath, the immensely strong one thought. 'This was an excellent strike with the arrow. My enemy deserves praise.' As he lowered himself on his arms, he thought in this way.[245] He mounted his chariot and roamed around on that chariot. The bull among rakshasas fixed one, three, five and seven arrows to his bow, stretched it and released them. Those arrows were like death and were shot from the bow of the Indra among rakshasas. They were tufted with gold and dazzled like the sun. They made the sky blaze. The rakshasa shot a flood of arrows. However, Raghava's younger brother wasn't scared. He severed these with many sharp arrows. Ravana's son saw that his arrows had been countered in the battle. The enemy of Indra of the gods angrily seized a sharp arrow. The immensely energetic one affixed and violently released

---

[245] The blow made him bend down and he probably got off the chariot.

this arrow. It approached Soumitri and struck him between the breasts. In the battle, Atikaya struck Soumitri in the chest. Like musth from a crazy elephant, a copious quantity of blood began to flow. The lord violently freed himself from that stake. He picked up a sharp arrow and affixed a weapon to it. When the great-souled one invoked agneyastra on that arrow, the bow and the arrow blazed. The extremely energetic Atikaya affixed the *sourastra*.[246] He affixed a gold-tufted arrow that resembled a serpent. Lakshmana shot that terrible and blazing arrow towards Atikaya and it was like the deadly staff of the Destroyer.[247] The roamer in the night saw that the arrow had been invoked with agneyastra. He shot a blazing arrow that had been invoked with suryastra. Those two arrows struck each other in the sky, blazing in their energy, like two wrathful serpents. They consumed each other and fell down on the ground. Their rays were reduced to ashes and those two excellent arrows were no longer radiant. Angry, Atikaya released the *aishika* weapon.[248] The valiant Soumitri severed this with aindrastra. On seeing that the aishika had been destroyed, the prince who was Ravana's son angrily invoked *yamyastra*[249] on an arrow. The roamer in the night shot this weapon towards Lakshmana and Lakshmana destroyed this with *vayavyastra*.[250] Angry, Lakshmana showered down arrows on Ravana's son, like rain pouring down from a cloud. They struck Atikaya and severed his armour, which was encrusted with diamonds. Shattered violently by the arrows, it fell down on the ground. Lakshmana, the slayer of enemy heroes, saw that the arrows had been rendered unsuccessful. The immensely illustrious one showered down thousands of arrows. Torrents of arrows were showered down on the immensely strong Atikaya and he was devoid of his armour. However, the rakshasa was not pained in the encounter. Moreover, the supreme among men was incapable of wounding him in the battle. At this, Vayu approached

---

[246] Divine weapon named after the sun god. Suryastra is a synonym.
[247] Yama.
[248] Another divine weapon, invoked on a blade of grass and associated with Tvashta.
[249] Named after Yama.
[250] Named after Vayu.

and spoke these words. 'He has obtained a boon from Brahma and is clad in armour that makes it impossible to kill him. He has to be splintered with brahmastra. There is no other means to kill him.' Soumitri's valour was like that of Indra and he heard Vayu's words. He affixed an arrow that was irresistible in its force and suddenly invoked brahmastra. Soumitri invoked that supreme weapon on an excellent arrow that was sharp at the tips. The directions, the moon, the sun, the giant planets, the sky and the earth were terrified and agitated. That well-tufted arrow was like Yama's messenger and brahmastra was affixed to the bow. That arrow was like the vajra. In the battle, Soumitri shot this towards the son of Indra's enemy. It was shot by Lakshmana and was irresistible in its force. It descended, blazing away, on an arrow that was colourfully tufted, embellished with excellent gold and diamonds. In the battle, Atikaya saw it approach. On seeing it, Atikaya violently struck it with many sharp arrows. However, that arrow possessed Suparna's force and with great speed, approached him. Atikaya saw that blazing arrow approach, resembling Death. He made vain efforts to strike it with spears, swords, clubs, battleaxes, javelins, ploughs[251] and bows. However, blazing like the fire, that arrow rendered all these extraordinary weapons futile. It struck and severed Atikaya's head, decorated with the diadem. The head, with the helmet on the head, was struck by Lakshmana's arrow and fell down violently on the ground, like one of Himalayas' peaks. With their faces resembling blooming lotuses, the many apes were delighted. They worshipped Lakshmana, who had accomplished his objective. The invincible enemy, terrible in his strength, had been killed.

Chapter 6(60)

The large number of rakshasas who had not been killed quickly went to Ravana and told him that the bulls among the

---

[251] Plough (*hala*) is probably a typo and should be arrow.

rakshasas, Devantaka, Trishira, Atikaya and the others had been
slain. Hearing that they had been violently killed, the king lost his
senses and tears flowed from his eyes. Because of the terrible news
of his sons being killed and the news that his brothers had been
killed, the king thought for a long time. The king was distressed
and was deeply submerged in an ocean of grief. Seeing this, Indrajit,
the son of the king of the rakshasas, addressed him in these words.
'O father! O Indra among the rakshasas! You should not lose your
senses, not as long as Indrajit is alive. In a battle, a person who has
been struck by the arrows of Indra's enemy will find it impossible
to protect his life. Today, you will see the bodies of Rama and
Lakshmana mangled and pierced by my arrows. They will lose their
lives and lie down on the ground. Their bodies will be completely
pierced by arrows. Listen to the pledge taken by Shakra's enemy.
This is properly based on manliness and has fortune to back it
up. Today, I will torment Rama and Lakshmana with a flood of
arrows. Today, in the sacrificial ground used by Bali, Vishnu's
fierce enemy, Indra, Vaivasvata, Vishnu, Mitra, the Sadhyas, the
Ashvins, Vaishvanara,[252] the sun god and the moon god will witness
my immeasurable valour.' The enemy of Indra of the gods said this.
Without his spirit being distressed, he sought the king's permission.
He mounted an excellent chariot that was like the wind in speed,
yoked to excellent donkeys.

The immensely energetic one mounted a chariot that was
like Indra's chariot. The scorcher of enemies swiftly went to the
place where the fighting was taking place. As the great-souled one
proceeded, many extremely strong ones followed him. They were
cheerful and wielded the best of bows in their hands. Some were
mounted on the backs of elephants and some were astride excellent
horses. They wielded spears, clubs, swords, battleaxes and maces.
There were the blaring of conch shells and the terrible and loud noise
of drums. Worshipped by the roamers in the night, the enemy of Indra
of the gods departed. The slayer of enemies had a white umbrella,
with the complexion of a conch shell or the moon. He was as radiant

---

[252] Agni.

as the full moon in the sky. The brave one was fanned with golden whisks that were also decorated with gold. He was handsome and foremost among all archers, fanned by the best of whisks. Indrajit left Lanka, like the sun in his energy. In his valour, as radiant as the shining sun in the sky, he illuminated the city. He left, surrounded by that large army. Seeing this, Ravana, lord of the rakshasas, spoke to his handsome son. 'O son! You have defeated Vasava and there is no charioteer who can stand before you, not to speak of a mortal human. You will slay Raghava.' Having said this, the Indra among the rakshasas pronounced great benedictions over him.

The greatly energetic one, the destroyer of enemies, reached the field of battle. He stationed the rakshasas all around his chariot. His complexion was like the one who devours oblations.[253] With the proper mantras, the best among rakshasas offered oblations into the fire. He prepared the oblations, with parched grain and clarified butter, and placed garlands and fragrances in front. The powerful Indra among rakshasas rendered these oblations into the fire. The weapons were used in place of reeds. *Vibhitaka*[254] was used as kindling. There were red garments and ladles made out of iron. He spread out javelins like a bed of reeds and lit a fire. He grasped the neck of a live goat that was completely black. With the kindling that was offered, a fire without smoke resulted. From the signs, it was seen that victory would be obtained. The fire itself arose in personified form and, with flames that were like molten gold in complexion, circumambulated and accepted the oblations. He was supreme among all those who possessed knowledge of the brahmastra. He invited all the weapons to remain on his bow and his chariot. The weapons were invited and oblations were offered into the fire. The sun, the planets, the moon, the nakshatras and the firmament were terrified. Blazing in energy like the fire and like the great Indra in his powers, he offered oblations into the fire. With his bow, arrows, sword, chariot, horses and charioteer, he assumed the unthinkable form of remaining invisible.

[253] The fire.
[254] A kind of myrobalan.

In the great battle, he left his soldiers behind and quickly attacked the army of the apes. Remaining invisible, he shot nets of fierce arrows. These rained down, like water from dark clouds. Their bodies were mangled by Shakrajit's[255] arrows. They were struck by maya and screamed in hideous tones. In the battle, the apes were like mountains. However, they were brought down, like excellent mountains shattered by Indra's vajra. In the battle, they could only see arrows that were sharp at the tips penetrate the soldiers of the apes. The rakshasa, the enemy of Indra of the gods, was deep in his use of maya and they were unable to see him. The great-souled lord of the rakshasas covered all the directions with innumerable arrows sharp at the tips. He shrouded the radiance of the sun and caused distress to the Indras among the apes. Spears, swords and battleaxes, resembling a blazing fire, pierced them. They were like raging fires, emitting sparks. This fierce shower rained down on the soldiers of the king of the apes. The leaders of the apes were struck by these blazing and sharp arrows. Afflicted by Shakrajit's arrows, they were like blossoming kimshukas. They clung to each other and roared in hideous tones. The weapons of the Indra among the rakshasas mangled the bulls among the apes and made them fall down. Struck and with their eyes torn out, some looked up into the sky. Some leaned on each other and fell down on the ground. Hanumat, Sugriva, Angada, Gandhamadana, Jambavat, Sushena, Vegadarshina, Mainda, Dvivida, Nila, Gavaksha, Gaja, Gomukha, Kesari, Hariloma, the ape Vidyuddamshtra, Suryanana, Jyotimukha, the ape Dadhimukha, Pavakaksha, Nala and the ape Kumuda—all of them were struck with spears, javelins and sharp arrows, all invoked with Indrajit's mantras. The supreme rakshasa pierced all those tigers among apes. The foremost leaders among the apes were mangled with clubs and pierced with arrows that were gold-tufted.

He next rained down arrows that are as radiant as the rays of the sun on Rama and Lakshmana. Rama's beauty was supreme and he did not think about this shower of arrows, regarding it as

---

[255] Shakrajit is the same as Indrajit.

no more than a shower of rain. However, looking at it, he spoke to Lakshmana. 'O Lakshmana! This Indra among rakshasas, the enemy of Indra of the gods, is resorting to the brahmastra again. He is fiercely bringing down the soldiers of the apes. He is engaging with us and afflicting us with these arrows. The great-souled one has obtained a boon from Svayambhu. He is in the sky and has made his terrible form invisible. How can one fight against someone who doesn't possess a body? How can one raise a weapon and kill Indrajit? I think that the illustrious Svayambhu cannot be thought of and this shows the power of his weapon. O intelligent one! Remain here with me and tolerate this shower of arrows now. This Indra among rakshasas has concealed himself and is enveloping all the directions with his nets of arrows. All the best among the valiant ones have fallen down and the army of the king of the apes is no longer resplendent. Let us fall down, unconscious. Let us abandon all anger and joy and withdraw from the battle. On seeing this, it is certain that this enemy of the immortals will return, having obtained success in the field of battle.' At this, they allowed themselves to be struck by Indrajit's nets of weapons. Having caused them distress in the field of battle, the Indra among rakshasas roared in delight. With Rama and Lakshmana, the soldiers of the king of the apes were suddenly immersed in misery in that encounter. He[256] returned to the city protected by Dashagriva's arms.

Chapter 6(61)

In the forefront of the field of battle, the soldiers and the leaders of the apes lost their senses. Sugriva, Nila, Angada and Jambavat did not know what they should do. Vibhishana was supreme among those who were intelligent and he saw that the soldiers were distressed. He spoke these unmatched words of assurance to the brave king of the apes. 'Do not be frightened. This is not the time

---

[256] Indrajit.

for despondency. The two noble ones are disabled and suffering because of the words uttered by Svayambhu.[257] That is the reason they have succumbed to the net of Indrajit's weapons. This supreme weapon was given by Svayambhu Brahma and its force is irresistible. The two princes have shown it respect and have fallen down. This is not the time for despondency.'

Hearing Vibhishana's words, the intelligent Maruti showed his respects to Brahma's weapon. Hanumat said, 'These spirited soldiers of the apes have been struck down. We must comfort those who are still alive.' In the night, those two brave ones, Hanumat and the supreme among the rakshasas,[258] roamed around in the field of battle, with torches in their hands. They had fallen down in every direction, with blood oozing from the wounds in their bodies. Their tails, hands, thighs, feet, fingers and heads had been mangled. The earth was strewn with fallen apes who were like mountains. Blazing weapons could also be seen, fallen down on the ground. Vibhishana and Hanumat also saw Sugriva, Angada, Nila, Sharabha, Gandhamadana, Jambavat, Sushena, Vegadarshina, Ahuka, Mainda, Nala, Jyotimukha, Dvivida and Panasa—brought down in the battle. Sixty-seven crores of spirited apes had been brought down by Svayambhu's beloved weapon in the fifth part of the day.[259]

Hanumat and Vibhishana searched for Jambavat and looked at the army that had been afflicted by the arrows, resembling the terrible waves of the ocean. He was naturally old and aged and had been pierced with hundreds of arrows. Prajapati's brave son[260] was like a fire that had been pacified. Having seen and met him, Poulastya[261] spoke these words. 'You have been shattered by these sharp arrows. Are you still alive?' Having heard Vibhishana's words, Jambavat, bull among the bears, managed to utter these

[257] The boon granted by Brahma.
[258] Vibhishana.
[259] A day of twelve hours was divided into five parts, each consisting of 144 minutes. This incident occurred in the fifth segment, the last part of the day.
[260] Jambavat.
[261] Vibhishana.

words with difficulty. 'O Indra among the nairittas! O immensely brave one! I have recognized you through your voice. My body has been pierced with sharp arrows and I am unable to see you with my eyes. O nairitta! Anjana had an excellent son through the wind god. He is Hanumat, supreme among the apes. Is he still alive?' Hearing Jambavat's words, Vibhishana asked, 'Ignoring the two noble ones,[262] why are you asking about Maruti? O noble one! The supreme affection you have displayed towards the son of the wind god is not shown towards King Sugriva, Angada or Raghava.' Hearing Vibhishana's words, Jambavat replied in these words. 'O tiger among nairittas! Listen to the reason why I asked about Maruti. If that brave one is alive, even if this army has been destroyed, we will be alive. If Hanumat has lost his life, even if we are alive, we will be as good as dead. O son![263] Maruti is like the wind. He is like the fire in his valour. As long as he is alive, there is still hope.'

At this, Hanumat, the son of the wind god, humbly approached the aged Jambavat and grasped his feet. The senses of the bull among bears were afflicted. However, on hearing Hanumat's words, he thought that he had got back his life again. The immensely energetic Jambavat spoke to Hanumat. 'O tiger among the apes! Come here. You must save the apes. There is no one else who possesses sufficient valour to be a supreme friend to them. This is the time to show that valour. I do not see anyone else. Bring joy to the brave armies of the bears and the apes. Free Rama and Lakshmana from their wounds and the stakes. O Hanumat! You must progressively travel beyond the ocean and go to the supreme spot, the Himalayas, best among mountains. O slayer of enemies! You will see the golden Mount Rishabha there, supreme among mountains, and also see Mount Kailasa. O brave one! In between those two summits, you will see a mountain that is full of herbs. It blazes and is unmatched in its radiance. It has all the herbs. O tiger among apes! You will see four herbs on the summit there. They

---

[262] Rama and Lakshmana.
[263] The word used is tata.

blaze and illuminate the ten directions. These are the great herbs—
mritasanjivani, vishalyakarani, souvarnakarani and *sandhani*.[264] O
Hanumat! You must get all of these and return swiftly. O son of the
one who conveys fragrances![265] You will thereby comfort them and
bring life back to the apes.'

Hearing Jambavat's words, Hanumat, bull among the apes,
was filled with strength, the way the ocean is filled with the force of
the waters. He stood on the summit of the mountain[266] and pressed
down on that excellent mountain.[267] The brave Hanumat was seen
to resemble a second mountain. The mountain was shattered and
suffered from the pressure of the ape's feet. It suffered from that
great burden and was incapable of bearing it. Suffering from the
force exerted by the ape, the mountain blazed and fell down on the
ground. Because of what Hanumat did, the peaks were shattered.
As that supreme among mountains was whirled around, the apes
were incapable of remaining there. The trees and the slopes of the
mountain were crushed and shattered. In the night, Lanka was
terrified. The large gates were whirled around and the houses and
the turrets were shattered. It was as if the city was dancing. He
was himself like a mountain on earth and crushed the earth. The
son of the wind god agitated the earth, with all its oceans. As he
pressed down on the mountain with his feet, his mouth resembled
the mouth of the subterranean fire. He opened it wide and roared
fiercely, terrifying the rakshasas. All the rakshasas in Lanka heard
the extraordinary sound of his roar and because of their fear, were
unable to move. Terrible in his valour, Maruti bowed down before
Rama. For Raghava's sake, the scorcher of enemies resolved to
undertake this supreme task. He raised up his tail, which resembled
a serpent. He bent his back and contracted his ears. He opened
his mouth, like the mouth of the subterranean fire. With terrible

---

[264] Mritasanjivani brings the dead back to life, vishalyakarani removes stakes and
heals wounds, souvarnakarani restores the original complexion of the body and sandhani
repairs broken bones.

[265] That is, the wind.

[266] Trikuta.

[267] Pressed down with his feet.

force, he leapt up into the sky. As he leapt up, because of the force and speed of his arms and his thighs, clumps of trees, boulders, rocks and ordinary apes were lifted up, and when the momentum was lost, these fell down into the water. He stretched out his arms, which looked like the coils of serpents. With a valour that resembled that of the enemy of the serpents,[268] the son of the wind god left for Meru, the excellent king of the mountains, seemingly dragging the directions away with his force. The garlands of waves in the ocean were agitated and all the creatures that dwelt there were severely hurled around. He was like the chakra released from Vishnu's arm and as he swiftly departed, he looked at all this. Without any exhaustion, he traversed the path followed by the sun.

The best among apes suddenly saw the Himalayas, supreme among mountains. There were diverse kinds of waterfalls there. There were many caverns and springs. The beautiful peaks were like masses of white clouds. He reached the great Indra among mountains. There were tall and terrible peaks that rose up. He saw the great and sacred hermitages, populated by supreme and divine rishis. He saw Brahma's treasure,[269] the abode of silver,[270] Shakra's abode, the place where Rudra released his bow, Hayanana,[271] the blazing Brahmashira,[272] the servants of Vaivasvata,[273] the abode of the vajra, the abode of Vaishravana,[274] Suryanibandhana, which blazes like the sun,[275] Brahma's abode, Shankara's bow and the navel of the earth.[276] In the Himalayas, there was the excellent and lofty Mount Kailasa and the excellent, lofty and golden Mount

---

[268] Garuda.

[269] Alternatively, Brahma's abode.

[270] Interpreted as Kailasa, Shiva's abode.

[271] Horse-faced, place where Vishnu is worshipped in his form of Hayagriva (horse-necked).

[272] There are stories about Rudra having severed Brahma's fifth head (shira).

[273] Probably meaning Yama.

[274] Kubera.

[275] Surya (the sun god) was excessively brilliant and Vishvakarma shaved off a part of this brilliance. The place where Surya was bound down, for this task to be done, is known as Suryanibandhana.

[276] This is the spot through where one enters the nether regions.

Rishabha. He saw the Indra among mountains that had all the herbs. It blazed and was illuminated because of all the herbs. The son of Vasava's messenger[277] was amazed to see this, blazing like the rays of the fire. That Indra among mountains was filled with herbs and he started to search for the right herbs. The great ape had travelled across thousands of yojanas. The son of the wind god roamed around the mountain that was full of divine herbs. However, knowing that someone had come, all the great herbs on that excellent mountain made themselves invisible. Unable to see them, the great-souled Hanumat became enraged and roared loudly. He was intolerant and his eyes turned as red as the fire.

He addressed the Indra among mountains in these words. 'O god! It is extremely evident that you do not have the least bit of compassion for Raghava. Behold the great strength of my arms today. O Indra among mountains! You will find yourself shattered.' There were peaks, summits and trees on that mountain. There were thousands of minerals, including gold. He seized it with force and leapt up. The summit of the mountain was dislodged and the peaks fragmented. He uprooted it and leapt up into the sky, scaring the worlds and the Indras among the gods and the asuras. With a speed and force that surpassed that of Garuda, he proceeded, praised by many creatures who resided in the sky. He seized the summit, which was as radiant as the sun and resorted to the path followed by the sun. He was himself as radiant as the sun and approached the sun, resembling a second sun. That mountain was extremely radiant and the son of the one who bears fragrances[278] was himself like a mountain. He resembled the chakra, with one thousand edges, hurled with a great gust by Vishnu into the sky.

The apes saw him and roared. On seeing them, he also roared back in delight. Hearing the roars that they let out, the residents of Lanka roared in even more terrible voices. The great-souled one descended on that excellent mountain,[279] amidst the soldiers of the apes. He lowered his head down and greeted the best among the

---

[277] Vayu is Indra's messenger.
[278] Vayu.
[279] Trikuta.

apes and embraced Vibhishana. The two human princes inhaled the fragrance of the great herbs and were freed from all their wounds. The brave apes also stood up. The ape who was the son of the bearer of fragrances used his fierce valour to carry back the mountain with herbs.[280] Using his force, he returned again to Rama.

Chapter 6(62)

Sugriva, the immensely energetic lord of the apes, addressed the immensely strong Hanumat, indicating the subsequent course of action. 'Kumbhakarna and the four princes have been killed. Therefore, it is not possible for Ravana to undertake any action now. There are apes who are extremely strong and dexterous. Let those bulls among apes swiftly take torches and attack Lanka.'

The sun had set and it was the start of a terrible night. The bulls among apes headed for Lanka, with torches in their hands. With torches in their hands, large numbers of apes attacked it from all sides. The guards, with malformed eyes, suddenly ran away. Cheerfully, they set fire to the turrets, floors of mansions, many roads and palaces. The fire burnt down and consumed thousands of houses and all the residences of rakshasas, who loved their homes. There was armour decorated with gold and vessels full of garlands and garments. Because they had been drinking, their eyes were unsteady and they lurched as they walked. Their garments were entwined with those of their lovers, though they were filled with intolerance because of the enemy. They had maces and spears in their hands, but they were eating and drinking. With their beloveds, they were lying down on extremely expensive beds. They swiftly grabbed their sons and fled in different directions. Thousands of houses of the residents of Lanka were burnt by the fire and blazed repeatedly. There were extremely firm and extremely expensive houses, with deep qualities. They were made out of gold, in shapes

[280] He returned it to the Himalayas.

of the moon and the half-moon. They were excellent and with many floors, shining like the moon. There were colourful windows and couches everywhere. Decorated with jewels and coral, they seemed to touch the sun. There was the sound of herons and peacocks and the jingling of ornaments. Those houses that were like mountains were burnt by the fire. Surrounded by the fire, the turrets looked like masses of clouds tinged by lightning, when summer is over. Beautiful women who were asleep in mansions were burnt. Throwing aside all their ornaments, they lamented, 'Alas!' Surrounded by the fire, the houses fell down. They were like the shattered summits of mountains, struck by the vajra of the wielder of the vajra. From a distance, as they were burnt, the houses resembled the summits of the Himalayas, blazing with groves of herbs. The tops of the mansions were burnt and blazed, engulfed in flames. In the night, Lanka seemed to be full of flowering kimshukas. The keepers of elephants set the elephants free. The keepers of horses set the horses free. Lanka was like the turbulent ocean at the time of the end of the worlds. On seeing a freed horse, an elephant was scared and retreated. On seeing a frightened elephant, a horse was scared and retreated. In a short while, the city was burnt by the apes. It seemed as if the earth was ablaze at the time of the terrible destruction of the worlds. From ten yojanas away, one could hear the sounds of the women screaming, as they were burnt and scorched and enveloped in smoke.

With their bodies burnt by the fire, the enemy rakshasas emerged. Desiring to fight, the apes attacked them violently. The sound emitted by the apes and the rakshasas resounded in the ten directions, the ocean and the earth. The great-souled Rama and Lakshmana had been freed of their wounds. With excellent bows in their hands, they fearlessly advanced. Rama twanged his excellent bow and this created a tumultuous sound that caused fear to the rakshasas. Stretching his giant bow, Rama was as radiant as the illustrious and enraged Bhava,[281] stretching a bow made out of the Vedas. The sound created by the apes, the roar of the rakshasas and

---

[281] Shiva.

the sound of Rama twanging his bow —these three pervaded the ten directions. Because of the arrows released from his bow, the main turrent of the city, resembling Kailasa's peak, was shattered and fell down on the ground. On witnessing Rama's arrows, in mansions and houses, the Indras among the rakshasas armoured themselves and created a tumult. As they prepared for battle, they roared like lions. To the Indras among the rakshasas, that night was terrible. The great-souled Sugriva, Indra among the apes, commanded, 'O apes! Approach the gates and fight. If someone is present there, but acts in a contrary way, he will slight the command of the king and should be killed.'

The foremost among the apes held blazing torches in their hands and were stationed at the gates. Ravana was filled with intolerance. The ten directions were agitated because of his yawning and stomping around. He was seen to resemble Rudra, with rage permeating his body. Angry, with many rakshasas, he sent Kumbha and Nikumbha, the two sons of Kumbhakarna. The lord of the rakshasas commanded all the rakshasas, 'O rakshasas! Roar like lions and advance.' Thus urged, the brave rakshasas emerged from Lanka, with blazing weapons and roaring repeatedly. There were terrible horses, chariots and elephants, with innumerable foot soldiers. They had blazing spears, clubs, swords, javelins, spikes and bows. That army of rakshasas was terrible and was filled with terrible valour and manliness. There were nets of golden armour on the arms and they brandished battleaxes. They whirled around great weapons and affixed arrows to their bows. The air was filled with the intoxicating scent of perfumes, garlands and liquor. With so many terrible and brave ones, the roar resembled that of a thundering cloud.

On seeing the invincible army of the rakshasas advance, the army of the apes stirred itself and roared. The army of the rakshasas also attacked the army of the enemy with great force, like insects heading towards a fire. There were iron clubs in their hands and bludgeons in their fists. That excellent army of the rakshasas was supremely radiant. The roamers in the night were terrible in form and their brave warriors used swords and sharp arrows to sever the heads of the enemy apes. A warrior who was striking someone else was killed.[282] A warrior who was bringing someone else down was brought down. A warrior who was censuring someone else was censured. A warrior who was biting someone else was bitten. Some said, 'Strike me.' Others said, 'You are being struck.' Someone else said, 'I will strike you.' Someone spoke to another and said, 'Why are you suffering this hardship by remaining here?' They raised giant spears, javelins, swords and fists. There was a great and tumultuous battle between the apes and the rakshasas. In the battle, the rakshasas killed apes in tens and sevens. The apes brought down rakshasas in tens and sevens. Hair and garments were dishevelled. Armour and standards were cast aside. The apes attacked and surrounded the army of the rakshasas.

Chapter 6(63)

There was a tumultuous battle that led to the slaughter of brave warriors. Desiring to fight, Angada approached the brave Kampana. Challenging Angada, the angry Kampana first struck him with the great force of a club. Severely struck, he reeled. When he regained his senses, the energetic one hurled the summit of a mountain. Afflicted by the blow, Kampana fell down on the ground. With the brave ones killed, the army of the Indra among the rakshasas was distressed. It retreated towards the spot where Kumbhakarna's son[283] was. Kumbha reassured the army and attacked with force. Controlling himself, the supreme among archers seized his bow. He shot excellent arrows that were like virulent serpents, capable of tearing the body apart. With excellent arrows affixed, his excellent bow was like a second bow of Indra, tinged with lightning, astride the radiant Airavata.[284]

[282] Signifying the violation of the rules of war and the chaos.
[283] Kumbha.
[284] There is a double image of Indra astride Airavata, wielding his bow, and of the rainbow as Indra's bow.

He drew his bow all the way back to his ears and using an arrow with a golden shaft, tufted with the feathers of birds, struck Dvivida. The excellent ape possessed the complexion of the summit of Trikuta. However, suddenly struck, his feet tottered. He was agitated and fell down, writhing. Mainda saw that his brother had been routed in the great encounter. He seized a giant boulder and attacked with force. The immensely strong one flung the boulder towards the rakshasas. However, Kumbha shattered the boulder with five sparkling arrows. He affixed another arrow with an excellent tip, resembling a virulent serpent. The immensely energetic one struck Dvivida's elder brother in the chest. The blow pierced Mainda, the leader of the apes, in his inner organs. Senseless, he fell down on the ground. Angada saw that his immensely strong maternal uncles had been brought down. He attacked Kumbha, who had his bow upraised, with force. As he descended, Kumbha pierced him with five iron arrows and three other sharp arrows, the way one strikes an elephant with a goad. Kumbha pierced the valiant Angada with many kinds of arrows, which were extremely sharp, pointed and keen, decorated with gold. Though he was pierced in his limbs, Angada, Vali's son, did not tremble. He rained down showers of boulders and trees on his head. Kumbhakarna's son sliced down all of them and all the boulders hurled by Vali's handsome son. Seeing that the leader of the apes was descending on him, Kumbha pierced him between the eyebrows with arrows, the way one strikes an elephant with a flaming torch. He was covered with blood, flowing from his eyes. Angada covered these with one hand and used the other hand to seize a sala tree. That tree was like Indra's standard, like Mandara. While all the rakshasas looked on, he hurled it with force. However, he shot it down with seven arrows that were capable of mangling the body. On seeing this, Angada was distressed. He lost his senses and sank down. The invincible Angada was distressed, as if he was submerged in an ocean. Witnessing this, the best among the apes went and informed Raghava.

Hearing that Vali's son was suffering in the great battle, Rama commanded the best among the apes, with Jambavat at the forefront. The tigers among the apes heard Rama's command. Extremely

enraged, they attacked Kumbha, who was brandishing his bow. Their
eyes red with rage, they held trees and boulders in their hands. The
bulls among the apes desired to protect Angada. Jambavat and the apes
Sushena and Vegadarshi angrily attacked Kumbhakarna's brave son.
Seeing those extremely strong apes advance, he countered them with
torrents of arrows, the way one dams a store of water with rocks. The
great-souled Indras among the apes were unable to breach his storm
of arrows, just as the great ocean cannot cross the shoreline. The large
number of apes were afflicted by these arrows. On seeing this, the lord
of the apes kept his brother's son, Angada, in the background. In the
battle, Sugriva attacked Kumbha with force, just as a powerful lion
attacks an elephant that is roaming around on the slope of a mountain.
He uprooted giant boulders and many ashvakarna and dhava trees.
The immensely strong one hurled many other trees. Kumbhakarna's
invincible son used his sharp arrows to sever that invincible downpour
of trees that enveloped the sky. Kumbha aimed his fierce and sharp
arrows at these trees. Shattered by them, they were as radiant as
terrible shataghnis. That shower of trees was severed by the valiant
Kumbha. On seeing this, the handsome and great-spirited lord of
the apes was not distressed. Though he was himself pierced by those
arrows, he tolerated it. He violently seized Kumbha's bow, which was
as resplendent as Indra's bow, and broke it. He swiftly attacked and
performed this extremely difficult deed. Kumbha was like an elephant
with its tusks broken and he angrily spoke to him. 'O Nikumbha's elder
brother! Your valour and the force of your arrows are extraordinary.
Both you and Ravana possess good intentions[285] and powers. You are
the equal of Prahlada, Bali, Vritra's destroyer,[286] Kubera and Varuna.
You have been born in the likeness of your father, who was supreme
in strength. O mighty-armed one! O slayer of enemies! If you wield
the spear in your hand, the gods cannot cross you, just as someone
who has conquered his senses cannot be agitated. Because of the boon
he received, your paternal uncle[287] can withstand the gods and the
danavas. However, Kumbhakarna could withstand the gods and the

---

[285] Towards rakshasas.
[286] Indra.
[287] Ravana.

asuras because of his valour. You are Indrajit's equal in the wielding
of the bow and Ravana's equal in powers. Because of your strength
and valour, you are now the best in the world of the rakshasas. Today,
let all the creatures witness the great and extraordinary encounter
between you and me, like that between Shakra and Shambara. You
have performed unmatched tasks and have shown your skill in the use
of weapons. You have brought down brave apes who were terrible in
their valour. O brave one! If I do not kill you, I am scared of being
censured. However, you are exhausted because of what you have
done. Rest and then behold my strength.' Sugriva's words sounded
like respect, but actually indicated disrespect. Like oblations rendered
into a fire, they served to enhance his energy. Kumbha leapt up and
attacked Sugriva. He angrily struck him on the chest with a fist that
had the force of the vajra. His skin was splintered and blood started
to flow out. With the great force of his fist, he struck him again on
the chest. It was as if the blazing vajra had struck Mount Meru.
However, the force of the blow ignited his energy again. Thus struck,
the immensely strong Sugriva, bull among apes, countered with his
own fist, which was like the vajra. His fist was as radiant as the solar
disc, emitting one thousand rays. He brought that clenched fist down
on the valiant Kumbha's chest. Struck by the fist, the rakshasa swiftly
fell down. His limbs were red,[288] like the sky when its radiance has
dissipated. Kumbha fell down, his chest shattered by the fist. His form
was like that of the earth when it is afflicted by Rudra. He was terrible
in his valour, but was killed in the battle by the bull among the apes.
The earth, with its mountains and forests, trembled. The rakshasas
were filled with greater fear.

Chapter 6(64)

Nikumbha saw that his brother had been brought down
by Sugriva. He glanced at the Indra among the apes, as

---

[288] Because of the blood, with an implicit comparison with the evening sky.

if he would burn him down in rage. The brave one grasped his club, which was like the peak of an excellent mountain. It was auspicious, decorated and plated and was five fingers in width. It was bound in a golden piece of cloth and studded with diamonds and rubies. It was as terrible as Yama's staff and dispelled the fear of the rakshasas. It was like Shakra's standard. In the battle, the immensely energetic Nikumbha, terrible in his valour, seized it and opening his mouth wide, roared. There was golden armour on his chest and armlets on his arms. He was adorned with earrings and decorated with a colourful garland. Because of the radiance of his ornaments and his club, Nikumbha was as resplendent as a cloud, tinged with lightning and a radiant rainbow. The tip of his club thundered like the gust of a storm. It blazed and roared, like a fire without smoke. As the great-souled one whirled his club, it was as if the city with the excellent residences of the gandharvas[289] was whirled around, or Amaravati with all its residences was whirled around. As Nikumbha whirled his club around, it was as if the firmament, with the stars, the planets, the nakshatras, the moon and the giant planets, was also whirled around. As he dazzled and whirled his club around, he became impossible to approach. Nikumbha was blind with rage, like the fire of destruction that arises at the end of a yuga. Because of their fear, the rakshasas and the apes were incapable of moving. However, with his chest bared, the strong Hanumat stood in front of him. His[290] arms were like clubs and his shining club dazzled. The strong one used his strength to bring it down on his chest. The club struck his steady and broad chest and shattered into one hundred fragments. Shattered, it fell down, like hundreds of meteors dislodged from the sky. Struck by the blow of the club, the great ape wavered a little. But he was like a mountain during an earthquake. Struck in this way, Hanumat, supreme among apes and immensely strong, used his strength to clench his fist. The immensely energetic one, like Vayu in valour,

[289] Meaning Alakapuri, Kubera's capital.
[290] Nikumbha's.

raised it and with force and strength, brought it down on the valiant Nikumbha's chest. At this, his skin splintered and blood started to flow. The fist seemed to blaze, like lightning in the sky. Nikumbha trembled because of the blow. However, he recovered and seized the immensely strong Hanumat. In that terrible battle, seeing that Nikumbha had raised the immensely strong Hanumat, the residents of Lanka roared. The son of the wind god was being carried off by Kumbhakarna's son. But he struck him with a fist that possessed the force of the vajra. Hanumat, the son of the wind god, quickly freed himself and flung Nikumbha down on the ground. Making great efforts, he flung Nikumbha down and crushed him. He flung him down with force and leapt on to the valiant one's chest. He seized him with his arms and twisted his head around. He tore off his head and emitted a loud and terrible roar. Suffering, Nikumbha roared in the encounter with the son of the wind god. An extremely terrible battle commenced between Dasharatha's son and the army of the Indra among the rakshasas and it was devastating.

Chapter 6(65)

Hearing that Nikumbha had been killed and Kumbha brought down, Ravana was greatly enraged and blazed like a fire. Because of both anger and sorrow, the nairitta became senseless. He commanded the large-eyed Makaraksha, Khara's son. 'O son! I am instructing you. Take an army with you and go. Slay Raghava and Lakshmana, together with the residents of the forest.' Hearing Ravana's words, Makaraksha, the roamer in the night who was Khara's son, prided himself on his bravery and signified his assent. He greeted Dashagriva and circumambulated him. Obeying Ravana's instructions, the strong one emerged from the auspicious house. The commander of the army was near him and Khara's son addressed him in these words. 'Swiftly bring a chariot and quickly summon the soldiers.' Hearing his words, the roamer in the night who was the commander of the army brought and presented the chariot and the army. The roamer in the night[291] circumambulated the chariot and ascended it. He instructed the charioteer to quickly drive the chariot away. Makaraksha spoke to all the rakshasas. 'O rakshasas! All of you remain in front of me and fight. The great-souled Ravana, the king of the rakshasas, has commanded me to kill Rama and Lakshmana in the battle. O roamers in the night! I will slay Rama and Lakshmana with my excellent arrows today and also the ape Sugriva and the other apes. Today, I will use my spear to bring down the large army of the apes. I will burn down those who approach, like a fire consuming dry kindling.' Hearing Makaraksha's words, the strong roamers in the night controlled themselves and armed themselves with many kinds of weapons. They were cruel and could assume any form at will. They were tawny eyed and armoured. They roared like elephants. With their dishevelled hair, they were fearful. Gigantic in form, they surrounded Khara's son, who was huge in size. They cheerfully attacked and made the earth tremble. Thousands of conch shells and drums were sounded in every direction. A great sound of beating and clapping arose.

The rakshasa's standard fell down violently. The whip was also dislodged from the charioteer's hand. The horses yoked to the chariot lost all their valour. Their feet wavered. They were distressed and there were tears in their eyes. A harsh and extremely terrible wind, mixed with dust, started to blow. This is what happened when the terrible and evil-minded Makaraksha marched out. The rakshasas were terrible in their valour. Despite witnessing these ominous portents, they paid no heed to them. All of them emerged and went to where Rama and Lakshmana were. Their complexions were like dense clouds, elephants and buffaloes. In the forefront of the battle, they had formerly been mangled by clubs and swords. They were accomplished in fighting and exclaimed, 'I', 'I'. As they roamed around, the roamers in the night roared.

[291] Makaraksha.

Chapter 6(66)

The bulls among the apes saw Makaraksha emerge. Desiring to fight, all of them leapt up and stood ready. An extremely great encounter commenced between the roamers in the night and the apes, like that between the gods and the danavas. It made the body hair stand up. They were brought down with trees and spears. They were brought down with clubs and maces. The apes and the roamers in the night crushed each other. In every direction, the roamers in the night used spears, javelins, clubs, swords, spikes, darts, bhindipalas and showers of arrows. With nooses, maces, staffs and other kinds of weapons, the roamers in the night caused carnage amidst the lions among the apes. The apes were afflicted by the torrents of arrows shot by Khara's son. All of them were scared and suffered from fear, resulting in flight. The rakshasas saw that all the residents of the forest were running away. Proud as lions and desiring victory, the rakshasas roared. In every direction, the apes fled. Rama comforted them and countered the rakshasas with a shower of arrows.

On seeing that the rakshasas had been restrained, Makaraksha, the roamer in the night, blazed in anger, like a fire. He spoke these words. 'O Rama! Wait. There will be a duel with me. The sharp arrows shot from my bow will take your life away. You slew my father in Dandakaranya. I remember your deed. On seeing you in front of me, my rage has increased. O evil-souled Raghava! My limbs are on fire, since at that time, I did not see you in the great forest. O Rama! It is good fortune that I am able to see you approach me now. Like a hungry lion that sees a deer, I have been craving for this. Today, the force of my arrows will dispatch you to the kingdom of the dead. You will then meet the brave ones you have killed earlier. O Rama! What is the need to speak much? Listen to my words. In the field of battle, all the worlds will behold me. O Rama! This great battle will use weapons, clubs, arms, or whatever that you are used to fighting with.' Hearing Makaraksha's words, Rama, Dasharatha's son, laughed. He replied in these words, though the other one continued to speak. 'In Dandaka, I killed fourteen thousand rakshasas, your father, Trishira and Dushana. O wicked one! Vultures, jackals and crows will use their sharp beaks, nails and goads[292] today and satisfy themselves with your flesh.'

Khara's son, the roamer in the night, was thus addressed by Rama. In the field of battle, he shot torrents of arrows towards Raghava. Rama severed that shower of arrows with many arrows. Severed, thousands of gold-tufted arrows fell down on the ground. As those two energetic ones clashed against each other, an encounter commenced between the rakshasa who was Khara's son and Dasharatha's son. The sound of bowstrings slapping against palms was like the roar of clouds in the sky. The sound emitted by twanging bows was heard in the field of battle. To witness the extraordinary encounter, all the gods, danavas, gandharvas, kinnaras and giant serpents assembled in the firmament. Though their bodies were pierced, their strength was doubled. In the field of battle, they sought to counter each other's deeds. In the battle, the rakshasa sliced down torrents of arrows that Rama shot. Using innumerable arrows, Rama also severed the arrows the rakshasa shot. All the directions and the sub-directions were covered with arrows. The earth was covered everywhere and nothing could be seen. The mighty-armed Raghava became angry and severed the rakshasa's bow. He used eight iron arrows to pierce his charioteer. Rama used his arrows to shatter his chariot and brought down the horses yoked to the chariot. Deprived of his chariot, Makaraksha, the roamer in the night, stationed himself on the ground. Stationed on the ground, the rakshasa seized a spear in his hand. With a radiance like that of the fire of destruction at the end of a yuga, he terrified all creatures. The roamer in the night whirled that blazing and great spear. In the great battle, he angrily hurled it towards Raghava. Released from the hand of Khara's son, it blazed as it descended. However, with four arrows, Raghava severed the spear in the sky. Decorated with divine gold, that spear was splintered into many parts. Struck by Rama's arrows, it was shattered and fell down on the ground, like a giant meteor. The spear was destroyed

---

[292] That is, claws like goads.

by Rama, the performer of extraordinary deeds. On seeing this, all the beings who were in the firmament uttered words of praise. Makaraksha, the roamer in the night, saw that the spear had been destroyed. He raised his fist and told Kakutstha, 'Wait. Wait.' On seeing him descend, the descendant of the Raghu lineage laughed. He affixed *pavakastra*[293] to his bow. In the battle, Kakutstha killed the rakshasa with this weapon. With his heart shattered, he fell down and died. All the rakshasas saw that Makaraksha had been brought down. Afflicted by their fear of Rama's arrows, they fled to Lanka. Using the force of his arrows, the son of King Dasharatha killed the roamer in the night who was Khara's son. It was as if a mountain had been struck by the vajra and had been shattered. On seeing this, the gods rejoiced.

Chapter 6(67)

Hearing that Makaraksha had been killed, Ravana, the victor in assemblies, was enraged. He instructed his son, Indrajit, to fight. 'O brave one! Slay those two extremely valiant brothers, Rama and Lakshmana. While they can be seen, you will remain invisible. Therefore, you are stronger in every way. You have performed the unrivalled deed of having defeated Indra in a battle. When you see two ordinary humans, how can you not slay them in a battle?' Thus addressed by the Indra among the rakshasas, he accepted his father's words. Following the prescribed rites, Indrajit offered oblations to the fire in the sacrificial ground. As he offered oblations into the fire, rakshasa women respectfully arrived at the spot where Ravana's son was, carrying red headdresses. The weapons were used as beds of reeds. Vibhitaka was offered as kindling. There were red garments and ladles made out of iron. All around the fire, beds of reeds were spread out. He seized a goat that

---

[293] Divine weapon named after Pavaka, the fire god. Therefore, pavakastra is a synonym for agneyastra.

was completely black and alive by the throat.[294] When the kindling was properly offered, the flames arose, without any smoke. The signs that manifested themselves indicated victory. Having accepted the oblations, the fire god himself arose.[295] The flames, which had the complexion of molten gold, circumambulated him. He offered oblations into the fire and satisfied the gods, the danavas and the rakshasas. He ascended the auspicious and excellent chariot that was capable of vanishing. The excellent chariot was yoked to four horses and stocked with sharp arrows. A great bow was placed in it and it was resplendent. With its golden embellishments, its form dazzled. The chariot was decorated with the marks of deer, full moons and half-moons. Indrajit's blazing form was like that of the fire, adorned with a giant necklace that was made out of molten gold. His standard was decorated with lapis lazuli. He was protected by Brahma's weapon, which was like the sun. Ravana's extremely strong son was extremely invincible.

Indrajit, the victor in assemblies, emerged from the city. He had offered oblations into the fire. He had uttered the rakshasa mantras that enabled him to become invisible. He said, 'Today, in the battle, I will kill the two who are false mendicants in the forest.[296] In the supreme encounter, I will give my father, Ravana, victory. I will destroy all apes on earth and kill Rama and Lakshmana. I will cause great delight.' Having said this, he vanished. He angrily descended, urged by Dashagriva's words. Indra's enemy came to the battle with a fierce bow and sharp iron arrows. In the midst of the apes, he saw those two extremely brave ones, like two three-hooded serpents. Those two brave ones were shooting nets of arrows. He thought, 'These are the ones.' He strung his bow and showered down arrows on them, enveloping them, like a cloud showering down rain. With his chariot, he reached the sky and could not be seen with the eyes. Remaining there, he pierced Rama and Lakshmana with sharp arrows. All around, Rama and Lakshmana were enveloped by the force of his arrows. They sought

---

[294] Indrajit seems to have offered the live goat as an offering into the fire.

[295] In personified form.

[296] In the sense that a true mendicant has no use for weapons.

to invoke divine weapons on the arrows on their bows. Those two immensely strong ones covered the sky with their nets of arrows. However, though those arrows were like weapons used by the gods, they could not touch him. He covered the firmament with a darkness that was like smoke. The handsome one enveloped the directions with a dark mist and rendered them invisible. The slap of his bowstring against his palm could not be heard. There was no sound from the axle of his chariot or the hooves of his horses. His movement could not be heard and his form could not be seen. Through that dark and dense cloud, there was the extraordinary downpour of his arrows. The mighty-armed one showered down iron arrows and rained down other arrows. Because of the boon he had obtained, he possessed arrows that were like the sun. Angrily, in the battle, Ravana's son used these to severely pierce Rama everywhere on his body. Like rain showering down on two mountains, those two were struck by floods of iron arrows. Those two tigers among men shot sharp arrows that were gold-tufted. Ravana's son was in the firmament and those arrows, tufted with the feathers of herons, reached and pierced him there. Covered with blood, they fell down on the ground. Those two supreme men were severely afflicted by these floods of arrows. As these descended, they severed them with many broad-headed arrows. Dasharatha's two sons shot their excellent weapons in whatever direction those sharp arrows were seen to descend from. However, Ravana's atiratha son roamed around in all the directions. Skilled in striking the objective, he used his sharp arrows to pierce Dasharatha's two sons. Those two brave ones were severely pierced with gold-tufted arrows that had been crafted well. Dasharatha's two sons looked like blossoming kimshukas. No one knew where he was. No one could see his bow or arrows. Like the sun when it is shrouded in clouds, no one could make out where he was. Pierced by him, the apes were killed and lost their lives. Hundreds of them fell down on the ground.

Extremely angry, Lakshmana addressed his brother in these words. 'To destroy all the rakshasas, I am going to invoke brahmastra.' Rama spoke to Lakshmana, the bearer of auspicious signs. 'For the sake of one, you should not destroy all the rakshasas on earth. You should not kill someone who is not fighting, is hiding, has joined his hands in salutation and is seeking refuge, is running away or is distracted. O immensely strong one! We must make efforts to kill this one alone. We will use immensely forceful weapons that are like venomous serpents. This inferior one uses maya. He is powerful because he is invisible. While all the leaders of the apes look on, this rakshasa will be killed. Whether he enters the ground or the sky, whether he is in the nether regions or in the firmament, irrespective of whether he hides himself, he will be scorched by my weapons. He will lose his life and fall down on the ground.' Surrounded by the bulls among the apes, the great-souled and brave descendant of the Raghu lineage spoke these words. The great-souled one swiftly searched for a means whereby the performer of terrible and cruel deeds might be killed.

Chapter 6(68)

He[297] discerned what was in the great-souled Raghava's mind. He withdrew from the battle and entered his own city. He remembered the deaths of the spirited rakshasas. His eyes coppery red in rage, the brave and immensely radiant one emerged. Surrounded by rakshasas, the immensely valiant Poulastya Indrajit, the thorn of the gods, emerged through the western gate. Indrajit saw those two brothers, Rama and Lakshmana. Those two brave ones were ready to fight. He resolved to use his maya. On his chariot, Indrajit placed an image of Sita that was made out of maya. Surrounded by a large army, he desired to kill her. The extremely evil-minded one made up his mind to confound everyone. In an attempt to kill Sita, he proceeded in the direction of the apes. The residents of the forest saw him emerge from the city. Enraged and desiring to fight, they attacked him, with boulders in their hands. Hanumat, tiger

[297] Indrajit.

among apes, was in the lead. He seized an extremely large peak of a mountain, impossible for others to grasp.

He saw the miserable Sita on Indrajit's chariot. Her hair was in a single braid. She was distressed and because of fasting, her face was emaciated. Raghava's beloved was without ornaments. She was clad in a single faded garment. Though she was the best among women, she was covered in filth and dust all over her body. For a while, he glanced towards her and thought that she was Maithilee. Her face was overflowing with tears. Hanumat was dejected. She did not say anything. She was afflicted by grief. The ascetic lady was devoid of any joy. He saw Sita in the chariot used by the son of the Indra among the rakshasas. The great ape thought, 'What is this?' With the best among the apes, he rushed towards Ravana's son. Seeing the army of the apes, Ravana's son became senseless with rage. He unsheathed his sword and seized Sita by the hair on her head. They saw that woman being oppressed by Ravana's son on the chariot. Because of the maya, she was shrieking, 'Rama! Alas, Rama!' Seeing that she had been seized by the hair, Hanumat was filled with misery. Tears of sorrow flowed from the eyes of the son of the wind god. In his rage, he spoke these harsh words to the son of the lord of the rakshasas. 'O evil-souled one! It is for your own destruction that you have touched a lock of her hair. You have been born in a lineage of *brahmarshi*s,[298] but have resorted to the womb of a rakshasi.[299] Shame on you. Since you possess such an inclination, you are wicked in conduct. You are cruel and ignoble. You are evil in conduct and inferior. Your valour is evil. Such an act is ignoble. You are cruel and there is no compassion in you. Maithilee has been dislodged from her home and her kingdom. She has been dislodged from Rama's arms. O cruel one! What crime has she committed that you wish to slay her? If you kill Sita, you will not remain alive for a long period of time. Because of this deed, you deserve to be killed and you have come into my hands. In this world, those who kill women are condemned and deserve to be

---

[298] A sage with knowledge of the supreme being (brahman).
[299] A reference to Ravana's parentage.

killed by people. You will give up your life in this world and not obtain any fruits after death.' Surrounded by apes with upraised weapons, Hanumat said this. He angrily rushed towards the son of the Indra among the rakshasas.

The immensely valiant army of the residents of the forest descended. Terrible in force, the army of the rakshasas countered them. Agitating the army of the apes with thousands of arrows, Indrajit replied to Hanumat, best among the apes. 'Sugriva, Rama and you came here for her. While you look on, I will kill that Vaidehi today. O ape! After killing her, I will take care of Rama, Lakshmana and you. I will slay Sugriva and the ignoble Vibhishana. O ape! You have said that women should not be killed. However, anything that causes misery to the enemy is a task that should be undertaken.' The Sita made out of maya was weeping. Having said this, Indrajit used his sharp-edged sword to kill her. That ascetic lady was sliced along the trail followed by the sacred thread.[300] The wide-hipped one, beautiful to see, fell down on the ground. Having killed the lady, Indrajit spoke to Hanumat. 'Behold. She was Rama's and I have killed her in my rage.' Indrajit himself killed her with his large sword. He sat cheerfully in his chariot and roared loudly. The apes who were nearby heard this sound. He was impossible to approach. He opened his mouth wide and roared. Thus, the evil-minded one killed Sita. Ravana's son was delighted in his mind. The apes saw his rejoicing form. With miserable appearances, they ran away.

Chapter 6(69)

They heard that terrible roar, which was like the sound of Shakra's vajra. Looking towards him, the bulls among the apes fled in all the directions. Hanumat, the son of the wind god, spoke to all of them. Their faces were dejected. They were miserable

---

[300] The sacred thread slopes down from the left shoulder towards the right. Hence, Sita was diagonally sliced from left to right.

and were separately running away. 'O apes! Why are you running away with dejected faces? Why have you lost all interest in fighting? Where has your bravery gone? I am marching to battle, ahead of you. Follow me at the rear. For brave ones who have been born in noble families, it is not proper to retreat.' Thus addressed by Vayu's intelligent son, they became angry. Delighted in their minds, they seized the summits of mountains and trees. The bulls among the apes roared and descended on the rakshasas. In the great battle, they surrounded and followed Hanumat. In every direction, Hanumat was surrounded by the foremost among the apes. Like a fire with flames, he began to consume the army of the enemy. The extremely large ape created carnage among the rakshasas. Surrounded by the soldiers of the apes, he was like Yama, the Destroyer. The great ape was filled with grief and rage. Hanumat hurled a large boulder towards the chariot of Ravana's son. On seeing it descend towards the chariot, the charioteer urged the well-trained horses and conveyed the chariot far away. The boulder was rendered unsuccessful and penetrated the earth. It could not reach Indrajit, his chariot, or his charioteer. The army of the rakshasas suffered because of the descending rocks. Hundreds of residents of the forest roared and attacked. They held aloft trees and summits of mountains that were gigantic in size. Terrible in their valour, the apes hurled these in the midst of the enemy. The apes were immensely valiant and struck them bravely with trees. The roamers in the night, terrible in form, were injured in the battle. Indrajit saw that his soldiers were afflicted by the apes. He angrily seized his weapons and advanced towards the enemy. Surrounded by his soldiers, he shot torrents of arrows. Firm in his valour, he slew many tigers among the apes. In the battle, his followers used spears, vajras, swords, javelins and heavy clubs to kill apes. The immensely strong Hanumat, terrible in his valour, caused carnage among the rakshasas, using sala trees with trunks and branches and boulders. Repulsing the army of the enemy, Hanumat said, 'O residents of the forest! Let us retreat. We need not strive against this army any more. We fought for the sake of Janaka's daughter. We strove and were ready to give up our lives because we sought to do what would bring Rama pleasure. But she

has been killed. We must inform Rama and Sugriva about this. We
will do what they ask us to do in retaliation.' The best among the
apes spoke to all the apes and restrained them in this way. Gently,
but fearlessly, he returned with his army.

Seeing that Hanumat was headed towards the spot where
Raghava was, Indrajit went to Nikumbhila,[301] to offer oblations
into the fire. Following the prescribed rites, the rakshasa lit the
fire in the sacrificial ground. On devouring the oblations of blood,
the fire blazed up. The flames were seen to be dense, satisfied by
the offerings of blood. Like the sun in the evening, fierce flames
arose. Indrajit knew about the rites. To ensure the prosperity of the
rakshasas, he followed the rites and offered oblations. The rakshasas
knew about what should be done, and what should not be done, at
sacrifices. They watched and stood around in large numbers.

Chapter 6(70)

Hearing the great sound of the battle between the rakshasas
and the residents of the forest, Raghava spoke to Jambavat.
'O amiable one! There is no doubt that Hanumat has performed
an extremely difficult deed. The terrible and extremely loud sound
of fighting can be heard. Therefore, surround yourself with your
own army. Go and help him. Go and quickly help the best among
the apes while he is fighting.' The king of the bears agreed and
surrounded himself with his own army. He approached the western
gate, where the ape Hanumat was. As he was advancing, the lord of
the bears saw Hanumat along the path. He was surrounded by apes
who had fought and were now sighing. Along the path, Hanumat
saw that ready army of bears. It was terrible and was like a dark
cloud. He met it and made it return.

With that army of the apes, the immensely illustrious one swiftly
went to Rama's presence. Miserable, he spoke these words. 'We

---

[301] The sacrificial ground.

were fighting in the battle and saw Indrajit, Ravana's son, kill the
weeping Sita. O slayer of enemies! On seeing this, I was distressed
and my senses were in a whirl. Therefore, I have come to you, to
tell you about what has occurred.' Hearing his words, Raghava
became senseless with grief. He fell down on the ground, like a
tree severed at the roots. Raghava was like a god and he fell down
on the ground. On seeing this, all the excellent apes leapt up and
approached from all directions. They sprinkled him with water that
was fragrant with the scent of lotuses and lilies, just as one sprinkles
an intolerable and consuming fire that has suddenly arisen.

Extremely miserable, Lakshmana engulfed the ailing Rama in
his arms and spoke words that were full of meaning. 'O noble one!
You have remained established on an auspicious path. You have
conquered your senses. But dharma is futile. It cannot save you
from adversities. Dharma is not like mobile and immobile objects
that can be seen. Therefore, it is my view that it does not exist.
Immobile objects are evident and mobile objects are also like that.
Artha is not like that. Otherwise, someone like you would not have
faced this catastrophe. Had adharma led to consequences, Ravana
would have gone to hell. Nor would someone like you, devoted
to dharma, have confronted this adversity. There is no hardship
for him and you have faced this hardship. The fruits of adharma
have become those of dharma and the fruits of dharma have
become those of adharma. If people are not attached to adharma
and unite themselves with dharma, if they follow dharma, they
should obtain the fruits of dharma. For those in whom dharma
is established, artha must be enhanced. But those who follow
dharma are suffering. Therefore, both of them[302] must be futile.
O Raghava! Those who are wicked in their deeds must be killed
because of their adharma. Who will slay the one who has killed
dharma because of his deeds? Perhaps someone follows the
recommended rituals and is killed, or kills someone else instead.
Perhaps this is ascribed to destiny and the person is not affected
by the wicked deed. O afflicter of enemies! How does one counter

---

[302] Dharma and adharma.

destiny? How can one be attached to what is not manifest? How
is one capable of attaining supreme dharma? O foremost among
those who are virtuous! If there is virtue, why are you suffering
from this vice? Why has someone like you faced this calamity?
Perhaps those who are weak in strength and suffer from lack of
virility follow dharma. It is my view that it[303] is weak in strength
and robbed of honour. It should not be served. If dharma is for the
strong, its qualities should manifest themselves in valour. Abandon
dharma and follow the principle that dharma exists where there
is strength. O scorcher of enemies! If dharma is indeed based on
speaking the truth, why did our cruel father bind you down to
a falsehood?[304] O scorcher of enemies! Had dharma or adharma
existed, Shatakratu, the wielder of the vajra, would not have killed
a sage and performed a sacrifice thereafter.[305] O Raghava! Those
who resort to adharma can destroy dharma. O Kakutstha! In
everything, a man does as he wishes. O father![306] O Raghava! It
is my view that dharma lies in this.[307] When you were deprived of
the kingdom, that was the time when dharma was severed at the
roots. Here and there, artha must be accumulated and made to
prosper. All the rites flow from this, like rivers from mountains. A
man who is deprived of artha is limited in energy. All his rites are
destroyed, like a small stream during the summer. A person used to
happiness may desire happiness and abandon artha. However, he
then indulges in evil acts and sins result. A person with artha has
friends. A person with artha has relatives. A person with artha is
a true man in this world. A person with artha is learned. A person
with artha is brave. A person with artha is intelligent. A person
with artha is immensely fortunate. A person with artha possesses
great qualities. I have told you about the great taints that come
about through the abandoning of artha. O brave one! By making

---

[303] Dharma.

[304] By not instating Rama as the heir apparent.

[305] Indra killed a sage named Vishvarupa. This was adharma, but he atoned for it by
performing a sacrifice.

[306] The word used is tata.

[307] In strength.

up your mind to abandon the kingdom, that is what you have done. A person who possesses artha is encircled by dharma, kama and artha. A person without riches cannot desire artha. He is incapable of searching out artha. O lord of men! Everything flows from artha—delight, desire, pride, dharma, anger, tranquility and self-control. If a person follows dharma in this world, but his artha is destroyed, as in you, all those are missing in him, like planets on a bad day. O brave one! Established in the words of your senior, you proceeded on an exile. Your wife, more loved than your own life, was abducted by a rakshasa. O brave one! Thus, today, Indrajit has brought about this great misery on you. O Raghava! Arise. I will dispel it with my deeds. O unblemished one! I will arise for the sake of your beloved. I am enraged at witnessing the death of Janaka's daughter. I will use my terrible arrows to bring down Lanka, with its horses, elephants, chariots and the Indras among the rakshasas.'

Chapter 6(71)

Lakshmana, devoted to his brother, comforted Rama. Instructing the divisions to remain in their places, Vibhishana arrived at the spot. He was surrounded by his four brave advisers, who were wielding many kinds of weapons. They looked like masses of dark collyrium, like a herd of elephants. He approached the great-souled Raghava, who was immersed in his grief. He also saw the apes, with tears streaming from their eyes. He saw the great-souled Raghava, the delight of the Ikshvaku lineage. He was senseless and was lying down on Lakshmana's lap. Vibhishana saw Rama, ashamed and tormented by grief. Distressed in his soul and suffering internally, he asked, 'What is this?' Lakshmana glanced at Vibhishana's face and at Sugriva and the apes. His voice choking with tears, he spoke these words. 'Raghava has heard that Indrajit has killed Sita. O amiable one! Having heard Hanumat's words, he has lost his senses.' As Soumitri was speaking, Vibhishana stopped him. Rama was

senseless, but he addressed him in words that were full of meaning.
'O Indra among men! In an afflicted state, Hanumat told you that.
But I think that what he said is like the ocean drying up. I know the
intention of the evil-souled Ravana. O mighty-armed one! He will
never kill Sita. Desiring his welfare, I beseeched him several times
that he should give up Vaidehi. But he never heeded those words.
It is impossible to see her through sama, bheda, dana, not to speak
of fighting. How could it be possible through any other means?[308]
That rakshasa departed after confounding the apes. He is offering
oblations in the sanctuary named Nikumbhila. On returning, he
will offer oblations and Ravana's son will become unassailable in
battle, even to the gods, with Vasava. That is indeed the reason
why he has used maya and caused confusion. O father![309] He did
not desire an obstruction caused through the valour of the apes.
Before it is completed, we should go there, with our soldiers. O tiger
among men! Cast aside this futile torment that has come over you.
On seeing you afflicted by sorrow, all the forces are suffering. Be
assured. Steady your heart and remain here. Resort to your spirit.
Send Lakshmana with the soldiers who will be summoned. Once
he abandons his task,[310] this tiger among men will slay him with
his sharp arrows. His arrows are sharp and fierce, with a speed
like that in the wings of birds. The arrows of this amiable one are
like birds and will drink his blood. O mighty-armed one! Instruct
Lakshmana for the destruction of the rakshasa, like the wielder of
the vajra using his vajra. He possesses the auspicious signs. O best
among men! There is no time to waste. One must now do whatever
is necessary to slay the enemy. Therefore, tell him that he should
kill the enemy. Release him, like the great Indra crushing the city
of the asuras. If he finishes his sacrifice, the Indra among rakshasas
will be invisible to gods and asuras. If he fights after completing his
sacrifice, there will be a great danger to even the gods.'

---

[308] The sense seems to be that it would have been impossible for Indrajit to bring Sita
out in public.
[309] The word used is tata.
[310] The sacrifice.

Chapter 6(72)

Afflicted by grief, Raghava heard these words. He was unable to clearly comprehend what the rakshasa had said. Rama, the victor of enemy cities, then resorted to his fortitude. He spoke to Vibhishana, who was seated near the apes. 'O lord of the nairittas! O Vibhishana! I wish to again hear the words that you have spoken. Tell me what you want.' Hearing Raghava's words, Vibhishana, eloquent in the use of words, carefully repeated the words again. 'O mighty-armed one! As you had instructed, I arranged the forces in different divisions. O brave one! I followed your words and progressively stationed them. In every direction, the entire army was apportioned out. The leaders and the others were properly laid out in separate parts. O immensely illustrious one! Listen to something else that I have to report. Because you are needlessly tormented, our hearts are also tormented. O king! Abandon this grief and the false torment that has come upon you. Abandon the worries that only enhance the delight of the enemy. O brave one! Be cheerful and exert yourself if you wish to obtain Sita and slay the roamers in the night. O descendant of the Raghu lineage! I am speaking to you. Listen to my beneficial words. It is best that Soumitri should surround himself with a large army and go there. He should reach Nikumbhila and kill Ravana's son in a battle, using arrows that are like venomous serpents, released from the circle of his bow. The great archer, the victor in assemblies, will kill Ravana's son with his arrows. Because of his austerities, that brave one has obtained a boon from Svayambhu. He has obtained the Brahmashira weapon and horses that can go wherever they want. "O Indra's enemy! If an enemy strikes you before you have reached Nikumbhila and before you have offered oblations into the fire, the person who strikes you will be the cause of your death."[311] O king! This is what the intelligent one ordained as a means of his death. O Rama! For the sake of killing Indrajit, command a large army. When he has been killed, know that Ravana and the large number of his well-wishers will also have been killed.'

[311] This is what Brahma told Indrajit.

Hearing Vibhishana's words, Rama spoke these words. 'O one who has truth as his valour! I know about his terrible maya. He is wise and knows about the use of brahmastra. He is immensely strong and great in his use of maya. In a battle, he can render the gods, together with Varuna, unconscious. On his chariot, the immensely illustrious one roams around in the firmament, invisible. O brave one! One cannot discern his movement, like the sun when it is enveloped in clouds.' Knowing about the valour and maya of the evil-souled enemy, Raghava addressed Lakshmana, who was accomplished in his deeds, in the following words. 'Surround yourself with the entire army of the Indra among the apes. O Lakshmana! Be with the leaders of the herds, with Hanumat at the forefront. Surround yourself with the soldiers of Jambavat, the lord of the bears. The son of the rakshasa possesses the strength of maya. Kill him. This great-souled roamer in the night knows about his maya. With his advisers, he will follow you at the rear.'

Hearing Raghava's words, Lakshmana, terrible in his valour, seized his excellent bow, accompanied by Vibhishana. He bound his armour, wielding a sword. He held arrows and a golden bow. Touching Rama's feet, Soumitri cheerfully said, 'Today, arrows will be released from my bow and piercing Ravana's son, will descend into Lanka, the way swans enter a pond. Today, my arrows will be released from the string of this great bow and pierce his terrible body, devastating him.' He spoke these words before his radiant elder brother. Having worshipped at his senior's feet, he circumambulated him. He then left for the Nikumbhila sanctuary, protected by Ravana's son. Having heard the benedictions from his brother, Lakshmana, the powerful prince, quickly left, together with Vibhishana. Hanumat was surrounded by many thousands of apes and with Vibhishana's advisers, followed Lakshmana. He[312] left with speed, surrounded by a large army of soldiers of the apes. Along the path, he saw that the army of the king of the bears was also stationed. Soumitri, the delight of his friends, travelled a long distance. From a distance, he saw the army of the Indra among the

---

[312] Lakshmana.

rakshasas, arrayed in the form of a vyuha. The scorcher of enemies reached, with the bow in his hand. Following Brahma's dictum, the descendant of the Raghu lineage was ready to defeat the one who invoked maya. The army of the enemy possessed many kinds of sparkling and radiant weapons. It was thick with standards and dense with large chariots. It was immeasurable in force and caused fear. It was like darkness, but he penetrated it.

Chapter 6(73)

In that situation, Ravana's younger brother[313] addressed Lakshmana in meaningful words that would ensure his success and cause injury to the enemy. 'O Lakshmana! Make efforts to break this large army. When it is shattered, the son of the Indra among the rakshasas will become visible. Shower down excellent arrows that are like Indra's vajra on the enemy. Quickly attack, before he accomplishes the sacrifice. O brave one! Slay the evil-souled one. Ravana's son is cruel in his deeds and causes fear to all the worlds.'

Hearing Vibhishana's words, Lakshmana, the possessor of the auspicious signs, showered down arrows in the direction of the son of the Indra among the rakshasas. Bears and apes, fighting with trees and excellent boulders, collectively attacked that army. Desiring to kill the soldiers of the apes, the rakshasas countered and attacked with sharp arrows, swords, spears and javelins. There was a tumultuous engagement between the apes and the rakshasas. A large sound was heard everywhere around Lanka. Enveloped with many kinds of weapons, sharp arrows, trees and raised summits of mountains, the sky looked terrible. In the encounter, the rakshasas, with malformed faces, hurled down weapons and created an extremely great fear among the apes. In a similar way, all the apes used trees and the summits of mountains to strike and kill the bulls

---

[313] Vibhishana.

among the rakshasas in the encounter. The foremost among the bears and the apes were gigantic in size and extremely strong. The rakshasas were slaughtered by them and a great fear was instilled in them.

Hearing that his own army was distressed and afflicted by the enemy, the invincible one[314] arose, without completing the sacrifice. With rage generated in him, Ravana's son emerged from amidst the trees and the darkness. The rakshasa mounted the chariot that had already been yoked and kept ready. He was like a mass of black collyrium and his bow and arrows were terrible. He was cruel and his mouth and eyes were red. He was like Death, the destroyer. On seeing him astride the chariot, the army of rakshasas, terrible in their force, returned, to fight with Lakshmana. Hanumat was like a mountain and extremely unassailable. At that time, the slayer of enemies seized a gigantic tree. He burnt down the soldiers of the rakshasas, like the fire of destruction. In the battle, the ape rendered many unconscious with that tree. The rakshasas saw that the spirited son of the wind god was destroying them. Thousands of them obstructed Hanumat. They wielded sharp spears and had javelins and swords in their hands. There were swords. Those with spears in their hands fought with spears. Those with javelins in their hands fought with javelins. There were maces, clubs and spikes that were auspicious to behold. There were hundreds of shataghnis and bludgeons that were made out of iron. The rakshasas used terrible battleaxes and bhindipalas. The force of the fists was like that of the vajra. The palms were like the vajra. From every direction, they advanced and attacked the one who was like a mountain, while he angrily created great carnage among them.

Indrajit saw that the best among the apes was like a mountain. The son of the wind god, the slayer of enemies, was killing the enemy. He told the charioteer, 'Take me to the spot where the ape is. If he is ignored, he will cause destruction to the rakshasas.' Thus addressed, the charioteer went to the spot where Maruti was. On the chariot,

---

[314] Indrajit.

he bore along the extremely invincible Indrajit. Approaching, the
rakshasa showered down arrows, swords, javelins, cutlasses and
battleaxes on the ape's head. Maruti received all those terrible
weapons. Overcome by great rage, he spoke these words. 'O evil-
minded son of Ravana! If you are brave, fight. If you approach
the son of the wind god, you will not return with your life. O evil-
minded one! In this battle, if you wish to have a duel with me, fight
with your arms and withstand me. You will then be supreme among
the rakshasas.' In a desire to slay Hanumat, Ravana's son raised his
bow and arrow. Vibhishana told Lakshmana, 'This is Ravana's son
and he has vanquished Vasava. He is now stationed on his chariot
and desires to kill Hanumat. Your arrows are unmatched and are
capable of shattering the enemy. O Soumitri! They are terrible and
can bring an end to life. Slay Ravana's son with these.' The great-
souled Vibhishana, who caused fright to the enemy, said this. He
saw that the invincible one, resembling a mountain and terrible in
his strength, was mounted on his chariot.

Chapter 6(74)

When Vibhishana said this, Soumitri was filled with delight.
He grasped a bow in his hand and quickly left. Having gone
a short distance away, he entered a large forest. Vibhishana showed
Lakshmana the ongoing sacrifice. Ravana's energetic brother
showed Lakshmana an extremely terrible nyagrodha that was like
a dark cloud. 'This is the spot where Ravana's strong son renders
offerings to creatures. After they have accepted these, he goes out
to fight. Thereafter, the rakshasa becomes invisible to all creatures.
He uses his excellent arrows to bind enemies down in the battle and
kill them. Ravana's strong son has not yet entered the nyagrodha.
Use your sharp arrows to destroy him, his charioteer, his horses
and his chariot.' The immensely energetic Soumitri, the delight of
his friends, agreed. He stood there, stretching his colourful bow.
Ravana's strong son was on a chariot that had the complexion of

the fire. Indrajit was armoured, with a sword and a standard. He showed himself.

The immensely energetic one spoke to the unvanquished Poulastya. 'In this encounter, I am challenging you. Give me a good fight.' Ravana's spirited and extremely energetic son was addressed in this way. On seeing Vibhishana there, he spoke these harsh words. 'You were born and reared here. You are my father's brother. O rakshasa! You are my paternal uncle. How can you cause injury to a son? O one with evil intelligence! Kinship, affection and relationships do not exist in you. There is no sign of fraternal affection. O defiler of dharma! There is no dharma in you. O one with evil intelligence! You are a person to be grieved over. You should be condemned by the virtuous. You have abandoned your own relatives and have become a servant to the enemy. This is not good behaviour or intelligence. You do not comprehend the great difference. How can one compare residence with one's relatives to the inferior state of seeking refuge with the enemy? Others may possess qualities and one's own relatives may be devoid of qualities. But relatives who are devoid of qualities are superior. An enemy is always an enemy. O roamer in the night! O Ravana's younger brother! Only a harsh person like you is capable of showing this ruthlessness towards your own relatives.' Thus addressed by his brother's son, Vibhishana replied, 'O rakshasa! Why are you indulging in self-praise? You do not seem to be aware of my good conduct. O son of the Indra among the rakshasas! O wicked one! Abandon the harshness that comes from insolence. I have been born in the lineage of rakshasas, the perpetrators of cruel deeds. However, the qualities and conduct that exist in me are primarily those of humans, not those of rakshasas. I find no pleasure in being terrible. I do not take delight in adharma. If a brother indulges in wicked conduct, how can such a brother be restrained? If a person indulges in stealing another person's possessions, if a person touches another person's wife and if a person does not trust his well-wishers—these three sins can bring about destruction. The terrible slaying of maharshis, the conflict with all the gods, arrogance, anger, enmity and perversity—these sins will destroy my brother's life and prosperity. They envelop and shroud his qualities, like clouds do to mountains. Because of these taints, my brother, your father, has been abandoned by me. The city of Lanka, you, and your father, will no longer exist. You are extremely insolent. You are childish. You are arrogant. O rakshasa! You are bound in the noose of destiny. Tell me whatever you wish. You are now facing a catastrophe here. Why are you speaking to me? O worst of rakshasas! You are incapable of entering the nyagrodha. The two Kakutsthas will oppress you and you are incapable of remaining alive. In this encounter, fight with Lakshmana, god among men. When you have been killed, you will perform the work of the gods in Yama's eternal abode. Raise yourself and exhibit your own strength. Use all the weapons and the inexhaustible arrows. Having come within the reach of Lakshmana's arrows today, you and your army will no longer remain alive.'

Chapter 6(75)

Hearing Vibhishana's words, Ravana's son became senseless with rage. He spoke harsh words and attacked forcefully. On the well-ornamented and giant chariot, yoked to black horses, he held up his weapons and sword. He was stationed, like Death. He was lofty and giant in size. His force was extensive and firm. He touched his terrible bow and the arrows that destroyed enemies. Extremely angry, he spoke to Soumitri, Vibhishana and the tigers among the apes, 'Behold my valour. Today, showers of invincible arrows will be released from my bow. Released, they will pour down in the encounter, like water from the sky. Today, arrows will be released from my large bow. They will destroy bodies, like fire does a mass of cotton. Sharp arrows, spears, javelins, swords and spikes will mangle you. Today, all of you will leave for Yama's eternal abode. In the battle, the dexterity of my hands will shoot torrents of arrows. I will roar like a cloud. Who will stand before me?'

Lakshmana heard the Indra among rakshasas roaring. With a fearless face, he angrily addressed Ravana's son in these words. 'O rakshasa! You have spoken about accomplishing the task of crossing over to the unapproachable distant shore. But the intelligent person is one who accomplishes the task of crossing over to the distant shore. O evil-minded one! You think you have accomplished the objective. But you have not accomplished it and the objective is extremely difficult to reach. Know that it cannot be accomplished through words alone. Be successful first. At that time, you followed the path of becoming invisible. But that is a path resorted to by thieves. It is not something that is patronized by brave people. O rakshasa! I have come and am stationed within range of your arrows. Demonstrate your energy today. Why are you indulging in words of self-praise?'

Having been thus addressed, the immensely strong Indrajit, the victor in assemblies, touched his terrible bow and shot sharp arrows. He released extremely forceful arrows that were like venomous serpents. They reached Lakshmana and fell down, sighing like serpents. In the battle, Indrajit, Ravana's son, pierced Lakshmana, who possessed the auspicious signs, with extremely swift and forceful arrows. His limbs were severely pierced by the arrows and blood started to flow. The handsome Lakshmana was resplendent, like a fire without smoke. Indrajit reflected on the deed he had achieved. He approached, roared loudly and spoke these words. 'O Soumitri! These arrows are sharp at the edges and have been shot from my bow. They can take lives away. They will now take away your life. O Lakshmana! When you lose your life and are killed by me today, herds of jackals and flocks of hawks and vultures will descend on you. The extremely evil-minded Rama is always a friend to kshatriyas, but is always ignoble. You are his devoted brother and he will see that you have been slain by me today. Your armour will be shattered and will fall down on the ground. Your bow will be fragmented. O Soumitri! Your head will be severed. You will be slain by me today.'

Angry, Ravana's son spoke these harsh words. Lakshmana, who knew about the meanings behind words, replied in words that were full of reasoning. 'O rakshasa! Why are you praising a deed you have not yet accomplished? Perform an act so that I can have faith in your self-praise. I will not speak any harsh words, nor will I abuse you in any way. O worst among beings! Behold. Without indulging in self-praise, I will kill you.' Having said this, Lakshmana affixed five iron arrows and drawing the bow back all the way up to his ear, struck the rakshasa on the chest with great force. Struck by those arrows, Ravana's son became angry. He aimed three arrows properly and pierced Lakshmana back. As they sought to slay each other, there ensued an extremely terrible and tumultuous clash in the battle between the lion among men and the lion among rakshasas. Both of them were full of strength. Both of them were valiant. Both of them were extremely brave. Both of them were accomplished in the use of all weapons. Both of them were extremely difficult to vanquish. Both of them were equal in strength and energy. Those two extremely brave ones fought, like two planets engaging in the firmament. Those two were impossible to assail and they fought like Bala and Vritra.[315] Those two great-souled ones fought like maned lions. Stationed there, those two shot arrows along many paths. The lion among men and the lion among rakshasas fought cheerfully. The supreme man and the supreme rakshasa were exceedingly happy. They wielded their bows and arrows, desiring victory. They severely showered down floods of arrows on each other, like clouds pouring down rain.

Chapter 6(76)

Dasharatha's son, the slayer of enemies, affixed an arrow and angrily shot it towards the Indra among rakshasas, sighing like a serpent. Ravana's son heard the noise of the palm slap against the bowstring. With his face pale, he glanced towards Lakshmana. Vibhishana saw that the face of the rakshasa who was Ravana's

---

[315] That is, Indra and Vritra.

son had turned pale. Soumitri was engaged in fighting and he spoke
to him. 'I can see the signs in Ravana's son. O mighty-armed one!
There is no doubt that he will be broken quickly.' At this, Soumitri
affixed arrows that were like the flames of the fire. He shot these
sharp arrows, like snakes emerging from their holes. Lakshmana's
arrows were like Shakra's vajra to the touch. Struck by these, he
was benumbed for a while and his senses were agitated. He regained
consciousness after some time and his senses recovered. The brave
one saw that Dasharatha's brave son was stationed there.

His eyes red with rage, he approached Soumitri. Having
approached, he again addressed him in harsh words. 'Do you not
remember my valour in the first encounter? In the encounter, you
and your brother were bound down and were writhing. My arrows
were like Shakra's vajra. In that first great battle, with all your
companions, you were lying down on the ground, unconscious. I
think that you do not retain any memory of that, or perhaps you
desire to go to Yama's abode. That is the reason you wish to attack
me. If you have not witnessed my valour in that first encounter, I will
show it to you today. Steady yourself now.' Saying this, he pierced
Lakshmana with seven arrows and used ten sharp-edged and excellent
arrows to strike Hanumat. With his rage doubled, he angrily used
one hundred well-aimed arrows to pierce the valiant Vibhishana. On
seeing what Indrajit had done, Rama's younger brother paid no heed
to it. He laughed and said, 'This is a trifle.' The bull among men
affixed and released terrible arrows. In the battle, with no fear on his
face, Lakshmana angrily shot these at Ravana's son. 'O roamer in
the night! Brave ones who come to fight do not strike like this. These
arrows of yours are light, limited in valour and pleasant. In a battle,
brave ones who seek victory do not fight like this.' Saying this, he
showered down arrows. Shattered by the arrows, a gold-embellished
armour was fragmented and fell down on the floor of the chariot,
like a net of stars dislodged from the sky. In the battle, the brave
Indrajit's armour was shattered by iron arrows and he was wounded.
But he was as firm as a mountain. As they engaged in that tumultuous
battle, they sighed and glanced at each other. All their limbs were
pierced by arrows and blood started to flow. They repeatedly

exhibited their excellence in use and knowledge of weapons. The high
and low trajectories of their arrows traced patterns in the sky. They
shot arrows with dexterity, aimed well and colourfully, without any
blemishes. Both of them, the man and the rakshasa, were terrible and
fierce. The terrible sounds of their palms slapping could be separately
heard. It was like the extremely terrible sound of thunderous clouds
in the sky. In the battle, gold-tufted arrows descended on their bodies.
Smeared with blood, they emerged again and penetrated the ground.
There were other extremely sharp weapons that clashed against each
other in the sky. Thousands of their arrows clashed and severed
each other. Piles of arrows accumulated in that terrible battle. They
resembled piles of blazing kusha grass at a sacrifice dedicated to the
fire. With wounds in their bodies, those two great-souled ones were
resplendent. They looked like blossoming *shalmali* and kimshuka
trees in the forest, devoid of leaves. Terrible and tumultuous clashes
repeatedly took place as Indrajit and Lakshmana sought to triumph
over each other. In the battle, Lakshmana struck Ravana's son and
Ravana's son struck Lakshmana. They struck each other and neither
suffered from exhaustion. Nets of arrows deeply pierced the bodies
of those two spirited ones. Those two immensely brave ones were
as radiant as mountains with emanating peaks. Severely wounded
by the arrows, they were smeared with blood. They dazzled in all
their limbs and were like blazing fires. As they fought against each
other, a long period of time elapsed. However, in the forefront of that
encounter, neither of them suffered from exhaustion.

Lakshmana had never been defeated in the field of battle. To
dispel any exhaustion he might suffer in the encounter, Vibhishana
arrived at the spot where the clash was taking place. The immensely
energetic one spoke agreeable and beneficial words.

Chapter 6(77)

On seeing that the man and the rakshasa were engaged with
each other and fighting, Ravana's brave brother presented

himself in the field of battle. He stood there and stretched his
giant bow, shooting large arrows, sharp at the tips, towards the
rakshasas. Well-aimed, those arrows, which were like flames
to the touch, descended. They shattered the rakshasas, like
the vajra shatters a large mountain. Vibhishana's companions,
supreme among rakshasas, used spears, javelins and swords to
sever brave rakshasas in the battle. Vibhishana was surrounded
by those rakshasas and looked like an elephant amidst proud
young tuskers. The apes loved to fight with the rakshasas. At
that time, the supreme among rakshasas, who knew about time,
urged them with these words. 'Stationed here is the only refuge
for the Indra among rakshasas. This is all that remains of his
army. O lords among the apes! Why are you waiting? When this
wicked rakshasa is killed in the forefront of the battle, with the
exception of Ravana, all the rest of his army will be destroyed. The
brave Prahasta has been killed and so has the immensely strong
Nikumbha. So have Kumbhakarna, Kumbha and Dhumraksha, the
roamer in the night. So have Akampana, Suparshva, the rakshasa
Chakramali, Kampana, Sattvavanta, Devantaka and Narantaka.
These extremely strong ones, many supreme rakshasas, have been
killed. When one has used one's arms to swim across the ocean and
cross it, this puddle[316] is a trifle. O apes! Only this much remains
to be defeated. All the rakshasas who approached, insolent of their
strength, have been killed. For Rama's sake, I will cast aside all
compassion and kill my brother's son. However, it is not proper
to kill a son one has given birth to.[317] Even if I desire to kill him,
the tears in my eyes will be an impediment. That is the reason the
mighty-armed Lakshmana must pacify him. O apes! Slay all those
of his servants who dare to approach.' They were thus urged by
that illustrious rakshasa. The Indras among apes were delighted
and lashed their tails. The tigers among apes roared repeatedly.
They uttered many kinds of sounds, like peacocks when they catch
sight of clouds.

[316] Goshpada.
[317] Though Indrajit is his brother's son, he is like a son.

Jambavat was surrounded by all of his own herds. They attacked the rakshasas with rocks, nails and teeth. The lord of the bears struck them and abandoning their fear, the immensely strong rakshasas surrounded him, with many kinds of weapons. In the battle, Jambavat was slaying the soldiers of the rakshasas and they attacked him with arrows, sharp battleaxes, javelins, staffs and spears. There was a tumultuous clash between the apes and the rakshasas, like the angry battle between the gods and the asuras. There was a loud and terrible noise. Enraged, Hanumat uprooted a sala tree from the mountain. He clashed against thousands of rakshasas and created carnage. In the battle, Indrajit had a tumultuous duel with his paternal uncle. The slayer of brave enemies then attacked Lakshmana again.

Those two brave ones, Lakshmana and the rakshasa, fought in the battle. Desiring to kill each other, they showered down floods of arrows. Those two extremely strong ones glanced at each other and covered each other with nets of arrows, just as swift clouds envelop the moon and the sun at the end of the summer. Because of their dexterity in the use of their hands, the acts of picking up the bow, affixing an arrow, aiming it, releasing it, stretching the bow, shooting the arrow, adjusting the hold or striking the target could not be seen. In every direction, there were nets of arrows, shot powerfully from the bows. The sky was covered and nothing could be seen. Everything was covered in great darkness and it seemed to be even more terrible. The wind did not blow then and the fire did not blaze. The maharshis exclaimed, 'May all be well with the worlds.' The gandharvas and the charanas came and assembled there.

The lion among rakshasas possessed four black horses adorned with gold. Soumitri used four arrows to pierce these four horses. As his charioteer was driving around, the dexterous Raghava used another broad-headed arrow to sever his handsome head from his body. Ravana's son saw that his charioteer had been slain in the battle. He was distressed and lost his cheer in the battle. The leaders of the apes saw that the rakshasa had distress written on his face. They were extremely delighted and worshipped Lakshmana. Four lords of the apes—Pramathi, Sharabha, Rabhasa and Gandhamadana, became intolerant and attacked powerfully. Those apes quickly leapt on to his excellent horses. Those four extremely brave ones, terrible in their valour, descended there. The apes, resembling mountains, stood on the backs of the horses and because of the pressure, blood started to flow from their mouths. The maharatha's horses were crushed and killed. With force, they[318] then leapt up and came to Lakshmana's side. His horses had been killed. His chariot had been crushed. His charioteer had been killed. However, Ravana's son showered down arrows and attacked Soumitri. Lakshmana was like the great Indra. He shot sharp and excellent arrows at the one who was on foot. He[319] also shot sharp and excellent arrows and he[320] countered them with his fierce storm of arrows.

Chapter 6(78)

With his horses slain, the immensely energetic roamer in the night was stationed on the ground. Indrajit became extremely angry and blazed in his energy. Those two archers wished to kill each other and shot fierce arrows. They were like two bull elephants in the forest, emerging in search of victory over each other. The rakshasas and the residents of the forest devastated each other. Here and there, they attacked each other, but did not forsake their masters in the battle. He resorted to his great dexterity and aiming towards Lakshmana, showered down arrows, like Purandara showering down rain. Indrajit shot these showers of arrows that were extremely difficult to repulse. However, Lakshmana, the slayer of enemies, fearlessly countered them. Ravana's son formed the view that Lakshmana was clad in impenetrable armour. Extremely angry, and displaying his dexterity in using weapons, Indrajit therefore pierced Lakshmana in the forehead with three well-tufted

[318] The four apes.
[319] Indrajit.
[320] Lakshmana.

arrows. With those arrows adhering to his forehead, the descendant of the Raghu lineage was resplendent. He took pride in fighting and in the forefront of the battle, he looked like a mountain with three peaks. In the great battle, he was afflicted by the rakshasa's arrows. Swiftly, Lakshmana struck him back with five arrows. Lakshmana and Indrajit were brave and possessed extremely strong bows. Terrible in their valour, they struck each other with sharp arrows. Those two archers clashed against each other, and desiring victory over each other, pierced each other's bodies with arrows everywhere.

Vibhishana became extremely angry and killed his horses.[321] He struck him in the chest with five arrows that were like the vajra to the touch. Those gold-tufted arrows reached their target and penetrated his body. They were smeared with blood and looked like giant red serpents. The immensely strong Indrajit became angry with his paternal uncle and attacked him in the midst of the excellent rakshasas, using an arrow given by Yama. The immensely energetic Lakshmana saw that he had picked up that great arrow and, terrible in his valour, picked up another arrow. In a dream, Kubera, immeasurable in his soul, had himself given him this. It was impossible to vanquish and impossible to withstand, even for Indra, the gods and the asuras. At the same time, those two excellent arrows were affixed to the excellent bows. As those two brave ones stretched them, they blazed in their great radiance. As those two arrows were released from their bows, they illuminated the sky. With great energy, the points struck each other and fell down. They crashed against each other like giant planets and fell down. In the battle, they shattered into a hundred fragments and fell down on the ground. Both of them saw that their arrows had been repulsed in the field of battle. Both Lakshmana and Indrajit were ashamed, but anger was generated in them. Angry, Soumitri affixed Varuna's weapon. In the battle, Indrajit stationed himself and released

---

[321] By excising shlokas, the Critical Edition breaks continuity. Indrajit's horses have already been killed. In the excised shlokas, Indrajit returns to Lanka and comes back with another chariot and horses. While fighting against Lakshmana, he then attacks Vibhishana. Those shlokas have also been excised.

Rudra's great weapon. There was an extremely tumultuous and wonderful clash. The beings who were in the firmament surrounded Lakshmana. A fearful and terrible engagement continued between the apes and the rakshasas. The many beings who were in the sky were astounded and gathered around. In the battle, the rishis, the ancestors, the gods, the gandharvas, Garuda and the serpents, with Shatakratu at the forefront, protected Lakshmana.

Raghava's brave younger brother affixed another excellent arrow that was like fire to the touch and would prove to be extremely terrible for Ravana's son. It was well tufted, with a rounded frame and excellent joints. It had been crafted well. The arrow was decorated with gold and would bring an end to the body. It was impossible to counter and impossible to withstand. It caused great fear to rakshasas. It was excellent, like venomous poison. It was worshipped in assemblies of the gods. In ancient times, in the battle between the gods and the asuras, the immensely energetic lord Shakra, borne by tawny steeds, had used this for victory over the danavas. In the battle, Soumitri invoked the unvanquished aindrastra. The best among men affixed this excellent arrow to the excellent bow. He affixed the arrow that could crush the enemy to the bow. The invincible one readied himself, like the Destroyer at the time of the destruction of the worlds. Lakshmana possessed the auspicious qualities. He affixed it to his excellent bow, drew it back and spoke meaningful words that were meant to accomplish his objective. 'If Rama has dharma in his soul, if he is devoted to the truth, if he is Dasharatha's son and if he is unmatched in his manliness, then slay Ravana's son.'[322] In the battle, the brave Lakshmana drew the bow all the way back up to his ear and released the arrow towards Indrajit. Lakshmana, the slayer of enemy heroes, invoked aindrastra. Indrajit's handsome head was clad in a helmet and was adorned with earrings. The head was severed from the body and fell down on the ground. The rakshasa's giant head was severed from his shoulders. It was seen on the ground, shining like gold and covered in blood. Slain, Ravana's son swiftly fell down on

---

[322] This is addressed to the arrow.

the ground. His armour and helmet were shattered and his bow was fragmented.

With Vibhishana, all the apes roared in joy at his death, just as the gods had when Vritra had been killed. In the firmament, the gods, the great-souled rishis and the gandharvas and the apsaras pronounced chants of victory. The large army of the rakshasas saw that he had fallen down. They were slaughtered by the apes who desired victory and fled in different directions. The rakshasas were slaughtered by the apes and cast aside their weapons. Deprived of their senses, all of them rushed towards Lanka. Terrified, many hundreds of rakshasas fled in different directions. All of them abandoned their weapons, the spears and the battleaxes. Afflicted by the apes, some were frightened and entered Lanka. Some fell down in the ocean and some sought refuge in the mountain. They saw that Indrajit was lying down, having been killed in the battle. Among the thousands of rakshasas, none could be seen. When the sun sets, its rays no longer remain. Like that, when he fell down, the rakshasas set in different directions. The rays of the sun had been pacified. The fire had been put out. The immensely energetic one had departed and his life had set. When the son of the Indra among the rakshasas fell down, many sufferings of the world were pacified and enemies who had been destroyed rejoiced. With the illustrious Shakra, all the bulls among the gods were delighted. The rakshasa, the perpetrator of wicked deeds, had been killed. The sky and the water were purified and the daityas and danavas rejoiced. Someone who had caused fear to all the worlds had fallen down.

Together, all the gods, the gandharvas and the danavas said, 'May the brahmanas roam around, devoid of anxiety and with all the sins cleansed.' The bull among the nairittas was supreme in his strength. On seeing that he had been slain in the battle, the leaders of the apes were delighted and applauded this. Vibhishana, Hanumat and Jambavat, the leader of herds of bears, were delighted at the victory and praised Lakshmana. The bulls among the apes leapt, shouted and roared. With the objective having been attained, they surrounded the descendant of the Raghu lineage. The apes lashed

their tails and slapped themselves. They exclaimed, 'Lakshmana
has been victorious.' Delighted in their minds, the apes embraced
each other. They conversed with each other about Raghava's many
qualities. The gods saw and heard that their beloved well-wisher,
Lakshmana, had accomplished an extremely difficult task in the
battle. They were happy and their minds were filled with great
delight, on hearing that Indra's enemy had been killed.

Chapter 6(79)

Lakshmana, the possessor of auspicious qualities, was covered
with blood all over his body. But he was delighted at having
been able to kill Shakrajit in the battle. The immensely energetic one
returned with Jambavat, the valiant Hanumat and all the residents
of the forest. Lakshmana leant on Vibhishana and Hanumat and
quickly reached the spot where Sugriva and Raghava were. Soumitri
greeted Rama and approached him. He drew near his brother,
just as Indra's younger brother[323] approaches Shakra. The brave
one told him that the terrible Indrajit had been killed. Delighted,
Vibhishana informed Rama that the great-souled Lakshmana had
severed the head of Ravana's son. He made him sit down on his lap
and embraced the injured one. He inhaled the fragrance of his head
and repeatedly touched him. The bull among men spoke these words
of assurance to Lakshmana. 'You have performed a supremely
beneficial deed, one that is extremely difficult to accomplish.
Since Ravana will emerge, I will be freed of my enemies today. On
hearing that his son has been brought down, he will come with a
large army with battle formations. The lord of the rakshasas will be
tormented by grief because his son has been killed and will emerge.
He will surround himself with a large army and will be difficult
to vanquish. But I will kill him. You have killed Shakrajit in the
battle today. O Lakshmana! With you as my protector, and of Sita

---

[323] Vishnu.

and this earth, nothing is very difficult for me to obtain.' Raghava comforted his brother and embraced him.

Happy, Rama addressed Sushena in these words. 'O immensely wise one! Soumitri is devoted to his friends and he is suffering from these wounds. Act so that he can be happy and well soon. Act quickly, so that Soumitri and Vibhishana are cured of their wounds. The brave soldiers of the bears and the apes fight with trees. There are others who have fought and are suffering from wounds and stakes. Make all the efforts so that they can be happy and well soon.' The leader of the apes was thus addressed by the great-souled Rama. Through the nose, Sushena gave Lakshmana a supreme medicine. Once he had inhaled its fragrance, all his wounds were healed. His pain was gone and all his injuries were cured. Following Raghava's command, he[324] also treated Vibhishana, best among the well-wishers, and all the other foremost apes. Soumitri attained his natural state. His wounds were healed and his pain was gone. In a short while, his fever disappeared and he was happy. Rama saw that the lord of the apes, Vibhishana, Jambavat, the lord of the bears, and Soumitri were hale and had got up, freed from injuries. With the soldiers, he rejoiced for a long period of time. Dasharatha's great-souled son worshipped the extremely difficult task that had been accomplished by Lakshmana. On hearing that Shakrajit had been brought down in the battle, the Indras among the herds rejoiced.

Chapter 6(80)

Poulastya's advisers heard that Indrajit had been killed. Distressed, they went and told Dashagriva the news. 'O great king! O immensely radiant one! In the battle, your son has been killed by Lakshmana, with Vibhishana's help, while all of us looked on. When he engaged in fighting, the brave one was invincible in encounters. Indrajit, your brave son, defeated the gods. But he

[324] Sushena.

has been slain by Lakshmana.' Hearing that fearful, dreadful and terrible news about his son's death in the battle, he lost his senses for a long period of time. After some time, the king, the bull among the rakshasas, regained his senses. He was afflicted by grief on account of his son and miserable. With his senses in a whirl, he lamented. 'O foremost in the army of the rakshasas! Alas! My child! O maharatha! Having defeated Indra, how could you have come under Lakshmana's subjugation today? Indeed, when you were angry in a battle, your arrows could have even penetrated Death and the peaks of Mandara, not to speak of Lakshmana. Today, I hold a great deal of respect for King Vaivasvata.[325] O mighty-armed one! It is because of him that you have been subjected to the dharma of time. This is the path followed by excellent warriors and large numbers of immortals too. If a man desires heaven, he should be killed for the sake of his lord. On seeing that Indrajit has been killed, the large number of gods, all the guardians of the world and the rishis will sleep happily today, freed from fear. Without Indrajit, all the three worlds and the earth with its groves seems lonely and empty to me today. Today, I will hear the screams of the nairitta maidens in the inner quarters, like the roars of herds of female elephants in mountain caverns. O scorcher of enemies! You were the heir apparent over the rakshasas in Lanka. Abandoning them, your mother and your wife, where have you gone? O brave one! When I had left for Yama's abode, you should have performed the funeral rites for me. But the opposite has happened. Sugriva, Lakshmana and Raghava are alive. Without uprooting my stakes, why have you abandoned us and left?' Ravana, the lord of the rakshasas, lamented in this and other ways. Because of the calamity over his son, he was immersed in great rage.

He was naturally terrible and the rage of his fire made him senseless. His form was like that of the angry and unassailable Rudra. Tears dropped from his enraged eyes, like drops of oil from the flames of blazing lamps. The loud sound of his gnashing his teeth could be heard, as if the danavas were dragging around

---

[325] Yama.

a mechanical contrivance. He was like the fire of destruction. In whichever direction he looked, the rakshasas were scared and terrified and hid themselves. As he looked at the directions, he was like an enraged Death, desiring to devour all mobile and immobile objects. All the rakshasas could not approach him. Ravana, the lord of the rakshasas, became extremely angry. Desiring to assign rakshasas to the field of battle, he spoke to them in their midst. 'I have performed supreme austerities for one thousand years and when these were over, Svayambhu was pleased with me. As a consequence of those austerities and because of Svayambhu's favours, I have never suffered any fear from asuras and gods. Brahma gave me armour that dazzles like the sun. When I crushed the gods and the asuras, the strength of the vajra could not shatter it. I will now wear that, astride my chariot in the battle. Even Purandara himself will be unable to act against me today. When he was pleased with me, Svayambhu gave me a great bow and arrows. I used those when I crushed the gods and the asuras. To the terrible sound of hundreds of trumpets, let that bow of mine be taken out for the great battle in which Rama and Lakshmana will be killed.'

The brave one was tormented because his son had been killed and fell prey to rage. Ravana thought about it in his mind and resolved to kill Sita. His eyes were coppery red and extremely terrible. He was horrible to behold. He was miserable and in a distressed voice, he glanced towards all the roamers in the night and addressed them. 'My child used maya to deceive the residents of the forest. He showed them the sight of Sita being killed. I will make that come true. This is pleasing to me. Vaidehi is devoted to the friend of the kshatriyas[326] and I will destroy her.' Having told his advisers this, he swiftly touched his sword and drew it out. It possessed all the qualities and was as radiant as a clear sky. Surrounded by his advisers, he left the assembly hall with great force. Ravana was afflicted by sorrow on account of his son and his eyes were full of grief. Having angrily seized the sword, he violently went to the spot where Maithilee was. On seeing the angry

---

[326] Rama.

rakshasa leave, the rakshasas roared like lions. They embraced each other and said, 'Today, those two brothers will see him and be agitated. When angry, he has vanquished the four guardians of the world. In battles, he has brought down many other enemies.' While they were conversing, he went to Ashokavana. Senseless with rage, Ravana rushed towards Vaidehi. He was extremely angry. His well-wishers, those who thought about his welfare, sought to restrain him. But he rushed forward angrily, like a planet in the sky heading towards Rohini. The unblemished Maithilee was guarded by the rakshasis. She saw the enraged rakshasa, holding the excellent sword. On seeing him with the sword, Janaka's daughter was distressed, though many well-wishers tried to restrain him and make him withdraw.

'This one is angry and is himself rushing towards me.[327] Though I have a protector, this evil-minded one will render me without a protector. I have been devoted to my husband and he has urged me many times. He has asked me to be his wife and seek pleasure. But he has been rebuffed by me. That is the reason he has come here. It is evident that he has lost hope. It is evident that he is full of anger and confusion and is ready to kill me. Or, for my sake, this ignoble one might have brought down the two brothers, Rama and Lakshmana, tigers among men, in the battle today. If the two princes were destroyed because of me, that would be a shame. I was inferior and did not act in accordance with Hanumat's words. I could have easily left on his back. Though I would have been censured, I would have been on my husband's lap and would not have had to grieve today. I think that Kousalya's heart will be shattered when she hears that her son has been destroyed in the battle. She has only a single son. When she remembers the great-souled one and weeps, she will think about his birth, his childhood, his youth and all the acts of dharma he has performed. On hearing about her son being killed, she will lose all hope. Though she will perform the funeral rites, she will be unconscious. It is certain that she will enter a fire or enter water. Shame on Kubja Manthara, the

---

[327] These are Sita's thoughts.

one with evil inclinations. It is because of her that Kousalya will suffer from this hardship.'

The ascetic Maithilee lamented in this way. She was like Rohini separated from the moon and under the subjugation of a planet. The lord of the rakshasas, had an intelligent adviser named Suparshva. He saw her. Though he was restrained by the other advisers, he spoke these words to Ravana. 'You are Dashagriva and you are the younger brother of Vaishravana himself. How can you forget dharma in your rage and desire to kill Vaidehi? You have studied the knowledge of the Vedas and have bathed thereafter.[328] You have always been devoted to your own dharma. O brave one! O lord of the rakshasas! How can you think of killing a woman? O king! Look at Maithilee. She possesses beauty. Therefore, with us, release your anger towards Raghava. You should arise now. It is the fourteenth day of *krishna paksha*. Surround yourself with an army and emerge on *amavasya*[329] for the sake of victory. You are brave and intelligent. You have a chariot and a sword. Station yourself on an excellent chariot. Kill Rama, Dasharatha's son, and you will obtain Maithilee.' The generous-souled well-wisher said this and Ravana accepted the words that were in conformity with dharma. The valiant one went to his residence. Then, surrounded by the well-wishers, he again went to the assembly hall.

Chapter 6(81)

Distressed and extremely miserable, the king entered the assembly hall. He sat down on his excellent seat and sighed like an angry lion. The extremely strong one spoke to all the commanders of the force. He was afflicted by hardship on account of his son. Ravana joined his hands in salutation and spoke these words. 'All of you surround yourselves with all the elephants and

---

[328] Bathing is an act of purification, performed after concluding a period of studies.
[329] The day of the new moon is amavasya, that is, the next day.

the horses. Emerge with hordes of chariots and surround yourselves with foot soldiers. In the battle, you should only surround Rama and kill him. Like clouds during the monsoon, cheerfully shower down arrows. Otherwise, in the great battle tomorrow, while all the worlds look on, I will pierce Rama's body with sharp arrows and kill him.' The Indra among rakshasas said this and the rakshasas accepted his words. They quickly emerged on chariots, surrounded by armies of elephants.

There was an extremely terrible battle just before sunrise. There was a tumultuous clash between the rakshasas and the apes. In the battle, the apes and the rakshasas struck each other with colourful clubs, spears, swords and battleaxes. Rivers of blood started to flow. The elephants and chariots were the banks, the horses were the fish and the standards were the trees. Large number of bodies were borne along. In the battle, the Indras among the apes leapt up and leapt down. They shattered the standards, armour, chariots, horses and many kinds of weapons. With their sharp teeth and nails, the apes tore out the hair, ears, foreheads and noses of the rakshasas. In the encounter, one hundred bulls among apes rushed towards a single rakshasa, like birds rush towards a tree with fruits. The terrible rakshasas were like mountains and slew the apes with heavy clubs, spears, swords and battleaxes. The large army of apes was slaughtered by the rakshasas and sought succour with Rama, Dasharatha's son, the one who provides refuge.

At this, the immensely energetic and valiant Rama seized his bow. He entered the army of the rakshasas and showered down floods of arrows. When the extremely terrible Rama entered, he was like the sun in the sky. He burnt them down with the flames of his arrows and they could not approach him. To the roamers in the night, the extremely terrible Rama was like Death. In the battle, they saw Rama perform deeds that were extremely difficult to achieve. He drove away that large army and shattered the giant chariots. They could not see Rama, just as one cannot see the wind in the forest. Rama was swift in his deeds. He severed, mangled and routed the army, afflicting them with his weapons and scorching them with his arrows. But they could not see him. Though they

were struck in their bodies, they could not see Raghava, just as
creatures are unable to see the inner soul that is established in the
senses. 'This is he, he is slaying the army of elephants. This is he,
he is destroying the giant chariots. This is he, he is devastating the
foot soldiers and horses with his sharp arrows.' In the encounter, all
the rakshasas saw Rama's likeness everywhere. Finding Raghava's
resemblance in each other, they angrily slew each other. The great-
souled one had confounded them with the supreme *gandharvastra*[330]
and scorched the army of the enemy. That is the reason they saw
Rama everywhere. In the battle, the rakshasas saw thousands of
Ramas. And, in the great battle, they next saw a single Kakutstha.
The great-souled one was roaming around with a bow with a
golden handle. He brandished it like a circle of fire and they could
not see Raghava. The bow was like the rim of a wheel, with the
arrows as spokes. The body was like a navel and emitted sparks
as the breath of life. There was the roar of the palm slapping
against the bowstring. The plucking of the bowstring was full of
energy and intelligence. Applying divine weapons to the bowstring,
he slaughtered the rakshasas in the encounter. They saw Rama's
wheel, like the subjects see the wheel of time. There was an army
of ten thousand chariots that were as fleet as the wind. There
were eighteen thousand spirited elephants. There were fourteen
thousand horses with riders. There was a complete complement of
two hundred thousand rakshasa foot soldiers. The rakshasas could
assume any form at will. Using arrows that were like the flames
of the fire, within the eighth part of a day,[331] Rama destroyed all
these. The horses were killed. The chariots were destroyed. They
were exhausted and their standards were shattered. The remaining
roamers in the night returned to the city of Lanka. The field of
battle was full of slain elephants, foot soldiers and horses. It looked
like a pleasure ground for the enraged Rudra, the wielder of the
Pinaka. The gods, the gandharvas, the siddhas and the supreme
rishis praised Rama's deeds and worshipped him.

[330] Divine weapon named after gandharvas.
[331] Three hours.

Rama spoke to Sugriva, who was near him. 'The strength of such divine weapons exists in me, or in Tryambaka.' The great-souled Rama, who was Shakra's equal and had cleansed all sins, slaughtered the army of the rakshasas, using his *astra*s and his *shastra*s.[332] He was praised by the large numbers of delighted gods.

Chapter 6(82)

There were thousands of elephants and horses with riders. There were chariots with the complexion of the fire. There were thousands of standards. There were thousands of rakshasas who fought with clubs and maces. There were golden and colourful standards. There were brave ones who could assume any form at will. They were slain with sharp arrows decorated with gold. Rama, the performer of unblemished deeds, did this to the army sent by Ravana. The remaining roamers in the night heard about, and saw, this devastation. They were distressed and overcome by thoughts.

The rakshasis had become widows. Their sons had been killed. They shrieked because their relatives had been killed. They met the rakshasas and lamented in their sorrow. 'Shurpanakha is aged and ugly. Her stomach hangs down. Rama is like Kandarpa[333] in his beauty. How could she have approached him in the forest? He is delicate and great in spirit. He is engaged in the welfare of all creatures. She should be killed by people. She is inferior in beauty. But she saw him and was smitten with desire. She is devoid of all the qualities. He possesses the qualities and is greatly energetic. His face is beautiful, her face is ugly. How could the rakshasi have desired Rama? These people are limited in their fortune. She is

---

[332] The text uses both the words astra and shastra. Both mean weapons. Broadly, an astra is hurled, while a shastra is held in the hand. Shastra is typically used for a human weapon, while astra is a term also used for a divine weapon, such as one invoked on an arrow.

[333] The god of love.

wrinkled and has grey hair. She committed a ridiculous misdeed, condemned by all the worlds. That led to the destruction of the rakshasas and Khara and Dushana. That ugly woman oppressed Raghava. Ravana contracted this great enmity because of her. The rakshasa Dashagriva brought Sita for his own destruction. Dashagriva will not get Sita, Janaka's daughter. However, he has been bound in an eternal enmity with the powerful Raghava. Rama single-handedly killed the rakshasa Viradha, who craved for Vaidehi. That spectacle is sufficient proof.[334] There were fourteen thousand rakshasas who were terrible in their deeds. He killed them in Janasthana, using arrows that were like the flames of fire. In the encounter, he used arrows that were like the sun to kill Khara, Dushana and Trishira. That is sufficient proof. Kabandha fed on blood and his arms were one yojana long. He was killed, while he was roaring in anger and suffering. That is sufficient proof. Vali was like a cloud and he was the son of the one with one thousand eyes. Rama killed Vali. That is sufficient proof. With his wishes destroyed, the distressed Sugriva resided on Mount Rishyamuka and he was established in the kingdom. That is sufficient proof. For the welfare of all the rakshasas, Vibhishana spoke words that were full of dharma and artha. However, because of his confusion, those did not appeal to him. Had the younger brother of the lord of treasure acted in accordance with Vibhishana's words, this city of Lanka wouldn't have become afflicted with grief and wouldn't have become a cremation ground. Despite hearing that Kumbhakarna had been killed by the immensely strong Raghava and about his beloved son, Indrajit, Ravana did not understand. Wails can be heard in family after family of the rakshasas. 'My son, my brother, my husband, has been killed in the battle.' Hundreds and thousands of chariots, horses and elephants have been killed and destroyed by the brave Rama in the battle, and so have rakshasa foot soldiers. Assuming Rama's form, Rudra, Vishnu, the great Indra Shatakratu, or Death himself is killing us. With the best among brave ones killed

---

[334] Of Rama's powers.

by Rama, there is no hope of our remaining alive. We do not
see an end to our fears. Therefore, we are lamenting. The brave
Dashagriva has obtained boons for the field of battle. Therefore,
he does not comprehend this extremely terrible fear that has
arisen from Rama's hands. When he engages in a battle against
Rama and is attacked, the gods, the gandharvas, the pishachas
and the rakshasas will not be able to save him. In every battle
that Ravana engages in, evil portents are seen. They are telling us
about Rama destroying Ravana. Pleased, the grandfather granted
Ravana freedom from fear through gods, danavas and rakshasas.
However, he did not ask about humans. Therefore, we[335] are
certain that there is a fear from humans. A terrible destruction
of life will occur for the rakshasa Ravana. Powerful because
of the boon he had obtained, the rakshasa caused oppression.
Blazing in their austerities, the gods worshipped the grandfather.
Satisfied, for the welfare of the gods, the great-souled grandfather
addressed all the gods in these great words. "From today, in the
three worlds, the danavas and the rakshasas will always be full
of fear and will wander around till eternity." All the gods, with
Indra at the forefront, went and propitiated Mahadeva, the one
with the bull on his banner, the destroyer of the city of Tripura.
Mahadeva was pleased and addressed the gods in these words.
"For your welfare, a woman will be born and she will ensure
the destruction of the rakshasas." Earlier, hunger consumed the
danavas. Like that, Sita has been engaged by the gods. She is the
slayer of rakshasas and will devour us, together with Ravana. The
evil-minded and insolent Ravana has brought this about through
his misdeeds. This terrible misfortune has occurred and we are
immersed in grief. We do not see anyone in the world who can
offer us protection from what Raghava has unleashed, like Death
at the time of the destruction of a yuga.' All the women of the
roamers in the night said this and embraced each other in their
arms. They sorrowed and grieved, afflicted by fear. They shrieked
in these extremely terrible voices.

[335] The text actually uses the singular, since the women are lamenting individually.

Chapter 6(83)

In every family in Lanka, there were the screams of the rakshasis. Ravana heard the piteous sounds of these lamentations. He sighed deeply and thought for a while. Ravana, terrible to behold, was extremely angry. He bit his lips with his teeth and his eyes were red with rage. He was like the fire of destruction. Even the rakshasas found him difficult to look at and lost their senses. The lord of the rakshasas spoke to the rakshasas who were near him. He seemed to burn them down with his eyes and because of their fear, they could not clearly make out what he said. 'Tell Mahodara, Mahaparshva and the rakshasa Virupaksha to obey my commands and ask the soldiers to swiftly depart.'[336] Hearing his words, the rakshasas were afflicted by fear. Following the king's orders, they urged the rakshasas who were still not agitated. All the rakshasas, terrible to behold, agreed to what he had said. All of them performed acts of benediction and advanced towards Ravana. As is proper, all the maharathas worshipped Ravana. They joined their hands in salutation and stood there, wishing for the victory of their master. Ravana was senseless with rage.

He laughed and spoke to Mahodara, Mahaparshva and the rakshasa Virupaksha. 'From my bow, I will today shoot arrows that are like the sun at the time of the destruction of a yuga. I will convey Raghava and Lakshmana to Yama's abode. By slaying the enemy, I will extract revenge for Khara, Kumbhakarna, Prahasta and Indrajit. The net of my arrows will go and cover everything and the firmament, the directions, the rivers and the ocean will no longer be seen. My arrows will be waves that arise from the bow that is the ocean. I will use these to crush the herds of apes, in their respective divisions and subdivisions. Their faces are like blooming lotuses and their complexions are like the filaments of lotuses. Those herds are like lotus ponds and I will crush them like an elephant. In the

[336] Mahodara and Mahaparshva have already been killed. However, Ravana may have been confused. There is also the hedge that the rakshasas couldn't clearly make out what he said. But since Mahodara and Mahaparshva are killed again, there is a clear case of inconsistency.

encounter, the leaders of the herds will have arrows embedded in
their faces today. They will be strewn around the earth, like lotuses
with stalks. Today, there will be a terrible fight against the apes who
use trees as weapons. Shooting a single arrow in the battle, I will
pierce hundreds. Husbands have been killed. Brothers have been
killed. Sons have been killed. By slaying their enemies today, I will
perform the act of wiping away their tears. They will be mangled
by my arrows today. They will be scattered around, senseless. In
the battle today, I will make efforts to cover the earth with apes,
so that the ground cannot be seen. Today, I will use my arrows to
cause affliction. I will satisfy jackals, vultures and all the others that
survive on flesh with the flesh of the enemy. Swiftly prepare my
chariot. Swiftly bring me my bow. Let the roamers in the night who
remain follow me into the battle.'

Hearing his words, Mahaparshva spoke to the commanders
who were present there. 'Let all the forces be readied.' The angry
commanders went around, from one house of a rakshasa to another
house. Light in their valour, they went all around Lanka and urged
the soldiers. In a short while, the rakshasas, terrible in their valour,
emerged. With horrible faces, they roared. They wielded many
kinds of weapons in their arms. There were swords, spears, javelins,
clubs, maces, ploughs, sharp-edged spikes and large and heavy
bludgeons. There were staffs, sparkling chakras, sharp battleaxes,
bhindipalas, shataghnis and many other excellent weapons.
Following Ravana's command, the commanders quickly brought a
chariot. They urged the charioteer to hurry and yoke eight horses
to this chariot. Blazing in his own energy, he ascended this divine
chariot. Ravana's spirit was deep and he seemed to shatter the
earth. Obtaining Ravana's permission, Mahaparshva, Mahodara
and the invincible Virupaksha climbed on to their chariots. They
roared cheerfully and seemed to shatter the earth. Desiring victory,
they emitted terrible roars and emerged. The energetic one[337] was
like Yama, the Destroyer. Advancing into battle, he held aloft his
bow and emerged, surrounded by an army of large numbers of

[337] Ravana.

rakshasas. The maharatha's chariot was yoked to swift horses. He emerged through the gate where Rama and Lakshmana were.

The sun lost its radiance. The directions were covered in darkness. Birds shrieked in terrible tones. The earth trembled. Blood showered down from the sky. The horses stumbled. A vulture descended on the top of the standard. Jackals howled in inauspicious tones. His left eye throbbed. His left arm twitched. His face turned pale. His voice was slightly distorted. The rakshasa Dashagriva proceeded to fight and these evil portents, signifying his death in the battle, manifested themselves. A meteor fell down from the sky, with a sound like that of a storm. Vultures called out in hideous tones. Crows cawed. These terrible portents manifested themselves, but he paid no heed to them. Ravana was confounded. He was urged by destiny, for the sake of his own destruction. He emerged.

Hearing the clatter of the chariots of the great-souled rakshasas, the apes returned and a clash commenced between the two armies. There was a tumultuous battle between the apes and the rakshasas. Desiring victory, they angrily slaughtered each other. Dashagriva was angry. He used arrows decorated in gold to cause great carnage in the army of the apes. Ravana sliced off the heads of the foremost ones in the army. Some were breathless and were killed. Some were shattered along the flanks. The heads of some were severed. Some lost their eyes. Dashanana dilated his eyes in rage. On his chariot, he wandered around here and there in the battle. Wherever he went, the leaders of the apes were unable to withstand the force of his arrows.

Chapter 6(84)

The earth was strewn with apes whose bodies had been mangled by Dashagriva's arrows. They were incapable of tolerating the descent of Ravana's arrows, just as insects are incapable of tolerating a blazing fire. They were afflicted by those sharp arrows. They screamed and fled in different directions. They were like elephants, consumed and surrounded by the flames of a fire. As

Ravana advanced in the battle and pierced them with his arrows,
he drove away the army of the apes, like the wind dispelling large
clouds. The Indra among the rakshasas created carnage among the
residents of the forest. In the battle, he then swiftly approached
Raghava. Sugriva saw that the apes were routed in the encounter
and were running away. He quickly urged Sushena to take care of
the divisions and made up his mind to fight. The brave ape[338] was
just like him and he put him in charge. Using a tree as a weapon,
Sugriva himself then marched in the direction of the enemy. With
large boulders and many kinds of large trees, all the leaders of
the herds followed him, staying by his side or at the rear. In the
encounter, Sugriva roared in a loud voice. He brought down and
killed many excellent rakshasas. Gigantic in size, the lord of the
apes crushed the rakshasas. He was like the wind at the time of
the destruction of a yuga, devastating large trees. He showered
down innumerable boulders on the rakshasa army, just as a cloud
showers down hail stones on a flock of birds in a grove. Showers
of boulders were hurled by the king of the apes. The heads of the
rakshasas were crushed. Mangled, they fell down like mountains. In
every direction, the rakshasas were devastated and brought down.
Shattering them, Sugriva roared.

The archer rakshasa, Virupaksha, announced his name. The
invincible one leapt down from his chariot and climbed astride an
elephant. The maharatha Virupaksha mounted that elephant. He
uttered a terrible roar and rushed towards the apes. At the head of
the army, he shot terrible arrows towards Sugriva. He cheered up the
anxious rakshasas and urged and assured them. The Indra among the
apes was severely pierced by the rakshasa's sharp arrow. He was angry.
In great rage, he made up his mind to kill him. The brave ape held
aloft a tree. He advanced in front of that large elephant and struck it.
Sugriva's blow struck that giant elephant. It retreated the distance of a
bow and trumpeted loudly. The valiant rakshasa descended from the
injured elephant. He quickly advanced towards his enemy, the ape.
Dextrous in his valour, he seized a shield made of oxhide and a sword.

---

[338] Sushena.

He approached Sugriva, who stood there, censuring him. Sugriva was angry. He seized a giant boulder that was like a cloud and hurled it towards Virupaksha. The bull among the rakshasas saw that the boulder was descending. Extremely brave, he struck him back with the sword. In front of the army, he angrily struck Sugriva with the sword. Struck by the sword, his armour was shattered and it fell down. The ape let go of what had fallen down. He leapt up and slapped him with his palm, making a terrible sound that was like that of thunder. Using his skills, the rakshasa freed himself from the blows Sugriva was ready with. He raised his fist and struck him in the chest. At this, Sugriva, lord of the apes, became angrier. He saw that the rakshasa had freed himself from his blows. The ape discerned an opportunity to strike Virupaksha. With his huge palm, he angrily struck him on the region around his temple. That blow of the palm was like the force of the great Indra's vajra and he fell down on the ground. He fell down, covered in blood, and vomited blood. His angry eyes were dilated and he was covered in froth and blood. Virupaksha was seen to have become even more disfigured.[339] He writhed and trembled, his sides were covered with blood. The apes saw that their enemy was roaring piteously. The spirited apes and the rakshasas engaged with each other properly. The two terrible armies were like two thundering oceans. They were like two oceans that had crossed their shorelines. They saw that the immensely strong one, with the disfigured eyes, had been killed by the king of the apes. All the soldiers of the apes and the rakshasas became as turbulent as the Ganga.

Chapter 6(85)

In the great battle, they swiftly killed each other's soldiers. Both the armies were diminished, like lakes during a strong summer. At the destruction of his army and at Virupaksha's death, Ravana,

---

[339] There is a pun. The word *virupaksha* means one with malformed or disfigured eyes. Virupaksha's eyes became more malformed.

the lord of the rakshasas, became twice as angry. In front of the
two armies, he saw that his soldiers were being slaughtered and
destroyed. He was distressed to see this reversal of fate in the battle.
Mahodara, the destroyer of enemies, was near him and he told him,
'O mighty-armed one! At at time like this, my hope of victory is
established in you. O brave one! Exhibit your valour now. Slay
the forces of the enemy. This is the time to repay the debt to your
master. Fight well.'

Thus addressed by the Indra among the rakshasas, Mahodara
signified his assent. Like an insect heading towards a fire, he entered
the forces of the enemy. The immensely strong one created carnage
among the apes. The energetic one was goaded by his master's words
and by his own valour. Sugriva saw that the large army of the apes
was routed in the battle. He immediately attacked Mahodara. The
immensely energetic one, the lord of the apes, seized a large and
terrible boulder that was like a mountain. He hurled this, so as to
kill him. Mahodara saw that the boulder was suddenly descending.
Though it was difficult to approach, he fearlessly pierced it with his
arrows. The rakshasa countered it with his storm of arrows. The
boulder was shattered into a thousand fragments and fell down on
the ground, like a flock of anxious vultures. Seeing that the boulder
had been fragmented, Sugriva became senseless with rage. In the field
of battle, he uprooted a sala tree and hurled it towards the rakshasa.
The brave one, the victor over enemy cities, shattered it with his
arrows. Angry, he[340] saw a club that had fallen down on the ground.
He whirled around that blazing club and brandished it. Striking with
force, he used the tip of the club to slay his excellent horses. With his
horses slain, the brave one leapt down from his large chariot. The
rakshasa Mahodara angrily seized a mace. In the battle, those two
brave ones faced each other with a club and a mace. They roared like
two excellent bulls, like clouds tinged with lightning. The roamer
in the night angrily hurled his mace. The lord of the apes struck
his mace with his club. The mace and the club were shattered and

---

[340] Sugriva. Apes using weapons is rare, suggesting that this incident about Mahodara
doesn't belong, Mahodara having already been killed.

fell down on the ground. From the ground, the energetic Sugriva picked up a terrible iron bludgeon that was decorated with gold. He raised it and hurled it. But his adversary also flung a mace. These two crashed against each other, were shattered and fell down on the ground. With their weapons shattered, they used their fists to engage with each other. They were full of energy and strength and were like blazing fires. They struck each other and roared repeatedly. They struck each other with their palms and fell down on the ground. They quickly leapt up again and struck each other. The brave and unvanquished ones used their arms to fling each other down. A sword was lying not far away and so was a shield. The rakshasa Mahodara was swift in his force and he seized these. There was another giant sword and shield that had fallen down. Sugriva, best among the apes, was quicker and he seized these. Their limbs were full of rage and they roared as they attacked each other. They were accomplished in the use of weapons. In the encounter, they cheerfully held up their swords. They swiftly circled and executed motions from the right. They both focused on being victorious and angrily attacked each other. The brave Mahodara was immensely swift and prided himself on his bravery. The evil-minded one brought his sword down on that giant shield. As he tried to extricate the sword, which was stuck, the elephant among apes used his own sword to sever his head, adorned with a helmet and with earrings. With his head severed, he fell down on the ground. On seeing this, the army of the Indra among the rakshasas did not remain there any longer. Having killed him, with the other apes, the ape[341] roared. Dashagriva was angry, while Raghava rejoiced.

Chapter 6(86)

When Mahodara was killed, the immensely strong Mahaparshva agitated Angada's army with his terrible arrows. He severed

---

[341] Sugriva.

the heads of all the foremost apes from their bodies and brought them down, like the wind severing fruits from their stems. The rakshasa used arrows to sever the arms of some and severed the shoulders of others. He angrily shattered the flanks of other apes. The apes were afflicted by the shower of Mahaparshva's arrows. All their faces were filled with distress and they lost their senses. Angada saw that his army was anxious and was afflicted by the rakshasa. The mighty-armed one resorted to his force, like the ocean on a day of the full moon. He seized an iron club that was as dazzling as the rays of the sun.[342] In the battle, the best among the apes attacked Mahaparshva. Mahaparshva lost his senses because of that blow. Senseless, with his charioteer, he fell down on the ground from the chariot. The energetic king of the bears was like a mass of black collyrium and his forces were like a mass of clouds. He angrily seized a giant boulder that was like the summit of a mountain. The extremely valiant one used this to swiftly slay his horses and shatter his chariot. In a short while, the immensely strong Mahaparshva regained his senses. He pierced Angada repeatedly with many arrows. He pierced Jambavat, the king of the bears, between the breasts with three arrows and struck Gavaksha with many arrows. Gavaksha and Jambavat were afflicted by these arrows. On seeing this, Angada became senseless with rage and seized a terrible club. The club was as radiant as the rays of the sun and was made out of iron. Standing at a distance, Angada angrily hurled the club towards the rakshasa. The powerful one seized the club in both his hands and whirled it around. To slay Mahaparshva, Vali's son hurled it towards him. The club was powerfully flung towards the rakshasa. It knocked off the bow and arrow from his hand and also brought down his helmet. Vali's powerful son attacked him with force. He angrily struck him on the temple with his palm, just below the earring. The immensely swift and immensely radiant Mahaparshva became angry. He seized an extremely large battleaxe in one hand. It was firm and had been washed in oil. It sparkled and its essence was

---

[342] The use of a weapon suggests the same interpolation about the Mahaparshva incident.

as hard as stone. Extremely angry, the rakshasa brought this down
on Vali's son. It had been severely struck towards his left shoulder.
However, the enraged Angada freed himself from the battleaxe. The
brave Angada was his father's equal in valour. Enraged, he tightened
his own fist, which was like the vajra. He knew about inner organs
and aimed it towards the rakshasa's chest and his heart. He brought
down the fist, which was like Indra's vajra to the touch. In the great
battle, he brought this down on the rakshasa. His heart was quickly
crushed. Slain, he fell down on the ground. When he fell down on
the ground, his soldiers were agitated. In the encounter, Ravana
became extremely angry.

Chapter 6(87)

In the great battle, Ravana saw that the two rakshasas, Mahodara
and Mahaparshva, had been killed and that the immensely strong
and brave Virupaksha had also been killed. He was filled with great
rage. He urged his charioteer and spoke to him in these words. 'My
advisers have been killed and the city has been barricaded. Slaying
Rama and Lakshmana, I will destroy this misery. Rama is the tree
and Sita is the flowers and fruits that result. I will kill him in the
battle. Sugriva, Jambavat, Kumuda and Nala are his branches.'
The atiratha was astride a giant chariot and its clatter sounded
in the ten directions. Roaring, he advanced and quickly attacked
Raghava. The rivers, mountains and forests were filled with that
sound. The earth, with all its boars, animals and elephants, quaked.
He used an extremely terrible and extremely fearful weapon known
as *tamasa*.[343] This scorched all the apes. In every direction, they fell
down. Hundreds of divisions in the army were shattered by Ravana's
excellent arrows. On seeing this, Raghava stationed himself.

He saw that the unvanquished Rama was stationed there. He
was with his brother, Lakshmana, like Vasava with Vishnu. He

---

[343] Meaning darkness.

seemed to be etching on the sky with his giant bow. His eyes were like the petals of lotuses and the scorcher of enemies was long-armed. The apes had been routed in the battle and had been brought down by Ravana. On seeing this, Raghava cheerfully grasped his bow at the middle. He started to stretch that excellent bow with great force. It emitted a loud noise and seemed to shatter the earth. Ravana came within the range of the arrows of the two princes. It was as if Rahu had come near the moon and the sun. The sound of the torrent of Ravana's arrows and of Rama stretching the bow made the rakshasas fall down in their hundreds. Lakshmana wished to fight with him first. He shot sharp arrows from his bow and these arrows were like the flames of a fire. No sooner had the archer Lakshmana shot these into the sky, than the immensely energetic Ravana countered these arrows with his own arrows. Displaying the dexterity of his hands, he severed one of Lakshmana's arrows with one arrow, three arrows with three arrows and ten arrows with ten arrows. Ravana, the victor in assemblies, passed over Lakshmana. He approached Rama, who was stationed like an immobile mountain.

His eyes red with rage, he approached him in that battle. Ravana showered down arrows on Raghava. There was a downpour of arrows, released from Ravana's bow. On seeing that these were falling down, Rama swiftly seized a broad-headed arrow. The flood of arrows blazed and were immensely forceful. They were like venomous serpents. Raghava severed these with sharp and broad-headed arrows. Raghava swiftly attacked Ravana and Ravana attacked Raghava. They showered down many kinds of sharp arrows on each other. Colourful circles of arrows zoomed around, to the left and to the right. Undefeated in battle, they countered each other's arrows. As they simultaneously fought with each other, all the creatures were terrified. It was as if Rudra and Yama were shooting arrows at each other. The air became thick with many kinds of arrows zooming around. It was as if it was dense with clouds, tinged with garlands of lightning, at the end of the summer. In the midst of these showers of arrows, the sky seemed to possess windows. Those arrows were swift in speed and exceedingly sharp.

They were speedy and tufted with the feathers of vultures. Because
of the arrows, there was a terrible and supreme darkness. It was as
if large clouds had arisen after the sun had set. As they desired to
slay each other, the battle was tumultuous. It was unapproachable
and unthinkable, like that between Vritra and Vasava. Both of them
were supreme archers and accomplished in the use of weapons. Both
of them were foremost among those who knew about weapons, and
they roamed around in the battle. Wherever both of them went, the
place became full of arrows. They were like waves in the ocean,
struck by the wind. Ravana, the one who made the worlds shriek,
was skilful in the use of his hands. He shot a garland of iron arrows
towards Rama's forehead. They were shot from a terrible bow and
possessed the complexion of dark lotuses. However, Rama bore it
on his head and was not pained. Rama was filled with anger. He
affixed an arrow, chanted mantras on it and invoked *roudrastra* on
it. The immensely energetic and valiant one shot this from his bow.
Severing the arrows of the Indra among the rakshasas, he shot more
arrows. Those arrows descended on his armour, which was like a
giant cloud. However, because the Indra among rakshasas could
not be killed,[344] these did not lead to any pain in him. Rama was
accomplished in the use of all weapons. The lord of the rakshasas
was mounted on his chariot and he struck him on the forehead with
a supreme weapon. However, Ravana countered these arrows. Like
five-hooded serpents that were in the form of arrows, these hissed
and penetrated the ground. Having destroyed Raghava's weapons,
Ravana became senseless with rage. He affixed the extremely terrible
asura weapon. This released sharp arrows. Some had the faces of
lions and tigers, others had the faces of herons and crows. Some
had the faces of vultures and hawks, others had the faces of jackals.
Some had the faces of wolves, others had gaping mouths and were
extremely fearful. Some had five heads with flickering tongues.
Some arrows had the faces of donkeys, others had faces that were
like those of boars. Some had faces like dogs and cocks, some had
faces like venomous makaras. The immensely energetic one used his

---

[344] Because of his invincible armour.

maya to shoot these towards Rama and they sighed like serpents. The descendant of the Raghu lineage confronted the asura weapon. Great in his endeavour, he released *pavakastra*, which was like the fire. There were arrows with faces like blazing fires, others with faces that resembled the sun. There were faces like the moon and the half-moon, other faces like comets. There were faces that possessed the complexions of planets and nakshatras, other faces resembling giant meteors. There were some with tongues like lightning. He shot these sharp arrows. Ravana's terrible arrows were repulsed by Raghava's weapon. They were destroyed in the sky and shattered into thousands of fragments. Rama, the performer of unblemished deeds, destroyed that weapon. On seeing this, all the apes, who could assume any form at will, roared.

Chapter 6(88)

When that weapon was countered, the rage of Ravana, the lord of the rakshasas, was doubled. Thereafter, he resorted to another weapon. The immensely radiant one resorted to another terrible weapon that had been fashioned by Maya.[345] Ravana released this terrible weapon towards Raghava. From the bow, blazing spears, clubs and maces, with essence as hard as the vajra, emerged in all the directions. There were bludgeons and deceptive nooses, blazing like thunder. Many kinds of sharp weapons descended, like the wind at the end of a yuga. The prosperous Raghava was supreme among those who knew about weapons. The immensely radiant one destroyed that weapon with the supreme gandharva weapon. When that weapon was countered by the great-souled Raghava, Ravana's eyes turned coppery red with rage and he invoked sourastra. From the intelligent Dashagriva's bow, which was terrible in force, large and radiant chakras descended. As these descended, the sky blazed everywhere. As these descended,

---

[345] The architect of the demons.

the directions were illuminated, as if by the moon, the sun and the planets. In the field of battle, Raghava countered Ravana's chakras with torrents of arrows and other diverse weapons. Ravana, the lord of the rakshasas, saw that the weapon had been destroyed. He pierced Rama in all the inner organs with ten arrows. He was pierced by ten arrows that emerged from Ravana's large bow. However, the immensely energetic Raghava did not tremble. Raghava, the victor in assemblies, became angry. He pierced Ravana, all over his body, with many arrows.

At this time, Raghava's powerful younger brother became angry. Lakshmana, the slayer of enemy heroes, seized seven arrows. Ravana's standard had the figure of a man atop it. The immensely radiant one used these extremely forceful arrows to sever that into many fragments. The nairitta's charioteer's head was handsome, with blazing earrings. The immensely strong Lakshmana used an arrow to sever this. Lakshmana used five sharp arrows to shatter the bow, which was like an elephant's trunk, of the Indra among the rakshasas.

Ravana's horses were like dark clouds. They were well trained and were like mountains. Vibhishana leapt up and killed them with his club. With the horses slain, Ravana leapt down with great force from that large chariot, filled with a terrible rage towards his brother. He picked up a javelin. That giant javelin blazed, it flamed like the vajra. The powerful Indra among the rakshasas hurled this towards Vibhishana. Lakshmana severed it with three arrows before it could reach Vibhishana, and the apes who were fighting roared. Shattered into three pieces, that javelin, with golden garlands, fell down, emitting sparks. It blazed like a giant meteor that has been dislodged from the firmament. The accomplished one then picked up a giant javelin that was as unassailable as Death. It blazed in its own energy. The evil-souled and strong Ravana prepared to hurl this blazing and extremely terrible javelin with force and its radiance was like that of Shakra's vajra. Vibhishana's life was in danger. The brave Lakshmana advanced quickly. To free him, the brave Lakshmana grasped his bow and showered down arrows on Ravana, with the javelin still held in his hand. The great-

souled one shot torrents of arrows. Having been neutralized in
his act of valour, he[346] made up his mind not to strike. Ravana
saw that his brother had been freed by Lakshmana. He turned his
face towards Lakshmana and spoke these words. 'Priding yourself
on your valour, you have freed this rakshasa Vibhishana. Now
escape from this javelin that will descend on you. This javelin is
smeared with blood and will pierce your heart. It will be hurled
from my arm, which is like a club. It will depart after robbing you
of your life.' That javelin was adorned with eight bells that made
a loud noise. It had been constructed by Maya. It was invincible
and killed the enemy. It seemed to blaze in its energy. Having said
this, extremely angry, Ravana hurled this towards Lakshmana and
roared. It was hurled with terrible force and made a sound like that
of Shakra's vajra. In the field of battle, the javelin descended on
Lakshmana with force. As the javelin descended through the sky,
Raghava entreated it, 'May all be well with Lakshmana. May you
fail. May your efforts be futile.' It descended with great force on
Lakshmana's broad chest. It blazed and was immensely radiant, like
the tongue of the king of the serpents.[347] Because of the force with
which Ravana had hurled it, the javelin penetrated extremely deep
into Lakshmana's heart and he fell down on the ground.

Raghava was nearby and saw the state Lakshmana was in.
Because of affection towards his brother, the immensely energetic
one was distressed in his heart. His eyes full of tears, he thought
for a while. He became greatly angry, like the fire at the end of a
yuga. Raghava thought that this was not the time to be despondent.
For the sake of killing Ravana, he continued in that extremely
tumultuous battle. In the great battle, Rama saw that Lakshmana
had been mangled by the javelin. His body was covered with blood
and he resembled a serpent in a mountain. The javelin had been
hurled by the powerful Ravana. The best among the apes made
efforts to pluck it out. However, they were unable to do so. The
rakshasa was dexterous in the use of his hands and he afflicted

---

[346] Ravana decided not to throw the javelin at Vibhishana.
[347] Vasuki.

and oppressed them with his floods of arrows. Having pierced
Soumitri, the javelin had penetrated the ground. Rama grasped that
fearful javelin in his arms and drew it out. Enraged in the battle,
the powerful one broke it. While he was drawing out the javelin,
the powerful Ravana showered down arrows, which penetrated the
inner organs, all over his body. Not thinking about these arrows, he
embraced Lakshmana.

Raghava spoke to Hanumat and Sugriva. 'O supreme among
the apes! Remain standing around Lakshmana. This is the time for
valour and I have desired this for a very long time. The evil-souled
Dashagriva, evil in his intentions, must be killed. Like a *chataka* bird
that wishes to see a cloud at the end of the summer, I have waited
for this. O apes! At this time, hear the truthful pledge that I am
taking. Before long, the world will be without Ravana or without
Rama. I have lost my kingdom, I have dwelt in the forest, I have
roamed around in Dandaka and the rakshasas have approached and
have oppressed Vaidehi. I have faced great hardships and the misery
has been like hell. Slaying Ravana in the battle today, I will free
myself from all of these. That is the reason why I have summoned
this army of the apes, killed Vali in the battle and instated Sugriva
in the kingdom. That is the reason a bridge was built across the
ocean and the ocean was crossed. In this battle today, the wicked
one has come within the range of my vision. Now that he has come
within the range of my vision, he does not deserve to remain alive.
The sight of Ravana is like the sight of a poisonous snake to me. O
invincible ones! O bulls among the apes! Be reassured and watch
this battle between me and Ravana. Seat yourselves on the peaks of
mountains. In my battle today, let the three worlds, the gandharvas,
the gods, the rishis and the charanas see Rama and witness what it
means to be Rama. Today, I will perform deeds that the worlds,
with their mobile and immobile objects, will always talk about, as
long as the earth exists.'

Having said this, Rama controlled himself. In the battle, he
struck Dashagriva with sharp arrows that were decorated in gold.
Ravana showered down blazing iron arrows and clubs on Rama,
the way a cloud pours down showers. Desiring to kill each other,

Rama and Ravana shot arrows at each other and these arrows created a tumultuous noise. Rama and Ravana's arrows were shattered and scattered. Their tips blazed in the sky and they then fell down on the ground. There was the great sound of Rama and Ravana slapping their palms against bowstrings. It was wonderful and all the creatures were terrified. The great-souled one[348] created a net through his showers of arrows and they issued from his bow, blazing. Afflicted by these and frightened, Ravana fled from the encounter, just as the wind drives away clouds.

Chapter 6(89)

He fought this tumultuous battle with the evil-souled Ravana. Shooting torrents of arrows, he addressed Sushena in these words. 'Because of Ravana's force, Lakshmana has fallen down on the ground. He is writhing like a serpent. O brave one! This is causing grief in me. This brave one is wet with blood and I love him more than my own life. Behold. My mind is so distressed that I am incapable of fighting. This brother of mine took pride in fighting and he possesses auspicious qualities. If he dies,[349] what happiness is there in my remaining alive? I am ashamed of my valour. The bow is falling down from my hand. My arrows are falling down. My sight is dimmed with tears. My terrible thoughts are increasing and I wish to die. I have seen my brother brought down by the evil-souled Ravana. I am overcome by great grief. I am lamenting and my senses are distracted. I have nothing to do with fighting. There is no purpose to my life and no use for Sita. I have seen my brother, Lakshmana, brought down in the battle, covered with dust. What will I do with the kingdom? What will I do with my life? I have nothing to do with this fight. In the field of battle, Lakshmana has been brought down and is lying down.'

[348] Rama.
[349] The text uses the expression 'attains panchatva'.

The brave Sushena comforted Rama and addressed him in these words. 'O mighty-armed one! Lakshmana, the extender of prosperity, is not dead. His mouth is not distorted. His face has not turned dark and dull. It can be seen that his face is extremely radiant and clear. The palms of his hands are like lotuses and his eyes are extremely clear. O lord of the earth! These are not the signs of someone who has lost his life. O brave one! O slayer of enemies! Do not grieve in vain. He is alive. Though he is lying down on the ground, with his body loose, these signs tell us that it is as if he is sleeping. O brave one! His heart is breathing and he is trembling repeatedly.' The one who knew about the use of words, Sushena, addressed Raghava in these words. Hanumat was near him and he then quickly addressed him in these words. 'O amiable one! Swiftly go to the mountain that has all the herbs. O brave one! The auspicious Jambavat has spoken to you about this earlier. Bring the herb that grows on its southern peak. There is the auspicious one named vishalyakarani, which cures all wounds. There are souvarnakarani, sanjivani and *sandhanakarani*.[350] Quickly go and bring these back. These are required to bring life back to the brave and great-souled Lakshmana.'

Thus addressed, Hanumat went to the mountain with the herbs with the speed of thought. However, the handsome one could not identify those great herbs. The infinitely energetic son of the wind god had a thought. 'Let me take the entire summit of the mountain and leave this place. If I go without taking vishalyakarani and waste time, there will be a sin. There may be a great calamity.' The immensely strong Hanumat thought in this way. Hanumat quickly seized and uprooted the summit of the mountain. 'O bull among the apes![351] I could not identify the herbs. Therefore, I have brought back the entire summit of the mountain.' Thus addressed, Sushena, the best among the apes, praised the son of the wind god. He pulled out the herbs. The supreme among apes crushed those herbs. Sushena, the extremely radiant one, applied these to Lakshmana,

---

[350] Referred to earlier as sandhani.

[351] On return, Hanumat is addressing Sushena. Because the Critical Edition has excised some shlokas, there is a break in continuity.

through the nose. Lakshmana, the slayer of enemy heroes, had been wounded. Inhaling these, he was cured of his wounds and relieved of his pain. He quickly arose from the ground. The apes saw that Lakshmana had stood up from the ground. Extremely delighted, they praised and worshipped Sushena.

Rama, the slayer of enemy heroes, told Lakshmana, 'Come. Come to me.' With tears flowing from his eyes, he embraced him, deep in his affection. Raghava embraced Soumitri and said, 'O brave one! It is good fortune that I see you again, having returned after dying. There would have been no purpose to my remaining alive, or to Sita, or to victory. Had you died, what would have been the purpose of remaining alive?' The great-souled Raghava told him this. With a weak and feeble voice, Lakshmana replied to him in these words. 'O one who has truth as his valour! You have taken a pledge earlier.[352] Having taken that pledge, you ought not to speak like someone who lacks spirit. O unblemished one! Virtuous ones do not take pledges that are falsified. The sign of greatness is to fulfil a pledge. O unblemished one! On my account, your army has faced a loss in hope. Fulfil your pledge now, by killing Ravana. If an enemy comes within the range of your arrows, he cannot remain alive, just as a giant elephant cannot escape from a roaring lion that has sharp teeth. I wish to quickly see the death of that evil-souled one. Before the sun has set, that task must be accomplished.'

Chapter 6(90)

Raghava heard the words that Lakshmana spoke. In front of the army, he shot terrible arrows towards Ravana. Dashagriva was astride his chariot and struck Rama with extremely terrible arrows that were like the vajra, like rain pouring down from a cloud. Rama controlled himself and used arrows that were like blazing fires, embellished with gold, to pierce Dashagriva in the encounter.

[352] Of killing Ravana.

Rama was on the ground, while the rakshasa was mounted on a chariot. The gods, the gandharvas and the danavas said that this was a fight among unequals. With the handsome and excellent chariot of the king of the gods, he descended from heaven, in front of Kakutstha.[353] The chariot was colourfully made out of gold and was decorated with hundreds of bells. It was like the rising sun and the kubara was made out of lapis lazuli. There were well-trained horses with golden harnesses and the whips were white. The horses were decorated in nets of gold that resembled the sun. There was a golden standard on a pole. Stationed on a chariot, with the goad in his hand, Matali, the charioteer of the one with one thousand eyes, joined his hands in salutation and addressed Rama in these words. 'O Kakutstha! For your victory, the one with the one thousand eyes has sent this chariot. O great-spirited one! O prosperous one! O destroyer of enemies! He has given it to you. This is Indra's great bow and this armour is like the fire. These arrows are like the sun and this javelin is sparkling and sharp. O brave one! Mount this chariot and slay the rakshasa Ravana, like the great Indra did to the danavas. O Rama! I will be your charioteer.' Thus addressed, Rama greeted him and circumambulated the chariot. He mounted it and was radiant, pervading the worlds with his prosperity.

There was an extraordinary battle between the mighty-armed Rama and the rakshasa Ravana, a duel that made the body hair stand up. Raghava was supreme in the knowledge of weapons. He destroyed the gandharvastra of the king of the rakshasas with his gandharvastra, divine weapons with his divine weapons. The roamer in the night, the lord of the rakshasas, became greatly angry and again shot the extremely terrible rakshasa weapon. Arrows embellished in gold were released from Ravana's bow. They turned into extremely virulent serpents and approached Kakutstha. Their mouths blazed. They vomited blazing fires from their mouths. Terrible and with mouths gaping, they approached Rama. They were like Vasuki to the touch. They were blazing serpents, extremely

---

[353] Because of excision of shlokas, the Critical Edition breaks the continuity. The 'he' is Matali, Indra's charioteer, who has been asked by Indra to bring Indra's chariot to Rama and act as Rama's charioteer.

poisonous. They covered all the directions and the sub-directions. In the battle, Rama saw that those serpents were descending. He applied the extremely terrible Garuda weapon. Gold-tufted and as resplendent as the fire, it was released from Raghava's bow. It turned into golden eagles, the enemies of serpents, and roamed around. They destroyed all those arrows that were in the form of extremely swift serpents. The arrows used by Rama were like eagles, but could assume any form at will. When his weapon was countered, Ravana, the lord of the rakshasas, became angry. He showered down extremely terrible torrents of arrows on Rama. He afflicted Rama, the performer of unblemished deeds, with thousands of arrows and used storms of arrows to pierce Matali. Ravana brought down the seat on the chariot and the chariot's standard. He also struck Indra's horses with nets of arrows. On seeing Rama afflicted, the gods, the gandharvas, the danavas, the charanas, the siddhas and the supreme rishis were distressed. The Indras among the apes and Vibhishana were also pained, on seeing that the moon that was Rama being devoured by the Rahu that was Ravana. The *prajapatya* nakshatra Rohini is loved by the moon.[354] It was as if it had been attacked by Budha,[355] signifying danger to all subjects. The ocean seemed to be on fire and its waves were circled in smoke. It seemed to angrily leap up and touch the sky. The rays of the sun were dimmed and an excellent man, with the complexion of a weapon, could be seen there, holding a headless torso on his lap and touched by a comet. The nakshatra Vishakha, presided over by the divinities Indra and Agni and the nakshatra of the Kosalas, could be seen in the sky, attacked by Angaraka.[356] The one with ten heads and twenty arms seized his bow and arrow. Dashagriva could be seen, resembling Mount Mainaka. Rama was restrained by the rakshasa Dashagriva and could not affix his arrows in the field of battle. He angrily knit his brows and his eyes turned red. He was filled with great rage, as if he would burn down with his eyes.

[354] The older name for Rohini used to be Prajapati. As such, Rohini is presided over by Prajapati.

[355] Mercury.

[356] Angaraka is Mangala (Mars).

Chapter 6(91)

Seeing that the intelligent Rama was enraged, all the beings were terrified and the earth trembled. The mountains, with their lions and tigers, quaked. The trees swayed. The ocean, the lord of the rivers, was agitated. Dense clouds thundered in the sky in harsh tones. Evil portents roared and manifested themselves in all the directions. On seeing that Rama was greatly angry, there were terrible omens. All the beings were terrified and Ravana was scared. The gods astride their vimanas, the gandharvas, the giant serpents, the rishis, the danavas, the daityas and the eagles roaming around in the sky witnessed the battle, which was like that of the world getting destroyed. Using many kinds of terrible weapons, those two brave ones fought against each other. All the gods and the asuras assembled in personified forms to witness the great encounter. Delighted, they spoke the following words. The asuras present said, 'Victory to Dashagriva.' The gods repeatedly said, 'Victory to Rama.'

At that time, Ravana was filled with rage. Desiring to strike Raghava, the evil-souled one picked up a great weapon. Its essence was as hard as the vajra. It emitted a loud roar and was capable of scorching all enemies. It was as heavy as the summit of a mountain and it was extremely terrible to behold. Its sharp tip was filled with smoke and it was like the fire that engulfs at the end of a yuga. He seized this extremely terrible weapon, which even Death found difficult to approach. In its capacity to tear and shatter, it caused fear to all creatures. In his anger, Ravana seized this blazing spear. Extremely angry, the valiant one seized the spear in the middle. In the battle, he was surrounded by an army of brave rakshasas. Raising it in the battle, the one who was gigantic in size roared horribly, delighting his own soldiers. He was angry and his eyes were red. The earth, the sky, the directions and the sub-directions trembled at the terrible noise emitted by the Indra among the rakshasas. The evil-souled one emitted an extremely loud roar. All the creatures were terrified and the ocean was agitated. The extremely valiant Ravana seized that giant spear. He emitted an extremely loud roar

and addressed Rama in these harsh words. 'O Rama! This spear
has an essence like that of the vajra. I have angrily raised it up. It
will now take away your life, since you sought to help your brother.
In front of the armies, you have slain brave rakshasas. You pride
yourself in fighting. Today, I will swiftly kill you and balance affairs.
O Raghava! Stay there now. I will kill you with this spear.' Having
said this, the lord of the rakshasas hurled the spear. As it descended,
Raghava countered it with a storm of arrows, just as Vasava
counters a fire of destruction that has arisen with a flood of water.
Ravana's giant spear was scorched by the arrows that emerged from
Rama's bow, just as insects are by a fire. However, in the sky, those
arrows touched the spear and were shattered and reduced to ashes.
At this, Raghava was filled with rage. Matali had brought a javelin
constructed by Vasava. Extremely angry, Raghava, the descendant
of the Raghu lineage, seized this. The powerful one raised it up and
the javelin resounded to the sound of bells. It blazed in the sky,
like a dazzling meteor at the end of a yuga. He flung this and the
spear of the Indra among the rakshasas fell down. The giant spear
was shattered by the javelin and fell down, robbed of its brilliance.
Rama then used sharp arrows that were extremely forceful, like the
vajra, to pierce his extremely swift steeds. He pierced Ravana in the
chest with sharp arrows. Raghava also struck him in the forehead
with three excellent arrows. The Indra among the rakshasas was
mangled all over his limbs with these arrows and blood started to
flow from his body. He was like a blossoming ashoka amidst other
trees. His body was pierced by Rama's arrows. The Indra among
the roamers in the night was wet with blood all over his body. In
the midst of that assembly, he was filled with regret. He was filled
with extremely great rage.

Chapter 6(92)

Ravana prided himself on fighting. But he was angry that he
had been worsted by Kakutstha in the battle. He was filled

with great rage. With his eyes blazing, the valiant one angrily seized his bow. In the great battle, he angrily attacked Raghava. Like a cloud showering down from the sky, Ravana rained down hundreds of torrents of arrows on Raghava, like a pond being filled up. In the battle, Kakutstha was covered with nets of arrows released from the bow. However, like an immobile large mountain, he did not tremble. Stationed in the battle, he used his arrows to counter those nets of arrows. The valiant one received them, as if they were the rays of the sun. The great-souled roamer in the night used the dexterity of his hands and angrily struck Raghava in the chest with thousands of arrows. In the battle, Lakshmana's elder brother was covered with blood. He was seen to be like a giant and blossoming kimshuka tree in the forest. The extremely energetic Kakutstha was angry at having been struck by these arrows. As radiant as the sun that arises at the end of a yuga, he grasped arrows. Both Rama and Ravana were extremely angry. In the battle, they were unable to see each other, because it was dark with arrows.

The brave Rama, Dasharatha's son, was filled with rage. He laughed and addressed Ravana in these harsh words. 'O worst among the rakshasas! When I did not know, you abducted my helpless wife from Janasthana. Therefore, you are hardly brave. In the great forest, she was without me and was miserable. You abducted her forcibly. Yet, you consider yourself to be brave. O brave one![357] You oppressed a woman, someone else's wife, when she was without a protector. You committed the deed of a coward. Yet, you consider yourself to be brave. You broke rules. You are shameless. You possess no character. In your insolence, you invited death. Yet, you consider yourself to be brave. As the brother of the lord of treasures, you are indeed full of bravery and strength. The deed that you committed is indeed praiseworthy. It is full of fame and greatness. Your insolent act was contemptible and vile. Because of what you did, you will now reap the great fruits. O evil-minded one! You consider yourself to be brave. Despite having abducted Sita like a thief, you have no shame. Had you used your strength

[357] In sarcasm.

to oppress Sita in my presence, you would have been slain with
my arrows at that very instant and seen your brother, Khara. O
evil-souled one! It is good fortune that you have now come within
the range of my vision. Today, I will use sharp arrows to convey
you to Yama's abode. Today, my arrows will sever your head, with
those radiant earrings. It will lie down in the dust of the battle field,
dragged around by predatory creatures. O Ravana! Your chest will
be flung down on the ground and vultures will descend on it. They
will drink the blood that flows out from the wounds that my arrows
will create. My arrows will mangle you today. You will lose your
life and fall down. Like Garuda against serpents, birds will drag
out your entrails.' The brave Rama, the slayer of enemies, said this.
The Indra among rakshasas was near him and he showered down
arrows on him. Rama desired to slay his enemy in the battle and
his valour, strength, delight and strength of weapons doubled. All
kinds of weapons manifested themselves before him. The immensely
energetic one was delighted and the dexterity of his hands increased.
He recognized these auspicious signs that manifested themselves
before him. Rama struck the rakshasa Ravana yet again.

Dashagriva was struck by a storm of boulders from the apes
and the shower of Raghava's arrows. His heart was in a whirl. He
could not use his weapons, stretch his bow or use his valour to
counter this. His inner soul was suffering. He did hurl arrows and
many kinds of weapons. However, because the time of his death had
arrived, these did not serve any purpose in the battle. His charioteer
saw that his leader was in such a state on the chariot. He wasn't
scared, but gently withdrew the chariot from the battle.

Chapter 6(93)

Urged by the strength of Death, he was confused and angry.
His eyes red with rage, Ravana spoke to the charioteer. 'O
one with evil intelligence! Am I inferior in valour? Am I incapable?
Am I bereft of manliness? Am I a coward? Am I light in spirit?

Am I devoid of energy? Has maya deserted me? Have my weapons
been cast away? You are resorting to your own intelligence and are
showing me disrespect. Why are you slighting me? Why are you
ignoring what I desire? In the sight of the enemy, you have brought
my chariot away. O ignoble one! Over a long period of time, I have
earned fame, valour, energy and trust. Because of you, these have
now been destroyed. My enemy is famous for his valour and his
valour causes delight. He saw that I had come to fight with him.
However, you have made me a coward. O evil-minded one! In your
confusion, you withdrew this chariot. This truth is beyond debate,
you have been bribed by the enemy. A well-wisher who desires to
ensure what is beneficial does not act in this way. What you have
done is just like what an enemy would do. Swiftly take this chariot
back, before my enemy withdraws. If you have been with me and if
you remember my qualities, do that.'

The charioteer had his welfare in mind, though he had been
harshly addressed by a foolish person. He entreated Ravana in these
beneficial words. 'I am not a coward. I am not stupid. Nor have I
been bribed by the enemy. I am not mad. I am not without affection.
Nor have I forgotten the good deeds you have done to me. I desired
your welfare and sought to protect your fame. My mind was full of
affection towards you. That is why I did something agreeable in the
guise of the disagreeable. O great king! I am devoted to ensuring
your pleasure. Therefore, you should not reprimand my faults, as
if by someone who is light and ignoble. Listen to the reason why I
withdrew the chariot from the battle, as one would from the force
of water in a river. Having performed great deeds in the battle, I
could understand that you were exhausted. O brave one! I take no
delight in preventing you from taking on a confrontation. These
steeds yoked to the chariot were tired from bearing the chariot
along. They were suffering, like cows during the summer when they
are lashed by rain. Many kinds of portents presented themselves
before us. As I circled around, I noticed all these different signs of
danger. One must know about the time and the place, the good
and the bad signs and the misery, delight, exhaustion, strengths and
weaknesses of the warrior on the chariot. One must know about the

nature of the ground—low, plain or uneven. One must know about the time of battle and the signs of weakness in the enemy. A person who wishes well for the warrior in the chariot must know about driving forward, remaining in one place and withdrawing and also everything about the warrior in the chariot. I did that so that you could rest and so could the horses yoked to the chariot and so that your terrible exhaustion might be reduced. O brave one! I did not withdraw the chariot on my own volition. O lord! Everything that I did is because I am full of affection towards my master. O slayer of enemies! Command me properly and tell me. O brave one! With a relieved mind, I will act accordingly.'

Ravana was satisfied at the words of the charioteer. He praised him in many ways. Since he loved fighting, he said, 'O charioteer! Swiftly drive my chariot in Raghava's direction. Ravana does not retreat without killing the enemy in the battle.' Ravana, the lord of the rakshasas, said this. Satisfied, he gave him an auspicious and excellent ornament for the hand. Urged by Ravana's words, the charioteer quickly goaded the horses. In a short while, the great chariot of the Indra among the rakshasas was stationed in front of Rama.

Chapter 6(94)

The king of men saw the chariot of the king of the rakshasas return suddenly. It possessed a huge standard and roared. It was yoked to black horses and was terrible in its radiance. It was like Indra's weapon[358] in the clouds, with flags of lightning, and was stocked with weapons. He[359] showered down arrows, like a cloud pouring down rain. He[360] saw his enemy descend on a chariot that was like a cloud. It possessed a clatter like that of the vajra shattering a mountain. Rama spoke to Matali, the charioteer of the

---

[358] The rainbow.
[359] Ravana.
[360] Rama.

one with the thousand eyes. 'O Matali! Look at the enraged enemy descending on his chariot. He is again descending with great force, from left to right.[361] It is my view that he has made up his mind to kill himself in the battle. Therefore, be attentive and proceed in the direction of the enemy's chariot. I wish to destroy it, just as a wind drives away clouds that have arisen. Do not be distracted. Do not be frightened. Let your grasp and sight be firm. Control the reins and the goad and drive the chariot quickly. You are used to driving Purandara's chariot and it is not desired that I should instruct you. I wish to fight single-mindedly. Therefore, I am reminding you, not teaching you.' Matali was satisfied with Rama's words. The excellent charioteer of the gods drove the chariot. He kept Ravana's great chariot on the left. The dust raised from the wheels of the chariot made Ravana quaver.

Dashagriva was angry and his coppery red eyes dilated. Rama was facing his chariot and he showered him with arrows. Rama tolerated this oppression, using his patience to overcome the rage. In the battle, he grasped Indra's bow, which possessed an extremely great force. In the great battle, they wished to kill each other. Those two extremely energetic ones used arrows that were as resplendent as the sun's rays and oppressed each other. Facing each other, they were like two proud lions. Desiring Ravana's destruction, the gods, the gandharvas, the siddhas and the supreme rishis gathered to witness the duel. Terrible portents that made the body hair rise up arose. They signified Ravana's destruction and Raghava's victory. The gods showered down blood on Ravana's chariot. Fierce winds circled around in a counterclockwise direction. A large flock of vultures roamed around in the sky. Wherever the chariot[362] proceeded, they accompanied it. Resembling a red hibiscus flower,[363] evening shrouded Lanka. But the ground was seen to blaze, as if it was day. Accompanied by storms, giant meteors fell down, with a loud noise. Since this signified harm to Ravana, the rakshasas were distressed. Wherever Ravana was, the earth trembled. The

---

[361] Counterclockwise, therefore, inauspicious.
[362] Ravana's chariot.
[363] The *japa* flower.

arms of rakshasas who tried to strike were seized.[364] Coppery, yellow, dark and white rays were seen to descend from the sun on Ravana's limbs, like minerals flowing from a mountain. Vultures followed him and vomited flames from their mouths. Facing him and looking towards him, terrified jackals howled in inauspicious tones. In the battle, a perverse wind started to blow and raised dust, so that the sight of the king of the rakshasas became unclear. Though there were no sounds from the clouds, in every direction, Indra's thunder descended on the soldiers, making a terrible noise that was impossible to tolerate. All the directions and sub-directions were enveloped in darkness. There was a shower of dust and it became extremely difficult to see the sky. Hundreds of sarika birds[365] quarrelled horribly with one another and fell down on his chariot, making a hideous sound and shrieking in terrible voices. The horses showered sparks from their loins and incessant drops of water from their eyes. In this way, there were many kinds of fearful portents, signifying Ravana's terrible destruction. For Rama, in every direction, pleasant and auspicious omens manifested themselves, indicating his victory. Raghava knew about the nature of portents. He saw the portents that manifested themselves in the field of battle and was filled with delight. In the battle, he exhibited greater valour and supreme conduct.

Chapter 6(95)

There was an extremely cruel and extremely great duel in the battle between Rama and Ravana then and it was fearful to all creatures. The soldiers of the rakshasas and the large army of the apes seized weapons. But they stationed themselves and did not move.[366] As they watched the powerful man and rakshasa engage with each other, all their hearts were filled with great wonder. They

---

[364] That is, they were rendered immobile.

[365] A sarika bird is a kind of thrush, *Turdus salica*.

[366] They were spectators to the duel.

anxiously held many weapons in their hands. But as they witnessed
the battle, their minds were filled with amazement and they did not
strike each other. The eyes of Ravana's rakshasas and Raghava's
apes were filled with amazement. The soldiers were like paintings.
Raghava and Ravana saw those portents. They were firm in their
intolerance and made up their minds to fight fearlessly. Kakutstha
was sure he would win. Ravana was certain he would die. They
displayed their fortitude and all their spirit in that battle.

The valiant Dashagriva was filled with rage. Raghava was on
his chariot and he shot his arrows in the direction of his standard.
Those arrows failed to reach the standard on Purandara's chariot.
They touched the pole of the chariot and fell down on the ground.
The valiant Rama drew his bow angrily. He made up his mind to
strike back at every strike. He shot a sharp arrow in the direction of
Ravana's standard. It was like a huge serpent and blazed in its own
energy. The arrow pierced Dashagriva's standard and penetrated
the ground. It severed the standard on Ravana's chariot and brought
it down on the ground. The extremely strong Ravana saw that his
standard had been destroyed. In the battle, because of the fire of
his rage, he seemed to blaze. Overcome with anger, he seemed to
vomit out large showers of arrows. Ravana pierced Rama's divine
horses with arrows. Though pierced, the horses did not lose their
feet. They were firm in their hearts and it was as if they had been
struck with the stalks of lotuses. Ravana saw that the horses were
not frightened. Extremely angry, he showered down arrows again.
Using his maya, he brought down showers of arrows that were in the
form of clubs, maces, chakras, bludgeons, summits of mountains,
trees, spears and battleaxes. With no exhaustion in his heart, he shot
thousands of arrows. It was terrible and tumultuous and generated
fear. There was a horrible echo. In that battle, there were many
great weapons that were invincible. Letting Raghava's chariot be, in
every direction, Dashagriva, whose mind had been made up about
his destruction, quickly shot continuous arrows on the army of the
apes. Kakutstha saw that in the battle, his enemy, Ravana, was
covering everything. Laughingly, he affixed sharp arrows. In the
encounter, he shot hundreds and thousands of arrows. On seeing

this, Ravana incessantly covered the sky with his own arrows. Both of them showered down radiant arrows. Consequently, there seemed to be a second dazzling sky that was made out of arrows alone. No arrow missed the target. Having pierced, no arrow failed in its purpose. In that battle, Rama and Ravana shot arrows. They incessantly fought against each other, to the left and to the right. They shot torrents of arrows and no space was left in the sky. Rama struck Ravana's horses. Ravana struck Rama's horses. They struck each other and countered what the other one had done.

Chapter 6(96)

In that battle, Rama and Ravana fought. On witnessing this, all the creatures were astounded in their hearts. They were engaged in killing each other and were terrible in form. In the encounter, they afflicted each other from their excellent chariots. The chariots moved in different modes—circular, straight, advancing and retreating. The charioteers, who knew about the techniques charioteers should follow, exhibited many kinds of movements. Rama wounded Ravana and Ravana wounded Rama. They used speed in forward movements and also used speed in rearward movements. From those two excellent chariots, they showered down nets of arrows. They roamed around in that battle, like clouds showering down rain on earth. They exhibited many kinds of movements in that encounter. They stood there again, facing each other. The carriage of one chariot met the carriage of the other. The mouth of one horse faced the mouth of another.[367] As they stood there, flags faced flags. With four sharp and blazing arrows shot from his bow, Rama made Ravana's four horses retreat. When his horses were forced to retreat, the roamer in the night was filled with rage and shot sharp arrows towards Raghava. Raghava was severely pierced by the strong Dashagriva. But there was no discomfiture in him, nor

---

[367] That is, the adversary's horse.

was he pained. The roamer in the night again shot arrows towards the charioteer of the one who holds the vajra in his hand and these made a noise like the clap of thunder. Those immensely forceful arrows descended on Matali's body. However, they did not cause the slightest bit of confusion or pain. Raghava was angry at this oppression of Matali, as if he himself had suffered. He shot a net of arrows and his enemy retreated. His enemy was on his chariot and the brave Raghava shot twenty, thirty, sixty, hundreds and thousands of arrows. The seven oceans were agitated by the sound of clubs, maces and bludgeons and the wind created by the tufts of the arrows. The residents of the ocean, in the nether regions of patala, were agitated. All the thousands of danavas and serpents were distressed. The entire earth, with its mountains, forests and groves, trembled. The sun lost its radiance and the wind did not blow.

All the gods, the gandharvas, the siddhas, the supreme rishis, the kinnaras and the giant serpents were worried. They said, 'May there be safety to cattle and brahmanas. May the worlds remain till eternity. In this battle, may Raghava be victorious over Ravana, the lord of the rakshasas.' The mighty-armed extender of the deeds of the Raghu lineage became angry. Rama affixed a kshura arrow, that was like virulent poison, to his bow. Ravana's handsome head blazed, with its earrings. While the three worlds looked on, he severed the head and it fell down on the ground. However, Ravana sprouted another head that was exactly similar. Rama, who was swift in action, became angry. Acting with a quick hand, he affixed an arrow and severed this second head of Ravana's. However, no sooner was this head severed, than another one was seen. Rama used arrows that were like the vajra to sever this too. In this way, one hundred heads that were equally radiant were severed. No signs were seen about Ravana's end, or his life being over. The brave extender of Kousalya's delight was accomplished in all weapons. Having used many arrows, Raghava started to think. 'All these arrows have killed Maricha, Khara, Dushana, Viradha in the Krouncha forest and Kabandha in the Dandaka forest. In this encounter, what is the reason for their being countered by Ravana, evil in his intelligence?'

While remaining attentive in the encounter, Raghava thought in this
way and showered down floods of arrows on Ravana's chest. On
his chariot, Ravana, the lord of the rakshasas, was also angry. In the
battle, he struck Rama back, showering down maces and clubs. The
gods, the danavas, the yakshas, the pishachas, the serpents and the
rakshasas witnessed this great encounter that continued through the
night. During night, day, *muhurta* or *kshana*,[368] there was no break
in the battle between Rama and Ravana.

Chapter 6(97)

At this, Matali reminded Raghava. 'O brave one! Why are you
acting towards him as if you don't know what is to be done?
O lord! To kill him, use the grandfather's weapon. The time for his
destruction, which the gods spoke about, has come now.' Rama
was reminded by Matali's words. He seized a blazing arrow that
sighed like a serpent. In the battle, the valiant one used an invincible
and great arrow given by Brahma, and which had been given to him
earlier by the illustrious rishi Agastya. For Indra's sake, the infinitely
energetic Brahma had fashioned this earlier. Earlier, he had given
it to the lord of the gods, when he had desired to conquer the three
worlds. The wind was in its feathers, the fire and the sun were in
its points. Its body was made out of space. It was as heavy as Meru
and Mandara. Its form blazed. It was well tufted and decorated
with gold. Its energy had been fashioned out of all the elements and
it was like the sun in its radiance. It was like the smoking fire of
destruction. It was as radiant as a venomous serpent. It was swift
in action and could shatter hordes of men, elephants and horses.
It could shatter gates, barricades and mountains. Many kinds of
blood were smeared on its limbs. Extremely terrible, it was smeared
with fat. Its essence was as firm as the vajra. It emitted a loud

---

[368] Kshana is a measurement of time, with differing interpretations. A second or an
instant is accurate enough. Muhurta is forty-eight minutes.

roar. It could shatter many assemblies. It was terrible and terrified everyone. It sighed like a serpent. It was fearful, with Yama's form. In a battle, it always provided food to herons, vultures, cranes, herds of jackals and rakshasas. It brought delight to the Indras among the apes and led to lassitude among the rakshasas. It was colourful and had many kinds of swift feathers, including those of Garuda. This was an excellent arrow that could destroy the fear of the worlds and of the Ikshvakus. It robbed the enemy of his deeds and caused delight to one's own self.

The immensely strong Rama chanted mantras over this great arrow, following the rites mentioned in the Vedas. The powerful one affixed it to his bow. Extremely angry, he stretched his terrible bow and attentively, shot this arrow, which could shatter the inner organs, towards Ravana. It was as invincible as the vajra and was released from an arm that was as strong as the vajra. It was as irresistible as Death and descended on Ravana's chest. The arrow, which could bring an end to the body, was released with great force. It shattered the evil-souled Ravana's heart. The forceful arrow could bring an end to life. It took away Ravana's life, and smeared with blood, penetrated the ground. Having killed Ravana, the arrow had a form that was wet with blood. Having performed its task, it quietly returned to the quiver. His breath of life was separated from his body and he fell down. The bow and arrows also fell down from his hand. The immensely radiant Indra among the nairittas, whose force was terrible, lost his life. He fell down on the ground from his chariot, like Vritra when he was slain by the vajra.

On seeing that he had fallen down on the ground, the remaining roamers in the night were terrified by fear. With their protector killed, they fled in different directions. On seeing that Dashagriva had been killed and that Raghava was victorious, the apes, who fought with trees, roared and attacked them. They were afflicted and routed by the apes. In their fear, they rushed towards Lanka. Their refuge had been killed. They were in a pitiable state and their faces were full of tears. Delighted and desiring victory, the apes roared. They proclaimed Raghava's victory and Ravana's death.

In the firmament, the pleasant drums of the gods were sounded. A wind that was extremely pleasant, with the scent of divine fragrances, started to blow. Lovely flowers were showered down from the sky and descended on the ground. Since he had performed an extremely difficult deed, they were showered down on Raghava's chariot. Praises of Raghava were heard in the sky. The great-souled gods uttered words of acclaim. At the terrible Ravana, who caused fear to all the worlds, being killed, the gods and the charanas were filled with great joy. Raghava was delighted at having been able to kill the bull among the rakshasas and having accomplished the desires of Sugriva and the immensely strong Angada. The storm was pacified. The directions were peaceful and the sky sparkled. The earth did not tremble and there was no strong wind. The sun's radiance became steady. Delighted at Raghava's victory, Sugriva, Vibhishana, the other well-wishers and Lakshmana surrounded the charming one. Following the rites, they worshipped him. The one who was steadfast in his pledge had killed the enemy. Surrounded by his own forces, he dazzled in the field of battle. The immensely energetic delight of the king of the Raghu lineage[369] was surrounded by them, like Indra by large numbers of gods.

Chapter 6(98)

On seeing that Ravana had been killed by the great-souled Raghava, the rakshasis who were in the inner quarters were afflicted by grief and rushed out.[370] Though they were restrained by many, they writhed around in the dust on the ground. Afflicted by sorrow, their hair was dishevelled. They were like cows, when the calves had been killed. With the rakshasas, they emerged from the northern gate. They entered the terrible field of battle and searched for their slain husbands. They lamented everywhere, 'Alas, noble

---

[369] Meaning Dasharatha.
[370] There were Ravana's wives and there were the wives of other rakshasas too.

one! Alas, protector!' They roamed amidst the headless torsos,
on the ground that was a mire of blood. They were crushed with
sorrow because of their husbands. Tears flowed from their eyes.
They shrieked and screamed like female elephants, when the leaders
of the herd had been killed.

They saw the immensely radiant Ravana lying down on the
ground. He was gigantic in size and great in bravery. He was like
a mass of dark collyrium. They suddenly saw their husband lying
down on the ground, in the dust of the battle. Like severed forest
creepers, they fell down on his body. One embraced him with a
great deal of respect, another wept. One embraced his feet, another
clung to his neck. Another raised her hands up and writhed around
on the ground. On seeing the face of the slain one, another was filled
with confusion. One took up his head on her lap, another looked
at his face and cried. Like dew on a lotus flower, another wiped his
face with her tears. They suffered on seeing their husband, Ravana,
slain and lying down on the ground. They shrieked in many ways.
Overcome by grief, they lamented repeatedly. 'He terrified Shakra.
He terrified Yama. He took Pushpaka away from King Vaishravana.
In battles, he created great fear for gandharvas, rishis and the great-
souled gods. Such a person is lying down, killed in the battle. He
knew no fear from asuras, gods or serpents. But he faced fear from
a human. He could not be killed by the gods, the danavas or the
rakshasas. But he is lying down, slain in the battle by a human
on foot. The gods, the yakshas and the asuras were incapable of
killing him. How could he have obtained his death at the hands
of a mortal, limited in spirit?' In this way, the women wept and
lamented. Afflicted by sorrow, they lamented again and again. 'You
did not listen to the well-wishers, who always spoke about what
was beneficial for you. With you killed, we have also been brought
down. Your brother, Vibhishana, spoke desirable and beneficial
words to you. However, because of your confusion and because
you desired your own death, you reprimanded him in harsh words.
Had you returned Sita Maithilee to Rama, this terrible catastrophe
wouldn't have occurred today. Our great foundation has been struck
down. Had you followed your brother's wishes, Rama would have

been one of our friends. All of us wouldn't have become widows and the desires of the enemy wouldn't have been fulfilled. You were repeatedly cruel towards Sita and used force to imprison her. The rakshasas, you and we—all three have been brought down in the same way. O bull among rakshasas! You acted out of your own desire, but that wasn't desirable. Everything is driven by destiny. Destiny decides the killer and the killed. O mighty-armed one! In the battle, the destruction of the apes, of the rakshasas and of you has been brought about because of the forces of destiny. In this world, when the results of destiny arise, artha, kama, valour or commands are incapable of resisting them.' Miserable, the wives of the lord of the rakshasas lamented in this way. With tears flowing from their eyes, they were as grief-stricken as female curlews.

Chapter 6(99)

The wives of the rakshasa lamented in this way. The eldest and beloved wife looked miserably at her husband. She saw that Dashagriva had been killed by Rama, whose deeds were unthinkable. Mandodari piteously lamented about her husband. 'O mighty-armed one! You were known as Vaishravana's younger brother. When you were angry, even Purandara was scared of standing before you. Anxious at hearing your name, the rishis, the gods of the earth, the illustrious gandharvas and the charanas fled in different directions. O king! O bull among rakshasas! Rama, a mere human, has vanquished you in the battle. Why are you not ashamed at this? Full of prosperity and valour, you invaded the three worlds. You could not be resisted. Yet, you have been slain by a man wandering around in the forest. Assuming any form at will, you roamed around in the dominion of men. In a battle, you should not have come about your destruction at the hands of Rama. In the field of battle, I do not believe that Rama performed this act. Nor do I think he attacked and invaded you in every possible way. In earlier times, you conquered your senses and vanquished the three

worlds. As remembrance of that, the senses have defeated you now.
In Rama's form, Vasava himself may have come to destroy your
maya beyond any possible doubt. As soon as your brother Khara,
surrounded by many rakshasas, was killed in Janasthana, it was
evident that he was no mere human. Even the gods find it extremely
difficult to penetrate the city of Lanka. As soon as Hanumat used
his valour to enter, we were distressed. I told you not to engage in
an enmity with Raghava. But since you did not heed that, this evil
has come upon us. O bull among the rakshasas! For the destruction
of your prosperity, your body and your own relatives, a sudden
desire for Sita came upon you. O evil-minded one! She is superior
to Arundhati[371] and Rohini. You oppressed the respected one. This
was not an act that was worthy of you. Maithilee is no match for
me in nobility of birth, beauty or gentleness. But because of your
confusion, you did not comprehend whether she was superior to me
or equal to me. In every way, among all beings, there is a reason for
death. As for you, Maithilee is the reason for your death. Maithilee
will find pleasure with Rama, freed from grief. I am limited in
fortune. That is the reason I am immersed in this terrible ocean of
grief. I have sported with you in Kailasa, Mandara, Meru and the
grove of Chaitraratha, in beautiful vimanas that were unmatched
in their prosperity. Clad in colourful garlands and garments, I
have seen many regions. O brave one! With your death, I am now
deprived of all those objects of pleasure. O immensely fortunate
one! My brother-in-law[372] speaks the truth and what he said was
true. "This one[373] has presented herself for the destruction of the
foremost among the rakshasas. Desire and anger have arisen and
addiction to them will bring about hardship." You have brought
about all this. The lineage of the rakshasas is without a protector.
You were famous for your strength and manliness and I should
not grieve over you. But because of my feminine nature, my mind
is whirling around in pity. You have accepted your good deeds
and bad deeds and have attained your own destination. Since I am

[371] Vasishtha's wife.
[372] Vibhishana.
[373] Sita.

miserable at being separated from you, I am grieving about myself.
You possess the complexion of a dark cloud. You are attired in
yellow garments. You wear auspicious armlets. Why are you lying
down, covered in blood, with your entire body stretched out?
I am afflicted by grief. You seem to be asleep. Why are you not
replying to me? You were immensely valiant and accomplished.
You did not run away from an encounter. I am the granddaughter
of a yatudhana.[374] Why are you not replying to me? Your club is as
radiant as the sun and you used it to oppress enemies in battles. It is
like the vajra of the wielder of the vajra and you always revered it. It
is polished with nets of gold and in battles, you have struck enemies
with this. Arrows have shattered it into a thousand fragments and
they are scattered around. Shame on my heart. It is not shattering
into a thousand fragments. You are dead and the consequence is
that I am afflicted by grief.'

At this time, Rama spoke to Vibhishana. 'Restrain the women
and perform funeral rites for your brother.' Having comforted them,
Vibhishana addressed Rama in the following words. He knew about
dharma and he used his intelligence to think about it. His beneficial
words were full of dharma and artha. Following what Rama had
said, he replied in these words. 'He abandoned the vows of dharma.
He was cruel. He was violent and followed falsehood. He was
attracted to the wives of others. I should not perform funeral rites
for him. He was an enemy in the form of a brother. He was always
engaged in what was injurious. Though the respect due to a senior
deserves worship, Ravana does not deserve to be worshipped. O
Rama! Men on earth will refer to me as someone cruel. However,
on hearing about all his qualities, they will subsequently say that I
performed a good deed.' On hearing this, Rama, supreme among
the upholders of dharma, was greatly delighted. The one who
knew about words and was eloquent in the use of words addressed
Vibhishana in these words. 'I have obtained victory because of your
powers. Therefore, I must do what is agreeable to you. O lord of
the rakshasas! You must certainly pardon the words that I use.

[374] Mandodari's grandfather was Sumali.

The roamer in the night followed adharma and falsehood. He was attached to desire. However, he was always energetic, strong and brave in battles. It has been heard that he could not be defeated by the gods, with Shatakratu at the forefront. The great-souled Ravana was full of strength and he made the worlds scream. With death, enmity ends and we no longer have any need for that. Therefore, let his funeral rites be performed. He belongs to me, just as he does to you. O mighty-armed one! Following the prescribed ordinances, his funeral rites should be performed by you. You will then obtain great dharma and fame.'

Hearing Raghava's words, Vibhishana hurried. He arranged for the proper funeral rites for Ravana. Following the ordinances, Vibhishana applied fire. He repeatedly entreated the women and comforted them. With all the rakshasis, Vibhishana entered.[375] He then approached Rama's presence and stood there humbly. With his soldiers and Sugriva and Lakshmana, Rama was delighted that his enemy had been killed, just as Vritra had been by Shatakratu.

Chapter 6(100)

On witnessing Ravana's death, the gods, the gandharvas and the danavas conversed about this auspicious account and left on their respective vimanas. Conversing about the terrible Ravana's death, Raghava's valour, the excellent fight put by the apes, Sugriva's counsel and the love and valour of Soumitri Lakshmana, those immensely fortunate ones happily returned to wherever they had come from. Raghava's divine chariot had been given by Indra and was as radiant as the fire. The mighty-armed one worshipped Matali and gave him leave to return with that. Having obtained Raghava's permission, Matali, Shakra's charioteer, ascended that divine chariot and ascended to heaven. When he ascended to heaven on that chariot, Raghava, supreme among warriors, was extremely

[375] The city of Lanka.

delighted and embraced Sugriva. He embraced Sugriva and was greeted by Lakshmana. Worshipped by the best among the apes, he went to the place where the forces were camped.

Soumitri Lakshmana, full of spirit and blazing in energy, was near him. Rama spoke to him. 'O amiable one! Vibhishana must be consecrated in Lanka. He is devoted and faithful and has done good deeds for me. Though he is Ravana's younger brother, this is my supreme desire. O amiable one! Let us see Vibhishana consecrated in Lanka.' Soumitri was thus addressed by the great-souled Raghava. He happily agreed and brought a golden pot. In the midst of the rakshasas in Lanka, following Rama's command, Soumitri used that golden pot to consecrate Vibhishana. The one with dharma in his soul consecrated Vibhishana, who was pure in his soul. On seeing that Vibhishana, Indra among rakshasas, had been consecrated in Lanka, the advisers[376] and the rakshasas who were devoted to him rejoiced. With Lakshmana, Raghava was filled with great delight. Granted by Rama, Vibhishana obtained that great kingdom. Having comforted the ordinary people, he came to Rama. Happy in their minds and content, the roamers in the night who were residents of the city brought and offered him[377] unbroken grain,[378] sweetmeats[379] and divine parched grain.[380] The invincible and valiant one accepted all these auspicious objects and offered them to Raghava and Lakshmana. Rama saw that Vibhishana had accomplished his objective and was now prosperous. Therefore, wishing to do what would bring him pleasure, he accepted everything.

The brave ape Hanumat, who was like a mountain, was standing near him, with his hands joined in salutation and his head bowed down. Rama addressed him in these words. 'Take the permission of this amiable and great king, Vibhishana. Resort to humility and enter Ravana's residence. Tell Vaidehi that I, Sugriva and Lakshmana are well. O supreme among victorious ones! Tell

[376] Vibhishana's four advisers.
[377] Brought Vibhishana.
[378] *Akshata*, unhusked grain.
[379] *Modaka*.
[380] *Laja*.

her that I have killed Ravana. O lord of the apes! Convey this agreeable news to Vaidehi. Ascertain her message and return.'

Chapter 6(101)

Hanumat, the son of the wind god, was instructed in this way. Worshipped by the roamers in the night, he entered the city of Lanka. The immensely energetic one entered Ravana's residence and saw her, terrified like Rohini separated from the moon. He approached her in secret, bowed his head down and greeted her. He started to tell her everything that Rama had said. 'O Vaidehi! Rama, Sugriva and Lakshmana are well. With the help of Vibhishana, Lakshmana and the apes, Rama, the destroyer of enemies, has accomplished his objective and has killed the enemy. He has said that he is well. O queen! The valiant Ravana has been made to die. The brave Rama, the descendant of the Raghu lineage, has asked about your welfare. Having accomplished his inner desires, extremely happy, he has told you this. "O queen![381] I am conveying this agreeable news and am also praising you. O one who knows about dharma! It is my good fortune that you are still alive after my victory in the battle. O Sita! We have obtained victory. Be at ease. Dispel your anxiety. The enemy, Ravana, has been killed and Lanka has been brought under subjugation. I have not slept. My resolution was firm that I would win you back. A bridge was built across the great ocean and the pledge has been accomplished. As long as you are in Ravana's residence, you need not have any fear. Everything in this prosperous Lanka is now under Vibhishana's control. Therefore, be comforted and at ease. It is as if you are in your own house. This one is going to you.[382] He is happy and eager to see you."'

[381] These are Rama's words, being stated by Hanumat. Hence, we have put them within quotes.

[382] This is probably a reference to Hanumat. But since the subject isn't mentioned, it is conceivable that Rama meant Vibhishana.

Thus addressed, with a face like the moon, Sita leapt up. Her joy constricted her and she was unable to say anything. Since Sita did not reply, the best among the apes spoke to her. 'O queen! What are you thinking? Why are you not replying to me?' Sita based herself on dharma and was thus addressed by Hanumat. Extremely delighted, and in a voice choking with tears, she replied. 'I have heard this pleasant news that my husband has obtained victory. I was overwhelmed with joy and, for a while, was unable to speak. O ape! You have brought me this agreeable news. However, though I have thought about it, I do not see anything here that I can give you and honour you with. O amiable one! O ape! You have brought me this agreeable news. However, I do not see anything on earth that can be given to someone like you. Gold, silver, many riches, a kingdom or the three worlds are not sufficient for someone who brings this news.' When Vaidehi Sita spoke in this way, stationed in front of her, the ape joined his hands in salutation and heard her words.

He replied, 'You are engaged in doing what brings your husband pleasure. You desire your husband's victory. It is only someone like you who can speak such gentle words. O amiable one! Your words are gentle and profound. They are superior to heaps of jewels and the kingdom of the gods. I have obtained my objective. I have seen Rama victorious, having slain the enemy. In qualities, that is superior to the kingdom of the gods and everything else. Earlier, all these rakshasis have censured you. If you permit it, I wish to kill them. They are terrible in form and conduct. They are cruel and their eyes are crueller. You are devoted to your husband and when you were in Ashokavana, they oppressed you. These rakshasis are extremely terrible and they are horrible in speech. Grant me this boon. I wish to kill them, using different kinds of blows. O beautiful one! I will strike them and bring them down with fists, hands, feet, teeth and terrible blows with the thighs. I will eat up their noses and ears. I will pull out their hair. When I strike, kill and make them suffer, their mouths will turn extremely dry. O illustrious one! In this way, I wish to strike them in many different ways. O queen! They have committed crimes towards you and I want to kill them.' Vaidehi, Janaka's daughter, was addressed by Hanumat in this way. The illustrious one replied to Hanumat in words that were full of dharma. 'O supreme among apes! They were dependent on the king and under his control. They acted in accordance with someone else's command. It is not proper to be angry with servant maids. Because of my former wicked deeds, this misfortune has come upon me. That is the reason I obtained all this. In this world, one reaps the consequences of one's own deeds. Destiny determined that this kind of misfortune had to be suffered. Ravana's servant maids are weak in strength and I am pardoning them. The rakshasis censured me because they were commanded by Ravana. O supreme among apes! Since he has been killed, they will no longer roar. In this connection, there is an ancient shloka that was chanted by a bear in a tiger's presence. It is full of dharma. O ape! Hear it. "The wicked acts committed by others are evil committed by others. They do not touch you. A pledge must be honoured. For virtuous people, good conduct constitutes ornaments."[383] O ape! The wicked do not deserve to be killed. Since there is no one who does not commit a crime, it is better and noble to show them compassion. The rakshasas can assume any form at will and roam around the world, causing injury. But though they act wickedly, one should not act inappropriately towards them.' Hanumat, accomplished in the use of words, was thus addressed by Sita. He replied to Sita, Rama's illustrious wife. 'You are indeed an illustrious and appropriate wife for Rama. O queen! Give me your message of reply, so that I can go to the spot where Raghava is.'

Thus addressed by Hanumat, Vaidehi, Janaka's daughter, replied, 'O supreme among apes! I wish to see my husband.' Hearing her words, Hanumat, the immensely radiant son of the

---

[383] The story is as follows. A tiger pursued a hunter. The hunter climbed a tree on which a bear was perched. The hunter and the bear agreed that they would not push each other down. The tiger asked the bear to push the hunter down, but he refused. When the tiger asked the hunter to push down the bear, he tried, but wasn't successful. The tiger repeated the request to the bear, citing violation of the pledge. However, the bear refused and chanted the shloka.

wind god, delighted Maithilee and addressed her in these words. 'O
noble one! You will see Rama, whose face is like the full moon, and
Lakshmana, like Shachi sees the lord of the gods. His friends stand
firm and his enemy has been killed.' He addressed Sita, who was as
radiant as Shri herself. With great speed, Hanumat went to the spot
where Raghava was.

Chapter 6(102)

Rama was supreme among all wielders of the bow. Having gone
there, the immensely wise ape, who knew about the meanings
of words, addressed him. 'This task was started because of her and
it has led to fruits. The queen, Maithilee, is tormented by grief. You
should see her. She is immersed in grief and her eyes are overflowing
with tears. Having heard about your victory, she has been filled
with joy. She trusted me because of the earlier occasion.[384] Because
of her trust in you, she said, "My husband has been successful
in his objective. I wish to see him, together with Lakshmana."'
Hanumat told the one who was supreme among the upholders of
dharma this. With his eyes full of tears, Rama suddenly started to
think. He emitted deep and warm sighs. He looked at the ground.
Vibhishana was like a cloud and was nearby. He told him, 'Let
Vaidehi be adorned in divine ornaments and let her be smeared with
celestial pastes. After she has bathed her head, let her be brought
here quickly.'

Thus addressed by Rama, Vibhishana hurried. Urged by his
master and accompanied by women, he entered the inner quarters,
where Sita was. 'O Vaidehi![385] Adorn yourself in divine ornaments
and smear yourself with celestial pastes. O fortunate one! Mount a
vehicle. Your husband desires to see you.' Thus addressed, Vaidehi
replied to Vibhishana, 'O lord of the rakshasas! I wish to see my

---

[384] When Hanumat visited her in Ashokavana.

[385] The Critical Edition excises a shloka where we are told that Vibhishana tells Sita
this, after greeting her.

husband without having had a bath.' Hearing her words, Vibhishana said, 'Rama is your husband and you should act in accordance with what he has said.' The virtuous Maithilee was faithful and devoted to her husband and treated her husband like a divinity. Hearing his words, she consented. Sita bathed her hair and young maidens ornamented her. She was adorned in extremely expensive ornaments. She was attired in extremely expensive garments. She ascended a dazzling palanquin that was covered with an extremely expensive spread. Protected by many rakshasas, Vibhishana took her there. He went there and made it known to the great-souled one that he had arrived. He bowed down and happily informed that Sita had arrived.

She had resided in the residence of a rakshasa for a long time. On hearing that she had arrived, Raghava was filled with all three of joy, misery and rage. He saw that Vibhishana was near him. He reflected and thought deeply. Raghava addressed him in these cheerless words. 'O lord of the rakshasas! O amiable one! You have always been engaged in ensuring my victory. Let Vaidehi be quickly brought into my presence.' Vibhishana heard Raghava's words of command. He endeavoured to ensure that everyone was swiftly cleared from that place. Men with cloaks[386] and headdresses, with staffs made of cane in their hands, roamed around everywhere, dispersing people. Everywhere, hordes of bears, apes and rakshasas were made to withdraw some distance away. When all of them were being withdrawn, a roar arose. It was like the sound of the ocean, when it is agitated by a storm. In every direction, the terrified people were being dispersed away. On seeing this, because of resentment and compassion, Raghava prevented this. Rama was angry and seemed to burn down with his sight. He addressed the immensely wise Vibhishana in words of censure. 'Ignoring me, why are you making these people suffer? Cease this attempt to disperse people. They are my own people. Women do not need houses, garments, walls, condemnation and this kind of royal treatment. Their covering is good conduct. There is no sin to women being

---

[386] *Kanchuka*, this can also be translated as jacket, upper garment, or armour.

seen at time of adversity, hardship, war, *svayamvara*,[387] sacrifice or marriage. She has simultaneously suffered from war and great hardship. There is no sin to her being seen, especially because this is in my presence. O Vibhishana! Let her be brought quickly before me. Let Sita see me stationed here, surrounded by all the large numbers of my well-wishers.'

Thus addressed by Rama, the distressed Vibhishana humbly brought Sita to Rama's presence. Hearing Rama's words, Lakshmana, Sugriva and the ape Hanumat were also extremely unhappy. They detected terrible signs in the way he was looking towards his wife. They debated[388] that Raghava was unpleasant towards his wife. Because of her shame, Maithilee seemed to shrink into her own body. Following Vibhishana, she approached her husband. In that assembly of people, because of her shame, she covered her face with her garment. As she approached her husband, she wept and exclaimed, 'O noble one!' Regarding her husband as a divinity, she was filled with amazement, delight and affection. With a face that was even more amiable, she glanced towards her husband's amiable face. She looked for a long time at her beloved's face, which was as handsome as the full moon when it has arisen. All her mental fatigue was dispelled. Her own face sparkled like the moon.

Chapter 6(103)

Rama glanced at Maithilee, who was bowed down, next to him. He started to express the anger that raged in his heart. 'O fortunate one! Having defeated the enemy in a battle, you have been won back by me. I have thus achieved what could be accomplished through manliness. My great intolerance has been quenched and I have cleansed the oppression. At the same time, I have removed

---

[387] When a maiden chooses her own husband.
[388] Within themselves, not publicly.

the disrespect that the enemy exhibited towards me. Today, my manliness has been seen. My efforts have been successful. Through my own powers, I have accomplished the pledge today. When you were alone, you were taken away by a fickle rakshasa. That was a taint brought about by destiny. As a human, I have vanquished it. If a man does not use his energy to cleanse the disrespect that has been shown to him, what is the point of his manliness? He is limited in his energy. In leaping over the ocean and crushing Lanka, Hanumat performed praiseworthy deeds that have been rendered successful today. Sugriva and his soldiers exhibited valour in the field of battle and provide beneficial counsel. Today, their exertions have met with success. The devoted Vibhishana abandoned his brother, who was devoid of qualities, and presented himself before me. His exertions have met with success.' Hearing such words, uttered by Rama, Sita's eyes widened, like those of a doe, and became full of tears.

Seeing her, Rama was again filled with rage. He blazed, like a fire into which an excessive quantity of clarified butter had been sprinkled. He knit his eyebrows in a frown. With his eyes, he glanced sideways at her. In the midst of the apes and the rakshasas, he addressed Sita in these harsh words. 'A man must act so as to cleanse any oppression caused to him. O Sita! I have been successful in that, cleansing the oppression at the hands of the enemy. Despite his austerities and despite cleansing his soul, the sage Agastya found the southern direction to be unassailable. I have conquered that world of the living. O fortunate one! Let it be known to you that this exertion in the field of battle, accomplished well because of the valour of my well-wishers, was not undertaken for your sake. My conduct has always been such as to ward off bad reputation in every possible way. I have cleansed the blemish that was associated with my famous lineage. You are standing in front of me and there is a doubt about your character. I am firm in my antipathy towards you, just as a person suffering in the eyes detests a lamp. O Janaka's daughter! Therefore, you have my permission to go wherever you want. O fortunate one! These ten directions exist. I have nothing to do with you. If a woman has resided in the house of another, which energetic man, who has been born in a noble lineage, will take her back again, in a happy frame of mind? You were on Ravana's lap.[389] He has looked at you with wicked eyes. When I mention my great lineage, how can I take you back again? I won you back for a reason and I have got that fame back. I have no attachment for you. You can go wherever you desire. O fortunate one! I have spoken to you in this way after making up my mind. If it makes you happy, you can turn your mind towards Lakshmana or Bharata, Sugriva, Indra among apes, or Vibhishana, Indra among rakshasas. O Sita! Turn your mind towards them, or whatever else makes you happy. Ravana saw your divine and lovely beauty. O Sita! When you were roaming around in his house for such a long time, he must have molested you.' Maithilee deserved to hear pleasant words, but heard these unpleasant ones spoken by her beloved. She released floods of tears and trembled severely for a very long time. She was like a creeper struck by the trunk of a gigantic elephant.

Chapter 6(104)

Vaidehi was thus addressed in harsh words by the enraged Raghava and they made the body hair stand up. She was gravely pained. Earlier, Maithilee had never heard such words in an assembly of people. Hearing her husband's harsh words, she was ashamed and mortified. Because of the stakes in those words, Janaka's daughter was like a dog impaled by spikes.[390] She shed copious tears. She wiped her face, which was overflowing with tears. Speaking in a slow and low voice, she addressed her husband in these words. 'Such words are extremely terrible to the ear. O brave one! Like an ordinary man speaking to an ordinary woman, why are you making me hear such harsh words? O mighty-armed one! I am not what you take me to be. You should have trust in me. I swear on my own character. Because

---

[389] While Sita was being abducted.
[390] Perhaps from the quills of a porcupine, though that is not necessary.

of the conduct of ordinary women, you are casting doubts on the entire species. If I have been tested by you, you should cast aside all doubt. O lord! I did not go to him. When he touched my body, I was incapacitated. I did not commit the crime out of my own desire. It was destiny. My heart was under my control and it was devoted to you. When one does not have a protector, what can one do with a body that comes under someone else's control? O one who grants honours! We have grown up in proximity. If you have not understood my sentiments from that, I have been destroyed for an eternity. O brave one! You sent Hanumat to look for me. I was in Lanka then. O brave one! Why did you not abandon me then? O brave one! In the presence of the Indra among the apes, had you abandoned me then, I would have given up my life. There would have been no need for the exertion, or the need to set lives at risk. There would have been no need for this pointless suffering borne by your well-wishers. O tiger among men! However, you only followed your rage. You were like a feeble man, placing importance on a feminine sentiment. I was not really born from Janaka. I was born from the earth. O one who knows about conduct! You did not set great score to my conduct. Though you accepted my hand in marriage when both of us were children, this was not sufficient proof. You have turned your back towards my devotion, good conduct and everything else.' Her voice choking with tears, she said this and wept.

Distressed and immersed in thought, Sita then spoke to Lakshmana. 'O Soumitri! Prepare a funeral pyre for me. That is the medication for a calamity. Having suffered from a false accusation, I am not interested in remaining alive. My husband is displeased with my qualities and has abandoned me in an assembly of people. It is better that I should enter a fire, the destination for those who do not have a destination.' Vaidehi told Lakshmana, the slayer of enemy heroes, this. Filled with great intolerance, she glanced towards Raghava. From the indicated signs, Soumitri understood what was in Rama's mind. Given the valiant Rama's inclination, Soumitri prepared a funeral pyre. With her face lowered, Vaidehi slowly circumambulated Rama and approached the blazing fire. Maithilee bowed down to the gods and the brahmanas. She joined her hands in salutation and approached the fire. 'If my heart has always been with Raghava and never wavered, let the fire, which is a witness to the world, save me in every possible way.' Having said this, Vaidehi circumambulated the fire. Without the slightest bit of hesitation in her mind, she entered the blazing flames.

There was an extremely large gathering of the young and the aged there and they saw Maithilee enter the fire. As she entered the fire, loud and extraordinary sounds of lamentation arose from the rakshasas and the apes.

Chapter 6(105)

King Vaishravana, Yama, with the ancestors, the thousand-eyed great Indra, Varuna, the scorcher of enemies, the handsome three-eyed Mahadeva, with the bull as his banner, and Brahma, the creator of all the worlds and supreme among those who know about the brahman—all of them arrived in vimanas that were as radiant as the sun. They arrived in the city of Lanka and approached Raghava. The best among the gods raised their large arms, their hands full of ornaments, and spoke to Raghava, while he stood there, his hands joined in salutation. 'You are the lord of all the worlds. You are supreme and best among those who know. How can you ignore Sita when she descends into the fire? Why don't you comprehend your nature as the best among all the gods? Among the Vasus, you are the foremost Vasu, Ritadhama, who was a Prajapati.[391] He was Svayambhu, the original creator of the three worlds. Among the Rudras, you are the eighth Rudra.[392] Among the Sadhyas, you are the fifth.[393] The two Ashvins are your ears and the sun and the moon

---

[391] There are eight Vasus. The names vary, though Ritadhama is not a name in the standard lists. Ritadhama means one whose abode is the truth.

[392] There are eleven Rudras. Since the names vary in different lists, the eighth Rudra cannot be given a specific name.

[393] There is no unambiguous number of Sadhyas, but a number of twelve is sometimes given.

are your eyes. O scorcher of enemies! You are seen at the beginning and the end of the worlds. Like an ordinary human, you are ignoring Vaidehi.' The guardians of the worlds addressed Raghava, the lord of the worlds, in this way. Rama, supreme among the upholders of dharma, replied to the best among the gods. 'I think of myself as human. I am Rama, Dasharatha's son. You illustrious ones should tell me who I am and what I am.'

When Kakutstha said this, Brahma, supreme among those who know about the brahman, responded. 'O Rama! O one for whom valour is the truth! Hear the truth. You are the god Narayana. You are the handsome lord who has the chakra as a weapon. You are the single-tusked boar. You are the one who has vanquished his enemies in the past and will in the future. You are without decay. You are the brahman. O Raghava! You are the truth in the middle and at the end.[394] You are supreme dharma in the worlds. You are Vishvaksena.[395] You are the four-armed one. You are the wielder of the Sharnga bow. You are Hrishikesha. You are Purusha.[396] You are Purushottama.[397] You have not been vanquished. You are the Vishnu who wields the sword. You are the immensely strong Krishna. You are the leader of armies and villages. You are intelligence. You are the spirit. You are forgiveness. You are self-control. You are the origin. You are the destruction. You are Upendra. You are Madhusudana. You perform deeds for Indra. You are the great Indra. You are Padmanabha.[398] You are the one who ends battles. You are the one who grants refuge. You are the refuge. The maharshis have spoken of you as the divine one. You are the one with one thousand horns. You are the soul of the Vedas. You are the one with one hundred tongues. You are the great bull. You are the sacrifice. O scorcher of enemies! You are *vashatkara*.[399] You are *omkara*.[400] No one knows about

---

[394] Of the universe.
[395] Vishnu's name, meaning one whose soldiers can go everywhere.
[396] The supreme being.
[397] The excellent being.
[398] One with a lotus in his navel.
[399] Vashatkara is the exclamation *'vashat'* made at the time of offering an oblation.
[400] The sound of *'om'/'aum'*.

your origin or your end. You are seen in all creatures, in cattle and in brahmanas. You are in all the directions, the sky, the mountains and the rivers. You possess a thousand feet. You are the one with Shri. You possess a hundred heads. You possess a thousand eyes. You bear the earth, with all its creatures and the mountains. You are the giant serpent,[401] seen in the water at the bottom of the earth. O Rama! You sustain the three worlds, with the gods, the gandharvas and the danavas. O Rama! I am your heart. The goddess Sarasvati is your tongue. O lord! The gods, created by Brahma, are your body hair. Night has been said to be the closing of your eyes and day the opening of your eyes. You are the pure speech of the Vedas. There is nothing without you. Everything in the universe is your body. The earth is your patience. The fire is your anger. Your equanimity is Soma.[402] You bear the *srivatsa* mark.[403] In ancient times, with three valorous strides, you traversed the three worlds. Having bound the great asura, Bali, you made the great Indra the king. Sita is Lakshmi and you are the god Vishnu. You are Krishna. You are Prajapati. You entered a human body in this world for the sake of killing Ravana. O supreme among the upholders of dharma! You have performed the task for us. O Rama! Now that Ravana has been killed, we can cheerfully return to heaven. Your strength and valour are invincible. Your power never fails. Men who are devoted to you never fail. O god! If men faithfully chant about you as the ancient Purushottama, it is certain that they will never be vanquished.'

Chapter 6(106)

Hearing the auspicious words spoken by the grandfather, the fire god arose, holding Vaidehi in his lap. She was like the rising sun, adorned in ornaments made out of molten gold. The young

---

[401] Shesha.

[402] The moon.

[403] Vishnu bears the srivatsa mark (or curl) on his chest. This is the place where Lakshmi resides.

one was attired in red garments. Her dark hair was curled. She was wearing garlands that did not fade and ornaments. That was the form of the spirited one. Holding Vaidehi in his lap, the fire god gave her to Rama. The fire, the witness of the world, told Rama, 'O Rama! This is Vaidehi and there is no sin in her. She possesses good conduct and her conduct is firm. In words, thoughts, intelligence and sight, she has always followed you. She was distressed, incapacitated and separated from you in the lonely forest. At that time, the rakshasa Ravana, full of valour, abducted her. Though she was protected and confined in the inner quarters, her mind was always devoted to you. She was guarded by terrible rakshasis who were terrible in their intelligence. They tempted and censured Maithilee in many ways. But her inner thoughts were always in you and she did not even think about that rakshasa. Her sentiments are pure. She is faultless. O Raghava! Accept her. She should not suffer in any way. I am commanding you.' The immensely energetic one, patient and firm in his valour, was addressed in this way.

Rama, supreme among the upholders of dharma, replied to the best of the gods. 'Before the three worlds, Sita certainly needed to be purified. The auspicious one has dwelt for a long period of time in Ravana's inner quarters. Had Janakee not been purified, virtuous people would have told me that Rama, Dasharatha's son, is foolish and is driven by desire. I know that Maithilee, Janaka's daughter, is single-mindedly devoted to me and that her mind is only on me. However, I am devoted to the truth. For the sake of persuading the three worlds, I ignored Vaidehi when she entered the fire. This large-eyed one was protected through her own energy and Ravana could not violate her, just as the great ocean does not cross the shoreline. The extremely evil-souled one was unable to approach Maithilee even in his thoughts. She was like the blazing flames of the fire and there was no question of his approaching and oppressing her. The auspicious one did not consider the prosperity in Ravana's inner quarters. Just as the sun is not separate from its radiance, Sita is not separate from me. Maithilee, Janaka's daughter, has been purified before the three worlds. No one is capable of sullying her deeds. I must certainly act in accordance with all the beneficial words you have spoken. The gentle guardians of the world have also spoken about what is beneficial.' When he spoke these words, because of his deeds, he was praised by the extremely strong ones. The immensely strong Rama was united with his beloved. Raghava, who deserved happiness, was happy.

Chapter 6(107)

Hearing the auspicious words spoken by Raghava, Maheshvara spoke words that were even more auspicious. 'O lotus-eyed one! O mighty-armed one! O broad-chested one! O scorcher of enemies! O supreme among those who wield weapons! It is good fortune that you have accomplished this task. On account of the fear of Ravana, a terrible darkness had spread over all the worlds. It is good fortune that you have dispelled this in the battle. You must see and comfort the distressed Bharata, the illustrious Kousalya, Kaikeyee and Sumitra, Lakshmana's mother. You must obtain the kingdom of Ayodhya and delight the well-wishers. O immensely strong one! You must establish the noble lineage of the Ikshvakus. You must perform a horse sacrifice and obtain excellent fame. You must donate riches to the brahmanas and go to heaven. Your father, King Dasharatha, is on this vimana. O Kakutstha! Your immensely illustrious senior has come to the world of men. Having been saved by you, his son, he went to Indra's handsome world. With your brother, Lakshmana, greet him.'

Their father was seated on the top of the vimana. Hearing Mahadeva's words, Kakutstha, with Lakshmana, bowed down before him. Their father blazed in his own prosperity. He was attired in dazzling garments. With his brother, Lakshmana, the lord saw his father. Astride the vimana, on seeing his son, whom he loved more than his own lives,[404] King Dasharatha was filled with great joy. When the lord approached that excellent seat, the mighty-

---

[404] Used in the plural.

armed one took him up on his lap. Embracing him in his arms, he
commended him in these words. 'In heaven, I receive a great deal
of respect from the gods and the rishis. O Rama! However, I am
telling you truthfully. Listen to me. Without you, this is nothing.
O supreme among eloquent ones! The words that Kaikeyee spoke,
for the sake of exiling you, are still impaled in my heart. I see that
you are well with Lakshmana and I have embraced you. Today, I
have been freed from my misery, like the sun from mist. O son! I
have been saved by you, my great-souled and excellent son, just as
the sage Ashtavakra, with dharma in his soul, saved a brahmana.[405]
O amiable one! O Purushottama! I now know that the lords of the
gods had ordained it that you would kill Ravana in this world. O
Rama! Kousalya will indeed attain her objective. She will see you
return home. O slayer of enemies! When she sees you return from the
forest, she will be happy. O Rama! The men who see you return to
the city will indeed be successful in their objectives. They will see you
consecrated as the king, sprinkled with water. The strong Bharata is
pure. He follows dharma and is devoted to you. I desire to see you
and he unite. O amiable one! You have spent fourteen years in the
forest, residing there with Sita and the intelligent Lakshmana. The
period of your exile in the forest is over. You have been successful
in accomplishing your pledge. You have also killed Ravana in the
battle and have satisfied the gods. O slayer of enemies! You have
performed a praiseworthy deed and have obtained fame. Instated in
the kingdom, may you have a long life, with your brothers.'

When the king said this, Rama joined his hands in salutation and
said, 'O one who knows about dharma! Show your favours towards
Kaikeyee and Bharata. You told Kaikeyee, "I am disowning you and
your son." O lord! That terrible curse should not touch Kaikeyee or
her son.' When Rama joined his hands in salutation and said this,
the great king agreed. He embraced Lakshmana and again spoke
these words.[406] 'Devotedly serve Rama and Vaidehi Sita. You will
then make me extremely happy and obtain the fruits of dharma.

---

[405] Ashtavakra's story is told in the Mahabharata. The brahmana in question is
Kahoda, Ashtavakra's father. Kahoda had been imprisoned, but Ashtavakra saved him.
[406] These are addressed to Lakshmana.

O one who knows about dharma! You will obtain dharma and great fame on earth. When Rama is pleased, you will also obtain greatness in heaven. O fortunate one! O extender of Sumitra's delight! Serve Rama. Rama is always engaged in ensuring what is auspicious for all the worlds. Indra, the three worlds, the siddhas and the supreme rishis approach the great-souled one and worship him as Purushottama. He has been spoken of as the unmanifest one, the one without decay. O amiable one! He is the heart of the gods, who were created by Brahma. Rama is the scorcher of enemies and is subtle. Having served at his feet, you will obtain dharma and great fame. Serve him and Vaidehi Sita with devotion.' The mighty-armed Lakshmana was standing there, his hands joined in salutation, and he was addressed in this way.

The king, with dharma in his soul, then addressed Vaidehi in these auspicious words. 'O Vaidehi! You should not harbour any anger towards him. Rama had your welfare in mind and wished to purify you. O one with the excellent brows! Though I must certainly mention it in my words, you need not be instructed about serving your husband. He is a supreme divinity to you.' He thus instructed his two sons and Sita, his daughter-in-law. In a blazing vimana, Dasharatha then went to Indra's world.

Chapter 6(108)

After Kakutstha[407] left, the great Indra, the chastiser of Paka, spoke in an extremely happy voice to Raghava, who was standing there, his hands joined in salutation. 'O Rama! O scorcher of enemies! Your seeing us should not be fruitless. I am full of affection for you. Tell me what you desire.' Kakutstha was addressed in this way. With his brother, Lakshmana, and his wife, Sita, he joined his hands in salutation and said, 'O lord of all the gods! O supreme among eloquent ones! If you are full of affection for me,

---

[407] Meaning Dasharatha.

I will tell you. Please act accordingly and make my words come true. There are valiant ones who have gone to Yama's abode on my account. Let all those apes regain their lives and stand up. Devoted to me and seeking to ensure my pleasure, they did not think about death. Through your favours, let them be united again. This is the boon I ask for. Let them be free of their pains. Let them be free of their wounds. Let them be full of strength and manliness. O one who grants honours! I desire to see the golangulas and the Indras among the bears. Wherever the apes are, let there be sparkling rivers and the best of roots and fruits, irrespective of the season.'

Hearing the words of the great-souled Raghava, the great Indra replied in words that bore signs of affection. 'O son![408] O descendant of the Raghu lineage! You have asked for a great boon. The apes will arise, as if they have awoken after being asleep. They will be filled with great delight and will meet their well-wishers, relatives, kin and near ones. O great archer! Even if the season isn't right, the trees will be colourful with flowers and laden with fruit. The rivers will be full of water.'

Earlier, their bodies had been covered with wounds. They were now hale, without any wounds. All the apes were astounded and exclaimed, 'What is this?' All the supreme gods saw that Kakutstha had completely attained his objective. They first praised him, who deserved praise, together with Lakshmana. 'O brave one! Take your leave of the apes and go to Ayodhya. Comfort the devoted and ascetic Maithilee. Meet your brother, Bharata. Grieving over you, he is observing vows. Go and consecrate yourself and delight the residents of the city.' Saying this, the gods took their leave of Rama and Soumitri. They cheerfully went to heaven in vimanas that were like the sun. Kakutstha honoured all the excellent gods. With his brother, Lakshmana, he instructed that the camps should be set up. Protected by Lakshmana, that illustrious and large army was full of joy. In every direction, it blazed and dazzled in its prosperity. Night set in, illuminated by cool beams.[409]

---

[408] The word used is tata.
[409] Of the moon.

Chapter 6(109)

Having slept during the night, Rama, the slayer of enemies, awoke happily. After having proclaimed his victory, Vibhishana joined his hands in salutation and addressed him in these words. 'O Raghava! Many objects for bathing, unguents for the body, garments, ornaments, sandalwood paste, diverse kinds of divine garlands and lotus-eyed women who know about ornaments have all been kept ready, so that you can bathe.' Thus addressed, Kakutstha replied to Vibhishana, 'Invite Sugriva and the best among the apes to have a bath. The mighty-armed and delicate prince is devoted to the truth. He is used to happiness. However, on my account, the one with dharma in his soul is suffering. With Bharata, Kaikeyee's son who follows dharma, I will now have a bath with extremely expensive garments and ornaments. See how we can swiftly return to that city. This route to return to Ayodhya is extremely difficult to travel on.'

Thus addressed by Kakutstha, Vibhishana replied, 'O son of a king! I will convey you to the city in a single day. O fortunate one! There is a vimana named Pushpaka and it is like the sun. This belonged to my brother, Kubera, but Ravana used his force to seize it. That vimana is like a cloud and it is here. Using that vehicle, without any anxiety, you can go to Ayodhya. O wise one! However, if you are favourably inclined towards me, if you remember my qualities and if you have any affection for me, reside here for some more time. With your brother, Lakshmana, and your wife, Vaidehi, you will be worshipped with all the objects of desire. O Rama! Leave after that. I am full of affection for you. My soldiers and the large number of my well-wishers have made arrangements so that you can be honoured properly. Accept everything that I have prepared. O Raghava! I am your well-wisher and am affectionately entreating you. I am your servant. Show me your favours. I am certainly not trying to order you.' While all the rakshasas and the apes heard this, thus addressed, Rama replied to Vibhishana. 'O brave one! O scorcher of enemies! I have been worshipped by you and your advisers. With supreme affection, you have made every

effort that you can. O lord of the rakshasas! Indeed, it is not that
I don't want to act in accordance with your words. However, my
mind is urging me to hurry, so that I can see my brother, Bharata.
He came to Chitrakuta to make me return. He bowed his head
down and beseeched me. But I did not act in accordance with his
words. Kousalya, Sumitra, the illustrious Kaikeyee, the seniors, the
well-wishers and the residents of the city are there, with their sons.
O lord of the rakshasas! Quickly present that vimana before me.
With my task accomplished, it is not proper that I should reside
here. O amiable one! O Vibhishana! I have been worshipped. Grant
me permission. You should not be angry with me. Bring it swiftly.'
      It had gold all over its body and its platform was made out
of lapis lazuli and jewels. There were deep chambers everywhere,
with the complexion of silver. It was ornamented with white flags
and standards. It was decorated with golden mansions that were
ornamented with golden lotuses. Nets of bells were strewn around.
The windows were embellished with pearls and jewels. Lattice work
with bells was everywhere and it made a pleasant sound. It was
like the summit of Meru and had been created by Vishvakarma. It
was decorated with many mansions, with hues of silver and gold.
The floors were made out of colourful crystal. Colourful in all its
parts, there were excellent seats made out of lapis lazuli. There
were extremely expensive and extremely thick and handsome
spreads. The invincible vimana, as swift as thought, was presented.
Vibhishana came and informed Rama that it was ready.

Chapter 6(110)

Rama saw that Vibhishana had presented Pushpaka and had
decorated it with flowers. He was standing nearby and spoke to
him.[410] Humbly, with his hands joined in salutation, the lord among
the rakshasas hurriedly asked, 'O Raghava! What will I do?' Having

---

[410] Vibhishana spoke to Rama.

thought a little, while Lakshmana heard, Raghava addressed him in words that were great in affection. 'O Vibhishana! Make careful efforts so that all these residents of the forest are honoured with gems, chariots and all kinds of ornaments. O lord of the rakshasas! It is with their help that Lanka has been attacked and won. They have been cheerful and have given up all fear of losing their lives. They did not retreat from the battle. O one who shows honours! They deserve honours. If these leaders of the apes are shown respect, they will be grateful and happy. Listen to me. All of them will come near you because you are generous, collect friends, are compassionate and are famous.' Thus addressed by Rama, Vibhishana divided up jewels and wealth and honoured all the apes. The leaders of the herds were worshipped with jewels and wealth.

Having seen this, Rama ascended that excellent vimana. He took the illustrious and ashamed Vaidehi on his lap. His valiant brother, the archer Lakshmana, was with him. From the vimana, Kakutstha spoke to all the apes, the immensely valorous Sugriva and the rakshasa Vibhishana. 'O supreme among apes! You have performed the task of friends. With my leave, all of you return wherever you wish. O scorcher of enemies! O Sugriva! You have always been scared of offending dharma. You have done everything that a friend and a well-wisher should do. Surrounded by all your soldiers, return quickly to Kishkindha. O Vibhishana! Reside in your own kingdom of Lanka, bestowed by me on you. Even the gods, with Indra, are incapable of assailing you. I will return to Ayodhya, my father's capital. I desire to take the permission and leave from all of you.'

Thus addressed by Rama, all the apes, the Indra among the apes, Vibhishana and all the rakshasas joined their hands in salutation and said, 'We wish to go to Ayodhya. Take all of us with you. O son of a king! After seeing you sprinkled in the course of the consecration and greeting Kousalya, we will quickly return to our own houses.' The one with dharma in his soul was thus addressed by the apes and Vibhishana. The handsome Raghava spoke to Sugriva and Vibhishana. 'This will bring me delight. I will obtain the greatest of joys if I go to the city with large numbers of my well-wishers. O

Sugriva! With the apes, swiftly ascend the vimana. O Vibhishana!
O Indra among the rakshasas! You also ascend, with your advisers.'
Delighted, Sugriva and his soldiers and Vibhishana and his advisers
swiftly ascended the divine Pushpaka. This was Kubera's supreme
resort. When all of them had ascended, with Raghava's permission,
it leapt up into the sky. The radiant vimana proceeded, yoked to
swans. Rama was delighted and resembled Kubera.

Chapter 6(111)

With Rama's permission, the excellent vimana leapt up. It was
like a giant cloud that seemed to be breathing. The descendant
of the Raghu lineage cast his eye around everywhere. Rama spoke
to Maithilee Sita, whose face was like the moon. 'O Vaidehi! Look
at Lanka, constructed by Vishvakarma. It is placed atop the summit
of Trikuta and is like the summit of Kailasa. Behold the field of
battle, covered with a mire made out of flesh and blood. O Sita!
There was a great destruction of apes and rakshasas. O large-eyed
one! On your account, this is where I killed Ravana. Kumbhakarna
and Prahasta, roamer in the night, were killed there. That is where
Lakshmana killed Indrajit, Ravana's son, in the battle. Other
powerful rakshasas were killed—Virupaksha, who was impossible
to look at, Mahaparshva, Mahodara, Akampana, Trishira, Atikaya,
Devantaka and Narantaka. His wife is named Mandodari. She is
lamenting there, surrounded by thousands and thousands of her co-
wives. O one with the beautiful face! Look at the *tirtha* on the ocean
there.[411] That is where we crossed over the ocean and spent the night.
O large-eyed one! That is the bridge I constructed over the ocean,
the abode of the waters. It was extremely difficult to build and it
was done for your sake. This is Nala Setu.[412] O Vaidehi! Behold the
ocean that cannot be agitated. It is Varuna's abode. It is roaring

---

[411] Tirtha means a place of pilgrimage. But etymologically, it means a place where one
descends into the water. In this context, the latter meaning is appropriate.

[412] *Setu* means bridge, the bridge being named after Nala.

and the distant shore cannot be seen. It is full of conch shells and oysters. O Maithilee! Behold that golden Indra among mountains.[413] It seems to possess a golden navel. When Hanumat leapt across the ocean, this is where he rested. That is where Vibhishana, the king of the rakshasas, arrived. O Sita! Kishkindha, with its beautiful groves, can be seen there. That is Sugriva's beautiful city, where I killed Vali. O Sita! Rishyamuka, the supreme and large mountain can be seen, as if it is a cloud tinged with lightning. It is covered with gold and other minerals. Sugriva, Indra among the apes, came and met me here. O Sita! I contracted a pledge for the sake of Vali's destruction. The lake of Pampa, with its colourful groves, can be seen there. Separated from you and extremely miserable, I lamented there. I met Shabaree, who followed dharma, along its shore. That is where I killed Kabandha. His arms were one yojana long. O Sita! Janasthana can be seen there, with the beautiful tree. O one who loves pleasure! On your account, that is where a great encounter raged between the cruel Ravana and the great-souled Jatayu. That is where I used my swift arrows to kill and bring down Khara, Dushana and the immensely valiant Trishira in a battle. O one who is beautiful to behold! The colourful cottage of leaves can be seen there. Ravana, Indra among the rakshasas, forcibly abducted you from there. That is the beautiful Godavari, with its sparkling and auspicious waters. O Maithilee! Behold. Agastya's hermitage can be seen. O Vaidehi! Sharabhanga's great hermitage can be seen there. That is where Shakra Purandara, with the one thousand eyes, arrived. O slender-waisted one! A residence of ascetics can be seen there. Atri, the leader of the group and like the sun and the fire in his splendour, was there. O Sita! That is where you met the ascetic lady who followed dharma.[414] That is the region where I killed Viradha, who was gigantic in size. O one with the excellent body! Chitrakuta has shown itself there. To seek my favours, Kaikeyee's son had come there. From a distance, Yamuna, with its colourful groves, can be seen. O Maithilee! Bharadvaja's beautiful hermitage

---

[413] Mainaka.
[414] Atri's wife, Anasuya.

has revealed itself. O one with the beautiful complexion! Ganga, with the three flows, can be seen. That is Shringaverapura, where Guha arrived. Ayodhya, my father's capital, can be seen there. O Vaidehi! We have returned to Ayodhya. Bow down before it.'

At this, all the apes, the rakshasas and Vibhishana leapt up, to see the city that was beautiful to behold. It was garlanded with white mansions. There were large roads, full of elephants and horses. The apes saw the city of Ayodhya. It was like Amaravati, the city of the great Indra.

Chapter 6(112)

After a full fourteen years were over, it was the fifth lunar day.[415] Lakshmana's elder brother reached Bharadvaja's hermitage. He controlled himself and worshipped the sage. After greeting him, he asked Bharadvaja, the store of austerities, 'O illustrious one! Have you heard that all is well with the city, that there is no disease and there are plenty of alms?[416] Is Bharata conducting himself well? Are my mothers alive?'

The great sage, Bharadvaja, was asked by Rama in this way. He smiled first. Cheerfully, he replied to the best among the Raghu lineage. 'Bharata has smeared himself with mud and is awaiting you with matted hair. He has your sandals in front of him. All is well in your house. A long time ago, attired in bark, you entered the great forest. You were dislodged from the kingdom and were only interested in undertaking tasks of dharma. Your wife was the third.[417] You followed the words of your father. You gave up everything and proceeded on foot. Like an immortal dislodged from heaven, you gave up all the objects of desire. O victor in assemblies! On seeing you, I was initially filled with compassion. You followed Kaikeyee's words and survived on wild roots and fruits. You

---

[415] Panchami in *shukla paksha*.

[416] If the city is prosperous, there will be plenty of alms to be distributed.

[417] Lakshmana was the second.

have now returned, having accomplished your objective. You are prosperous, with large numbers of friends and well-wishers. On seeing you, having triumphed over the enemy, my heart is filled with great delight. O Raghava! I know everything about your joy and misery. You obtained a great deal of this. For the sake of the brahmanas and to protect all the ascetics, you undertook that great slaughter in Janasthana. I know about the sighting of Maricha, Sita's oppression, the sighting of Kabandha, the arrival in Pampa, the friendship with Sugriva and that you killed Vali because of that. I know about searching for Vaidehi, the deed performed by the son of the wind god, the building of Nala Setu for Vaidehi's sake and about the delighted leaders of the apes setting Lanka on fire. In a battle, you killed Ravana, the thorn of the gods, with his sons, relatives, advisers, soldiers and mounts. The gods came before you and granted you a boon. O one who is devoted to dharma! Through my austerities, I know all this. O supreme among those who wield weapons! I will also grant you a boon. I will offer you *arghya*.[418] Accept it and go to Ayodhya tomorrow.'

The son of the king bowed his head down and accepted these words. Having cheerfully agreed, the handsome one asked for a boon. 'O illustrious one! As I proceed towards Ayodhya, may all the trees along the road overflow with honey. May they yield unseasonal fruits.' Trees without fruit became full of fruit. Trees without flowers became full of flowers. All the trees with dry leaves started to flow with honey.

Chapter 6(113)

Looking towards Ayodhya, Raghava was thoughtful. While he was thinking, he saw the apes. Rama was swift in his valour and sought to do what brought pleasure. He wished to do something

---

[418] Objects always offered to a guest—*padya* (water to wash the feet), *achamaniya* (water to wash the mouth/face), *arghya* (a gift) and *asana* (a seat).

pleasant.[419] The intelligent and energetic one spoke to the ape Hanumat. 'O supreme among the apes! Swiftly and quickly, go to Ayodhya. Find out if all is well with the people and in the king's palace. Go to Guha in Shringaverapura. It is in an impenetrable part of the forest. Convey my words and news about my welfare to the lord of the *nishada*s.[420] On hearing that I am well, without disease and free from anxiety, Guha will be happy. He is a friend who is like my own self. Happy, Guha, the lord of the nishadas, will tell you about the road towards Ayodhya and about Bharata's conduct. Convey my words and news about my welfare to Bharata too. Tell him that I, with my wife and Lakshmana, have been successful in our objective. Tell him about Vaidehi's abduction by the powerful Ravana, the conversation with Sugriva and Vali's death in the battle, the search for Maithilee and you finding her after leaping over the great and inexhaustible waters of the ocean, our reaching the ocean and seeing the ocean, the construction of the bridge, Ravana's death, the boons granted by the great Indra, Brahma and Varuna and my meeting with my father because of Mahadeva's favours. Tell him that I have vanquished a great number of enemies and have obtained supreme fame and that I have returned successful in my objective, with immensely strong friends. On hearing all this, the expression Bharata wears on his face will reveal to you his inclinations towards me. Everything will be known through Bharata's limbs. The truth will be discerned through the complexion of his face and what he says. If one is prosperous with all the objects of desire in a kingdom, full of elephants, horses and chariots, obtained from the father and grandfathers, which person's mind will not change? Having been associated with this prosperous kingdom, if Bharata desires it for himself, let that descendant of the Raghu lineage rule over the entire earth. O ape! Get to know his inclination and conduct. You must return swiftly, before we proceed too far.'[421] Hanumat, the son of the wind god, was commanded in this way. He assumed a human form and hurried towards Ayodhya.

[419] Conveying the news that day, instead of waiting for the next day.
[420] The nishadas were hunters who dwelt in mountains and forests.
[421] Towards Ayodhya.

He leapt across his father's path,[422] the auspicious residence of the Indras among the serpents. He crossed the terrible confluence of the Ganga and the Yamuna and descended. The valiant one reached Shringaverapura and approached Guha. Hanumat cheerfully addressed him in these auspicious words. 'Kakutstha Rama, with truth as his valour, is your friend. With Sita and Soumitri, he has asked about your welfare. After obtaining Bharadvaja's permission, he followed the words of the sage and has spent the night of the fifth lunar day there. You will see Raghava today.' The immensely energetic one, his body hair standing up in delight, said this. The powerful one leapt up with great force and without even thinking about it, departed. He saw Rama's[423] tirtha, the rivers Valukini and Gomatee and the extremely terrible forest of sala trees. The tiger among elephants swiftly traversed a long distance.

He approached the flowering trees near Nandigrama. When he was one *krosha*[424] away from Ayodhya, he saw the miserable Bharata, attired in bark and black antelope skin. From having resided in the hermitage, he was emaciated. He had filth on his limbs and wore matted hair. He was grieving because of the hardship his brother had suffered. He was controlled, surviving on roots and fruits. He was following the dharma of ascetics. Matted hair was coiled high on his head. His garments were of bark and deerskin. He was controlled and had cleansed his soul. His energy was like that of a brahmana rishi. With the sandals in front, he ruled over the earth. In the world, he protected the four varnas from all kinds of fear. Pure advisers and priests were present with him. There were also commanders of the forces, attired in ochre garments. The citizens were devoted to dharma. Since the prince was attired in rags and black antelope skin, they had also given up objects of pleasure. He[425] knew about dharma and was like a second Dharma in embodied form. Hanumat, the son of the wind god, joined his hands in salutation and addressed him in these words. 'Kakutstha

---

[422] The sky, the path followed by Vayu.
[423] Parashurama's.
[424] One krosha is two miles, however, the definition was not standardized.
[425] Bharata.

resided in Dandakaranya, attired in bark and sporting matted hair. You are grieving over him. He has asked about your welfare. O lord! I am conveying pleasant news. Abandon this terrible sorrow. You will be united with your brother, Rama, this very instant. Having slain Ravana, Rama has got Maithilee back. Having been successful in his objective, he has arrived, with his immensely strong friends. The immensely energetic Lakshmana has also come and so has the illustrious Sita of Videha, like Shachi with the great Indra.'

Bharata, Kaikeyee's son, was thus addressed by Hanumat. He was delighted. But that joy also led to confusion and he suddenly fell down. In a short while, Raghava[426] reassured himself and arose. Bharata spoke to Hanumat, who had brought the pleasant news. Freed from sorrow and full of joy, he respectfully embraced the ape. The handsome Bharata made him wet with large drops of tears. 'Out of compassion, you have come here. Are you a god or a man? O amiable one! You have brought me pleasant tidings and I will give you what is agreeable—one hundred thousand cows, one hundred excellent villages and sixteen maidens who are auspicious in conduct as your wives. They wear earrings and are golden in complexion. These women are as amiable as the moon. They are decorated in all the ornaments. They are accomplished and have been born in noble families.' From the supreme among the apes, the prince heard the extraordinary news about Rama's arrival. He was delighted at the prospect of seeing Rama. Rejoicing, he again spoke these words.

Chapter 6(114)

'It has indeed been several years since he left for the great forest. I have now heard delightful news about my lord being recounted. The popular saying occurs to me. "If a man is alive, there will be fortune, even after one hundred years." How did the meeting

---

[426] Bharata.

between Raghava and the apes take place? Where did it happen? What was the reason? I am asking you. Tell me the truth.'

Asked by the prince, he sat down on a mat and told him everything about Rama's conduct in the forest. 'Because of the boon granted to your mother, Rama left on an exile. Grieving over his son, King Dasharatha died. O lord! Messengers quickly brought you to the royal residence. You entered Ayodhya, but did not desire the kingdom. You went to Mount Chitrakuta and invited your brother, the afflicter of enemies, to accept the kingdom. But he followed the path of dharma and virtue. He stuck to the king's words and refused the kingdom. You accepted the noble one's sandals and returned. O mighty-armed one! Everything about what occurred till then is known to you. Hear from me about what happened after you returned. You returned and he entered the desolate and extremely large forest of Dandaka, full of animals and birds and extending all the way up to the ocean. As they proceeded through that desolate forest, the powerful Viradha was seen and he roared extremely loudly. He raised his hands up high and emitted an extremely loud roar. However, while he was trumpeting like an elephant, they flung him down into a pit, with his face hanging downwards. Those brothers, Rama and Lakshmana, performed this extremely difficult deed. In the evening, they went to Sharabhanga's beautiful hermitage. After greeting Rama, for whom truth is valour, the sage, Sharabhanga went to heaven. All of them reached Janasthana. There were fourteen thousand rakshasas who were terrible in their deeds. While he was residing there, the great-souled Raghava killed them.[427] After this, Shurpanakha arrived in Rama's presence. Commanded by Rama, Lakshmana suddenly arose. The immensely strong one seized his sword and sliced off her nose and ears. The suffering child approached Ravana. The terrible rakshasa named Maricha was Ravana's follower. Assuming the form of a bejewelled deer, he tempted Vaidehi. Seeing this, Vaidehi told Rama, "Seize it. This handsome and beautiful one should be in our hermitage." Wielding

---

[427] The Critical Edition has the wrong sequence of events. Non-Critical versions preserve the right sequence.

a bow and arrows, Rama rushed after it. Rushing after it, he slew
it with arrows with drooping tufts. O amiable one! When Raghava
rushed after the deer and Lakshmana had also left, Dashagriva
entered the hermitage. He quickly seized Sita, like a planet seizes
Rohini in the sky. In an encounter, he killed the eagle Jatayu, who
desired to save her. Violently seizing Sita, the rakshasa departed
quickly. Apes who were like mountains were based on the summit of
a mountain and they witnessed the extraordinary sight of Sita being
seized. They were amazed to see Ravana, the lord of the rakshasas,
rush away. Ravana, the one who made the worlds shriek, entered
Lanka. He entered his large and auspicious residence, embellished
all around with gold. Having entered, Ravana sought to comfort
Maithilee with his words. When Kakutstha returned, he saw the
eagle and was distressed. When the eagle was killed, Rama cremated
his father's beloved friend. They wandered in the region around
the Godavari, filled with blossoms. In the great forest, the rakshasa
named Kabandha approached. Following Kabandha's words, Rama,
for whom truth is his valour, went to Mount Rishyamuka and met
Sugriva. Even before they met, affection had been generated in their
hearts.[428] When they met and conversed, a great love was generated
between them. With the valour of his own arms, Rama killed the
immensely large and immensely strong Vali in a battle and returned
his own kingdom to him.[429] With all the apes, Sugriva was instated
in the kingdom. He gave a pledge to prince Rama that he would
search out the trail. The Indras among the apes were commanded
by the great-souled Sugriva. Ten crores of apes were sent in all the
directions. Among them, we got lost in Vindhya, supreme among
mountains. We were tormented by great grief and a long period of
time elapsed. The valiant brother of the king of the eagles is named
Sampati. He informed us that Sita was dwelling in Ravana's abode.
My relatives were overcome by sorrow, but I overcame the misery
that was engulfing me. I resorted to my own valour and leapt across
one hundred yojanas. I went to the rakshasa's Ashokavana and saw

[428] Hanumat had been used as a messenger before Rama and Sugriva actually met.
That must be the explanation for this statement.
[429] To Sugriva.

her alone there. She was clad in a faded silken garment. She was miserable, but was firm in her vows. I met the unblemished one in the proper way and asked her everything. I obtained the jewel as a sign. Successful in the objective, I returned. I went to Rama, who is unblemished in his deeds. I gave him the token, the giant jewel that radiated rays. Hearing about Maithilee, he rejoiced and like an afflicted person who drinks amrita and regains his life, he too recovered his hopes of remaining alive. He arose and made arrangements for victory, making up his mind to destroy Lanka. Like the fire that destroys all the worlds, he wished to destroy the world. Reaching the ocean, Nala constructed a bridge. Using that bridge, the army of brave apes crossed. Nila killed Prahasta and Raghava killed Kumbhakarna. Lakshmana killed Ravana's son and Rama himself killed Ravana. Kakutstha, the scorcher of enemies, met Shakra, Yama, Varuna and the divine sages and received boons. Having obtained the boons, he was delighted and met the apes.[430] Astride the Pushpaka vimana, he went to Kishkindha.[431] Having reached the Ganga again, he is residing in the presence of the sages. Tomorrow, when it is the conjunction of the nakshatra Pushya, without any impediments, you will see Rama.'

Hearing about the great and truthful words from Hanumat, Bharata was delighted and joined his hands in salutation. With his mind rejoicing, he spoke these words. 'What I have desired for a long time has indeed become completely fulfilled.'

Chapter 6(115)

On hearing this, Bharata, for whom truth was valour, was supremely delighted. Rejoicing, the slayer of enemy heroes

---

[430] Who had been revived.

[431] As they were returning from Lanka to Ayodhya in the Pushpaka vimana, the Critical Edition excises some shlokas. In those excised shlokas, they stopped in Kishkindha to pick up the wives of the apes, who also came to Ayodhya to join in the festivities. With those shlokas excised, this reference to Kishkindha is unnecessary.

commanded Shatrughna. 'To the sound of musical instruments, let pure men offer worship of extremely fragrant flowers at all the temples[432] and chaityas of the city. Let the wives of the king,[433] the advisers, the soldiers and the wives of the soldiers emerge, so that they can see Rama, whose face is like the moon.' Hearing Bharata's words, the valiant Shatrughna, the slayer of enemy heroes, divided artisans into groups of thousands and urged them. 'Let the entire stretch up to Nandigrama be levelled. Level the low spots. Level the uneven spots. Sprinkle the entire ground with water that is as cool as ice. Let others spread parched grain and flowers everywhere. Let flags be raised along the roads of this supreme and excellent city. Before the sun rises, let all the houses be decorated. Let garlands of extremely fragrant flowers, in the five colours,[434] be strewn around. Let hundreds of men sprinkle the walls along the royal road.'

There were thousands of crazy elephants and these were decorated with gold. There were other elephants and female elephants with golden harnesses. Yoking their chariots, excellent maharathas quickly emerged. All of Dasharatha's wives mounted vehicles. With Kousalya and Sumitra at the forefront, they emerged. The earth seemed to tremble from the sound of the hooves of the horses, the clatter of the wheels of the chariots and the noise of conch shells and drums. The entire city reached Nandigrama. There were the best among brahmanas, with dharma in their souls. There were the chiefs of the shrenis,[435] with all their divisions. There were ministers, with garlands and sweetmeats in their hands. In addition to the sound of conch shell and drums, there were the sounds of bards singing panegyrics. He[436] was surrounded by all these. The one who knew about dharma placed the noble one's sandals on his head. He took a white umbrella that was decorated with white

---

[432] The word 'temple' should not convey the wrong impression. A better translation is 'houses of the gods'. In all probability, these were in individual residences and were not collective places of worship.

[433] Dasharatha's wives.

[434] Since these are flowers, this probably means red, blue, white, yellow and pink.

[435] A shreni is like a guild, it is an association of traders or artisans who follow the same line of business. The word means a rank or line.

[436] Bharata.

garlands. He also took white whisks made out of hair, decorated
with gold, and appropriate for a king. He was lean and emaciated
because of his fasting. He was attired in bark and black antelope
skin. Having already heard about his brother's arrival, he was
filled with joy. With his advisers, the great-souled one advanced to
receive Rama.

Looking towards the son of the wind god, Bharata addressed
him in these words. 'I hope the fickleness that characterizes monkeys
has not taken hold of you. I cannot see the noble Kakutstha Rama,
the scorcher of enemies.' Hearing the words spoken, Hanumat
replied to Bharata, for whom truth was his valour, in words that
were indicative of deep meaning. 'Because of Bharadvaja's favours,
trees that always yield fruits and flowers and flow with honey have
been obtained. The sound of crazy humming bees can be heard. O
scorcher of enemies! That was the boon conferred by Vasava. That
is how hospitality, with all the qualities, was offered to the soldiers.
The terrible and joyous sound of the residents of the forest can be
heard. I think that the army of the apes is crossing the river Gomatee.
Behold. A lot of dust has arisen in the direction of the Valukini. I
think the apes are shaking the beautiful forest of sala trees. From a
distance, the divine Pushpaka vimana can be seen. It sparkles like
the moon. Using his mental powers, Brahma constructed it. Having
slain Ravana and his relatives, the great-souled one obtained it
through the favours of the lord of treasure. It is divine and possesses
the speed of thought. The two brave Raghavas, with Vaidehi, the
immensely energetic Sugriva and Vibhishana, Indra among the
rakshasas, are in it.'

A great sound of rejoicing arose and seemed to touch the
sky. Women, children, the young and the aged shouted, 'Rama is
coming.' They descended from their chariots, elephants and horses
and took to the ground. Like the moon in the sky, the men saw
the vimana. Delighted, they joined their hands in salutation in
Raghava's direction. They welcomed him in the proper way and
worshipped Rama. Lakshmana's elder brother was on a vimana
that had been constructed by Brahma with his mental powers. With
long and large eyes, he was radiant, like a second wielder of the

vajra. His brother, Rama, was in the front of the vimana, like the sun atop Meru. Bharata lowered his head down and worshipped him.

When the vimana touched down, Bharata, for whom truth was his valour, happily approached Rama and greeted him again. Kakutstha had seen him after a long time. Full of joy, he made Bharata rise, embraced him and placed him on his lap. The scorcher of enemies, Bharata, then happily approached Lakshmana and Vaidehi, greeted them and announced his name. Kaikeyee's son also embraced Sugriva, Jambavat, Angada, Mainda, Dvivida, Nila and Rishabha. The apes, who could assume any form at will, assumed human forms. Cheerfully, they asked Bharata about his welfare. Bharata addressed Vibhishana in words of conciliation. 'It is good fortune that this extremely difficult task has been accomplished with your help.' Shatrughna greeted Rama and Lakshmana. Full of humility, he subsequently worshipped at Sita's feet.

Rama approached his miserable mother, who was afflicted by grief. He bowed and seized her feet, delighting his mother's mind. He greeted Sumitra and the illustrious Kaikeyee. With all his mothers, he then approached the priest.[437]

Joining their hands in salutation, all the residents told Rama, 'O mighty-armed one! O extender of Kousalya's delight! Welcome.' When the citizens joined their hands in salutation, Bharata's elder brother saw that it was like an array of blooming lotuses.

Bharata, who knew about dharma, himself took Rama's sandals and inserted the feet of the Indra among men into these. Joining his hands in salutation, Bharata told Rama, 'I have protected this kingdom in trust and I am returning it to you. My birth has become successful today and my wishes have also been fulfilled. I have seen the king of Ayodhya return. I have taken care of your treasury, stores of grain, the city and the army. Because of your energy, everything is ten times what it used to be.' The apes and the rakshasa Vibhishana witnessed Bharata's devotion to his brother and heard him. They shed tears. Delighted, Raghava placed Bharata on his lap.

---

[437] Vasishtha.

With the soldiers, they used that vimana to go to Bharata's hermitage. With the soldiers, Raghava reached Bharata's hermitage. They got down from the vimana and stood on the ground, before it. Rama told the excellent vimana, 'I give you permission to go to the god Vaishravana.' Having obtained Rama's permission, the excellent vimana headed in a northward direction and went to the residence of the lord of treasures.

Like Shakra, the lord of the immortals, approaching Brihaspati, Raghava approached his own priest.[438] He pressed his feet. The valiant one sat down with him, but on a separate auspicious seat.

Chapter 6(116)

Bharata, the extender of Kaikeyee's delight, placed his hands in salutation above his head. He spoke to his elder brother Rama, for whom truth was his valour. 'Honouring my mother's words, you gave me the kingdom. I have given it back to you, just as you had given it to me. I cannot bear this burden alone, which has been imposed on me by a stronger bull. I am like one who is young and am not interested in bearing this heavy load. I think that this prosperous kingdom is similar to a dam being shattered by a great flood of water. It is difficult to bridge. This is like a donkey trying to follow the footsteps of a horse, or a crow that of a swan. O lord! O scorcher of enemies! I am not interested in following in your footsteps. A tree that has been planted inside one's house may grow up and become large, extremely difficult to climb, with a large trunk and branches. Its flowers may dry up and it may not show any flowers. Nothing may indeed be obtained by the person who planted it. O mighty-armed one! I wish to make this analogy known to you.[439] O Indra among men! I am devoted to you and am your servant. Instruct me. Let the universe, all around, see you

---

[438] Vasishtha.

[439] The analogy probably means that Bharata has planted the tree. But now that the tree has grown up, it requires Rama to look after it.

consecrated today. Blazing in your energy, scorch like the midday sun. After sleeping, awake to the sounds of many trumpets blaring, the sounds of girdles and anklets and the sweet sounds of singing. As long as the wheel revolves[440] and as long as the earth is here, may you be the lord of everything on this extensive earth.'

Hearing Bharata's words, Rama, the victor over enemy cities, accepted these words and sat down on an auspicious seat. Following Shatrughna's words, accomplished tenders of the beard,[441] who were pleasant in the use of their hands, swiftly surrounded Raghava. Bharata, the immensely strong Lakshmana, Sugriva, Indra among the apes, and Vibhishana, Indra of the rakshasas, bathed first. The matted hair was cleaned. He bathed and wore colourful garlands, with unguents smeared. Donning extremely expensive garments, he blazed in his prosperity. The valiant extender of the lineage of the Ikshvakus[442] arranged for the personal care of Rama and the prosperous Lakshmana. All of Dasharatha's wives arranged for Sita's personal care. Those spirited ones also made themselves look beautiful. Kousalya, delighted and affectionate towards her son, also took care to make all the other wives of the Raghavas[443] look beautiful.

On Shatrughna's words, the charioteer named Sumantra yoked a chariot that was beautiful in all its parts. The chariot was like the divine solar disc. On seeing it, the mighty-armed Rama, for whom truth was valour, mounted it. Placing the priest at the forefront, King Dasharatha's advisers prepared everything properly in Ayodhya. They consulted about the conduct, so that the city might become prosperous. 'Arrange everything for the consecration so that the great-souled one becomes worthy of victory. For Rama's sake, you should perform everything in an auspicious manner.' In this way, all the ministers requested the priest. Making up their minds to see Rama, they then quickly emerged from the city. Like the one with the thousand eyes on a chariot yoked to tawny

---

[440] The wheel of time.
[441] Barbers.
[442] Presumably meaning Shatrughna.
[443] The wives of the other three brothers.

horses, the unblemished Rama mounted the chariot and left for the supreme city. Bharata seized the reins and Shatrughna grasped the umbrella. Lakshmana fanned the whisk atop his head. Sugriva, lord of the apes, held a whisk that was made out of white hair. Vibhishana, Indra among the rakshasas, held another one that was like the moon. Large numbers of rishis, the gods and large numbers of Maruts praised Rama from the sky and the sweet sounds of these were heard. There was an elephant named Shatrunjaya and it was like a mountain. The immensely energetic Sugriva, lord of the apes, mounted this. The apes proceeded on nine thousand elephants. They assumed the forms of humans and adorned themselves in all the ornaments. There was the sound of conch shells being blown and drums were sounded.

The tigers among men went to the city that was garlanded with mansions. They[444] saw the atiratha Raghava arrive, radiant in form, on a chariot, with attendants in front. They honoured Kakutstha and were greeted back by Rama. As he was surrounded by his brothers, they followed the great-souled one. Surrounded by advisers, brahmanas and ordinary people, like the moon by nakshatras, Rama blazed in his prosperity. Minstrels proceeded in front, with svastikas[445] in their hands. Trumpets were sounded rhythmically. They surrounded him and proceeded, chanting auspicious songs. Maidens and brahmanas proceeded in front, with gold-hued unhusked grain in their hands. There were also men holding sweetmeats. Rama told the ministers about his friendship with Sugriva, the powers of the son of the wind god and the deeds of the apes. On hearing this, the residents of the city of Ayodhya were astounded. Having told them this, Rama entered Ayodhya, full of happy and healthy people, surrounded by the apes. In every house, the residents of the city raised auspicious flags.

He entered the beautiful palace, his father's residence and the abode of the Ikshvakus. The great-souled one reached and entered his father's residence. He greeted Kousalya, Sumitra and Kaikeyee.

444 The citizens.
445 A svastika is a kind of musical instrument.

The prince, the descendant of the Raghu lineage, spoke to Bharata, supreme among those who followed dharma, in sweet words full of meaning. 'This excellent residence has a large Ashokavana. It is full of pearls and lapis lazuli. Make Sugriva stay here.' Hearing his words, Bharata, for whom truth was his valour, took Sugriva by the hands and entered that residence. They entered and urged by Shatrughna, oil lamps, couches and spreads were quickly brought. Raghava's immensely energetic younger brother spoke to Sugriva, 'O lord! Command the messengers about Rama's consecration.' Sugriva quickly gave four Indras among apes four pots that were decorated with all kinds of jewels. 'O apes! In the morning, go to the four oceans and collect water and fill these pots. Act according to my command.' The great-souled apes, who resembled elephants, were addressed in this way. As swift as Garuda, they quickly leapt up into the sky. Jambavat, Hanumat, the ape Vegadarshi and Rishabha filled and brought four pots of water. They brought a fifth pot, filled with water from one hundred rivers. Sushena,[446] full of spirit, brought a pot, decorated with all kinds of jewels, filled with water from the eastern ocean. Rishabha swiftly brought water from the southern ocean. Gavaya brought water from the great western ocean and covered the water in the golden pot with red sandalwood powder and *karpura*.[447] The one who was like the wind god in valour, the one who was like Garuda and the wind in valour[448] quickly brought cool water from the northern ocean in a large pot that was decorated with jewels.

For the sake of Rama's consecration, with the advisers, Shatrughna reported this to the supreme priest and his well-wishers. With the brahmanas, the aged Vasishtha proceeded. With Sita, he asked Rama to sit down on a seat encrusted with gems. Vasishtha, Vamadeva, Jabali, Kashyapa, Katyayana, Suyajna, Goutama and Vijaya sprinkled the tiger among men with water, just as the Vasus did to Vasava, the one with the thousand eyes.

---

[446] There is an obvious inconsistency in the names of the four apes who went to the four oceans.

[447] Camphor.

[448] That is, Hanumat.

The officiating priests who were brahmanas did this first. They were then followed by maidens, ministers, warriors and merchants, who cheerfully consecrated him too, with the juices of all the herbs, while the gods were stationed in the sky. The four guardians of the world were there, with all the gods. Shatrughna held a white and auspicious umbrella. Sugriva, lord of the apes, held a whisk made out of white hair, while Vibhishana, Indra among the rakshasas, held another one that was like the moon. Urged by Vasava, Vayu gave Raghava a golden garland that blazed in form and was made out of one hundred lotuses. Urged by Shakra, he also gave the Indra among men a necklace made out of pearls. It was encrusted with all the jewels and was decorated with gems and jewels. At the well-deserved consecration of the intelligent Rama, divine gandharvas sang and large numbers of apsaras danced. The earth was full of succulent grain. The trees were full of fruits and fragrant flowers. This is what happened at the festivities for Raghava. The bull among men first gave brahmanas one hundred bulls and followed it up with one hundred thousand horses and also cows with calves. Raghava also gave brahmanas thirty crores of gold,[449] many kinds of ornaments and extremely expensive garments. The bull among men gave Sugriva a divine garland. It was golden, studded with gems and resembled the rays of the sun. He gave the patient Angada, Vali's son, a bracelet that was colourful with lapis lazuli and gems and was decorated with diamonds and jewels. Rama gave Sita an excellent necklace made out of pearls. It was decorated with the best of jewels and was like the beams of the moon. While Vaidehi looked on, he gave Vayu's son a radiant and divine garment and auspicious ornaments. While all the apes and her husband repeatedly looked on, Janaka's daughter took off her necklace.[450] Since he[451] knew about signs, he looked at Janaka's daughter and spoke to her. 'O immensely fortunate one! O beautiful one! Give this necklace to whoever you are satisfied with. He has always possessed manliness, valour, intelligence and other qualities. Give it to Vayu's son.'

---

[449] Golden coins.
[450] Probably not the one Rama had just given her.
[451] Rama.

The dark-eyed one gave the necklace to Vayu's son. Wearing that necklace, Hanumat, bull among apes, was radiant. It was as white and pure as the moon and he looked like a mountain with white clouds. Glancing towards Mainda, Dvivida and Nila, the scorcher of enemies, the lord of the earth, gave them all the objects of desire. He honoured all the aged apes and all the other bulls among the apes, as they deserved, and gave them garments and ornaments. All of them were worshipped, as they deserved, with all the desired ornaments. Delighted, all of them returned to wherever they had come from.

Full of great joy, the extremely generous Raghava ruled. Rama knew about dharma and was devoted to dharma. He told Lakshmana, 'O one who knows about dharma! Remain here with me. This earth has been powerfully ruled by former kings and the burden has been borne by our forefathers. You are like me. Be the heir apparent and bear this burden with me.' Though he repeatedly entreated Soumitri with all his soul, Soumitri did not accept this assignment. At this, the great-souled one instated Bharata as the heir apparent. Raghava, with dharma in his soul, obtained that excellent kingdom. With his well-wishers, brothers and relatives, he performed many kinds of rites and sacrifices. The bull among kings performed *poundarika, ashvamedha, vajapeya* and many other sacrifices. Raghava ruled the kingdom for ten thousand years. He sacrificed excellent horses at one hundred ashvamedha sacrifices and gave away copious quantities of dakshina. The powerful one possessed arms that stretched all the way down to his thighs. He had broad shoulders. With Lakshmana as his follower, Rama ruled the earth. As long as Rama ruled the kingdom, no widows lamented. There was no fear from predatory beasts. There was no fear on account of disease. There were no bandits in the world. No one suffered from lack of riches. The aged did not have to perform funeral rites for the young.[452] Everyone was cheerful. Everyone was devoted to dharma. They looked towards Rama and did not cause violence towards each other. As long as Rama ruled the kingdom,

---

[452] That is, the young did not die before the old.

people were without disease and devoid of sorrow. They lived for one thousand years and had one thousand sons. The trees extended their trunks and always had flowers. They always had fruit. The rain showered down at the right time. The breeze had a pleasant touch. People were satisfied with their own tasks and performed their own duties. As long as Rama ruled, there was no falsehood in the subjects and they were devoted to dharma. All of them possessed the qualities and all of them were devoted to dharma. Rama ruled the kingdom for ten thousand years.

This ends Yuddha Kanda.

CHAPTER SEVEN

Uttara Kanda

Sarga (1): 27 shlokas
Sarga (2): 29 shlokas
Sarga (3): 31 shlokas
Sarga (4): 31 shlokas
Sarga (5): 41 shlokas
Sarga (6): 55 shlokas
Sarga (7): 50 shlokas
Sarga (8): 25 shlokas
Sarga (9): 37 shlokas
Sarga (10): 42 shlokas
Sarga (11): 41 shlokas
Sarga (12): 29 shlokas
Sarga (13): 39 shlokas
Sarga (14): 25 shlokas
Sarga (15): 31 shlokas
Sarga (16): 31 shlokas
Sarga (17): 31 shlokas
Sarga (18): 33 shlokas
Sarga (19): 26 shlokas
Sarga (20): 25 shlokas
Sarga (21): 29 shlokas
Sarga (22): 43 shlokas
Sarga (23): 46 shlokas
Sarga (24): 35 shlokas
Sarga (25): 50 shlokas

Sarga (26): 47 shlokas
Sarga (27): 42 shlokas
Sarga (28): 46 shlokas
Sarga (29): 40 shlokas
Sarga (30): 42 shlokas
Sarga (31): 40 shlokas
Sarga (32): 72 shlokas
Sarga (33): 23 shlokas
Sarga (34): 44 shlokas
Sarga (35): 65 shlokas
Sarga (36): 46 shlokas
Sarga (37): 14 shlokas
Sarga (38): 17 shlokas
Sarga (39): 24 shlokas
Sarga (40): 18 shlokas
Sarga (41): 27 shlokas
Sarga (42): 23 shlokas
Sarga (43): 19 shlokas
Sarga (44): 22 shlokas
Sarga (45): 28 shlokas
Sarga (46): 18 shlokas
Sarga (47): 18 shlokas
Sarga (48): 20 shlokas
Sarga (49): 18 shlokas
Sarga (50): 20 shlokas

Chapter 7(1)

When the rakshasas had been slain and Rama had obtained the kingdom, all the rishis came to congratulate Raghava. Koushika, Yavakrita, Raibha, Chyavana, and Medhatithi's son, Kanva—these were the ones who resided in the eastern direction. Svastyatreya, the illustrious Namuchi, Pramuchi and Agastya were the ones who came from the southern direction. Prishadgu,

Kavasha, Dhoumya and the great rishi, Roudreya, were the ones who came with their disciples, from the western direction. Vasishtha, Kashyapa, Atri, Vishvamitra, Goutama, Jamadagni and Bharadvaja—there were these seven maharshis.[453] Those great-souled ones reached Raghava's residence, radiant as the fire, and waited for the *pratihara*.[454] Following their words, the great-souled pratihara quickly went. He swiftly entered and approached Raghava. He suddenly saw Rama, who was like the full moon when it has arisen, and told him that Agastya and the other rishis had arrived. The king was like the rising sun in his radiance. Hearing that the sages had come, he told the gatekeeper to ensure they were comfortable and to make them enter. On seeing the sages arrive, Rama stood up and joined his hands in salutation. He controlled himself, greeted them and offered them seats. Those bulls among rishis sat down, as they deserved, on comfortable seats with golden and colourful spreads. Rama asked them about their welfare, together with that of their disciples and their companions.

The maharshis, who knew about the Vedas, addressed Rama in these words. 'O descendant of the Raghu lineage! We are well in every possible way. It is good fortune that we see you are well, having slain your enemies. O Rama! We no longer suffer from the burden of Ravana, lord of the rakshasas. There is no doubt that you can conquer the three worlds with your bow. O Rama! It is good fortune that you killed Ravana, with his sons and grandsons. It is good fortune that we see you victorious today, with your wife. It is good fortune that Prahasta, Vikata, Virupaksha, Mahodara and the invincible Akampana, the roamers in the night, have been killed by you. O Rama! Kumbhakarna was gigantic in size and there was no one as large as him in this world. It is good fortune that you brought him down in the battle. It is good fortune that the Indra among rakshasas turned up to have a duel with you. The gods could not kill him, but you were victorious over him. However, Ravana's defeat in the encounter was hardly surprising. After all, it is good fortune

---

[453] By implication, from the northern direction.

[454] The pratihara is the gatekeeper or doorkeeper. They waited for the gatekeeper to announce their arrival to Rama.

that you killed Ravana's son, when he turned up to have a duel with you. O mighty-armed one! O brave one! It is good fortune that you could free yourself from the enemy of the gods, who was like Death. You were victorious. O amiable one! On hearing that Indrajit had been killed, we were amazed. All the creatures found it impossible to kill him. He could invoke great maya in a battle. O brave one! O amiable one! You gave us something sacred. As dakshina, you gave us freedom from fear. O Kakutstha! O afflicter of enemies! It is good fortune that you are prospering in your victory.'

Rama was greatly astounded. He joined his hands in salutation and said, 'Passing over the two immensely valiant Kumbhakarna and Ravana, the roamer in the night, why are you praising Ravana's son? Passing over the immensely valiant Mahodara, Prahasta and the rakshasa Virupaksha, why are you praising Ravana's son? What were his powers? What was his strength and his valour? What was the reason for his being superior to Ravana? If I am capable of hearing it, if you are indeed capable of telling me and if this is not a secret account, I wish to hear the story. How did he defeat Shakra and how did he obtain a boon?'

Chapter 7(2)

Hearing the words of the great-souled Raghava, the immensely energetic Kumbhayoni[455] spoke these words. 'O king! Hear about his conduct and about his great energy and strength, about how he killed enemies in battle, though enemies couldn't kill him. O Raghava! However, I will start by telling you about Ravana's lineage and birth. I will tell you about how a boon was bestowed on him. O Rama! Earlier, in krita yuga, the lord Prajapati[456] had a son. He was a brahmana rishi named Pulastya and he was like the grandfather himself. It is impossible to recount the qualities about his conduct in following dharma. One can only say that he

---

[455] Agastya's name.
[456] Brahma.

was Prajapati's son and mention his name. To observe dharma, he went to the slopes of the large mountain, Meru. The bull among sages went to Trinavindu's hermitage and resided there. The one with dharma in his soul performed austerities there. He studied and controlled his senses. But maidens went to that hermitage and created obstructions. They were the maidens of gods and serpents, daughters of royal sages and apsaras. They went to that region and sported there. The objects of desire of all the seasons were present there and the grove was beautiful. Those maidens always went to that region and sported. The immensely energetic and great sage became angry and said, "Anyone who comes within my range of vision will become pregnant." They returned after hearing the great-souled one's words. Scared of the brahmana's curse, they did not go to that region again. However, the daughter of the royal sage, Trinavindu, had not heard this. Not scared at all, she went to that hermitage and began to roam around. At that time, the great rishi who was Prajapati's son was studying there. Because of his austerities, he was radiant and blazed. She heard the sounds of the Vedas being chanted and she saw the store of austerities. Her body turned pale and the signs of her being pregnant were clearly visible. On seeing her form, she became greatly anxious. "How did this happen?" Finding out her state, she went and stood before her father. Seeing her in that state, Trinavindu asked, "How have you come to assume a form like this?" The maiden was distressed. She joined her hands in salutation and spoke to the store of austerities.[457] "O father! I do not know the reason why my form has become like this. However, earlier, I was searching for my friends and went alone to maharshi Pulastya's hermitage. But when I went to the hermitage of the one with the cleansed soul, I did not see any of my friends there. Seeing my distorted form, I came here." The royal sage, Trinavindu, dazzled in radiance because of his austerities. Meditating, the rishi perceived the act which led to this consequence. He got to know about the curse that the maharshi with the cleansed soul had imposed. Taking his daughter with him, he went to Pulastya and addressed him thus. "O illustrious one! My daughter is adorned

---

[457] Meaning Trinavindu.

with her own qualities. O maharshi! I am myself offering her to you as alms. Accept her. When you engage in austerities, your senses will become exhausted. There is no doubt that she will always serve you devotedly." Hearing the words of the royal sage who followed dharma, the brahmana agreed and accepted the maiden. Having given her away, the king went to his own hermitage. Since then, the maiden resided there and satisfied her husband with her qualities. The immensely energetic one was pleased and addressed her in these words. "O fortunate one! You possess an abundance of qualities and I am pleased with you. Therefore, I will now grant you a son who will be like me in qualities. He will extend both lineages and will be famous as Poulastya. You heard me chanting the Vedas. Therefore, there is no doubt that his name will be Vishrava."[458] Thus addressed, the maiden was delighted in her inner soul. Within a short period of time, that daughter had a son named Vishrava.[459] He was full of purity and dharma and was famous in the three worlds. Vishrava, bull among sages, observed austerities, just like his father.'

Chapter 7(3)

Within a short period of time, Vishrava, Pulastya's son and bull among sages, started to perform austerities, just like his father. He was truthful, accomplished, devoted to studying, pure, always devoted to dharma, unattached to all objects of pleasure and possessed good conduct. On knowing about his good conduct, the great rishi, Bharadvaja, bestowed his own daughter, Devavarnini, on Vishrava as a wife. Vishrava, bull among sages, was filled with great delight. Following dharma, he accepted Bharadvaja's daughter. The one with dharma in his soul had an energetic son who was extraordinary, possessing all the qualities of a brahmana.

---

[458] From *vishruta* (heard). The son's name was Vishrava. Poulastya means Pulastya's son. Therefore, he was also Poulastya.

[459] The same as Vishravasa.

When he was born, his paternal grandfather[460] was extremely happy. With the other celestial rishis, he happily gave him a name. "Since he is Vishrava's son and is like Vishrava himself, he will therefore be known by the name of Vaishravana." The immensely energetic Vaishravana began to grow up in that hermitage, like a fire into which oblations have been offered. While he was in that hermitage, the great-souled one arrived at the determination, "Since dharma is the supreme objective, I will also control myself and follow dharma." In the great forest, he tormented himself through austerities for one thousand years. He followed the rituals for a full one thousand years. He lived only on water, he survived only on air, or he ate nothing. In this way, he passed one thousand years as if it was only one year. With large numbers of extremely energetic gods and with Indra, Brahma went to the hermitage and spoke these words. "O child! O one who is good in vows! I am pleased with your deeds. Ask for a boon. It is my view that you are fortunate and deserve to be granted a boon." The grandfather was in front of him and Vaishravana replied, "O illustrious one! I wish to be a guardian of the world and look after all treasures." Content in his mind and happy, with the large number of gods, Brahma told Vaishravana that he agreed to this. "After Yama, Indra and Varuna, I was about to create a fourth guardian of the world. That is the status you have asked for. O one who knows about dharma! Therefore, go and become Dhanesha.[461] From now, you will become a fourth, after Yama, Indra and Varuna. This Pushpaka vimana is like the sun. Accept this as a vehicle you can move around in, so that you can travel just as the gods do. May you be fortunate. All of us will return to wherever we came from. O son! Having granted you a great boon, we have also become successful."

'With Brahma at the forefront, all the gods left through the sky. Dhanesha went to his father and bowed down in humility, addressing him in these words. "O illustrious one! I have obtained a boon from the one who was generated from a lotus.[462] O lord!

---

[460] Pulastya.

[461] The lord of riches, *dhana + isha*, Kubera.

[462] Brahma.

However, Prajapati has not indicated a place for me to live in. O illustrious one! O lord! Therefore, search out and indicate a residence for me, so that no suffering of any type is caused to any being there." Thus addressed by his son, Vishrava, bull among sages, replied in these words. "O one who knows about dharma! O one who is learned about dharma! Listen. Vishvakarma constructed a beautiful city named Lanka for the rakshasas to reside in. It is like Indra's Amaravati. It is a beautiful city, with turrets made out of gold and lapis lazuli. In earlier times, because they were afflicted by fear of Vishnu, the rakshasas abandoned it and it is empty. All the large number of rakshasas have gone to the nether regions of rasatala. Make your mind agreeable to the prospect of dwelling there. There will be no taint associated with your residing there and no one will be obstructed in any way." The one who had dharma in his soul heard the words of his father, who abided by dharma. He dwelt in Lanka, on the summit of a mountain. Within a short period of time, thousands of happy and delighted nairittas gathered around and filled the place up, under his rule. Vishrava's son, the lord of the nairittas, happily resided there, in Lanka, with the ocean as the frontier. From time to time, the lord of treasures, humble in his soul, used Pushpaka to happily go and visit his father and his mother. He would be praised by gods, large numbers of gandharvas, siddhas and charanas. Prosperous and surrounded by them, like the sun with the energy of its rays, he would travel to his father's presence.'

Chapter 7(4)

Hearing Agastya's words, Rama was filled with surprise. He repeatedly looked towards Agastya, whose form was like that of *tretagni*.[463] How was it possible for the rakshasas to have resided in Lanka earlier? He shook his head, smiled and said, 'O illustrious one! The devourers of flesh used to live in Lanka earlier. Hearing

---

[463] The three fires, *garhapatya, ahavaniya* and *dakshinagni*.

you say this, I am filled with wonder. We have heard that the rakshasas were born from Pulastya's lineage. However, on the basis of what you have recounted, I now think their origins lie elsewhere. Were they stronger than Ravana, Kumbhakarna, Prahasta, Vikata and Ravana's sons? O brahmana! Who was their ancestor? What was his name? What was the strength of his austerities? What were the crimes they committed that they were driven away by Vishnu earlier? O unblemished one! You should tell me everything about this. You have generated a curiosity in me. Dispel it, the way the sun drives away darkness.'

Hearing Raghava's words, embellished with cleansed speech, Agastya seemed a little surprised and spoke to him. 'In ancient times, Brahma was born from the lotus in the waters.[464] He first created the waters and to protect them, created various creatures. Those creatures humbly presented themselves before the one who had created the creatures.[465] They were scared and afflicted because of hunger and thirst and asked, "What shall we do?" Prajapati smiled at all of them. The one who confers honours said, "Take care and protect." Among those hungry creatures, there were some who said, "We shall protect." There were some, who despite being devoured, said, "We shall be swift." "Those of you who said we shall protect shall be rakshasas. Those of you who said we shall be swift shall be yakshas."[466] There were two brothers who were bulls among rakshasas and they were Heti and Praheti. Those two scorchers of enemies were like Madhu and Kaitabha.[467] Praheti was devoted to dharma and did not desire a wife. However, for the sake of obtaining a wife, Heti undertook supreme efforts. There was a maiden named Bhaya and she caused great fear. She was Kala's[468] sister. The immensely intelligent one, immeasurable in his soul, himself went and sought to marry her. Through her, Heti, bull among rakshasas, had a son. He was best among sons and

[464] The lotus in Vishnu's navel, Vishnu resting in the waters.

[465] That is, Brahma.

[466] These are Brahma's words. 'We shall protect' is *rakshama*. Hence, rakshasas. 'We shall be swift' is *yakshama*. Hence, yakshas.

[467] Demons killed by Vishnu.

[468] Kala means time, destiny, death.

he was known as Vidyutkesha. Heti's son, Vidyutkesha, was as radiant as a blazing fire. The immensely energetic one started to grow up, like a lotus in the water. When the fortunate roamer in the night became a youth, his father sought to get him married off. Sandhya's daughter was like Sandhya herself in powers. For his son, Heti, the bull among rakshasas, sought her. O Raghava! Sandhya thought, "She will certainly have to be given to someone else." Therefore, she bestowed her on Vidyutkesha. Vidyutkesha, the roamer in the night, obtained Sandhya's daughter. Like Maghavan with Poulami, he pleasured with her. O Rama! Within a short time, through Vidyutkesha, Salakantakata[469] was conceived, just as dense clouds are conceived from the waters of the ocean. The foetus in the rakshasi's womb was as radiant as a cloud. She went to Mandara and delivered, like Ganga delivering Agni's son.[470] Having delivered, she desired Vidyutkesha again. Forgetting her own son, she found pleasure with her husband. The child she delivered was like the autumn sun in his radiance. He covered his face in his hands and wept as loudly as a cloud. For a beneficial purpose, the lord Hara was proceeding on his bull. With Uma, he saw the weeping son of the rakshasa. Parvati was overcome by compassion. Therefore, the destroyer of Tripura[471] made the son of the rakshasa as old as his mother. Mahadeva is without decay and without change. He also made the child immortal. To cause pleasure to Parvati, he also gave him a city[472] that could travel through the sky. O son of a king! Uma also gave boons to rakshasis. They would deliver as soon as they conceived and the infant would instantly acquire the same age as that of the mother. Sukesha[473] became insolent because of the boons he received. Thanks to that proximity with the lord Hara, he obtained prosperity. Having obtained the city that travelled through the sky, like Purandara, the immensely intelligent one travelled everywhere in the sky.'

[469] Sandhya's daughter.

[470] Agni's son means Skanda. There are different stories about the birth of Skanda, Kartikeya or Kumara. In some of these, Ganga figures.

[471] Shiva.

[472] A vimana that was like a city.

[473] Vidyutkesha's son.

Chapter 7(5)

'There was a gandharva named Gramani and he was like Vishvavasu[474] in his resplendence.[475] He had a daughter named Devavati and she was like a second Shri. He saw that the rakshasa Sukesha followed dharma and had obtained boons. Following dharma, he bestowed her on Sukesha, like Daksha bestowing Shri.[476] She obtained a beloved husband who was prosperous because he had obtained boons. Devavati was content, like a poor person who has got riches. United with her, the roamer in the night was also resplendent. He was like a giant elephant born from Anjana,[477] in the company of a female elephant. O Raghava! Through Devavati, Sukesha, lord of the rakshasas, had three sons who were like three eyes to the rakshasa. They were Malyavat, Sumali and Mali—supreme among strong ones. Like the three worlds, they were without any anxiety. They were as stable as the three fires. They were as sharp as the three mantras.[478] They were as terrible as the three that cause disease.[479] Sukesha's three sons dazzled like the three fires. They grew up without any impediments, just as a disease that is ignored does. They realized that their father had obtained great prosperity because of his boons. Therefore, the brothers made up their minds to go to Meru and torment themselves through austerities. O supreme among kings! The rakshasas resorted to terrible rituals. They observed terrible austerities that terrified all creatures. Resorting to truth, uprightness and self-control, they performed austerities that are extremely difficult to undertake on earth. The three worlds, with the gods, the asuras and humans, were tormented. The lord with the four faces[480] was on a supreme

---

[474] The king of the gandharvas.

[475] This is still Agastya speaking.

[476] There is an allusion to Daksha marrying off his daughters to Dharma. Though the names of the daughters married to Dharma varies, Shri/Lakshmi typically figures in the list.

[477] One of the dishagajas.

[478] Mantras associated with the Rig Veda, Sama Veda and Yajur Veda.

[479] *Vata, pitta* and *kapha*. These can be loosely translated as wind, bile and phlegm. In Ayurveda, these are the three *doshas* or humours in the body and they are always striving against each other.

[480] Brahma.

vimana. He came before Sukesha's sons and invited them, "I will grant boons."[481] Knowing that Brahma was about to grant boons, with all the large number of gods, together with Indra, surrounding him, they trembled like trees. They joined their hands in salutation and said, "O god! If we have worshipped you, if you wish to grant us boons, let us be invincible. Let us slay our enemies and let us live forever. Through the powers of Vishnu, let us be devoted to each other." The lord Brahma, devoted to brahmanas, told Sukesha's sons that it would indeed be that way. He then went to Brahma's world. O Rama! All those roamers in the night obtained the boon. Because they had obtained the boon, they became fearless and started to oppress the gods and the asuras. The gods, the large number of rishis and the charanas were slaughtered by them. Like men in hell, they could not find a protector. O supreme among the Raghu lineage! The undecaying Vishvakarma was an excellent artisan. Happy, the rakshasas went to him and said, "You are the one who builds residences for the gods, according to what they want. O immensely wise one! Build a similar residence for us too, on the Himalayas, Meru or Mandara. Create a great residence for us that is like Maheshvara's residence." The mighty-armed Vishvakarma told them about a residence for the rakshasas that would be like Shakra's Amaravati. "There is a mountain named Trikuta on the shores of the southern ocean. There is a peak in the middle of that mountain and it is like a cloud. Even the birds find it extremely difficult to approach, since there are ragged slopes on four sides. It[482] extends for thirty yojanas and has golden ramparts and gates. Following Shakra's command, I will construct the city of Lanka. O excellent rakshasas! You will reside in that impenetrable city, just as Indra and the gods dwell in Amaravati. O slayers of enemies! When you reach the fortified city of Lanka and are surrounded by many rakshasas, enemies will find it impossible to assail you." O Rama! Hearing Vishvakarma's words, the rakshasas went to Lanka with one thousand followers and started to reside there. There were firm walls and moats. The place was full of hundreds of golden

---

481 Invited them to ask for boons.
482 The residence, that is, the city.

houses. Having reached Lanka, those cheerful roamers in the night found pleasure there. There was a *gandharvi*[483] named Narmada and she followed all kinds of dharma. She had three daughters who were as radiant as Hri, Shri and Kirti.[484] The rakshasi[485] followed the order, eldest downwards, and bestowed them on the rakshasas. The daughters possessed faces that were like the full moon and having bestowed them, she was delighted. The three Indras among the rakshasas obtained the three daughters of the gandharvi. The immensely fortunate mother bestowed them in the nakshatra when Bhaga is the divinity.[486] O Rama! O lord! Thus, Sukesha's sons obtained wives. They sported with those wives, like the immortals do with apsaras. Malyavat's wife was the beautiful Sundari.[487] O Rama! Hear about the offspring Sundari had. The sons were Vajramushti, Virupaksha, the rakshasa Durmukha, Suptaghna, Yajnakopa, Matta and Unmatta, and there was a beautiful daughter, Anala. Sumali's wife had a face that was like the full moon. Her name was Ketumati and he loved her more than his own life. O great king! In due order, hear about the offspring that Sumali, roamer in the night, had through Ketumati—Prahasta, Kampana, Vikata, Kalakarmuka, Dhumaraksha, Danda, the immensely strong Suparshva, Sahladi, Praghasa and the rakshasa Bhasakarna. Sumali's daughters were Raka, Pushpotkata, the sweet-smiling Kaikasi and Kumbhinasi. Mali's wife was the gandharvi Vasuda and she was beautiful in form. Her eyes were like the petals of lotuses and these eyes made her resemble an excellent *yakshi*.[488] O Raghava! Hear about the offspring Sumali's younger brother had through her. I will recount them. Mali's sons were Anala, Anila, Hara and Sampati and they are Vibhishana's advisers.[489] Thus, those three roamers in the night, bulls among rakshasas, were surrounded by hundreds of sons.

[483] Gandharva lady.

[484] Hri is the personification of modesty and Kirti is the personification of deeds.

[485] The gandharvi is being described as a rakshasi.

[486] Each nakshatra has an associated divinity, which is often the original Vedic name of the nakshatra. Bhaga is the divinity for Uttara Phalguni nakshatra and Bhaga is also the god for marital prosperity.

[487] Since *sundari* means beautiful, there is a pun.

[488] Yaksha lady.

[489] Earlier, these names have been given as Anala, Sharabha, Sampati and Praghasa.

Insolent because of their strength and valour, they oppressed the gods, together with Indra, the rishis, the serpents and the danavas. Like the wind, they roamed around the entire universe. They were controlled and in battles, they were like Death. They were extremely insolent because of the boons they had received. They destroyed all the sacrifices and rituals.'

Chapter 7(6)

'The gods and the rishis, the stores of austerities, were slaughtered by them. Afflicted by grief, they went and sought refuge with Maheshvara, the god of the gods. They approached Kamari,[490] Tripurari,[491] the one with the three eyes. The gods joined their hands in salutation. Suffering from fear, they stuttered in their words. "O illustrious one! O one who causes an impediment to enemies! Sukesha's sons, having obtained a boon from the grandfather, face no hurdles. O lord of subjects! They are oppressing all the subjects. O one who provides a refuge! They have destroyed our refuges and our hermitages. They have driven Shakra away from heaven and are sporting in heaven, like Shakra. O god! The rakshasas are insolent because of the boon and say, 'I am Vishnu.' 'I am Rudra.' 'I am Brahma.' 'I am the king of the gods.' 'I am Yama.' 'I am Varuna.' 'I am the moon god.' 'I am the sun god.' Invincible in battle, they obstruct all those who advance in front of them. O god! That is the reason we are afflicted by fear. You should grant us freedom from fear. Assume an inauspicious form[492] and slay the thorns of the gods." Thus addressed by all the gods, Kapardi Nilalohita,[493] the lord of large numbers of gods, took Sukesha's side and said, "I will not slay them. Those asuras cannot be killed by me. However,

---

[490] The enemy (*ari*) of Kama (the god of love). Since Shiva burnt down Kama, this means Shiva.

[491] The enemy (ari) of Tripura, meaning Shiva.

[492] There is a reason for the use of this expression. *Shiva* means auspicious and the word used for inauspicious is *ashiva*.

[493] Kapardi and Nilalohita are Shiva's names.

I will counsel you about how they can be killed. O bulls among the gods! Place the following kind of effort at the forefront. Go and seek refuge with Vishnu. That lord will slay them." At this, they praised Maheshvara, uttering sounds of victory. Afflicted by fear on account of those who roamed around in the night, they approached Vishnu. With a great deal of respect, they bowed down before the god who holds the conch shell and the chakra. Scared and suffering from Sukesha's sons, they spoke these words. "O god! Sukesha's three sons are like the three fires. Because of the boon they obtained, they attacked us and took away our positions. There is an impenetrable city named Lanka and it is located on the summit of Trikuta. Based there, those roamers in the night oppress all of us. O Madhusudana! Therefore, for bringing us pleasure, slay them. Their faces are like lotuses. Use your chakra to sever them and offer them to Yama. We are scared and there is no one who can dispel our fear like you. O god! Destroy our fear, the way the sun destroys mist." Janardana, the god of the gods, was addressed by the gods in this way. The one who grants freedom from fear, the one who offers fear to the enemy, replied to the gods. "I know the rakshasa Sukesha. He is insolent because of the boon he has received from Ishana.[494] I know Malyavat, the eldest among the sons. I will slay the worst among the rakshasas. They have transgressed all agreements. O gods! I will kill them in a battle. Be without anxiety." All the gods were addressed in this way by Vishnu. They praised Janardana, the lord Vishnu. Happy, they returned to their residences.

'Malyavat, the roamer in the night, heard about the efforts made by the gods. He addressed his two brave brothers in these words. "The immortals and the rishis assembled and went to Shankara. Desiring our deaths, they addressed the one with the three eyes in these words. 'O god! Sukesha's sons have become strong because they obtained a boon. At every step, they assume terrible forms and are engaged in obstructing us. O Uma's lord! We have been overcome by those rakshasas and are incapacitated. Because of those evil-souled ones, we are scared of remaining in our own residences. O three-eyed one! Therefore, for our benefit, slay

---

[494] Mahadeva.

them. O supreme among those who strike! Burn those rakshasas
down with your *humkara*.[495] The slayer of Andhaka[496] heard the
words spoken by the gods. He touched his head with his hand and
addressed them in these words. 'O gods! Sukesha's sons cannot be
slain by me in a battle. However, I will counsel you about how
they can be killed. Janardana holds the chakra and the conch shell
in his hand. He is attired in a yellow garment. He will slay them
in a battle. Resort to that refuge.' They heard what they desired
from Hara and greeted Kamari. They went to Narayana's residence
and told him everything. At this, Narayana spoke to the gods, with
Indra at the forefront. 'O gods! Do not suffer from anxiety. I will
slay the enemies of the gods.' O bulls among rakshasas! The gods
are afflicted by fear and Hari has pledged to kill us. Therefore, think
about what is best. Narayana has caused misery by vanquishing
Hiranyakashipu, Mrityu and other enemies of the gods. He desires
to kill us." Hearing Malyavat's words, Mali and Sumali replied to
their elder brother, like the two Ashvins[497] speaking to Vasava. "We
have studied, donated at sacrifices and protected our prosperity.
We have obtained health and long lifespans. We are established in
our own dharma. The ocean that is the gods cannot be agitated,
but with innumerable weapons, we have immersed ourselves in
that. We have always vanquished the gods in battles. Death has
no fear for us. Narayana, Rudra, Shakra and Yama are always
scared of standing in front of us. O lord of the rakshasas! There
is no crime we have committed towards Vishnu. Vishnu's mind is
disturbed because of the crimes we have committed towards the
gods. Therefore, let us arise and surround ourselves with all the
soldiers. Let us kill the gods. This taint has arisen because of them."
Mali and Sumali said this to the lord Malyavat, their elder brother.

'All the rakshasas announced the preparations. They angrily
emerged to fight, like Jambha,[498] Vritra and Bala. They were astride

---

[495] Humkara means to utter the sound 'hum', a sound believed to possess special powers.

[496] Shiva killed a demon named Andhaka.

[497] The word used in the text translates as the two sons of the sun god. The Ashvins are sons of the sun god.

[498] Alternatively, Jrimbha. These are names of famous demons.

chariots, Indras among elephants and horses that were as large as mountains. Their mounts were donkeys, bulls, camels, dolphins, serpents, makaras, tortoises, fish, birds that were like Garuda, lions, tigers, boars, *srimara*s and *chamara*s.[499] Proud of their valour, all the rakshasas left Lanka. To fight, the enemies of the gods left for the world of the gods. All the other residents of Lanka saw that Lanka's destruction was imminent. All the creatures saw reason for fear and were mentally disturbed. Fearful and ominous portents manifested themselves on earth and in the sky, signifying the swift destruction of the Indras among the rakshasas. Clouds showered down bones and warm blood. The ocean crossed its shoreline and mountains moved. Thousands of bhutas were tormented and danced, laughing out aloud in voices like the thundering of clouds. Large flocks of vultures, emitting flames from their mouths, circled among the rakshasas, like the wheel of time. The rakshasas were proud of their strength and paid no attention to these great portents. Entangled in the noose of death, they did not retreat from their journey. The roamers in the night, blazing like sacrificial fires, placed Malyavat, Mali and Sumali at their forefront. Like embodied creatures seeking refuge with the Creator, all of them sought refuge with Malyavat, who was like Mount Malyavat. The army of Indras among the rakshasas roared like a large and dense cloud. Desiring victory and commanded by Mali, they went to the world of the gods. Through messengers of the gods, the lord Narayana heard about the preparations made by the rakshasas and made up his mind to fight. Wielding a chakra, a sword and excellent weapons, he advanced towards the soldiers of the enemies of the gods. Gods, siddhas, rishis, giant serpents, best among gandharvas and apsaras sung his praises. The wind generated from Suparna's wings whirled around and shattered the weapons in that army of the king of the rakshasas. It resembled a dark and large mountain and it stared to quake. Thousands of roamers in the night surrounded Madhava and pierced him with supreme weapons that were sharp and smeared with flesh and blood. Their forms were like the fire of destruction that comes at the end of a yuga.'

[499] A srimara is a kind of animal that is found in marshy places, similar to deer. A chamara is a yak.

Chapter 7(7)

'The rakshasas roared like clouds and approached the mountain that was Narayana. They showered down torrents of arrows, like clouds pouring down on mountains. Vishnu was dark blue and those excellent roamers in the night were also dark blue. It seemed as if clouds were showering down on a mountain made out of dark collyrium. The arrows released from the rakshasa bows penetrated Hari, like locusts on a field, gnats on a mountain, makaras in the ocean and creatures around a pot of amrita. They were as swift as the vajra and the wind. It was as if the destruction of the worlds had arrived. Chariot riders were on chariots. Elephant riders were mounted on the tops of elephants. Horse riders used excellent horses. Others were on foot or in the sky. Those Indras among rakshasas were like mountains and used hundreds of arrows, swords and spears. Like a brahmana undertaking *pranayama*,[500] Hari seemed to lose his breath. In that great battle, like a giant whale attacked by fish, he was struck all over his body by the roamers in the night. He used the Sharnga bow against the rakshasas. He stretched the bow all the way back and shot arrows that were as swift as thought, with faces like the vajra. Vishnu shattered hundreds and thousands into fragments as small as sesamum seeds. Like a rising wind drives away clouds, that shower of arrows drove them away. Purushottama then blew on his giant conch shell, Panchajanya. This king of conch shells was born from the water and Hari blew on it with all his strength. There was a terrible roar, like a cloud thundering at the end of a yuga. The sound of that king of conch shells terrified the rakshasas, like elephants in musth are scared by a lion in the forest. The horses were incapable of remaining there. The elephants lost their musth. Because of the blare of the conch shell, the warriors became weak and were dislodged from their chariots. The arrows released from Sharnga bow had faces that were like the vajra and possessed excellent tufts. They shattered

---

[500] Yoga has eight elements—*yama* (restraint), *niyama* (rituals), *asana* (posture), pranayama (control of the breath), *pratyahara* (withdrawal), *dharana* (retention), *dhyana* (meditation) and *samadhi* (liberation).

the rakshasas and penetrated the ground. Other terrible rakshasas were mangled by arrows released from Narayana's bow and fell down, like mountains struck by the vajra. They were wounded by Adhokshaja's[501] arrows. Blood began to exude from these wounds, like golden ore oozing out in mountains. The rakshasas were roaring, but this was surpassed by the blare of the king of conch shells, the sound created by Sharnga bow and Vishnu's roaring. The arrows released from Narayana's Sharnga were as terrible as the rays of the sun, the waves of the ocean and storms from clouds battering large mountains. Hundreds and thousands of arrows were shot swiftly. *Sharabha*s drive away lions.[502] Lions drive away elephants. Elephants drive away tigers. Tigers drive away leopards. Leopards drive away dogs. Dogs drive away cats. Cats drive away snakes. Snakes drive away mice. Like that, in that battle, Vishnu's powers drove the rakshasas away. Vishnu drove them away and they lay down on the ground. Madhusudana killed thousands of rakshasas. He made the conch shell roar, like the king of the gods makes clouds roar. They were devoured by Narayana's arrows. Because of the blaring of the conch shell, they lost their senses. Routed, the army of the rakshasas fled towards Lanka. The army of the rakshasas was shattered by Narayana's arrows and routed.

'In the encounter, Sumali sought to counter Hari with his shower of arrows. His arms were decorated with golden ornaments and he raised them, like an elephant raising its trunk. Like a cloud tinged with lightning, the rakshasa roared in delight. His charioteer's head blazed with earrings. While Sumali was roaring, he[503] severed it and without the charioteer, the horses dragged the rakshasa around, here and there. A man without control is whirled around by his senses, which are like horses. In that way, those distracted horses dragged around Sumali, lord of the rakshasas. In the battle, Mali seized his bow and arrows and attacked. Mali's arrows were decorated with gold. Released from his bow, they penetrated Hari the way *krouncha* birds enter the water. He was struck by thousands of

---

[501] One of Vishnu's names.

[502] A sharabha is a mythical animal and the concept has evolved over time. A sharabha has eight legs, lives in the mountains, slays lions and lives on raw flesh.

[503] Vishnu.

arrows shot by Mali in the encounter. However, just as a person who has conquered his senses is not agitated, Vishnu was not disturbed. The illustrious one, the creator of all beings, twanged his bow. The wielder of the mace shot torrents of arrows in Mali's direction. Those arrows were as radiant as lightning and like the vajra, penetrated Mali's body. They drank his blood, like serpents drinking amrita in ancient times. Having countered Mali, Hari used his force to bring down Mali's diadem, chariot, standard, bow and horses. Having been deprived of his chariot, Mali, supreme among those who roam around in the night, seized a club. With the club in his hand, he leapt up, like a lion springing on a mountain. He was like Indra striking a mountain with his vajra, or like Yama striking Ishana.[504] In the battle, he struck Garuda on the forehead with this. Garuda was severely struck by Mali's club. Suffering from the pain, he bore the god away from the fight. When the god was thus withdrawn because of what Mali had done, a giant clamour arose, because the rakshasas roared. The younger brother of the one with tawny horses[505] heard the sound of the rakshasas roaring. Having been made to withdraw,[506] he wished to kill Mali and released his chakra. It was as radiant as the solar disc and illuminated everything with its own radiance. The chakra was like the wheel of time and brought down Mali's head. The terrible head of the Indra among the rakshasas was severed by the chakra. It fell down, covered with blood, like Rahu's head in ancient times. The gods were extremely delighted. With all their strength, they roared like lions and uttered words of praise for the god.[507] Seeing that Mali had been killed, Sumali and Malyavat were tormented by grief. With all their soldiers, they rushed towards Lanka. Having gained his composure, the great-minded Garuda returned. Enraged, he used the force of his wings to drive away the rakshasas. Narayana's arrows were like the vajra and were released from his bow. With dishevelled hair, the roamers in the night were driven away by these, as if struck by the great Indra's vajra. Their arrows were shattered, their weapons fell

---

[504] Shiva.
[505] Indra is the one with tawny horses and Vishnu is Indra's younger brother.
[506] The Critical Edition excises a shloka where Vishnu looks angrily at Garuda.
[507] Vishnu.

down. Their bodies were struck and mangled by the arrows. Their eyes rolled around in fear and their entrails emerged. The army seemed to have gone mad. They were like elephants afflicted by lions. With their elephants, the roamers in the night screamed loudly. It was just as they had been crushed by a lion in ancient times.[508] Routed by the net of Hari's arrows, they flung aside the nets of their own arrows. Resembling clouds of destruction, those roamers in the night fled, just as dark clouds are dispelled by the wind. Their heads were severed by blows from the chakra. Their limbs were crushed by blows from the mace. Many were sliced down by blows from the sword. The Indras among the rakshasas fell down, like mountains. Their faces were severed by the chakra. Their chests were crushed by the club. Their necks were broken by the plough.[509] Their heads were shattered by the club. Some were sliced down with the sword. Others suffered because of the arrows. From the sky, the rakshasas were swiftly brought down into the waters of the ocean. Their garments were dislodged. Their necklaces and earrings were strewn around. The roamers in the night, resembling dark clouds, were seen to be continuously brought down. They were like dark mountains that were being brought down.'

Chapter 7(8)

'They were slaughtered by Padmanabha[510] and turned their backs. Malyavat retreated, like the ocean when it confronts the shoreline. His eyes red with rage, the roamer in the night shook his head. He addressed Padmanabha in these harsh words. "O Narayana! You do not know about the eternal dharma of kshatriyas. We do not wish to fight. There are others who have been routed. Even then, as you please, you are killing us. O lord of the gods! You have committed the sin of killing those who have

---

[508] This is a reference to Vishnu's *narasimha* (half-man, half-lion) incarnation. In that form, Vishnu killed Hiranyakashipu.

[509] A plough is typically Balarama's weapon.

[510] Vishnu, the one with the lotus in his navel.

retreated. A person who kills in this way does not attain heaven and does not reap the fruits of his good deeds. O wielder of the conch shell and the chakra! If you love the idea of fighting, I am stationed in front of you. Exhibit your strength. I will see it." The powerful younger brother of the king of the gods replied to the Indra among the rakshasas. "The gods were terrified on account of their fear of you and I have granted them freedom from fear. By destroying the rakshasas, I am fulfilling my pledge. I have always preferred doing something agreeable for the gods to my own lives.[511] Even if you go to rasatala, I will kill you." The god said this, his eyes as red as lotuses. Enraged, the Indra among the rakshasas pierced him with a javelin and roared. Adorned with bells, the javelin roared and was released from Malyavat's hand. It was radiant on Hari's chest, like lightning inside a cloud. The one who is loved by the wielder of the spear plucked out the javelin.[512] The lotus-eyed one then flung it towards Malyavat. Released from Govinda's hand, that javelin was like one hurled by Skanda, desiring to kill the rakshasa. It was like a giant meteor unleashed on a mountain of collyrium. His broad chest was radiant because of a sparkling necklace. It shattered it and brought down the Indra among the rakshasas, like the summit of a mountain by the vajra. It shattered his armour and he was immersed in great darkness.[513] However, like an immobile mountain, Malyavat regained his composure again. He picked up a spear that was completely made out of iron, embellished with many spikes. Seizing this, he firmly struck the god between the breasts. Engaged in the battle, the roamer in the night next struck Vasava's younger brother with his fist and retreated a bow length away. At this, loud sounds of praise were heard in the sky. Having struck Vishnu, the rakshasa struck Garuda. Vinata's son angrily struck the rakshasa with the force of his wings, the way a powerful wind scatters away a heap of dry leaves. Sumali saw that his elder brother had been driven away by the force of the wings of the Indra among birds. With all his forces, he left for Lanka. The rakshasa Malyavat was routed by the

---

[511] The text uses the plural.
[512] The wielder of the spear is Kartikeya. That is, Vishnu is loved by Kartikeya.
[513] That is, he lost his senses.

force of the wings. Ashamed, he collected his own force and also left for Lanka. O Rama! In this way, the lotus-eyed Hari killed many rakshasas in the battle and routed the best among their leaders. Afflicted by fear, they were incapable of fighting back against Vishnu. With their wives, they left Lanka. They went to patala and started to reside there. O descendant of the Raghu lineage! All the rakshasas approached Sumali, who was famous for his valour and had been born in Salakantakata's lineage, and resorted to him.[514] You slew the rakshasas named Poulastya. Sumali, Malyavat and Mali were their ancestors. O immensely strong one! All of them were stronger than Ravana. O victor over enemy cities! No one other than the lord of the gods, the god Narayana, the wielder of the conch shell, chakra and mace, could have slain those rakshasas. You are the eternal four-armed god, Narayana. O unvanquished one! O lord! O one without decay! You have been born to slay the rakshasas.'

Chapter 7(9)

'After some time, the rakshasa named Sumali emerged from rasatala and started to wander around everywhere in the world of the mortals. He was like a dark cloud and his earrings were made out molten gold. He had his daughter with him and this maiden was like Shri without the lotus. He saw the lord of treasures, proceeding on Pushpaka. He saw him proceeding through the sky, resembling a fire. The rakshasa spoke to his daughter, who was known by the name of Kaikasi. "O daughter! This is the time to give you away. Your youth is passing. O daughter! You are like Shri with the lotus and possess all the qualities. With dharma in our minds, all of us are like puppets in your cause.[515] Scared of being refused, you have not approached any grooms so far. All those who

---

[514] There is no indication that Malyavat had been killed.
[515] Searching for an appropriate groom. According to dharma, the daughter has to be given away to someone in marriage.

desire respect are always miserable on account of their daughters. O daughter! They do not know who will be a groom for their daughter. A maiden always places three families in uncertainty— the mother's lineage, the father's lineage and the lineage into which she is bestowed. O daughter! Therefore, you should yourself go and accept Vishrava, born in the Poulastya lineage, as your husband. He is best among the supreme sages and has been born in Prajapati's lineage. In this way, there is no doubt that sons and daughters will be born who are like the sun in their energy, just as this lord of treasures is." O Rama! At that time, the brahmana who was Pulastya's son was engaged in agnihotra, looking like a fourth fire. It was a terrible time of the day.[516] However, out of respect for her father, she did not think about this. She approached him and stood there, her eyes cast downwards, towards her feet. He saw the one with the excellent hips, with a face like the full moon. The extremely generous one, who blazed in his energy, asked, "O fortunate one! Whose daughter are you? Where have you come from and what is the reason why you have come here? O beautiful one! Tell me the truth about this." Thus addressed, the maiden joined her hands in salutation and replied, "O sage! Through your own powers, you are capable of knowing what is in my mind. O brahmana! Know that I have come here because I have been commanded by my father. My name is Kaikasi. The remaining bit is only known to you." At this, the sage meditated and determined the reason. He addressed her in these words. "O fortunate one! I have got to know the reason that is in your mind. You have come to me at a terrible time of the day. O fortunate one! Therefore, listen to the kind of sons you will give birth to. They will be terrible. They will perform terrible deeds. They will love terrible people. O one with excellent hips! You will give birth to rakshasas who are cruel in their deeds." Hearing his words, she bowed down before him and replied in these words. "O illustrious one! You are descended from Brahma and such sons should not be born from someone like you." At this, the sage said, "The son who will be born after this will be appropriate for my lineage. He will have dharma in his soul."

[516] The evening.

'O Rama! The maiden was addressed in this way. After some time, she gave birth to a horrible and extremely terrible son in the form of a rakshasa. He had ten heads and large teeth. He was like a mass of black collyrium. His lips were coppery red and he had twenty arms. His mouth was large and his hair blazed. As soon as he was born, jackals spouted out flames from their mouths. Predatory creatures started to circle in a counterclockwise direction. The gods showered down blood. Clouds thundered harshly. In the sky, the sun's lustre faded. Giant meteors fell down on the ground. His father, who was like the grandfather, gave him a name. "Since he has been born with ten heads, he will be known as Dashagriva." After this, the immensely strong Kumbhakarna was born. There was no one else who was as gigantic as him in size. After this, the one with the malformed face was born and she was named Shurpanakha. Vibhishana, with dharma in his soul, was a son who was born to Kaikasi later. Those extremely energetic ones grew up in that great forest. Among them, the cruel Dashagriva was the one who caused anxiety to the worlds. The maharshis were engaged in pursuits of dharma. Without thinking about it, the crazy and wicked Kumbhakarna devoured them and terrified the three worlds. Vibhishana possessed dharma in his soul and always remained on the path of dharma. He studied, was controlled in his diet, fasted and controlled his senses.

'On some occasion, the immensely energetic god who was the lord of treasures came to see his father, mounted on Pushpaka. Kaikasi saw him, blazing in his energy. Because of the rakshasi nature of her intelligence, she told Dashagriva, "O son! Look at your brother, Vaishravana. He is enveloped in energy. You are brothers and should be similar. But look at yourself and look at him. O Dashagriva! O one who is infinitely brave! O son! Act so that you can quickly become Vaishravana's equal." Hearing his mother's words, the powerful Dashagriva was filled with unlimited intolerance and took a pledge. "Know that this is my true pledge. I will become like my brother or superior to him. O mother! I will soon be like that. Abandon the torment in your heart." Angry with his younger brother, Dashagriva resolved, "I have decided that I will perform austerities to obtain what I desire." To accomplish the objective, he went to the auspicious hermitage of Gokarna.'

Chapter 7(10)

Rama asked the brahmana, 'What did the brothers do in the forest? O brahmana! Great in their vows, what kind of austerities did they undertake?'

Controlled in his mind, Agastya replied to Rama. He told him about the rites of dharma the brothers observed. 'Kumbhakarna was always devoted to dharma. In the heat of the summer, he tormented himself amidst the five fires.[517] During the monsoon, despite being drenched by rain, he was in *virasana*.[518] During the winter, he was always submerged in water. Ten thousand years passed in this way. He was controlled in his pursuit of dharma and always based himself on the path of virtue. Vibhishana, with dharma in his soul, was always pure and devoted to dharma. For five thousand years, he stood on one foot. When the rites were over, large numbers of apsaras danced. Flowers showered down and the gods were agitated. For another five thousand years, he raised his hands up. He studied and controlled his mind. With his head raised, he looked at the sun. In this way, Vibhishana spent ten thousand years, controlled in his mind, as if he was in Nandana, in heaven. For ten thousand years, Dashanana ate nothing. At the end of every thousand years, he offered one of his heads as an oblation into the fire. Nine thousand years passed in this way. Nine heads were offered into the fire. At the end of ten thousand years, the one with dharma in his soul wished to sever his tenth head. However, the grandfather arrived there. Extremely happy, the grandfather arrived, with the other gods. He said, "O son! O Dashagriva! O son! I am pleased with you. O one who knows about dharma! Quickly seek the boon that you desire. What do you wish for? What can I do for you now, so that your efforts are not in vain?" Delighted in his soul, Dashagriva replied. He bowed his head down before the god and his voice choked in joy. "O illustrious one! For creatures, there never is a fear that is as great as that of death. There is no enemy like death. I desire to be immortal. O supervisor of creatures! Till eternity, let birds, serpents, yakshas, daityas, danavas, rakshasas and gods be unable

---

[517] Four fires in four directions and the sun overhead.
[518] Literally, posture of a hero. A seated position used by ascetics.

to kill me. O one who is worshipped by the immortals! There is no other creature I need to think about. All other creatures, humans and others, are like grass." The rakshasa Dashagriva, with dharma in his soul, said this. O Rama! With the gods, the grandfather replied in these words. "O bull among rakshasas! It shall be as you say. I am pleased with you. Therefore, listen to my auspicious words. O unblemished one! O rakshasa! You have already offered your heads into the fire and they will again be restored, as they used to be." The grandfather said this to the rakshasa Dashagriva and the heads that had been offered as oblations into the fire sprouted again. O Rama! After having said this to Dashagriva, Prajapati, the grandfather of the worlds, addressed Vibhishana in these words. "O Vibhishana! O child! Your intelligence is in conformity with dharma. O one who knows about dharma! O one who is excellent in vows! I am pleased with you. Ask for a boon." Vibhishana, with dharma in his soul, joined his hands in salutation and replied in these words. "May I always be surrounded by all the qualities, just as the moon is by its beams. O one who is excellent in vows! Since the preceptor of the worlds is satisfied with me and has offered to grant me a boon, I am successful. Let my intelligence be in accordance with the *ashrama* I am in.[519] Let me be devoted to that kind of dharma and let me observe that kind of dharma. O extremely generous one! This is the only supreme boon that I have in mind. In this world, if a person is devoted to dharma, there is nothing that he cannot obtain." Prajapati was delighted and told Vibhishana, "O child! You already follow dharma and it will be as you say. O one who afflicts enemies! Though you have been born in the lineage of rakshasas, there will be no adharma in your intelligence. I grant you immortality." O scorcher of enemies! After this, he prepared to confer a boon on Kumbhakarna. At this, all the gods joined their hands in salutation and addressed Prajapati in these words. "You should not grant a boon to Kumbhakarna. You know that the evil-minded one will terrify the worlds. O Brahma! He has already devoured seven apsaras from Nandana, ten of the great Indra's followers, rishis and humans. O one who is infinite in radiance! Give him a boon that will confuse him. Let the worlds be

---

[519] The four ashramas of *brahmacharya, garhasthya, vanaprastha* and *sannyasa.*

secure and let him also be satisfied." Addressed in this way by the gods, Brahma, born from the lotus, started to think. As he thought of her, the goddess Sarasvati presented herself by his side. Standing next to him, Sarasvati joined her hands in salutation and spoke to him in these words. "O god! I have come here. What shall I do?" When she arrived, Prajapati addressed Sarasvati in these words. "For that Indra among rakshasas, become the speech that the gods desire." Thus addressed by Prajapati, she agreed and entered.[520] "O Kumbhakarna![521] O mighty-armed one! Ask for the boon that is in your mind." Hearing these words, Kumbhakarna replied in these words. "O god of the gods! I desire that I may be able to sleep for many years." With the gods, the grandfather said that it would indeed be like that. Having got him to say this, the goddess Sarasvati left for heaven. The evil-souled Kumbhakarna was miserable and thought, "What are these words that emerged from my mouth now?" Thus, the brothers, blazing in their energy, received boons. They went to a *shleshmataka*[522] forest and happily resided there.'

Chapter 7(11)

'Sumali got to know that the roamers in the night had obtained boons. Abandoning his fear, with his companions, he emerged from rasatala. The rakshasa's advisers were Maricha, Prahasta, Virupaksha and Mahodara. Extremely angry, they emerged. Sumali was surrounded by these bulls among the rakshasas. He went to Dashagriva, embraced him and said, "O son! It is good fortune that the wish we thought about has materialized. You have obtained a boon like this. It is the best in the three worlds. O mighty-armed one! We suffered from great fear on account of Vishnu. Because of that, we abandoned Lanka and went to rasatala. We were routed and slighted and had to abandon our own residences. All

---

[520] Entered Kumbhakarna's tongue.
[521] This is Brahma speaking.
[522] The Assyrian plum, *Cordia myxa*.

of us collectively fled and entered rasatala. This city of Lanka is ours and is desired by the rakshasas. However, your brother, the intelligent lord of treasures, resides there. O mighty-armed one! If you are capable of swiftly obtaining it back, using sama or dana, that should be done. O son! There is no doubt that you should be the lord of Lanka. O immensely strong one! You will be the lord of all of us." Dashagriva spoke to his maternal grandfather, who had presented himself. "The lord of treasures is our senior and one should not speak about him in this way." Dashagriva, the roamer in the night, spoke these words. At this, Prahasta humbly replied, citing reasons. "O Dashagriva! O mighty-armed one! You should not speak in this way. There is no fraternal relationship for brave ones. Listen to my words. Aditi and Diti were sisters and they were together. Those two extremely beautiful ones were the wives of Kashyapa Prajapati. Aditi gave birth to the gods, the lords of the three worlds. Diti gave birth to the daityas and they were born from Kashyapa himself. O one who knows about dharma! O brave one! Before Vishnu exhibited his powers, everything, the forests, the oceans and the earth, with all its mountains, used to belong to the daityas. However, exhibiting his powers, Vishnu killed them in a battle and brought the undecaying three worlds under the subjugation of the gods. You are not the only one who will cause such a transgression.[523] The gods have done this earlier. Therefore, act in accordance with my words." Dashagriva was thus addressed by the evil-souled Prahasta. Having thought for a while, he signified his assent. Full of delight, that very night, with those roamers in the night, the valiant Dashagriva went to the forest. Dashagriva, the roamer in the night, based himself in Trikuta. He sent Prahasta, accomplished in the use of words, as an emissary. "O Prahasta! O bull among nairittas![524] Go quickly and convey my words to the lord of riches. First speak words that are in conformity with sama. 'O king! This city of Lanka belongs to the great-souled rakshasas. O amiable one! O unblemished one! It is not proper for

[523] Of enmity with a brother.
[524] There seems to be a typo in the Critical Edition. Kubera is referred to as a bull among the nairittas.

you to reside here. O infinitely brave one! Therefore, you should follow my words, uttered in conformity with sama, and return it. You will then show affection and also follow dharma.'" Having gone there, Prahasta, accomplished in the use of words, said this. He conveyed all of Dashagriva's words to the lord of treasures. The god Vaishravana heard Prahasta's words. The one who was accomplished in the use of words replied to Prahasta in these words. "Go and tell Dashagriva this. 'O mighty-armed one! The city and kingdom that are with me belong to you. Enjoy them, bereft of thorns. O fortunate one! I will soon act completely in accordance with the rakshasa's words. But can you wait until this has been reported to our father?'" Having said this, the lord of riches went to his father's presence. He greeted his senior and told him what Dashagriva desired. "O father! Dashagriva has sent a messenger to me. He wants me to give him the city of Lanka, which was formerly populated by large numbers of rakshasas. O one who is good in vows! Instruct me about what I should do in this situation." Thus addressed, the brahmana rishi Vishrava, bull among sages, addressed the lord of treasures in these words. "O son! Listen to my words. The mighty-armed Dashagriva has also said this in my presence. However, I have reprimanded that extremely evil-minded one several times. In anger, I have repeatedly told him that he will be destroyed. O son! Listen to my beneficial words, which are full of dharma. That extremely evil-minded one is confused because he obtained a boon. He cannot distinguish between who should be respected and who should not be respected. Having succumbed to his terrible nature, he did not comprehend my curse. O mighty-armed one! Therefore, go to Mount Kailasa and construct your residence there. With your followers, abandon Lanka. There is the beautiful river Mandakinee there, supreme among rivers. The waters are covered with golden lotuses that are like the sun. O lord of treasures! Without this, you will not obtain peace from this enmity with the rakshasas. You know that he has obtained a supreme boon." Thus addressed, he showed respect towards his father and accepted these words. He left with his wives, the citizens, his advisers, the mounts and the riches. Prahasta went to Dashagriva and told him everything. "The city of Lanka is empty and it is thirty

yojanas in expanse. With us, enter it and follow your own dharma.'
The rakshasa Prahasta addressed Ravana in this way and with his
brothers, his forces and his followers, he entered the city of Lanka.
The roamers in the night consecrated him and Dashanana started
to live in that city. The roamers in the night, who resembled dark
clouds, obtained their objects of desire in that city. The lord of
treasures showed respect to his father's words. On that mountain,
he resided in a city that sparkled like the moon. There were the best
of ornamented and decorated residences. It was like Purandara's
Amaravati.'

Chapter 7(12)

'Once the Indra among rakshasas had been consecrated, with
his brothers, he thought about whom to bestow his rakshasi
sister on. He gave the rakshasi, his sister Shurpanakha, to the Indra
among danavas named Vidyujjihva,[525] from the Kalakeya lineage.
O Rama! Having bestowed his sister, the king was roaming around
on a hunt and saw Maya, Diti's son. Dashagriva, roamer in the
night, saw that he was with a maiden. "Why are you wandering
around alone in this forest, where there are no humans to hunt?"
Thus addressed, Maya told the roamer in the night, "I will tell
you everything that has occurred. Listen to my words. O son![526]
Earlier, you may have heard about the apsara named Hema. Just
as Poulami was given to Shatakratu, the gods bestowed her on me.
O son! I was attached to her for five hundred years. After that, to
accomplish some task of the gods, she has been away for fourteen
years. For Hema's sake, I have constructed a city made out of gold.
I have fashioned it out of maya and it is colourful with diamonds
and lapis lazuli. However, separated from her and extremely
miserable, I did not find the slightest bit of attachment to that place.
Therefore, I abandoned the city. Taking my daughter with me, I

---

[525] Vidyut-jihva.
[526] The word used is tata.

have come to this forest. O king! This is my daughter and she has been reared by her.[527] With her, I am looking around for a groom for her. For all respectable men who are fathers, a daughter is the source of unhappiness. A daughter always causes uncertainty in two families.[528] O son! Through my wife, two sons have been born to me. Mayavi is the first and Dundubhi followed later. I have told you the truth about everything that you asked. O son! Having said this, who are you? Let me know who you are." Thus addressed, the Indra among rakshasas humbly replied. "I am the son of Poulastya and my name is Dashagriva." Hearing that he was the son of a brahmana rishi, Maya was filled with joy. The idea of bestowing his daughter on him appealed to him. Smiling, the Indra among daityas addressed the Indra among rakshasas in these words. "O king! This daughter of mine has been born from the apsara Hema. This maiden's name is Mandodari. Accept her as your wife." O Rama! Dashagriva replied, signifying his agreement. He lit a fire there and accepted her hand. O Rama! Maya did not know about the curse imposed by the store of austerities.[529] Even if he had, he would have bestowed her on someone born in the grandfather's lineage. He also gave an invincible and extremely wonderful javelin, obtained through supreme austerities. This was the one he struck Lakshmana with. In this way, the lord and master of Lanka obtained a wife. He went to the city with his wife and got his two brothers married off. Vairochana's granddaughter was named Vajrajvala.[530] Ravana wedded her to Kumbhakarna, as his wife. Shailusha, the great-souled king of the gandharvas had a daughter. Her name was Sarama. Vibhishana, who knew about dharma, obtained her as a wife. She was born along the shores of Lake Manasa. O son! At the time of the moon, the water in Lake Manasa started to overflow. Out of affection towards her daughter, the mother shouted out these words. "O lake! Do not extend further." That is the reason she became Sarama.[531] In this way, the rakshasas obtained wives

---

[527] By Hema.
[528] Probably meaning the father's and the mother's.
[529] On Ravana, by Vishrava.
[530] Vairochana is Bali. Vajrajvala was Bali's daughter's daughter.
[531] Derived from *sara/sarasa* (lake) and *ma* (do not).

and found pleasure with their respective wives, like the gandharvas in Nandana. Mandodari gave birth to a son named Meghanada. All of you know him by the name of Indrajit. In earlier times, as soon as he was born, this son of a rakshasa wept in a loud voice. This sounded like the thunder of a cloud. All of Lanka seemed to be stupefied by the sound. Thus, his father himself named him Meghanada.[532] O Rama! He grew up in Ravana's auspicious inner quarters. He was protected by excellent women, like fire hidden inside wood.'

Chapter 7(13)

'After some time, the fierce sleep created by the creator of the worlds manifested itself before Kumbhakarna. His brother was seated nearby and Kumbhakarna addressed him in these words. "O king! I am suffering from sleep. Get a residence created for me." The king engaged artisans who were like Vishvakarma and they constructed a residence for Kumbhakarna that was like Kailasa. It was white and one yojana wide. Its length was double that. It was a sight to be seen and was constructed for Kumbhakarna, freed of all obstructions. Everywhere, it was decorated with pillars, made out of crystal and colourful with gold. It was made beautiful with lapis lazuli and there were nets of bells. The gates were encrusted with ivory and the platforms were made out of diamonds and crystal. It was always pleasant everywhere, like a sacred cave inside Meru. Kumbhakarna, roamer in the night, went to sleep there. He slept for many thousands of years and did not wake. When Kumbhakarna was overcome by sleep, Dashanana continuously obstructed the gods, the rishis, the yakshas and the gandharvas. Extremely enraged, Dashanana went to the wonderful groves, Nandana and the others, and devastated them. He sported like an elephant in the river, like the wind flinging away trees and like the vajra shattering mountains. He always caused devastation.

[532] One whose roar (*nada*) is like that of a cloud (*megha*).

'The lord of treasures got to know about Dashagriva's conduct. Displaying his fraternal affection, Vaishravana, who knew about dharma, reminded him about his own lineage, sending a messenger to Lanka for Dashagriva's benefit. He[533] went to the city of Lanka and met Vibhishana, who followed dharma, showed him respect and asked about the reason for his arrival. He asked about the king's[534] welfare and that of his kin and relatives. He then showed him the assembly hall where Dashanana was seated. He saw the king there, blazing in his own energy. He uttered pronouncements of victory and worshipped him. Thereafter, he was silent for a while. He then approached Dashagriva, who was seated on a couch covered with excellent spreads. The messenger addressed him in these words. "O king! O amiable one! I will tell you everything that your brother has said, relevant and appropriate for both your conduct and your lineage. 'Everything that you have done so far is sufficient. Be virtuous, so that it adds to your character. If you are capable, be established in virtue and act in accordance with dharma. I have seen Nandana destroyed. I have heard that the rishis have been killed. O king! I have heard about the gods making preparations against you. O lord of the rakshasas! You have shown me disrespect in many ways. However, if crimes are committed by children, they must be protected by their own relatives. I have gone to the slopes of the Himalayas and am engaged in following dharma. I have controlled myself and have resorted to fierce vows. I have controlled my senses. I have seen the lord god[535] there, together with the goddess Uma. There, my left eye was brought down by the goddess.[536] Parvati was sporting there, assuming an unmatched form. I only wanted to find out who this auspicious one was. There was no other fraudulent reason. However, because of the powers of the goddess, my left eye was burnt down. Like a stellar body covered

---

[533] The messenger.
[534] Kubera's.
[535] Mahadeva.
[536] Since Kubera looked at Shiva and Parvati with envy, his eye was destroyed. Subsequently, this lost eye was replaced with a yellow eye. This is the standard story, with a slight variation given here.

in mist, my eye turned yellow. Thereafter, I went to that extensive slope on the mountain. I observed a great vow for a full eight hundred years. When the rituals were over, the god Maheshvara was pleased with me. Happy in his mind, the lord addressed me in these words. "O one who knows about dharma! O one who is good in vows! O lord of treasures! I am pleased with your austerities, since you have undertaken this vow and have completed it. There is no third person who can accomplish a vow like this. This vow is extremely difficult to observe and I accomplished it in ancient times. O lord of treasures! Therefore, the idea of a friendship with me should appeal to you. O unblemished one! You have won me over with your austerities. Be my friend. Your left eye was burnt down because of the powers of the goddess. Your name as the one with a single yellow eye will remain for eternity." Through Shankara's permission, I thus obtained his friendship. Having returned, I have heard about your wicked resolutions. O defiler of the lineage! Withdraw from this association with those who follow adharma. With large numbers of rishis, the gods are thinking about a means to get you killed.'" Thus addressed, Dashagriva's eyes turned red with rage. He wrung his hands, bit his lips and spoke these words. "O messenger! I have understood what you are trying to say through these words. You and my brother, who sent you, will no longer exist and nor will your residences. What the protector of riches has spoken about will bring no benefit to me. That foolish one has told me about a friendship with Maheshvara. I think that a senior and an elder brother must not be killed. Therefore, having heard his words, this is what I have decided. Resorting to the valour in my arms, I will conquer the three worlds. Because of what he[537] has done, right this instant, I will convey the four guardians of the world to Yama's eternal abode." Having said this, the lord of Lanka killed the messenger with his sword and gave the body to the evil-souled rakshasas to devour. Performing the auspicious rites, Ravana ascended his chariot. Desiring to conquer the three worlds, he went to the place where the lord of treasures was.'

[537] Kubera.

Chapter 7(14)

'He was with six advisers who were always insolent because of their strength—Mahodara, Prahasta, Maricha, Shuka, Sarana and the brave Dhumraksha. They always loved to fight. Surrounded by them, the prosperous one proceeded to burn down the worlds in his rage. He crossed cities, rivers, mountains, forests and groves and reached Mount Kailasa in an instant. Those who were in the mountain[538] heard the Indra among rakshasas announce, "I am the king's brother." They went to where the lord of treasures was. They went and told him everything about what his brother had decided to do. Dhanada[539] gave them permission to go and fight. The army of the king of the nairittas was turbulent, like a waxing ocean. It seemed to make the mountain quake. A battle ensued between the yakshas and the rakshasas. Soon, the yakshas' advisers were distressed. On seeing that the soldiers were in this state, Dashagriva, the roamer in the night, uttered roars of delight and angrily attacked. The Indra among rakshasas possessed advisers who were terrible in valour. Each one of them fought against one thousand. Dashagriva immersed himself in the soldiers, killing them with clubs, maces, swords, spears and javelins. Without pausing to breathe, Dashanana slaughtered them. He showered down like a dense cloud and countered the Indra among the yakshas. The evil-souled one raised a club that was like the staff of Death. He penetrated the yaksha soldiers and conveyed them to Yama's eternal abode. Those soldiers were like an extensive mass of dry kindling. In extremely terrible fashion, he consumed them, like a fire fanned by the wind. The advisers, Mahodara, Shuka and the others, were in the middle. They drove away the few remaining yakshas, like the wind dispelling clouds. The limbs of some were mangled in the clash. In the battle, others fell down on the ground. Some bit their lips with their teeth. Others were bitten with teeth and fell down on the ground. In the field of battle, they clung to each other in fear and their weapons were dislodged. The yakshas lost all enterprise, like a bank destroyed by the waters. Those who were killed went to heaven, though they had fought on

---

[538] The yakshas who were there.
[539] The lord of treasures, Kubera.

earth. The large number of rishis looked on and there was no space left in the firmament.[540] O Rama! At this time, the extremely great yaksha named Samyodhakantaka arrived there, with a large army and mounts. Like Vishnu striking, the yaksha struck Maricha and he fell down on the ground, like one whose merit has been exhausted falling down from the sky. In a short while, the roamer in the night regained his senses and assured himself. He fought against the yaksha and made him run away. O Rama! Doorkeepers protected the gate, which was golden all over and was embellished with lapis lazuli and silver. At this time, Dashagriva, roamer in the night, entered through there. The doorkeeper known as Suryabhanu tried to restrain him. The yaksha uprooted the gate and struck him with that. The yaksha struck him severely with the gate. O Rama! However, because of the boon he had obtained from the one who was born from the waters,[541] no harm was done to him. He then struck the yaksha with that gate. The yaksha could no longer be seen. It was as if he had consumed him. On witnessing his valour, all the yakshas fled. Afflicted by fear, they entered rivers and caves.'

Chapter 7(15)

'On seeing that hundreds and thousands of yakshas had been driven away, the lord of treasures himself emerged to fight. There was a yaksha named Manichara and he was extremely difficult to vanquish. Surrounded by thousands of yakshas with the four kinds of forces, he started to fight. In the battle, the yakshas struck the rakshasas with clubs, maces, spears, javelins, spikes and bludgeons and drove them away. Prahasta killed one thousand in the encounter. Using his club, Mahodara killed another one thousand. O Rama! The evil-souled Maricha became enraged. In the twinkling of an eye, be brought down two thousand. In that great encounter, Dhumraksha attacked Manibhadra.[542] He angrily struck him in the chest with a

---

[540] It was dense with spectators.
[541] Brahma.
[542] Manibhadra is the same as Manichara.

club. However, Manibhadra did not tremble. He too picked up a
club and struck the rakshasa. Struck on the head, Dhumraksha lost
his senses and fell down. Struck, Dhumraksha fell down, covered
with blood. On seeing this, Dashanana became extremely angry and
attacked Manibhadra. He was like the fire that arises at the time
of the destruction of a yuga. The bull among rakshasas angrily
attacked and struck him with three javelins. In the battle, the king
of the rakshasas next struck him with a club. Because of that blow,
his crown was dislodged to one side. Since that time, the yaksha has
been known as Parshvamouli.[543] Having repulsed the great-souled
yaksha, Manibhadra, in the battle, he pronounced his name with an
extremely loud roar and this resounded in that mountain.

'From a distance, the lord of treasures could be seen, wielding a
club. Shukra, Proshthapada, Shamkha and Padma were with him.[544]
He saw his brother in the battle, dislodged from his respectability
because of the curse. The intelligent one addressed him in words
that were appropriate for the grandfather's lineage. "O evil-minded
one! Though I try to restrain you, you do not understand. When
you go to hell later, you will realize the consequences. A stupid
man who is confused and drinks poison will understand the
consequences of his deeds in the form of fruits. Nothing that you do
is in conformity with dharma, which would have delighted the gods.
You do not comprehend where your present sentiments are taking
you. A person who shows disrespect to his mother, father, brother
or preceptor, will see the consequences when he comes under the
subjugation of the king of the dead. This body is temporary. If a
foolish person does not perform austerities, he is tormented later.
When he is dead, he sees the state he has reduced himself to. No
one who is evil in intelligence can ever cultivate true intelligence.
He reaps the consequences according to the acts he has undertaken.

---

[543] Meaning, one whose crown leans towards one side.

[544] Kubera is accompanied by treasures (*nidhi*) named Padma and Shamkha, in
personified form. Padma emerges from a *padma* (lotus) and Shamkha emerges from a
shamkha (conch shell). Manibhadra is usually Kubera's general. Proshthapada is a
nakshatra. More accurately, it is a collective name for two nakshatras, Purva Bhadrapada
and Uttara Bhadrapada. Presumably, this nakshatra and Shukra (Venus) were with
Kubera, in embodied form.

Through the deeds they have themselves undertaken earlier, men obtain intelligence, beauty, strength, riches, sons, advisers and everything else. Your intelligence is such that you will go to hell. However, I will not converse with you. It is my decision that one should not do that with those who are evil in conduct." Having said this, he struck all the advisers, Maricha and the others, such that they were repulsed and forced to run away. After this, the great-souled Indra among the yakshas struck Dashagriva on the head with a club. However, he did not waver from the spot. O Rama! In that great battle, they then struck each other. They did not fall unconscious. Nor were they exhausted. Both of them became even more intolerant. In the battle, Dhanada[545] released agneyastra. Dashagriva countered the weapon with *varunastra*. The lord of the rakshasas then immersed himself in the maya of the rakshasas. He struck Dhanada on the head with his gigantic club. Thus struck, he lost his senses and blood started to flow. The lord of treasures fell down, like an ashoka tree severed at the root. Padma and the other nidhis took the lord of treasures to the grove of Nandana and revived Dhanada. O Rama! Thus, Dhanada was vanquished by the lord of the rakshasas. As a sign of his victory, he seized Pushpaka vimana. It was full of golden pillars and its doors were made of gems and lapis lazuli. There were nets of pearls and trees with fruits that yielded all the objects of desire. It could travel wherever it wished. Having won it through his valour, the king mounted it. Having defeated the god Vaishravana, he descended from Kailasa.'

Chapter 7(16)

'O Rama! The lord of rakshasas defeated his brother, Dhanada. He then went to the clump of reeds where Mahasena was born.[546] Dashagriva saw that golden clump of reeds. He saw that net of rays, resembling a second sun. O Rama! He ascended the

---

[545] Kubera, the lord of treasures, the one who grants treasures.
[546] Mahasena is Kartika. As a child, he was left in a clump of reeds.

mountain and in the beautiful extremity of a forest, saw that in the sky, Pushpaka's progress was impeded. On seeing that Pushpaka couldn't move, surrounded by his advisers, the rakshasa began to think. "This can go wherever it wants. How has its movement been impeded? What is the reason why Pushpaka cannot advance? This must be the act of someone who is on this mountain." The intelligent Maricha spoke to Dashagriva. "O king! There must be some reason why Pushpaka cannot advance." Bhava's follower, the powerful Nandishvara[547] arrived by his side and fearlessly addressed the Indra among the rakshasas. "O Dashagriva! Return. Shankara is sporting on this mountain. Therefore, this mountain has been made impassable for birds, serpents, yakshas, daityas, danavas, rakshasas and all creatures." His eyes turned coppery red with rage and he descended from Pushpaka. Saying, "Who is this Shankara?" he went to the bottom of the mountain. He saw the lord Nandishvara standing not far away, holding a spear and resembling a second Shankara. The rakshasa saw that he was an odd kind of human[548] and ignored him. In his foolishness, he laughed, like a cloud filled with water. The illustrious Nandi was like a second body of Shankara's and became angry. He spoke to the rakshasa Dashagriva, who had presented himself there. "O evil-minded rakshasa! You have seen my odd kind of human form and in your foolishness, have slighted me. You have laughed at me. Therefore, in the lineage of the vanaras, there will be born those who are like me in form, so as to ensure your destruction. They will be my equal in bravery and energy. O roamer in the night! Because of what you have done, I am capable of killing you right now. But I do not wish to kill you. Because of your own former deeds, you have already been killed." The roamer in the night paid no heed to Nandi's words.

'He approached the mountain and spoke these words. "O lord of the earth![549] This mountain has prevented my progress and has

---

[547] Often known simply as Nandi.

[548] The text uses the word *vanara*. Nandi doesn't have the face of an ape. He has the face of a bull, with a human body. Therefore, vanara should not be translated as ape. Vanara actually means a special kind of man. This explains our translation.

[549] The word used is Gopati. Go means cattle, as well as the earth. Gopati can therefore be translated both as lord of the earth and lord of cattle.

impeded Pushpaka's movement. I will destroy its foundation. O
Bhava! What powers allow you to sport like a king? It should be
known to me. I do not know why I should be scared." O king!
Having said this, he inserted his arms under the mountain and tried
to raise it, the way a predatory beast raises a tree with an animal on
it. O Rama! At this, Mahadeva laughed at what he had done. As if
he was sporting, he pressed down on the mountain with the big toe
of his foot. Thus pressed, the hands that were under the mountain
were crushed. The rakshasa's advisers who were present were
astounded. The rakshasa became angry at his hands being crushed.
He emitted an extremely loud roar that filled up the three worlds.
Thinking that the worlds were about to end, humans were terrified
at the sound. The gods were also agitated and were distracted from
their own tasks. Mahadeva, seated on the summit of the mountain,
was pleased.[550] Freeing his hands, he addressed Dashanana in these
words. "O roamer in the night! I am pleased with your valour and
your ferocity. You let out a roar in your pain and that one was
extremely terrible. Therefore, your name should be Ravana and this
will be your name. Gods, humans, yakshas and others who are on
the surface of this world will address you by this name—Ravana,
who makes the worlds scream.[551] O Poulastya! Confidently proceed
along whichever path you want to follow. O lord of the rakshasas! I
am giving you permission to leave." Ravana obtained his name from
Maheshvara himself. Having greeted Mahadeva, he mounted the
vimana. O Rama! After this, Ravana roamed around on earth. Here
and there, he started to obstruct the extremely brave kshatriyas.'

Chapter 7(17)

'O king! After this, the mighty-armed one wandered around
on earth. Ravana reached a forest in the Himalayas and

---

[550] The Critical Edition excises shlokas and breaks the continuity. Ravana prayed to
Mahadeva. That is the reason Mahadeva was pleased.
[551] The word *rava* means shriek/yell. Hence, Ravana can be interpreted in two
ways—someone who himself shrieks, or someone who makes the worlds shriek.

roamed around there. There, he saw a maiden with matted hair, clad in black antelope skin. Like a goddess, she was observing noble rituals and performing austerities. He saw the beautiful maiden who was observing that extremely great vow. His soul was confused because of desire. He smiled and asked her, "O fortunate one! Acting against your youth, why are you behaving in this way? This kind of reaction is not right for someone who possesses your beauty. O fortunate one! Whose daughter are you? O unblemished one! Who is your husband? I am asking you. Tell me. Why are you performing austerities in this secluded place?" The maiden was thus asked by the ignoble rakshasa. The store of austerities followed the due rituals of hospitality and said, "A brahmana rishi who follows dharma is my father and his name is Kushadhvaja. The prosperous one is Brihaspati's son and he is like Brihaspati in intelligence. The great-souled one always practises the Vedas. I have been born as his eloquent daughter.[552] I am known by the name of Vedavati. Desiring to accept me as a bride, gods, gandharvas, yakshas, rakshasas and serpents have gone to my father. O lord of the rakshasas! However, my father did not bestow me on them. O mighty-armed one! I will tell you the reason. Listen. My father intended that Vishnu, supreme among the gods and the lord of the three worlds, should be his son-in-law. My father did not want anyone else. There was a king of the daityas, named Shambhu, and he was insolent because of his strength. On hearing that the one with dharma in his soul wished to bestow me in this way, he was filled with rage. While my father was asleep during the night, the evil one killed him. My distressed mother embraced my father's head. With him, the immensely fortunate one entered the funeral pyre. My desire is to make my father's wish about Narayana come true. That is the virtuous intention in my heart. Even if I have to die, I will accomplish my father's wish. I have taken that pledge and am therefore undertaking these pervasive austerities. O bull among rakshasas! I have thus told you everything. Know that I have resorted to this dharma because I desire Narayana as my husband. O king! O Poulastya's descendant! I know about you. Because of

---

[552] Alternatively, speech has been born to him as a daughter.

my austerities, I can know everything that goes on in the three worlds." At this, Ravana spoke to the maiden who was observing this extremely great vow. Suffering from Kandarpa's arrows, he alighted from the top of the vimana. "O one with the excellent hips! Since your inclinations are like that, you are blind. O one with eyes like a fawn! It is the aged who should seek to accumulate dharma. You possess all the qualities. You should not act in this way. O timid one! You are the most beautiful in the three worlds. It is a rule that youth does not last. Who is this Vishnu that you have spoken about? O fortunate one! O beautiful one! You desire him. But he is not my equal in valour, austerities, pursuing pleasure or strength." Without any fear, the maiden replied to the roamer in the night, though the rakshasa had used his hand to seize her by the hair. Angry, Vedavati cut off the bit of hair with her hand.[553] Having lit a fire and made up her mind to die, the supreme one said, "O ignoble one! Having been oppressed by you, I no longer wish to remain alive now. O rakshasa! While you look on, I will enter this fire. I am faultless and am without a protector. Since you have oppressed me, for the sake of your destruction, I will be born again. This is especially because women are incapable of killing evil ones. If I curse you, my store of austerities will be diminished.[554] If I have performed good deeds, if I have given donations and I have rendered oblations, I will be born as the virtuous daughter of someone who follows dharma, but not through the womb." Having said this, she entered the blazing fire. From the firmament, divine flowers rained down in every direction. Using your superhuman bravery, you attacked and killed an enemy who was like a mountain. However, in her rage, she had already killed him. In this way, the immensely fortunate one was born on earth again, from the mouth of a plough in the field, like the flame of a fire from a sacrificial altar. In krita yuga, her name was Vedavati. For the destruction of that rakshasa, she was born in treta yuga. She was born from a plough and people referred to her as Sita.'

[553] The Critical Edition excises a shloka that says one of her hands had turned into a sword.

[554] Any act of cursing reduces the accumulated merits of austerities.

Chapter 7(18)

'When Vedavati entered the fire, Ravana ascended Pushpaka and started to roam around the earth. The rakshasa reached Ushirabija[555] where, with the gods, King Marutta was performing a sacrifice. There was a brahmana rishi named Samvarta and he was just like his brother, Brihaspati. Surrounded by all the large numbers of brahmanas, the one who knew about dharma was officiating at the sacrifice. The gods saw that the rakshasa was invincible because of the boon he had obtained. Scared of being oppressed, they assumed the forms of other species. Indra turned into a peacock, Dharmaraja into a crow, the lord of treasures into a lizard and Varuna into a swan. Ravana, the lord of the rakshasas, approached the king and said, "Give me a fight or say that you have been vanquished by me." At this, King Marutta asked him, "Who are you?" The rakshasa laughed out aloud and addressed him in these words. "O king! I am pleased at your ignorance. You do not know about Ravana, Dhanada's younger brother. Who in the three worlds does not know about my strength? I have defeated my brother and have seized his vimana." King Marutta replied to the rakshasa, "You are indeed blessed that you have vanquished your elder brother in a battle. This is not an act that is in conformity with dharma and is condemned by the worlds. It is not something to boast about. Having performed the evil-minded act of defeating your brother, you are boasting about it. Earlier, what act of dharma have you accomplished that you obtained this boon and strength? You are praising yourself through words, but I have never heard of you before." The king seized his bow and arrow and angrily emerged to fight. However, the great rishi, Samvarta obstructed his path and addressed Marutta in words filled with affection. "If you listen to my words, this clash will not be good for you. If this sacrifice to Maheshvara is not completed, your lineage will be destroyed. How can someone who has consecrated himself for a sacrifice fight? How can someone who has consecrated himself for a sacrifice be cruel? The outcome of a battle is always uncertain and the rakshasas are

---

[555] This is described as a mountain and as a place where King Marutta performed a sacrifice.

extremely difficult to defeat." Hearing his preceptor's words, King
Marutta desisted. He cast aside his bow and arrows. Composing
himself, he stationed himself near the sacrifice. Shuka[556] decided that
he had been defeated and announced, "Ravana is victorious.' He
uttered a roar of delight. He[557] devoured the great rishis who had
assembled for the sacrifice. Satisfying himself with their blood, he
again wandered around the earth.

'When Ravana had left, Indra and the gods, the residents of
heaven, assumed their own forms and spoke to the respective species.
Delighted, Indra spoke to the peacock with the blue feathers. "O
bird! O one who knows about dharma! O bird! I am pleased with
you because of the good deed you have done. My one thousand eyes
will be displayed on your feathers. When I shower down, as a mark
of my affection, you will also be delighted." O lord of men! Before
this, the feathers of all peacocks used to be blue. Having obtained
the boon from the lord of the gods, all of them became multi-hued.
O Rama! Dharmaraja spoke to the crow who was standing in front
of him. "O bird! I am extremely pleased with you. Hear my words
of affection. I afflict other creatures with various kinds of disease.
But because of my affection towards you, they will have no powers
over you. There is no doubt about this. O bird! Because of the boon
I am granting you, you will have no fear of death. Until men kill
you, you will not die. Men who are in my dominion will be afflicted
by hunger. With their relatives, they will be satisfied whenever you
eat." Varuna spoke to the swan who wanders around in the waters
of the Ganga. O lord of those who use their wings to travel! Hear my
words. They are full of affection. O amiable one! Your complexion
will be beautiful, like that of the lunar disc. Your excellent radiance
will be like that of white foam. When you approach my body,[558] your
form will always be handsome. As a mark of my affection, you will
always enjoy unmatched joy." O Rama! In earlier times, swans did
not possess a complexion that was white all over. Their wings were
blue at the tips and their breasts were smooth, but like tender grass

---

[556] Ravana's adviser.
[557] Ravana.
[558] Varuna's body is the water.

at the ends. Vaishravana spoke to the lizard who was seated on the
mountain. "I am pleased with you and am granting you a golden
complexion. Till eternity, your head will always be golden in hue.
Because of my affection, you will possess this golden complexion."
At the sacrifice, the gods thus bestowed these boons on them. With
the king, they again returned to their own residences.'

Chapter 7(19)

'Having defeated Marutta, the lord of the rakshasas left.
Dashanana wished to fight in the cities of the Indras among
men. He approached all the Indras among kings who were like the
great king or Varuna. The Indra among rakshasas told them, "Give
me a fight. Alternatively, say that you have been defeated by me.
This is my firm determination. If you do not act in this way, you will
not be able to escape from me." O son! There were many wise kings
who followed dharma. Knowing about the strength the enemy had
obtained through the boon, they said that they had been defeated.
Dushyanta, Suratha, Gadhi, Gaya, Pururava—all these kings
said that they had been defeated. After this, Ravana, lord of the
rakshasas, approached Ayodhya. Like Shakra protects Amaravati,
it was protected extremely well by Anaranya. He approached this
king and said, "Grant me a battle. Otherwise, say that you have
been defeated by me. That is my command." Anaranya became
extremely angry and told the Indra among the rakshasas, "O lord
of the rakshasas! I will grant you a duel." The Indra among men
had heard about him and had already collected an extremely large
army. He emerged with this, ready to slay the rakshasa. There
were thousands of elephants and tens of thousands of horses. He
emerged instantly, covering the earth with his foot soldiers and
chariots. Ravana's forces clashed against the king's forces. O king!
Like oblations rendered into a fire, these lives were destroyed. The
Indra among men saw that his large army was being destroyed, like
the waters of the five rivers when they reach the great ocean. He
himself brandished his bow, which was like Shakra's excellent bow.

Senseless with rage, the Indra among men attacked Ravana. The descendant of the Ikshvaku lineage brought down eight hundred arrows on the head of the king of the rakshasas. Though the arrows descended on him, they did not wound him even a bit. They were like torrents of rain pouring down from a cloud on the summit of a mountain. The king of the rakshasas became angry and struck the king on the head with his palm, bringing him down from the chariot. Suffering in his limbs and trembling, the king fell down on the ground. He was like a large sala tree, struck by a bolt of lightning in the forest and brought down. The rakshasa laughed and spoke to the king of the Ikshvaku lineage. "Having fought against me, what are the fruits you have obtained now? O lord of men! There is no one in the three worlds who can grant me a duel. I have a suspicion that you have been intoxicated by addiction to objects of pleasure and have not heard about my strength." The king's life was weakened and he uttered these words. "What can I possibly do? Destiny is difficult to cross. O rakshasa! You are praising yourself, but I have not been defeated by you. I have suffered because of destiny and you are only an instrument. What am I capable of doing now? My life is ebbing away. O rakshasa! Listen to the words that I am speaking. You have slighted the lineage of the Ikshvakus. If I have given donations, if I have offered oblations, if I have performed good deeds, if I have observed austerities and if I have protected my subjects properly, my words will come true. A great-souled one will be born in this lineage of the Ikshvakus. He will be an extremely energetic king and he will take away your life." At this, the drums of the gods were sounded from the tops of the clouds. When this curse was pronounced, flowers were showered down from the sky. O Indra among kings! The king went to his due position in heaven. O Rama! When the king went to heaven, the rakshasa returned.'

Chapter 7(20)

'The lord of the rakshasas terrified all the mortals on earth. In a dense forest, he approached Narada, supreme among

sages. The immensely energetic divine rishi, Narada, was infinite
in his radiance. Seated atop a cloud, he spoke to Ravana, who was
astride Pushpaka. "O lord of the rakshasas! O amiable one! O
Vishrava's son! Wait. I am pleased with your noble lineage, your
valour and your energy. Just as I was satisfied when Vishnu killed
the daityas, I am extremely content that you have afflicted and
crushed eagles and serpents in battles. However, I have something
to tell you. If you wish to listen, it is worth hearing. O bull among
the rakshasa! After hearing, it is for you to decide on your next
course of action. You cannot be killed by the gods. Why are you
killing people on earth? People on earth are under the subjugation
of death and have already been killed. O mighty-armed one! O lord
of the rakshasas! Behold humans on earth. Because they pursue
different objectives, they do not know about their destination. Some
people are delighted in pursuit of musical instruments and dancing.
Some others are miserable, with tears flowing down from their eyes.
People are confused because of their affection towards mothers,
fathers, sons, wives and other loved ones, destroying themselves.
They do not even understand their own hardships. These people
are already devastated because of their confusion. What is the point
of causing them suffering? O amiable one! There is no doubt that
you have already conquered the world of the mortals." Blazing in
his energy, the lord of Lanka was thus addressed. He bowed down
before Narada, smiled and said, "O maharshi! O one who sports
with gods and gandharvas! O one who loves fights! Indeed, for the
sake of being victorious, I will go to rasatala. Having conquered
the three worlds, I will bring the serpents and the gods under my
subjugation. Thereafter, I will churn the ocean, the store of juices,
for the sake of amrita." The illustrious rishi Narada spoke to
Dashagriva. "If that is where you want to go, why follow any other
path now? This extremely difficult path goes towards the city of the
king of the dead. O extremely invincible one! O afflicter of enemies!
Follow this path to Yama." Dashanana was like an autumn cloud.
Thus addressed, he smiled and said that he would do what he had
been asked to. He said, "O great brahmana! Therefore, I will head
towards the southern direction, so as to kill Vaivasvata, the king
who is the son of the sun god. O illustrious one! O lord! Desiring

to fight, I have already taken a pledge that I will defeat the four
guardians of the world. Hence, I will proceed towards the city of
the king of the dead. I will engage with Death, the one who causes
suffering to all creatures." Having said this, Dashagriva greeted
the sage. Cheerful, with his ministers, he left towards the southern
direction. The immensely energetic Narada thought for a while.
Resembling a fire without smoke, the Indra among brahmanas
thought. "How can one cause injury to Death? He follows dharma
and afflicts the three worlds, with Indra included, and the mobile
and immobile objects, when their lifespans decay. He always drives
away the three worlds and makes them suffer with fear. How can
the Indra among rakshasas voluntarily go to him? He[559] is the
ordainer and arranges destiny for the performers of good and bad
deeds. He is the conqueror of the three worlds. How can he be
conquered? And if that happens, who will be the ordainer? Full of
curiosity, I will also go to Yama's abode."'

Chapter 7(21)

'The Indra among brahmanas was light in his valour. Having
thought, he headed for Yama's abode, intending to tell him
what had occurred. He saw Yama there, with the god Agni at the
forefront. Depending on what they deserved, he was ordaining
the destiny for all creatures. Yama saw that maharshi Narada
had arrived. Following dharma, he welcomed him with a seat and
arghya and said, "O celestial rishi! Is all well? I hope dharma is
not suffering. O one who is worshipped by gods and gandharvas!
Why have you come?" The illustrious rishi, Narada, addressed him
in these words. "Listen to what I have to say and then determine
what needs to be done. O king of the dead! There is a roamer in
the night named Dashagriva. He is extremely difficult to defeat.
He is coming here, intending to use his valour to subjugate you.
O lord! That is the reason I have swiftly come here. You exert

[559] Yama.

the staff of chastisement. What will you do now?" At this time,
the rakshasa's vimana could be seen, advancing through the sky.
It could be seen from a distance, like the rays of the rising sun.
The immensely strong one illuminated the spot with Pushpaka's
radiance, driving away all the darkness. He approached. The
mighty-armed Dashagriva cast his eye around, here and there. He
saw creatures enjoying the fruits of their good deeds and suffering
from their bad deeds. Those who had committed wicked deeds
were being slaughtered because of what they themselves had done.
Ravana, strongest among the strong, freed them. Using his superior
strength, the rakshasa freed the dead. The ones who were meant to
protect the dead[560] became extremely angry and attacked the Indra
among the rakshasas. Those brave ones showered down hundreds
and thousands of spears, clubs, javelins, bludgeons, spikes and darts
on Pushpaka. Like speedy bees, they started to shatter Pushpaka's
seats, mansions, platforms and gates. Pushpaka vimana possessed
a divine origin. Because of Brahma's energy, it was indestructible.
Though shattered in the battle, it became whole again. Together
with King Dashanana, Ravana's immensely valiant advisers also
freely fought, resorting to their strength. The advisers of the Indra
among the rakshasas fought in that great battle. Their bodies were
covered with blood and they were struck with all kinds of weapons.
Yama's large forces and the rakshasa's immensely fortunate advisers
fought against each other in the clash, striking with different kinds
of weapons. Then they[561] abandoned the rakshasa's immensely
energetic advisers and attacked Dashanana with a shower of spears.
The best among rakshasas was on the vimana and was mangled
with these blows, blood flowing from his body. He looked like a
blossoming ashoka tree. However, he was strongest among the
strong and showered down spears, maces, javelins, spikes, darts,
arrows, clubs, trees, mountains and other weapons. They countered
all these with their own weapons. Hundreds and thousands of them
attacked the terrible rakshasa who was fighting alone. Resembling
mountains and clouds, all of them surrounded him. They incessantly

560 Yama's servants.
561 Yama's soldiers.

showered down catapults and spears. With his armour shattered, he became angry. He became wet because of the blood that was flowing. He abandoned Pushpaka and stood on the ground. With the bow in his hand, the lord of the rakshasas stood on the ground. Having regained his senses in an instant, he was like another Death. He affixed the divine *pashupata* weapon to his bow. Saying, "Wait, wait," he stretched his bow. In the battle, that arrow was garlanded by flames and was followed by predatory beasts.[562] It was shot towards those forces, intending to burn them down like trees. Its energy consumed Vaivasvata's soldiers. They fell down in the battle, like trees burnt by a conflagration. Surrounded by his advisers, the rakshasa, terrible in his valour, emitted an extremely loud roar and seemed to make the earth tremble.'

Chapter 7(22)

'Vaivasvata Yama heard his loud roar. He thought that the enemy had been victorious and that his own forces had been destroyed. He decided that his warriors had been killed and his eyes became red and dilated with rage. He asked his charioteer to quickly ready his chariot and bring it. The charioteer brought the divine chariot, which made a loud noise. The immensely energetic one mounted that large chariot and was astride it. Death was mounted in front, with a noose and a club in his hands, just as he does when he is about to destroy the three worlds, with their mobile and immobile objects. The personified form of Kaladanda[563] was stationed next to him on the chariot. This was Yama's divine weapon and blazed in its energy. The three worlds were terrified and the residents of heaven trembled. They saw that Death was enraged and this brought fear to the three worlds. The advisers of the Indra among rakshasas saw the gruesome chariot, with Death mounted on it. It was a sight that brought fear to the three worlds.

[562] Which would eat the dead bodies.
[563] Yama's rod of chastisement.

All of them lost their spirits and their senses. They were afflicted by fear. "We are not capable of fighting." Saying this, they fled. The rakshasa also saw the chariot that brought fear to the three worlds. However, he was not agitated or distressed. Yama approached Ravana and showered down spears and javelins, angrily piercing the rakshasa in his inner organs. Ravana remained steady and released showers of arrows on Vaivasvata's chariot, like a cloud pouring down rain. He[564] brought down one hundred large javelins on his broad chest. The rakshasa was incapable of countering these and suffered from these wounds. Yama, the afflicter of enemies, struck him with many weapons. The battle raged for seven nights and neither one was routed or defeated. The battle between Yama and the rakshasa continued again. Both wished to be victorious and neither one retreated from the encounter. With Prajapati at the forefront, the gods, the gandharvas, the siddhas and the supreme rishis assembled as spectators in the field of battle. As the foremost among the rakshasas and the lord of the dead fought, it was as if the destruction of the worlds had arrived. The Indra among rakshasas became angry in the encounter. He incessantly shot arrows from his bow and enveloped the sky. He quickly struck Mrityu with four arrows and the charioteer with seven arrows.[565] He struck Yama in the inner organs with one thousand arrows.

'Yama became violently angry. Garlands of flames issued from his mouth. There were angry flames in his mouth and his breath. The gods, the danavas and the rakshasas witnessed this extraordinary sight. The blazing fire of anger was about to burn down the enemy's army. Mrityu became extremely angry and spoke to Vaivasvata. "O god! Quickly grant me permission, so that I can slay this enemy in the battle. Naraka, Shambara, Vritra, Shambhu, the powerful Kartasvara, Namuchi, Virochana, Madhu, Kaitabha and many other powerful and extremely invincible ones have become distressed on seeing me. Why worry about this roamer in the night? O one who knows about dharma! It is best to grant me

---

[564] Yama.

[565] Mrityu (Death) is usually a synonym for Yama, but is being described separately here.

permission, so that I can kill him now. After seeing me, no one is capable of remaining alive even for an instant. This is not because of my strength. It is because of the importance that has been given to me. If I touch anyone, that person can no longer remain alive." The powerful Dharmaraja heard his words and told Mrityu, "I will kill him." The lord Vaivasvata's eyes turned red with rage. He raised the invincible Kaladanda in his hand. Death's solid noose was right next to it and so was the personified form of the club, like fire to the touch. As soon as they saw these, the lives of creatures started to dry up, not to speak of embodied beings being struck by these and suffering from these. Surrounded by flames, it was about to consume the roamer in the night. Angry, the powerful one touched the extremely terrible Kaladanda with his hand. All the creatures fled from the field of battle. On seeing that Yama had raised his Kaladanda, the gods were agitated. As soon as he raised this Kaladanda in Ravana's direction, the grandfather showed himself and spoke these words. "O Vaivasvata! O mighty-armed one! O one who is infinite in valour! You should indeed withdraw the Kaladanda and not use it against the roamer in the night. O bull among the gods! I have granted him a boon. You should not render the words I spoke false. Placing Mrityu at the forefront, I had fashioned this Kaladanda earlier and in bringing down all creatures, it will be invincible. O amiable one! Therefore, you should not bring it down on this rakshasa's head. If it is brought down, no one is capable of remaining alive even for an instant. If it is brought down and the rakshasa does not die, or if Dashagriva dies, in either case, a falsehood will be committed. Therefore, control the Kaladanda, which you have raised to bring about the death of the Indra among the rakshasas. While all the worlds look on, make my words come true." Thus addressed, with dharma in his soul, Yama replied. "I have withdrawn the Kaladanda. You are like the lord Vishnu to us. However, now that I am engaged in this battle, what am I capable of doing? This rakshasa is insolent because of his boon and I cannot kill him. Therefore, in the eyes of this rakshasa, I should be destroyed." Having said this, he vanished with his chariot and his horses. Dashagriva announced that he had become victorious. Cheerful, he left Yama's abode on Pushpaka. With the gods and with Brahma at the forefront, Vaivasvata went to heaven. Narada, the great sage, was delighted.'

Chapter 7(23)

'Thus, Dashagriva defeated Yama, the bull among the gods. Proud at his victory, Ravana saw his own aides. Maricha and the others were emboldened by his victory.[566] Ravana comforted them and took them up on Pushpaka. He happily entered rasatala, the store of the waters. This was full of large numbers of daityas and serpents and was Varuna's well-protected dominion. He went to the city of Bhogavati,[567] protected by Vasuki. He went to the city that was full of jewels and brought the serpents under his subjugation. Daityas known as Nivatakavachas had obtained boons and resided there. The rakshasa approached them and challenged them in a battle. All those daityas were extremely brave and full of strength. Invincible in fighting, they wielded many kinds of weapons and started to fight. They fought with each other for more than a year. However, they could not defeat each other. Nor was either side destroyed. The undecaying grandfather could travel anywhere in the three worlds. Astride his excellent vimana, the god swiftly arrived there. He restrained the Nivatakavachas who were engaged in fighting. Knowing about the truth, the aged grandfather addressed them in these words. "The gods and the asuras are incapable of defeating this Ravana in a battle. Nor are the gods and the asuras, with Indra included, capable of bringing about your destruction. The idea of your friendship with this rakshasa appeals to me. There is no doubt that you should be united and should be each other's well-wishers." With the fire as a witness, Ravana contracted an alliance of friendship with the Nivatakavachas and became happy. They honoured each other and spent one year in bliss. Dashanana obtained honours that were superior to what he got in his own

---

[566] They had run away earlier.
[567] The capital city of the nagas.

city. From them, he learnt more than one hundred different kinds of maya. He roamed around in rasatala, the city of the Indra of the waters.

'He reached a city named Ashma,[568] protected by the Kalakeyas. He conquered it in an instant and killed four hundred daityas. The lord of the rakshasas then saw Varuna's divine abode. It possessed the complexion of a white cloud and was stationed like Kailasa. He saw the cow named Surabhee there. Milk continuously flowed from her. The milk that flows from her gives rise to the ocean named Kshiroda.[569] The powerful Chandra,[570] whose cool beams bring welfare to subjects, was generated from there and the supreme rishis, the Phenapas,[571] survive on this. Amrita was generated there and the *sura*[572] the gods subsist on. Men on earth know her by the name of Surabhee. Ravana circumambulated the supremely wonderful being. He then entered the extremely terrible city, protected by many kinds of forces. There were hundreds of different kinds of flows, with hues like those of autumn clouds. He saw Varuna's excellent house, which was always cheerful. In an encounter, he attacked and killed the commander of the forces. He said, "Go and quickly tell the king that I have come. Ravana has come here, desiring to fight. Grant him a fight. If you do not wish to be terrified, join your hands in salutation and say that you have been vanquished." At this time, the great-souled Varuna became angry. He emerged with his sons and grandsons and with Gou and Pushkara.[573] They possessed the qualities of valour and surrounded themselves with their own forces. They yoked chariots that could travel wherever they willed, as radiant as the sun, and emerged to fight. There was an extremely terrible clash that made the body hair stand up, between the sons of the Indra of the waters and the rakshasa Ravana. In a short while, the immensely brave advisers of the rakshasa Dashagriva brought down all of Varuna's forces.

---

[568] *Ashma* means made of stone.

[569] An ocean whose water is made out of milk.

[570] The moon, the moon god.

[571] Phenapas are sages who survive on foam.

[572] A kind of liquor.

[573] Gou and Pushkara are the names of two of Varuna's commanders.

Varuna's sons saw that the net of arrows had afflicted their own forces in the battle and withdrew from the field of battle. Ravana was on the ground, but now returned to Pushpaka. On seeing this, they[574] mounted swift chariots and advanced through the sky. They were now in comparable situations[575] and a terrible and great clash commenced in the sky, like that between the gods and the danavas. In that battle, they used arrows that were like the fire to make Ravana retreat and cheerfully emitted many kinds of roars. On seeing that his king was suffering in this way, Mahodara became angry. The brave one wished to fight and gave up all fear of death. He saw that their horses were like the wind and could go wherever they willed. Therefore, Mahodara struck them with his club and made them fall down on the ground. In the battle, he killed the horses of Varuna's sons. Having seen that they had thus been deprived of their chariots, he quickly emitted a loud roar. Destroyed and killed by Mahodara, their chariots, horses and excellent charioteers fell down on the ground. The great-souled Varuna's sons abandoned their chariots. Though they were distressed, because of their own powers, those brave ones remained stationed in the sky.[576] They strung their bows and pierced Mahodara. Enraged in the battle, they collectively attacked Ravana. Angry, Dashagriva was stationed like the fire of destruction. He showered down immensely forceful arrows and struck them in their inner organs. The invincible one brought down many kinds of clubs, hundreds of broad arrows, spears, javelins, shataghnis and spikes on them. Those brave ones were driven away and the foot soldiers were crushed. Having struck Varuna's sons, the rakshasa let out a loud roar. He showered down many terrible weapons, like floods of rain from a cloud. All of them were repulsed and fell down on the ground. Servants swiftly withdrew them from the field of battle and delivered them to their houses. The rakshasa told them to convey his message to Varuna. Varuna's minister was named Prabhasa and he told Ravana, "The immensely energetic lord of the waters has gone to Brahma's

---

[574] Varuna's sons.
[575] Because Varuna's sons were also on chariots travelling through the sky.
[576] They did not fall down on the ground.

world.[577] You have challenged him to a battle, but Varuna has gone there, to listen to the gandharvas.[578] O brave one! With the king gone, why are you unnecessarily exerting yourself? The brave princes assembled here, but they have been defeated." Hearing this, the Indra among rakshasas announced his name. Uttering roars of delight, he emerged from Varuna's abode. He returned along the route he had used to come. Proceeding through the sky, the rakshasa headed in the direction of Lanka.'

Chapter 7(24)

'The evil-souled Ravana returned cheerfully. Along the path, he abducted the daughters of royal sages, gods and gandharvas. If the rakshasa saw any beautiful woman or maiden, he slew her relatives and placed her in his vimana. In this way, Ravana seized the daughters of serpents, yakshas, men, rakshasas, daityas and danavas. Their hair was long. Their limbs were beautiful. Their faces were like the full moon. All of them were young. Afflicted by fear, their breasts hung down. They were like the rays of the fire. Their fear gave rise to a fire of grief. Suffering from misery, they trembled and shed warm tears. As they sighed, their breathing seemed to ignite everything. It was as if the fire of an agnihotra sacrifice had been lit inside Pushpaka. Some were afflicted by great sorrow and wondered, "When will he kill me?" Overwhelmed by sorrow and misery, the women remembered their mothers, fathers, brothers, sons and fathers-in-law and collectively lamented. "What will my son do without me? What will my mother and my brother do?" They were immersed in an ocean of grief. "Alas! What will I do without my divinity, my husband? O Death! Show me your favours and convey me to Yama's abode. In earlier times, in a different body, what evil deeds have been committed by me? That

---

[577] There is an inconsistency, since we have earlier been told that Varuna had emerged to fight.

[578] The gandharvas were going to sing in Brahma's presence.

is the reason I have been oppressed in this way and am submerged in an ocean of grief. Indeed, I do not see any end to my present sorrows. Since this wicked one has proved to be supreme, shame on this world of men. Ravana is powerful and is stronger than my relatives. He is like a rising sun that has destroyed the stars. Alas! This rakshasa is extremely strong. If I know about the means of his death, I will be delighted. Alas! He is evil in conduct and does not understand this himself. This evil-souled one is strong in every possible way. This act of oppressing other people's wives is an act that is worthy of him. This evil-minded one always finds delight in the wives of others. Therefore, because of what he has done to women, Ravana deserves to be killed." Because of the curses of the women, he lost his energy and his radiance was diminished. They were virtuous and devoted to their husbands. They based themselves on the path of virtue.

'While they lamented in this way, Ravana, the lord of the rakshasas, entered the city of Lanka and was worshipped by the roamers in the night. The sister of the king of the rakshasas was extremely miserable. She fell down at his feet and attempted to speak. Ravana raised his sister and comforted her. He said, "O fortunate one! What is it? Tell me quickly." Her eyes overflowing with tears, the rakshasi replied in these words. "O king! Because of your strength, I have become a widow. O king! Because of your valour, the daityas have been slain in the battle. They were known as the Kalakeyas and were immensely strong and brave. O brother! I loved my husband more than my own life. But at that time, because he was regarded as an enemy, he was killed. O king! When you killed this relation of mine, it is as if you killed me too. It is because of you that the appellation of 'widow' is being applied to me and I have been forced to suffer this. You should certainly have protected your brother-in-law in the battle. O king! However, you have slain him in the battle and are not ashamed." The rakshasa was addressed and reprimanded by his sister in this way. He comforted her and spoke to her in words of conciliation. "O child! Enough of this grieving. You should not be scared in any possible way. In particular, I will always satisfy you with honours and gifts. I was intoxicated in the battle. Desiring victory,

I shot arrows. O auspicious one! In the heat of the battle, I did
not distinguish friend from foe. O sister! That is how I killed your
husband in the battle. That being the case, right now, I will do
whatever is beneficial for you. Go and reside with your prosperous
brother, Khara. I will grant your brother the gift that he will be
the lord of fourteen thousand greatly energetic rakshasas. The lord
Khara is your brother. He is the son of your mother's sister. You
will see that he will himself always do whatever you ask him to
do. For the sake of protecting Dandaka, quickly go to that brave
one. The immensely strong Dushana will be the commander of the
forces. Earlier, the enraged Ushanas had cursed him that he would
reside in this part of the forest, inhabited by rakshasas. There is
no doubt that this will happen."[579] Having said this, Dashagriva
commanded his soldiers, fourteen thousand rakshasas who could
assume any form at will. Fearless, Khara surrounded himself with
these rakshasas, who were terrible to behold, and quickly left for
Dandaka. With all his thorns destroyed, he established a kingdom
there. Happy, Shurpanakha started to live in the forest of Dandaka.'

Chapter 7(25)

'**D**ashagriva bestowed that terrible forest on Khara. Having
comforted his sister, he was happy and also reassured
himself. With his followers, the great-souled Indra among the
rakshasas entered a giant grove in Lanka, known by the name
of Nikumbhila. O amiable one! It was filled with hundreds of
sacrificial altars and adorned with chaityas. He saw a sacrifice,
blazing in prosperity, going on there. He saw his own son,
Meghanada, the scorcher of enemies, there. He was attired in black
antelope skin, his hair was tied in a knot on the top of his head
and he held a water pot. The lord of the rakshasas approached and
embraced him in his arms. He asked, "O child! What are you doing

---

[579] More accurately, Ushanas (Shukracharya) had cursed Danda, from the lineage of
the Ikshvakus, that he would be destined to live in this way.

here? Tell me." For the sake of extending the prosperity of the
sacrifice, his preceptor, the great ascetic Ushanas, foremost among
brahmanas, replied to Ravana, best among rakshasas. "O king! I
will tell you. Listen to everything. Your son has performed seven
extremely pervasive sacrifices—agnishtoma, ashvamedha sacrifice,
bahusuvarnaka, *rajasuya* sacrifice, *gomedha*, and *vaishnava*.[580]
He has now engaged in *maheshvara* sacrifice, something that any
man finds extremely difficult to undertake. After this, your son has
obtained a boon from Pashupati himself. He has obtained a divine
chariot that can travel in the firmament at will. He has obtained
the maya named *tamasi*. Through this, one can create darkness. O
lord of the rakshasas! If one fights with the use of this maya, not
even the gods or the asuras are capable of knowing how to fight
against such a person in a battle. He has also obtained a quiver
filled with inexhaustible arrows and an extremely invincible bow.
O amiable one! He has also got a powerful weapon that can crush
the enemy in a battle. O Dashanana! Your son has obtained all
these boons. The sacrifice was completed today and I was waiting
here for you." At this, Dashagriva replied, "What you have done is
not good.[581] You have used various objects to worship the enemy,
with Indra at the forefront. However, what has been done is
done. One cannot undo it. O amiable one! Come. Let us proceed
towards our own residence." With his son and with Vibhishana,
Dashagriva left. He made the women, who were distressed and
weeping, descend.[582] They possessed all the auspicious signs and
were ornamented with jewels. They were the maidens of the gods,
the danavas and the rakshasas. They were adorned in many kinds
of ornaments and blazed in their own energies. Vibhishana saw
that those women were overwhelmed by grief. Knowing what
his[583] intentions were, the one with dharma in his soul addressed
him in these words. "This kind of action destroys fame, prosperity
and the lineage. You act according to your caprices and cause

---

[580] Ashvamedha is a horse sacrifice, rajasuya is a royal sacrifice. A cow is sacrificed in
gomedha, bahusuvarnaka means that a lot of gold is donated.
[581] Dashagriva is speaking to Meghanada, not to Shukracharya.
[582] From Pushpaka.
[583] Ravana's.

oppression to beings. You oppressed their relatives and abducted these beautiful women. O king! This is exactly the way Madhu crossed you and abducted Kumbhinasi." Ravana replied in these words. "I do not understand this. What have you said? Who is the one named Madhu?" Vibhishana angrily replied in these words. "Hear about the fruits that result from wicked acts. Our maternal grandfather is Sumali and his elder brother is Malyavat. That famous roamer in the night is aged and wise. He is the elder father[584] of our mother and is thus our senior. His daughter's daughter is named Kumbhinasi. Our mother's sister is Anala and she is her daughter. Therefore, following dharma, she is a sister to us brothers. O king! The rakshasa Madhu used force to abduct her. Your son was engaged in this sacrifice then and I was performing austerities in the water. He slew the best among the rakshasas, your revered advisers. O king! She was protected in your inner quarters, but he forcibly abducted her. O great king! On hearing about this, I forgave him and did not kill him. A brother must always bestow a maiden on a groom. Know that the fruits of what one does is reaped in this world."[585] At this, Dashagriva's eyes turned red with rage. He said, "Let my chariot be readied quickly. Let the brave ones prepare. Let my brother, Kumbhakarna, and the other foremost roamers in the night ascend their mounts. Let them arm themselves with many kinds of weapons. In the battle today, I will kill Madhu, since he is not scared of Ravana. I desire to fight and, surrounded by well-wishers, I will go to Indra's world. I will conquer heaven and bring Purandara under my subjugation. I will sport on my return, adorning myself with the riches of the three worlds." Four thousand akshouhinis of rakshasas proceeded in the front. They left quickly, armed with many kinds of weapons and wishing to fight. Indrajit was at the forefront of the soldiers and the commanders were with him. Ravana was in the middle and the brave Kumbhakarna was at the rear. Vibhishana, with dharma in his soul, remained in Lanka, performing acts of dharma.

---

[584] Meaning father's elder brother.

[585] Vibhishana is implying that Madhu's act is the consequence of Ravana's wicked deeds.

'All those immensely fortunate ones proceeded towards
Madhupura.[586] All those rakshasas left with chariots, elephants,
donkeys, camels, horses and blazing and large serpents, and there
was no space left in the sky. There were hundreds of daityas who
were firm in their enmity towards the gods. On seeing that Ravana
was proceeding, they followed him at the rear. Dashanana went to
Madhupura and entered. He didn't see Madhu there, but he saw his
sister. She joined her hands in salutation and bowed her head down
at his feet. His sister, Kumbhinasi, was terrified of the king of the
rakshasas. Ravana, the best among the rakshasas, raised her and
said, "Do not be frightened. What can I do for you?" She replied,
"O king! O immensely strong one! O one who grants honours! If
you are pleased with me, you should not kill my husband now. O
Indra among kings! I am faithful to my husband. Look towards me
and make your words come true. O mighty-armed one! You have
yourself told me that I should not be scared." On seeing that his
sister was standing there, Ravana asked, "Who is your husband?
Quickly tell me that. For the sake of conquering the world of the
gods, I will take him with me. Because of compassion and affection
towards you, I will refrain from the act of killing Madhu." Thus
addressed, she awoke the roamer in the night,[587] who was asleep.
Cheerfully, the rakshasi spoke to the extremely learned one. "My
brother, Dashagriva, the roamer in the night, has come here. He
desires to conquer the world of the gods and is asking for your help.
O rakshasa! For the sake of helping him, go with your relatives. He
has been gentle and has honoured you. You should do what he has
thought of." Hearing her words, Madhu agreed. He saw the best
among the rakshasas and as is proper, welcomed him. Following
dharma, he worshipped Ravana, the lord of the rakshasas. The
valiant Dashagriva was worshipped in Madhu's residence. Having
spent the night there, he prepared to leave. He went to Mount
Kailasa, Vaishravana's abode. The Indra among rakshasas, whose
complexion was like that of the great Indra, made his forces
camp there.'

[586] Madhu's city.
[587] Madhu.

Chapter 7(26)

'When the sun was about to set, the valiant Dashagriva reached the spot and made his soldiers set up camp there. The sparkling moon arose, as radiant as the mountain itself. Because of the radiance of the moon, he saw the many qualities of the trees there. There were groves of divine karnikaras and dense growth of *kadamba*. There were ponds with blooming lotuses and the waters of the Mandakinee. He heard the sweet sounds of bells being rung. Large numbers of apsaras sang in Dhanada's abode. Driven by the wind, the trees released showers of flowers. Residence on that mountain was intoxicating, with the scent of spring flowers. A pleasant breeze blew, mixed with the sweet fragrance and pollen from the *madhupushpa*[588] flower. This enhanced Ravana's desire. There was singing. There were many flowers. There was a cool breeze. The mountain possessed all the qualities. The night progressed, illuminated by a moon that had arisen. The extremely valiant Ravana succumbed to the arrows of desire. He sighed and sighed and looked towards the moon. At that time, Rambha, supreme among all the apsaras, was seen there. She was adorned in celestial flowers and her face was like the full moon. She was adorned in wet flowers that belonged to all the six seasons. She was covered in a blue garment that had the complexion of a cloud full of water. Her face was like the moon and her auspicious eyebrows were like bows. Her thighs were like the trunks of elephants and her hands were as delicate as petals. She passed through the midst of the soldiers and Ravana noticed her. Suffering from the arrows of desire, the Indra among rakshasas seized her. As she was passing, he seized her by the hand. He smiled and asked, "O one with the beautiful hips! Where are you going? What objective are you striving for? Who will rise[589] and enjoy pleasure with you? Your lips possess the fragrance of blooming lotuses. Who will inhale that? Who will obtain satisfaction from the amrita that is in your lips?

---

[588] The wild croton tree. Alternatively, this can be taken to be the honey tree, or the ashoka.

[589] The imagery is of the moon rising.

O timid one! Your auspicious and full breasts are like golden pots
and there is no space between them. Whose chest will you allow
them to be crushed against? Your thighs are round and golden.
They are thick and ornamented with a golden girdle. Your hips are
like heaven. Today, whom will you allow to mount them? There
is no man who is superior to me, not even Shakra, Vishnu and the
Ashvins. O timid one! Therefore, it is not proper that you should
go to anyone other than me. O one with the plump hips! Come
and rest on this auspicious slope of the mountain. There is no other
lord in the three worlds who is my equal. Dashanana is joining his
hands in salutation and is beseeching you. I am the lord and the
master of the three worlds. Serve me." Thus addressed, Rambha
joined her hands in salutation, trembling. She said, "Show me your
favours. You should not speak to me in this way. You are my senior.
Indeed, if anyone else seeks to oppress me, you should protect me.
Following dharma, I am your daughter-in-law. I am telling you
the truth." With her face cast downwards, she looked towards
her feet and addressed Dashagriva in this way. He said, "You can
be my daughter-in-law only if you are my son's wife." Agreeing,
Rambha replied to Ravana in these words. "O bull among the
rakshasas! Following dharma, I am your son's wife. Your brother,
Vaishravana, has a son whom he loves more than his own life. He
is famous in the three worlds as Nalakubara. In following dharma,
he is like a brahmana. In valour, he is a kshatriya. In his anger, he
is like the fire. In forgiveness, he is the equal of the earth. Because
the son of the guardian of the world gave me a sign, I am going to
him, adorning myself in all the ornaments. The sentiments I possess
towards him are not like those I have towards anyone else. O king!
O scorcher of enemies! That is the truth. Therefore, you should let
me go. The one with dharma in his soul is eagerly waiting for me to
reach. You should not be an impediment for your son.[590] Therefore,
you should release me. O bull among rakshasas! Follow the path
pursued by the virtuous. You should be respected by me. In that
way, I should be protected by you." Rambha spoke these words and
they were full of dharma.

[590] By extension.

'The rakshasa was reprimanded in this way. However, the strongest of the strong was overcome by confusion and seized her. He was angry and confounded by desire. He thus started to have intercourse with her. Rambha was deprived of her ornaments. Her garlands were cast aside. She was like the bank of a river, when it had been destroyed by a sporting elephant. She was trembling and ashamed. Terrified, she went to Nalakubara and joined her hands in salutation, falling down at his feet. The great-souled Nalakubara saw the state she was in. He asked, "O fortunate one! Why have you fallen down at my feet?" She sighed and trembled. Joining her hands in salutation, she started to tell him everything, exactly as it had happened. "O god! This Dashagriva had come here, headed towards heaven. His soldiers and aides were spending the night here. O scorcher of enemies! He saw me going to meet you. The rakshasa seized me and asked me who I was and whom I belonged to. I told him the entire truth. However, his soul was overwhelmed by desire and he did not listen to my words. O god! O lord! I entreated him, telling him that I was his daughter-in-law. However, he ignored all that and forcibly raped me. O one who grants honours! Thus, you should pardon me my crime. O amiable one! The strength of a woman is not the same as that of a man." Hearing this, Vaishravana's son became enraged. Hearing about this severe act of rape, he started to meditate. In this way, Vaishravana's son got to know everything about that deed. His eyes became coppery red with rage and he instantly took some water in his hand. Having touched water, he followed the rituals and flung it up into the sky.[591] He then pronounced a terrible curse on the Indra among the rakshasas. "She did not desire it, yet you forcibly raped her. Therefore, you will not be able to approach any other maiden who does not desire it. If a woman does not desire it and you rape her because of your desire, your head will shatter into seven fragments." As resplendent as a blazing fire, he pronounced this curse. The drums of the gods were sounded and flowers rained down from the sky. All the gods, with Prajapati as the foremost, were delighted. They got to know about the death of a rakshasa

---

[591] Flung the water up into the air as part of the ritual of invoking a curse.

who oppressed all the worlds. Dashagriva heard the curse that made the body hair stand up. The idea of having intercourse with a woman who did not desire it no longer appealed to him.'

Chapter 7(27)

'Having crossed Kailasa with the other rakshasas, the immensely energetic Dashagriva, roamer in the night, reached Indra's world. The soldiers of the rakshasas approached it from every direction. The sound that arose in the world of the gods was like that of the ocean being shattered. Hearing that Ravana had reached, Indra's throne started to wobble. He spoke to all the assembled gods. "O Adityas, Vasus, Rudras, Vishvadevas, Sadhyas and Maruts! Get ready to fight against the evil-souled Ravana." The gods, Shakra's equal in battle, were thus addressed by Shakra. Faithful to the prospect of fighting, those great-spirited ones armoured themselves. The great Indra was distressed and scared of Ravana. He approached Vishnu and addressed him in these words. "O Vishnu! O one who is great in valour and bravery! What will I do? This rakshasa is powerful and has come here, desiring to fight. He is powerful because of the boon that he has obtained. Indeed, there is no other reason.[592] O god! O Prajapati![593] Tell us the truth about what must be done. Namuchi, Vritra, Bali, Naraka and Shambara were stupefied and consumed. Do something like that. O god of the gods! O extremely strong one! There is no one other than you. You are the supreme refuge. O Purushottama! There is no one other than you. You are the prosperous Narayana. You are the eternal Padmanabha. You are the one who has established me in this eternal kingdom of the gods. O god of the gods! Therefore, you should yourself tell me the truth. Will you use a sword and a chakra to fight against this enemy in the battle?" The god and lord, Narayana, was addressed by Shakra in this way. He replied, "Do

---

[592] For his strength.
[593] This word is being used for Vishnu.

not be frightened. Hear from me about what must be done. No
god or danava is capable of fighting against this evil-acting one,
or advancing against him and slaying him in a battle. Because of
the boon that has been conferred on him, he is extremely difficult
to vanquish. Intoxicated because of his strength, in every possible
way, he will perform great deeds. The rakshasa also has his son as
his aide. I can foresee all this through my divine sight. O Shakra!
You have asked whether I will fight against him in the battle. I will
not fight against Ravana, the lord of the rakshasas. Vishnu does
not retreat from a battle without slaying the enemy. However, this
rakshasa has obtained a boon and it is extremely difficult for me to
accomplish that objective now. O Indra of the gods! O Shatakratu!
But I am taking a pledge before you. I will be the reason for the
death of this rakshasa in a battle. In an encounter, I will slay Ravana
and his son. Once I know that the time has arrived, I will satisfy the
gods."

'At this time, night was over and a roar was heard. In every
direction, Ravana's soldiers started to fight. A battle commenced
between the gods and the rakshasas. It was terrible, with tumultuous
roars. Many kinds of weapons were used in the battle. The rakshasas
were cruel and were terrible to behold. Following Ravana's
command, his advisers rushed out to fight. There were Maricha,
Prahasta, Mahaparshva, Mahodara, Akampana, Nikumbha,
Shuka, Sarana, Sahlada, Dhumaketu, Mahadamshtra, Mahamukha,
Jambumali, Mahamali and the rakshasa Virupaksha. Surrounding
himself with these extremely strong ones, Sumali, Ravana's senior
and bull among rakshasas, entered amidst the soldiers. With those
other roamers in the night, he angrily used many kinds of sharp
weapons to devastate all the large numbers of gods. At this time, the
eighth Vasu, the Vasu known as Savitra, entered the great field of
battle.[594] A battle raged between the gods and the rakshasas. They[595]
angrily tolerated the deeds of the rakshasas and did not retreat
from the battle. In the encounter, the brave rakshasas also faced the

---

[594] The names of the eight Vasus vary from text to text. The one referred to as Savitra
is more commonly known as Prabhasa.

[595] The gods.

gods. They struck each other with hundreds and thousands of many different kinds of terrible weapons. The gods were extremely brave. Using their own energies, they used many kinds of terrible weapons in the battle and conveyed the rakshasas to Yama's abode. At this time, the brave rakshasa named Sumali angrily used many kinds of weapons and attacked in the battle. He wrathfully struck all the forces of the gods with many kinds of sharp weapons and destroyed them, like the wind dispelling clouds. He oppressed all the gods with showers of large arrows, spears and terrible javelins. Though they tried to control themselves, they could not stand before him. The gods were driven away by Sumali. However, the eighth of the Vasus, the god Savitra, remained there. He surrounded himself with his own forces and struck the roamer in the night. Brave and extremely energetic, he countered him in the battle. There was an extremely crazy and extremely terrible encounter between their forces. Neither Sumali, nor the Vasu, retreated from the battle. The extremely great-souled Vasu used large arrows to instantly bring down his gigantic chariot, which was yoked to serpents. Using hundreds of sharp arrows, he destroyed his chariot in that battle. Then, to kill him, the Vasu seized a club in his hand. He swiftly seized that auspicious club, which blazed like Kaladanda. Savitra struck Sumali on the head with this and brought him down. Blazing like a meteor, it descended on his head and brought him down, just as the great vajra, released by the one with one thousand eyes, shatters a mountain. His bones, body or flesh could no longer be seen. In that encounter, the club reduced him to ashes and brought him down. On seeing that he had been killed in the battle, in every direction, all the rakshasas collectively fled, shrieking in loud tones.'

Chapter 7(28)

'Sumali was killed, reduced to ashes by the Vasu. In the battle, Ravana's son saw this and also saw that his own soldiers had been driven away, afflicted by the arrows. The powerful one became angry. Meghanada remained there and made all the rakshasas return. His chariot possessed the complexion of the fire. His giant chariot could go anywhere at will. Like a blazing conflagration in the forest, he attacked all those soldiers. He entered, wielding many kinds of weapons. On seeing him, all the gods fled in different directions. There was no one who was capable of remaining in front of him and fighting. Seeing that all of them were pierced and terrified, Shakra spoke to them. "You should not be frightened. Nor should you run away. Return to the field of battle. This son of mine has never been vanquished. He is advancing to fight." Shakra's son was the god known as Jayanta. On a chariot that had been wonderfully crafted, he advanced into the battle. All the gods surrounded Shachi's son. They remained there and clashed against Ravana's son in the battle. The great clash between the god, the son of the great Indra, and the rakshasa, the son of the Indra among the rakshasas, was one between two equals. The rakshasa's son used arrows that were embellished with gold to bring down the charioteer, Matali's son, from his seat.[596] In the field of battle, Shachi's son, Jayanta, also angrily pierced back the charioteer of Ravana's son. Enraged, the extremely energetic rakshasa dilated his eyes. Ravana's son repulsed Shakra's son with showers of arrows. Ravana's son seized and brought down large and firm weapons— shataghnis, spears, javelins, clubs, swords, battleaxes and extremely large summits of mountains. The worlds were distressed and a great darkness was generated. Ravana's son continued to strike the enemy. Shachi's son was surrounded by the forces of the gods on all sides. However, they suffered in many kinds of ways and fled. They were incapable of differentiating each other, distinguishing the enemy from the gods. Here and there, in every direction, they were routed and ran away.

'There was a brave and valiant daitya named Puloma. At this time, he seized Shachi's son and ran away. He seized his grandson and entered the great ocean. This noble Puloma was Shachi's father and his[597] maternal grandfather. The gods witnessed this extremely terrible sight of Jayanta being destroyed. They were cheerless

---

[596] Matali is Indra's charioteer and Matali's son is Jayanta's charioteer.
[597] Jayanta's.

and distressed and fled in different directions. Ravana's son was delighted and surrounded himself with his own forces. Emitting a loud roar, he rushed against the gods. On seeing that his son had been destroyed and witnessing the valour of Ravana's son, Indra of the gods asked Matali to bring him his chariot. Matali readied that divine, extremely terrible and large chariot. It was borne along at the speed of thought. Clouds that thundered loudly and lightning were attached to the chariot. As it proceeded, turbulent and noisy winds preceded it. As Vasava headed for the battle, many musical instruments were sounded and there were controlled sounds of praise. Large numbers of apsaras danced. The Rudras, Vasus, Adityas, Sadhyas and large numbers of Maruts armed themselves with diverse weapons, surrounded the lord of the gods and emerged. As Shakra emerged, a harsh wind started to blow. The sun lost its radiance and giant meteors started to fall down.

'At this time, the brave and powerful Dashagriva mounted a divine chariot that had been constructed by Vishvakarma. It made the body hair stand up and was yoked to extremely large serpents. The wind generated from their breathing ignited the field of battle. Brave daityas and roamers in the night surrounded the divine chariot and advanced against the great Indra in the battle. He restrained his son[598] and himself advanced into the battle. Ravana's son sat down.[599] A battle commenced between the gods and the rakshasas. Terrible weapons that resembled clouds were showered down in the battle. The evil-souled Kumbhakarna raised many kinds of weapons. However, in the encounter, he did not know whom he should fight against. He used his teeth, arms, feet, spears, javelins, arrows and anything to angrily strike the gods. The roamer in the night approached the immensely fortunate Rudras and Adityas and started to fight against them, incessantly showering down weapons. In that battle, using many kinds of sharp weapons, the gods and the large number of Maruts drove away all the rakshasa soldiers. Some were killed by weapons. Others writhed around on the

---

[598] Ravana asked Meghanada not to fight against Indra.
[599] He withdrew from the battle.

ground. Others remained in the battle, clinging to their mounts—chariots, donkeys, camels, serpents, horses, dolphins, boars and others with faces like pishachas. Some clung to these with their arms. Others were stupefied and uprooted. The roamers in the night were pierced by the weapons of the gods and died. The field of battle seemed to be a painting. Dead and crazy rakshasas were strewn around on the ground. A river of blood started to flow. The place was full of herons and vultures. A river began to flow in the field of battle and the weapons were like crocodiles. Meanwhile, the powerful Dashagriva became angry. He saw that his entire army had been brought down by the gods. He swiftly submerged himself in the army, which resembled a waxing ocean. He slew the gods in the encounter and approached Shakra. Shakra stretched his large bow, which emitted an extremely large sound. The sound of it being twanged resounded in the ten directions. Indra stretched that great bow and brought down arrows that were as radiant as the sun on Ravana's head. However, the mighty-armed Dashagriva remained there. He showered down arrows and dislodged Shakra's bow. They fought against each other and showered down arrows in every direction. Nothing could be discerned then. Everything was covered in darkness.'

Chapter 7(29)

'When that darkness was generated, the rakshasas and the gods, intoxicated by their strength, fought and killed each other. Out of the large armies of the gods and the rakshasas, only one-tenth remained in the battle. This is all that was left. The rest had been conveyed to Yama's abode. Submerged in that darkness, all the gods and the rakshasas could not distinguish each other, but fought against each other. However, three were not confused, despite being immersed in that net of darkness—Indra, Ravana and Ravana's immensely strong son. Ravana saw that all those forces had been slain in the battle. He was suffused with a fierce anger and emitted a loud roar. Filled with rage, the invincible one spoke to his

son, who was astride his chariot.[600] "Take me to the midst of the
enemy soldiers. Today, I will myself use my valour against all the
gods. I will strike them with extremely firm weapons, destroy them
and dislodge them from the firmament. I will slay Indra, Varuna,
Dhanada and Yama. I will myself kill all the gods and establish
myself above them. This is not the time for sorrow. Convey my
chariot quickly. I have already told you twice. Take me right up to
the end. Any place that we are in is like Nandana. Take me now to
the spot where Mount Udaya is." Hearing his words, the charioteer
urged the horses, which possessed the speed of thought, and took
him to the midst of the enemy. Ascertaining his intention, Shakra,
the lord of the gods, stationed in the battle on his chariot, addressed
the gods in these words. "O gods! Listen to my words. This is what
appeals to me. It is best that we seize the rakshasa Dashagriva while
he is alive. Because of these soldiers, he is exceedingly strong and
he is on a chariot that is as energetic as the wind. He is waxing,
like the waves of the ocean during the full moon. He is fearless
because of the boon he has obtained and it is impossible to kill
him now. Therefore, in this battle, we must endeavour to capture
him. When Bali was seized, I enjoyed the three worlds. In that
way, the idea of capturing this wicked one appeals to me." After
this, Shakra abandoned Ravana and went to a different spot. The
immensely energetic one fought against the rakshasas and destroyed
them in the battle. Dashagriva did not retreat and penetrated from
the north. Shatakratu penetrated from the southern flank. The lord
of the rakshasas penetrated one hundred yojanas. He showered
down arrows and countered the entire army of the gods. Shakra
saw that his own forces had been penetrated. He did not retreat
and fearlessly approached Dashanana. At this time, on discerning
that Ravana was being devoured by Shakra, the danavas and the
rakshasas emitted roars of, "Alas! He will be killed." At this,
senseless with rage, Ravana's son ascended his chariot. Enraged,
he penetrated that extremely terrible army. He entered, using the
maya that had been given to him by Gopati[601] earlier. Invisible to

---

[600] However, the words are directed more towards the charioteer.

[601] Lord of the earth or lord of cattle. Here, it means Shiva.

all creatures, he countered those soldiers. After this, abandoning the gods, he swiftly rushed towards Shakra. The immensely energetic and great Indra saw his enemy's son. He afflicted Matali and the horses with excellent arrows. Using the dexterity of his hands, he then countered the great Indra with showers of arrows. Shakra abandoned the chariot and Matali. Ascending Airavata, he started to look around for Ravana's son. However, because of the strength of his maya, the rakshasa could not be seen in the battle. He enveloped the infinitely energetic and great Indra with torrents of arrows. Ravana's son thought that Indra was exhausted. He used his maya to bind him up and took him amidst his own soldiers. Using the strength of his maya, he seized the great Indra in the battle. On seeing this, all the gods exclaimed, "Who has taken him away? The learned one cannot be seen. Someone has used maya to take him away." Meanwhile, all the large numbers of angry gods attacked Ravana and showered down weapons on him. In the battle, Ravana clashed against the Vasus, the Adityas and the Maruts. Afflicted by weapons, he was incapable of remaining there and fighting. He was exhausted and his form was of one suffering from those blows. Remaining invisible in the battle, Ravana's son spoke to his father. "O father! Come. Let us leave and withdraw from this fight. Our victory is evident. Assure yourself and be devoid of any anxiety. Shakra, the lord of the three worlds and of the soldiers of the gods, has been captured by me. The gods have been routed. With the energetic enemy captured, enjoy the three worlds as you wish. Why unnecessarily exert yourself in this battle? It is futile." The army of the gods also retreated from the field of battle. Hearing the words of Ravana's son, Dashanana also assured himself. The master and lord of roamers in the night thus lost anxiety in the battle and was victorious. He cheerfully left for his own residence and addressed his son in these words. "Your valour is like that of an extremely strong person and you have extended the respect towards my lineage. Your valour is like that of the immortals and you have vanquished the lord of the gods and the gods. Quickly fetch Vasava. Surrounding yourself with the soldiers, head for the city.[602] With

602 Lanka.

the advisers following me, I will also quickly leave for that place."
Thus, Ravana's son captured the lord of the gods. Surrounded by
his forces and his mounts, the rakshasa reached his own residence.
Thereafter, cheerful in his mind, he gave the rakshasas permission
to leave.'

Chapter 7(30)

'Ravana's extremely strong son vanquished the great Indra.
With Prajapati at the forefront, all the gods went to Lanka.
They approached Ravana, who was surrounded by his sons and
brothers. Remaining stationed in the sky, Prajapati addressed him
in a conciliatory tone. "O child! O Ravana! I am pleased with your
son in the battle. His valour and generosity are amazing. They
are like yours, or superior to yours. With your own energy, you
have conquered all the three worlds. You have made your pledge
come true. I am pleased with my own son.[603] O Ravana! Your
son, Ravana's son, is extremely strong. He will be famous in the
world as Indrajit.[604] This rakshasa will vanquish strong enemies.
O king! With his support, you have brought the gods under your
subjugation. You should release the mighty-armed and great Indra,
the chastiser of Paka. In return for setting him free, what should the
gods give you?" At this, the immensely energetic Indrajit, the victor
in assemblies, said, "O god! In return for setting him free, I desire
immortality." The god who was born from the lotus replied to
Ravana's son. "There is no creature on earth who can be immortal."
Thereupon, Indrajit replied to the one who was born from the lotus.
"Then hear about the kind of success I want for setting Shatakratu
free. O god! Whenever I worship the fire and render oblations into
it, prior to advancing into battle, desiring to defeat the enemy, if
I fight before completing the rituals and before offering oblations
into the fire, let it be possible for me to be killed only then. All men

---

[603] Because Ravana was descended from Brahma.
[604] Someone who has vanquished Indra.

seek the boon of immortality through austerities. Let immortality
be conferred on me through my valour." The god Prajapati replied
in words signifying his assent. Having been freed by Indrajit, Shakra
and the gods went to heaven.

'Meanwhile, Shakra was distressed. His garments and garlands
were dislodged. O Rama! He was overcome by thoughts and was
immersed in deep reflection. On seeing him in that state, the god
Prajapati spoke to him. "O Shatakratu! Why are you suffering from
this anxiety? Remember the wicked deed you committed earlier.
O Indra of the immortals! O lord! In earlier times, I created many
subjects. Their complexion was identical. Their languages were the
same. All of them were identical in form. There was no distinction
between them, in appearance or in signs. With single-minded
attention, I thought about these subjects. To create some kind of
distinction between them, I fashioned a woman. From the existing
subjects, I used the best of their limbs to create her. I constructed
a woman without blemish, with beauty and qualities.[605] Because
she was without blemish, her name became Ahalya. O Indra of the
gods! O bull among the gods! Having created the woman, a thought
then occurred to me. Whom would she belong to? O Shakra! O lord!
O Purandara! You got to know about the woman and because of
your sense of superiority, you thought that she would be your wife.
However, I bestowed her on the great-souled Goutama. After she
had been with him for many years, she was oppressed by you.[606] At
that time, I got to know about the great sage's fortitude. Through
the fruits of his austerities, he got to know that his wife had been
touched by you. Even then, the great sage, with dharma in his
soul, continued to find pleasure with her. When I bestowed her on
Goutama, the gods lost all hope of obtaining her. However, you were
angry and overcome by desire, you went to the sage's hermitage. You
saw that woman, who blazed like the flame of a fire. O Shakra! You
were full of desire and intolerance and oppressed her. The supreme
rishi saw you in the hermitage then. Supremely energetic, he cursed

---

[605] The word *ahalya* means without being ploughed, without being furrowed.
Therefore, it means one without blemish. That is the reason she was known as Ahalya.

[606] Adopting Goutama's appearance, Indra seduced her.

you in his rage. 'O Indra of the gods! You will face catastrophe and misfortune. O Vasava! Without any fear, you oppressed my wife. O king! Therefore, in a battle, you will be captured by the enemy's hand. O evil-minded one! There is no doubt that the sentiments you have brought into currency will also be prevalent among humans. If an extremely strong person perpetrates this great act of adharma, half of that will therefore devolve on you and half will be borne by the perpetrator. O Purandara! Since you have started this practice of adharma, your status will not be permanent. No one who becomes Indra of the gods will ever be permanent. This is the curse I pronounce.' This is what he told you. The extremely great ascetic also reprimanded his wife. 'O one who has not been modest! You will remain near my hermitage, but will be disfigured. You are the one who possesses youth and beauty. However, in this world, you will no longer be the only one who is beautiful in this way. Your beauty was extremely difficult to obtain and all the subjects approached you. This confusion resulted because it only existed in you.' Since then, all the subjects started possessing beauty. All this, including the new kind of creation, occurred because of that sage's curse. O mighty-armed one! Remember the evil deed that you committed. O Vasava! You have been seized by the enemy because of that and not because of any other reason. Control yourself and quickly perform a vaishnava sacrifice. You will go to heaven after you have purified yourself through that sacrifice. O Indra of the gods! Your son has not been destroyed in the great battle. His grandfather has taken him and hidden him inside the great ocean." Hearing this, the great Indra performed a vaishnava sacrifice. The gods again went to heaven and brought it under their control. O Rama! I have recounted the kind of strength Indrajit possessed. He defeated Indra of the gods and other creatures. What next?'

Chapter 7(31)

At this, the immensely energetic Rama was astounded. He bowed down and again addressed Agastya, supreme among sages, in these words. 'O illustrious one! O supreme among brahmanas! Was the world empty then? Was Ravana, lord of the rakshasas, not rebuffed by anyone? Or perhaps all the lords of the earth were deprived of valour. Since the kings were deprived of excellent weapons, many of them were vanquished.'

Hearing Raghava's words, the illustrious rishi, Agastya, smiled and spoke to Rama, as if the grandfather was speaking to Ishvara.[607] 'O bull among kings! In this way, he obstructed the kings. O Rama! O lord of the earth! Ravana roamed around the earth. There was a city named Mahishmati[608] and it was as resplendent as the city in heaven. He reached the place inhabited by the supreme Vasuretas.[609] In his powers, the king who was there was the equal of Vasuretas. His name was Arjuna and he was like a fire kindled on a bed of reeds. The lord Arjuna, the powerful king of the Haihayas went to the Narmada, to sport with the women. Ravana, the Indra among the rakshasas, reached the region on that very day. He asked the advisers, "Where is King Arjuna? You should quickly tell me that. I am Ravana and I have come here today to fight against the best among men. Without any hesitation, you should go and tell him about my arrival." The learned advisers were addressed by Ravana in this way. They told the lord of the rakshasas, "The king is not here." Vishrava's son heard from the citizens that Arjuna had left. He withdrew and went to the Vindhyas, the mountains that were like the Himalayas. It was covered with clouds and seemed to have sprouted out of the ground. Ravana saw the Vindhyas, etched like a painting in the sky. It possessed one thousand peaks and its caverns were full of lions. Waterfalls with cool water descended and they seemed to be laughing. The lofty peaks rose up towards heaven. Gods, danavas, gandharvas and kinnaras sported there with their wives and there were large numbers of apsaras. Unmatched sparkling water flowed along the rivers. It was as if serpents with flickering tongues were in the waters. With radiant caverns, the mountain was like the Himalayas. Having seen the Vindhyas, Ravana proceeded towards

---

[607] Meaning Maheshvara.

[608] The capital of the Chedi kingdom, adjacent to Avanti. In today's Madhya Pradesh.

[609] Vasuretas is the name of the fire god.

the Narmada. The river flowed downwards towards the western ocean and its sacred waters moved continuously. Buffaloes, srimaras, lions, tigers, bears and excellent elephants suffered from the heat. Becoming thirsty, they agitated that store of waters. *Chakravakas*, *karandavas*, swans, waterfowls and cranes were always crazy and called everywhere. The river was stretched out like a woman. The flowering trees were like ornaments, the chakravakas were like her two breasts, the extensive banks were like hips and the flocks of swans were like a girdle. Her limbs were smeared with pollen from the flowers, the foam from the water was like a garment. Bathing there was like touching her and the blooming lotuses were like her auspicious eyes. Reaching the Narmada, supreme among rivers, Dashanana quickly descended from Pushpaka and bathed there, like approaching a desirable and beautiful woman. He sported along its banks, adorned with many kinds of flowers. With his advisers, the bull among the rakshasas sat down. Having reached and seen Narmada, the lord of the rakshasas was delighted.

'Ravana, the lord of the rakshasas, laughed in sport and spoke to his advisers—Maricha, Shuka and Sarana. "Behold. The one with the one thousand rays has made the world golden. The sun, whose fierce rays radiate heat, is located in the middle of the sky. However, on knowing that I am seated here, the sun is behaving like the moon.[610] The waters of the Narmada are cool and fragrant, destroying all exhaustion. Because of its fear of me, the wind is also blowing in a restrained way. The Narmada is the best among rivers and is one that enhances pleasure. With fish and birds hidden in the waters, it is stationed like a frightened woman. In encounters, you have been wounded by the weapons of kings who are Indra's equal. Blood has flowed out, like the juices from red sandalwood. All of you also bathe in Narmada, just as large and crazy elephants bathe in the Ganga, holding large lotuses in their trunks. It brings pleasure to men. Bathe in this great river and cleanse yourselves of your sins. This bank is like the autumn moon in its radiance. I will slowly put together a garland of flowers for Umapati."[611] Having been

---

[610] The sun's rays are cool and not hot.
[611] Shiva.

instructed by Ravana, Maricha, Shuka and Sarana, with Mahodara
and Dhumraksha, immersed themselves in the Narmada. Like the
giant elephants Vamana, Anjana and Padma bathing in the Ganga,
the elephants of the Indra among the rakshasas also agitated the
river Narmada. The rakshasas bathed in the excellent waters of the
Narmada. They ascended from the waters and started to collect
offerings of flowers for Ravana. Narmada's beautiful bank was
as radiant as a white cloud. In a short while, those Indras among
rakshasas created a pile of flowers that resembled a mountain.
Ravana, the lord of the rakshasas, held those accumulated flowers
and descended into the river, like a giant elephant wishing to bathe
in the Ganga. Having bathed, Ravana emerged from the waters of
the Narmada. He followed the rituals and chanted excellent hymns.
As Ravana joined his hands in salutation and advanced, those seven
rakshasas[612] followed Ravana, the lord of the rakshasas, wherever
he went. They carried a golden *linga*[613] everywhere. Ravana set up
that linga in the middle of an altar made out of sand and worshipped
it with fragrant flowers and immortal scents. The supreme Hara
removes the afflictions of all virtuous people. He is the one who
grants boons. He is the one who wears the moon as an adornment.
The roamer in the night worshipped him. He then stretched out his
large hands and danced.'

Chapter 7(32)

'Ravana, Indra among the rakshasas, rendered that offering of
flowers at a spot on the banks of the Narmada. Arjuna, best
among victorious ones, was the lord and master of Mahishmati.
Not very far from that spot, he was submerged in the waters of the
Narmada, sporting with his women. In their midst, King Arjuna
was radiant. He was like a male elephant in the midst of one

---

[612] Maricha, Shuka, Sarana, Mahodara and Dhumraksha are obviously five of these.
The other two are probably Mahaparshva and Prahasta.
[613] Shiva linga.

thousand female elephants. He wished to test the supreme strength
of his one thousand arms. Therefore, Arjuna used his arms to stem
Narmada's flow. The sparkling waters reached the dam created by
Kartavirya's arms. Flooding the bank, the force started to flow in
the reverse direction. The flood of Narmada's waters was full of
fish, crocodiles and makaras and spread over the flowers and laid
out kusha grass,[614] as if it was the monsoon. The flood of waters
created by Kartavirya carried away all the offerings of flowers
Ravana had gathered. Ravana had only completed half of the
rituals and had to abandon them. He saw that Narmada was like
a beautiful and beloved woman who had turned perverse. He saw
that the increasing flood of waters resembled an ocean. However,
instead of heading westwards, it was flowing in an easterly
direction. Ravana saw that the waters of the river were behaving
like a wanton woman. The birds were also disturbed from their
natural and excellent state. Making a sound, Ravana pointed with
the fingers of his left hand and commanded Shuka and Sarana to
determine the reason for this sudden increase in flow. The brothers,
Shuka and Sarana, were commanded by Ravana. Those brave ones
left through the sky, heading in the western direction. Those two
roamers in the night travelled for only half a yojana and saw a
man sporting in the waters with women. He resembled a giant sala
tree. His loosened hair was as turbulent as the waters. His eyes
were red with intoxication. His form was as resplendent as that
of Madana. The scorcher of enemies had barricaded the river with
his one thousand arms, as if the mountain with the one thousand
feet[615] had barricaded the earth. There were one thousand young
and excellent women around him. They were like one thousand
maddened female elephants around a bull elephant. The rakshasas,
Shuka and Sarana, saw this extraordinary sight. They returned and
told Ravana what they had seen. "O lord of the rakshasas! There is
a man who resembles a giant sala tree. He is sporting with women
and has barricaded Narmada. The waters of the river have been
obstructed with his one thousand arms. That is the reason these

[614] Prepared by Ravana.
[615] This is a reference to Mount Meru.

torrents, resembling waves in the ocean, have been created." He
heard what Shuka and Sarana had to say. "That is Arjuna." Saying
this, Ravana arose, desiring to fight. The lord of the rakshasas left
in Arjuna's direction. He roared loudly and red rain showered
down from clouds. Mahodara, Mahaparshva, Dhumraksha, Shuka
and Sarana surrounded the Indra among rakshasas and went to the
spot where Arjuna was.

'The terrible and powerful rakshasa dazzled like a mass of
collyrium. In a short while, he reached the pool in Narmada. He
saw the Indra among men, surrounded by the women, resembling a
bull elephant filled with desire. King Arjuna also saw the rakshasas.
Filled with strength, the eyes of the Indra among rakshasas turned red
with rage. In a rumbling voice, he told his advisers, "This is Arjuna.
O advisers! Quickly tell the king of the Haihayas that the one who
is named Ravana has arrived to fight." Hearing Ravana's words,
holding their weapons, Arjuna's ministers arose and addressed
Ravana in these words. "O Ravana! You are virtuous and you have
determined an opportune time to fight. You wish to fight against
our king, who has been drinking and is surrounded by women. He
is intoxicated and is in the midst of those who are full of desire. You
are like a tiger that has approached an elephant. O Dashagriva!
Pardon us now. O son![616] Sleep during the night. If you like the idea
of fighting, you can fight tomorrow with Arjuna. Alternatively, if
you are filled with thirst for a fight and you must do it now, slay
us. You can then approach Arjuna and fight with him." At this,
Ravana's advisers killed the king's advisers in the encounter. Hungry,
they devoured them. As those who followed Arjuna clashed against
Ravana's ministers, a tumultuous sound arose along the banks of
the Narmada. With arrows, spears, javelins that were like the vajra
to the touch and weapons that could drag, they roared with Ravana
and powerfully attacked the warriors on the side of the lord of the
Haihayas. There was an extremely terrible sound, like that made by
crocodiles, fish and makaras in the ocean. With an energy that was
like that of the fire, Ravana's advisers, Prahasta, Shuka and Sarana,
angrily consumed Kartavirya's forces. Arjuna was still sporting. The

---

[616] The word used is tata.

men who were supposed to guard the gate went and told Arjuna what Ravana and his ministers had done. Arjuna told them and the women, "Do not be frightened." Like Anjana getting out of the waters of the Ganga, he arose from the water. Arjuna was like a fire and his eyes were filled with rage. He was extremely terrible and blazed like the fire that arrives at the end of a yuga. Wearing excellent and golden armlets, he quickly climbed up the bank. Seizing a club, he rushed against the rakshasas, just as the sun attacks darkness. He flung his arms around and raised that giant club. Using a force that was like that of Garuda, Arjuna descended on them. Prahasta fought with a mace and stood in his way, just as Mount Vindhya obstructs the path of the sun. He was stationed like Vindhya and did not waver. Maddened, he raised that terrible mace, which was plated with iron. Thundering like a cloud, Prahasta angrily hurled this. The tip of that mace blazed with flames, resembling a flowering ashoka. Hurled from Prahasta's hand, it seemed to burn everything down. Kartavirya Arjuna was like an elephant in his valour. As the mace headed towards him, he used his club to skilfully counter it. The lord of the Haihayas then attacked Prahasta. He whirled the heavy club around in five hundred of his arms. Prahasta was struck by the great force of that club. He fell down, like a stationary mountain struck by the vajra wielded by the wielder of the vajra. On seeing that Prahasta had fallen down, Maricha, Shuka, Sarana, Mahodara and Dhumraksha withdrew from the field of battle.

'When the advisers withdrew and Prahasta was brought down, Ravana quickly attacked Arjuna, supreme among kings. There was an extremely terrible battle between the king with one thousand arms and the rakshasa with twenty arms. It made the body hair stand up. They were like two agitated oceans, two mountains that began to move at the foundations, two suns that were full of energy and two fires that consumed everything. They were like two powerful elephants, like two bulls filled with desire. They roared like clouds and were as strong as lions. The rakshasa and Arjuna were as angry as Rudra and Death. They severely struck each other with their clubs. The man and the rakshasa tolerated those terrible blows of the clubs, just as mountains withstand the blow of the vajra. Echoes result when there is thunder. Like that, the sound of the clubs descending were heard in all the directions. When Arjuna's club descended on his chest, the sky was filled with a golden tinge, as if through a flash of lightning. In a similar way, Ravana repeatedly brought down the radiant club on Arjuna's chest, like a meteor descending on a large mountain. Arjuna did not suffer. Nor did the lord of large numbers of rakshasas. The encounter between them was between two equals, like that between Bali and Indra in earlier times. They were like two bulls fighting with their horns, or like two elephants fighting with their tusks. The man and the best among rakshasas struck each other. In the great duel, Arjuna wrathfully used all his strength and brought the club down between Ravana's breasts. However, he possessed an armour because of the boon. But the club descended on Ravana's chest and weakened him. It was shattered into two pieces and fell down on the ground, where the soldiers were. The club released by Arjuna struck Ravana. He was benumbed and roared, withdrawing only the distance of one bow length. Arjuna saw that Dashagriva was suffering. He violently seized him, the way Garuda seizes a serpent. Dashanana was forcibly seized in those one thousand arms. The powerful king bound him down, like Narayana did to Bali. On seeing that Dashagriva had thus been captured, the siddhas, charanas and gods uttered words of praise and showered down flowers on Arjuna's head. It was like a tiger seizing a deer, or a lion seizing an elephant. The king of the Haihayas repeatedly roared in delight, like a cloud. Regaining his senses, Prahasta saw that Dashanana had been bound. With the other rakshasas, he angrily rushed towards the king. The roamers in the night powerfully descended on him, just as at the end of the summer, clouds rush towards the ocean. They said, "Release him. Let him go. Wait. Wait for us." Saying this, they showered down clubs and spears on Arjuna. However, Arjuna was not scared. The slayer of enemies deftly avoided and seized the weapons of the enemy. He used extremely excellent weapons to shatter and drive away the rakshasas, just as the wind drives away clouds. Kartavirya Arjuna terrified the rakshasas. Seizing Ravana and surrounded by his well-wishers, he entered his city. He was like Puruhuta[617] and the brahmanas and citizens showered down flowers

[617] Indra.

on him. Arjuna entered the city with him, just as the one with one thousand eyes captured Bali.'

Chapter 7(33)

'This act of seizing Ravana was like that of capturing the wind. The rishi Pulastya heard the gods conversing about this in heaven. Out of affection towards his son's son, the one with great fortitude trembled. The great rishi went to see the lord of Mahishmati. The brahmana resorted to the path followed by the wind, travelling at a speed that was like that of the wind. With his valour and speed like that of thoughts, he reached the city of Mahishmati. He saw that it was like Amaravati, populated by happy and well-nourished people. Like Brahma entering Indra's Amaravati, he entered the city. It was as if the sun had descended and arrived on foot. It was a sight that was extremely difficult to behold. The news about his arrival was conveyed to Arjuna. The lord of the Haihayas heard the news about Pulastya. He joined his hands above his head in salutation and went forward to receive the best among brahmanas. Like Brihaspati before Indra, the priest advanced ahead of the king, carrying arghya and *madhuparka*.[618] The rishi arrived, like a sun that has arisen. On seeing this, Arjuna approached and worshipped him, like Indra honouring Ishvara.[619] He offered him padya, arghya and madhuparka. In a voice that was filled with delight, the Indra among kings spoke to Pulastya. "Today, you have made Mahishmati just like Amaravati. O Indra among all the Indras among brahmanas! I have seen you today. It is a sight that is extremely difficult to behold. O god! I am fortunate today. My lineage has been uplifted today. Your feet are worshipped by large numbers of gods and I have been able to worship them today. O brahmana! This kingdom, my sons, my wives and all of us belong to you. What is the task that needs to be done? Command us." Pulastya asked King Arjuna of the Haihayas about whether all was

---

[618] Madhuparka is a mixture comprising of honey, customarily offered to a guest.
[619] Maheshvara.

well with dharma, the fire[620] and the servants. He told the king, "O
Indra among kings! O one with eyes like the petals of a lotus! O one
with a face like the full moon! Since you have vanquished Dashagriva,
your strength is infinite. My grandson is extremely difficult to defeat.
The oceans and the winds remain immobile and stationary, out of
their fear for him. But you have captured him today. O son! Your
fame has been enhanced and your name has been heard everywhere.
O child! However, pay heed to my words and release Dashanana."
Without uttering any words to counter this, Arjuna accepted Pulastya's
command. Cheerfully, the Indra among Indras among kings released
the Indra among the rakshasas. Arjuna released the enemy of the gods
and honoured him with divine ornaments, garlands and garments.
With the fire as a witness, he contracted a pact of non-violence
and friendship with him. Bowing down before Brahma's son,[621] he
returned to his residence. Pulastya met the powerful Indra among the
rakshasas. Though he had been embraced[622] and treated like a guest
and released thereafter, he was ashamed. Having freed Dashagriva,
Pulastya, supreme among sages and the grandfather's son, went to
Brahma's world. Thus, Ravana was afflicted by Kartavirya. Because
of Pulastya's words, he subsequently released him. O descendant of
the Raghava lineage! If someone is strongest among the strong and
desires his own welfare, he should never disrespect others. Thus the
king with one thousand arms contracted friendship with the devourer
of flesh. However, he[623] was insolent and continued to roam around
the entire earth, causing carnage among men.'

Chapter 7(34)

'Ravana, the lord of the rakshasas, was freed by Arjuna. He
roamed around the earth, slighting everyone. Ravana was
insolent. Whenever he heard that any rakshasa or human was

[620] Meaning whether sacrifices were being properly conducted.
[621] Pulastya.
[622] By Arjuna.
[623] Ravana.

superior in strength, he approached him and challenged him to a fight. The city of Kishkindha was protected by Vali. On one occasion, he went there and challenged Vali, who wore a golden garland, to a fight. The adviser among the apes, the lord Tara, Tara's father,[624] addressed Ravana, who had arrived with a desire to fight, in these words. "O Indra among the rakshasas! Vali is your equal in strength. But he is not here. No other ape is capable of standing before you. O Ravana! Remain here for a while. Having performed sandhya[625] in the four oceans, Vali will soon return. Behold these piles of bones that are as white as conch shells. These belong to those who came here with a desire to fight against the energetic lord of the apes. O Ravana! O rakshasa! Clash against Vali only if you have drunk the juices of amrita. Otherwise, your life will be over. Alternatively, if you wish to die quickly, go to the southern ocean. You will see Vali there, bowing down before the sun." Ravana, the lord of the rakshasas, was reprimanded by Tara. He mounted Pushpaka and left for the southern ocean.

'Ravana saw Vali there, engaged in the sandhya worship. He was like a golden mountain, like the rising sun in his complexion. Resembling a mass of dark collyrium, Ravana descended from Pushpaka. Desiring to quickly seize Vali, he silently advanced on foot. However, at ease, Vali opened his eyes and saw Ravana. Though he got to know about his evil intentions, he was not scared. He was like a lion that sees a hare, like Garuda seeing a serpent. Ravana's intentions were wicked. Vali thought, "Evil in his intentions, he wishes to seize me now. I will grasp him by my side and go to the great oceans.[626] This enemy will be seen to dangle from my lap, like a garment dangling from my side. Dashagriva will be like a serpent seized by Garuda." Having made up his mind, Vali continued to listen.[627] He was like a king of the mountains

---

[624] The male ape is Tara and is the father of Taraa, Vali's wife.

[625] The evening rituals.

[626] To perform sandhya, Vali had to progressively go to the four oceans.

[627] The text of the Critical Edition causes a problem of translation here. Non-Critical editions use the word *mounam*. This simply means Vali waited silently. The Critical Edition uses the word *karnam* instead, meaning ear. We have hence interpreted it as Vali listening with his ears, since his eyes were closed. But the word also means diagonal or the diameter of a circle. It is possible that as part of the sandhya rituals, Vali had drawn auspicious signs on the ground.

and chanted mantras from the sacred texts. The king of the apes and the king of the rakshasas wished to seize each other. They were insolent and strong and exerted themselves to accomplish this task. Through the sound of the footsteps, Vali decided that Ravana was about to seize him. Without looking backwards, he extended his arms and grasped him, like the one born from the egg[628] seizes a serpent. The lord of the rakshasas desired to seize the ape, but was captured by him instead. Grasping him close to his side, the ape powerfully leapt up into the sky. He struck and pierced him repeatedly with his nails. Vali seized Ravana, like the wind seizing a cloud. The advisers of the rakshasa saw that Dashanana was being abducted. Desiring to free him, they roared in terrible voices and rushed behind them. They followed Vali, who was radiant in the middle of the sky. It was as if clouds in the sky were following the one with the rays.[629] Those excellent rakshasas tried to reach Vali. However, because of the force of his arms and his thighs, they were exhausted and fell down. Vali's trail was impossible to follow, even if Indras among mountains had attempted it. The Indra among apes was extremely swift and followed a path that even the birds couldn't follow. He progressively reached all the oceans and performed the sandhya rites there. Travelling through the sky, the ape was worshipped by all the creatures who roamed around in the sky. With Ravana, Vali went to the western ocean. The ape performed the sandhya worship there, bathed and chanted. Bearing Ravana, he then went to the northern ocean. He performed the sandhya worship in the northern ocean. Bearing Dashanana, Vali then went to the eastern ocean, the great store of waters. Vasava's son, the lord of the apes, performed the sandhya worship there. Seizing Ravana, he then returned towards Kishkindha. The ape had performed the sandhya rites in the four oceans. Exhausted at having had to bear Ravana, he descended in a grove in Kishkindha. The supreme ape freed Ravana from his flank and laughing at Ravana, asked him, "Where have you come from?" Ravana had been filled with great amazement. He was tired and his eyes rolled around. The lord of the rakshasas

---

[628] Garuda.
[629] The sun.

addressed the lord of the apes in these words. "O Indra among the apes! O one whose complexion is like that of the great Indra! I am Ravana, Indra among the rakshasas. I had come here, desiring to fight, but have suffered at your hands. Your strength is amazing. Your valour and depth are amazing. You seized me like an animal and travelled around the four oceans. O brave ape! I do not see any other brave one who could have borne me and travelled around like this, without suffering from exhaustion. O bull among apes! There are only three creatures who possess this kind of movement— thought, the wind and Suparna. There is no doubt about this. O bull among the apes! I have witnessed your strength. In front of the fire, I desire to contract an everlasting and affectionate pact of friendship with you. O lord of the apes! Wives, sons, the city, the kingdom, all the objects of pleasure, garments, food and everything else that I possess, will be divided and belong to both of us." After this, the ape and the rakshasa lit a fire. With fraternal sentiments, they embraced each other. The ape and the rakshasa stretched out their hands and cheerfully entered Kishkindha, like two lions entering a cave in the mountains. Like Sugriva, Ravana resided there for a month. His advisers were interested in oppressing the three worlds. They arrived and took him away. O lord! This is the former conduct of Vali towards Ravana. Having made him suffer, in the presence of the fire, he behaved towards him like a brother. O Rama! Vali's unmatched strength was extraordinary. However, he was consumed by you, like an insect by a flame.'

Chapter 7(35)

Rama humbly joined his hands in salutation before the sage who dwelt towards the south. He spoke to him in words that were full of meaning. 'Vali and Ravana were unmatched in their strength. However, it is my view that they were not Hanumat's equal in valour. Prowess, skill, strength, patience, wisdom, the attainment of good policy, valour and power—all of these found a home in Hanumat. On seeing the ocean, the army of the apes was distressed. However, comforting them, the ape leapt across one hundred yojanas. He made the city of Lanka suffer. In Ravana's inner quarters, he saw and spoke to Sita, comforting her. Single-handedly, Hanumat brought down the best of the soldiers, the sons of the ministers, the kimkaras and Ravana's son. He then freed himself from the bondage and addressed Dashanana. Like the fire does to the earth, he burnt down Lanka. The deeds that Hanumat accomplished in the battle are unheard of, even among Death, Shakra, Vishnu and the lord of treasures. It is because of the strength of his arms that I obtained Lanka, Sita, Lakshmana, victory, the kingdom, friends and relatives. Had Hanumat, lord of the apes, not been my friend, who knows what would have happened? It would not have been possible to find Janakee. In a desire to bring pleasure to Sugriva, when there was an enmity with Vali, why did he not burn him[630] down like a herb? I think Hanumat did not know about his own strength then. Though he could see the lord of the apes[631] suffering, despite being alive, he did not try. O illustrious one! O great sage! O one who is worshipped by the immortals! Tell me everything about Hanumat in detail, the complete truth.'

The rishi heard Raghava's words, which were full of reason. In Hanumat's presence, he addressed him in these words. 'O best among the Raghu lineage! What you have said about Hanumat is indeed true. There is no one else who is his equal in strength, speed and intelligence. However, in earlier times, the rishis imposed an inviolate curse on him. That is the reason this powerful one, the afflicter of enemies, did not know about his strength. O Rama! O immensely strong one! In his childhood, because of childishness, he did something. I am incapable of even describing it. O Raghava! O Rama! But if it is your intention to hear this, then listen with single-minded attention. I will tell you. There is a mountain named Sumeru. Because of a boon bestowed on it by the sun, its complexion is golden. His father, named Kesari, used to rule over the kingdom there. His beloved wife was known as Anjana. She gave birth to Vayu's excellent son. Anjana gave birth to a son whose

---

[630] Vali.
[631] Sugriva.

complexion was like that of a grain of paddy.[632] Desiring to collect
some fruit, she then left and wandered around in that desolate
region. Separated from his mother, he was afflicted by severe
hunger. The child wept, like the child in a clump of reeds.[633] The sun
was rising, resembling a japa flower.[634] On seeing it and desiring
some fruit, he leapt up towards the sun. The child's form was like
that of the rising sun and he leapt up in the direction of the rising
sun. Wishing to seize the rising sun, he leapt up into the middle
of the sky. Thus, overcome by childish sentiments, Hanumat leapt
up. The gods, the danavas and the siddhas were struck by great
wonder. "Vayu, Garuda and thought does not possess the kind of
speed with which Vayu's son is travelling through the excellent sky.
If this is the kind of speed and valour he possesses as a child, what
will his force be when he is strong and young?" As he leapt, Vayu
also leapt behind his son. He wished to protect him from the fear of
being burnt down by the sun and there was a wind that was as cool
as ice. Through the strength of his father, the child progressively
travelled through many thousands of yojanas across the sky and
easily reached the sun. The sun saw him approach, but took him
to be a child who cannot commit a crime. Therefore, the sun did
not burn him down. On the day he leapt up to seize the sun, on
the same day, Rahu desired to seize the sun. O Rama! Astride the
sun's chariot, he was severely seized by him.[635] Attacked, Rahu, the
afflicter of the moon and the sun, was terrified. In rage, Simhika's
son[636] went to Indra's abode. His eyebrows knit in a frown, he
spoke to the god, who was surrounded by a large number of gods.
"O Vasava! To satisfy my hunger, you have given me the moon
and the sun. O slayer of Bala and Vritra! Why have you now given
them to someone else? Today is the right time[637] and I approached
the sun, to seize it. Though Rahu was approaching, someone else
violently seized the sun." Hearing Rahu's words, Vasava was filled

---

[632] *Shalishuka,* a variety of rice.
[633] Meaning Kartikeya.
[634] The red hibiscus.
[635] Rahu was seized by Hanumat.
[636] Rahu.
[637] For an eclipse.

with fear. He leapt up from his throne, abandoning it. He cast aside his golden garland. Indra mounted the Indra among elephants.[638] Its complexion was like that of Mount Kailasa. It possessed four tusks and exuded musth. It was tall and was decorated with golden bells that seemed to laugh out aloud. With Rahu leading the way, he went to the place where the sun and Hanumat were. There, leaving the elephant and Rahu behind, he approached and saw the one whose form was like the summit of a mountain. He[639] let go of the sun and glanced towards Rahu. Desiring to seize Simhika's son, he leapt up into the sky again. O Rama! Letting go of the sun, the ape advanced. On seeing his large form, Rahu, who was only a mouth,[640] retreated. Terrified, Simhika's son sought a protector in Indra and repeatedly spoke to him. "O Indra! Save me. O Indra!" When Rahu was shrieking, Indra heard the words that he spoke and replied, "Do not be scared. I will kill him." At that time, Maruti saw the gigantic Airavata. Taking it to be some kind of fruit, he rushed towards the king of elephants. He rushed towards Airavata, wishing to seize it. In an instant, his form became terrible, as radiant as that of Indra or Agni. When he rushed forward in this way, Shachi's lord wasn't greatly enraged.[641] He released the vajra from his hand and struck him with that. Struck by Indra's vajra, he fell down on the mountain. When he fell down, his left jawbone was shattered. Struck by the vajra, the child lost his senses and fell down. Angry at Indra, Vayu wished to cause harm to the subjects. The lord is inside all creatures. Just as Vasava obstructs the rain, he obstructed the excretory organs of all creatures. Suffering from Vayu's rage, all the creatures were incapable of breathing. All the joints in their bodies became like pieces of wood. There was no svadha[642] and no sounds of vashatkara. There were no rites and dharma was abandoned. Because of Vayu's rage, the three worlds

---

[638] Airavata.

[639] Hanumat.

[640] Rahu is only a mouth, the body having been chopped off by Vishnu at the time of the churning of the ocean, when Rahu disguised himself as a god and had a bit of the amrita.

[641] That is, he struck him a mild blow.

[642] Svadha is an oblation offered to the ancestors.

became like hell. Afflicted by unhappiness and desiring happiness, the subjects, the gandharvas, the gods, the asuras and men rushed to Prajapati. The gods were suffering. They joined their hands in salutation and spoke to the one who had been born from the navel. "O illustrious one! You have created the four kinds of subjects.[643] Through Vayu, you have given us our lifespans. O excellent one! You have made him the lord of life. Why is he hating us now? In their misery, people are weeping, like women in the inner quarters. O lord! We are suffering because of Vayu and are seeking refuge with you. O slayer of enemies! We are oppressed and suffering because the wind has been obstructed." Prajapati, the lord of subjects, heard the subjects. Having been addressed, he spoke to the subjects. "There must be some reason. There must be a reason why Vayu is angry and has caused this obstruction. O subjects! You must listen to everything. Having heard, you must pardon him. The lord of the immortals, Indra, has brought down his son today, listening to the words that Rahu spoke. That is the reason, Vayu, your king, is angry. Vayu does not possess a body. But he roams around in bodies and nurtures them. Without Vayu, all bodies will be reduced to dust. Vayu is the breath of life and happiness. Vayu is everywhere in this world. Abandoned by Vayu, there will be no happiness in the world. Today, abandoned by Vayu, the world has lost its lifespan. There is no breath of life today and everyone is stationed like a piece of wood. All this has happened to us because of Vayu's obstruction. By causing displeasure to Aditi's son,[644] you should not head towards destruction." With the subjects, the gods, the gandharvas, the serpents and the guhyakas, Prajapati went to the spot where Vayu was, clasping his son, who had been struck by Indra of the gods. The one who perpetually moves[645] was embracing his son, whose complexion was as golden as that of the fire. With the gods, the siddhas, the rishis, the serpents and the rakshasas, the one with the four faces[646] looked compassionately towards him.'

[643] Those born from wombs, those born from eggs, plants and those born from sweat (insects and worms).

[644] Vayu.

[645] Vayu.

[646] Brahma.

Chapter 7(36)

'The grandfather saw that Vayu was afflicted because his son had been killed. Raising the child in his lap, he arose and stood in front of the creator. His earrings, diadem, garland and golden ornaments moved.[647] He prostrated himself thrice at the creator's feet. The one who knew about the Vedas stretched out his long hand that was adorned with ornaments and raised Vayu. He touched the child. As soon as he was touched by the one who was born from the waters and from the lotus, like crops that are sprinkled with water, he regained his life. On seeing that the one who had seemed to lose his life was full of life, the one who bore fragrances[648] rejoiced. As in earlier times, he started to move around in all creatures. Freed from the disease that had been brought about by Vayu, all the subjects were delighted. They were like lotuses in a pond, freed from cold winds. Brahma Triyugma, Trikaku, Tridhama, worshipped by the Tridashas, spoke to the gods, desiring to bring pleasure to Vayu.[649] "O great Indra, Agni, Varuna, lord of treasures and Maheshvara! You know everything. Even then, I will tell you what is beneficial. In future, this child will perform deeds for you. To satisfy Vayu, all of us should therefore confer boons on him." At this, the one with the one thousand eyes and auspicious face was filled with affection. He flung a garland made out waterlilies around his neck and said, "Your jawbone was shattered because of the vajra released from my hand. O tiger among apes! Your name will be Hanumat.[650] I will also grant you a supreme and excellent boon. From now, my vajra will not be able to kill you." Martanda[651] told the illustrious

[647] Because he suddenly stood up.

[648] Vayu.

[649] *Tridasha* is an expression used for the gods in general. Tridasha means thirty and refers to twelve Adityas, eleven Rudras and eight Vasus, adding up to thirty-one. *Triyugma* means three pairs, that is, one possessing the three pairs. The three pairs are *yasha* (fame) and *virya* (valour); *aishvarshya* (prosperity) and *shri* (riches); and *jnana* (knowledge) and *vairagya* (detachment). *Trikaku* means one with three peaks and is used to signify that a person possesses thrice the usual excellence. *Tridhama* means someone who is glorified in the three worlds.

[650] Literally, the one with the jaw.

[651] Surya, the sun god.

grandfather. "I will give him a hundredth part of my energy, so that he possesses the capability to study the sacred texts. I will grant him sacred texts so that he becomes eloquent in speech." Varuna granted him the boon that for a million years, he would not die from Varuna's noose or waters. Yama said that his staff would not be able to kill him and that he would never suffer from disease. "I also give him the boon that he will never be distressed and will be happy in battles." The one who grants boons[652] said, "My club will not be able to kill him, the possessor of tawny pupils, in a battle." Shankara granted him the supreme boon, "My weapons, or weapons that come from me, will not bring about his death." The great-souled Brahma spoke these words. "Under no circumstance, will Brahma's staff be able to kill him. He will have a long lifespan." Vishvakarma looked at the child, who was like the rising sun. The immensely intelligent one, supreme among artisans, spoke about the following boon. "I have fashioned all kinds of weapons for the gods. At the time of battle, these will not be able to kill him." Thus, the gods ornamented him with boons. The one with the four faces, the preceptor of the worlds, was happy and spoke to Vayu. "He will cause fear to the enemy and grant his friends freedom from fear. O Maruta![653] This son of yours, Maruti, will be invincible. In battles, to bring suffering to Ravana and to do what brings Rama pleasure, he will perform deeds that will make the body hair stand up." Saying this, with the grandfather at the forefront, all the immortals took their leave of Vayu and went away, to wherever they had come from.

'The bearer of scents clasped his son and brought him home. He told Anjana about the boons that had been conferred and left. O Rama! He obtained boons and those boons added to his strength. This was added to his own strength and he became as full as the ocean. The bull among apes was filled with strength. Without any fear, he started to cause harm to maharshis in their hermitages.

---

[652] The Critical Edition uses the expression Varada, one who grants boons. Non-Critical Editions say Dhanada, Kubera. In any event, this boon is being conferred by Kubera.

[653] Maruta is a specific term for Vayu, not to be confused with Marut. Maruti means Maruta's son.

He shattered and destroyed the ladles and vessels for agnihotra sacrifices and the piles of bark. What could those peaceful ones do? Because of what Brahma had done, he could not be killed by all the Brahmadandas.[654] Knowing this, the rishis always pardoned him. Even when Kesari, Vayu and Anjana tried to restrain him, the ape continued to transgress the boundaries. O best among the Raghu lineage! Moderately angry, they cursed him. "O ape! Using your strength, you are obstructing us. Therefore, confounded by our curse, you will not remember it for a long period of time." Because of the energy in the curse of the maharshis, his energy vanished. Mild in form, he roamed around in the hermitages. Vali and Sugriva's father was named Riksharaja. He was the king of all the apes and in his energy, he was like the sun. The lord of the apes ruled over the kingdom of the apes for a long time. After this, the one named Riksharaja succumbed to the dharma of time. The ministers, skilled in counselling, consecrated Vali in the ancestral kingdom and Sugriva at Vali's feet.[655] His[656] friendship with Sugriva was deep, without any blemishes, like that between Vayu and Agni. O Rama! At the time of the enmity between Vali and Sugriva, since he had succumbed to the curse, he did not know about his own strength. O Rama! Vali made Sugriva wander around. At that time, Maruti did not know about his own strength. In this world, there is no one who is superior to Hanumat in valour, enterprise, intelligence, power, good conduct, gentleness, good policy, depth, skill, bravery and patience. In earlier times, this Indra among the apes desired to learn grammar from Surya's mouth. To learn this great text, the immeasurable one followed Surya from Mount Udaya to Mount Asta. He is as fathomless as the ocean. He is like the fire in his ability to burn down the worlds. In his ability to destroy the worlds, he is like Death. Who can stand before Hanumat? There are other great Indras among the apes—Sugriva, Mainda, Dvivida, Nila, Tara, Tareya, Anala and Rambha. O Rama! The gods created them for your sake. I have told you everything that you asked

---

[654] Brahmadanda means Brahma's staff (*danda*). But it also means punishment and curses levied by brahmanas.

[655] Sugriva was instated as the heir apparent.

[656] Hanumat's.

about. I have recounted Hanumat's conduct as a child. O Rama! I
have happily conversed with you. We will now leave.'

Having said this, all the rishis went away to wherever they had
come from.

Chapter 7(37)

Taking leave of them, Rama embraced his friend Pratardana,
the fearless king of Kashi, and addressed him in these words.
'O king! I have met you. You have exhibited supreme friendliness
and affection. With Bharata, you have made great efforts.[657] You can
now leave for the city of Varanasi, in Kashi. It is beautiful and is
protected by you, possessing excellent walls and gates.' Saying this,
Kakutstha arose from this excellent seat. The one with dharma in his
soul embraced him close to his bosom. He took leave of his friend
and greeted the other lords of the earth. Raghava smiled at them
and spoke to them in words that were full of sweet syllables. 'Your
affection is deep and your energy protects. You are always controlled
and devoted to dharma and the truth. It is because of the powers
and energy of you great-souled ones that the evil-minded and evil-
souled Ravana, lord of the rakshasas, has been killed. I am only the
instrument. Your energy has slain Ravana, his companions, his sons
and his relatives in the battle. On hearing that the daughter of King
Janaka had been abducted in the forest, the great-souled Bharata
had summoned you here. All of you great-souled kings assembled to
make efforts. A long period of time has elapsed and the idea of your
return appeals to me.' The kings were filled with great delight and
replied, 'O Rama! It is good fortune that you have been victorious
and are established in this kingdom. It is good fortune that Sita has
been got back. It is good fortune that the enemy has been defeated.
This constitutes a great deed for us. This was our supreme desire.
O Rama! We wanted to see you victorious and the enemy killed. O

---

[657] This hangs loose. It is not clear what Pratardana has helped Bharata about. (It
is not clear from non-Critical Editions either.) The interpretation is that Pratardana had
offered (Bharata) that he would help Rama fight against Ravana.

Kakutstha! You have praised us because of your generosity. It is only someone who deserves to be praised who can praise in this way. We seek your leave to depart. You will always remain in our hearts. O great king! We will always be affectionate towards you.'

Chapter 7(38)

The great-souled kings left in different directions. The earth trembled as those brave ones cheerfully left for their own cities. For Raghava's sake, many thousands of akshouhinis had come and assembled. All of them happily returned. Full of strength and pride, all the kings said, 'We were unable to remain in front and witness the encounter with Ravana. Bharata summoned us later and it was a futile exercise. Had the kings been there, there is no doubt that they would have killed the rakshasa. Protected by the strength of the arms of Rama and Lakshmana, without any anxiety, we would have happily fought on the other shore of the ocean.' Thousands of kings conversed in this and other ways. Conversing, the maharathas went to their own kingdoms. Having gone to their cities, to bring pleasure to Rama, the kings donated many kinds of jewels. There were horses, gems, garments, elephants crazy with musth, divine sandalwood and celestial garments. Bharata, Lakshmana and maharatha Shatrughna collected those treasures and returned again to Ayodhya. Those bulls among men returned to the beautiful city of Ayodhya and gave all those jewels to the great-souled Raghava. Filled with joy, Raghava accepted all those and gave all those to the great-souled Sugriva. He gave them to Vibhishana, other bears and apes, other brave ones with Hanumat as the foremost and the immensely strong rakshasas. Cheerful in their minds, they accepted everything that Rama had given them. The immensely strong ones wore them on their heads, necks and arms. They drank many kinds of extremely fragrant liquor.[658] They ate meat and extremely sweet fruit. All of them resided there for more than a month. But

[658] Madhu. Therefore, alternatively, honey.

because of their affection towards Rama, it seemed to be only an instant. Rama found pleasure with the apes who could assume any form at will, with the immensely valiant kings[659] and the extremely strong rakshasas. The pleasant and second month of Shishira[660] also passed. All the apes and rakshasas were delighted.

Chapter 7(39)

The bears, apes and rakshasas resided there. The immensely energetic Raghava spoke to Sugriva. 'O amiable one! Go to Kishkindha, which is impossible for even the gods and the asuras to assail. Without any thorns and with the advisers, rule over the kingdom. O mighty-armed one! Filled with great affection, look towards Angada, Hanumat, the immensely strong Nala, the brave Sushena, your father-in-law, Tara, supreme among strong ones, the invincible Kumuda, the extremely strong Nila, the brave Shatabali, Mainda, Dvivida, Gaja, Gavaksha, Gavaya, the immensely strong Sharabha and the immensely strong and invincible Jambavat, the king of the bears. Look towards Gandhamadana with affection. Filled with affection, look towards all the other extremely great-souled ones who were ready to give up their lives for my sake. Do not do anything disagreeable to them.' Saying this, he repeatedly praised Sugriva.

In sweet words, Rama addressed Vibhishana in these words. 'O king! You are revered. Follow dharma and rule Lanka. It is the city of the rakshasas and of your brother, Vaishravana. O king! You should never turn your mind towards adharma. Indeed, it is certainly intelligent kings who enjoy the earth. O king! Always remember me and Sugriva with great affection. Go, devoid of any anxiety.' Hearing Rama's words, the bears, the apes and the rakshasas repeatedly lauded Kakutstha in words of praise. 'O mighty-armed one! Your intelligence and valour are extraordinary. O Rama! Your sweetness has always been supreme, like that of Svayambhu.'

---

[659] However, the kings had already left.
[660] Shishira is winter, the months of Magha and Phalguna.

While all the apes and rakshasas were speaking in this way, Hanumat bowed down and addressed Raghava in these words. 'O king! I have always had great affection for you. O brave one! I have always been controlled in my devotion towards you. I do not feel like going elsewhere. O brave one! There is no doubt that as long as Rama's account is heard on earth, until that time, life will reside in my body.' Thus addressed, the Indra among kings arose from his seat and raising and embracing Hanumat, addressed him in these words. 'O best among apes! There is no doubt that this will happen. As long as the worlds remain, my account will also remain. As long as my account travels around in the worlds, there is no doubt that until that time, life will reside in your body.' Raghava took off the necklace from around his neck. It was made of lapis lazuli and possessed the complexion of the moon. Affectionately, he fastened it around Hanumat's neck. The great ape clasped the necklace close to his chest. He was as radiant as the Himalaya mountains, when the moon adorns the crest. Hearing Raghava's words, all the apes arose. The immensely strong ones bowed their heads down at his feet and departed. Rama embraced the mighty-armed Sugriva and clasped Vibhishana, with dharma in his soul, close to his bosom. All their voices choked with tears. There were tears in their eyes and they were almost senseless. They took their leave of Raghava with a great deal of sorrow, as if they were confounded.

Chapter 7(40)

The mighty-armed one gave leave to the bears, apes and rakshasas. Rama was happy and with his brothers, found joy in this happiness. On one afternoon, with his brothers, Raghava heard sweet speech being spoken from the sky. 'O amiable one! O Rama! Look towards my face with a peaceful glance. O lord! Know me to be Pushpaka. I have come here from Mount Kailasa. Following your command, I went to Dhanada. O best among men! However, when I presented myself before him, he told me, "Having slain the invincible Ravana, lord of the rakshasas in a battle, the great-souled Raghava, Indra among men, has won you. O amiable one! I am greatly delighted that he has killed that evil-souled one, Ravana, with his companions, sons, advisers and relatives. Rama, supreme in his soul, has conquered Lanka and you. O amiable one! I am commanding you. You should bear him. It is my supreme desire that you should belong to the descendant of the Raghava lineage. Be his vehicle and bear him to all the worlds. Without any anxiety, go there." Knowing the instructions of the great-souled Dhanada, I have again come to your presence. Therefore, accept me.' Kakutstha agreed and honoured Pushpaka with parched grain, fragrant flowers and excellent perfumes. 'Go where you wish. Come when I remember you.' Saying this, Rama released Pushpaka again. Adorned with flowers, Pushpaka left for the desired direction. Thus, knowing about its own soul, Pushpaka vanished.

Bharata joined his hands in salutation and addressed the descendant of the Raghu lineage in these words. 'When you are ruling over the kingdom, all kinds of extraordinary creatures who aren't human are repeatedly seen. A little more than a month has passed, but there is no disease among mortals. O Raghava! Even creatures who are old and decayed do not die. Women give birth to sons. The men are healthy. O king! The people who are residents of the city are filled with great joy. At the right time, Vasava showers down rain that is like amrita. The wind that blows is extremely pleasant to the touch. O lord of men! There has not been a king like this for a long time. This is what the inhabitants of the city and the countryside are talking about.' Bharata spoke these extremely sweet words. On hearing them, Rama was delighted. He was filled with pleasure, happiness and joy.

Chapter 7(41)

Having let go of Pushpaka, decorated with gold, the mighty-armed Rama entered Ashokavana.[661] The place was adorned

---

[661] To state the obvious, this is not the Ashokavana in Lanka.

with sandalwood, aloe, mango, *tunga*,[662] *kalayeka*[663] and *devadaru* trees in every direction. It was covered with *priyangu*s, kadambas, *kurubaka*s, jambus, patalas and *kovidara*s. There were beautiful flowers and pleasant fruits everywhere. The beautiful leaves and flowers fluttered and it was full of intoxicated bees. There were birds of many hues—cuckoos and *bhringaraja*s. Hundreds of other kinds of colourful birds resided on the branches of mango trees and decorated them. Some trees were like molten gold. Other trees were like the flames of the fire. There were other radiant trees that possessed the complexion of blue collyrium. There were many kinds of ponds and they were filled with excellent water. The extremely expensive stairs were made out of jewels, with crystal deep inside them. There were clumps of blossoming lotuses, adorned with chakravaka birds. There were many kinds of walls and the platforms made out of stone were decorated. Here and there, parts of the grove were like lapis lazuli and gems. The grass was excellent and the trees were laden with flowers. It was like Indra's Nandana, or like Brahma's Chaitraratha. In that spot, Rama's grove had a form like that. There were seats outside the houses and the houses were covered with creepers. The descendant of the Raghu lineage entered that prosperous Ashokavana. He sat down on an auspicious seat that was decorated with bouquets of flowers.

Rama sat down on a seat that was covered with a spread of kusha grass. Kakutstha clasped Sita in his arms and like Indra offering Shachi amrita, made her drink excellent *maireya* liquor. Rama asked the servants to quickly bring different kinds of meat, various types of fruit and other objects to be used. Young and beautiful women who were under the influence of drink, accomplished in singing and dancing, danced before the king. Thus, with Sita, whose face was beautiful, Rama was delighted. Like a god, he spent many days finding pleasure with Vaidehi. While the great-souled Raghava, king among men, sported himself in this way, the auspicious winter season passed. In the forenoon, following dharma, the one who knew about dharma performed all the tasks that had to be

---

[662] Tree with red flowers, *Mallotus phillippensis*.
[663] A kind of fragrant wood.

done for the city. In the remaining half of the day, he was in the inner quarters. In the forenoon, Sita performed the tasks meant for the gods. In particular, she joined her hands in salutation and served her mothers-in-law. Thereafter, adorned in many colourful ornaments, she went to Rama, just as in heaven Shachi goes to the one with the one thousand eyes when he is seated. On seeing that his wife was expecting, Raghava was infinitely delighted and uttered words of praise. He said, "O Vaidehi! These are signs of my getting an offspring. Tell me. What do you wish for? What should I do to satisfy your wishes?" Vaidehi smiled and addressed Rama in these words. "O Raghava! I wish to see the sacred forests where the hermitages are. The rishis, sacred in their deeds, reside along the banks of the Ganga. O brave one! I wish to survive on fruits and roots and live near their feet. O Kakutstha! This is my supreme desire, that even if it is for one night, I should reside with those sacred ones who subsist on roots and fruits." Rama, unblemished in his deeds, promised that he would act in this way. "O Vaidehi! Be assured. There is no doubt that you will go there tomorrow." Kakutstha said this to Maithilee, Janaka's daughter. With his well-wishers, Rama then left for the chambers that were in the middle.[664]

Chapter 7(42)

Learned people came and seated themselves near the king on all sides. They spoke about many kinds of things and laughed. Vijaya, Madhumatta, Kashyapa, Pingala, Kusha, Suraji, Kaliya, Bhadra, Dantavakra and Sumagadha—they conversed about many kinds of things that made them laugh. In the course of one such conversation, Raghava asked, 'O Bhadra! What is being talked about in the city? What is happening in the kingdom? What do the residents of the city and the countryside, who are dependent on me, say about me? What do the dependents say about Sita, Bharata and Lakshmana? What do the dependents say about Shatrughna

[664] He emerged from the inner quarters.

and my mother, Kaikeyee? If there are complaints about a king, the residents leave for a new kingdom.'

Thus addressed by Rama, Bhadra joined his hands in salutation and said, 'O king! The residents who are in the city speak auspicious words. O amiable one! They speak about the victory you earned after killing Dashagriva. O bull among men! In their own cities, the citizens repeatedly converse about this.' Thus addressed by Bhadra, Raghava replied in these words. 'The residents of the city may utter agreeable words and disagreeable ones too. Hearing about what they say, I will perform auspicious deeds and avoid inauspicious ones. Do not be scared. Have no fear or anxiety. Tell me what people in the city and the countryside speak about.' Hearing the words spoken by the great-souled Raghava, Bhadra joined his hands in salutation. He controlled himself and uttered these extremely beautiful words in reply. 'O king! Hear about the agreeable and disagreeable words citizens speak in the crossroads, the forests and the groves. "Rama performed the extremely difficult task of building a bridge across the ocean. No gods or danavas had ever done this earlier. He killed the invincible Ravana, with his forces and his mounts. He brought the apes, the bears and the rakshasas under his subjugation. Raghava killed Ravana in the battle and got Sita back. Turning his back on any intolerance, he again brought her back to his own house. But what kind of a heart does he possess? He finds pleasure and happiness with Sita. Though Ravana had forcibly abducted her earlier, he takes her up on his lap. She had been taken to Lanka and had been confined in Ashokavana. She had been under the subjugation of the rakshasas. Why does Rama not find this reprehensible? We will also have to tolerate this from our wives. Subjects follow whatever a king does." O king! The residents of the city say this and many other things, in all the cities and the countryside.' Hearing the words that he spoke, Raghava was greatly afflicted. He asked all the well-wishers, 'Do they say this?' All of them lowered their heads down on the ground and bowed before him. Despondent, they replied to Raghava, 'There is no doubt about this.' Kakutstha heard the words that all of them spoke. The scorcher of enemies gave all of them permission to leave.

Chapter 7(43)

Having allowed the well-wishers to go, Raghava thought and made up his mind. He spoke these words to the gatekeeper who was near him. 'Quickly fetch Soumitri Lakshmana, the one with the auspicious signs, the mighty-armed Bharata and the unvanquished Shatrughna. Hearing Rama's words, the gatekeeper joined his hands in salutation above his head. Without being barred, he went to Lakshmana's house and entered. Joining his hands in salutation again, he addressed him in these words. 'The king wishes to see you. Go there without any delay.' Hearing Raghava's command, Soumitri agreed. Mounting his chariot, he went to Raghava's residence. Seeing that Lakshmana had left, the gatekeeper went to Bharata's presence. Joining his hands in salutation, he spoke these words. 'The king desires to see you.' Bharata heard the words that the gatekeeper had spoken. He swiftly got up from his seat and went there on foot. Seeing that Bharata had left, he[665] quickly went to Shatrughna's residence. Joining his hands in salutation, he addressed him in these words. 'O best among the Raghu lineage! Come. Let us go. The king wishes to see you. Lakshmana and the immensely illustrious Bharata have already left.' Hearing his words about what Rama had commanded, Shatrughna bowed his head down on the ground and went to where Raghava was.

Hearing that the princes had come, he[666] was overcome by thoughts and his senses were distracted. He lowered his head and with a disturbed mind, addressed the gatekeeper in these words. 'Quickly make the princes enter and bring them before me. My life depends on them. They are like my breath of life outside my body.' The princes were attired in white garments. Hearing the commands of the Indra among men, they carefully controlled themselves and entered, joining their hands in salutation. They glanced at his face, which was like the moon when it is grasped by a planet. It was like the setting sun, bereft of all radiance. They saw that the intelligent Rama's eyes were full of tears. They glanced at his face,

---

[665] The gatekeeper.
[666] Rama.

which resembled a lotus with its lustre lost. They quickly lowered their heads at Rama's feet and greeted him. All of them controlled themselves and stood there. However, Rama's eyes were only full of tears. The mighty-armed one embraced them with his arms and raised them. Asking them to be seated, he addressed them in these words. 'You are everything to me. You are my life. O lords of men! I rule over this kingdom because of what you have done. You are accomplished in the sacred texts. You are full of intelligence. O lords of men! Therefore, for my sake, again make efforts.'

Chapter 7(44)

All of them sat down, distressed in their minds. With his mouth dry, Kakutstha addressed them in these words. 'O fortunate ones! All of you listen to what is in my mind. Do not act in a contrary way. Hear what the citizens are saying about me and Sita. There is great and terrible condemnation among the residents of the city and the countryside. It has shattered my inner organs. I have been born in the lineage of the great-souled Ikshvakus. In the city, they are conversing about Sita's evil conduct. O amiable ones! You know that Ravana abducted Sita in the desolate Dandaka forest and that he was destroyed by me. O Soumitri! You yourself saw that the bearer of oblations to the gods[667] and Vayu, who travels in the sky, declared Sita to be devoid of sin. In earlier times, in the presence of the gods and all the rishis, the moon and the sun also averred that Janaka's daughter was devoid of all sin. In the presence of the gods and the gandharvas, in the island of Lanka, the great Indra delivered the one who is pure in conduct into my hands. In my inner soul, I know that the illustrious Sita is pure. That is the reason I accepted Vaidehi and returned to Ayodhya. However, grief because of this great condemnation is shattering my heart now. This great condemnation is spoken about in the cities and in the countryside. In this world, if a person's bad deeds are spoken about, that person

[667] The fire.

is destined for the inferior worlds as long as this recital takes place.
The gods condemn bad deeds. The gods honour deeds. Therefore,
great-souled ones undertake all acts that lead to deeds. O bulls
among men! Scared and terrified of condemnation, I am prepared
to give up my life and all of you, not to speak of Janaka's daughter.
That is the reason you see me immersed in this ocean of grief. I do
not see any other misery that can be greater. O Soumitri! Tomorrow
morning, ask Sumantra to prepare the chariot. Ascend it with Sita
and leave her at the end of the kingdom. The extremely great-souled
Valmiki has a hermitage on the other bank of the Ganga. It is like
heaven and is located on the banks of the Tamasa. O descendant of
the Raghu lineage! Leave her in that desolate region. O Soumitri!
After doing this, return quickly. Act in accordance with my words.
Do not at all answer me back about Sita. If you try to restrain me,
I will be greatly displeased. I am urging all of you, on my arms and
on my life, that after I have stopped speaking, you do not entreat me
in any way. If you respect me, if you follow my commands, you will
now take Sita away from here. Act in accordance with my words.
She has earlier told me that she wants to see the great hermitages
located on the banks of the Ganga. Her wish will also be satisfied.'
With tears flowing from his eyes, Kakutstha said this. Surrounded
by his brothers, the one with dharma in his soul then entered.

Chapter 7(45)

Miserable in his mind, Lakshmana spent the night. His
mouth dry, he addressed Sumantra in these words. 'O
charioteer! Swiftly yoke the horses to the excellent chariot. Cover
the auspicious seat with spreads so that Sita can come there from
the king's residence. From the king's residence, I will take Sita to
the hermitage of the maharshis, the performers of sacred deeds.
Quickly fetch the chariot.' Sumantra acted as he was told and yoked
the excellent steeds. The extremely beautiful and excellent chariot
was equipped with a pleasant couch with spreads. He brought it
to Soumitri, who brought delight to his friends, and said, 'O lord!

The chariot has arrived. Do what you have to.' Thus addressed by Sumantra, Lakshmana entered the royal residence. The bull among men approached Sita and told her, 'O queen! We have been commanded by the king. I am to take you and quickly go to the auspicious hermitage of the sages on the banks of the Ganga.' Vaidehi was thus addressed by the great-souled Lakshmana. Filled with unmatched delight, the idea of going appealed to her. Taking extremely expensive garments and many kinds of jewels, Vaidehi prepared to go. 'I will give these ornaments to the wives of the sages.' Soumitri agreed to what she had said and made Maithilee mount the chariot. Remembering Rama's command, they quickly left on those horses.

At that time, Sita spoke to Lakshmana, who enhanced prosperity. 'O descendant of the Raghu lineage! I can see many inauspicious signs. My eye is twitching and there is a trembling in my body. O Soumitri! A sense of disquiet can be discerned in my heart. Though I am extremely eager, I am also suffering from a great lack of fortitude. O large-eyed one! To my eyes, the earth seems to be empty. With his brothers, I hope your brother is well. O brave one! In particular, I hope so are my mothers-in-law. I hope all the creatures in the city and the countryside are well.' Joining her hands in salutation, Sita sought this from the gods. Hearing this, Lakshmana bowed his head down and honoured Maithilee. With his heart dry, he said, 'All is well.' They reached a hermitage on the banks of the Gomatee where they could dwell.[668] Arising in the morning, Soumitri spoke to the charioteer. 'Quickly yoke the chariot. Like Tryambaka[669] in the mountain, I will today bear the waters of the Bhageerathee on my head.'[670] Without thinking about it, the charioteer swiftly yoked the horses, which possessed the speed of thought, to the chariot. He joined his hands in salutation and told Maithilee, 'Mount.' Hearing the charioteer's words, Sita ascended that excellent chariot, together with Soumitri and the intelligent Sumantra. After they had travelled for half a day, Lakshmana saw

[668] For the night.
[669] Shiva.
[670] That is, Lakshmana wants to bathe in the Ganga.

the Bhageerathee, the store of waters. Miserable, he wept loudly. Sita saw that Lakshmana was greatly afflicted and spoke these words. 'O one who knows about dharma! Why are you weeping? We have reached the banks of the Jahnavee and I have wished this for a long time. O Lakshmana! This is the time for joy. Why are you distressed? O bull among men! You have always remained at Rama's feet. Are you filled with grief because you have been away from him for two nights? O Lakshmana! I also love Rama, more than my own life. However, I am not grieving in this way. Do not be childish. Make me cross the Ganga and make me see the ascetics. I will give them these expensive garments and ornaments. I will honour the maharshis, as they deserve. After spending a night there, we will return to the city again.' Hearing her words, he wiped his auspicious eyes. Using a boat, Lakshmana crossed the sacred Ganga.

Chapter 7(46)

The nishadas prepared and brought an extremely large boat. Raghava's younger brother first made Maithilee climb on to it and then ascended it himself. Lakshmana told Sumantra, 'Stay with the chariot.' Tormented by grief, he asked the boatman to steer the boat. Lakshmana reached the other bank of the Bhageerathee. Joining his hands in salutation and with his voice choking with tears, he addressed Maithilee in these words. 'O Vaidehi! As a result of what people are saying, the noble and intelligent one has asked me to do something that is driving a great stake into my heart. It is better for me to die now. Death would be superior to this. He has engaged me in this kind of task, condemned by the world. O one who is good in vows! Show me your favours and do not be angry with me.' Joining his hands in salutation and prostrating himself on the ground, Lakshmana said this. He desired death for himself and was weeping, his hands joined in salutation. On seeing this, Maithilee became extremely anxious and addressed Lakshmana in these words. 'O Lakshmana! I do not understand this. Tell me the truth. I can see that you are not well. Is everything well with the king? I am urging you in the name of the king among men. What is the truth behind you being tormented? In my presence, you are being commanded by me. Tell me.' When Vaidehi took a pledge in this way, Lakshmana's senses were distressed. With his face and with his words choking because of the tears, he spoke these words. 'O Janaka's daughter! In the midst of the courtiers, he heard the extremely terrible condemnation being voiced about you by the residents of the city and the countryside. O queen! I cannot utter those words in front of you. I have turned my back on those intolerant words[671] that were in the king's heart. As far as I am concerned, you are innocent. But because of those words, the king has cast you aside. O queen! Scared, he has accepted the words spoken by the residents of the city and the countryside and there can be no countering of that decision. I will have to leave you at the end of this hermitage. Though you are expecting, the king has instructed me through his commands. O auspicious one! I will have to leave you here in this sacred and beautiful grove with the hermitages of the brahmana rishis. Do not grieve. King Dasharatha was my father. The brahmana Valmiki, the extremely illustrious bull among sages, was his great friend. Happily seek refuge at the feet of the great-souled one. O Janaka's daughter! Fast and with great attentiveness, reside there with him. Be devoted to your husband and always have Rama in your heart. O queen! That is the way you will obtain great benefit.'

Chapter 7(47)

Janaka's daughter heard Lakshmana's terrible words. Overcome by great sorrow, Vaidehi fell down. She regained her senses after a while, but her eyes were full of tears. With a distressed voice, Janaka's daughter addressed Lakshmana in these words. 'O Lakshmana! The creator has certainly created my body for the sake of suffering grief. Therefore, today, misery has manifested itself in embodied form

[671] I am ignoring them. I have forgotten them.

before me. What crime have I committed in an earlier life? Whom
have I separated from his wife? I am pure in conduct. Nevertheless,
the king has abandoned me. Earlier, I resided in a hermitage,
following Rama's footsteps. O Soumitri! The misery put me into
turmoil, but I controlled it.[672] O amiable one! How will I dwell
alone in a hermitage? Tell me. Overcome with sorrow, how will I
handle this grief? How will I tell the sage about the injury the king
has done to me? What is the reason why the great-souled Raghava
has abandoned me? O Soumitri! Indeed, I should not remain alive.
I should give up my life in the waters of the Jahnavee. But if I do
that, my husband's royal lineage will laugh at me. O Soumitri! Do
what you have been commanded to. I will suffer misery. Abandon
me. Follow the instructions of the king. However, listen to my
words. In particular, I am joining my hands in salutation before my
mothers-in-law. Ask them to accept this honour. I am bowing my
head down and worshipping at their feet. Ask about their welfare
and that of the king. "Always behave towards the citizens as you
behave towards your brothers. This is your supreme dharma and
you will obtain excellent fame because of this. O bull among men!
Let the citizens benefit from the king following dharma. I am not
grieving over my own body. O descendant of the Raghu lineage!
Free yourself from the condemnation of the citizens."[673] Thus
addressed by Sita, Lakshmana's senses were afflicted. He bowed his
head down on the ground and was incapable of saying anything.
Weeping in a loud voice, he circumambulated her. Then he again
mounted the boat and urged the boatman. Bearing the burden of
sorrow, he reached the northern bank. Confounded by grief, he
quickly ascended the chariot. Like one without a protector, he
repeatedly glanced back towards Sita. As he proceeded, Lakshmana
saw that she was writhing around on the other bank. From the
chariot and from a distance, Lakshmana repeatedly looked back
towards her. Anxious, he repeatedly looked back towards Sita, who
was overwhelmed with grief. The ascetic lady was overcome by the

[672] Because I was with Rama.
[673] The text doesn't suggest any reason for this part to be put within quotes. Sita
might have directed these words at Lakshmana too. But it seems as if this is a message to
Rama, to be conveyed by Lakshmana. Therefore, we have put it within quotes.

burden of grief. The illustrious one could not see her protector.[674] She was filled with misery and wept in a loud voice, like a peahen in the forest.

Chapter 7(48)

The sons of the sage saw Sita weeping there. They rushed to the illustrious Valmiki, supreme in intelligence. The sons of the sage worshipped the feet of the sage, the maharshi. All of them told him about a lady weeping in a loud voice. 'O illustrious one! O great-souled one! We have never seen anything like this before. There is a wife who is like Shri. She is confounded and is shrieking in a distorted tone. O illustrious one! It is best that you come and see for yourself. She is like a goddess who has been dislodged from the sky. We do not think she is human. You should go and welcome her with proper rites.' Hearing their words, the one who knew about dharma used his intelligence to determine what should be done. He used the insight obtained through his austerities and went to the spot where Maithilee was. Walking on foot for a short while, the great sage reached the place. Taking excellent arghya, he reached the banks of the Jahnavee. He saw Raghava's beloved wife there, like one who was without a protector. Sita was overcome by the burden of grief. Valmiki, bull among sages, addressed her in sweet words, as if delighting her with his energy. 'O queen! O Dasharatha's daughter-in-law! O Rama's queen! O Janaka's daughter! O one who is devoted to her husband! Welcome. Because of the fruits of dharma, I have got to know that you have come. My heart has got to know about all the reasons. O Sita! Through the insight obtained through austerities, I know that you are devoid of sin. O Vaidehi! You are pure in sentiments and you have now come to me. My hermitage is not very far from here. Ascetics engaged in austerities are there. Reside there. They will always nurture you, like their own children. Accept this arghya. Do not be scared and have no anxiety.

[674] This could mean either Rama or Lakshmana.

Do not grieve. It is as if you are in your own home.' Sita heard the extraordinary words uttered by the sage. She bowed her head down at his feet. Joining her hands in salutation, she agreed. The sage left. Joining her hands in salutation, she followed him at the rear towards the spot where the controlled ascetics, always devoted to dharma, were. They saw the sage coming, with Vaidehi following him. Extremely happy, they came there and spoke these words. 'O best among sages! O lord! You have come after a long time.[675] All of us are greeting you. Tell us what we should do.' Hearing their words, Valmiki replied, 'Sita, the wife of the intelligent Rama, has arrived. She is Dasharatha's daughter-in-law and Janaka's daughter. Though she is innocent, she has been abandoned by her husband. She must always be protected by me. Look towards her with great affection. Pay heed to my words. In particular, honour her.' The immensely illustrious one repeatedly assured Vaidehi. Surrounded by his disciples, the greatly ascetic one returned to his own hermitage.[676]

Chapter 7(49)

After seeing that Maithilee Sita had entered the hermitage, Lakshmana was distressed in his mind. He was overcome by a terrible and severe torment. The greatly energetic one spoke to Sumantra, the charioteer who was also a counsellor. 'Because of the torment on account of Sita, you will behold the intelligent Rama's misery. What can be a greater misery for Raghava than having to give up Janaka's daughter, his wife who is pure in conduct? It is evident this is destiny. O charioteer! I think the separation of Raghava from Vaidehi is because of that. Destiny is impossible to cross. When he is angry, Raghava can kill the gods, the gandharvas, the asuras and the rakshasas. But he has to follow destiny. Earlier, because of my father's command, he had to reside for fourteen years

---

[675] Obviously, Valmiki had gone to meet Sita from his own hermitage. The other sages, in their respective hermitages, had not met him for some time.

[676] He left Sita with the other ascetics.

in the extremely terrible and desolate forest. On hearing the words of the citizens, this exile of Sita is a greater grief than that. It seems to me to be cruel. O charioteer! This is a deed that destroys fame. How can it be based on dharma? He acted in this way towards Maithilee only because citizens spoke injurious words.' Lakshmana said this and many other things.

Hearing these, Sumantra joined his hands in salutation and said the following words. 'O Soumitri! You should not be tormented about Maithilee. O Lakshmana! In front of your father, the brahmana had mentioned this earlier. He said that Rama's misery would be lasting and that he would have few friends. After some time, this great one, with dharma in his soul, would abandon you, Maithilee, Shatrughna and Bharata. O Soumitri! You should mention this to Bharata. When the king[677] had asked, Durvasa had told him this. O bull among men! In the presence of the great king, Vasishtha and me, the rishi had spoken these words. On hearing the rishi's words, the bull among men[678] had told me, "O charioteer! Never reveal this in front of people." O one who is amiable to behold! I controlled myself and never acted contrary to the words spoken by that guardian of the world. O amiable one! I should not have revealed it in front of you either. O descendant of the Raghu lineage! However, if you wish to hear it, listen. The Indra among men had told me about this secret earlier. Nevertheless, I can recount it before you.' Destiny is extremely difficult to transgress. Hearing these great words, filled with grave meaning, Soumitri replied in the following words. 'O charioteer! Tell me the truth.'

Chapter 7(50)

The charioteer was thus urged by the great-souled Lakshmana. He began to speak the words that had been uttered by the rishi. 'In ancient times, there was a great sage named Durvasa and he was

[677] Dasharatha.
[678] Dasharatha.

Atri's son. He resided in Vasishtha's sacred hermitage during the rainy season. To see the great-souled priest,[679] your greatly energetic and immensely illustrious father had himself gone to that hermitage. He saw the great sage[680] seated to Vasishtha's left, blazing in his energy and resembling the sun. Humbly, he greeted those two sages, best among ascetics. Thus worshipped, both of them welcomed the king. Having been offered padya, fruits and roots, he sat down with the sages. Having sat down with them, he engaged in an extremely pleasant conversation with the supreme rishis. It was midday and the sun was in the middle of the sky. After some time, in the course of the conversation, the king joined his hands in salutation and spoke to Atri's great-souled son, the store of austerities. "O illustrious one! How long will my lineage last? What will be Rama's lifespan? What will be the lifespans of my other sons? What will be the lifespan of Rama's daughter? O illustrious one! I wish to know what will happen to my lineage. Please tell me."

'Hearing the words spoken by King Dasharatha, the extremely energetic Durvasa started to speak. "Rama will be the lord of Ayodhya for a long period of time. His followers will be happy and prosperous. However, for some reason, the one with dharma in his soul, will abandon the illustrious Maithilee for a long period of time. After ruling the kingdom for eleven thousand years, Rama will go to Brahma's world. The destroyer of enemy cities will perform many prosperous horse sacrifices. Kakutstha will establish many royal lineages."[681] After telling the king about these lineages that would come, the extremely energetic and immensely radiant one became silent. When the sage became silent, King Dasharatha honoured those two great-souled ones and returned to his excellent city. I heard what the sage had said in those earlier times. Having heard, I secreted it in my heart. There can be no violation of what he said. O Raghava! That being the case, you should not be tormented. O supreme among men! For Sita's sake and for Raghava's sake, be firm.'

679 Vasishtha.
680 Durvasa.
681 The Critical Edition excises a shloka where Durvasa said Rama would have two sons.

Hearing the extremely astounding words spoken by the charioteer, he[682] uttered words of praise and obtained unmatched delight. Lakshmana and the charioteer conversed with each other along the route. Since the sun had set, they spent the night near the Gomatee.

Chapter 7(51)

The descendant of the Raghu lineage spent the night near the Gomatee. Having woken in the morning, Lakshmana departed. When half of the day was over, the maharatha entered Ayodhya, full of jewels and inhabited by healthy and happy people. The extremely intelligent Soumitri was filled with great despondency. 'What will I say when I go there and approach Rama's feet?' While he was thinking this, he saw Rama's residence in front of him. It was extremely large and was like the moon. The supreme among men descended near the gate of the royal residence. He entered without being obstructed, his face hung downwards and distress in his mind. He saw the miserable Raghava, seated on his excellent seat. He saw his elder brother in front of him, his eyes full of tears. With his senses afflicted, Lakshmana grasped his feet. He controlled himself and joining his hands in salutation, spoke these miserable words. 'O noble one! Placing your command at the forefront, I have abandoned Janaka's daughter. As commanded, I have left her on the banks of the Ganga, in Valmiki's auspicious hermitage. O brave one! I have returned thereafter, to serve at your feet. O tiger among men! Do not grieve. The progress of time is like this. Therefore, someone who is spirited and learned like you should not sorrow. All stores of riches are exhausted. Everything that rises up must fall down. Any association ends in disassociation. Life ends in death. You are capable of assuring your soul yourself. You can conquer your mind and all the worlds. O Kakutstha! Why are you then sorrowing like this? Bulls among men who are like you are not confounded in this

[682] Lakshmana.

way. O king! You abandoned Maithilee because of the censure. O tiger among men! Control yourself and resort to your fortitude. Cast aside this feeble intelligence. Do not be tormented.' Kakutstha was addressed by the great-souled Lakshmana in this way. Filled with great affection, he spoke to Soumitri, who was devoted to his friends. 'O Lakshmana! O best among men! It is indeed as you have said. O brave one! I am satisfied that you have acted in accordance with my command. O amiable one! My torment has been dispelled and I have withdrawn from it. O Lakshmana! You have entreated me in extremely sweet words.'

Chapter 7(52)

Sumantra arrived and addressed Raghava in these words. 'O king! Some ascetics are waiting at the gate, having been stopped there. At the forefront of those maharshis is one who is named Bhargava Chyavana. O great king! They have urged that they wish to see you. O tiger among men! They reside along the banks of the Yamuna and seek your favours.' Hearing his words, Rama, who knew about dharma, replied, 'Let the great-souled brahmanas, with Bhargava at the forefront, enter.' Placing the king's command at the forefront, he[683] joined his hands in salutation above his head and asked the many revered ascetics who were at the gate to enter. There were more than one hundred of them, blazing in their own energies. Those great-souled ascetics entered the royal residence. Those brahmanas held pots filled with water from all the tirthas. They held many kinds of fruits and roots that they had brought for Rama. Rama accepted everything that had been offered with affection—all the water from the tirthas and the many kinds of fruit. The mighty-armed one spoke to all those great sages, 'As you deserve, please sit down on these excellent seats.' Hearing the words spoken by Rama, all those maharshis sat down on those beautiful and golden seats, spread with cushions. The destroyer of enemy

---

[683] Sumantra.

cities saw that the rishis had seated themselves. Controlling himself and joining his hands in salutation, Raghava addressed them in these words. 'O stores of austerities! Why have you come here? What can I do for you? All the commands of the maharshis will be cheerfully undertaken. Everything in this kingdom and the life that is in my heart is all for the sake of the brahmanas. I am stating this truthfully.' On hearing his words, loud words of praise arose from the rishis who resided along the banks of the Yamuna, fierce in their austerities. Filled with great delight, those great-souled ones said, 'O best among men! Other than you, there is no one on earth who could have said this. O king! We have been to many kings who are extremely strong. Despite hearing about the importance of the task, the idea of taking a pledge to accomplish it did not appeal to them. However, displaying the due respect to brahmanas, you have taken a pledge without ascertaining the reason. There is no doubt that you will do what you have promised to. You will certainly save the rishis from a great fear.'

Chapter 7(53)

When the rishis said this, Kakutstha addressed them in these words. 'Tell me what task must be done for you. I will destroy your fear.' When Kakutstha said this, Bhargava spoke these words. 'O lord of men! Hear the reason for our fear and it is the foundation of the country's fear too. O Rama! Earlier, in krita yuga, there was an extremely strong daitya. He was the eldest son of Lola and the great asura's name was Madhu. He was the refuge of brahmanas and possessed great intelligence. He had unmatched affection for the extremely generous gods. Madhu was full of valour, extremely controlled and devoted to dharma. Revering him a lot, Rudra gave him an extraordinary boon. Extremely delighted, the great-souled one gave the immensely valiant one an extremely radiant trident that was superior to his own trident and addressed him in these words. "You possess unmatched dharma. I am greatly delighted with you. Therefore, as a mark of my favours, I am giving you this excellent and auspicious weapon. O great asura! As long as you do not act against the gods and the brahmanas, till that time, this trident will remain with you. However, if you act in a contrary way, you will no longer possess it and it will be destroyed. As long as you possess it, you can fight without any anxiety. The trident will consume[684] and again return to your hand." Having obtained this boon from Rudra, the great asura again bowed down before Mahadeva and addressed him in these words. "O illustrious one! O god! O lord of the gods! Let this excellent trident also remain in my lineage." When Madhu said this, the god Shiva Mahadeva, the lord of all creatures, replied, "This cannot be. However, because of my auspicious favours, your words cannot be futile either. Therefore, this trident will pass on to one of your sons. As long as the trident is in the hand of that son and as long as he holds the trident in his hand, he cannot be killed by any creature." Thus, Madhu obtained this great and extraordinary boon from the god. The best among the asuras created an extremely radiant residence.[685] His immensely fortunate and beloved wife was Kumbhinasi. The immensely radiant one was the daughter of Visvavasu and Anala. Her son was the terrible and extremely valiant one named Lavana. Since childhood, he was evil in his soul and wicked in his conduct. On seeing that his son was insolent, Madhu became filled with sorrow. However, though he grieved, he did not tell him anything. Having left his world, he entered Varuna's abode. He gave Lavana the trident and told him about the boon. Thanks to the powers of the trident and his own evil-souled nature, he tormented the three worlds, especially the ascetics. These are the powers of Lavana and his trident. O Kakutstha! Having heard about it, determine what is best for us. O Rama! O brave one! Earlier, because of our fear, we have sought freedom from fear from many kings. But we have not been able to find a protector. We heard that you have killed Ravana, with his forces and mounts. We seek a protector in you. There is no other king on earth. We are afflicted by fear on account of Lavana and desire that you should save us.'

[684] The enemy.
[685] For housing the trident.

Chapter 7(54)

Thus addressed by the rishi, Rama joined his hands in salutation and replied. 'What does Lavana eat? What is his conduct? Where does he reside?' Hearing Raghava's words, all the rishis told him how Lavana had grown up. 'He eats all creatures, especially ascetics. His conduct is always terrible. He always resides in Madhuvana. Every day, he always kills and eats ten thousand lions, tigers, deer, leopards and humans. The immensely strong one eats many other creatures. They face destruction, as if they face Death with a gaping mouth.' Hearing this, Raghava addressed the great sages in these words. 'Let your fear be dispelled. I will slay that rakshasa.' He thus took a pledge before the sages, fierce in their austerities. The descendant of the Raghu lineage summoned all his brothers and asked them, 'O brave ones! Who will slay Lavana? Whose share does he belong to? Is he meant for the mighty-armed Bharata or Shatrughna?' When Raghava said this, Bharata replied in these words. 'I will kill him. He should be part of my share.' Hearing Bharata's words, Lakshmana's younger brother,[686] who was full of power and valour, got up from his golden seat. Bowing down before the lord of men, Shatrughna spoke these words. 'The mighty-armed middle one[687] among the descendants of Raghu has performed his appointed task. O noble one! Earlier, the noble one has protected the empty city of Ayodhya, despite his heart being tormented while he waited for your return. O king! He had to tolerate many kinds of hardship. In Nandigrama, the great-souled one slept on a bed of misery. He ate fruits and roots. He had matted hair and was attired in bark. The descendant of the Raghava lineage undertook such kinds of hardships. O king! If you send me, while he remains here, he will not have to face a hardship again.' Thus addressed by Shatrughna, Raghava again said, 'O Kakutstha! Then let it be that way. Act according to my instructions. O mighty-armed one! I am conferring the kingdom of the auspicious city of Madhu on you, since it is your wish that Bharata should reside here. You are brave and accomplished in learning. You are capable

---

[686] Shatrughna.
[687] The brother in the middle.

of establishing a prosperous city and an auspicious countryside
in Madhu's dominion. When a lineage is uprooted and a king is
also slain, a person who does not set up a king there goes to hell.[688]
Pay heed to my words. Having killed Madhu's son, Lavana, who
is wicked in his determination, follow dharma and rule over that
kingdom. O brave one! You should not speak any words in reply
that contradict mine. Since I am older and since you are a child,
there is no doubt that you must act in this way. O Kakutstha! With
Vasishtha at the forefront, and with the other brahmanas following
the rituals and pronouncing mantras, it is my desire that I should
make efforts to consecrate you.'[689]

Chapter 7(55)

When Rama spoke in this way, Shatrughna, who was full of
valour, was filled with great shame. In a soft and gentle voice,
he replied, 'O bull among men! One must certainly act in accordance
with your command. O immensely fortunate one! It is impossible to
cross your instructions. O king! O bull among men! I will indeed do
what you desire.' When the brave and great-souled Shatrughna said
this, Rama was delighted and spoke to Lakshmana and Bharata.
'Control yourselves and bring all the objects required for the
consecration. I will consecrate the invincible tiger among men today.
O Katkusthas![690] Convey my command and summon the priest, the
priests who will offer oblations, the priests who will officiate and all
the ministers.' Thus commanded by the king, the maharathas acted
in that way. With the priest at the forefront, they made arrangements
for the consecration and entered the royal palace, which was like
Purandara's residence. After this, the great-souled Shatrughna's
consecration was undertaken, delighting everyone who was in
Raghava's prosperous city. Having performed the consecration,

---

[688] To prevent anarchy, a king is needed. Therefore, a person who kills an existing
king must ensure that there is a subsequent king.
[689] As the king of Madhu's dominion.
[690] In the dual, addressing Lakshmana and Bharata.

Raghava took Shatrughna up on his lap and addressed him in these sweet words, filling him with energy. 'O destroyer of enemy cities! O amiable one! O descendant of the Raghu lineage! I am giving you this divine and invincible arrow. Kill Lavana with it. O Kakutstha! When he was lying down on the great ocean and could not be seen by the gods and the asuras, the god Svayambhu[691] created this arrow. While he was invisible to all creatures and was filled with rage in a desire to kill the evil-souled Madhu and Kaitabha, the brave one fashioned this excellent arrow. Desiring to create the three worlds, he used this excellent arrow to kill those two in the battle and created the worlds. O Shatrughna! Desiring to kill Ravana earlier, I did not shoot this arrow because there would have been great fear among creatures. The great-souled Tryambaka gave Madhu the excellent weapon of a giant trident for the sake of slaying the enemy. Keeping it in that residence and repeatedly worshipping it, he[692] looks towards all the directions, seeking to obtain food for himself. Whenever anyone wishes to challenge him to a battle, the rakshasa seizes the trident and reduces him to ashes. O tiger among men! When he is outside the city, he is without a weapon.[693] With your weapon, remain at the gate, before he has entered the city. O bull among men! O mighty-armed one! Challenge him to a fight before he has entered the residence. You will thereby slay the rakshasa. If you act in any other way, he cannot be killed. O brave one! If you do what I have said, he will be destroyed. I have told you everything about the calamity that resulted from the trident. The prosperous Shitikantha[694] gave it and it is invincible.'

Chapter 7(56)

Kakutstha said this and repeatedly praised him. The descendant of the Raghu lineage again spoke these words. 'O bull among

[691] Vishnu.
[692] Lavana.
[693] When he is hunting for food outside the city, he doesn't have the trident with him.
[694] The one with the blue throat, Shiva.

men! There are four thousand horses, two thousand chariots and
one hundred elephants here. The shops along the roads have
many kinds of merchandise.[695] O Shatrughna! Let dancers and
actors follow you. O bull among men! Take ten thousand golden
coins. O Shatrughna! Go with sufficient quantities of riches and
mounts. O brave one! Take excellent, cheerful and healthy forces
who are armed properly. O supreme among men! Address them,
give them gifts and make them happy. O Raghava! In a place
where there are no wives and relatives, large numbers of servants
reside only when they are happy. Therefore, depart with a lot of
happy people and a large army. However, approach Madhuvana
alone, with a bow in your hand. That way, the subjects will not
know that you are going there to fight. Without arising suspicion,
you will be able to approach Lavana, Madhu's son. O bull among
men! There is no one else who can bring about his death. As
soon as he sees anyone approach, Lavana kills him. O amiable
one! Lavana should be killed when summer is over and it is a
night in the rainy season. That is the time for the evil-minded
one's death. Let your soldiers advance with the maharshis at the
forefront. When there is a little bit of summer left, the waters
of the Jahnavee can be crossed. Control yourself and make all
the forces camp along the banks of the river. O one who is light
in valour! With your bow, advance ahead.' Rama spoke in this
way to the immensely strong Shatrughna. He[696] summoned the
foremost commanders and addressed them in these words. 'These
are the camps earmarked for you to reside in. Dwell there, without
any conflicts. But make sure there are no impediments.' Having
been commanded in this way, the large army departed. He greeted
Kousalya, Sumitra and Kaikeyee. Circumambulating Rama, he
bowed his head down before him. Shatrughna, the scorcher of
enemies, took Rama's leave. He joined his hands in salutation
and bowed down before Lakshmana and Bharata. Controlling
himself, Shatrughna circumambulated the priest, Vasishtha. The
immensely strong one departed.

[695] Take those with you.
[696] Shatrughna.

Chapter 7(57)

After the entire army had left, it resided for one month along the path. Shatrughna left quickly, alone and speedily. After residing for two nights along the way, the brave descendant of the Raghava lineage reached Valmiki's excellent and sacred hermitage. He greeted the great-souled Valmiki, supreme among sages. He joined his hands in salutation and addressed him in these words. 'O illustrious one! I have come here, wishing to do something for my senior. Tomorrow morning, I will leave for the west, Varuna's direction.' Hearing Shatrughna's words, the bull among sages smiled and replied, 'O great-souled one! O immensely illustrious one! Welcome. O amiable one! My hermitage is for the lineage of the Raghavas. Without any hesitation, accept a seat, padya and arghya from me. Accept the honours and fruits and roots as food. O Kakutstha! Eat and be filled with great satisfaction.' After eating, the mighty-armed one asked the maharshi. 'Near the hermitage, there are signs of a former sacrifice. Whom does this belong to?'

Hearing what he said, Valmiki replied in these words. 'O Shatrughna! Listen to whom this place belonged to in earlier times. Your ancestor was the son of the great-souled King Sudasa. His son was named Mitrasaha. He was valiant and devoted to dharma. Even when he was a child, Soudasa[697] started to hunt. While he was roaming around, the brave one saw two rakshasas. They were in the form of two terrible tigers. Even when they devoured thousands of deer, they were not satisfied. It was not sufficient for them. He saw that those two rakshasas had emptied the forest of all deer. Filled with rage, he used a large arrow to kill one of them. Soudasa, bull among men, brought down one. Without anxiety and with his intolerance over, he looked towards the slain rakshasa. While he was thus looking, the rakshasa's companion was filled with great and terrible torment. He told Soudasa, "You have slain my companion, though he has committed no crime. O wicked one! Therefore, I will give you the reaction to your action." Having said this, the rakshasa vanished from the spot. When time passed,

[697] Sudasa's son, Mitrasaha.

Mitrasaha became the king. The king performed a sacrifice near that hermitage.[698] He performed a great horse sacrifice, tended to by Vasishtha. There was a great sacrifice there and it lasted for an extremely large number of years. It was extensive and greatly prosperous and was like a sacrifice of the gods. When the sacrifice was over, the rakshasa remembered the former enmity. It assumed Vasishtha's form, came before the king and said, "Now that the sacrifice is over, give me some flesh to eat. Quickly give it to me. You should not think about it." He heard the words spoken by the rakshasa who could assume any form at will. The lord of the earth spoke to those who were skilled in preparing food. "Swiftly prepare tasty oblations[699] that are mixed with meat, so that the preceptor is satisfied." Hearing the king's command, the cook was scared in his mind. But the rakshasa assumed the form of a cook and did what had been asked. It offered the flesh of a human to the king and said, "These are tasty oblations with meat, prepared by me." O tiger among men! He,[700] with his wife, Madayanti, offered the meat prepared and brought by the rakshasa and offered it to Vasishtha. The brahmana got to know that food with human flesh had been brought. He was filled with great rage and started to say the following. "O king! Since you wish to serve this kind of food to me, there is no doubt that this will be your food." The king and his wife repeatedly prostrated themselves before him. They told Vasishtha what the one in the form of a brahmana[701] had told them. Learning from the lord of men that the rakshasa had distorted everything, Vasishtha again spoke to the king, lord of men. "I spoke those words when I was overcome by rage. I am incapable of rendering them false. However, I will grant you a boon. The duration of this curse will be for twelve years. O Indra among kings! Because of my favours, you will not remember the past." Thus the king, the destroyer of enemies, was cursed in this way. He got his kingdom back and protected the subjects. O

---

[698] Where the rakshasa had been killed.

[699] *Havishya.*

[700] Soudasa.

[701] The rakshasa.

Raghava! This is the auspicious and extensive sacrificial ground of Kalmashapada.[702] You asked about it. His hermitage is nearby.'

Having heard the extremely terrible account about that Indra among kings, he[703] honoured the maharshi and entered the cottage made out of leaves.

Chapter 7(58)

On the night when Shatrughna entered the cottage made out of leaves, Sita gave birth to two sons that very night. In the middle of the night, the children who were sons of the sages came and gave Valmiki the agreeable news about Sita's auspicious delivery. 'O immensely energetic one! Protect her and destroy the evil demons.' Hearing their words, the sage was filled with delight. He protected her by performing the rituals that would kill demons and destroy rakshasas. The brahmana took some kusha grass in his fist and cut it.[704] To protect them and destroy demons, Valmiki gave each of the two one half. To the pronouncement of mantras, the one who was born first was named Kusha. He was cleansed with kusha grass. That is the reason he was named Kusha. The one who was born later was carefully cleansed with the cut off bit that was left. The aged one thus gave him the name of Lava. Hence, those two twin sons obtained the names of Lava and Kusha. He[705] said, 'Because of what I have done, they will be famous by these two names. They were protected in this way at the hands of the controlled sage. They were protected and were cleansed of all sin. They[706] performed the rites to protect them and gave them their gotras and their names. They pronounced that these two auspicious ones were the sons of Rama and Sita.' In the middle of the night,

---

[702] Soudasa's name. He was thus known as Kalmashapada, because his feet (pada) had a blemish (kalmasha). The story has been recounted earlier.

[703] Shatrughna.

[704] The word lava means to cut off.

[705] Valmiki.

[706] The sages.

Shatrughna heard this extremely pleasant news. In the night, he went to the cottage of leaves and said, 'This is good fortune. It is fortunate.' In this way, the great-souled Shatrughna rejoiced. Swift in speed, the monsoon night in the month of Shravana passed. In the morning, the immensely valiant one performed the morning rituals in due order. He joined his hands in salutation and took the sage's permission. He then again left for the western direction. Spending seven nights along the way, he reached the banks of the Yamuna. There, he resided in the hermitage of the rishis who are auspicious in their deeds. Residing with the immensely illustrious sages, with Bhargava at the forefront, the king[707] heard many kinds of accounts.

Chapter 7(59)

When night commenced, Shatrughna asked the brahmana Chyavana, the descendant of the Bhrigu lineage, about Lavana's strengths and weaknesses. 'O brahmana! Using the strength of the trident, whom has he brought down earlier? Who are the ones who came to have a duel with the one who possesses the excellent trident?'

Hearing the words spoken by the great-souled Shatrughna, the immensely energetic Chyavana replied to the descendant of the Raghu lineage. 'O bull among men! It[708] has performed innumerable deeds. There was the conduct of the powerful one from the Ikshvaku lineage.[709] Hear about it. Earlier, in Ayodhya, there was a powerful king who was Yuvanashva's son. The valiant one was famous in the three worlds as Mandhata. That lord of the earth brought the entire earth under his rule. The king then made efforts to conquer the world of the gods. Indra and the great-souled gods suffered from terrible fear, because

---

[707] Shatrughna.
[708] The trident.
[709] Mandhata.

Mandhata was making efforts, wishing to conquer the world of the gods. The king took a pledge, "I will take away half of Shakra's throne and half of his kingdom. I will bind down large numbers of gods." The chastiser of Paka got to know about his wicked intention. He addressed Yuvanashva's son in these comforting words. "O bull among men! You have still not been able to become the king of the human world. Without bringing the earth under your subjugation, you desire the kingdom of the gods. O brave one! After having brought the entire earth under your subjugation, use your servants, forces and mounts to obtain the kingdom of the gods." Thus addressed by Indra, Mandhata replied in these words. "O Shakra! Where on earth is my rule countered?" The one with the one thousand eyes said, "There is the rakshasa named Lavana. O unblemished one! He is Madhu's son and in Madhuvana, he does not follow your commands." The one with the one thousand eyes spoke these disagreeable and terrible words. Hearing these, the king was unable to say anything in reply. Ashamed, he lowered his face. The lord of men was ashamed. With a lowered face, he did not say anything. Taking his leave of the one with one thousand eyes, he again returned to this prosperous world.

'His heart was filled with intolerance. With his servants, forces and mounts, the unblemished one arrived to bring Madhu's son under his subjugation. The bull among men desired to fight against Lavana. He sent a messenger to Lavana. He went to Madhu's son and spoke many disagreeable words. Consequently, the rakshasa ate up the messenger. When the messenger did not return for a long time, the king was filled with rage. From every direction, he afflicted the rakshasa with a shower of arrows. Lavana laughed and seized the trident in his hand. To slay the king and his followers, he hurled that excellent weapon. Blazing, the trident reduced the king, his servants, his forces and his mounts to ashes and returned to Lavana's hand. Thus, the extremely great king was slain with his forces and mounts. O brave one! The strength of that excellent trident is immeasurable. There is no doubt that you will kill Lavana tomorrow morning, as long as he has not taken up his weapon. If you are swift, your victory is certain.'

Chapter 7(60)

The great-souled Shatrughna desired the auspicious victory.
While they were talking and conversing, the night passed
quickly. The morning sparkled. Goaded by hunger and searching
for food, at that time, the brave rakshasa emerged from his city.
Meanwhile, the brave Shatrughna crossed the river Yamuna. With
a bow in his hand, he stood at the gate of Madhupura.[710] The
rakshasa was cruel in his deeds. When half the day was over, he
returned with a large burden of many thousands of creatures he had
killed. He saw Shatrughna stationed at the gate, holding a weapon.
The rakshasa asked him, 'Why are you acting in this way? O worst
among men! In my rage, I have eaten thousands who have wielded
weapons like this. Do you wish for your death? O worst of men!
Today, I have not collected my complete quota of food. O evil-
minded one! How have you managed to enter my mouth on your
own?' Having said this, he laughed repeatedly. Shatrughna was full
of valour. Filled with anger, tears started to fall from his eyes. The
great-souled Shatrughna was filled with anger towards him. Rays of
energy began to emerge from all over his body. Extremely enraged,
Shatrughna spoke to the roamer in the night. 'O one who is evil in
intelligence! I wish to fight against you. There will be a duel with
you. I am Dasharatha's son and the intelligent Rama's brother. My
name is Shatrughna. I am the slayer of enemies.[711] I have come here
wishing to kill you. Therefore, I wish to fight against you. Grant
me a duel. You are the enemy of all creatures. You will not escape
from me with your life.' Thus addressed, the rakshasa laughed and
replied to the best of men, 'O evil-minded one! It is good fortune
that you have come here. The rakshasa named Ravana was my
brother through my mother's side.[712] O worst among men! On
account of a woman, he was slain by the evil-minded Rama. Earlier,
I have pardoned and ignored that destruction of Ravana's lineage.
However, in particular, you are standing in front of me now. I have

---

[710] Madhu's city.

[711] Since *shatrughna* means a slayer of enemies, there is a play on words.

[712] Lavanasura's mother was Kumbhini, Madhu's wife. Kumbhini was Ravana's sister.

not only defeated all these creatures. You, and these worst among men, are like grass to me. O evil-minded one! You desire to fight. I will grant you a fight. I will give you what you want. Let me prepare my weapon.' Shatrughna told him, 'Clinging on to your life, where will you go? A person who has cleansed his soul does not let go of an enemy who has arrived, even if he happens to be weak. If a person is weak in intelligence and lets an enemy go, that foolish-minded one is killed, like a coward.'

Chapter 7(61)

He heard what the great-souled Shatrughna had spoken. Filled with fierce anger, he said, 'Wait. Wait.' He wrung one hand with another hand and gnashed his teeth. Lavana challenged the tiger of the Raghu lineage. Shatrughna, the slayer of the enemies of the gods, addressed Lavana, who was terrible in his valour, in these words. 'When you defeated the others, Shatrughna had not yet been born. Today, struck by arrows, you will go to Yama's abode. Just as the gods witnessed Ravana being killed in the battle, the rishis, the brahmanas and the learned ones will see a wicked one like you killed by me today. O roamer in the night! You will fall down today, burnt by my arrows. The city and the countryside will obtain peace. Today, an arrow that is like the vajra will be shot from my hand and will penetrate your heart, like the rays of the sun entering a lotus.' Thus addressed, Lavana became senseless with rage and hurled a giant tree at Shatrughna's chest. The brave one shattered this into one hundred fragments. The rakshasa saw that his attempt had been rendered futile. The powerful one again seized many trees and hurled them towards Shatrughna. As the large number of trees descended, the energetic Shatrughna used three and four arrows with drooping tufts to sever each of these. Shatrughna shot a shower of arrows towards the rakshasa's chest. However, the rakshasa was full of valour and was not distressed. Lavana laughed and playfully uprooted a tree. He struck him on the head with this and with his limbs affected, he lost his senses.

When the brave one fell down, great sounds of lamentation arose among the rishis, the large number of gods, the gandharvas and the apsaras.

Shatrughna had fallen down on the ground. Thinking that he had been killed, the rakshasa ignored him. He found the opportunity to enter his own residence. However, on seeing that he had fallen down on the ground, he did not seize his trident. Taking him to be dead, he raised up that burden of food. Honoured by the rishis, at the gate of the rakshasa's house, he regained his senses in an instant and again seized his weapons. He grasped the divine, invincible and excellent arrow. It was terrible, blazing in energy, and filled the ten directions. It resembled the vajra. It was like the vajra in force. It was like Meru and Mandara in its powers. It was covered everywhere with drooping tufts and was invincible in battle. The revered arrow was smeared all over with sandalwood paste. Its feathers were beautiful. It was extremely terrible to Indras among danavas, Indras among mountains and asuras. It scorched like the fire of destruction that manifests itself at the end of a yuga. On seeing it, all the creatures were filled with terror. The gods, the asuras, the gandharvas, large numbers of apsaras and the entire universe were troubled. They presented themselves before the grandfather. They spoke to the god, the lord of the gods, the one who grants boons, the great grandfather. 'O god! Has the destruction of the worlds arrived? Is this the end of the yuga? O great grandfather! We have not seen anything like this before, or heard of it. O lord! The gods are filled with fear and confusion. It is the destruction of the worlds.' Hearing their words, Brahma, the grandfather of the worlds, told them that there was no reason to fear. There was nothing for the gods to be scared about. 'Shatrughna has picked up this arrow to kill Lavana. O supreme among the gods! All of you have been confounded by its energy. O children! This arrow is full of energy and you are scared because of that. Earlier, this belonged to the eternal god who is the creator of the worlds.[713] The great-souled one created this great arrow to slay the two daityas, Madhu and Kaitabha. Only Vishnu knows

[713] Vishnu.

about this arrow, which is filled with energy. Earlier, it was the embodied form of the great-souled Vishnu himself. Go and behold how Rama's great-souled and brave younger brother uses it to slay Lavana, best among rakshasas.' They heard the pleasant words of the god of the gods. They went to the spot where Shatrughna and Lavana were fighting.

The divine arrow was held in Shatrughna's hand. All the creatures saw it, like the fire that arises at the time of the destruction of a yuga. The descendant of the Raghu lineage saw that the sky was covered with gods. He repeatedly roared like a lion and again glanced towards Lavana. The great-souled Shatrughna challenged him and filled with rage, Lavana presented himself for the encounter. The best among archers stretched his bow all the way back up to his ears and shot that large arrow towards Lavana's broad chest. Swiftly penetrating his chest, it entered rasatala. Having gone to rasatala, the celestial arrow was worshipped by the gods. It then quickly returned to the descendant of the Ikshvaku lineage. Lavana, the roamer in the night, was shattered by Shatrughna's arrow. He suddenly fell down on the ground, like a mountain struck by the vajra. When the rakshasa Lavana was killed, while all the creatures looked on, that divine and giant trident returned again to Rudra. With a single arrow, the brave one of the Raghu lineage brought down and killed the terror of the three worlds. With his bow and arrow raised, he was as dazzling as the one with the one thousand rays, when it dispels darkness.

Chapter 7(62)

When Lavana was killed, the gods, with Indra and Agni at the forefront, spoke these extremely sweet words to Shatrughna, the scorcher of enemies. 'O child! It is good fortune that you have been victorious. It is good fortune that the rakshasa Lavana has been killed. O tiger among men! O Raghava! Ask for a boon. O mighty-armed one! All of us have assembled here to confer a boon on you, desiring that you should be victorious. The sight of us cannot be futile.' Hearing the words spoken by the gods, the brave one raised his hands in salutation above his head. Controlling himself, the mighty-armed Shatrughna replied, 'This Madhupura[714] is beautiful. It is splendid and has been constructed by the gods. It is my desired boon that it should be quickly populated.' Pleased in their minds, the gods agreed to what Raghava had said. 'There is no doubt that this beautiful city will be full of Shurasenas.'[715] Having said this, the great-souled ones went to heaven. The immensely energetic Shatrughna summoned his soldiers. Hearing Shatrughna's command, the soldiers arrived quickly. Instructed by Shatrughna, they started to construct residences. In twelve years, an auspicious city that was like heaven was constructed. Without any fear, the Shurasenas started to reside in this dominion. The fields were full of crops and Vasava rained at the right time. The brave men were without disease and it was protected by Shatrughna's arms. Located on the banks of the Yamuna, it was ornamented and was in the shape of a half moon. It was adorned with the best of houses. It was adorned with quadrangles and shops. Earlier, the place had been rendered empty by Lavana. It was now beautiful, filled with those brave ones and prosperous with many kinds of merchandise. Shatrughna, Bharata's brother, did everything to make it wealthy and prosperous. Greatly delighted, he looked at it and was filled with supreme joy. After having resided in that beautiful and auspicious city for twelve years, his mind turned towards the idea of seeing Rama's feet again.

Chapter 7(63)

After twelve years had passed, followed by a few servants, forces and followers, Shatrughna went to Ayodhya, protected by Rama. He asked the ministers, the foremost commanders and the priest to return. He proceeded on an excellent chariot, yoked

---

[714] Identified with Mathura.
[715] Literally, *shurasenas* mean brave soldiers.

to radiant steeds. As he proceeded, the descendant of the Raghu lineage resided in seven or eight places. Anxious to see Raghava, he quickly proceeded to Ayodhya. The handsome descendant of the Ikshvaku lineage entered the beautiful city. The mighty-armed one entered the place where the immensely radiant Rama was. He greeted the great-souled one, who seemed to blaze in his energy. Joining his hands in salutation, he spoke to Rama, for whom, truth was his valour. 'O great king! I have done everything, just as you had asked me to do. I have killed the wicked Lavana and I have populated that city. O descendant of the Raghu lineage! Separated from you, twelve years have passed. O king! Separated from you, I am not interested in residing there any more. O Kakutstha! O one who is infinite in valour! Show me your favours. Without you, my residence there is like that of a calf without its mother.' When Shatrughna said this, he embraced him and said, 'O brave one! Do not grieve in this way. A kshatriya should not act in this fashion. O Raghava! Kings do not suffer when they have to live somewhere else. O Raghava! The dharma of kshatriyas is to protect the subjects. O brave one! From time to time, come to Ayodhya to see me. O best among men! Having come here, return to your own city again. There is no doubt that I love you greatly, more than my own life. However, the protection of the kingdom is a task that must certainly be undertaken. O Kakutstha! Therefore, reside here with me for five nights. After that, with your servants, forces and mounts, go to Madhura.'[716] Rama's words were full of dharma and agreeable to the mind. Though Shatrughna was distressed at these words, he uttered words of agreement. As commanded by Raghava, Kakutstha[717] resided there for five nights. After that, the great archer made arrangements to depart. He took his leave from the great-souled Rama, for whom, truth was his valour, and also from Bharata and Lakshmana. He ascended his great chariot. The great-souled Lakshmana and Bharata followed him for some distance. Thereafter, Shatrughna quickly went to the city.

[716] Madhupura or Mathura.
[717] Shatrughna.

Chapter 7(64)

After Shatrughna had left, Raghava happily sported with his brothers. Following dharma, he protected the kingdom. After some days, an aged brahmana from the countryside came to the king's gate, holding the dead body of a male child. He lamented in many kinds of words and the syllables were filled with affection. He said, 'Alas, son! Your rites have not been performed. What wicked deed did I commit in an earlier life? I have had to see you, my only son, face death. You are a child and have not attained youth. You are only five years old. O son! Causing me grief, you have faced death before your appointed time. O son! Grieving over you, there is no doubt that I, and your mother, will also die within a few days. I do not remember having spoken anything false. Nor do I remember having caused injury. What is the evil act I have committed? Today, my son, yet a child, has been conveyed to Vaivasvata's eternal abode, without having performed the rites for his father. In Rama's dominion, this has not been seen, or heard of, earlier. It is terrible to behold. Someone is dying before his appointed time. There is no doubt that Rama has committed some wicked deed. O king! Bring this child, who has come under the subjugation of death, back to life. O king! With your brothers, you will enjoy a long lifespan. O extremely strong one! Till now, we have happily slept in your kingdom. This dominion of the great-souled Ikshvakus is without a protector now. The child has had to go because we have now obtained Rama as a protector and a king. If the subjects are not protected in the proper way, the taint devolves on the king. Because of the evil deeds of a king, people die before their time. Alternatively, people in your city and the countryside are performing inappropriate tasks and you are not protecting them. That is the reason this fear has resulted before its time. It is extremely evident and certain that this has happened because of the king's transgression in the city or in the countryside. That is the reason this child has died.' Tormented by sorrow on account of his son, he repeatedly censured and reprimanded the king with many kinds of words.

Chapter 7(65)

The brahmana lamented in this piteous way, filled with misery and grief. Raghava heard everything. Sorrowing and extremely tormented, he summoned his ministers, Vasishtha, Vamadeva, his brothers and the merchants. With Vasishtha, eight brahmanas entered. They told the king, who was like a king, 'May you prosper.' Markandeya, Moudgalya, Vamadeva, Kashyapa, Katyayana, Jabali, Goutama and Narada—all these bulls among brahmanas sat down on seats. As they deserved, the ministers and the merchants were honoured. All of them sat down, blazing in their energy. After honouring the brahmanas, Raghava told them everything.

Hearing the king's miserable words, in the presence of the rishis and the king, Narada replied in these auspicious words. 'O king! Listen to the reason why this child died before his appointed time. O brave one! O descendant of the Raghu lineage! After listening, do what must be done. O Rama! Earlier, in krita yuga, only brahmanas were ascetics. O king! Someone who was not a brahmana never became an ascetic then. In that yuga, all of them openly blazed with the power of the brahman. All of them were far-sighted and no one died before his time. After that, in treta yuga, men possessed bodies.[718] Kshatriyas, who had performed austerities in their earlier lives, were born.[719] Because of valour and austerities, in treta yuga, these great-souled men were superior to those who had been born in the earlier yuga.[720] All the brahmanas and the kshatriyas were both equal in valour.[721] No particular superiority could be distinguished between the two sets. At that time, the four varnas were established everywhere. Adharma established one foot on the ground.[722] Touched by adharma, brahmanas became wicked. Because of the wicked deeds, the former lifespans became limited. However, there were also people in the world who continued to

---

[718] In krita yuga, there were those who did not possess bodies.

[719] By implication, there were no kshatriyas in krita yuga.

[720] The kshatriyas were superior to the brahmanas who had been born in krita yuga.

[721] The brahmanas and kshatriyas of treta yuga.

[722] Dharma declines as one goes down the cycle of four yugas. Dharma has four feet in krita yuga, three in treta yuga, two in dvapara yuga and one in kali yuga.

follow and were devoted to the true dharma. In treta yuga, there were brahmanas and kshatriyas who tormented themselves through austerities. All the other people served them. That was the supreme dharma of vaishyas and shudras. In particular, shudras worshipped all the varnas. When dvapara yuga presented itself, a second foot of adharma descended again. At the end of the present yuga, dvapara is approaching. O bull among men! Adharma and falsehood are prospering. When dvapara approached, vaishyas started to engage in austerities. O bull among men! However, shudras did not obtain the right to perform the fierce austerities of dharma. O best among men! Those inferior in varna are tormenting themselves through great austerities. However, those born in shudra wombs will only obtain the right to perform austerities in kali yuga. O Rama! O king! In dvapara, a shudra is performing a great act of adharma. Within the limits of your kingdom, he is performing great austerities. An evil-minded shudra is performing austerities. That is the reason this child has died. O tiger among kings! If an evil-minded man performs an act of adharma within a king's kingdom or city, there is no doubt that the king swiftly goes to hell. O tiger among men! Therefore, carefully search within your own dominion to find out where the evil-acting one is. This is the way dharma and lifespans will increase among men. O best among men! The child will also come back to life.'

Chapter 7(66)

It was as if Narada's words were full of amrita. Hearing them, he obtained infinite delight and addressed Lakshmana in these words. 'O amiable one! O Lakshmana! Go and comfort the best among brahmanas. Place the child's dead body in a pot filled with oil. O amiable one! Use perfumes, extremely expensive oil and fragrances to ensure that the child's body does not decay. Let the body of the child, whose deeds are unblemished, be protected. Act so that his muscles and joints do not suffer.' Kakutstha commanded Lakshmana, the one with the auspicious signs, in this way. In his mind, the immensely illustrious one thought of Pushpaka and asked it to come. Discerning the indication, in an instant, Pushpaka, decorated with gold, arrived near Raghava. It bowed down and said, 'O lord of men! O mighty-armed one! I am under your control. Your servant has arrived.' Hearing the beautiful words spoken by Pushpaka, the lord of men greeted the maharshis and mounted it. He grasped his bow, his quivers and his swords, beautiful in its resplendence. He entrusted the city to the two brave ones, Soumitri and Bharata. He headed in the western direction and searched everywhere in the desert. He went to the beautiful northern direction, covered by the Himalayas. He could not find the slightest bit of misdeed there. The lord of men searched everywhere in the eastern direction. The descendant of a royal sage then went to the southern direction. He saw a great lake on the northern slope of Shaivala.[723] Near that lake, an ascetic was tormenting himself through great austerities. Raghava saw the handsome one, hanging face downwards. He approached the one who was tormenting himself through these excellent austerities. Raghava spoke these words. 'O one who is excellent in vows! You are blessed. O one who is firm in valour! You are pervasive in austerities. Whose womb have you been born in? I am asking you out of curiosity. I am Rama, Dasharatha's son. Why do you wish to do this? Is it to obtain heaven or get a boon? Why are you tormenting yourself through these austerities? O ascetic! I wish to hear. O fortunate one! Are you a brahmana or an invincible kshatriya? Are you a vaishya or a shudra? Tell me the truth.'

Chapter 7(67)

Rama, the performer of unblemished deeds, spoke these words. Hearing them, with his face hanging downwards, he replied in these words. 'I have been born in the womb of a shudra and have resorted to these fierce austerities. O Rama! O immensely

[723] A peak in the Vindhyas.

illustrious one! I wish to go to heaven in my own physical body.
O king! I do not utter a falsehood. I wish to conquer the world
of the gods. O Kakutstha! Know me to be a shudra. My name
is Shambuka.' Hearing the shudra's words, Raghava unsheathed
his sparkling sword, extremely beautiful in its radiance, from its
scabbard and severed his head. In that instant, the child came
back to life. The lotus-eyed Rama went to Agastya's hermitage.
Delighted and happy, he bowed down in humility and greeted the
great-souled one, who seemed to be blazing in his energy. After
having obtained supreme hospitality, the lord of men sat down.
The immensely energetic and great sage, Kumbhayoni,[724] spoke
to him. 'O best among men! O Raghava! Welcome. It is good
fortune that you have come here. O Rama! I respect you a lot.
You possess many excellent qualities. O king! You are a guest
and should be honoured. You are always in my heart. The gods
have said that you have arrived, after killing the shudra. Because
you have acted in accordance with dharma, the brahmana's son
has come back to life. O Raghava! Spend the night here with
me. When it is morning, you can use Pushpaka to return to
your own city. O amiable one! This ornament was constructed
by Vishvakarma. It is divine and celestial in form. It blazes in its
own energy. O Kakutstha! O Raghava! Do something that will
bring me pleasure and accept it. Great fruits are obtained if one
gives away what has been given to one's own self earlier. O bull
among men! Therefore, I am following the rituals and giving it to
you. Accept it.' The great-souled Rama accepted it from the sage.
The colourful and celestial ornament blazed like the sun. Rama
accepted that excellent ornament. He then asked, 'O brahmana!
This divine ornament is extremely wonderful. It has an excellent
form. Where did it come from? O illustrious one! How did you get
it? Who brought it to you? O brahmana! O immensely illustrious
one! I am asking you out of curiosity. There are many kinds of
supreme and wonderful treasures with you.' When Kakutstha said
this, the sage replied in these words. 'O Rama! Hear about what
happened in the treta yuga that has just passed.'

---

[724] Agastya's name.

Chapter 7(68)

'Earlier, in treta yuga, there was an extremely large forest. It extended for one hundred yojanas in every direction. It was devoid of animals and birds. There were no men in the forest. O amiable one! Wishing to perform excellent austerities, I went to that forest. I was incapable of discerning the expanse of that forest. There were roots and many kinds of trees with pleasant fruits to eat. In the midst of the forest, there was a lake that was one yojana wide. It was full of lotuses and waterlilies and covered everywhere with lichen. The excellent water was pleasant and extremely tasty. There was no mud. It was not agitated and it was full of beautiful birds. Near that lake, there was a large and extraordinary hermitage. It was ancient and extremely sacred. However, there were no ascetics there. O bull among men! I resided there for a summer night. When it was morning, I arose and approached the lake. I saw a dead body there. It was well-nourished and without any decay. O king! It was near that store of waters, full of great beauty. O Raghava! O lord! I remained there for a while, thinking. Who was this on the shore of the lake and why? In a short while, I saw a divine and extraordinary sight. An extremely large vimana arrived, yoked to swans and possessing the speed of thought. O descendant of the Raghu lineage! There was an extremely divine being on that vimana. O brave one! A thousand apsaras, adorned in divine ornaments, were worshipping him. There were others who were singing beautiful songs and playing on musical instruments. O Rama! While I looked on, he descended from the vimana. O descendant of the Raghu lineage! The divine being started to eat the dead body. As he wished, he devoured many bits of that flesh and was satiated. After this, the divine being descended into the lake. O bull among men! As is proper, the divine being touched the water.[725] He then started to mount that supreme and excellent vimana. I saw the one, who resembled a god, ascend. O bull among men! I addressed him in these words. "You resemble a god. Who are you? Why did you eat this condemned food? O amiable one!

---

[725] He washed his hands and mouth.

Why did you eat it? You should tell me the reason. You are radiant and are like a revered god. Such inclinations are extraordinary. O amiable one! This food is condemned. I wish to hear the truth about this."'

Chapter 7(69)

'O Rama! He heard the words I had spoken, uttered with auspicious syllables. O descendant of the Raghu lineage! The divine being joined his hands in salutation and replied. "O brahmana! Listen to my account, as it occurred. It is full of both joy and misery. O brahmana! You have asked me about it. This is impossible for me to cross. In earlier times, my immensely illustrious father was the king of Vidarbha. He was valiant and was famous in the three worlds as Sudeva. O brahmana! He had two sons, born from two different wives. I was known as Shveta and my younger brother was Suratha. When my father went to heaven, the citizens consecrated me. Controlling myself, I followed dharma and ruled over the kingdom. O one good in vows! In this way, one thousand years passed. O brahmana! I ruled over the kingdom and following dharma, protected the subjects. O supreme among brahmanas! Through some means, I got to know about my lifespan. Taking the dharma of time to heart, I went to the forest. That forest was impenetrable and was devoid of animals and birds. I entered it near this auspicious lake and started to perform austerities. I instated my brother, Suratha, as the king over the kingdom. Having approached this lake, I performed austerities for a long time. O great sage! I performed austerities for three thousand years. After having performed these extremely difficult austerities, I obtained Brahma's excellent world. O supreme among brahmanas! While I was in heaven, I was overcome by hunger and thirst. O extremely generous one! They obstructed me and my senses were afflicted. I went to the grandfather, the best in the three worlds, and spoke to him. 'O illustrious one! In Brahma's worlds, there should not be any hunger or thirst. Since I have come under the subjugation

of hunger and thirst, what deed have I committed? O god! O
grandfather! Tell me. What should be my food?' The grandfather
told me, 'O Sudeva's son! Your food is your own succulent flesh.
You will always eat that. While you were performing those excellent
austerities, you nourished your own body. O Shveta! O immensely
intelligent one! Without sowing, nothing is reaped. You did not
give the slightest bit to creatures who resided in the forest. O child!
Therefore, despite being in heaven, you are suffering from hunger
and thirst. You nourished your own excellent body through food.
You will devour it, as if it is the juice of amrita. That is what will
satiate you. O Shveta! When the extremely great and invincible
rishi, Agastya, arrives in that forest, you will be freed from this
hardship. O amiable one! O mighty-armed one! He is capable of
saving large numbers of gods, not to speak of someone like you who
has succumbed to hunger and thirst.' I heard the decision of the
illustrious one, the god of the gods. O supreme among brahmanas!
I thus eat this condemned food, my own body. O brahmana! I have
been eating it and many years have passed. O brahmana rishi! It
does not decay and I obtain excellent satisfaction. This is how my
hardship came about. You should free me from this hardship. Who
can save me, other than the brahmana Kumbhayoni? O supreme
among brahmanas! O brahmana rishi! You should show me your
favours. In return for saving me, accept this ornament." I heard
the words of the divine being, full of grief. In return for saving
him, I accepted that excellent ornament. I accepted that auspicious
ornament. Immediately, the former human body of the royal sage
was destroyed. When the body was destroyed, the royal sage was
greatly delighted. Content and delighted, the king went to heaven
again. O Kakutstha! He was like Shakra. Because of what I did, he
gave me this extraordinary and divine ornament.'

Chapter 7(70)

Raghava heard Agastya's extraordinary words. Showing him
respect and astounded, he again started to ask. 'O illustrious

one! This forest, where Shveta, the king of Vidarbha, tormented himself through austerities, is terrible. There are no animals and birds. Why is that the case? There are no creatures in the forest that he entered to undertake austerities in. It is desolate and there are no humans here. How did this happen? I wish to hear the truth about this.'

Rama's words were full of curiosity. The immensely energetic one heard these words and started to speak. 'O Rama! In earlier times, in krita yuga, the lord Manu held the rod of chastisement. He had a great son, Ikshvaku, who was the extender of the lineage. He instated this eldest son, invincible on earth, in the kingdom and said, "Be the originator of royal lineages on earth." O Raghava! The son promised his father that he would do this. Extremely delighted, Manu again said, "O extremely generous one! I am greatly pleased with you. There is no doubt that you will be the originator. Protect the subjects using the rod. However, do not use the rod of chastisement without valid reason. If the rod is brought down on men when they commit crimes, that punishment is sanctioned and conveys the king to heaven. O mighty-armed one! O son! Therefore, be careful in using the rod. A person who acts in this way obtains supreme dharma in this world." Manu instructed his attentive son about many other things. Happy, he then proceeded to heaven, to Brahma's supreme world. When he went to heaven, the infinitely radiant Ikshvaku was filled with a serious thought. "How will I have sons?" Manu's son performed many kinds of rituals. The one with dharma in his soul then had one hundred sons who were like the sons of the gods. O son![726] O descendant of the Raghu lineage! The youngest among them was foolish and unaccomplished in learning. He did not serve his seniors. His father gave this one, who was limited in energy, the name of Danda. He knew the rod of chastisement would descend on his body.[727] O Raghava! He saw a terrible taint in his son. O scorcher of enemies! He gave him the kingdom that was between the mountains Vindhya and Shaivala. Danda became the king of the beautiful region between the slopes

---

[726] The word used is tata.
[727] The word danda means both rod and punishment.

of the two mountains. O Rama! He constructed an unmatched and excellent city there. O lord! He named this city Madhumanta. As his priest, he brought Ushanas, who was excellent in his vows. In this way, the king made him the priest of the kingdom, which was full of delighted people. It was like a kingdom of the gods in heaven.'

Chapter 7(71)

The maharshi who was born from the pot told Rama this. He then started to speak subsequent words to him. 'O Kakutstha! In this way, Danda, evil in his soul, ruled over that kingdom, which was bereft of thorns, for an innumerable number of years. On one occasion, in the beautiful month of Chaitra,[728] he went to Bhargava's[729] beautiful hermitage. Bhargava's daughter was unmatched on earth in her beauty. Danda saw the excellent one roaming around in the region of the forest. On seeing her, the one who was extremely evil in his intelligence, was afflicted by the arrows of Ananga.[730] Extremely eager, he approached the maiden and addressed her in these words. "O one with the beautiful hips! Where have you come from? O beautiful one! Whose daughter are you? O one with the excellent waist! I am asking you because I am suffering on account of Ananga." He was confused and crazy with desire. When he said this, Bhargava's daughter beseeched the king and replied in these words. "Know me to be the eldest daughter of Bhargava, the lord who is unblemished in his deeds. O Indra among kings! My name is Araja and I live in this hermitage. O Indra among kings! My father is your preceptor. You are the great-souled one's disciple. If the great ascetic is extremely angry, he will impose a hardship on you. O best among king! If this is your intention, you should follow the virtuous path indicated by dharma, and seek my hand from my immensely radiant father. Otherwise, you will have to reap terrible fruits. If my father

[728] March–April.
[729] Shukracharya.
[730] The god of love.

is angry, he can burn down the three worlds." Danda was suffering from the arrows of desire and was addressed by Araja in this way. Crazy with desire, he joined his hands in salutation above his head and replied, "O one with the beautiful hips! Show me your favours. You should not waste time in this way. O one with the beautiful face! Because of you, my life is being shattered. To get you, I am ready to be killed and ready to perform an extremely terrible and vile act. O timid one! I am devoted to you. Serve me. I am completely distracted by my attachment towards you." Having said this, the strongest of the strong seized the maiden with both of his hands. Though she writhed, he started to have intercourse with her, as he desired. Danda perpetrated this extremely horrible and extremely terrible and injurious act. He then quickly left for his excellent city of Madhumanta. Not far from the hermitage, Araja started to weep. Greatly terrified, she waited for her father, who was like a god.'

Chapter 7(72)

'In a short while, the divine sage, infinite in his radiance, returned to his own hermitage. He was surrounded by his disciples and was suffering from hunger. He saw the miserable Araja, smeared all over with dust. She was like the moonlight in the morning, no longer radiant because the sun was in front. Especially because he was suffering from hunger, he was filled with rage. About to burn down the three worlds, he spoke to his disciples. "Behold these perverse signs. I know that this has been done by Danda. Like the angry flames of a fire, I will bring down a terrible hardship on him. With his followers, the evil-minded and evil-souled one will head towards destruction. He is like a person who desires to touch the blazing flames of a fire. He has performed such an evil act, terrible to behold. Therefore, the evil-minded one will reap the fruits of his wicked deed. The evil-minded one has perpetrated a vile act. Within seven nights, with his servants, forces and mounts, the king will be killed. In every direction, an expanse of one hundred yojanas around the evil-minded one's dominion will be destroyed. The chastiser of Paka will bring down a great shower of dust. Everywhere, all creatures and all mobile and immobile objects will be destroyed by this great shower of dust. Within seven nights, everyone who resides within Danda's kingdom will be reduced to dust and will vanish." Blazing in his anger, he said this to the residents of the hermitage and asked the people to go to regions that were beyond the frontiers of this country. Hearing the words spoken by Ushanas, all the people who resided in the hermitage left that kingdom and started to reside in regions that were outside its limits. Having told the people this, the sage spoke to Araja. "O evil-minded one! Control yourself and dwell here, in this hermitage. There is an extremely beautiful and dazzling lake that extends for one yojana. O Araja! Do not suffer from anxiety. Enjoy it and wait for your time. During those nights, all creatures who reside near you will never be killed by that shower of dust." Having said this, Bhargava went to live somewhere else. As the one who knew about the brahman had said, within a week, everything was reduced to ashes. The area between the slopes of Vindhya and Shaivala are Danda's kingdom. Because of the act of adharma that had been done, it had been cursed by the brahmana rishi in earlier times. O Kakutstha! Since that time, it has been known as Dandakaranya.[731] Because the ascetics reside here, it is also known as Janasthana.[732] O Raghava! I have thus told you everything that you had asked me about. O brave one! The time for performing the sandhya rituals is passing. O tiger among men! In every direction, all the maharshis are holding full pots of water, to perform the water rites and worship the sun. O Rama! The sun has set. Go with the excellent brahmana rishis and perform the water rites.'

Chapter 7(73)

Following the rishi's words, Rama worshipped the sandhya, near the sacred waters of the lake, populated by apsaras. Rama

[731] Danda's/Dandaka's forest (*aranya*).
[732] Literally, place where people reside.

touched the water and worshipped the western sandhya. He then
entered the hermitage of the great-souled Kumbhayoni. For food,
Agastya arranged roots and fruits with many kinds of qualities,
herbs and sacred green leaves. The best among men ate the food
that was like amrita. Happy and content, he spent the night there.
In the morning, the scorcher of enemies arose and performed the
ablutions. The supreme of the Raghu lineage went to the rishi
to seek permission to leave. Rama greeted the maharshi who
had been born from the pot. He said, 'I seek your permission to
depart. Please grant me leave. O great-souled one! I am blessed and
favoured at having seen you. To purify myself, I will come here to
see you again.' Kakutstha spoke these words to the one who was
extraordinary to behold. With his eye towards dharma, the store of
austerities was greatly delighted. He said, 'O Rama! These words of
yours are extremely wonderful and are full of auspicious syllables.
O descendant of the Raghu lineage! You are the one who will purify
all the worlds. O Rama! Even if someone sees you for an instant,
that person is purified and goes to heaven. He is worshipped in
heaven by the gods. Creatures on earth who glance at you with
terrible eyes are immediately slain by Yama's staff and go to hell.
Without any anxiety, proceed along the path you desire, without
any fear. Follow dharma and rule over the kingdom. You are the
refuge of the universe.' When the sage said this, the king joined
his hands in salutation. He honoured the wise and sacred sage. He
greeted the best among sages and all the other stores of austerities.
Without any anxiety, he mounted Pushpaka, which was decorated
with gold. As he left, in every direction, large numbers of sages
pronounced benedictions. With a complexion like that of the great
Indra, it was as if the immortals were worshipping the one with
the thousand eyes. When Rama was firmly seated in Pushpaka,
decorated with gold, he was like the moon amidst clouds, at the
onset of the rainy season.

After half a day, Kakutstha reached Ayodhya and was
worshipped in every direction. He descended from the vimana.
He allowed the beautiful Pushpaka, which could go wherever it
wished, to leave. Rama went to the inner chambers and addressed
the gatekeeper in these words. 'Go to Lakshmana and Bharata, who

are light in their valour. Without any delay, go and tell them that I
have arrived.'

Chapter 7(74)

The gatekeeper heard the words spoken by Rama, the performer
of unblemished deeds. He told them what Raghava had said
and brought the princes there. Raghava saw that his beloved
Bharata and Lakshmana had come. Rama embraced them and
addressed them in these words. 'I have performed the brahmana's
excellent task exactly. O Raghavas! I again want to build a bridge
for dharma.[733] With the two of you, I wish to perform an excellent
rajasuya sacrifice. Eternal dharma is vested in this. Mitra, the slayer
of enemies, performed a rajasuya sacrifice. Having performed
that excellent sacrifice and having offered excellent oblations, he
obtained the status of being Varuna. Soma, who knows about
dharma, followed dharma and performed a rajasuya sacrifice. He
obtained fame in all the worlds and an eternal position. Today, with
me, the two of you should think about what is best and beneficial.
Control yourselves and tell me about our welfare.' Raghava was
accomplished in the use of words. Hearing his words, Bharata joined
his hands in salutation and spoke the following words. 'O virtuous
one! Supreme dharma is vested in you. O mighty-armed one! The
entire earth is vested in you. O infinitely valiant one! So is fame. O
great-souled one! All the kings look towards you, as the immortals
do towards Prajapati. You are the protector of the world. O king!
O immensely strong one! The subjects look towards you, as they do
towards a father. O Raghava! You are the refuge of the earth and
that of all living beings. O king! Why do you want to undertake
this kind of a sacrifice? It can be seen that all the royal lineages on
earth will be destroyed because of this. O king! When you are filled
with rage, all the men on earth who are filled with manliness will

[733] That is, he wants to perform a sacrifice.

be destroyed because of this.[734] O tiger among men! O one who is infinite in qualities and valour! You should not destroy the earth. It is already under your subjugation.' Rama, for whom truth was his valour, heard Bharata's words, which were like amrita, and was filled with great delight. He spoke these auspicious words to the one who extended Kaikeyee's delight. 'Because of the words you have spoken today, I am delighted. I am content. These words are not the result of impotence. They are full of dharma. O tiger among men! You have spoken about how the earth can be protected. O one who knows about dharma! Because of what you have said, I am giving up my desire to undertake a rajasuya sacrifice. The dharma of a respected king is to undertake sacrifices whereby the subjects are protected. Therefore, I am listening to your words. You have controlled yourself and spoken words that are full of virtue.'

Chapter 7(75)

When Rama said this to the great-souled Bharata, Lakshmana also addressed the descendant of the Raghu lineage in these auspicious words. 'The great sacrifice of ashvamedha purifies from all sins. O invincible one! If you wish to purify yourself, you should undertake this, the best among sacrifices. The ancient account of the extremely great-souled Vasava has been heard. When he committed the act of killing a brahmana,[735] Shakra purified himself through a horse sacrifice. O mighty-armed one! In ancient times, there was a clash between the gods and the asuras. There was a great daitya named Vritra and he was revered by the worlds. He was one hundred yojanas wide and three yojanas tall. Filled with attachment towards the three worlds, he always looked towards them with affection. He knew about dharma. He was grateful and he possessed great intelligence. Extremely controlled, he followed dharma and ruled over the entire earth. When he ruled, the earth

---

[734] If they do not accept Rama's overlordship, they will have to fight and will be killed.
[735] Vritra was the son of a brahmana.

could be milked for all the objects of desire. It yielded succulent roots and fruits. Without being tilled, the earth yielded extremely large quantities of crops. When the great-souled one ruled, the kingdom could be enjoyed in this fashion. It was prosperous and was extraordinary to behold. The thought arose in his mind, "I will perform supreme austerities. Austerities represent the supreme benefit. Austerities represent supreme happiness." He instated his eldest son, Parameshvara, in the city. He resorted to fierce austerities and tormented all the gods. When Vritra tormented himself through these austerities, Vasava was greatly afflicted. He went to Vishnu and addressed him in these words. "O mighty-armed one! Through his austerities, Vritra has conquered all the worlds. The one with dharma in his soul is powerful and I am incapable of countering him. O lord of the gods! As long as he undertakes these austerities, he will hold sway over these worlds and they will remain under his subjugation. O immensely strong one! You are ignoring this extremely pervasive one. O lord of the gods! If you are angry with him, Vritra will be destroyed in an instant. O Vishnu! When he approaches you, as long as you look towards him with affection, till then, he will remain the protector of the worlds. It is because of the favours you have done that he obtains this extremely great fame in the worlds. It is because of what you have done that everything in the universe is peaceful and without decay. O Vishnu! All these residents of heaven are looking towards you. You should render great assistance in slaying Vritra. You have always aided these great-souled ones. No one else can withstand him. You are the refuge of all those who do not have a refuge."'

Chapter 7(76)

The slayer of enemies heard Lakshmana's words and said, 'O Lakshmana! Complete the account about Vritra being killed.' Hearing what Raghava had said, Lakshmana, the extender of Sumitra's delight, again started to speak about the divine account. 'Vishnu heard the words of the one with one thousand eyes and

those of all the residents of heaven. He spoke to all the gods, with
Indra at the forefront. "I am already bound in affection towards the
extremely great-souled Vritra. Therefore, to bring you pleasure, I
cannot slay the great asura. However, I must certainly do what will
bring you great happiness. Hence, I will tell you about the means
whereby you can kill Vritra. O supreme among gods! I will divide
myself into three parts. O one with one thousand eyes! There is no
doubt that Vritra can be killed through this means. One part will
enter Vasava, the second part will be in the vajra, while the third
part will be in the earth. O Shakra! Thereby, Vritra will be killed."
Addressed by the lord of the gods in this way, the gods replied in
these words. "O slayer of daityas! There is no doubt that what you
have said will transpire. May you be fortunate. Desiring to slay
the asura Vritra, we will depart now. O extremely pervasive one!
Pervade Vasava with your own energy." Thereafter, with the one
with one thousand eyes at the forefront, all those great-souled ones
went to the forest where Vritra, the great asura, was. They saw
the supreme asura tormenting himself. Full of energy, he seemed to
drink up the three worlds and burn up the sky. On seeing the best
among asuras, all the gods were terrified. "How can we kill him?
How can we not be defeated?" While they were thinking in this
way, Purandara, the one with one thousand eyes, seized the vajra in
his hands and brought it down on Vritra's head. It was as terrible as
the fire of destruction, blazing in its great rays. It scorched Vritra's
head and the universe was terrified. The lord of the gods[736] thought
that this killing of Vritra should not have been done. The immensely
illustrious one went to the end of the worlds. However, wherever
Indra went, the sin of killing a brahmana followed him. It entered
his body and Indra was filled with misery. With the enemy dead
and Indra also destroyed, the gods, with Agni at the forefront, went
to Vishnu, the best in the three worlds, and repeatedly worshipped
him. "O god! You are the supreme refuge. You are the lord who
predated the creation of the universe. You have assumed the form
of Vishnu for the sake of protecting all creatures. You have ensured
that Vritra was killed. However, Vasava has been contained because

[736] Indra.

of the sin of killing a brahmana. O tiger among the gods! Instruct
a way for him to be freed." Hearing their words, Vishnu spoke to
the gods. "If Shakra, the wielder of the vajra, performs a sacrifice
to me, he will be purified. Let the chastiser of Paka perform the
sacred horse sacrifice for me. He will be freed from fear and will
again become Indra of the gods." The gods were commanded by
his words, which were like amrita. Praised by the gods, Vishnu, the
lord of the gods, departed.'

Chapter 7(77)

Lakshmana recounted everything about Vritra being killed. The
best among men then started to speak about whatever was left
of the account. 'The immensely valiant Vritra, who caused fear to
the gods, was thus killed. However, because he had killed Vritra
and was surrounded by the sin of killing a brahmana, Shakra did
not regain his senses for some time. Having lost his senses and
unconscious, he sought refuge in the end of the worlds. Writhing
like a serpent, he resided there for some time. When the one with
one thousand eyes was destroyed, the universe became anxious.
The earth was destroyed. The forests were dry and without any
juices. There were no flows in the stores of waters, lakes and rivers.
Because there were no rains, all living beings were agitated. When
the worlds were being destroyed, the gods were scared in their minds.
As they had been told by Vishnu earlier, they started to perform the
sacrifice. All the large numbers of gods, with the preceptors and the
rishis, collectively went to the spot where Indra was, confounded by
his fear. They saw the one with the one thousand eyes, confounded
by the sin of having killed a brahmana. With the lord of the gods[737]
at the forefront, they commenced the horse sacrifice. O lord of
men! For the sake of purifying himself from the sin of killing a
brahmana, the great-souled and extremely great Indra undertook
the prosperous horse sacrifice. When the sacrifice was over, the

[737] Indra.

sin of killing a brahmana emerged from the great-souled one's body and asked, "What place has been ordained for me?" The gods were satisfied. Filled with joy, they told it, "O invincible one! Divide yourself into four parts." Hearing the words spoken by the great-souled gods, in their presence, the sin of killing a brahmana, which was finding it difficult to find a place to reside in, said the following. "These are the places I have chosen. One of my parts will dwell in rivers, when they are full of water. The second part will reside in trees. I am stating this to you truthfully. Young women are full of pride. To destroy their pride, my third part will reside in them for three nights.[738] O bulls among gods! My fourth part will resort to those who kill brahmanas, without first considering whether they have been injured by them." Thus addressed, all the gods replied, "O one who is finding it difficult to find a place to dwell in! Everything shall be exactly as you have stated it. May you accomplish what you desire." Delighted, the gods worshipped the one with one thousand eyes. Vasava was cured of his fever and cleansed of his sin. The entire universe was pacified and found a refuge in the one with one thousand eyes. Shakra worshipped that extraordinary sacrifice. O descendant of the Raghu lineage! Such are the powers of the horse sacrifice. O extremely fortunate one! O king! Perform a horse sacrifice.'

Chapter 7(78)

Lakshmana, eloquent in the use of words, spoke these words. Hearing them, the immensely energetic Raghava smiled and replied in these words. "O best among men! O Lakshmana! It is indeed as you have said, the complete story of Vritra's death and the fruits of a horse sacrifice. O amiable one! I have heard that in ancient times, Kardama Prajapati's son was named Ila. He was handsome and was extremely devoted to dharma. He was the lord of Bahlika. The immensely illustrious king brought the entire

[738] During the menstrual cycle.

earth under his subjugation. O tiger among men! He protected the
kingdom as if it was his own son. O amiable one! O descendant
of the Raghu lineage! The gods, the extremely large daityas, the
giant asuras, the serpents, the rakshasas, the gandharvas and the
extremely great-souled yakshas always worshipped him. They
were scared of him. The three worlds were scared of the great-
souled one's rage. The king was like that, established in dharma
and valour. His intelligence was extremely pervasive and the
immensely illustrious one ruled over Bahlika. The mighty-armed
one went on a hunt to a beautiful forest, with his servants, forces
and mounts. It was the pleasant month of Chaitra. In the forest, the
king killed hundreds of thousands of animals. Despite having killed
them, the great-souled king was not satisfied. The great-souled one
killed tens of thousands of many kinds of animals. He then reached
the spot where Mahasena[739] was born. At that time, the invincible
Hara, the lord of the gods, was sporting there with the daughter
of the king of the mountains and with his own companions. To
please the goddess, in a waterfall in the mountain there, Uma's
lord, the one with the bull on his banner, had transformed himself
into a woman. In that part of the forest, all the creatures which
were male in nature had also got transformed into female forms.
At this time, King Ila, Kardama's son, reached the place, having
killed thousands of animals. O descendant of the Raghu lineage!
He saw that the predatory creatures, the birds and the animals,
and he and his companions, had all become feminine. On seeing
what had happened to himself, he was filled with great sorrow.
Knowing that this had happened because of Umapati,[740] he was
terrified. With his servants, forces and mounts, the king sought
refuge with the great-souled god, Shitikantha Kapardi.[741] With the
goddess, the immensely illustrious granter of boons laughed. The
granter of boons himself addressed Prajapati's son in these words.
"Arise! O royal sage! O Kardama's son! O immensely strong
one! Arise! O amiable one! O one who is good in vows! Ask for

---

[739] Kartikeya.

[740] Uma's lord, Uma's husband, Shiva.

[741] Shitikantha and Kapardi are Shiva's names, Kapardi meaning the one with matted
hair.

any boon other than that of becoming a man." Having been thus
refused by the great-souled one, the king was afflicted by sorrow.
In the form of a woman, he did not ask for any other boon from
that excellent god. Filled with great sorrow, the king prostrated
himself before the daughter of the king of the mountains. "O great
goddess! O one who is in everyone's heart! O granter of boons!
O beautiful one! You are the one who grants boons to the worlds
and even to Isha.[742] O goddess! O amiable one! O one who should
be worshipped! Your sight cannot be futile. I am bowing down
before you." She was near Hara and got to know what was in the
mind of the royal sage. Honouring Rudra, the goddess replied in
these auspicious words. "The god, the granter of boons, will grant
you half of your boon and I will grant you the other half. As you
wished, between a man and a woman, therefore accept half." He
heard the excellent and extraordinary boon granted by the goddess.
Delighted, the king replied in these words. "O goddess! If you are
pleased with me, let me be a woman for one month, sought after
because she is unmatched in beauty on earth. For the next month,
I can become a man." The goddess with the extremely beautiful
face got to know his desire. She replied in auspicious words. "It
will be that way. O king! When you are in the form of a man, you
will not remember what happened as a woman. In the next month,
when you are a woman, you will not remember what happened as
a man." In this way, the king who was Kardama's son remained
a man for one month. In the next month, he became the woman
Ila,[743] most beautiful in the three worlds.'

Chapter 7(79)

Rama recounted this account about Ila. Hearing this, Lakshmana
and Bharata were greatly surprised. Wishing to know about
the great-souled king in detail, they joined their hands in salutation

[742] Shiva.
[743] Ila as man and Ilaa as woman.

and asked again. 'How did the king bear the hardship of being a woman? When he was a man, how did he conduct himself?'

Their words were full of curiosity. Hearing them, Kakutstha started to recount what happened to the king. 'In the first month, she was a woman, most beautiful in the worlds. She surrounded herself with her former followers, who also became women. Most beautiful in the worlds, she quickly entered that forest, full of trees, shrubs and creepers. With eyes like a lotus, she wandered around on foot. She abandoned all the mounts that had surrounded her from all sides. Ila roamed around in the caverns in the mountains. Not very far from the mountain, in that part of the forest, there was the best of lakes, extremely beautiful. It was full of many kinds of birds. Ila saw Soma's son, Budha, there. His form was radiant, like the full moon when it rises. Difficult to approach, he was tormenting himself through fierce austerities in the midst of the water. He was famous, desirable and young. O descendant of the Raghu lineage![744] With her companions, who were formerly male but were now female, she was surprised to see him. All of them started to agitate the waters of the lake. On seeing her, Budha was also afflicted by the arrows of Kama. He was disturbed and started to advance through the water. He saw Ila, most beautiful in the three worlds. He started to think, "Who is this? She is superior to a goddess. Earlier, I have not seen such wonderful beauty in a goddess, a naga or asura lady, or an apsara. If she has not been married already, she is just right for me." Arriving at this conclusion, he arose from the waters on to the land. Having reached his hermitage, he summoned four of those women. They arrived and worshipped the one with dharma in his soul. The one with dharma in his soul asked them, "Who is she? She is the most beautiful in the worlds. Why has she come here? Without any delay, tell me the truth." His words were auspicious. They were sweet, with sweet syllables. Hearing them, all those women replied in sweet words. "The one with the beautiful hips has always been our mistress. She doesn't have a husband. With us, she roams

---

[744] In the singular, though it should be dual, since both Bharata and Lakshmana are being spoken to.

around in the forest and the extremities of the forest." Hearing the words spoken by those women, the brahmana recalled the sacred learning known as *avartani*.[745] He got to know everything about what had happened to the king. The bull among sages spoke to all those women. "O fortunate ones! Become kimpurushas[746] and reside on the slopes of this mountain. Construct residences wherever you can find a spot on this mountain. All kinds of roots, leaves and fruits can always be found here. As women, you will also find husbands who will be known as kimpurushas." They heard the words of Soma's son, to the effect that they had become kimpurushas. They constructed many kinds of residences on that mountain and started to reside there.'

Chapter 7(80)

Hearing about the origin of kimpurushas, Lakshmana and Bharata told Rama, the lord of men, that this was extraordinary. The immensely illustrious Rama continued to speak about the great-souled son of Prajapati. 'The supreme among rishis saw that all those kinnara ladies had left. He seemed to smile and spoke to that extremely beautiful lady. "O one with an extremely beautiful face! I am Soma's son and he loves me dearly. O beautiful one! Serve me. Glance towards me with gentle and affectionate eyes." Alone and without her friends, she heard his words. Ila, best among beautiful ones, replied to the great planet. "O amiable one! I am also driven by desire and am under your control. O Soma's son! Command me. Do whatever you want with me." Hearing her extremely wonderful words, he was filled with delight. Driven by desire, the son of the moon found his pleasure with her. While Budha found his pleasure with Ila, the one with the beautiful face, the month of Madhava[747] passed. However, he was so driven by

[745] The brahmana means Budha. Avartani means a crucible, a place where things are whirled around. Specifically, it is a kind of learning that facilitates memory retention.

[746] Also known as kinnaras, semi-divine species described as Kubera's companions.

[747] The month of Magha.

desire that it seemed to be only an instant. When the month was over, Prajapati's handsome son,[748] with a face like that of the full moon, arose from his bed. He saw Soma's son there, tormenting himself in the lake. His arms were raised up and he was without any support. The king spoke to him. "O illustrious one! With my followers, I entered this impenetrable mountain. I cannot see those soldiers. Where have my companions gone?" Having been deprived of his senses,[749] the royal sage said this. Hearing this, he[750] replied in auspicious and greatly comforting words. "Because of a great shower of hailstones, your servants have been brought down. You were scared because of the storm and the shower and slept in the hermitage. O fortunate one! Be reassured and do not fear, or have any anxiety. O brave one! Eat roots and fruits and dwell wherever you wish." The immensely illustrious king was comforted by these words, though he was distressed that his servants and companions had been destroyed. He replied in these auspicious words. "With my servants gone, I will abandon my own kingdom. O brahmana! I seek your permission to reside here for some time. O brahmana! My eldest son is immensely illustrious and is devoted to dharma. He is known by the name of Shashabindu. He will receive my kingdom. With my servants and wives gone, I am sad and cannot remain here either. O immensely energetic one! Your words are not agreeable either."[751] When the Indra among kings spoke these supremely extraordinary words, Budha first comforted him and then said, "If it pleases you, dwell here.[752] O Kardama's immensely strong son! You should not be tormented. If you reside here for a year, I will do what will be beneficial for you." Budha was unblemished in his deeds and knew about the brahman. Hearing what he had said, he made up his mind to reside there. During the months when she was a woman, the auspicious one incessantly found pleasure with him. During the months when he was a man, he turned his mind towards dharma. In the ninth month, Ila, the one with the beautiful hips,

---

[748] Ila, in the form of a man.
[749] Having lost his memory.
[750] Budha.
[751] Of residing there.
[752] For some time.

delivered Soma's son's son. This was Pururava, who was like his father in energy. As soon as he was born, the one with the beautiful hips handed him over to his father. Ila's son was extremely strong and was like Budha in complexion. The king had assumed the form of a man and Budha comforted him. The one with the cleansed soul delighted him by telling him accounts that were full of dharma.'

Chapter 7(81)

Rama told them about this extraordinary birth. The immensely illustrious Lakshmana and Bharata spoke to him again. 'O best among men! Beloved by Soma's son, she resided there for one year. You should tell us the truth about what she did next.' Hearing the sweet words in which he had been asked, Rama started to again recite the account of Prajapati's son. 'After one year, when the brave one had again become a man, the extremely intelligent and extremely pervasive Budha summoned the extremely illustrious Samvarta, Bhrigu's son, Chyavana, the sage Arishtanemi, Pramodana, Modakara and the sage Durvasa. He was accomplished in the use of words and knew about the truth. He summoned all these well-wishers. He controlled himself and patiently told them, "This mighty-armed king is Ila, the son of Kardama. All of you know what happened to him. Therefore, decide what is best for him." While they were conversing in this way, the extremely energetic Kardama came to the hermitage, with many great-souled brahmanas—Pulastya, Kratu, Vashatkara and the immensely energetic Omkara.[753] Those immensely energetic ones came to the hermitage. Since all of them had come, they were delighted in their minds. Desiring the welfare of the lord of Bahlika, they started to say different things. For the sake of the supreme welfare of his son, Kardama spoke these words. "O brahmanas! Listen to my words. This is what is best for the king. I do not see any medication other than the one with the bull on his banner. There is no sacrifice the

---

[753] Here, both Vashatkara and Omkara are proper names.

great-souled one[754] loves more than a horse sacrifice. Therefore, for the king's sake, let all of us perform this extremely difficult sacrifice." After Kardama had said this, the idea appealed to all the bulls among the brahmanas, that they should perform a sacrifice to worship Rudra. Samvarta's disciple was the royal sage, who was the destroyer of enemy cities. He was famous as Marutta and he made the arrangements for the sacrifice. Near Budha's hermitage, this great sacrifice took place. Those immensely illustrious ones sought to greatly satisfy Rudra. When the sacrifice was over, Umapati was filled with great delight. He told all the brahmanas the following about Ila. "O supreme among brahmanas! I am delighted with your devotion and this horse sacrifice. What can I do that is agreeable and auspicious for the lord of Bahlika?" When the lord of the gods said this, the brahmanas controlled themselves and replied, "Show your favours and let Ila be a man, as he used to be." Pleased, Rudra again conferred manhood on the extremely energetic Ila and having given him this, he vanished. When the horse sacrifice was over and Hara could no longer be seen, all the far-sighted brahmanas returned to wherever they had come from. The king abandoned Bahlika. In the excellent middle part of the country, he populated the city of Pratishthana,[755] which brought him fame. Shashabindu, the destroyer of enemy cities, was the king of Bahlika. Ila, Prajapati's powerful son, was the king in Pratishthana. In due course, Ila obtained Brahma's supreme world and Ila's son, Pururava, became the king in Pratishthana. O bulls among men! Such are the powers of a horse sacrifice. Someone who was a woman became a man, something that is extremely difficult to achieve.'

Chapter 7(82)

Kakutstha recounted this to his infinitely radiant brothers. He again addressed Lakshmana in words that were filled with

---

[754] Shiva.
[755] Identified as Jhusi, near Prayaga.

dharma. 'O Lakshmana! Vasishtha, Vamadeva, Jabali, Kashyapa and all the other foremost brahmanas—summon them, consult with them and place them at the forefront for a horse sacrifice. I will worship and release a horse that possesses qualities.' Hearing the words spoken by Raghava, the one who was swift in his valour summoned all the brahmanas and made them meet Raghava. Raghava saw those extremely invincible ones, who were like gods. He worshipped at their feet and they pronounced benedictions on him. Raghava joined his hands in salutation before those excellent brahmanas and spoke to them about the horse sacrifice, in words that were filled with dharma. Those foremost brahmanas heard those extraordinary words about the horse sacrifice and were extremely happy. Discerning their views, Rama told Lakshmana, 'O mighty-armed one! Send for the great-souled Sugriva. Let the fortunate one quickly come here with the many great apes who seek refuge with him and enjoy the excellent sacrifice. O mighty-armed one! Let Vibhishana, light in his valour, come to the horse sacrifice, surrounded by many rakshasas who can travel anywhere at will. O tiger among men! Let the kings who wish to bring me pleasure swiftly come to the sacrificial arena, with their followers. O Lakshmana! There are brahmanas, devoted to dharma, who are in the kingdom.[756] Invite all of them to the horse sacrifice. O mighty-armed one! There are rishis who are stores of austerities and maharshis who are in the kingdom. Invite them, with their wives. O mighty-armed one! Issue instructions for a large sacrificial ground being prepared on the banks of the Gomatee, in the Naimisha forest. That is an exceedingly sacred spot. O immensely strong one! In advance, let one hundred thousand vehicles with beautiful rice[757] and ten thousand vehicles with sesamum and black gram[758] be despatched. Let the immensely intelligent Bharata proceed in advance, with many crores of gold and many hundreds of silver.[759]

[756] This requires explanation. There are ascetics who have left for the forest. Technically, those are outside the kingdom. Those who are in the kingdom are thus in the householder stage (garhasthya).

[757] Beautiful in the sense of being whole and not having cracked.

[758] *Mudga.*

[759] Meaning coins.

Let there be shops along all the roads, dancers and actors, merchants, the young and the old, controlled brahmanas, skilled artisans and learned craftsmen. Let all my mothers and the princes who are in the inner quarters leave. For the sake of being consecrated in the sacrifice, let a golden image of my wife be prepared.[760] Let the immensely intelligent Bharata leave in advance.'

Chapter 7(83)

Bharata's elder brother made everyone leave in advance. He then released a black horse that possessed all the qualities. He engaged Lakshmana and the officiating priests to leave with the horse. With his soldiers, Kakutstha followed it towards Naimisha. The mighty-armed one saw the extremely wonderful sacrificial arena. The prosperous one obtained great delight and said, 'Let all the kings reside in Naimisha.' Rama was honoured and honoured back those who had assembled from all the kingdoms. The immensely radiant, best among men, instructed that all those great-souled kings and their followers should be presented with extremely expensive gifts. With Shatrughna,[761] he quickly engaged Bharata to offer food, drinks and garments to those great-souled ones and their followers. With Sugriva, the great-souled apes were engaged in bowing down to all the brahmanas and serving them. Vibhishana was surrounded by many rakshasas wearing garlands. Like a servant, he presented himself before the rishis, fierce in their austerities. In this way, the well-arranged horse sacrifice commenced. Lakshmana was engaged to protect and tend to the horse. At the great-souled one's horse sacrifice, no words other than the following were heard. 'Do not stop giving until the seekers are satisfied.' The apes and rakshasas were seen to give them everything. At the king's excellent sacrifice, there was no one who was dirty, distressed, diseased or thin. It was surrounded by happy and healthy people. There were great-souled

[760] A sacred task must always be performed with one's wife.
[761] Shatrughna naturally returned for the sacrifice.

sages who had lived for a long time. They said, 'We have not seen a sacrifice like this, with its flood of gifts. Silver, gold, jewels and garments are being incessantly given and no end can be seen to this. We have not seen anything like this, at sacrifices by Shakra, Soma, Yama or Varuna.' This is what the stores of austerities said. There were apes everywhere. There were rakshasas everywhere. They could be seen, their hands laden with garments, riches and objects of desire. The sacrifice of the lion among kings was like this, with all the qualities. Undiminished, it continued for more than a year.

Chapter 7(84)

While that extremely wonderful sacrifice was being conducted, with his disciples, Valmiki, bull among sages, swiftly arrived there. He saw that sacrifice, which was almost divine and was extraordinary to behold. He went to the secluded spot where the rishis were residing in their auspicious cottages. He told his disciples, 'Both of you[762] control yourselves and go to the place where the sacrifice is being held. Filled with great delight, chant the entire Ramayana *kavya*[763] in the sacred residences of the rishis, the abodes of the brahmanas, the paths, the royal roads, the houses of the kings and the gate of Rama's mansion, where the rituals are being held. In particular, sing it before the officiating priests. There are many kinds of succulent fruit from the best of mountains. Eat and taste them and then sing. O children! If you eat those fruit, you will not be exhausted. Eat the extremely tasty roots from the city. King Rama is seated amidst the rishis. On hearing the sound, if he summons you, sing and make him hear it too. Earlier, I have instructed you about the different segments I have measured out. Filled with joy, sing twenty *sarga*s[764] every day. You must not be

---

[762] Lava and Kusha.

[763] A long poem.

[764] A sarga is a section. Since we are later told that the Valmiki Ramayana has 500 sargas, one can deduce that a sarga has roughly fifty shlokas. Therefore, sarga roughly corresponds to a chapter (*adhyaya*).

greedy and desire the slightest bit of riches. What use have those who live in hermitages, surviving on fruits and roots, for riches?[765] If Kakutstha asks you whose sons you are, tell the king that you are Valmiki's disciples. These strings[766] are extremely melodious and you have been instructed about the positions.[767] Without any worries, sing in extremely melodious and sweet tones. Sing right from the beginning and do not ignore the king. Following dharma, the king is the father of all creatures. Be attentive and cheerful. From tomorrow morning, sing the sweet songs, observing rhythm and metre.' The sage Prachetas[768] instructed them in these and many other ways. After this, the immensely illustrious and extremely powerful Valmiki became silent. Those two princes placed the wonderful and auspicious words uttered by the rishi in their hearts. Eager, they happily slept during the night, like the two Ashvins instructed by Bhargava's[769] polished teaching.

Chapter 7(85)

When the night was over, those two bathed in the morning and offered oblations to the fire. As the rishi had instructed them earlier, they first sung in those respective places. Kakutstha heard them sing in spots that their preceptor had instructed them about. They sung in those melodious tones and such a recital had never been heard before. It had been composed in many different segments and was full of rhythm and metre. Hearing this from the two children, Raghava was filled with curiosity. In between the tasks, the king, tiger among men, summoned the great sages, the kings, the learned ones, the merchants, the reciters of ancient accounts, those who were accomplished in the use of sounds and aged brahmanas. When all of them had assembled, he summoned

---

[765] Do not accept any riches as a reward for the singing.
[766] Of the musical instruments, the veena.
[767] Of the chords.
[768] Valmiki was the son of Prachetas, one of the Prajapatis.
[769] Shukracharya's.

the two singers. The large number of delighted rishis and the immensely energetic kings seemed to drink up the king and the two singers with their eyes. They told each other, 'All of them are similar. The two are like Rama and it is as if they are his mirror images. Had they not had matted hair and had they not been attired in bark, we would not have discerned any difference between the two singers and Raghava.' Hearing this conversation, which caused delight, the two sons of the sage[770] started to sing. The sweet and superhuman singing, like that of the gandharvas, commenced. The singing was so rich that none of the listeners were content. It started at the beginning, with the first sarga, about the sighting of Narada. They continued singing the other sargas, until twenty had been completed. When it was afternoon, Raghava, devoted to his brother, spoke to Bharata. 'We have heard twenty sargas. O Kakutstha! Quickly give eighteen thousand gold coins to the two great-souled ones. They are children and their efforts should not be in vain.' Kusha and Lava did not accept the gold that was given to them. Surprised, those two great-souled ones asked, 'What will we do with these? We are residents of the forest and survive on wild roots and fruits. In the forest, what will we do with gold and silver?' When they said this, all the listeners and Rama were curious and extremely surprised. Extremely eager to hear the learned recital of the kavya, Rama asked those two immensely energetic sons of a sage. 'O great-souled ones! How long is this kavya? How long has it been in existence? Who is the composer of this great kavya? Where does that bull among sages dwell?' When Raghava asked this, the sons of the sage replied, 'The illustrious Valmiki is the composer and he obtained this treasure through a sacrifice. He instructed us, so that we could recite this account to you, in its entirety. O Indra among kings! Including the beginning, it has five hundred sargas. O king! It has all the good and bad things about your birth and life. O king! O maharatha! If your thoughts are inclined towards hearing it, where there are gaps in the sacrifice, hear it from me and my younger brother.'[771] Rama agreed to this. Taking their leave

---

[770] Lava and Kusha.
[771] Thus, this reply is by Kusha.

of Raghava, they happily went to the spot where the bull among sages was residing. With the sages and the great-souled kings, Rama heard the sweet singing and went to the arena where the rituals were being performed.

Chapter 7(86)

With the sages, the kings and the apes, Rama heard that extremely wonderful song for several days. Through the song,[772] he got to know that Lava and Kusha were Sita's sons. In the midst of the courtiers, Rama spoke these words.[773] 'Go to the presence of the infinitely illustrious one[774] and tell him my words. If she is pure in conduct and if the great sage imagines her to be devoid of sin, then let her establish her purity. Go and ascertain whether the sage is comfortable with this and also find out Sita's wishes. After this, to assure me, return quickly and tell me. Tomorrow morning, for the sake of purifying herself and me, let Maithilee, Janaka's daughter, take a pledge in the midst of the courtiers.' Hearing Raghava's extremely extraordinary words, the messengers quickly went to the spot where the bull among sages was residing. The messengers prostrated themselves before the great-souled one, blazing in his infinite splendour. They repeated Rama's gentle and sweet words. Hearing what they said and ascertaining what was in Rama's mind, the extremely energetic sage replied in these words. 'O fortunate ones! It will be that way and Raghava will be satisfied. Sita will do that. For a woman, a husband is the divinity.' Thus addressed by the sage, all of Rama's greatly energetic messengers returned to Raghava, assured him, and told him all the sage's words. On hearing the great-souled one's words, Kakutstha was delighted. He spoke to the rishis and kings who were assembled there. 'O illustrious ones! Come with your disciples. O kings! Come

---

[772] The 'Uttara Kanda' part.
[773] To messengers.
[774] Valmiki.

with your followers. Let all the others who desire it also come and
see Sita take the pledge.' Hearing the words of the great-souled
Raghava, there were loud words of praise from all the best among
rishis. The great-souled kings applauded Raghava. 'O best among
men! Other than you, no one else on earth could have said this.'
Having made up his mind about what would happen the next day,
the slayer of enemies gave everyone permission to leave.

Chapter 7(87)

When night was over, the king, Raghava, went to the sacrificial
ground and summoned all the immensely energetic rishis.
Vasistha, Vamadeva, Jabali, Kashyapa, Vishvamitra, Dirghatapa,
the great ascetic Durvasa, Agastya, Bhargava, Shakti, Vamana,
Markandeya, the great ascetic Moudgalya, Bhargava Chyavana,
Shatananda, who knew about dharma, the energetic Bharadvaja,
Suprabha, Agni's son, many other sages who were firm in their
vows and all the kings who were tigers among men assembled. Filled
with curiosity, the extremely valiant rakshasas and the immensely
strong apes—all these great-souled ones also assembled. Kshatriyas,
vaishyas and thousands of shudras—all of them also assembled,
to see Sita take the pledge. All of them came there and were like
mountains made out of stone.

They heard the sage coming quickly, accompanied by Sita.
With her face cast downwards, Sita followed the rishi at the
rear. Her voice choked with tears and in her mind, she joined her
hands in salutation before Rama. The beautiful one could be seen
to advance, following the brahmana. Sita was behind Valmiki
and loud roars of praise arose. There were sounds of uproar
everywhere. On seeing her immersed in this great misery, they
were overcome by grief. Some praised Rama. Others praised Sita.
There were yet others who praised both of them. The bull among
sages entered in the midst of that crowd of people, with Sita as his
companion. Valmiki spoke to Raghava. 'O Dasharatha's son! This
is Sita. She is excellent in her vows and follows dharma. Without

having committed a crime, she was abandoned near my hermitage.
O Rama! O one who is great in vows! That was because you
were scared about people censuring you. You should grant your
permission, so that Sita can establish your trust in her. These twins
were born as Janakee's sons. These invincible ones are your sons. I
am telling you this truthfully. O descendant of the Raghava lineage!
I am the tenth son of Prachetas. I do not remember having uttered
a falsehood. These are your sons. I have performed austerities for
many thousands of years. If Maithilee isn't innocent, I will not reap
the fruits of those. O Raghava! Had I not known Sita to be pure
through my five senses and through my mind as the sixth, I would
not have accepted her near that waterfall in the mountain. She is
pure in conduct. She is devoid of sin. Her husband is her divinity.
However, you are scared because people condemned you. She will
instil confidence in you.'

Chapter 7(88)

When Valmiki said this, Raghava replied with his hands in
salutation, noticing the one with the complexion of a goddess
in the midst of the assembly. 'O greatly fortunate one! O one who
knows about dharma! It is indeed exactly as you have stated it. O
brahmana! I have confidence in your unblemished words. In the
presence of the gods, Vaidehi had instilled confidence in me earlier.
O brahmana! I know that she is innocent. However, scared because
of the condemnation of the people, I abandoned Sita. You should
pardon me. I know the twins who have been born, Lava and Kusha,
are my sons. However, I will be delighted if Maithilee establishes
her purity in the midst of the world.' Getting to know about Rama's
intention, all the supreme gods, with the grandfather at the forefront,
assembled. The Adityas, the Vasus, the Rudras, the Vishvadevas,
the large number of Maruts, the Ashvins, the rishis, the gandharvas,
the large number of apsaras, the Sadhyas, all the gods and all the
supreme rishis arrived. An auspicious, sacred and pleasant breeze
started to blow, with a divine fragrance, and delighted the hearts of

all the large numbers of best among the gods. Controlled, the men from all the kingdoms saw this wonderful and unthinkable event and thought that it was like during the former krita yuga.

Sita was dressed in an ochre garment. Her face was cast downwards. On seeing that all of them had assembled, she joined her hands in salutation and said, 'If I have not thought of anyone other than Raghava in my mind, then let the goddess earth open up a chasm for me.' When Vaidehi took this pledge, something extraordinary occurred. A divine and excellent throne arose from the middle of the earth. Infinitely valiant serpents held it up on their hoods. It was divine, with a celestial form, and was ornamented with every kind of jewel. The goddess earth was seated on it and engulfed Maithilee in her arms. Welcoming and honouring her, she made her sit on that throne. Seated on that throne, without any kind of obstruction, Sita started to enter the earth and a downpour of flowers showered down from the sky. Suddenly, extremely loud words of praise arose from among the gods. 'O Sita! You are to be praised. Such is your good conduct.' Stationed in the sky, the gods uttered many such words. Cheerful in their hearts on seeing Sita enter, they said this. All the sages and the tigers among kings who were in the sacrificial ground were greatly surprised. So were all the mobile and immobile objects in the sky and on earth, the immensely gigantic danavas and the lords of the serpents who were in patala. Some roared in joy. Some were immersed in thought. Some glanced towards Rama. The minds of some were on Sita. For a while, on seeing Sita enter, all those assembled ones from the world were confounded.

Chapter 7(89)

When the sacrifice was over, Rama was extremely distressed. Unable to see Vaidehi, he thought that the universe was empty. He was overcome by great grief and could not find any peace in his mind. He gave loads of riches to all the kings, the bears, the apes, the rakshasas, the large crowds of people and the best

among brahmanas and gave them leave to depart. The lotus-eyed
Rama gave all of them leave. With Sita in his heart, he entered
Ayodhya. The descendant of the Raghu lineage said, 'After Sita, I
will not take another wife.' From one sacrifice to another sacrifice,
the golden image of Janakee represented his wife. He performed
vajapeya, with ten times as many qualities, and gave away a lot of
gold.[775] The prosperous one performed many other great sacrifices—
agnishtoma, *atiratra* and *gosava* and gave away a lot of dakshina.
In this way, the great-souled Raghava ruled over the kingdom for
a very long period of time, carefully ensuring dharma. The bears,
apes and rakshasas always obeyed Rama's command. From one
day to another day, Raghava delighted all the kings. The rain god
showered down at the right time. The directions were clear and
sparkled. The city and the countryside were full of large numbers
of people who were happy and healthy. No one died at the wrong
time. Creatures did not suffer from disease. As long as Rama ruled
over the kingdom, there were no acts of adharma. After a long
period of time had passed, surrounded by her sons and grandsons,
Rama's illustrious mother followed the dharma of time. Sumitra
and the illustrious Kaikeyee followed her. Having performed many
acts of dharma, they went to heaven. All of them were established
in heaven, with King Dasharatha. Those immensely fortunate ones
met him and obtained the fruits of performing dharma together.
Especially addressed to his mothers, from time to time, Rama gave
away a lot of gifts to brahmanas and ascetics. Addressed to his
ancestors, he performed many extremely difficult sacrifices. Rama,
with dharma in his soul, did this to enhance the prosperity of the
gods and the ancestors.

Chapter 7(90)

After some time, Yudhajit, the king of Kekaya, sent his own
preceptor to the great-souled Raghava. This infinitely radiant

---

[775] The vajapeya sacrifice has ten times the qualities of an ashvamedha sacrifice.

brahmana rishi, Gargya, was the son of Angiras. He came with a gift
of ten thousand excellent horses, offered as a token of affection. The
king also sent Rama blankets, colourful jewels, excellent garments
and many ornaments. Raghava heard that maharshi Gargya had
come. He was the beloved messenger, of Ashvapati, his maternal
uncle.[776] Kakutstha arose and with his followers, advanced one
krosha to honour Gargya and accept those riches. He affectionately
asked all the relevant questions about the welfare of his maternal
uncle. After the immensely fortunate one had seated himself, Rama
started to ask, 'O illustrious one! What are the words spoken by
my maternal uncle, as a result of which, you have come here? You
are the best among those who know the use of words and you have
come here, like Brihaspati himself.' Hearing the words spoken by
Rama, the brahmana rishi started to tell Raghava about the task
at hand in detail and it was extraordinary. 'O mighty-armed one!
O bull among men! Your maternal uncle, Yudhajit,[777] has spoken
these words. If it appeals to you, listen to them affectionately. The
kingdom of the gandharvas is adorned with roots and fruits. It is
an extremely beautiful country and is located on both sides of the
Sindhu. The gandharvas, armed with weapons and accomplished in
fighting, protect it. There are three crores of the immensely strong
ones and those brave ones are the sons of Shailusha. O Kakutstha!
O mighty-armed one! If the idea appeals to you, control yourself,
conquer those two auspicious gandharva cities and populate them.
There is no one else who can be the refuge for those two extremely
beautiful dominions. O mighty-armed one! I am not telling you
a lie.'

    Hearing these words, Raghava was pleased with the maharshi
and with his maternal uncle. He looked towards Bharata and
spoke words of agreement. Delighted, Raghava joined his hands
in salutation before the brahmana and said, 'O brahmana rishi!
These two princes will conquer that country. Bharata has two
brave sons, Taksha and Pushkala. They will attentively follow

---

[776] Bharata's maternal uncle was Ashvapati, by extension, Rama's maternal uncle.
Yudhajit was Ashvapati's son.

[777] Since Yudhajit is not the maternal uncle, this is a misstatement.

dharma and protect my maternal uncle well. Placing Bharata at the forefront, these two princes and their forces and followers will slay the sons of the gandharva and populate those two cities. The one who is extremely devoted to dharma[778] will instate his two sons in those two excellent cities and again return to my presence.' Having told the brahmana rishi this, he commanded Bharata, his forces and his followers, and consecrated those two princes. At the time of an agreeable nakshatra, they placed the son of Angiras at the forefront. With the soldiers and the two princes, Bharata departed. As they left the city, the soldiers seemed to be led by Shakra. They were invincible to the gods and the asuras and followed Raghava[779] at some distance. Creatures that fed on flesh and extremely large rakshasas also followed Bharata, thirsty for blood. There were many extremely terrible creatures at the front, those that subsisted on flesh. Thousands of them wished to eat the flesh of the sons of the gandharva. Many thousands of lions, tigers, jackals and birds that roamed in the sky preceded the army at the front. Not suffering from any disease, the army spent one and a half months along the route. They then reached Kekaya, full of happy and healthy people.

Chapter 7(91)

The lord of Kekaya heard that Bharata had come as the commander. With Gargya, Yudhajit was filled with great delight. With a large crowd of people, Yudhajit emerged. He swiftly advanced against the gandharvas, who were like the gods in their forms. Light in their valour, Bharata and Yudhajit met. With their forces and foot soldiers, they reached the city of the gandharvas. Hearing, that Bharata had arrived, the immensely brave gandharvas assembled, desiring to fight. They roared in every direction. A tumultuous battle that made the body hair

[778] Meaning Bharata.
[779] Bharata.

stand up commenced. It was extremely terrible and continued for seven nights, but neither side could defeat the other. There was an extremely terrible weapon made out of black iron and it was named Samvarta. Enraged, Bharata, Rama's younger brother, invoked it against the gandharvas. Shattered by Samvarta, they were bound in the nooses of death. In an instant, three crores of great-souled ones were struck. The residents of heaven could not remember a strike which was this terrible. In an instant, those great-souled ones were reduced to this state. Bharata, Kaikeyee's son, slew those brave ones and populated two excellent and prosperous cities there. Taksha became the king of Takshashila and Pushkara[780] of Pushkaravata. These were two beautiful cities in the land of Gandhara, in the dominion of the gandharvas. They were full of heaps of jewels and adorned with groves. They were extensive in their qualities and sought to rival each other. Both of these were the best among beautiful places and unblemished in their conduct. There were well-laid-out shops and filled with gardens and vehicles. Both these beautiful and excellent cities were large and splendid. There were lofty, beautiful and excellent houses, similar to each other in complexion. There were large temples and these made the beautiful cities even more beautiful. Bharata, Raghava's younger brother, resided there for five years. Then Kaikeyee's mighty-armed son returned to Ayodhya again. Bharata greeted the great-souled Raghava, who was like another Dharma, just as Vasava greets the prosperous Brahma. He told him the excellent account about the gandharvas being killed and the populating of that country. Hearing this, Raghava was delighted.

Chapter 7(92)

Hearing this, with his brothers, Raghava was delighted. Raghava addressed his brother in these extraordinary words. 'O Soumitri! These two sons of yours, Angada and Chandraketu,

---

[780] Pushkara is the same as Pushkala.

are accomplished in dharma. They are firm in wielding bows and deserve kingdoms. I will consecrate them in virtuous and beautiful kingdoms that are appropriate, without any obstructions. Let these two archers find pleasure there. They should not suffer from any other king there. Nor should the hermitages there be destroyed. O amiable one! Search for such a country, so that we do not commit a crime.' Thus addressed by Rama, Bharata replied, 'There is the land of Karapatha. It is beautiful and without any disease. Instate the great-souled Angada in that city. Instate Chandraketu in beautiful Chandrakanta, which is also without disease.' Raghava accepted the words that Bharata had spoken. He brought that country under his subjugation and instated Angada there. The beautiful city of Angadiya was populated by Angada. It was beautiful and was protected by Rama, who was unblemished in his deeds. Chandraketu populated the Malla kingdom[781] with wrestlers. It was divine, like a city in heaven and became famous by the name of Chandrakanta. Rama, Bharata and Lakshmana were filled with great delight. They consecrated the princes and the two of them left with their forces and followers. Angada occupied the territory towards the west and Chandraketu towards the north. Soumitri followed Angada and Bharata followed Chandraketu, to help them along the flanks. Lakshmana resided in Angadiya for one year. When his invincible son was instated, he returned again to Ayodhya. Bharata resided there for more than a year. He then returned to Ayodhya, near Rama's feet. Both of them, Soumitri and Bharata, served at Rama's feet. Both of them were exceedingly devoted to dharma. Though time passed, because of their affection, they did not discern it. In this way, they spent ten thousand years, attentively pursuing dharma and always engaged in tasks meant for the citizens. Fulfilled in their minds, they spent this time, established along the path of supreme dharma and surrounded by prosperity. The three of them were prosperous and blazed in their energy. They were like three fires at virtuous sacrifices, when oblations had been offered into the fire.

[781] The Malla kingdom was in between Kosala and Videha. The word *malla* means wrestler or boxer.

Chapter 7(93)

Rama was established along the path of dharma. After some
time, Time[782] arrived at the king's gate, adopting the form
of an ascetic. He addressed the patient and illustrious Lakshmana
in these words. 'Go and tell the king that I have come here for
an important task. I am the messenger of Atibala, the infinitely
energetic maharshi. O immensely strong one! Because of something
that needs to be done, I have come here to see Rama.' Hearing his
words, Soumitri hurried and went and told Rama what the ascetic
had urged. 'O king! O immensely radiant one! Because of your
pursuit of dharma, may you be triumphant in both the worlds.[783]
An ascetic's messenger, like the sun in radiance, has come here to
meet you.' Hearing the words that Lakshmana had uttered, Rama
replied, 'O son![784] Let the immensely energetic ascetic messenger,
who will convey the words, enter.' Soumitri assented and made the
sage enter. He seemed to blaze in his energy and burn down with his
rays. Radiant in his own energy, he approached the best among the
Raghu lineage. The rishi spoke these sweet words to Raghava. 'May
you prosper.' The immensely energetic one was in front of him and
Rama worshipped him with arghya. Having given him that, he
eagerly started to ask about his welfare. Rama, supreme among
eloquent ones, asked about his welfare. The immensely illustrious
one then sat down on a divine and golden seat. Rama said, 'O great
sage! Welcome. Let me know about the message that has brought
you here as a messenger.' Urged thus by the lion among kings, the
sage spoke the following words. 'This can only be uttered between
the two of us. Anyone who witnesses these words has to be killed.
O Raghava! Anyone who hears or sees must be killed. It is only then
that I will tell you about the words of the best among sages.' Rama
pledged this and told Lakshmana, 'O mighty-armed one! Send the
doorkeeper away and remain at the door. O Soumitri! Anyone who
hears or sees the conversation between the two of us, me and the

---

[782] *Kala,* also Death or Destiny.
[783] This world and the world hereafter.
[784] The word used is tata.

rishi, will be killed.' Thus, Kakutstha engaged Lakshmana at the door. Raghava then told the sage, 'Speak. Attentively, tell me about the words spoken by the learned one. Do not worry. It will remain only in my heart.'

Chapter 7(94)

'O Rama! O mighty-armed one! Hear the reason why I have come here. O immensely strong one! I have been sent by the grandfather of the gods. O destroyer of enemy cities! O brave one! I am your eldest son, created out of your own maya. I am the Destroyer who gathers up everything. O mighty-armed one! The illustrious grandfather, the lord and master of all the worlds, has said that it is time for you to protect your own world. "In earlier times, when all the worlds were drawn in, you used your own maya to lie down on the great ocean.[785] In those ancient times, I was born from you. You used your maya to generate the handsome serpent Ananta who lies down in the water and two extremely strong creatures. They were Madhu and Kaitabha and their bones covered everything and constituted mountains. The earth was formed from their fat. I was also born from a divine lotus, as resplendent as the sun, originating in your navel. You said that creation was my task and invested everything in me. O lord of the universe! Having taken up the burden invested on me, I worshipped you. Because you are more energetic than me, I asked you to protect creatures. Since that time, for the sake of protecting all creatures, you gave given up your eternal and invincible form and assumed the form of Vishnu. Having been born as Aditya's valiant son, you delighted your brothers[786] and helped them and the worlds in every possible way. O supreme in the universe! Terrified and desiring Ravana's death, they came to you and you made up your mind to become human. You have resided here for eleven thousand years. Now destiny requires you

---

[785] These are Brahma's words, being repeated.
[786] The Adityas, the gods.

to return to your own ancient city. It is only because of your mental powers that you became the son of a human and have spent a full lifespan. O best among excellent men! It is time for you to return to our presence." O great king! O brave one! O fortunate one! If you still desire to rule over the subjects, reside here. I have conveyed the grandfather's words. O Raghava! Alternatively, conquer that wish and become Vishnu, the protector of the world of the gods. Let the gods be devoid of their anxiety.' He heard the words spoken by the grandfather, as repeated by Time. Raghava laughed and addressed the one who destroys everything in the following words. 'I have heard the extremely wonderful words of the god of the gods. I am greatly delighted that you have happened to come here. O fortunate one! I will go where you have come from. There is nothing to think about, since the thought had already occurred to me. I am under the control of the gods and I must do everything that they want. O one who destroys everything! What the grandfather has mentioned, will happen.'

Chapter 7(95)

While the two were conversing in this way, the illustrious rishi, Durvasa, arrived at the royal gate, desiring to see Rama. The excellent rishi approached Soumitri and said, 'Before my purpose is defeated, quickly make me see Rama.' Hearing the sage's words, Lakshmana, the slayer of enemy heroes, greeted the great-souled one and addressed him in these words. 'O illustrious one! Tell me about the task. What is the purpose? What can I do? O brahmana! Raghava will eagerly do it. Please wait for a while.' Hearing these words, the tiger among rishis became polluted with rage. As if burning him down his eyes, he addressed Lakshmana in these words. 'O Soumitri! Present me before Rama this very instant. Otherwise, I will curse the kingdom, the city, you and Raghava. O Soumitri! I will not spare Bharata's sons and yours. I am incapable of restraining the rage in my heart any longer.' The great-souled one's words were terrible. He thought about those words in his mind and determined what he should do. 'Let all creatures not be destroyed. One person's death is superior.' Having decided this, he went and told Raghava. Hearing Lakshmana's words, Rama gave Time permission to leave. The king swiftly emerged and saw Atri's son. He greeted the great-souled one, who seemed to blaze in his energy. Kakutstha joined his hands in salutation and asked, 'What needs to be done?' The lord, best among sages, heard the words Raghava had spoken. Durvasa replied, 'O Rama! O one who is devoted to dharma! Listen. O Raghava! My one thousand years are over today.[787] O unblemished one! Therefore, I wish to eat whatever has been cooked by you.' Hearing his words, Rama was filled with great delight. He offered the best among sages whatever had been cooked. The best among sages ate the food, which was like amrita. 'O Rama! This is virtuous.' Having said this, he returned to his own hermitage. When the immensely energetic one had gone, Raghava was pleased in his mind. However, remembering the words uttered by Time, he was filled with sorrow. Remembering those terrible words, he was greatly tormented by grief. He was distressed in his mind. With his face cast downwards, he was incapable of saying anything. Raghava thought about the words spoken by Time. The immensely illustrious one said, 'There is no other way', and was silent.

Chapter 7(96)

Lakshmana saw that the miserable Raghava's face was cast downwards, like the moon when it is eclipsed. He cheerfully addressed him in sweet words. 'O mighty-armed one! You should not be tormented on my account. The progress of destiny is like this and has been ordained earlier. O amiable one! Slay me without hesitation and fulfil your pledge. O Kakutstha! Men who do not keep their promises go to hell. O great king! O Raghava! If you are pleased with me and if you are favourably disposed towards

---

[787] Durvasa had taken a vow not to eat for one thousand years.

me, slay me without any hesitation. Make dharma flourish.' When Lakshmana said this, Rama's senses were in a whirl. He summoned his ministers and his priest. In their midst, the lord of men recounted what had happened—the pledge before the ascetic and Durvasa's arrival. Hearing this, all the ministers looked towards the preceptor. The greatly energetic Vasishtha spoke these words. 'O mighty-armed one! I had already foreseen this incident that makes the body hair stand up. O Rama! You will be separated from the immensely illustrious Lakshmana. Destiny is powerful. Do not make your pledge false. If pledges are destroyed, dharma also heads towards destruction. When dharma is destroyed, there is no doubt that everything in the three worlds, mobile and immobile objects and gods and rishis, are also destroyed. O tiger among men! For the sake of protecting the three worlds, kill Lakshmana today and make the universe safe.' In the midst of that assembly of courtiers, Rama heard these words, which were full of dharma and artha. He told Lakshmana, 'O Soumitri! Let there not be a catastrophe. Therefore, I am casting you away. Virtuous ones have decreed that killing and abandoning are both regarded as the same.' Rama spoke these words, his eyes overflowing with tears. Lakshmana quickly left and entered his own residence. He went to the Sarayu, joined his hands in salutation and touched the water. He controlled all the flows in his body and did not release his breaths. When he stopped breathing, Shakra, large numbers of apsaras, the gods and large numbers of rishis showered down flowers. Unseen by all men, Shakra seized the immensely strong Lakshmana and made him enter heaven in his physical body. The supreme among the gods were delighted that Vishnu's fourth part had arrived. Happy and full of joy, with the rishis, they worshipped him.

Chapter 7(97)

Having let Lakshmana go, Rama was overwhelmed by sorrow and grief. He told the priest, the ministers and the merchants, 'Today, I will consecrate Bharata, who is devoted to dharma, in the kingdom. Let the brave one be the lord of Ayodhya. After that, I will leave for the forest. Before time passes, let all the arrangements be made. Today, I will go to the destination that Lakshmana has gone to.' Hearing the words spoken by Raghava, all the ordinary subjects were severely afflicted. They bowed their heads down on the ground. It was as if they had lost their lives. On hearing what Rama had said, Bharata also lost his senses. He condemned the kingdom and told Raghava, 'O king! O descendant of the Raghu lineage! I am taking a pledge on the truth. Without you, I do not desire the world of heaven, or the kingdom. O king! O lord of men! Instate Kusha and Lava. Let the brave Kusha rule Kosala and Lava rule the north.[788] Let messengers who are swift in their valour go to Shatrughna. Let them tell him about our imminent departure for heaven and ask him to come here.' Hearing what Bharata had said, all the citizens were miserable and tormented. Their faces were downcast. On seeing this, Vasishtha spoke these words. 'O Rama! O child! Behold the people on earth. They are overcome by ordinary sentiments. Knowing what they desire, you should not do something that is disagreeable to them.' Hearing Vasishtha's words, he made those ordinary people rise up. Kakutstha asked all of them, 'What shall I do?' All the ordinary people addressed Rama in these words. 'O Rama! We will go wherever you go. This is our supreme delight. In our view, this is our supreme dharma. We are firm in following you. Our hearts will always be satisfied at that. O Kakutstha! If you have affection for the citizens and if you are extremely fond of them, let them proceed along the same virtuous path as you, with their sons and wives. O lord! If you do not wish to abandon us, take us with you, to the forest for asceticism, to impenetrable places, to rivers and to oceans.' Hearing their determination, he considered what should be done. Since the devotion of the citizens was firm, he told them that he agreed. Having decided this, on that very day, Raghava instated the brave Kusha in Kosala and Lava in the north. The great-souled one consecrated Kusha and Lava. He gave each of them one thousand chariots, thirty thousand elephants, ten thousand horses and riches. They were surrounded by many jewels

---

[788] That is, North Kosala.

and riches and happy and healthy people. Having been consecrated, those two brave ones left for their own cities. The great-souled one then sent a messenger to Shatrughna.

Chapter 7(98)

Urged by Rama's words, the messenger, light in his valour, swiftly left for Madhura and did not spend any nights during the journey.[789] He reached Madhura in three days and nights and told Shatrughna everything about what had transpired—the abandonment of Lakshmana, Raghava's pledge, the consecration of the two sons and the decision of the citizens to follow. The intelligent Rama had created a beautiful city for Kusha to the north of the Vindhya mountains and it was named Kushavati. The beautiful city that was referred to as Shravati[790] was for Lava. Leaving Ayodhya empty, Bharata intended to follow Raghava. He reported all this to the great-souled Shatrughna. The messenger stopped and added, 'O king! Hurry.' The news was terrible and the destruction of the lineage was nigh. Hearing this, the descendant of the Raghu lineage summoned the ordinary people and the priest, Kanchana, and told all of them about what had happened. He also said that with his brothers, he too would be destroyed.[791] Therefore, the valiant lord of men instated his two sons. Subahu obtained Madhura and Shatrughati obtained Vaidisha. He divided the forces in Madhura among the two sons. With riches and grain, he established these two kings. He took his leave from the king of Vaidisha, Shatrughati.[792] Alone on a chariot, Raghava left for Ayodhya.

He saw the great-souled one,[793] blazing like a fire. He was attired in a thin silken garment, with the undecaying sages. He

[789] That is, did not waste any time in resting along the way.

[790] Alternatively, Shravasti.

[791] Would die.

[792] Non-Critical versions also mention Subahu of Madhura. In the Critical version, this is left implicit.

[793] Rama.

controlled his senses, joined his hands in salutation and greeted Rama. The one who knew about dharma thought about dharma and spoke these words. 'I have instated my two sons, the warriors of the Raghava lineage. O king! Know that I have made up my mind about following you. Since your command is impossible to cross, please do not say anything contrary. O brave one! You should not abandon me, especially because I am devoted to you.' The descendant of the Raghu lineage realized that he had firmly made up his mind. Agreeing with Shatrughna, Rama spoke words of agreement. When he had finished speaking, innumerable apes, who could assume any form at will, bears and large numbers of rakshasas assembled. Knowing that Rama was about to be destroyed, all the sons of the gods, the sons of the rishis and the sons of the gandharvas also assembled. All of them assembled and greeted Rama. 'O king! O immensely illustrious one! We have come to follow you. O Rama! O bull among men! If you go without taking us, it will be as if you have raised Yama's staff and brought us down.' Hearing the words of the bears, apes and rakshasas, he spoke these sweet and gentle words to Vibhishana. 'O Vibhishana! O Indra among rakshasas! O immensely valiant one! As long as there are subjects, please hold up Lanka.[794] Follow dharma and protect the subjects. Do not say anything back in reply.' After this, Kakutstha spoke to Hanumat. 'You have already made up your mind to remain alive. Do not make that pledge of yours come false. O lord of the apes! As long as my account is spoken about in the world, till then, remain alive and follow your pledge.' Kakutstha Raghava then told all the apes and bears, 'Come with me.'

Chapter 7(99)

When night was over and it was morning, the broad-chested, immensely illustrious and lotus-eyed Rama spoke to the priest. 'Let the fires of agnihotra and vajapeya sacrifices proceed in front,

---

[794] That is, rule over Lanka.

with the flames blazing because of clarified butter and decorating the large road.' The energetic Vasishtha looked towards everything and ensured that all the rituals connected with the great journey[795] were properly observed. Wearing a silken garment and to the chanting of the name of the brahman, he[796] proceeded along the decorated road, holding some kusha grass in his hand. He said nothing. He did not try to avoid the difficult stretches along the path.[797] Like the blazing sun, he emerged from his house. Extremely controlled, Padma Shri[798] was on Rama's left. The large-eyed Hri[799] was to his right, stationed slightly ahead. Many kinds of arrows and the bow that was used in battles followed Kakutstha. All of these were in embodied form. The Vedas, Savitree, the protector of everything, Omkara, Vashatkara—all of these followed Rama, in the form of brahmanas. The great-souled rishis and all the brahmanas followed Kakutstha and reached the gate to heaven. All the women from the inner quarters followed them, the aged and young female servants and the servants who were eunuchs. Bharata and Shatrughna also proceeded, with those from their inner quarters. With Rama having taken that vow, they also took the same vow as Raghava. All the controlled and great-souled brahmanas were with the agnihotra fire. With their sons and wives, they followed the immensely intelligent Kakutstha. Cheerfully, all the ministers and the array of servants, with their sons and relatives, followed Raghava. All the ordinary people, happy and healthy, surrounded them. Delighted with his qualities, they followed Raghava as he proceeded. All of them were supreme in their happiness and health, and bathed. As all of them followed Rama's vow, a proud tumult arose. No one there was miserable. No one there was ashamed or sad. All of them were happy and delighted. It was extremely extraordinary. The inhabitants of the countryside wished to see the king emerge. They were tormented to see him and all of them followed him. Extremely

[795] Mahaprasthana, death.

[796] Rama.

[797] He did not try to avoid stones etc. and seek out the most comfortable stretch of the path.

[798] In embodied form. Padma is another name for Lakshmi/Shri, since she is on a lotus.

[799] The embodied form of modesty.

controlled, the bears, the apes, the rakshasas and the residents of the city followed him at the rear, filled with great devotion.

Chapter 7(100)

Sarayu, with the sacred waters, flowed in a westward direction. After having travelled for more than half a yojana, the descendant of the Raghu lineage saw the river. At that instant, surrounded by all the gods and the great-souled rishis, Brahma, the grandfather of the worlds, arrived at the spot where Kakutstha had presented himself at the gate to heaven. All of them came to the spot where Kakutstha had presented himself before heaven. They arrived on one hundred crores of celestial vimanas. Flowers showered down. A strong wind started to blow. Hundreds of trumpets blared and gandharvas and apsaras assembled. On foot, Rama approached the waters of the Sarayu. From the sky, the grandfather spoke these words. 'O Vishnu! O fortunate one! O Raghava! Come. It is good fortune that I have met you. Enter with your brothers and with the gods, in your own bodies. Enter your own eternal and great Vaishnavi energy, which is like the sky. O god! You are the refuge of the world. O large-eyed one! With the exception of your own maya, which you have resorted to earlier, there is no one who is capable of knowing you. You cannot be thought of. You are the great being. You are without decay and accumulate everything. O immensely energetic one! As you wish, enter your own body.' Hearing the grandfather's words, the immensely intelligent one made up his mind. In his own body and with his younger brothers, he entered his Vaishnava energy. When the god assumed his form of Vishnu, the gods, the Sadhyas and the large number of Maruts, with Indra and Agni at the forefront, worshipped him. So did the large number of divine rishis, the gandharvas, the apsaras, the birds, the serpents, the yakshas, the daityas, the danavas and the rakshasas. All of them were happy and delighted. All their wishes had come true. Uttering words of praise and without any blemishes, all of them went to heaven.

The immensely energetic Vishnu spoke to the grandfather. 'O one who is good in vows! You should also grant these large numbers of people.[800] All of these spirited ones have followed me, out of affection. They are devoted and you should honour them. For my sake, they have given up their bodies.' Hearing Vishnu's words, Brahma, the lord and preceptor of the worlds, said that all the assembled people could go to the world known as Santanika. 'O Rama! If anyone born as inferior species thinks of you and gives up his life out of devotion, that person will also reside in Santanika. It possesses all the qualities and is only next to Brahma's world. The apes will return to whichever gods they had been born from and so will the bears. The rishis, the serpents and the yakshas will also regain their own portions.' When the lord of the gods said this, they reached the place from where they would leave the earth. Their eyes filled with tears of joy and without any lassitude, they went to the Sarayu. Full of joy, all those creatures submerged themselves in the water. They gave up their bodies as humans and ascended vimanas. Those born as inferior species also approached the waters of the Sarayu. Their forms became divine and celestial. They were as radiant as gods. All mobile and immobile objects also went to the waters of the Sarayu. From those unblemished waters, they went to the world of the gods. There were apes, bears and rakshasas that had been born from the portions of the gods. All of them gave up their bodies in the water and entered their own portions. The preceptor of the worlds and heaven thus ensured that all of them obtained heaven. Thereafter, with the happy and delighted gods, the immensely intelligent one also went to heaven. The Uttara Kanda account, worshipped by Brahma, ends here. It is part of the famous and excellent Ramayana composed by Valmiki.

This ends the Uttara Kanda.

This ends the Valmiki Ramayana.

---

[800] Entry into heaven.